David Pickering has written and contributed to over 150 reference books. These include *The Macmillan Encyclopedia* (1984–92), *Cassell Dictionary of Abbreviations* (1996), *The Cassell Thesaurus* (1998), *The Oxford Guide to British and American Culture* (1999), *The Penguin Dictionary of First Names* (1999) and *Brewer's Dictionary of Modern Phrase and Fable* (2000). He lives in Buckingham.

Pears Factfinder

Edited by David Pickering

PENGUIN BOOKS

PENGUIN BOOKS

Published by the Penguin Group
Penguin Books Ltd, 80 Strand, London, WC2R ORL, England
Penguin Putnam Inc., 375 Hudson Street, New York, New York 10014, USA
Penguin Books Australia Ltd, 250 Camberwell Road, Camberwell, Victoria 3124, Australia
Penguin Books Canada Ltd, 10 Alcorn Avenue, Toronto, Ontario, Canada M4V 3B2
Penguin Books India (P) Ltd, 11 Community Centre, Panchsheel Park, New Delhi – 110 017, India
Penguin Books (NZ) Ltd, Private Bag 102902, NSMC, Auckland, New Zealand
Penguin Books (South Africa) (Pty) Ltd, 5 Watkins Street, Denver Ext 4, Johannesburg 2094, South Africa

Penguin Books Ltd, Registered Offices: 80 Strand, London, WC2R ORL, England

First published 2001
1

Set in TheSans and TheAntiqua B
Typeset by Rowland Phototypesetting Ltd, Bury St Edmunds, Suffolk
Printed in England by William Clowes Ltd, Beccles and London

Foreword

The *Pears Factfinder* has been designed as a companion volume to the best-selling *Pears Cyclopaedia* to provide quick and easy access to thousands of facts and figures about the world around us. Every effort has been made to ensure facts are as accurate and up-to-date as possible, including a wealth of international material as well as comprehensive coverage of the English-speaking world. The breadth of subjects covered makes the book equally useful for both general and specialized reference; it contains much information relevant to general knowledge, school and university studies, quizzes, and everyday home and office use.

The text has largely been compiled in the form of lists and tables, in the interests of clarity and accessibility, and organized into twelve broad fields covering all aspects of human knowledge and endeavour: the Universe; the World; Natural History; Human Geography; Human Society; Politics, Law and Economics; History; Mythology, Religion and Folklore; Science and Technology; Transport, Communication and Media; Art and Culture; and Sports and Games. The lists and tables included under each heading are detailed at the front of the book, guiding the reader in search of the answer to a particular query to the relevant page.

David Pickering

Contents

3 Natural History

4 Human Geography

5 *Human Society*

6 *Politics, Law and Economics*

6.2 *Administrative Organization*

6.3 *Law and Legislation*

6.4 *Economics*

7 *History*

7.1 *Historical Events*

7.2 *Ancient History*

7.3 *Monarchs and Emperors*

8 *Mythology, Religion and Folklore*

9 *Science and Technology*

10 *Transport, Communication and Media*

11 *Art and Culture*

12 *Sports and Games*

1
The Universe

1.1 *Astronomy*

Constellations

Constellation	Informal name
Andromeda	Andromeda
Antlia	Air Pump
Apus	Bird of Paradise
Aquarius	Water Bearer
Aquila	Eagle
Ara	Altar
Aries	Ram
Auriga	Charioteer
Boötes	Herdsman
Caelum	Chisel
Camelopardalis	Giraffe
Cancer	Crab
Canes Venatici	Hunting Dogs
Canis Major	Great Dog
Canis Minor	Little Dog
Capricornus	Sea Goat
Carina	Keel
Cassiopeia	Cassiopeia
Centaurus	Centaur
Cepheus	Cepheus
Cetus	Whale
Chamaeleon	Chameleon
Circinus	Compasses
Columba	Dove
Coma Berenices	Berenice's Hair
Corona Australis	Southern Crown
Corona Borealis	Northern Crown
Corvus	Crow

Constellation	Informal name
Crater	Cup
Crux	Southern Cross
Cygnus	Swan
Delphinus	Dolphin
Dorado	Swordfish
Draco	Dragon
Equuleus	Little Horse
Eridanus	River Eridanus
Fornax	Furnace
Gemini	Twins
Grus	Crane
Hercules	Hercules
Horologium	Clock
Hydra	Sea Serpent
Hydrus	Water Snake
Indus	Indian
Lacerta	Lizard
Leo	Lion
Leo Minor	Little Lion
Lepus	Hare
Libra	Scales
Lupus	Wolf
Lynx	Lynx
Lyra	Harp
Mensa	Table
Microscopium	Microscope
Monoceros	Unicorn
Musca	Fly
Norma	Level
Octans	Octant
Ophiuchus	Serpent Bearer
Orion	Orion
Pavo	Peacock
Pegasus	Winged Horse
Perseus	Perseus
Phoenix	Phoenix
Pictor	Easel
Pisces	Fishes
Piscis Austrinus	Southern Fish
Puppis	Ship's Stern
Pyxis	Mariner's Compass
Reticulum	Net
Sagitta	Arrow
Sagittarius	Archer
Scorpius	Scorpion
Sculptor	Sculptor
Scutum	Shield
Serpens	Serpent
Sextans	Sextant
Taurus	Bull
Telescopium	Telescope

Triangulum	Triangle
Triangulum Australe	Southern Triangle
Tucana	Toucan
Ursa Major	Great Bear
Ursa Minor	Little Bear
Vela	Sails
Virgo	Virgin
Volans	Flying Fish
Vulpecula	Fox

Star distances

Star	Distance (light years)
Proxima Centauri	4.24
Alpha Centauri A	4.34
Alpha Centauri B	4.34
Barnard's Star	5.97
Wolf 359 (CN Leonis)	7.80
Lalande 21185	8.19
UV Ceti A	8.55
UV Ceti B	8.55
Sirius A	8.67
Sirius B	8.67
Ross 154	9.52
Ross 248 (HH Andromedae)	10.37
Epsilon Eridani	10.63
Ross 128 (F1 Virginis)	10.79
L 789-6	11.12
GX Andromedae	11.22
GQ Andromedae	11.22
61 Cygnus A	11.22
61 Cygnus B	11.22
HD 173739	11.25
Epsilon Indi	11.25
Tau Ceti	11.41

Star magnitudes

Star	Magnitude	Distance (light years)
Alpha Canis Majoris (Sirius)	−1.47	8.7
Alpha Carinae (Canopus)	−0.72	98
Alpha Centauri (Rigil Kentaurus)	−0.29	4.3
Alpha Boötes (Arcturus)	−0.04	36
Alpha Lyrae (Vega)	0.03	26
Alpha Aurigae (Capella)	0.08	45
Beta Orionis (Rigel)	0.12	815
Alpha Canis Minoris (Procyon)	0.34	11
Alpha Orionis (Betelgeuse)	0.50 (variable)	520

Star	Magnitude	Distance (light years)
Alpha Eridani (Achernar)	0.5	118
Beta Centauri (Hadar)	0.60 (variable)	490
Alpha Crucis (Acrux)	0.76	370
Alpha Aquilae (Altair)	0.77	16
Alpha Tauri (Aldebaran)	0.85 (variable)	68
Alpha Scorpii (Antares)	0.96	520
Alpha Virginis (Spica)	0.98	220
Beta Geminorum (Pollux)	1.15	35
Alpha Piscis Austrini (Fomalhaut)	1.16	23
Beta Crucis (Mimosa)	1.20 (variable)	490
Alpha Cygni (Deneb)	1.25	1600

Comets

Comet	First recorded sighting	Period of orbit (years)
Halley	240 BC	76
Tycho	1577	unknown
Kirch/Newton	1680	8814
De Chéseaux	1744	unknown
Lexell	1770	5.6
Encke	1786	3.3
Flauergues	1811	3094
Pons-Winnecke	1819	6.34
Great Comet	1843	512.6
Donati	1858	1950
Tebbutt	1861	409.1
Swift-Tuttle	1862	125
Cruls	1882	758.4
Wolf	1884	8.4
Morehouse	1908	unknown
Daylight Comet	1910	unknown
Schwassmann–Wachmann 1	1925	15
Arend–Roland	1957	unknown
Mrkos	1957	unknown
Humason	1961	3 000
Seki–Lines	1962	unknown
Ikeya–Seki	1965	880
Tago–Sato–Kosaka	1969	420 000
Bennett	1970	1 680
Kohoutek	1973	75 000
Kobayashi–Berger–Milon	1975	unknown
West	1975	500 000
IRAS–Araki–Alcock	1983	unknown
Hale–Bopp	1995	2 400
Hyakutake	1996	18 000

Annual meteor showers

Name	Dates	Height of intensity	Approaching from (star region)
Quadrantids	1–6 January	3–4 January	Beta Boötis
Lyrids	19–22 April	22 Apr	Nu Herculis
Eta Aquarids	1–8 May	05 May	Eta Aquarii
Delta Aquarids	15 July–10 August	28 July–5 August	Delta Aquarii
Perseids	27 July–17 August	11–14 August	Eta Persei
Andromedids	25 September–6 December	14 November	Gamma Andromedae
Orionids	15–25 October	21 October	Nu Orionis
Leonids	14–20 November	17–18 November	Zeta Leonis
Geminids	8–14 December	13–14 December	Castor
Ursids	20–24 December	22–23 December	Kocab

The Sun

Age	4 700 000 000 years
Predicted lifespan	10 000 000 000 years
Diameter	1 392 530 km (864 950 mi)
Components	70% hydrogen, 30% helium, other elements less than 1%
Volume	1.414×10^{18} km^3
Mass	2×10^{30} kg
Mean density	1.4 g/cm^3
Luminosity	3.9×10^{27} kW
Surface temperature	5 770 K/5 496.8°C
Core temperature	15 000 000 K/15 000 000°C
Average orbital velocity	107 210 kph/66 620 mph
Rotation	26.8 days (at equator)

Solar eclipses 1995–2020

Date	Type of eclipse	Visible from
29 April 95	Annular*	S Pacific, S America
24 October 95	Total	Middle East, S Asia, S Pacific
09 March 97	Total	C and N Asia, Arctic
26 February 98	Total	Mid-Pacific, C America, N Atlantic
22 August 98	Annular	Indonesia, S Pacific, Indian Ocean
16 February 99	Annular	Indian Ocean, Australia
11 August 99	Total	N Atlantic, N Europe, Middle East, N India
21 June 01	Total	S Atlantic, S Africa, Madagascar
14 December 01	Annular	Pacific, C America
10 June 02	Annular	Indonesia, Pacific, Mexico
04 December 02	Total	S Africa, Indian Ocean, Australia

Date	Type of eclipse	Visible from
31 May 03	Annular	Iceland, Greenland
23 November 03	Total	Antarctic
08 April 05	Annular/Total	Pacific, Panama, Venezuela
03 October 05	Annular	Atlantic, Spain, Libya, Indian Ocean
29 March 06	Total	Atlantic, Libya, Turkey, Russia
22 September 06	Annular	Guyana, Atlantic, Indian Ocean
07 February 08	Annular	Antarctic
01 August 08	Total	Arctic, Siberia, China
26 January 09	Annular	S Atlantic, Indian Ocean, Borneo
22 July 09	Total	India, China, Pacific
15 January 10	Annular	Africa, Indian Ocean, China
11 July 10	Total	Pacific, S Chile
20–21 May 12	Annular	China, N Pacific, N America
13 November 12	Total	N Australia, Pacific
9–10 May 13	Annular	Australia, Pacific
03 November 13	Total	Atlantic, C Africa, Ethiopia
20 March 15	Total	N Atlantic, Arctic
09 March 16	Total	Indonesia, Pacific
01 September 16	Annular	Atlantic, Africa, Madagascar, Indian Ocean
26 February 17	Annular	Pacific, S America, Atlantic, Africa
21 August 17	Total	Pacific, N America, Atlantic
02 July 19	Total	Pacific, S America
26 December 19	Annular	Arabia, Sri Lanka, Indonesia, Pacific
21 June 20	Annular	Africa, Arabia, China, Pacific
12 December 20	Total	Pacific, S America, Atlantic

Note In an annular eclipse a narrow ring of the Sun remains visible around the Moon

Planets

Mercury

Maximum distance from the sun	69.4 million km (43.0 million mi)
Minimum distance from the sun	46.8 million km (29.0 million mi)
Planet year	88 days
Planet day	58 days 16 hours
Diameter at equator	4 878 km (3 031 mi)
Atmosphere	Hydrogen, helium, neon
Satellites	0

Venus

Maximum distance from the sun	109.0 million km (67.6 million mi)
Minimum distance from the sun	107.6 million km (66.7 mi)
Planet year	224.7 days
Planet day	243 days
Diameter at equator	12 104 km (7 521 mi)
Atmosphere	Carbon dioxide
Satellites	0

Earth

Maximum distance from the sun	152.6 million km (94.6 million mi)
Minimum distance from the sun	147.4 million km (91.4 million mi)
Planet year	365.26 days
Planet day	23 hours 56 mins 4 secs
Diameter at equator	12 756 km (7 927 mi)
Atmosphere	Nitrogen, oxygen
Satellites	1

Mars

Maximum distance from the sun	249.2 million km (154.5 million mi)
Minimum distance from the sun	207.3 million km (128.5 million mi)
Planet year	687 days
Planet day	24 hours 37 mins 23 secs
Diameter at equator	6 794 km (4 222 mi)
Atmosphere	Carbon dioxide
Satellites	2

Jupiter

Maximum distance from the sun	817.4 million km (506.8 million mi)
Minimum distance from the sun	741.6 million km (459.8 million mi)
Planet year	11.86 years
Planet day	9 hours 50 mins 30 secs
Diameter at equator	142 800 km (88 800 mi)
Atmosphere	Hydrogen, methane
Satellites	16

Saturn

Maximum distance from the sun	1 512 million km (937.6 million mi)
Minimum distance from the sun	1 346 million km (834.6 million mi)
Planet year	29.46 years
Planet day	10 hours 14 mins
Diameter at equator	120 000 km (74 600 mi)
Atmosphere	Hydrogen, helium
Satellites	18 or more

Uranus

Maximum distance from the sun	3 011 million km (1 867 million mi)
Minimum distance from the sun	2 740 million km (1 699 million mi)
Planet year	84.01 years
Planet day	16–28 hours (variable by latitude)
Diameter at equator	51 000 km (31 600 mi)
Atmosphere	Methane, helium, hydrogen
Satellites	15

Neptune

Maximum distance from the sun	4 543 million km (2 817 million mi)
Minimum distance from the sun	4 466 million km (2 769 million mi)
Planet year	164.79 years
Planet day	18–20 hours (variable by latitude)
Diameter at equator	49 500 km (30 800 mi)
Atmosphere	Methane, hydrogen
Satellites	2

Pluto

Maximum distance from the sun	7 346 million km (4 566 million mi)
Minimum distance from the sun	4 461 million km (2 766 million mi)
Planet year	247.7 years
Planet day	6 days 9 hours
Diameter at equator	2 300 km (1 430 mi)
Atmosphere	Methane
Satellites	1

Planetary satellites

Satellite	Year dis-covered	Diameter	Distance from planet	Orbital period (days)
Earth				
Moon		3 476 km (2 155 mi)	384 000 km (238 000 mi)	27.322
Mars				
Phobos	1877	27 km (17 mi)	938 000 km (583 000 mi)	0.319
Deimos	1877	15 km (9 mi)	2 346 000 km (1 458 000 mi)	1.262
Jupiter				
Metis	1979	40 km (25 mi)	128 000 km (79 000 mi)	0.295
Adrastea	1979	24 km (15 mi)	129 000 km (80 000 mi)	0.298
Amalthea	1892	270 km (168 mi)	181 000 km (112 000 mi)	0.498
Thebe	1979	100 km (60 mi)	222 000 km (138 000 mi)	0.675
Io	1610	3 650 km (2 260 mi)	422 000 km (262 000 mi)	1.769
Europa	1610	3 104 km (1 950 mi)	671 000 km (417 000 mi)	3.552
Ganymede	1610	5 260 km (3 270 mi)	1 070 000 km (665 000 mi)	7.155
Callisto	1610	4 800 km (3 000 mi)	1 883 000 km (1 170 000 mi)	16.689
Leda	1974	20 km (12 mi)	11 100 000 km (6 900 000 mi)	239
Himalia	1904	186 km (116 mi)	11 480 000 km (7 134 000 mi)	251
Lysithea	1938	40 km (25 mi)	11 720 000 km (7 283 000 mi)	259
Elara	1905	80 km (50 mi)	11 740 000 km (7 295 000 mi)	260
Ananke	1951	30 km (19 mi)	21 200 000 km (13 174 000 mi)	631
Carme	1938	40 km (25 mi)	22 600 000 km (14 044 000 mi)	692
Pasiphae	1908	50 km (30 mi)	23 500 000 km (14 603 000 mi)	735
Sinope	1914	40 km (25 mi)	23 700 000 km (14 727 000 mi)	758
Saturn				
Pan	1990	10 km (6 mi)	134 000 km (83 000 mi)	0.575
Atlas	1980	40 km (25 mi)	138 000 km (86 000 mi)	0.602
Prometheus	1980	100 km (60 mi)	139 000 km (86 000 mi)	0.613
Pandora	1980	100 km (60 mi)	142 000 km (88 000 mi)	0.629
Epimetheus	1980	140 km (90 mi)	151 000 km (94 000 mi)	0.695
Janus	1966	200 km (120 mi)	151 000 km (94 000 mi)	0.695
Mimas	1789	390 km (240 mi)	186 000 km (116 000 mi)	0.942
Enceladus	1789	500 km (310 mi)	238 000 km (148 000 mi)	1.37
Calypso	1980	30 km (19 mi)	295 000 km (183 000 mi)	1.888
Telesto	1980	30 km (19 mi)	295 000 km (183 000 mi)	1.888
Tethys	1684	1 050 km (650 mi)	295 000 km (183 000 mi)	1.888
Dione	1684	1 120 km (700 mi)	377 000 km (234 000 mi)	2.737

Helene	1980	15 km (9 mi)	1 378 000 km (235 000 mi)	2.737
Rhea	1672	1 530 km (950 mi)	1 527 000 km (327 000 mi)	4.518
Titan	1655	5 150 km (3 200 mi)	1 222 000 km (759 000 mi)	15.945
Hyperion	1848	480 km (300 mi)	1 481 000 km (920 000 mi)	21.277
Iapetus	1671	1 460 km (910 mi)	3 560 000 km (2 212 000 mi)	79.33
Phoebe	1898	220 km (137 mi)	12 950 000 km (8 047 000 mi)	550.48

Uranus*

Cordelia	1986	15 km (9 mi)	49 000 km (31 000 mi)	0.335
Ophelia	1986	20 km (12 mi)	53 000 km (33 000 mi)	0.376
Bianca	1986	50 km (31 mi)	59 000 km (37 000 mi)	0.435
Cressida	1986	70 km (43 mi)	62 000 km (38 000 mi)	0.464
Desdemona	1986	50 km (31 mi)	63 000 km (39 000 mi)	0.474
Juliet	1986	70 km (43 mi)	64 000 km (40 000 mi)	0.493
Portia	1986	90 km (56 mi)	66 000 km (41 000 mi)	0.513
Rosalind	1986	50 km (31 mi)	70 000 km (43 000 mi)	0.558
Belinda	1986	50 km (31 mi)	75 000 km (47 000 mi)	0.624
S/1986U10	1999	40 km (25 mi)	77 000 km (48 000 mi)	0.638
Puck	1948	170 km (110 mi)	86 000 km (53 000 mi)	0.762
Miranda	1851	480 km (300 mi)	130 000 km (81 000 mi)	1.413
Ariel	1851	1 160 km (720 mi)	191 000 km (119 000 mi)	2.52
Umbriel	1787	1 170 km (730 mi)	266 000 km (165 000 mi)	4.144
Titania	1787	1 580 km (980 mi)	436 000 km (271 000 mi)	8.706
Oberon	1986	1 500 km (950 mi)	583 000 km (362 000 mi)	13.463
Caliban	1997	40 km (25 mi)	7 165 000 km (4 452 000 mi)	579
Sycorax	1997	80 km (50 mi)	12 175 000 km (7 565 000 mi)	1 289

Neptune

Naiad	1989	50 km (31 mi)	48 000 km (30 000 mi)	0.294
Thalassa	1989	90 km (56 mi)	50 000 km (31 000 mi)	0.311
Despina	1989	150 km (93 mi)	53 000 km (33 000 mi)	0.335
Galatea	1989	160 km (99 mi)	62 000 km (39 000 mi)	0.429
Larissa	1989	200 km (120 mi)	74 000 km (46 000 mi)	0.555
Proteus	1989	420 km (260 mi)	118 000 km (73 000 mi)	1.122
Triton	1846	3 800 km (2 400 mi)	355 000 km (221 000 mi)	5.877
Nereid	1949	300 km (190 mi)	5 510 000 km (3 424 000 mi)	360.136

Pluto

Charon	1978	1 200 km (745 mi)	20 000 000 km (12 500 000 mi)	6.387

Note Three more satellites were discovered in orbit around Uranus in 1999, but await confirmation and naming

Lunar seas

Latin name	English name
Lacus Mortis	Lake of Death
Lacus Somniorum	Lake of Dreams
Mare Australe	Southern Sea
Mare Crisium	Sea of Crises
Mare Fecunditatis	Sea of Fertility
Mare Frigoris	Sea of Cold
Mare Humboldtianum	Humboldt's Sea
Mare Humorum	Sea of Humours
Mare Imbrium	Sea of Showers
Mare Ingenii	Sea of Geniuses
Mare Marginis	Marginal Sea
Mare Moscoviense	Moscow Sea
Mare Nectaris	Sea of Nectar
Mare Nubium	Sea of Clouds
Mare Orientale	Eastern Sea
Mare Serenitatis	Sea of Serenity
Mare Smythii	Smyth's Sea
Mare Spumans	Foaming Sea
Mare Tranquillitatis	Sea of Tranquillity
Mare Undarum	Sea of Waves
Mare Vaporum	Sea of Vapours
Oceanus Procellarum	Ocean of Storms
Palus Epidemiarum	Marsh of Epidemics
Palus Nebularum	Marsh of Mists
Palus Putredinis	Marsh of Decay
Palus Somnii	Marsh of Sleep
Sinus Aestuum	Bay of Heats
Sinus Iridum	Bay of Rainbows
Sinus Medii	Central Bay
Sinus Roris	Bay of Dew

Lunar eclipses 1995–2020

Date	Type of eclipse	Visible from
15 April 95	Partial	Pacific, Australia, SE Asia
04 April 96	Total	Africa, SE Europe, S America
27 September 96	Total	C and S America, N America, W Africa
24 March 97	Partial	C and S America, N America, W Africa
16 September 97	Total	S Africa, E Africa, Australia
28 July 99	Partial	Pacific, Australia, SE Asia
21 January 00	Total	N America, S America, SW Europe, W Africa
16 July 00	Total	Pacific, Australia, SE Asia
09 January 01	Total	Europe, Asia, Africa
05 July 01	Partial	Asia, Australia, Pacific

16 May 03	Total	Americas, Europe, Africa
09 November 03	Total	Americas, Europe, Africa, W Asia
04 May 04	Total	Europe, Africa, Asia
28 October 04	Total	Americas, Europe, Africa
17 October 05	Partial	E Asia, Pacific, N America
07 September 06	Partial	Australia, Asia, E Africa
03 March 07	Total	Europe, Asia, Africa
28 August 07	Total	Australia, Pacific, N America
21 February 08	Total	Americas, Europe, Africa
16 August 08	Partial	Europe, Africa, W Asia
31 December 09	Partial	Asia, Africa, Europe
26 June 10	Partial	Pacific
21 December 10	Total	N and S America
15 June 11	Total	Asia, Africa, Europe
10 December 11	Total	Pacific, Australia, E Asia
04 June 12	Partial	Pacific, Australasia
25 April 13	Total	Asia, Africa, Europe
14 April 14	Total	N and S America
08 October 14	Partial	Pacific, Australia, W Americas
04 April 15	Total	Pacific, Australasia
28 September 15	Partial	Africa, Europe, Americas
07 August 17	Total	Asia, Africa, Australia
31 January 18	Total	Pacific, Australia, Asia
27 July 18	Total	Asia, Africa, Europe
21 January 19	Partial	Americas, Europe
16 July 19	Partial	Asia, Africa, Europe

Astronomers Royal

Name	Period in office
John Flamsteed	1675–1719
Edmond Halley	1720–42
James Bradley	1742–62
Nathaniel Bliss	1762–64
Nevil Maskelyne	1765–1811
John Pond	1811–35
George Airy	1835–81
William Christie	1881–1910
Frank Dyson	1910–33
Harold Spencer Jones	1933–55
Richard Woolley	1956–71
Martin Ryle	1972–82
F. Graham Smith	1982–90
Arnold Wolfendale	1991–

1.2 *Space Exploration*

Chronology of space exploration

Date	Event
2300–2000 BC	Chinese and Babylonian astronomers conduct early studies of the heavens
1608	Telescope invented by Hans Lippershey
1632	First official observatory set up at Leiden (Netherlands)
1633	The Inquisition condemns the theories of Galileo
1675	Royal Greenwich Observatory instituted in London
1687	Publication of Isaac Newton's *Principia*
1705	Edmond Halley predicts return of Halley's comet
1781	William Herschel discovers Uranus
1846	Johann Galle identifies Neptune
1887	First photographic charts of the stars made
1923–30	Edwin Hubble confirms theory of expanding universe
1930	Clyde Tombaugh discovers Pluto
1931	Karl Jansky develops radio astronomy
1957	Jodrell Bank telescope completed; launch of first earth satellite, Sputnik 1, by USSR
1958	Discovery of Van Allen radiation belts
1963	First quasar discovered
1965	First spacewalk (USSR)
1967	First pulsar discovered
1969	First manned landing on the moon (USA)
1971	First unmanned landing on Mars (USA)
1977	Discovery of rings of Uranus; launch of space probes Voyager 1 and 2
1978	Space probes Pioneer 1 and 2 reach Venus; discovery of Pluto's satellite Charon
1981	First launch of US space shuttle
1986	Return of Halley's comet; Voyager 2 passes Uranus; loss of Challenger space shuttle
1988	Detection of a supernova five billion light years distant from earth
1989	Voyager 2 passes Neptune
1990	Launch of Hubble Space Telescope (USA)
1991	Space probe Galileo flies past asteroid Gaspra
1992	NASA begin 10-year search for alien radio signals
1996	Mars Pathfinder explores surface of Mars
1997	Mars Global Surveyor conducts photographic survey of Mars
2000	Construction of international space station started

Significant space missions

Launch date	Mission	Country/Agency	Details
04 October 57	Sputnik 1	USSR	First earth satellite
03 November 57	Sputnik 2	USSR	Carried live dog Laika as passenger
31 January 58	Explorer 1	USA	Discovered Van Allen radiation belts
02 January 59	Luna 1	USSR	Escaped gravity of earth; discovered solar wind
17 February 59	Vanguard 2	USA	First photograph of earth from space
12 September 59	Luna 2	USSR	First lunar impact
04 October 59	Luna 3	USSR	Photographed far side of moon
01 April 60	TIROS 1	USA	Weather satellite
13 April 60	Transit 1B	USA	Navigation satellite
12 August 60	ECHO 1	USA	Communications satellite
19 August 60	Sputnik 5	USSR	Two dogs survived orbit
12 April 61	Vostok 1	USSR	Yuri Gagarin became first man in orbit
20 February 62	Mercury	USA	John Glenn became first US astronaut in orbit
26 August 62	Mariner 2	USA	Venus flyby
01 November 62	Mars 1	USSR	Mars flyby
16 June 63	Vostok 6	USSR	Valentina Tereshkova became first woman in orbit
28 July 64	Ranger 7	USA	Took first close-up television pictures of the moon
28 November 64	Mariner 4	USA	Mars flyby photographs
18 March 65	Voskhod 2	USSR	A. A. Leonov conducts first spacewalk
06 April 65	Early Bird	USA	Commercial geostationary communications satellite
16 November 65	Venera 3	USSR	Venus impact
26 November 65	A-1 Asterix	France	French-launched satellite
04 December 65	Gemini 7	USA	Manned rendezvous
15 December 65	Gemini 6	USA	Manned rendezvous
31 January 66	Luna 9	USSR	Transmitted pictures from surface of the moon
16 March 66	Gemini 8	USA	First manned docking
31 March 66	Luna 10	USSR	Lunar orbiter
30 May 66	Surveyor 1	USA	Soft landing on moon
10 August 66	Lunar Orbiter 1	USA	Lunar orbiter
17 April 67	Surveyor 3	USA	Lunar surface sampler
22–28 Oct 67	Cosmos 186/188	USSR	Automatic docking
29 November 67	WRESAT	Australia	Australian-launched satellite
14 September 68	Zond 5	USSR	Put animals in orbit
21 December 68	Apollo 8	USA	Manned orbit of moon
14 January 69	Soyuz 4	USSR	Transfer of crews
15 January 69	Soyuz 5	USSR	Transfer of crews
16 July 69	Apollo 11	USA	Neil Armstrong became first man to walk on the moon
11 February 70	Oshumi	Japan	Japanese-launched satellite
24 April 70	Long March	China	Chinese-launched satellite

Launch date	Mission	Country/Agency	Details
17 August 70	Venera 7	USSR	Soft landing on Venus
12 September 70	Luna 16	USSR	Unmanned sample return
10 November 70	Luna 17	USSR	Unmanned lunar rover
19 May 71	Mars 2	USSR	Orbited Mars
28 May 71	Mars 3	USSR	Soft landing on Mars
30 May 71	Mariner 9	USA	Orbited Mars
28 October 71	Prospero	UK	UK-launched satellite
03 March 72	Pioneer 10	USA	Jupiter and Pluto flyby; left solar system
1973	Skylab 1–4	USA	Took X-ray pictures of solar corona
06 April 73	Pioneer 11	USA	Saturn flyby
03 November 73	Mariner 10	USA	First detailed photographs of Mercury
08 June 75	Venera 9	USSR	Orbit and photographs of Venus
15 July 75	Apollo/Soyuz	USA/USSR	First joint international manned space mission
Aug/Sep 75	Viking 1, 2	USA	First photographs from surface of Mars
Aug/Sep 77	Voyager 1, 2	USA	Flyby of Jupiter, Saturn, Uranus and Neptune
1978	IUE	USA/UK/ESA*	First international space observatory
12 August 78	ISEE C	USA	Comet intercept
24 December 79	Ariane/CAT	ESA	European launcher
18 July 80	Rohini	India	Indian-launched satellite
12 April 81	STS 1	USA	First launch of Columbia space shuttle
04 April 83	STS 6	USA	First launch of Challenger space shuttle
27 June 83	Soyuz T9	USSR	Construction in space
28 November 83	STS 9	USA	First launch of ESA spacelab
30 August 84	STS 41 D	USA	First launch of Discovery space shuttle
08 November 84	STS 51 A	USA	Recovery of two satellites in orbit
15 December 84	Vega 1	USSR	Flyby of Halley's Comet
02 July 85	Giotto	ESA	Photographs of nucleus of Halley's Comet
03 October 85	STS 51 J	USA	First launch of Atlantis space shuttle
13 March 86	Soyuz T15	USSR	Ferry between space stations
21 December 87	Soyuz TM4/6	USSR	In space for a year
12 January 88	Phobos 2	USSR	Rendezvous with Phobos
29 September 88	STS 26	USA	Resumption of shuttle programme after loss of Challenger
15 November 88	Buran	USSR	Unmanned space shuttle
05 May 89	Magellan	USA	Radar map of Venus
18 October 89	STS 34	USA	Launch of Galileo space probe
24 January 90	Muses A	Japan	Two satellites placed in lunar orbit
05 April 90	Pegsat	USA	First airborne launch
24 April 90	STS 31	USA/ESA	Launch of Hubble Space Telescope
06 October 90	STS 41	USA/ESA	First flight over solar poles
02 December 90	Soyuz TM11	USSR	First flight with paying passengers
08 March 91	Lacrosse 2	USA	Radar surveillance

30 March 91	Almaz 1	USSR	Survey mapping
05 April 91	STS 37	USA	Launch of Compton Gamma Ray Observatory
07 May 92	STS 47	USA	First launch of Endeavour space shuttle
31 July 92	STS 49	USA/ESA	First launch of Eureca recoverable spacecraft
10 August 92	Topex/Poseidon	ESA	Geodetic mapping
02 December 93	STS 59	USA	Repair of Hubble Space Telescope
25 January 94	Clementine	USA	Lunar/asteroid exploration
29 June 95	STS 69	USA/Russia	Docking of Atlantis space shuttle and Mir space station
17 November 95	ISO	ESA	Infrared space observatory
02 December 95	SOHO	USA	Study of solar activity
17 February 96	NEAR	USA	Rendezvous with asteroid
07 November 96	MGS	USA	Global survey of Mars
04 December 96	MPF	USA	Exploration of Mars surface
12 February 97	Haruka	Japan	Radio astronomy
05 May 97	Iridium	USA	Communication constellation
15 October 97	Cassini/Huygens	USA	Study of Saturn and Titan in 2004
06 January 98	Lunar Prospector	USA	Study of lunar surface
24 October 98	Deep Space 1	USA	Flyby of Asteroid 1992 KD in 1999
11 December 98	Mars Climate Orbiter	USA	Mars probe
03 January 99	Mars Polar Lander	USA	Mars probe (contact lost in late 1999)
07 February 99	Stardust	USA	Interception of Comet Wild-2 in 2004
07 April 2001	Mars Surveyor Orbiter	USA	Mineralogical mapping of Mars

Note ESA = European Space Agency

Space agencies

Agency	Headquarters	Members
Agenzia Spaziale Italiana (ASI)	Rome	Italy
British National Space Centre (BNSC)	London	UK
Centre National d'Etudes Spatiales (CNES)	Paris	France
Deutsche Agentur für Raumfahrtangelegenheiten (DARA)	Bonn	Germany
European Space Agency (ESA)	Paris	Austria, Belgium, Denmark, France, Germany, Ireland, Italy, Netherlands, Norway, Spain, Sweden, Switzerland, UK
Forbairt Science and Technology Directorate	Dublin	Ireland
National Aeronautics and Space Administration (NASA)	Washington	USA
Russian Space Agency (RKA)	Moscow	Kazakhstan, Russia, Ukraine

Ground-based telescopes

Telescope	Observatory	Type	Mirror/dish size	Date
Anglo-Australian Telescope (AAT)	Anglo-Australian Observatory (Sliding Spring Mountain, NSW, Australia)	Optical	3.9 m	1974
Arecibo Telescope	National Astronomy and Ionosphere Centre (Puerto Rico)	Radio	304.8 m	1963
Australia Telescope	Commonwealth Scientific and Industrial Research Organization (NSW, Australia)	Radio	7 × 22m, 1 × 64 m	1990
Bol'shoi Teleskop Azimutal'nyi	Special Astrophysical Observatory (Mt Pastukhov, Zelenchukskaya, Russia)	Optical	6 m	1976
	Byurakan Astrophysical Observatory (Mt Aragatz, Armenia)	Optical	2.6 m	1976
C. Donald Shane Telescope	Lick Observatory (Mt Hamilton, California, USA)	Optical	3.05 m	1959
California Submillimetre Observatory	California Institute of Technology (Mauna Kea, Hawaii, USA)	Submillimetre	10.4 m	1986
Canada–France–Hawaii Telescope (CFHT)	Canada–France–Hawaii Telescope Corporation (Mauna Kea, Hawaii, USA)	Optical	3.6 m	1979
	Cerro Tololo Inter-American Observatory (Cerro Tololo, Chile)	Optical	4 m	1976
Effelsberg Radio Telescope	Max Planck Institut für Radioastronomie (Effelsberg, Bonn, Germany)	Radio	100 m	1971
ESO New Technology Telescope	European Southern Observatory (Cerro Tololo, Chile)	Optical	3.6 m	1990
ESO 3.6 m	European Southern Observatory (Cerro La Silla, Chile)	Optical	3.6 m	1976
	Five College Radio Astronomy (New Salem, Massachusetts, USA)	Radio	14 m	1969
George Ellery Hale Telescope	Palomar Observatory (Palomar Mountain, California, USA)	Optical	5.08 m	1948
	German–Spanish Astronomical Centre (Calar Alto, Spain)	Optical	3.5 m	1985
Irenee du Pont Telescope	Mt Wilson and Las Campanas Observatories (Cerro Las Campanas, Chile)	Optical	2.57 m	1977
IRAM Array	Institut de Radio Astronomie Millimétrique (Plateau de Bure, France)	Millimetre	4 × 15 m	1979
Isaac Newton Telescope	Observatory Roque de los Muchachos (La Palma, Canary Isles)	Optical	2.54 m	1984
James Clerk Maxwell Telescope (JCMT)	Royal Observatory, Edinburgh (Mauna Kea, Hawaii, USA)	Submillimetre	15 m	1987
Keck I	California Association for Research and Astronomy (Mauna Kea, Hawaii)	Optical/infrared	10 m	1993
Keck II	California Association for Research and Astronomy (Mauna Kea, Hawaii)	Optical	10 m	1996

Lovell Telescope	Nuffield Radio Astronomy Laboratory (Jodrell Bank, Cheshire, UK)	Radio	76 m	1957
	McDonald Observatory (Mt Locke, Texas, USA)	Optical	2.7 m	1968
MERLIN (Multi-Element Radio-Linked Interferometer Network)	Nuffield Radio Astronomy Laboratory (Jodrell Bank), University of Manchester (UK)	Radio	5 × 25 m, 1 × 32 m, 1 × 76 m	1980
Multiple Mirror Telescope	Whipple Observatory (Mt Hopkins, Arizona, USA)	Optical	4.5 m	1979
NASA Infrared Telescope Facility (IRTF)	NASA (Mauna Kea, Hawaii, USA)	Infrared	3 m	1979
	National Radio Astronomy Observatory (Kitt Peak, Arizona, USA)	Millimetre	12 m	1982
Nicholas U. Mayall Telescope	Kitt Peak National Observatory (Kitt Peak, Arizona, USA)	Optical	4 m	1973
Nobeyama Millimetre Array	Nobeyama Radio Observatory (Nobeyama, Japan)	Millimetre	5 × 10 m	1986
Nobeyama Radio Telescope	Nobeyama Radio Observatory (Nobeyama, Japan)	Radio	45 m	1970
Parkes Radio Telescope	Australian National Radio Observatory (Parkes, NSW, Australia)	Radio	64 m	1961
Shajin Telescope	Crimean Astrophysical Observatory (Simeis, Ukraine)	Optical	2.6 m	1961
Swedish/European Submillimetre Telescope	European Southern Observatory (Cerro Tololo, Chile)	Submillimetre	10 m	1987
United Kingdom Infrared Telescope (UKIRT)	Royal Observatory, Edinburgh (Mauna Kea, Hawaii, USA)	Infrared	3.8 m	1979
Very Large Array (VLA)	National Radio Astronomy Observatories (Socorro, New Mexico, USA)	Radio	27 × 25 m	1980–1
William Herschel Telescope	Observatory Roque de los Muchachos (La Palma, Canary Isles)	Optical	4.2 m	1987

2
The World

2.1 *The Earth*

Earth data

Age	4 500 000 000 years
Area	509 600 000 sq km (197 000 000 sq mi)
Mass	$5\,976 \times 10^{27}$ grams
Land surface	148 000 000 sq km (57 000 000 sq mi) (c. 29% of total)
Water surface	361 600 000 sq km (140 000 000 sq mi) (c. 71% of total)
Circumference (equator)	40 076 km (24 902 mi)
Circumference (meridian)	40 000 km (24 860 mi)
Diameter (equator)	12 757 km (7 927 mi)
Diameter (meridian)	12 714 km (7 900 mi)
Period of axial rotation	23 hours 56 mins 4.0996 secs
Temperature at core	4 500°C

Geological time scale

Era	Period	Epoch	Million years before present	Events
Precambrian	Archaean (Azoic)		4500	Formation of Earth's crust and oceans
	Early Proterozoic		2500	Formation of carbonate sediments
	Riphean	Early Middle Late	1600 1300 900	Appearance of first marine life
	Vendian		650	Appearance of first algae and invertebrates

Palaeozoic		Caerfai	590	Appearance of shelled invertebrates and trilobites
		St David's	540	
		Merioneth	525	
	Ordovician	Tremadoc	505	Volcanic activity; appearance of first vertebrates
		Arenig	488	
		Llanvirn	478	
		Llandeilo	468	
		Caradoc	458	
		Ashgill	448	
	Silurian	Llandovery	438	Formation of new mountain ranges; appearance of first leafless land plants
		Wenlock	428	
		Ludlow	421	
		Pridoli	414	
	Devonian	Early	408	Abundant sea life; appearance of first insects
		Middle	387	
		Late	374	
	Carboniferous	Mississippian	360	Amphibians and sharks; first land reptiles
		Pennsylvanian	320	
	Permian	Early	286	Glaciation of southern hemisphere
		Late	258	
Mesozoic	Triassic	Early	248	Climate becomes warm and wet; Gondwanaland super-continent breaks up into continents; first appearance of mammals, dinosaurs, crustaceans, and flies
		Middle	243	
		Late	231	
	Jurassic	Lias	213	Separation of continents continues; reptiles thrive; appearance of first birds and flowers
		Dogger	188	
		Malm	163	
	Cretaceous	Early	144	Extinction of dinosaurs
		Late	98	
Cenoxoic	Tertiary	Palaeocene	65	Appearance of first primates
		Eocene	55	Widespread jungle; mammals thrive
		Oligocene	38	Seas recede; appearance of first snails, pachyderms, canines, and felines
		Miocene	25	Europe and Asia join; giant sharks; grazing mammals thrive
		Pliocene	5	Ice caps form; disappearance of many species
	Quaternary	Pleistocene	2	Appearance of primitive humans
		Holocene	0.01	Glaciers recede; humans develop agriculture and technology

Ice ages

Years before the present	Name
1 800–2 700 million	Huronian
880–940 million	Gnejso
770–820 million	Sturtian
570–615 million	Verangian
430–440 million	Ordovician
250–330 million	Permo-Carboniferous (Gondwanan)
10 000–1.64 million	Pleistocene (the Ice Age)

Continents

Continent	Area	Percentage of total landmass	Highest point (above sea level)	Lowest point (below sea level)
Asia	44 493 000 sq km (17 179 000 sq mi)	29.60%	Mt Everest 8 848 m (29 028 ft)	Dead Sea 400 m (1 312 ft)
Africa	30 293 000 sq km (11 696 000 sq mi)	20.20%	Mt Kilimanjaro 5 895 m (19 340 ft)	Lake Assal 156 m (512 ft)
North America	24 454 000 sq km (9 442 000 sq mi)	16.30%	Mt McKinley 6 194 m (20 320 ft)	Death Valley 86 m (282 ft)
South America	17 838 000 sq km (6 887 000 sq mi)	11.90%	Mt Aconcagua 6 960 m (22 831 ft)	Peninsular Valdez 40 m (131 ft)
Antarctica	13 975 000 sq km (5 396 000 sq mi)	9.30%	Vinson Massif 5 140 m (16 864 ft)	Bently subglacial trench 2 538 m (8 327 ft)
Europe*	10 245 000 sq km (3 956 000 sq mi)	6.80%	Mt Elbrus 5 642 m (18 510 ft)	Caspian Sea 29 m (94 ft)
Oceania	8 945 000 sq km (3 454 000 sq mi)	5.90%	Puncak Jaya 5 030 m (16 500 ft)	Lake Eyre 15 (49 ft)

Note Europe here includes the former USSR west of the Urals

Oceans

Ocean	Area	Percentage of total oceans	Average depth	Deepest point
Pacific	166 240 000 sq km (64 186 300 sq mi)	46%	4 300 m (14 100 ft)	Mariana Trench 11 040 m (36 220 ft)
Atlantic	86 550 000 sq km (33 420 000 sq mi)	24%	3 700 m (12 100 ft)	Puerto Rico Trench 8 648 m (28 372 ft)
Indian	73 427 000 sq km (28 350 500 sq mi)	20%	3 900 m (12 800 ft)	Java Trench 7 725 m (25 344 ft)
Arctic	9 485 000 sq km (3 662 000 sq mi)	3%	1 330 m (4 400 ft)	Eurasia Basin 5 122 m (16 804 ft)

Seas

Sea	Area
Coral Sea	4 791 000 sq km (1 850 000 sq mi)
Arabian Sea	3 863 000 sq km (1 492 000 sq mi)
S China Sea	3 685 000 sq km (1 423 000 sq mi)
Mediterranean Sea	2 516 000 sq km (971 000 sq mi)
Bering Sea	2 304 000 sq km (890 000 sq mi)
Bay of Bengal	2 172 000 sq km (839 000 sq mi)
Sea of Okhotsk	1 590 000 sq km (614 000 sq mi)
Gulf of Mexico	1 543 000 sq km (596 000 sq mi)
Gulf of Guinea	1 533 000 sq km (592 000 sq mi)
Barents Sea	1 405 000 sq km (542 000 sq mi)
Norwegian Sea	1 383 000 sq km (534 000 sq mi)
Gulf of Alaska	1 327 000 sq km (512 000 sq mi)
Hudson Bay	1 232 000 sq km (476 000 sq mi)
Greenland Sea	1 205 000 sq km (465 000 sq mi)
Arafura Sea	1 037 000 sq km (400 000 sq mi)
Philippine Sea	1 036 000 sq km (400 000 sq mi)
Sea of Japan	978 000 sq km (378 000 sq mi)
E Siberian Sea	901 000 sq km (348 000 sq mi)
Kara Sea	883 000 sq km (341 000 sq mi)
E China Sea	664 000 sq km (256 000 sq mi)
Andaman Sea	565 000 sq km (218 000 sq mi)
North Sea	520 000 sq km (201 000 sq mi)
Black Sea	508 900 sq km (196 000 sq mi)
Red Sea	453 000 sq km (175 000 sq mi)
Baltic Sea	414 000 sq km (160 000 sq mi)
Arabian/Persian Gulf	238 000 sq km (92 200 sq mi)
Gulf of St Lawrence	238 300 sq km (92 000 sq mi)

Island groups

Name	Country	Ocean/Sea	Number of islands	Main islands
Aeolian	Italy	Mediterranean	7	Stromboli, Lipari, Vulcanö, Salina
Åland	Finland	Gulf of Bothnia	6 554	Eckerö, Lemland, Vardö, Lumparland
Aleutian	USA	Pacific	150	Andreanof, Adak
Alexander	Canada	Pacific	1 100	Baranof, Prince of Wales
Andaman	India	Bay of Bengal	over 300	N Andaman, S Andaman
Antilles, Greater		Caribbean		Cuba, Jamaica, Haiti and the Dominican Republic, Puerto Rico
Antilles, Lesser		Caribbean		Windward, Leeward, Netherlands Antilles
Arctic Archipelago	Canada	Arctic		Baffin
Azores	Portugal	Atlantic	9	São Miguel, Flores

Name	Country	Ocean/Sea	Number of islands	Main islands
Bahamas	Bahamas	Atlantic	700	New Providence, Grand Bahama
Balearic	Spain	Mediterranean	5	Mallorca, Menorca, Ibiza
Bismarck	Papua New Guinea	Pacific	2 000	New Britain, New Ireland, Admiralty Island
Bijagos	Guinea-Bissau	Atlantic	15	Orango, Formoza, Caravela, Roxa
Canary	Spain	Atlantic	7	Tenerife, Gomera, Lanzarote, Las Palmas
Cape Verde	Cape Verde	Atlantic	10	Barlavento group, Sotavento group
Caroline	USA	Pacific	680	Yop, Pohnpei, Truk
Channel	UK	English Channel	4	Guernsey, Jersey, Sark, Alderney
Commander	Russia	Bering Sea	4	Bering, Medny
Comoros	Republic of Comoros	Mozambique Channel	4	Grand Mohore, Anjouan, Moheli, Mayotte
Cook	New Zealand	Pacific	15	Palmerston, Rarotonga, Mangaia
Cyclades	Greece	Aegean	c.220	Andros, Mikonos, Paros
Dodecanese	Greece	Aegean	12	Rhodes, Kos
Falkland	UK	Atlantic	200	W Falkland, E Falkland, S Georgia
Faroe	Denmark	Atlantic	22	Strømø, Østerø
Fiji	Fiji	Pacific	844	Viti Levu, Vanua Levu
Galapagos	Ecuador	Pacific	16	Santa Cruz, Santiago
Gotland	Sweden	Baltic	2	Gotland, Fårö
Greenland	Denmark	N Atlantic, Arctic	2	Greenland, Disko
Hawaiian	USA	Pacific	8	Hawaii, Oahu
Hebrides	UK	Atlantic	500	Lewis, Skye, Mull
Ionian	Greece	Aegean	7	Kerkira, Levkas
Japan	Japan	Pacific	over 1 000	Honshu, Hokkaido, Kyushu, Shikoku
Juan Fernandez	Chile	Pacific	3	Mas a Tierra, Santa Clara
Kuril	Russia/Japan	Pacific	56	Shumsu, Iturup
Laccadive	India	Arabian Sea	27	Laccadive, Amaindivi
Lofoten	Norway	Norwegian Sea	5	Hinnoy, Austvagoy
Madeira	Portugal	Atlantic	4	Madeira
Malay Archipelago	Indonesia/ Malaysia/ Philippines	Pacific/Indian	20 000	Borneo, New Guinea, Sumatra, Java, Philippine Islands
Maldives	Republic of Maldives	Indian	1 190	Male
Malta	Republic of Malta	Mediterranean	5	Malta, Gozo
Mariana	Mariana Islands	Pacific	14	Saipan, Tinian, Rota
Marquesas	France	Pacific	10	Nukultiva
Marshall	Marshall Islands	Pacific	more than 1 200	Bikini
Mascarene	France	Indian	3	Réunion, Mauritius, Rodrigues
Melanesia		Pacific		Solomon, Bismarck, Fiji, New Guinea

Micronesia		Pacific		Caroline, Gilbert, Marshalls, Kiribati
New Hebrides	Republic of Vanuatu	Pacific	72	Espiritu Santo
Newfoundland	Canada	Atlantic		Newfoundland
New Zealand	New Zealand	Pacific	over 4	North, South
Nicobar	India	Bay of Bengal	over 300	Great Nicobar
Novaya Semlya	Russia	Arctic	5	North, South
Orkney	UK	North Sea	20	Mainland, Ronaldsay
Philippines	Republic of the Philippines	Pacific	7100	Luzon, Mindanao, Samar
Polynesia		Pacific		Hawaii, Tonga, Kiribati, Easter, Samoa
Queen Charlotte	Canada	Pacific	150	Prince Rupert
São Tomé and Príncipe	Republic of São Tomé and Príncipe	Atlantic	2	São Tomé, Príncipe
Scilly	UK	English Channel	140	St Mary's, Tresco, St Martin's
Seychelles	Republic of Seychelles	Indian	115	Mahé, La Digue
Shetland	UK	North Sea	over 500	Mainland, Yell, Unst
Society	France	Pacific	2	Tahiti
Solomon	Solomon Islands	Pacific	over 6	New Georgia, San Cristobal
South Orkney	UK	Atlantic	2	Coronation, Laurie
Sri Lanka	Republic of Sri Lanka	Indian	2	Sri Lanka, Mannar
Taiwan	Republic of China	China Sea/Pacific		Taiwan
Tasmania	Australia	Tasman Sea	over 5	Tasmania, King Flinders, Bruny
Tierra del Fuego	Argentina/ Chile	Pacific		
Tristan da Cunha	UK	Atlantic	5	Gough, Inaccessible, Nightingale
Tuamotu	France	Pacific	80	Rangiroa, Hao, Fakarava
Tuvalu	Tuvalu	Pacific	9	Funafuti Atoll, Nanumea
Virgin	USA	Caribbean	over 50	St Croix, St Thomas
Virgin	UK	Caribbean	36	Tortola, Virgin Gorda
Zanzibar	Tanzania	Indian	3	Zanzibar, Tumbatu

Largest islands

Island	Area
Greenland (N Atlantic)	2 175 600 sq km (830 780 sq mi)
New Guinea (SW Pacific)	790 000 sq km (305 000 sq mi)
Borneo (SW Pacific)	737 000 sq km (285 000 sq mi)
Madagascar (Indian Ocean)	587 000 sq km (227 600 sq mi)
Baffin (Canadian Arctic)	507 000 sq km (196 000 sq mi)
Sumatra (Indian Ocean)	425 000 sq km (164 900 sq mi)

Island	Area
Honshu (NW Pacific)	228 000 sq km (88 000 sq mi)
Great Britain (N Atlantic)	219 000 sq km (84 400 sq mi)
Victoria (Canadian Arctic)	217 300 sq km (83 900 sq mi)
Ellesmere (Canadian Arctic)	196 000 sq km (75 800 sq mi)
Sulawesi (Indian Ocean)	174 000 sq km (67 400 sq mi)
South Island, New Zealand (SW Pacific)	151 000 sq km (58 200 sq mi)
Java (Indian Ocean)	129 000 sq km (50 000 sq mi)
North Island, New Zealand (SW Pacific)	114 000 sq km (44 200 sq mi)
Cuba (Caribbean Sea)	110 860 sq km (42 790 sq mi)
Newfoundland (NW Atlantic)	109 000 sq km (42 000 sq mi)
Luzon (W Pacific)	105 000 sq km (40 400 sq mi)
Iceland (N Atlantic)	103 000 sq km (40 000 sq mi)
Mindanao (W Pacific)	94 600 sq km (36 500 sq mi)
Novaya Zemlya islands (Barents Sea)	90 600 sq km (35 000 sq mi)
Hokkaido (NW Pacific)	78 500 sq km (30 300 sq mi)
Hispaniola (Caribbean Sea)	77 200 sq km (29 800 sq mi)
Sakhalin (NW Pacific)	75 100 sq km (29 000 sq mi)
Tierra del Fuego (S Atlantic)	71 200 sq km (27 500 sq mi)
Ireland (N Atlantic)	70 280 sq km (27 100 sq mi)

Largest lakes

Lake	Area
Caspian Sea (Iran/Azerbaijan/Russia/ Turkmenistan/Kazakhstan)	371 000 sq km (143 240 sq mi)
Superior (USA/Canada)	82 260 sq km (31 760 sq mi)
Aral Sea (Kazakhstan)	64 500 sq km (24 900 sq mi)
Victoria (E Africa)	62 940 sq km (24 300 sq mi)
Huron (USA/Canada)	59 580 sq km (23 000 sq mi)
Michigan (USA)	58 020 sq km (22 400 sq mi)
Tanganyika (E Africa)	32 000 sq km (12 350 sq mi)
Baikal (Russia)	31 500 sq km (12 160 sq mi)
Great Bear (Canada)	31 330 sq km (12 100 sq mi)
Great Slave (Canada)	28 570 sq km (11 030 sq mi)
Erie (USA/Canada)	25 710 sq km (9 920 sq mi)
Winnipeg (Canada)	24 390 sq km (9 420 sq mi)
Malawi/Nyasa (E Africa)	22 490 sq km (8 680 sq mi)
Ontario (Canada/USA)	19 270 sq km (7 440 sq mi)
Balkhash (Kazakhstan)	18 300 sq km (7 000 sq mi)
Ladoga (Russia)	18 130 sq km (7 000 sq mi)
Chad (W Africa)	10 000–26 000 sq km (4 000–10 000 sq mi)
Maracaibo (Venezuela)	13 010 sq km (5 020 sq mi)
Patos (Brazil)	10 140 sq km (3 920 sq mi)
Onega (Russia)	9 800 sq km (3 800 sq mi)

Longest rivers

River	Source	Outflow	Length
Nile	River Luvironza (Burundi)	E Mediterranean	6 690 km (4 160 mi)
Amazon	Lago Villafro (Peru)	S Atlantic	6 570 km (4 080 mi)
Mississippi	Missouri (S USA)	Gulf of Mexico	6 020 km (3 740 mi)
Chang Jiang (Yangtze)	Kunlun Mountains (W China)	Yellow Sea	5 980 km (3 720 mi)
Yenisey	Angara (W Mongolia)	Kara Sea	5 870 km (3 650 mi)
Amur	Khingan Mountains (N China)	Tartar Strait	5 780 km (3 590 mi)
Ob	Irtysh (W Mongolia)	Kara Sea	5 410 km (3 360 mi)
Plata	Paraná (central Brazil)	S Atlantic	4 880 km (3 030 mi)
Huang Ho (Yellow)	Bayan Har Shan range (central China)	Yellow Sea	4 840 km (3 010 mi)
Congo	River Lualaba (Congo)	Atlantic	4 630 km (2 880 mi)
Lena	River Kirenga (W of Lake Baykal)	Laptev Sea	4 400 km (2 730 mi)
Mackenzie	Tatlatui Lake (British Columbia)	Beaufort Sea	4 240 km (2 630 mi)
Mekong	Lants'ang (Tibet)	S China Sea	4 180 km (2 600 mi)
Niger	Loma Mountains (Guinea)	Gulf of Guinea	4 100 km (2 550 mi)
Murray–Darling	SE Queensland (Australia)	Lake Alexandrina (S Australia)	3 717 km (2 310 mi)

Highest waterfalls

Waterfall	Height*
Angel (Venezuela)	807 m (2 648 ft)
Itatinga (Brazil)	628 m (2 060 ft)
Cuquenan (Guyana–Venezuela)	610 m (2 000 ft)
Ormeli (Norway)	563 m (1 847 ft)
Tysse (Norway)	533 m (1 749 ft)
Pilao (Brazil)	524 m (1 719 ft)
Ribbon (USA)	491 m (1 612 ft)
Vestre Mardola (Norway)	468 m (1 535 ft)
Roraima (Guyana)	457 m (1 500 ft)
Cleve–Garth (New Zealand)	450 m (1476 ft)

Note Figures relate to longest individual fall

Highest mountains

Mountain	Height	First ascent
Everest (China–Nepal)	8 850 m (29 030 ft)	1953
K2 (Kashmir–Jammu)	8 610 m (28 250 ft)	1954
Kangchenjunga (India–Nepal)	8 600 m (28 210 ft)	1955
Lhotse (China–Nepal)	8 510 m (27 920 ft)	1956
Yalung Kang (India–Nepal)	8 500 m (27 890 ft)	1973
Kangchenjunga S Peak (India–Nepal)	8 490 m (27 850 ft)	1978

Mountain	Height	First ascent
Makalu I (China–Nepal)	8 480 m (27 820 ft)	1955
Kangchenjunga Middle Peak (India–Nepal)	8 470 m (27 800 ft)	1973
Lhotse Shar (China–Nepal)	8 380 m (27 500 ft)	1970
Dhaulagiri (Nepal)	8 170 m (26 810 ft)	1960
Manaslu (Nepal)	8 160 m (26 760 ft)	1956
Cho Oyu (China–Nepal)	8 150 m (26 750 ft)	1954
Nanga Parbat (Kashmir–Jammu)	8 130 m (26 660 ft)	1953
Annapurna I (Nepal)	8 080 m (26 470 ft)	1950
Gasherbrum I (Kashmir–Jammu)	8 070 m (26 470 ft)	1958
Broad Peak (Kashmir–Jammu)	8 050 m (26 400 ft)	1957
Gasherbrum II (Kashmir–Jammu)	8 030 m (26 360 ft)	1956
Gosainthan (China)	8 000 m (26 250 ft)	1964
Broad Peak (Kashmir–Jammu)	7 950 m (26 090 ft)	1975
Gasherbrum III (Kashmir–Jammu)	7 940 m (26 040 ft)	1975

Largest deserts

Desert	Area
Sahara (N Africa)	8 600 000 sq km (3 320 000 sq mi)
Arabian (SW Asia)	2 330 000 sq km (900 000 sq mi)
Gobi (Mongolia/NE China)	1 166 000 sq km (450 000 sq mi)
Patagonian (Argentina)	673 000 sq km (260 000 sq mi)
Great Basin (SW USA)	492 000 sq km (190 000 sq mi)
Chihuahuan (Mexico)	450 000 sq km (175 000 sq mi)
Great Sandy (NW Australia)	450 000 sq km (175 000 sq mi)
Sonoran (SW USA)	310 000 sq km (120 000 sq mi)
Kyzyl-Kum (Kazakhstan/Uzbekistan)	300 000 sq km (115 000 sq mi)
Takla Makan (N China)	270 000 sq km (105 000 sq mi)
Kalahari (SW Africa)	260 000 sq km (100 000 sq mi)
Kara-Kum (Turkmenistan)	260 000 sq km (100 000 sq mi)
Kavir (Iran)	260 000 sq km (100 000 sq mi)
Syrian (Saudi Arabia/Jordan/Syria/Iraq)	260 000 sq km (100 000 sq mi)
Nubian (Sudan)	260 000 sq km (100 000 sq mi)
Great Victoria (SW Australia)	235 000 sq km (125 000 sq mi)
Thar (India/Pakistan)	200 000 sq km (77 000 sq mi)
Ust'-Urt (Kazakhstan/Uzbekistan)	160 000 sq km (62 000 sq mi)
Bet-Pak-Dala (Kazakhstan)	155 000 sq km (60 000 sq mi)
Simpson (C Australia)	145 000 sq km (56 000 sq mi)

Deepest caves

Cave	Depth
Jean Bernard (France)	1 494 m (4 900 ft)
Snezhnaya (Russia)	1 340 m (4 397 ft)
Puertas de Illamina (Spain)	1 338 m (4 390 ft)
Pierre-Saint-Martin (France)	1 321 m (4 334 ft)
Sistema Huautla (Mexico)	1 240 m (4 067 ft)

Berger (France)	1 198 m (3 930 ft)
Vqerdi (Spain)	1 195 m (3 921 ft)
Dachstein-Mammuthöhle (Austria)	1 174 m (3 852 ft)
Zitu (Spain)	1 139 m (3 737 ft)
Badalona (Spain)	1 130 m (3 707 ft)
Batmanhöhle (Austria)	1 105 m (3 626 ft)
Schneeloch (Austria)	1 101 m (3 612 ft)
GES Malaga (Spain)	1 070 m (3 510 ft)
Lamprechtsofen (Austria)	1 024 m (3 360 ft)

Major volcanoes

Volcano	Height	Major eruptions	Last eruption
Aconcagua (Argentina)	6 959 m (22 831 ft)		extinct
Ararat (Turkey)	5 137 m (16 853 ft)	Holocene	extinct
Awu (Sangihe Island, Indonesia)	1 327 m (4 355 ft)	1711, 1856, 1892, 1968	1992
Bezymianny (Russia)	2 800 m (9 186 ft)	1955–6, 1981	1997
Coseguina (Nicaragua)	847 m (2 779 ft)	1835	1835
Cotopaxi (Ecuador)	5 897 m (19 347 ft)	1877	1975
El Chichón (Mexico)	1 350 m (4 430 ft)	1982	1982
Erebus (Antarctica)	4 023 m (13 200 ft)	1947, 1972, 1980, 1986, 1991	1995
Etna (Italy)	3 239 m (10 625 ft)	122, 1169, 1329, 1536, 1669, 1928, 1964, 1971, 1981, 1986, 1992	1999
Fuji (Japan)	3 776 m (12 388 ft)	1707	1707
Galunggung (Java)	2 181 m (7 155 ft)	1822, 1918	1982
Hekla (Iceland)	1 500 m (4 920 ft)	1693, 1845, 1947–8, 1970, 1981	1991
Helgafell (Iceland)	215 m (706 ft)	1973	1973
Hudson (Chile)	1 750 m (5 742 ft)	1971, 1973	1991
Jurullo (Mexico)	1 330 m (4 355 ft)	1759–74	1774
Katmai (Alaska)	2 047 m (6 715 ft)	1912, 1920, 1921, 1931, 1962	1974
Kilauea (Hawaii)	1 250 m (4 100 ft)	1823–4, 1952, 1955, 1960, 1967 8, 1968–74, 1983–7, 1988, 1991, 1992, 1994	1998
Kilimanjaro (Tanzania)	5 928 m (19 450 ft)	Pleistocene	extinct
Klyuchevskoy (Russia)	4 850 m (15 910 ft)	1700–1966, 1984, 1985, 1993	1997
Krakatoa (Sumatra)	818 m (2 685 ft)	1680, 1883, 1927, 1952–3, 1969, 1980	1996
La Soufrière (St Vincent)	1 234 m (4 048 ft)	1718, 1812, 1902, 1971–2	1979
Laki (Iceland)	500 m (1 642 ft)	1783, 1784, 1938	1996
Lamington (Papua New Guinea)	1 781 m (5 844 ft)	1951	1956
Lassen Peak (USA)	3 186 m (10 543 ft)	1914–15	1921
Mauna Loa (Hawaii)	4 171 m (13 685 ft)	1750, 1859, 1880, 1887, 1919, 1950, 1984	1987
Mayon (Philippines)	2 464 m (8 084 ft)	1616, 1766, 1814, 1897, 1968, 1978	1993

Volcano	Height	Major eruptions	Last eruption
Nyamuragira (Congo, Democratic Republic of)	3 056 m (10 026 ft)	1884, 1921–38, 1971, 1980, 1984, 1988	1998
Paricutín (Mexico)	3 188 m (10 460 ft)	1943–52	1952
Pelée, Mont (Martinique)	1 397 m (4 584 ft)	1902, 1929–32	1932
Pinatubo, Mt (Philippines)	1 759 m (5 770 ft)	1391, 1991	1995
Popocatèpetl (Mexico)	5 483 m (17 990 ft)	1347, 1920	1998
Rainier, Mt (USA)	4 394 m (14 416 ft)	1st century BC, 1820, 1825	1882
Ruapehu (New Zealand)	2 797 m (9 175 ft)	1945, 1953, 1969, 1975	1997
St Helens, Mt (USA)	2 549 m (8 364 ft)	1800, 1831, 1835, 1842–3, 1857, 1980, 1982, 1987	1991
Santorini/Thira (Greece)	566 m (1 857 ft)	1470 BC, 197 BC, AD 46, 1570–73, 1707–11, 1866–70, 1950	1998
Soufrière Hills (Montserrat)	968 m (3 176 ft)	1995–	1999
Stromboli (Italy)	931 m (3 055 ft)	1768, 1882, 1889, 1907, 1930, 1936, 1941, 1950, 1952, 1975, 1986, 1990	1998
Surtsey (Iceland)	174 m (570 ft)	1963–7	1967
Taal (Philippines)	1 448 m (4 752 ft)	1906, 1911, 1965, 1969, 1977	1988
Tambora (Sumbawa, Indonesia)	2 868 m (9 410 ft)	1815	1880
Tarawera (New Zealand)	1 149 m (3 770 ft)	1886	1973
Unzen (Japan)	1 360 m (4 461 ft)	1360, 1791, 1991	1996
Vesuvius (Italy)	1 289 m (4 230 ft)	79, 472, 1036, 1631, 1779, 1906	1944
Vulcano (Italy)	503 m (1 650 ft)	antiquity, 1444, 1730–40, 1786, 1873, 1888–90	1890

Earthquake severity scales

Richter Scale*

Magnitude	Relative amount of energy released
1	1
2	31
3	960
4	30 000
5	920 000
6	29 000 000
7	890 000 000
8	28 000 000 000
9	850 000 000 000

Note Named after US seismologist Charles Richter (1900–1985)

Mercalli scale

Intensity	Effects
I	Not felt
II	Felt by persons at rest on upper floors etc.
III	Felt indoors; vibrations similar to that of a passing truck; hanging objects swing; duration estimated
IV	Felt indoors by many; sleepers awoken; jolt similar to heavy truck striking building; windows, dishes, doors rattle; walls and frames creak; standing cars rock
V	Felt by most people; dishes and windows broken; doors swing; unstable objects overturned; pictures move
VI	Felt by everyone; slight damage; weak plaster and masonry crack; heavy furniture moved
VII	Difficult to stand; slight damage to good buildings; considerable damage to poor housing; some chimneys broken
VIII	Considerable damage to most buildings; poor housing badly affected; fall of walls and chimneys; branches broken off trees; cracks in ground
IX	General panic; considerable damage to all buildings; buildings shifted off foundations; underground pipes break; major cracks in ground
X	Most masonry and frame structures destroyed with foundations; rails bent; serious damage to dams, dykes, embankments; major landslides
XI	Few structures left standing; bridges destroyed; rails bent greatly; underground pipelines destroyed
XII	Damage total; objects thrown into the air; lines of sight and level distorted

Note Named after Italian seismologist Giuseppe Mercalli (1850–1914)

| *Major earthquakes*

Year	Location	Magnitude	Estimated number of deaths
526	Antioch (Turkey)		250 000
856	Corinth (Greece)		45 000
1268	Silicia (Asia Minor)		60 000
1290	Chihli (China)		100 000
1556	Shensi (China)		830 000
1667	Caucasia (Caucasus)		80 000
1693	Catania (Italy)		60 000
1730	Hokkaido (Japan)		137 000
1737	Calcutta (India)		300 000
1755	Lisbon (Portugal)		70 000
1783	Calabria (Italy)		50 000
1868	Ecuador/Colombia		70 000
1906	San Francisco (USA)	8.3	500
1906	Valparaiso (Chile)	8.6	20 000
1908	Messina (Italy)	7.5	120 000
1915	Avezzano (Italy)	7.5	30 000
1920	Gansu (China)	8.6	180 000
1923	Kwanto (Japan)	8.3	143 000
1927	Nan-shan (China)	8.3	200 000
1932	Gansu (China)	7.6	70 000
1935	Quetta (India)	7.5	60 000
1939	Chillan (Chile)	7.8	30 000

Year	Location	Magnitude	Estimated number of deaths
1939	Erzincan (Turkey)	7.9	23 000
1960	Agadir (Morocco)	5.8	12 000
1962	NW Iran	7.1	12 000
1964	Anchorage (USA)	8.5	131
1968	NE Iran	7.4	11 600
1970	Chimbote (Peru)	7.7	66 000
1972	S Iran	6.9	5 000
1972	Managua (Nicaragua)	6.2	5 000
1974	Kashmir	6.3	5 200
1976	Guatemala City	7.5	22 778
1976	Tangshan (China)	8.2	242 000
1978	NE Iran	7.7	25 000
1980	El Asnam (Algeria)	7.3	5 000
1980	S Italy	7.2	4 500
1982	N Yemen	6.0	2 800
1985	Mexico City	8.1	7 200
1988	Nepal/India	6.9	900
1988	SW China	7.6	1 000
1988	Armenia	7.0	25 000
1989	San Francisco	6.9	100
1990	Philippines	7.7	1 600
1990	Romania	6.6	70
1990	N Peru	5.8	200
1990	NW Iran	7.5	40 000
1990	Cabanatuan City	7.7	1 653
1991	Pakistan	6.8	300
1991	Afghanistan	6.8	1 000
1991	Georgis	7.2	100
1991	Costa Rica/Panama	7.5	80
1991	Uttar Pradesh (India)	6.1	1 000
1992	Nusa Tenggara Island (Indonesia)	6.8	2 500
1992	Erzincan (Turkey)	6.8	500
1992	Kyrgyzstan		c. 50
1992	Joshua Tree and Yucca Valley, California (USA)	7.4	2
1992	Cairo (Egypt)	5.9	552
1992	Maumere, Flores Island (Indonesia)	7.5	1 232
1993	Papua New Guinea	6.8	60
1993	Okushiri and Hokkaido Islands (N Japan)	7.8	185
1993	Guam (Mariana Islands)	8.1	
1993	Maharashta State (India)	6.5	22 000
1994	Los Angeles, California (USA)	6.8	61
1994	Halmahera Island (Indonesia)	6.8	c. 7
1994	Sumatra Island (Indonesia)	7.2	215
1994	Java (Indonesia)	7.7	200
1994	Paez River Valley (SW Colombia)	6.8	269
1994	Bolivia	8.2	5
1994	NW Algeria	5.6	c. 171
1994	Hokkaido (Japan) and Kuril Island (Russia)	8.2	c. 16
1994	Mindoro Island (Philippines)		60

1995	Kobe (Japan)	7.2	6 300
1995	W Colombia	6.4	31
1995	Neftegorsk, Sakhalin Island (Russia)	7.5	2 000
1995	Egion, Gulf of Corinth (Greece)	6.1	c. 20
1995	S Mexico	7.3	
1995	Sungai Penuh, S Sumatra (Indonesia)	6.7	84
1995	Manzanillo (Mexico)	7.6	66
1995	Dinar (Turkey)	6	c. 71
1995	Kuril Island (Russia)	7.9	0
1996	Lijiang, Yunan Province (China)	7	304
1996	Andreanof Island (Alaska)	7.9	
1996	Samar (Philippines)	7.9	
1996	Flores Sea (Indonesia)	7.9	
1996	Biak Island (Indonesia)	7.9	108
1996	Xinjiang Region (China)	6.9	26
1996	Inner Mongolia (China)	6.4	c. 14
1997	Ardabil (NW Iran)	5.5	c. 965
1997	Qayen (E Iran)	7.1	2 400
1997	Assisi (central Italy)	6	9
1998	Rustaq (Afghanistan)	6.1	c. 4 000
1999	Armenia (Colombia)	6	c. 2 000
1999	Izmit (Turkey)	7.4	c. 15 000
1999	Taiwan	7.6	c. 2 000
2000	NW Japan	7.1	
2001	Gujarat (India)	7.9	c. 30 000
2001	El Salvador	7.9	c. 1 000

Major tsunamis

Year	Location	Deaths
1498	Japan	5 000
1605	Japan	4 000
1611	Japan	5 000
1629	Indonesia	
1692	Jamaica	2 000
1707	Japan	30 000
1724	Peru	
1737	Kamchatka, Kuril Islands	
1741	Japan	c. 1 000
1746	Peru	5 000
1775	W Europe, Morocco, West Indies	60 000
1771	Ryukyu Islands	11 941
1783	Italy	30 000
1792	Japan	9 745
1800	Indonesia	400–500
1854	Japan	3 000
1868	Hawaii	81
1868	Chile, Hawaii	25 000
1877	Chile, Hawaii	many
1883	Java, Sumatra	36 000

Year	Location	Deaths
1896	Japan	27 122
1918	Kuril Islands, Russia, Japan, Hawaii	23
1923	Kamchatka, Hawaii	3
1933	Japan, Hawaii	3 000
1944	Japan	998
1946	Japan	1 997
1946	Aleutian Islands, Hawaii, California	165
1952	Kamchatka, Kuril Islands, Hawaii	many
1957	Hawaii, Japan	0
1960	Chile, Hawaii, Japan	1 260
1964	Alaska, Aleutian Islands, California	122
1976	Philippines	5 000
1979	Indonesia	187
1983	Japan, Korea	103
1990	Bangladesh	370
1992	Nicaragua	167
1992	Indonesia	400
1993	Japan, Russia	202
1994	Java	223
1994	Skagway, Alaska	1
1996	Indonesia	9
1996	Indonesia	161
1996	Peru	12
1998	Papua New Guinea	c. 2 000

Major hurricanes, typhoons, cyclones, and storms

Year	Storm	Location	Deaths
1588	Winter Storm	UK (sinking of Spanish Armada)	20 000
1737	Cyclone	Calcutta (India)	300 000
1780	Hurricane	West Indies, Barbados, Martinique, St Vincent, Guadeloupe	24 000
1791	Hurricane	Cuba	3 000
1822	Cyclone	Bakarganj (Bangladesh)	50 000
1864	Cyclone	Calcutta (India)	50 000
1876	Cyclone	Bakarganj (Bangladesh)	215 000
1881	Typhoon	China	300 000
1882	Cyclone	Bombay (India)	100 000
1884	Typhoon	W Japan	2 000
1893	Hurricane	S Carolina, Georgia	1 000
1897	Typhoon	Leyte (Philippines)	10 000
1899	Hurricane	San Ciriaco	3 369
1900	Hurricane	Galveston (N Texas)	6 000
1906	Hurricane	Mississippi, Alabama, Florida	134
1906	Hurricane	SE Florida	164
1906	Typhoon	Hong Kong	10 000
1909	Hurricane	Louisiana	350
1912	Typhoon	Wenchang (China)	50 000
1913	Tornado	Ohio, Indiana	700

1915	Hurricane	Galveston (N Texas), New Orleans (Louisiana)	550
1917	Typhoon	Honshu (Japan)	4 000
1919	Hurricane	Florida Keys, S Texas	600–900
1922	Typhoon	Shantou (China)	28 000
1926	Hurricane	Miama (Florida)	243
1928	Hurricane	Lake Okeechobee (Florida)	1 836
1930	Hurricane	San Zenon, Santo Domingo, Dominican Republic	2 000
1931	Hurricane	Belize	2 000
1932	Hurricane	Cuba	2 500
1932	Hurricane	Freeport (Texas)	40
1933	Hurricane	S Texas	40
1935	Hurricane	Florida Keys	408
1938	Hurricane	New England	600
1940	Hurricane	Georgia, S Carolina, N Carolina	50
1942	Cyclone	Bangladesh	61 000
1944	Hurricane	NE USA	390
1945	Typhoon	Makurazaki (Japan)	3 756
1947	Hurricane	SE Florida, Louisiana, Mississippi	51
1954	Typhoon	Toyama, N Honshu (Japan)	3 000
1954	Hurricane Carol	NE USA	60
1954	Hurricane Hazel	S Caroline, N Carolina	95
1955	Hurricane Diane	NE USA	184
1957	Hurricane Audrey	Louisiana, N Texas	390
1959	Typhoon Vera	Ise Bay (Japan)	5 098
1960	Hurricane Donna	Florida, E USA	50
1961	Hurricane Carla	Texas	46
1963	Hurricane Flora	Haiti, Cuba, Dominican Republic	7 000
1964	Hurricane Cleo	SE Florida	154
1964	Hurricane Hilda	Central Louisiana	38
1964	Typhoon Louise	Mindanao (Philippines)	58
1965	Hurricane Betsy	SE Florida, SE Louisiana, Mississippi	75
1967	Hurricane Beulah	S Texas	15
1969	Hurricane Camille	Mississippi, Louisiana	256
1970	Cyclone	Bangladesh	300 000
1972	Hurricane Agnes	E USA	117
1974	Cyclone Tracy	Darwin (Australia)	65
1974	Hurricane Fifi	Honduras	10 000
1974	Tornadoes	Central USA	322
1975	Hurricane Eloise	NW Florida	100
1979	Hurricane Frederic	Alabama, Mississippi	31
1979	Hurricane David	Florida, E USA	2 400
1980	Hurricane Allen	S Texas	235
1983	Hurricane Alicia	N Texas	18
1984	Tornadoes Ike and June	Mindanao (Philippines)	1 000
1985	Cyclone	Bangladesh	11 000
1985	Hurricane Kate	Florida Keys, NW Florida	16
1985	Hurricane Gloria	E USA	15
1985	Hurricane Juan	Louisiana	63
1987	Winter storm	S England, NW France	17
1988	Hurricane Joan	Caribbean	216

Year	Storm	Location	Deaths
1988	Hurricane Gilbert	Caribbean, Mexico	318
1989	Hurricane Hugo	S Carolina	71
1991	Cyclone	Bangladesh	200 000
1991	Hurricane Bob	NE USA	17
1992	Hurricane Andrew	S Florida, Bahamas	88
1994	Hurricane Gordon	Haiti, SE USA	1 130
1995	Hurricane Opal	NW Florida	19
1995	Typhoon Angela	Philippines	c. 500
1995	Hurricane Luis	Caribbean	12
1995	Tornado	Bangladesh	34
1995	Hurricane César	Panama, El Savador, Costa Rica	c. 600
1995	Typhoon Herb	Taiwan	50
1996	Hurricane Fran	N Carolina	37
1996	Cyclone	Andhra Pradesh (India)	c. 1 000
1997	Storms	Brazil	68
1997	Cyclone	Bangladesh	112
1997	Cyclone	Bangladesh	c.47
1997	Hurricane Pauline	W Mexico	217
1997	Typhoon Linda	S Vietnam, Thailand	3 500
1998	Tornadoes	Central Florida	38
1998	Tornadoes	Alabama, Georgia, Mississippi	c.41
1998	Hurricane Georges	Caribbean	602
1998	Typhoons Vickie, Zeb, and Babs	Philippines	c.1 000
1998	Storms Chip, Dawn, and Elvis	Central Vietnam	c. 265
1998	Hurricane Mitch	Central America, Caribbean	c. 11 000
1998	Typhoon Faith	Central Vietnam, Philippines	c. 45
1999	Cyclone Dani	Vanuatu, Fiji	c. 10
1999	Hurricane Floyd	Caribbean, E USA	c. 75
1999	Cyclone	Orisste (India)	c. 9000
1999	Tornadoes	Oklahoma, Kansas	46
1999	Storm	N Europe	c. 60
2000	Typhoon Bilis	Taiwan	11
2000	Typhoon Maria	China	c. 50

Note A hurricane is a windstorm in the N hemisphere with winds in excess of 74 mph (called a typhoon in the S hemisphere); a tornado is a column of air rotating around a low pressure centre; a cyclone is a circulation of winds around a depression (anticlockwise in N hemisphere; and clockwise in the S hemisphere))

2.2 *Climate and Environment*

Atmosphere

Atmospheric layers

Region	Layer	Altitude
Ionosphere	Troposphere	sea level–7 km (4.5 mi)/16 km (10 mi) at equator
	Stratosphere	7 km (4.5 mi)–50 km (31 mi)
	Mesosphere	50 km (31 mi)–80 km (50 mi)
	Thermosphere	80 km (50 mi)–400 km (248 mi)
Exosphere		above 400 km (248 mi)

Ionospheric layers

Layer	Altitude
D layer	50 km (31 mi)–90 km (56 mi)
E layer (Kennelly-Heaviside layer)	90 km (56 mi)–160 km (100 mi)
F layer (Appleton layer)	160 km (100 mi)–400 km (248 mi)

Atmospheric gases

Gas	Percentage by volume
Nitrogen	78.1
Oxygen	20.95
Argon	0.934
Carbon dioxide	0.031
Neon	0.00182
Helium	0.00052
Methane	0.0002
Krypton	0.00011
Hydrogen	0.00005
Nitrous oxide	0.00005
Ozone	0.00004
Xenon	0.000009

Climatic zones

Zone	Character	Area
Tropical	Average temperature above 18°C; often subject to monsoons	Chiefly within 15° of equator: Amazon, Malaysia, SE Asia, India, Africa, Congo Basin, Indonesia, Australia
Subtropical	Arid or semi-arid; desert or steppe	Sahara, central Asia, Mexico, Australia, Kalahari
Mediterranean	Average temperature in coolest months between 0°C and 18°C; rainy, with mild winters	California, S Africa, S Europe, parts of Chile, SW Australia

Zone	Character	Area
Temperate	Average temperature between 3°C and 18°C; rainy	Europe, E Asia, N USA, New Zealand, S Chile
Boreal	Wide range of temperature and rainfall according to time of year	Prairies of USA and parts of S Africa, Russia, and Australia
Arctic	Very cold; average annual temperature between 0°C and 10°C; brief summers	Polar regions

Meteorological records

Category	Record	Location
Highest temperature	58°C (136°F)	El Aiziza (Libya)
Highest annual average temperature	34°C (94°F)	Dallol (Ethiopia)
Lowest temperature	–89°C (–129°F)	Vostok (Antarctica)
Lowest annual average temperature	–58°C (–72°F)	Polyus Nedostupnosti (Antarctica)
Highest wind speed	372 kph (231 mph)	Mount Washington, New Hampshire (USA)
Highest monthly average wind speed	104 kph (65 mph)	Port Martin (Antarctica)
Highest rainfall (in 24 hours)	1 870 mm (74 in)	Cilaos (La Réunion Island)
Highest annual rainfall	26 990 mm (905 in)	Cherrapunji (India)
Longest drought	14 years	Arica (Chile)
Largest hailstone	1 kg (2.2 lbs)	Gopalganj (Bangladesh)
Heaviest snowfall (in 24 hours)	1 930 mm (76 in)	Silver Lake, Colorado (USA)

Wind speeds (Beaufort scale)*

Beaufort number	Wind force	Speed
0	calm	0–1 mph (0–1 knots)
1	light air	1–3 mph (1–3 knots)
2	light breeze	4–7 mph (4–6 knots)
3	gentle breeze	8–12 mph (7–10 knots)
4	moderate breeze	13–18 mph (11–16 knots)
5	fresh breeze	19–24 mph (17–21 knots)
6	strong breeze	25–31 mph (22–27 knots)
7	moderate gale	32–38 mph (28–33 knots)
8	fresh gale	39–46 mph (34–40 knots)
9	strong gale	47–54 mph (41–47 knots)
10	whole gale	55–63 mph (48–55 knots)
11	storm	64–72 mph (56–63 knots)
12–17	hurricane	73–82 mph (64–71 knots)
		83–92 mph (72–80 knots)
		93–103 mph (81–89 knots)
		104–114 mph (90–99 knots)
		115–125 mph (100–108 knots)
		126–136 mph (109–118 knots)

Note The Beaufort scale was named after Admiral Sir Francis Beaufort in 1805

Cloud types

Type	Height	Characteristics
Cirrus	5–10 km	Wispy, mares' tails
Cirrostratus	5–10 km	Halo cloud
Cirrocumulus	3–7.5 km	Mackerel sky
Altostratus	3–7.5 km	Overcast
Altocumulus	3–7.5 km	Widespread, resembling cotton balls
Nimbostratus	1–2.5 km	Dark grey, low
Stratocumulus	1–2.5 km	Widespread, heavy rolls
Stratus	1–2.5 km	Flattened, hazy
Cumulus	1.5–6 km	Rounded, fluffy, billowy
Cumulonimbus	1.5–6 km	Anvil-shaped, flat-bottomed, rain-carrying

Environmental disasters

Year	Location	Event	Result
1940s–1952	Love Canal, New York (USA)	Dumping of drums containing hazardous waste	Contamination and evacuation of surrounding area
1953	Minimata Bay (Japan)	Dumping of methyl mercury and other hazardous chemicals	Over 300 deaths by 1983 from 'Minimata disease'; thousands affected by serious genetic abnormalities and other health problems
1957	Kasli (Russia)	Chemical explosion in nuclear waste tanks	Radioactive contamination and evacuation of surrounding area
1957	Cumbria (UK)	Fire in Windscale plutonium production reactor	At least 39 deaths caused by radioactive contamination
1961	Idaho Falls, Idaho (USA)	Accident at experimental nuclear reactor	Three deaths
1967	Cornwall coast (UK)	Wreck of Torrey Canyon oil tanker	Spillage of 34 986 000 gallons of oil affecting coast of Cornwall
1968	Coast of South Africa	Hull failure of World Glory oil tanker	Spillage of 13 524 000 gallons of oil
1969	Off Massachusetts (USA)	Hull failure of Keo oil tanker	Spillage of 88 200 000 gallons of oil
1969	Lucens Vad (Switzerland)	Accident in experimental underground nuclear reactor	Escape of radioactive material necessitating sealing of cavern
1970	Tralhavet Bay (Sweden)	Collision involving Othello oil tanker	Spillage of 17 640 000–29 400 000 gallons of oil
1971	Monticello, Minnesota (USA)	Overflow of radioactive water at Northern States Power Company reactor	Contamination of Mississippi River and St Paul water system
1974	Gulf of Oman	Collision involving Sea Star oil tanker	Spillage of 33 810 000 gallons of oil
1975	Flixborough (UK)	Explosion of cyclohexane container	28 deaths

Year	Location	Event	Result
1976	Decatur, Alabama (USA)	Fire at Brown's Ferry nuclear reactor	$100 million damage
1976	Seveso (Italy)	Leak of toxic gas	Contamination of topsoil
1976	La Coruña (Spain)	Grounding of Urquiola oil tanker	Spillage of 29 400 000 gallons of oil
1977	North Sea	Blowout of well at Ecofisk oil field	Spillage of 8 200 000 gallons of oil
1977	Northern Pacific	Fire on Hawaiian Patriot oil tanker	Spillage of 29 106 000 gallons of oil
1978	Portsall (France)	Grounding of Amoco Cadiz oil tanker	Spillage of 65 562 000 gallons of oil affecting the coast of France
1979	Erwin, Tennessee (USA)	Release of uranium from nuclear fuel plant	Radioactive contamination of at least 1 000 people
1979	Galveston Bay, Texas (USA)	Collision involving Burmah Agate oil tanker	Spillage of 10 700 000 gallons of oil
1979	Three Mile Island, Pennsylvania (USA)	Partial meltdown of nuclear reactor core	Pollution by radioactive gases
1979	Gulf of Mexico	Blowout of Ixtoc 1 oil well	Spillage of 176 400 000 gallons of oil
1979	Trinidad and Tobago	Collision involving Atlantic Empress and Aegean Captain oil tankers	Spillage of 88 200 000 gallons of oil
1980s	Cubatão (Brazil)	Release of radioactive pollution from nuclear plants	Genetic deformities and serious health problems among local population
1980	Basel (Switzerland)	Fire at Sandoz factory	Pollution of River Rhine
1983	Cape Town (South Africa)	Fire on Castillo de Beliver oil tanker	Spillage of 73 500 000 gallons of oil
1983	Persian Gulf	Blowout in Nowruz oil field	Spillage of 176 400 000 gallons of oil
1984	Bhopal (India)	Leak of toxic gas at Union Carbide pesticide plant	Death of around 10 000 people
1986	Gore, Oklahoma (USA)	Explosion of cylinder of nuclear material	Death of one person and numerous injuries
1986	Chernobyl (Ukraine)	Explosion of nuclear reactor	At least 50 deaths and radioactive contamination of Ukraine and much of W Europe; evacuation of surrounding area and long-term health problems worldwide
1987	Goiana (Brazil)	Leak of radioactive material from disused radiotherapy unit	Radioactive contamination of 249 people
1988	Camelford, Cornwall (UK)	Accident at water-treatment works	Contamination by aluminium sulphate causing death of thousands of fish and health problems among local population
1988	Monongahela River, Pennsylvania (USA)	Rupture of oil storage tank	Spillage of 3 800 000 gallons of oil into Monongahela river

1989	Prince William Sound, Alaska (USA)	Grounding of Exxon Valdez oil tanker	Spillage of 10 080 000 gallons of oil severely affecting coast of Alaska
1989	Atlantic Ocean, north of Canary Islands	Explosion in Iranian Khark 5 oil tanker	Spillage of 19 000 000 gallons of oil
1991	Cervantes (W Australia)	Wreck of Greek Kiriki oil tanker	Spillage of 5 880 000 gallons of oil
1991	Kuwait	Oil released by Iraqi troops during Gulf War	Spillage of 25 000 000–130 000 000 gallons of oil
1992	La Coruña (Spain)	Grounding of Greek Aegean Sea oil tanker	Spillage of around 16 000 000 gallons of oil affecting coast of Spain
1993	Shetland (Scotland)	Wreck of Braer oil tanker	Spillage of 26 000 000 gallons of oil
1994	Usinsk (Russia)	Rupture of oil pipeline	Spillage of 4 300 000 gallons of oil affecting Arctic habitat
1996	Pembrokeshire coast (S Wales)	Grounding of Sea Empress oil tanker	Spillage of more than 19 000 000 gallons of oil
1996	Rhode Island (USA)	Grounding of North Cape oil tanker	Spillage of 300 000 gallons of oil
1997	Tokyo Bay (Japan)	Grounding of Diamond Grace oil tanker	Spillage of 13 400 tons of oil
2000	River Danube (Hungary)	Release of cyanide from gold mine	Contamination of rivers by 100 000 gallons of cyanide
2001	Galapagos Islands	Grounding of Jessica oil tanker	Spillage of 240 000 gallons of oil

Air pollution

Pollutant	Sources	Effects
Sulphur dioxide (SO_2)	Oil, coal combustion in power stations	Acid rain
Oxides of nitrogen (NO, NO_2)	Vehicle and power station emissions	Acid rain
Lead compounds	Combustion of leaded petrol in vehicles	Nerve poison
Carbon dioxide (CO_2)	Oil, coal, petrol, diesel combustion	Greenhouse effect
Carbon monoxide (CO)	Combustion of oil, coal, petrol, diesel fuels	Photochemical smog and poisons
Nuclear waste	Emissions from nuclear power plants, nuclear weapon testing, waste	Radioactivity leading to serious health and environmental problems

Greenhouse gases

Constituent gas	Pre-industrial concentration (1860)	Tropospheric concentration in the year 2000	Atmospheric lifetime (years)
Carbon dioxide	288 ppm*	368.4 ppm	120
Methane	848 ppb*	1690–1800 ppb	12
Nitrous oxide	285 ppb	311–12 ppb	120

Constituent gas	Pre-industrial concentration (1860)	Tropospheric concentration in the year 2000	Atmospheric lifetime (years)
CFC–11 (trichlorofluoromethane)	Zero	260–64 ppt*	50
CFC–12 (dichlorodifluoromethane)	Zero	528–38 ppt	102
CFC–113 (trichlorotrifluoroethane)	Zero	83 ppt	85
Carbon tetrachloride	Zero	97–100 ppt	42
Methyl chloroform	Zero	73–78 ppt	5
HCFC–22 (chlorodifluoromethane)	Zero	110–126 ppt	12
Sulphur hexafluoride	Zero	3.4–3.6 ppt	3 200
Trifluoromethyl sulphur pentafluoride	Zero	0.12 ppt	1 000
Perfluoroethane	Zero	4 ppt	10 000
Surface ozone	25 ppb	25–26 ppb	hours

Note ppm = parts per million; ppb = parts per billion; ppt = parts per trillion

Carbon dioxide emissions

Year	Annual carbon dioxide emissions (million tonnes)
1950	6 000
1955	7 000
1960	9 000
1965	11 000
1970	14 640
1975	15 744
1980	18 792
1985	19 580
1990	21 562
1995	23 900

Tropical deforestation

Country	Lost forest (hectares)
Brazil	2 554 000
Indonesia	1 084 000
Congo, Democratic Republic of	740 000
Bolivia	581 000
Mexico	508 000
Venezuela	503 000
Malaysia	400 000
Myanmar	387 000
Sudan	353 000
Thailand	329 000
Paraguay	327 000
Tanzania	323 000
Zambia	264 000
Colombia	262 000
Philippines	262 000
Angola	237 000

Peru	217 000
Ecuador	189 000
Cambodia	164 000
Nicaragua	151 000

Note Figures relate to the amount of forest lost in the years 1990–95

2.3 *Protected Areas*

World Heritage Sites

Country	Site
Albania	Butrinti
Algeria	Al Qal'a of Beni Hammad
	Tassili n'Ajjer
	M'Zab Valley
	Djémila
	Tipasa
	Timgad
	Kasbah of Algiers
Argentina	Los Glaciares
	Iguazu National Park
	Cueva le las Manos, Río Pinturas
	Península Valdés
Argentina/Brazil	Jesuit Missions of the Guaranis
Armenia	Monastery of Haghpat
Australia	Kakadu National Park
	Great Barrier Reef
	Willandra Lakes Region
	Tasmanian Wilderness
	Lord Howe Island Group
	Australian East Coast Temperate and Sub-Tropical Rainforest Parks
	Uluru-Kata Tjuta National Park
	Wet Tropics of Queensland
	Shark Bay, Western Australia
	Fraser Island
	Australian fossil mammal sites (Riversleigh/Naracoorte)
	Heard and McDonald Islands
	Macquarie Island
Austria	Historic centre of the city of Salzburg
	Palace and gardens of Schönbrunn
	Hallstatt–Dachstein Salzkammergut cultural landscape
	Semmering railway
	Historic centre of the city of Graz

Country	Site
Bangladesh	Historic Mosque City of Bagerhat
	Ruins of the Buddhist Vihara at Paharpur
	The Sundarbans
Belarus/Poland	Belovezhskaya Pushcha/Bialowieza Forest
Belgium	Flemish Béguinages
	Four Lifts on the Canal du Centre and their environs, La Louvière and Le Roeulx (Hainault)
	Grand-Place, Brussels
	Belfries of Flanders and Wallonia
Belize	Belize Barrier Reef Reserve System
Benin	Royal Palaces of Abomey
Bolivia	City of Potosi
	Jesuit Missions of the Chiquitos
	Historic city of Sucre
	El Fuerte de Samaipata
Brazil	Historic town of Ouro Preto
	Historic centre of the town of Olinda
	Historic centre of Salvador de Bahia
	Sanctuary of Bom Jesus do Congonhas
	Iguaçu National Park
	Brasilia
	Serra da Capivara National Park
	Historic centre of São Luis
	Historic centre of the town of Diamantina
	Discovery Coast Atlantic Forest Reserves
	Atlantic Forest Southeast Reserves
Bulgaria	Boyana Church
	Madara Rider
	Thracian tomb of Kazanlak
	Rock-hewn churches of Ivanovo
	Ancient city of Nessebar
	Rila Monastery
	Srebarna Nature Reserve
	Pirin National Park
	Thracian tomb of Sveshtari
Cambodia	Angkor
Cameroon	Dja Faunal Reserve
Canada	L'Anse aux Meadows National Historic Park
	Nahanni National Park
	Dinosaur Provincial Park
	Anthony Island
	Head-Smashed-In Buffalo Jump
	Wood Buffalo National Park
	Canadian Rocky Mountains Parks
	Quebec (historic area)
	Gros Morne National Park
	Tatshenshini-Alsek/Kluane National Park, Wrangell–St Elias National Park and Reserve, and Glacier Bay National Park
	Lunenburg old town
	Miguasha Park

Canada/USA	Waterton Glacier International Park
	Kluane National Park/Wrangell–St Elias National Park and Reserve, and Glacier Bay National Park
Central African Republic	Manovo-Gounda Saint Floris National Park
Chile	Rapa Nui National Park
China	Mount Taishan
	The Great Wall
	Imperial Palace of the Ming and Qing Dynasties
	Mogao Caves
	Mausoleum of the First Qin Emperor
	Peking Man site at Zhoukoudian
	Mount Huangshan
	Wulingyuan scenic and historic interest area
	Jiuzhaigou Valley scenic and historic interest area
	Huanglong scenic and historic interest area
	Mountain resort and outlying temples, Chengde
	Temple and cemetery of Confucius, and the Kong family mansion in Qufu
	Ancient building complex in the Wudang Mountains
	Potala Palace, Lhasa
	Lushan National Park
	Mount Emei and Leshan Giant Buddha
	Old town of Lijiang
	Ancient city of Ping Yao
	Classical gardens of Suzhou
	Summer Palace, imperial garden in Beijing
	Temple of Heaven, imperial sacrificial altar in Beijing
	Mount Wuyi
	Dazu rock carvings
Colombia	Port, fortresses and group of monuments, Cartagena
	Los Katios National Park
	Historic centre of Santa Cruz de Mompox
	Archaeological national park of Tierradentro
	Archaeological park of San Augustin
Congo, Democratic Republic of the	Virunga National Park
	Kahuzi–Biega National Park
	Garamba National Park
	Salonga National Park
	Okapi Wildlife Reserve
Costa Rica	Cocos Island National Park
	Area de Conservación Guanacaste
Costa Rica/Panama	Talamanca Range–La Amistad Reserves/La Amistad National Park
Côte d'Ivoire	Tai National Park
	Comoé National Park
Croatia	Old city of Dubrovnik
	Historical complex of Split with the Palace of Diocletian
	Plitvice Lakes National Park
	Episcopal complex of the Euphrasian Basilica in the historic centre of Porec
	Historic city of Trogir

Country	Site
Cuba	Old Havana and its fortifications
	Trinidad/Valley de los Ingenios
	San Pedro de la Roca Castle, Santiago de Cuba
	Desembarco del Granma National Park
	Viales Valley
Cyprus	Paphos
	Painted churches at Troodos region
	Choirokoita
Czech Republic	Historic centre of Prague
	Historic centre of Ceský Krumlov
	Historic centre of Telc
	Pilgrimage church of St John of Nepomuk at Zelena Hora
	Historic centre of Kutna Hora, with Sainte-Borbe church and the cathedral of Notre Dame de Sedlec
	Lednice–Valtice cultural landscape
	Holaovice historical village reservation
	Gardens and castle at Kromeríz
	Litomyl Castle
Denmark	Roskilde Cathedral
	Jelling mounds, runic stones, and church
Dominica	Morne Trois Pitons National Park
Dominican Republic	Colonial city of Santo Domingo
Ecuador	Galapagos Islands
	City of Quito
	Sangay National Park
	Historic centre of Santa Ana de los Rios de Cuenca
Egypt	Memphis and its necropolis
	Ancient Thebes with its necropolis
	Nubian monuments from Abu Simbel to Philae
	Islamic Cairo
	Abu Mena
El Salvador	Joya de Caren archaeological site
Estonia	Historic centre (old town) of Tallinn
Ethiopia	Simen National Park
	Rock-hewn churches, Lalibela
	Fasil Ghebbi, Gondar Region
	Lower valley of the Awash
	Tiya
	Aksum
	Lower valley of the Omo
Finland	Old Rauma
	Fortress of Suomenlinna
	Petäjävesi old church
	Verla Groundwood and Board Mill
	Bronze Age burial site of Sammallahdenmäki
France	Mont-Saint-Michel and its bay
	Chartres Cathedral
	Palace and park of Versailles
	Vézelay, church and hill
	Decorated grottoes, Vézère Valley

	Palace and park of Fontainebleau
	Château and estate of Chambord
	Amiens Cathedral
	The Roman theatre and its surroundings and the 'Triumphal Arch' of Orange
	Roman and romanesque monuments of Arles
	Cistercian abbey of Fontenay
	Royal Saltworks of Arc-et-Senans
	Place Stanislas, Place de la Carrière and Place d'Alliance in Nancy
	Church of Saint-savin sur Gartempe
	Cape Girolata, Cape Porto, and Scandola Nature Reserve in Corsica
	Pont du Gard (Roman aqueduct)
	Strasbourg–Grand Ile
	Paris, banks of the Seine
	Cathedral of Notre-Dame, former Abbey of Saint-Remi and Tau Palace, Cathedral of Reims
	Bourges Cathedral
	Historic centre of Avignon
	Canal du Midi
	Historic fortified city of Carcassonne
	Routes of Santiago de Compostela in France
	Historic site of Lyons
	Jurisdiction of Saint-Emilion
France/Spain	Pyrénées–Mount Perdu
Georgia	City-museum reserve of Mtskheta
	Bagrati Cathedral and Gelati Monastery
	Upper Svaneti
Germany	Aachen Cathedral
	Speyer Cathedral
	Würzburg Residence with the court gardens and Residence Square
	Pilgrimage church of Wies
	The Castles of Augustusburg and Falkenlust at Brühl
	St Mary's Cathedral and St Michael's Church at Hildesheim
	Roman monuments, cathedral and Liebfrauen-Church in Trier
	Hanseatic city of Lübeck
	Palaces and parks of Potsdam and Berlin
	Abbey and Altenmünster of Lorsch
	Mines of Rammelsberg and the historic town of Goslar
	Town of Bamberg
	Maulbronn Monastery complex
	Collegiate church, castle, and old town of Quedlinburg
	Völklingen Ironworks
	Fossil site of Messel
	Cologne Cathedral
	Bauhaus and its sites in Weimar and Dessau
	Luther memorials in Eisleben and Wittenberg
	Classical Weimar
	Museumsinsel (Museum Island), Berlin
	Wartburg Castle
Ghana	Forts and castles, Volta, Greater Accra, Central and Western Regions
	Ashanti traditional buildings

Country	Site
Greece	Temple of Apollo Epicurius at Bassae
	Archaeological site of Delphi
	The Acropolis, Athens
	Mount Athos
	Meteora
	Paleochristian and Byzantine monuments of Thessalonika
	Archaeological site of Epidaurus
	Medieval city of Rhodes
	Archaeological site of Olympia
	Mystras
	Delos
	Monasteries of Daphni, Hossios Lukas, and Nea Moni of Chios
	Pythagoreion and Heraion of Samos
	Archaeological site of Vergina
	Archaeological sites of Mycenae and Tiryns
	Historic centre (Chorá) with the Monastery of Saint John 'the Theologian' and the Cave of the Apocalypse on the Island of Pátmos
Guatemala	Tikal National Park
	Antigua Guatemala
	Archaeological park and ruins of Quirigua
Guinea/Côte d'Ivoire	Mount Nimba Strict Nature Reserve
Haiti	National History Park–Citadal, Sans Souci, Ramiers
Holy See	Vatican City
Honduras	Maya site of Copan
	Rio Platano biosphere reserve
Hungary	Budapest, the banks of the Danube with the district of Buda Castle
	Hollokö
	Millenary Benedictine monastery of Pannonhalma and its natural environment
	Hortobágy National Park
Hungary/Slovakia	Caves of the Aggtelek and Slovak Karst
India	Ajanta Caves
	Ellora Caves
	Agra Fort
	Taj Mahal
	The Sun Temple, Konarak
	Group of monuments at Mahabalipuram
	Kaziranga National Park
	Manas Wildlife Sanctuary
	Keoladeo National Park
	Churches and convents of Goa
	Khajuraho group of monuments
	Group of monuments at Hampi
	Fatehpur Sikri
	Group of monuments at Pattadakal
	Elephanta Caves
	Brihadisvara Temple, Thanjavur
	Sundarbans National Park
	Nanda Devi National Park
	Buddhist monuments at Sanchi

	Humayun's Tomb, Delhi
	Qutb Minar and its monuments, Delhi
	Darjeeling Himalayan railway
Indonesia	Komodo National Park
	Ujung Kulon National Park
	Borobudur Temple compound
	Prambanan Temple compound
	Sangiran early man site
	Lorentz National Park
Iran	Tchogha Zanbil
	Persepolis
	Meidan Emam, Esfahan
Iraq	Hatra
Ireland	Archaeological ensemble of the Bend of the Boyne
	Skellig Michael
Italy	Rock drawings in Valcamonica
	The Church and Dominican convent of Santa Maria delle Grazie with 'The Last Supper' by Leonardo da Vinci
	Historic centre of Florence
	Venice and its lagoon
	Piazza del Duomo, Pisa
	Historic centre of San Gimignano
	I Sassi di Matera
	Vicenza, city of Palladio
	Historic centre of Siena
	Historic centre of Naples
	Crespi d'Adda
	Renaissance town of Ferrara
	Castel del Monte
	The trulli of Alberobello
	Early Christian monuments of Ravenna
	Historic centre of the city of Pienza
	18th-century royal palace at Caserta with the park, the aqueduct of Vanvitelli and the San Leucio complex
	Residences of the Royal House of Savoy
	Botanical garden (Orto Botanico), Padua
	Portovenere, Cinque Terre and the Islands (Palmaria, Tino and Tinetto)
	Cathedral, Torre Civica and Piazza Grande, Modena
	Archaeological areas of Pompeii, Herculaneum and Torre Annunziata
	Costiera Amalfitana
	Archaeological area of Agrigento
	Villa Romana del Casale
	Su Nuraxi di Barumini
	Cilento and Vallo di Diano National Park with the archaeological sites of Paestum and Velia, and the Certosa di Padula
	Historic centre of Urbino
	Archaeological area and the Patriarchal Basilica of Aquileia
	Villa Adriana (Tivoli)
Italy/Holy See	Historic centre of Rome, the properties of the Holy See in that city enjoying extraterritorial rights, and San Paolo Fuori le Mura

Country	Site
Japan	Buddhist monuments in the Horyuji area
	Himeji-jo
	Yakushima
	Shirakami-Sanchi
	Historic monuments of ancient Kyoto, Uji, and Otsu cities
	Historic villages of Shirakawa-go and Gokoyama
	Hiroshima Peace Memorial (Genbaku Dome)
	Itsukushima Shinto shrine
	Historic monuments of ancient Nara
	Shrines and temples of Nikko
Jordan	Old City of Jerusalem and its walls
	Petra
	Quseir Amra
Kenya	Mount Kenya National Park/Natural Forest
	Sibiloi/Central Island National Parks
Korea, South	Sokkuram Grotto
	Temple of Haiensa Changgyong P'ango
	Chongmyo sanctuary
	Ch'angdokkung palace complex
	Hwasong fortress
Laos	Town of Luang Prabang
Latvia	Historic centre of Riga
Lebanon	Anjar
	Baalbek
	Byblos
	Tyre
	Ouadi Qadisha (the Holy Valley) and the Forest of the Cedars of God (Horsh Arz el-Rab)
Libya	Archaeological site of Leptis Magna
	Archaeological site of Sabratha
	Archaeological site of Cyrene
	Rock-art sites of Tadrart Acacus
	Old town of Ghadamès
Lithuania	Vilnius historic centre
Luxembourg	Old quarters and fortifications of Luxembourg city
Macedonia	Ohrid Region with is cultural and historical aspect and its natural environment
Madagascar	Tsingy de Bemaraha Strict Nature Reserve
Malawi	Lake Malawi National Park
Mali	Old towns of Djenné
	Timbuktu
	Cliff of Bandiagara (Land of the Dogons)
Malta	Hal Saflieni Hypogeum
	City of Valletta
	Megalithic temples of Malta
Mauritania	Banc d'Arguin National Park
	Ancient ksour of Ouadane, Chinguetti, Tichitt and Oualata
Mexico	Sian Ka'an
	Pre-Hispanic city and national park of Palenque
	Historic centre of Mexico City and Xochimilco
	Pre-Hispanic city of Teotihuacan

	Historic centre of Oaxaca and archaeological site of Monte Alban
	Historic centre of Puebla
	Historic town of Guanajuato and adjacent mines
	Pre-Hispanic city of Chichen-Itza
	Historic centre of Morelia
	El Tajin, Pre-Hispanic City
	Whale Sanctuary of El Vizcaino
	Historic centre of Zacatecas
	Rock paintings of the Sierra de San Francisco
	Earliest 16th-century monasteries on the slopes of Popocatepetl
	Pre-Hispanic town of Uxmal
	Historic monuments zone of Querétaro
	Hospicio Cabaas, Guadalajara
	Historic monuments zone of Tlacotalpan
	Archaeological zone of Paquimé, Casas Grandes
	Historic fortified town of Campeche
	Archaeological monuments zone of Xochicalco
Morocco	Medina of Fez
	Medina of Marrakesh
	Ksar of Aït-Ben-Haddou
	Historic city of Meknes
	Archaeological site of Volubilis
	Medina of Tétouan (formerly known as Titawin)
Mozambique	Island of Mozambique
Nepal	Sagarmatha National Park
	Kathmandu Valley
	Royal Chitwan National Park
	Lumbini, the birthplace of Buddha
Netherlands	Schokland and its neighbourhood
	Defence line of Amsterdam
	Mill network at Kinderdijk-Elshout
	Historic area of Willemstad, inner city and harbour, the Netherlands Antilles
	Ir.D.F. Woudagemaal (D.F. Wouda Steam Pumping Station)
	Droogmakerij de Beemster (Beemster Polder)
New Zealand	Te Wahipounamu–South West New Zealand
	Tongariro National Park
	New Zealand Sub-Antarctic Islands
Niger	Aïr and Ténéré Natural Reserves
	W National Park of Niger
Nigeria	Sukur cultural landscape
Norway	Urnes Stave Church
	Bryggen
	Røros
	Rock drawings of Alta
Oman	Bahla Fort
	Archaeological sites of Bat, Al-Khutm, and Al-Ayn
	Arabian oryx sanctuary
Pakistan	Archaeological ruins of Mohenjo Daro
	Taxila
	Buddhist ruins of Takht-i-Bahi and neighbouring city remains at Sahr-i-Bahlol

Country	Site
	Historical monuments of Thatta
	Fort and Shalamar Gardens in Lahore
	Rohtas Fort
Panama	Fortifications on the Caribbean side of Panama: Portobelo-San Lorenzo
	Darien National Park
	Historic district of Panamá, with the Saló Bolivar
Paraguay	Jesuit Missions of La Santisima Trinidad de Parana and Jesus de Tavarangue
Peru	City of Cuzco
	Historic sanctuary of Machu Picchu
	Chavin archaeological site
	Huascaran National Park
	Chan Chan Archaeological Zone
	Manu National Park
	Rio Abiseo National Park
	Historic centre of Lima
	The lines and geoglyphs of Nasca and Pampas de Jumana
Philippines	Tubbataha Reef Marine Park
	Baroque churches of the Philippines
	Terraced rice-fields of the Philippines cordilleras
	Historic town of Vigan
	Puerto-Princesa Subterranean River National Park
Poland	Kraków's historic centre
	Wieliczka Salt Mine
	Auschwitz Concentration Camp
	Historic centre of Warsaw
	Old City of Zamosc
	Medieval town of Torun
	Castle of the Teutonic Order in Malbork
	Kalwaria Zebrzydowska: the Mannerist architectural and park landscape complex and pilgrimage park
Portugal	Central zone of the town of Angra do Heroismo in the Azores
	Monastery of the Hieronymites and Tower of Belem in Lisbon
	Monastery of Batalha
	Convent of Christ in Tomar
	Historic centre of Evora
	Monastery of Alcobaça
	Cultural landscape of Sintra
	Historic centre of Oporto
	Prehistoric rock-art sites in the Côa Valley
	Laurisilva of Madeira
Romania	Danube Delta
	Biertan and its fortified church
	Monastery of Horezu
	Churches of Moldavia
	Historic centre of Sighisoara
	Dacian fortresses of the Orastie Mountains
	Wooden churches of Maramures

Russia	Historic centre of Saint Petersburg and related groups of monuments
	Khizi Pogost
	Kremlin and Red Square in Moscow
	Historic monuments of Novgorod and surroundings
	Cultural and historic ensemble of Solovetsky Islands
	The White Monuments of Vladimir and Suzdal
	Architectural ensemble of the Trinity Sergius Lavra in Sergiev Pasad
	Church of the Ascension, Kolomenskoye
	Komi virgin forests
	Lake Baikal
	Volcanoes of Kamchatka
	Golden Mountains of Altai
	Western Caucasus
Saint Christopher and Nevis	Brimstone Hill Fortress National Park
Senegal	Island of Gorée
	Niokolo-Koba National Park
	Djoudj National Bird Sanctuary
Seychelles	Aldabra Atoll
	Vallée de Mai Nature Reserve
Slovakia	Vlkolinec
	Aggtelek caves and the Slovak Karst
	Banská Stiavnica
	Spissky Hrad and its associated cultural monuments
Slovenia	Skocjan Caves
Solomon Islands	East Rennell
South Africa	Greater St Lucia Wetland Park
	Robben Island
	Fossil hominid sites of Sterkfontein, Swartkrans, Kromdraai and environs
Spain	Historic centre of Córdoba
	The Alhambra Generalife, and Albaicin, Granada
	Burgos Cathedral
	Monastery and site of the Escorial, Madrid
	Parque Güell, Palacio Güell, and Casa Mila, in Barcelona
	Altamira Cave
	Old town of Segovia and its aqueduct
	Churches of the Kingdom of the Asturias
	Santiago de Compostela (Old Town)
	Old town of Avila with its extra-muros churches
	Mudejar architecture of Teruel
	Historic city of Toledo
	Garajonay National Park
	Old town of Cáceres
	The Cathedral, the Alcazar, and the Archivo de Indias, in Seville
	Old city of Salamanca
	Poblet Monastery
	Archaeological ensemble of Mérida
	Royal Monastery of Santa Maria de Guadalupe
	The Route of Santiago de Compostela
	Doana National Park
	Historic walled town of Cuenca

Country	Site
	La Lonja de la Seda de Valencia
	Las Médulas
	Palau de la Música Catalana and the Hospital de Saint Pau, Barcelona
	San Millán Yuso and Suso monasteries
	University and historic precinct of Alcaláde Henares
	Rock-art of the Mediterranean basin on the Iberian peninsula
	Ibiza, biodiversity and culture
	San Cristóbal de La Laguna
Sri Lanka	Sacred city of Anuradhapura
	Ancient city of Polonnaruva
	Ancient city of Sigiriya
	Sinharaja Forest Reserve
	Sacred city of Kandy
	Old town of Galle and its fortifications
	Golden Temple of Dambulla
Sweden	Royal Domain of Drottningholm
	Birka and Hovgården
	Engelsberg Ironworks
	Rock carvings in Tanum Skogskyrkogården
	Hanseatic town of Visby
	Church village of Gammelstad, Luleå
	Laponian area
	Naval port of Karlskrona
Switzerland	Convent of Saint Gall
	Benedictine convent of Saint John at Müstair
	Old city of Berne
Syria	Ancient city of Damascus
	Ancient city of Bosra
	Site of Palmyra
	Ancient city of Aleppo
Tanzania	Ngorongoro conservation area
	Ruins of Kilwa Kisiwani and Songo Mnara
	Serengeti National Park
	Selous Game Reserve
	Kilimanjaro National Park
Thailand	Thungyai-Huai Kha Khaeng wildlife sanctuaries
	Historic town of Sukhothai and associated historic towns
	Historic city of Ayutthaya and associated historic towns
	Ban Chiang archaeological site
Tunisia	Medina of Tunis
	Site of Carthage
	Amphitheatre of El Djem
	Ichkeul National Park
	Punic town of Kerkuane and its necropolis
	Medina of Sousse
	Kairouan
	Dougga/Thugga
Turkey	Historic areas of Istanbul
	Göreme National Park and the rock sites of Cappadocia
	Great Mosque and hospital of Divrigi
	Hattusha

	Nemrut Dag
	Xanthos-Letoon
	Hierapolis-Pamukkale
	City of Safranbolu
	Archaeological site of Troy
Turkmenistan	State historical and cultural park 'Ancient Merv'
Uganda	Bwindi Impenetrable National Park
	Rwenzori Mountains National Park
Ukraine	Kiev: Saint Sophia Cathedral and related monastic buildings, and Lavra of Kiev-Pechersk
United Kingdom	The Giant's Causeway and Causeway coast
	Durham Castle and Cathedral
	Ironbridge Gorge
	Studley Royal Park including the ruins of Fountains Abbey
	Stonehenge, Avebury, and associated sites
	The castles and town walls of King Edward in Gwynedd
	Saint Kilda
	Blenheim Palace
	City of Bath
	Hadrian's Wall
	Palace of Westminster, Abbey of Westminster, and Saint Margaret's Church
	Henderson Island
	The Tower of London
	Canterbury Cathedral, Saint Augustine's Abbey, and Saint Martin's Church
	Edinburgh old and new towns
	Gough Island Wildlife Reserve
	Maritime Greenwich
	The heart of neolithic Orkney
United States of America	Mesa Verde
	Yellowstone
	Grand Canyon National Park
	Everglades National Park
	Independence Hall
	Redwood National Park
	Mammonth Cave National Park
	Olympic National Park
	Cahokia Mounds state historic site
	Great Smoky Mountains National Park
	La Fortaleza and San Juan historic site in Puerto Rico
	The Statue of Liberty
	Yosemite National Park
	Chaco Culture National Historical Park
	Monticello and University of Virginia in Charlottesville
	Hawaii Volcanoes National Park
	Pueblo de Taos
	Carlsbad Caverns National Park
	Waterton Glacier International Park (with Canada)
Uruguay	Historic quarter of Colonia del Sacramento
Uzbekistan	Itchan Kala
	Historic centre of Bukhara

Country	Site
Venezuela	Coro and its port
	Canaima National Park
Vietnam	The complex of Hué monuments
	Ha Long Bay
	Hoi An ancient town
	My Son sanctuary
Yemen	Old walled city of Shibam
	Old city of Sana'a
	Historic town of Zabid
Yugoslavia	Stari Ras and Sopocani
	Natural and culturo-historical region of Kotor
	Durmitor National Park
	Studenica Monastery
Zaïre	Virunga National Park
	Garamba National Park
	Kahuzi-Biega National Park
	Salonga National Park
Zambia/Zimbabwe	Victoria Falls/Mosi-oa-Tunya
Zimbabwe	Mana Pools National Park, Sapi, and Chewore Safari Areas
	Great Zimbabwe National Monument
	Khami Ruins National Monument

Note World Heritage Sites are internationally recognized under the aegis of the World Heritage Convention founded by UNESCO in 1972

Major National Parks

Park	Location	Area
Canada		
Banff	Alberta	6 641 sq km (2 564 sq mi)
Jasper	Alberta	10 878 sq km (4 200 sq mi)
Wood Buffalo	Alberta/Northwest Territories	44 800 sq km (17 297 sq mi)
England and Wales		
Brecon Beacons	Wales	1 351 sq km (522 sq mi)
The Broads	Norfolk	303 sq km (117 sq mi)
Dartmoor	Devon	954 sq km (368 sq mi)
Exmoor	Somerset, Devon	693 sq km (268 sq mi)
Lake District	Cumbria	2 292 sq km (885 sq mi)
The New Forest	Hampshire	376 sq km (117 sq mi)
Northumberland	Northumberland	1 049 sq km (405 sq mi)
North York Moors	North Yorkshire, Cleveland	1 436 sq km (554 sq mi)
Peak District	N England	1 438 sq km (555 sq mi)
Pembrokeshire Coast	Wales	584 sq km (225 sq mi)
Snowdonia	N Wales	2 142 sq km (817 sq mi)
Yorkshire Dales	Yorkshire, Cumbria	1 769 sq km (683 sq mi)
Other European		
Abruzzi	Italy	392 sq km (151 sq mi)
Bialowieski/Belovezhskaya	Poland/Belarus	928 sq km (358 sq mi)
Cévennes	France	844 sq km (326 sq mi)

Gran Paradiso	Italy	700 sq km (270 sq mi)
Hohe Tauern	Austria	2 589 sq km (1 000 sq mi)
Hortobágyi	Hungary	520 sq km (201 sq mi)
Pallas-Ounastunturi	Finland	500 sq km (193 sq mi)
Pfälzerwald	Germany	1 793 sq km (692 sq mi)
Rodane	Norway	572 sq km (221 sq mi)
Sarek	Sweden	1 940 sq km (749 sq mi)
Skaftafell	Iceland	500 sq km (193 sq mi)
Vanoise	France	528 sq km (204 sq mi)

South America

Amazonia	Brazil	10 000 sq km (3 861 sq mi)
Canaima	Venezuela	30 000 sq km (11 583 sq mi)
Galápagos	Ecuador	6 790 sq km (2 622 sq mi)
Manu	Peru	15 328 sq km (5 918 sq mi)

USA

Arcadia	SE Maine	158 sq km (61 sq mi)
Arches	E Utah	297 sq km (115 sq mi)
Badlands	SW South Dakota	985 sq km (380 sq mi)
Big Bend	W Texas	2 866 sq km (1 106 sq mi)
Biscayne	SE Florida	729 sq km (281 sq mi)
Bryce Canyon	SW Utah	145 sq km (56 sq mi)
Canyonlands	SE Utah	1 366 sq km (527 sq mi)
Capitol Reef	S Utah	979 sq km (378 sq mi)
Carlsbad Caverns	SE New Mexico	189 sq km (73 sq mi)
Channel Islands	S California	1 009 sq km (390 sq mi)
Crater Lake	SW Oregon	649 sq km (250 sq mi)
Death Valley	California, Nevada	8 368 sq km (3 231 sq mi)
Denali	S Alaska	16 452 sq km (6 352 sq mi)
Everglades	S Florida	5 661 sq km (2 186 sq mi)
Gates of the Arctic	N Alaska	28 540 sq km (11 019 sq mi)
Glacier	NW Montana	4 102 sq km (1 584 sq mi)
Glacier Bay	SE Alaska	15 695 sq km (6 060 sq mi)
Grand Canyon	NW Arizona	4 931 sq km (1 904 sq mi)
Grand Teton	NW Wyoming	1 257 sq km (485 sq mi)
Great Smoky Mountains	SW North Carolina, SE Tennessee	2 106 sq km (813 sq mi)
Guadalupe Mountains	W Texas	309 sq km (119 sq mi)
Haleakala	Maui Island, Hawaii	120 sq km (46 sq mi)
Hawaii Volcanoes	Hawaii Island, Hawaii	927 sq km (358 sq mi)
Hot Springs	C Arkansas	24 sq km (9 sq mi)
Isle Royale	NW Michigan	2 314 sq km (893 sq mi)
Katmai	SW Alaska	17 928 sq km (6 922 sq mi)
Kenai Fjords	S Alaska	2 295 sq km (886 sq mi)
Kings Canyon	E California	1 862 sq km (719 sq mi)
Kobuk Valley	N Alaska	6 920 sq km (2 672 sq mi)
Lake Clark	S Alaska	9 870 sq km (3 811 sq mi)
Lassen Volcanic	N California	430 sq km (166 sq mi)
Mammoth Cave	C Kentucky	212 sq km (82 sq mi)
Mesa Verde	SW Colorado	211 sq km (81 sq mi)
Mount Rainier	SW Washington	953 sq km (368 sq mi)
North Cascades	N Washington	2 043 sq km (789 sq mi)

Park	Location	Area
Olympic	NW Washington	3 703 sq km (1 430 sq mi)
Petrified Forest	E Arizona	378 sq km (146 sq mi)
Redwood	NW California	443 sq km (171 sq mi)
Rocky Mountain	C Colorado	1 068 sq km (412 sq mi)
Sequoia	E California	1 629 sq km (629 sq mi)
Shenandoah	N Virginia	788 sq km (304 sq mi)
Theodore Roosevelt	W North Dakota	285 sq km (110 sq mi)
Virgin Islands	St John, Virgin Islands	59 sq km (23 sq mi)
Voyageurs	N Minnesota	887 sq km (342 sq mi)
Wind Cave	SW South Dakota	114 sq km (44 sq mi)
Wrangell-St Elias	SE Alaska	32 970 sq km (12 730 sq mi)
Yellowstone	Idaho, Montana, Wyoming	8 984 sq km (3 469 sq mi)
Yosemite	E California	3 079 sq km (1 189 sq mi)
Zion	SW Utah	593 sq km (229 sq mi)

Country Code

Guard against the risk of fire

Fasten all gates

Keep dogs under control

Keep to the paths across farm land

Avoid damaging fencing, hedges, and walls

Leave no litter

Safeguard water supplies

Protect wild like, plants, and trees

Go carefully on country roads

Respect the life of the countryside

3
Natural History

3.1 *Flora and Fauna*

Evolution of species

1 600 million years BC	Appearance of first marine life and fossils
650 million years BC	Appearance of first seaweed, algae and invertebrates
590 million years BC	Appearance of shelled invertebrates and trilobites
505 million years BC	Appearance of first vertebrates; development of coral reefs
438 million years BC	Appearance of large vertebrates and first leafless land plants
408 million years BC	Appearance of many species of fish and primitive sharks; appearance of first amphibians and first insects
360 million years BC	Appearance of further amphibians and sharks and of first winged insects
286 million years BC	Extinction of some species of shelled fish; dominance of reptiles; appearance of deciduous plants
248 million years BC	Appearance of first ichthyosaurs, flying fish, crustaceans, mammals, dinosaurs and flies
213 million years BC	Reptiles become dominant species; appearance of first flowers and birds
144 million years BC	Appearance of turtles, rays and modern fish species; extinction of the dinosaurs
65 million years BC	Extinction of many reptile species; appearance of first primates
38 million years BC	Evolution of crabs, mussels, and snails; appearance of woolly mammoths and other pachyderms, canines, sabre-toothed tigers and other felines and grasses
25 million years BC	Appearance of giant sharks and grazing mammals
5 million years BC	Extinction of giant sharks; appearance of numerous modern fish species; primates flourish
2 million years BC	Primitive humans and many other modern species become established; extinction of many plant species

Classification of plants and animals

Level
Kingdom
Phylum (animals)/Division (plants)
Class
Order
Family
Genus
Species

3.2 *Plants*

Classification of plants

Phylum	Number of species	Examples
Angiospermophyta/ Magnoliophyta	More than 230 000	Flowering plants, trees and shrubs
Bryophyta	24 000	Liverworts, hornworts, mosses
Coniferophyta/Pinatae	550	Conifers, evergreen shrubs
Cycadophyta	100	Cycads
Filicinophyta/Pteridophyta	12 000	Ferns
Ginkgophyta	1	Gingko
Gnetophyta	70	Cone-bearing desert plants
Psilophyta	12	Whiskferns
Lycopodophyta	1 000	Club mosses
Sphenophyta/Equisetophyta	20	Horsetails, scouring rushes

Cereals

Cereal	Species	Origin
Barley	*Hordeum vulgare*	Middle East
Maize/corn	*Zea mays*	Central America
Millet (common)	*Panicum miliaceum*	Tropics
Millet (foxtail/Italian)	*Setaria italica*	Tropics
Millet (bulrush)	*Pennisetum americanum*	Tropics

Oats	*Avena sativa*	Mediterranean basin
Rice	*Oryza sativa*	Asia
Rye	*Secale cereale*	Mediterranean/SW Asia
Sorghum/Kaffir corn	*Sorghum bicolor*	Africa/Asia
Wheat	Genus *Triticum*	Mediterranean/W Asia

Vegetables

Vegetable	Species	Origin
Artichoke (Chinese)	*Stachys affinis*	China
Artichoke (globe)	*Cynara scolymus*	Mediterranean
Artichoke (Jerusalem)	*Helianthus tuberosus*	N America
Asparagus	*Asparagus officinalis*	Europe/Asia
Aubergine/eggplant	*Solanum melongena*	Asia/Africa
Avocado	*Persea americana*	Central America
Bean sprouts	*Vigna radiata*	China
Beans (black-eyed)	*Vigna unguiculata*	India/Iran
Beans (borlotti)	*Phaseolus vulgaris*	America
Beans (broad)	*Vicia faba*	Africa/Europe
Beans (flageolet)	*Phaseolus vulgaris*	America
Beans (French)	*Phaseolus vulgaris*	America
Beans (haricot)	*Phaseolus vulgaris*	America
Beans (kidney)	*Phaseolus vulgaris*	America
Beans (runner)	*Phaseolus coccineus*	America
Beans (soya)	*Glycine max*	E Asia
Beetroot	*Beta vulgaris*	Mediterranean
Broccoli	*Brassica oleracea*	Europe
Brussels sprouts	*Brassica oleracea (Gemmifera)*	N Europe
Cabbage	*Brassica oleracea (capitata)*	Europe/W Asia
Cardoon	*Cynara cardunculus*	Mediterranean
Carrot	*Daucus carota*	Asia
Cauliflower	*Brassica oleracea (Botrytis)*	Middle East
Celeriac	*Apium graveolens var. rapaceum*	Mediterranean
Celery	*Apium graveolens var. dulce*	Europe/N Africa/America
Chayote/chocho	*Sechium edule*	America
Chickpea	*Cicer arietinum*	W Asia
Chicory	*Cichorium intybus*	Europe/W Asia
Chinese leaf	*Brassica pekinensis*	E Asia/China
Chives	*Allium schoenoprasum*	Europe/N America
Courgette/zucchini	*Cucurbita pepo*	S America/Africa
Cucumber	*Cucumis sativus*	S Asia
Endive	*Cichorium endivia*	S Europe/East Indies/Africa
Fennel	*Foeniculum vulgare var. azoricum*	Europe
Kale/borecole	*Brassica oleracea (Acephala)*	Europe
Kohlrabi	*Brassica oleracea (Gongylodes)*	Europe
Laver	*Porphyra leucosticta/Porphyra umbilicalis*	Europe

Vegetable	Species	Origin
Leek	*Allium porrum*	Europe/N Africa
Lentil	*Lens culinaris*	S Asia
Lettuce	*Lactuca sativa*	Middle East
Marrow	*Cucurbita pepo*	America
Mooli	*Raphanus sativus*	E Africa
Mushroom	*Agaricus campestris*	Worldwide
Okra	*Abelmoschus esculentus*	Africa
Onion	*Allium cepa*	Central Asia
Parsnip	*Pastinaca sativa*	Europe
Pea	*Pisum sativum*	Asia/Europe
Pepper	*Capsicum annuum*	S America
Potato	*Solanum tuberosum*	S America
Pumpkin	*Cucurbita pepo*	S America
Radish	*Raphanus sativus*	China/Japan
Salsify	*Tragopogon porrifolius*	S Europe
Sorrel	*Rumex acetosa*	Europe
Spinach	*Spinacea oleracea*	Asia
Squash (winter)	*Cucurbita maxima*	America
Squash (summer)	*Cucurbita pepo*	America
Swede	*Brassica napus 'Napobrassica'*	Europe
Sweet potato	*Ipomoea batatas*	Central America
Swiss chard	*Beta vulgaris subsp. cicla*	Europe
Tomato	*Lycopersicon esculentum*	S America
Turnip	*Brassica rapa*	Middle East
Watercress	*Nasturtium officinale*	Europe/Asia
Yam	Genus *Dioscorea*	Tropics

Edible fruits

Fruit	Species	Origin
Acerola	*Malpighia glabra*	America
Apple	*Malus pumila*	Temperate regions
Apricot	*Prunus armenaica*	Asia
Avocado	*Persea americana*	Central America
Banana	*Musa acuminata*	India/S Asia
Bilberry	*Vaccinium myrtillus*	Europe/N Asia
Blackberry	*Rubus fruticosis*	N hemisphere
Blackcurrant	*Ribes nigrum*	Europe/Asia/Africa
Blueberry	*Vaccinium corymbosum*	America/Europe
Breadfruit	*Artocarpus altilis*	Malaysia
Carambola	*Averrhoa carambola*	S China
Cherimoya	*Annona cherimola*	Peru
Cherry (sour)	*Prunus cerasus*	Temperate regions
Cherry (sweet)	*Prunus avium*	Temperate regions
Clementine	*Citrus reticulata*	W Mediterranean
Cranberry	*Vaccinium oxycoccus*	N America

Damson	*Prunus institia*	Temperate regions
Date	*Phoenix dactylifera*	Persian Gulf
Fig	*Ficus carica*	W Asia
Gooseberry	*Ribes uva-crispa*	Europe
Grape	*Vitis vinefera*	Asia
Grapefruit	*Citrus paradisi*	West Indies
Greengage	*Prunus domestica*	Temperate regions
Guava	*Psidium guajava*	S America
Kiwi fruit	*Actinidia chinensis*	China
Kumquat	*Fortunella margarita*	China
Lemon	*Citrus limon*	India/S Asia
Lime	*Citrus aurantiifolia*	SE Asia
Loganberry	*Rubus loganobaccus*	America
Loquat	*Eriobotrya japonica*	China/Japan
Lychee	*Litchi chinensis*	China
Mandarin/tangerine	*Mangifera indica*	China
Mango	*Citrus reticulata*	S Asia
Medlar	*Mespilus germanica*	SE Europe/Asia
Melon	*Cucumis melo*	Egypt
Mulberry	*Morus nigra*	W Asia
Nectarine	*Prunus persica*	China
Orange	*Citrus sinensis*	China
Papaya	*Carica papaya*	Tropics
Passion fruit	*Passiflora edulis*	S America
Peach	*Prunus persica var. nectarina*	China
Pear	*Pyrus communis*	Middle East/E Europe
Persimmon/date-plum	*Diospyros kaki*	S America
Physalis/Cape gooseberry	*Physalis alkekengi*	E Asia
Pineapple	*Ananas comosus*	S America
Plum	*Prunus domestica*	Temperate regions
Pomegranate	*Punica granatum*	Persia
Pomelo	*Citrus maxima*	Malaysia
Quince	*Cydonia oblonga*	Iran
Raspberry	*Rubus idaeus*	N hemisphere
Redcurrant	*Ribes rubrum*	Europe/Asia/Africa
Rhubarb	*Rheum rhabarbarum*	Asia
Sapodillo plum	*Manilkara zapota*	Central America
Satsuma	*Citrus reticulata*	Japan
Soursop	*Annona muricata*	America
Strawberry	*Fragaria*	Europe/Asia
Tamarind	*Tamarindus indica*	Africa/S Asia
Tangelo/ugli	*Citrus tangelo*	N America
Water melon	*Citrullus lanatus*	Africa
White currant	*Ribes rubrum*	W Europe

Herbs

Herb	Species	Origin
Aconite/monkshood	*Aconitum napellus*	Europe/NW Asia
Agrimony	*Agrimonia eupatoria*	Europe
Alecost/costmary	*Balsamita major*	E Mediterranean
Aloe	*Aloe vera*	Africa
Anise	*Pimpinella anisum*	Egypt
Basil	*Ocimum basilicum*	Middle East
Borage	*Borago officinalis*	Mediterranean
Celandine	*Chelidonium majus*	Europe
Celery	*Apium graveolens*	Europe
Chamomile	*Chamaemelum nobile*	Europe/Asia
Chervil	*Anthriscus cerefolium*	Europe/Asia
Chicory	*Cichorium intybus*	Europe
Chives	*Allium schoenoprasum*	Europe/America
Coriander	*Coriandrum sativum*	N Africa/W Asia
Dandelion	*Taraxacum officinalis*	Europe
Deadly nightshade	*Atropa bella-donna*	Europe/Asia
Dill	*Anethium graveolens*	S Europe
Elder	*Sambucus nigra*	Europe
Epazote	*Chenopodium ambrosioides*	Central and S America
Fennel	*Foeniculum vulgare var. azoricum*	Mediterranean
Feverfew	*Tanacetum parthenium*	SE Europe/W Asia
Foxglove	*Digitalis purpurea*	Europe
Garlic	*Allium sativum*	Asia
Gentian	*Gentiana lutea*	Europe
Ginseng	*Panax pseudo-ginseng*	China
Guaiacum	*Guaiacum officinale*	Caribbean
Heartsease/wild pansy	*Viola tricolor*	Europe
Hemlock	*Conium maculatum*	Europe
Hemp	*Cannabis sativa*	Asia
Henbane	*Hyoscyamus niger*	Europe/W Asia/N Africa
Henna	*Lawsonia inermis*	Asia/Africa
Horseradish	*Armoracia rusticana*	SE Europe/W Asia
Hyssop	*Hyssopus officinalis*	S Europe
Juniper	*Juniperus communis*	Mediterranean
Lavender	*Lavandula officinalis*	Mediterranean
Leek	*Allium porrum*	Europe
Lemon	*Citrus limon*	Asia
Lemon balm	*Melissa officinalis*	S Europe
Lily of the valley	*Convallaria majalis*	Europe/N America
Lime (small-leaved)	*Tilia cordata*	Europe
Liquorice	*Glycyrrhiza glabra*	Egypt
Lovage	*Levisticum officinale*	W Asia
Mandrake	*Mandragora officinarum*	Himalayas/SE Europe/ W Asia
Marjoram	*Origanum majorana*	Africa/Asia/Mediterranean
Marsh mallow	*Althaea officinalis*	Europe/Asia
Maté	*Ilex paraguariensis*	S America
Mugwort	*Artemisia vulgaris*	Europe/Asia

Myrrh	*Commiphora myrrha*	Arabia/Africa
Myrtle	*Myrtus communis*	Asia/Mediterranean
Nasturtium	*Tropaeolum majus*	Peru
Onion	*Allium cepa*	Asia
Oregano	*Origanum vulgare*	Mediterranean
Parsley	*Petroselinum crispum*	Mediterranean
Peony	*Paeonia officinalis*	Europe/Asia/N America
Peppermint	*Mentha piperita*	Europe
Poppy	*Papaver somniferum*	Asia Minor
Purslane	*Portulaca oleracea*	Europe
Rosemary	*Rosmarinus officinalis*	Mediterranean
Rue	*Ruta graveolens*	Mediterranean
Saffron	*Crocus sativus*	Asia Minor
Sage	*Salvia officinalis*	N Mediterranean
Sorrel	*Rumex acetosa*	Europe
Spearmint	*Mentha spicata*	Europe
Tansy	*Tanacetum vulgare*	Asia
Tarragon	*Artemisia dracunculus*	Asia/E Europe
Thyme	*Thymus serpyllum*	Mediterranean
Valerian	*Valeriana officinalis*	Europe/Asia
Vervain	*Verbena officinalis*	Europe/Asia/N Africa
Watercress	*Nasturtium officinale*	Europe/Asia
Witch hazel	*Hamamelis virginiana*	N America/E Asia
Wormwood	*Aretemisia absinthium*	Europe
Yarrow/milfoil	*Achillea millefolium*	Europe/W Asia

Spices

Spice	Species	Origin
Allspice	*Pimenta dioica*	America/West Indies
Annatto	*Bixa orellana*	S America/West Indies
Asafoetida	*Ferula assa-foetida*	W Asia
Bay	*Laurus nobilis*	Mediterranean/Asia Minor
Caraway	*Carum carvi*	Europe/Asia
Cardamom	*Elettaria cardamomum*	SE Asia
Cayenne	*Capsicum annuum*	America/Africa
Chilli pepper	*Capsicum annuum*	America
Cinnamon	*Cinnamomum verum*	Sri Lanka
Cloves	*Syzygium aromaticum*	Moluccas
Cocoa	*Theobroma cacoa*	S America
Coconut	*Cocos nucifera*	Polynesia
Coriander	*Coriandrum sativum*	S Europe
Cumin	*Cuminum cyminum*	Mediterranean
Curry leaf	*Murraya koenigii*	India
Fennel	*Foeniculum vulgare*	S Europe
Fenugreek	*Trigonella foenum-graecum*	India/S Europe
Horseradish	*Armoracia rusticana*	E Europe
Ginger	*Zingiber officinale*	SE Asia
Mace	*Myristica fragrans*	Moluccas

Spice	Species	Origin
Mustard (black)	*Brassica nigra*	Europe/Africa/Asia/America
Mustard (white)	*Sinapis alba*	Europe/Asia
Nutmeg	*Myristica fragrans*	Moluccas
Paprika	*Capiscum annuum*	S America
Pepper	*Piper nigrum*	India
Sandalwood	*Santalum album*	India/Indonesia/Australia
Sassafras	*Sassafras albidum*	N America
Sesame	*Sesamum indicum*	Tropics
Soya	*Glycine max*	China
Tamarind	*Tamarindus indica*	Africa
Turmeric	*Curcuma longa*	SE Asia
Vanilla	*Vanilla planifolia*	Central America

Fungi

Phylum	Number of species	Examples
Ascomycota	15 000	Yeasts, morels, truffles, parasites of insects
Basidiomycota	25 000	Jelly fungi, rusts, smuts, common mushrooms, coral fungi, shelf fungi, puffballs
Deuteromycota	25 000	Pathogenic yeasts
Zygomycota	600	Black bread mould, parasites of insects and animals

Flowers

Flower	Genus/family	Origin
Acanthus	*Acanthus*	Europe
African lily/lily-of-the-Nile	*Agapanthus*	S Africa
African violet	*Saintpaulia*	Africa
Agapanthus	*Agapanthus*	S Africa
Allium	*Allium*	Asia/Europe
Alum root	*Heuchera*	N America
Alyssum	*Alyssum*	S Europe
Amaryllis/belladonna lily	*Amaryllis*	S Africa/tropical America
Anchusa	*Anchusa*	Asia/S Europe
Anemone	*Hepatica*	Europe/Caucasus
Asphodel	*Asphodelus*	S Europe
Aster	*Aster*	Europe/Asia/N America
Astilbe	*Astilbe*	Asia
Aubrietia	*Aubrietia*	SE Europe
Begonia	*Begonia*	S America/the Pacific
Bellflower	*Campanula*	N hemisphere
Bergamot	*Monarda*	N America
Bistort	*Polygonum*	Japan/Himalayas
Bleeding heart	*Dicentra*	China/Japan/N America
Bluebell	*Hyacinthoides*	Europe

Bugbane	*Cimicifuga*	N America/Japan
Busy lizzie	*Impatiens*	Tropics
Buttercup	*Ranunculus*	Temperate regions
Camassia	*Camassia*	N America
Carnation	*Dianthus*	Temperate regions
Catmint	*Nepeta*	Europe/Asia
Celandine	*Ranunculus*	Europe
Chionodoxa/glory of the snow	*Chionodoxa*	Greece/Turkey
Christmas rose	*Helleborus*	Europe
Chrysanthemum	*Chrysanthemum*	China
Cinquefoil	*Potentilla*	Europe/Asia
Columbine	*Aquilegia*	Europe
Crinum	*Crinum*	S Africa
Crocosmia	*Crocosmia*	S Africa
Crocus	*Crocus*	Mediterranean/Asia/ Africa
Crown imperial	*Fritillaria*	N India
Cupid's dart	*Catananche*	Europe
Cyclamen	*Cyclamen*	Asia/Mediterranean
Daffodil/narcissus	*Narcissus*	Mediterranean/Europe
Dahlia	*Dahlia*	Mexico
Daisy	*Bellis*	Europe
Delphinium	*Delphinium*	Europe/N America
Echinacea	*Echinacea*	N America
Edelweiss	*Leontopodium*	Europe/Asia
Erythronium/dog's tooth violet	*Erythronium*	Europe/Asia
Evening primrose	*Oenothera*	N America
Everlasting flower	*Helichrysum*	Australia
Everlasting flower (pearly)	*Anaphalis*	N America/Himalayas
Fleabane	*Erigeron*	Australia
Forget-me-not	*Myosotis*	Europe
Foxglove	*Digitalis*	Europe/Asia
Fraxinella	*Dictamnus*	Europe/Asia
Fritillaria	*Fritillaria*	Europe/Asia/N America
Galtonia	*Galtonia*	S Africa
Gentian	*Gentiana*	Temperate regions
Geranium	*Pelargonium*	Temperate regions/ subtropics
Geum	*Geum*	S Europe/N America
Gladiolus	*Gladiolus*	Europe/Asia/NE Africa
Goat's beard	*Aruncus*	N Europe
Golden rod	*Solidago*	Europe
Gypsophila	*Gypsophila*	Europe/Asia
Harebell	*Campanula*	N hemisphere
Hattie's pincushion	*Astrantia*	Europe
Heliopsis	*Heliopsis*	N America
Hellebore	*Helleborus*	Asia/Greece
Herb Christopher	*Actaea*	N America
Hippeastrum	*Hippeastrum*	Tropical America
Hollyhock	*Alcaea*	Europe/China
Hosta	*Hosta*	China/Japan
Hyacinth	*Hyacinthus*	S Europe/Asia

Flower	Genus/family	Origin
Hyacinth (grape)	*Muscari*	Europe/Mediterranean
Hyacinth (wild)	*Scilla*	Asia/S Europe
Iris	*Iris*	N hemisphere
Ithuriel's spear	*Brodiaea*	N America
Kaffir lily	*Schizostylis*	S Africa
Kirengeshoma	*Kirengeshoma*	Japan
Lapeirousia	*Lapeirousia*	S Africa
Liatris	*Liatris*	N America
Lily	*Lobelia*	China/Europe/America
Lily-of-the-valley	*Convallaria*	Europe/Asia/America
Lobelia	*Lobelia*	Africa/N America/Australia
Loosestrife	*Lysimachia*	Europe
Lotus	*Lotus*	Asia/America
Lupin	*Lupinus*	N America
Marigold (African, French)	*Tagetes*	Central America
Marigold (pot)	*Calendula*	(Obscure)
Meadow rue	*Thalictrum*	Europe/Asia
Mullein	*Verbascum*	Europe/Asia
Naked ladies	*Colchicum*	Asia/Europe
Nasturtium	*Tropaeolum*	S America/Mexico
Nerine	*Nerine*	S Africa
Orchid	*Orchidaea*	Tropics
Ornithogalum	*Ornithogalum*	S Africa
Ox-eye	*Buphthalmum*	Europe
Pansy	*Viola*	Temperate regions
Peacock/tiger flower	*Tigridia*	Asia
Peony	*Paeonia*	Asia/Europe
Peruvian lily	*Alstroemeria*	S America
Petunia	*Petunia*	S America
Phlox	*Phlox*	America
Poppy	*Papaver*	N hemisphere
Primrose	*Primula*	N hemisphere
Primula	*Primula*	N hemisphere
Red-hot poker	*Kniiphofia*	S Africa
Rouge (giant)	*Tigridia*	Mexico
Salvia	*Salvia*	S America/Europe/Asia
Sea holly	*Eryngium*	Europe/S America
Sidalcea	*Sidalcea*	N America
Snake's head	*Fritillaria*	Europe
Snapdragon	*Antirrhinum*	Europe/Asia/S America
Snowdrop	*Galanthus*	Europe
Snowflake	*Leucojum*	S Europe
Solfaterre	*Crocosmia crocosmiflora*	S Africa
Solomon's seal	*Polygonatum*	Europe/Asia
Speedwell	*Veronica*	Europe/Asia
Spiderwort	*Tradescantia*	N America
Squill	*Scilla*	Europe/Asia/S Africa
Sternbergia	*Sternbergia*	Europe
Stokesia	*Puschkinia*	N America
Striped squill	*Stokesia*	Asia

Sunflower	*Helianthus*	N America
Sweet pea	*Lathyrus*	Mediterranean
Sweet william	*Dianthus*	S Europe
Thistle (globe)	*Echinops*	Europe/Asia
Thistle (Scotch, cotton)	*Onopordum*	Europe
Tiger lily	*Lilium*	Asia
Tulip	*Tulipa*	Europe/Asia
Violet	*Viola*	N hemisphere
Wand flower	*Dierama*	S Africa
Water chestnut	*Trapa*	Asia
Water lily	*Nymphaea*	(Worldwide)
Winter aconite	*Eranthis*	Greece/Turkey
Wolfsbane	*Aconitum*	Europe/Asia
Yarrow	*Achillea*	Europe/W Asia

Shrubs

Shrub	Genus/family	Origin
Abelia	*Abelia*	Asia/China/Mexico
Abutilon	*Abutilon*	S America
Acacia/mimosa/wattle	*Acacia*	Australia/tropics
Almond (dwarf)	*Prunus*	Asia/Europe
Ampelopsis	*Ampelopsis*	Far East
Anthyllis	*Anthyllis*	Europe
Azalea	*Rhododendron*	N hemisphere
Berberis	*Berberis*	Asia/America/Europe
Bottle brush	*Callistemon*	Australia
Bougainvillea	*Bougainvillea*	S America
Broom	*Cytisus*	Europe
Buckthorn	*Rhamnus*	N hemisphere
Buddleia	*Buddleja*	China/S America
Cactus	*Cactaceae*	America
Calico bush/mountain laurel	*Kalmia*	China
Camellia	*Camellia*	Asia
Caryopteris	*Caryopteris*	Asia
Ceanothus	*Ceanothus*	N America
Ceratostigma	*Ceratostigma*	China
Chinese lantern	*Physalis*	Japan
Cistus	*Cistus*	Europe
Clematis	*Clematis*	N hemisphere
Clerodendrum	*Clerodendrum*	China
Colquhonia	*Colquhounia*	Himalayas
Cornelian cherry	*Cornus*	Europe
Coronilla	*Coronilla*	S Europe
Corylopsis	*Corylopsis*	China/Japan
Cotoneaster	*Cotoneaster*	Asia
Currant (flowering)	*Ribes*	N America
Desfontainia	*Desfontainia*	S America
Deutzia	*Deutzia*	Asia
Diplera	*Diplera*	China

Shrub	Genus/family	Origin
Dogwood	*Cornus*	Europe/SW Asia
Embothrium	*Embothrium*	S America
Escallonia	*Escallonia*	S America
Euchryphia	*Euchryphia*	Chile/Australasia
Euryops	*Euryops*	S Africa
Fabiana	*Fabiana*	S America
Firethorn	*Pyracantha*	China
Forsythia	*Forsythia*	China
Frangipani	*Plumeria*	Tropical America
Fuchsia	*Fuchsia*	Central and S America/ New Zealand
Gardenia	*Gardenia*	Tropics
Garland flower	*Daphne*	Europe/Asia
Garrya	*Garrya*	America
Gorse/furze	*Ulex*	Europe
Hawthorn	*Crataegus*	N America/Europe/ N Africa
Heath (winter-flowering)	*Erica*	Africa/Europe
Heather	*Calluna*	Europe/W Asia
Hebe	*Hebe*	New Zealand
Helichrysum	*Helichrysum*	Australia/S Africa
Hibiscus	*Hibiscus*	China/India
Honeysuckle	*Lonicera*	Temperate regions
Hydrangea	*Hydrangea*	Asia/America
Hyssop	*Hyssopus*	S Europe/W Asia
Indigofera	*Indigofera*	Himalayas
Ipomoea/morning glory	*Ipomoea*	Tropical America
Japonica	*Chaenomeles*	N Asia
Jasmine	*Jasminum*	Asia
Jerusalem sage	*Phlomis*	Europe
Kerria	*Kerria*	China
Kolkwitzia	*Kolkwitzia*	China
Laburnum	*Laburnum*	Europe/Asia
Lavender	*Lavandula*	Europe
Leptospermum	*Leptospermum*	Australasia
Lespedeza	*Lespedeza*	China/Japan
Leycesteria	*Leycesteria*	Himalayas
Lilac/syringa	*Syringa*	Europe
Lion's tail	*Leonotis*	S Africa
Magnolia	*Magnolia*	China/Japan
Mahonia	*Mahonia*	Japan
Malus	*Malus*	N America/Asia
Mensiesa	*Menziesa*	Japan
Mimulus	*Mimulus*	N America
Mock orange	*Philadelphus*	Europe/Asia/N America
Moltkia	*Moltkia*	Greece
Mother-of-pearl	*Symphoricarpus*	N America
Myrtle	*Myrtus*	Europe
Oleander	*Nerium*	Mediterranean
Olearia	*Olearia*	New Zealand

Oleaster	*Eleagnus*	Europe/Asia/N America
Osmanthus	*Osmanthus*	China
Pearl bush	*Exochorda*	China
Peony	*Paeonia*	Europe/Asia/N America
Pieris	*Pieris*	China
Poinsettia	*Euphorbia*	Mexico
Potentilla	*Potentilla*	Asia
Rhododendron	*Rhododendron*	S Asia
Rhus	*Rhus*	Europe/N America
Ribbon woods	*Hoheria*	New Zealand
Robinia	*Robinia*	N America
Rock rose/sun rose	*Helianthemum*	Europe
Rose	*Rosa*	N hemisphere
Rosemary	*Rosmarinus*	Europe/Asia
Rowan/mountain ash	*Sorbus*	Europe/Asia
Sage (common)	*Salvia*	S Europe
St John's wort	*Hypericum*	Europe/Asia
Sea buckthorn	*Hippophae*	SW Europe
Senecio	*Senecio*	New Zealand
Skimmia	*Skimmia*	Japan/China
Snowberry	*Symphoricarpos*	N America
Spiraea	*Spiraea*	China/Japan
Stachyurus	*Stachyurus*	China
Staphylea	*Staphylea*	Europe/Asia
Tamarisk	*Tamarix*	Europe
Thyme	*Thymus*	Europe
Veronica	*Veronica*	New Zealand
Viburnum	*Viburnum*	Europe/Asia/Africa
Virginia creeper	*Parthenocissus*	N America
Weigela	*Weigela*	N China
Winter sweet	*Chimonanthus*	China
Wisteria	*Wisteria*	China/Japan
Witch-hazel	*Hamamelis*	China/Japan

Trees

Tree	Species	Origin
Alder (common)	*Alnus glutinosa*	Europe
Almond	*Prunus dulcis*	W Asia/N Africa
Apple	*Malus pumila*	Europe/W Africa
Apple (crab)	*Malus sylvestris*	Europe/Asia
Ash	*Fraxinus excelsior*	Europe
Aspen	*Populus tremula*	Europe
Bean tree	*Catalpa bignonioides*	America/SE Asia
Beech (common)	*Fagus sylvatica*	Europe
Beech (copper)	*Fagus purpurea 'Atropunicea'*	Europe
Beech (roble)	*Nothofagus obliqua*	S America
Birch (silver)	*Betula pendula*	Europe/America/Asia
Box	*Buxus sempervirens*	Europe/N Africa

Tree	Species	Origin
Brazil nut	*Bertholletia excelsa*	S America
Camellia	*Stewartia pseudo-camellia*	Asia
Castor-oil (prickly)	*Eleutherococcus pictus*	Tropics
Cedar of Lebanon	*Cedrus libani*	Asia
Cedar (smooth Tasmanian)	*Arthrotaxis cupressoides*	Australia
Cedar (white)	*Thuja occidentalis*	America
Cherry (morello/sour)	*Prunus cerasus*	Europe/Asia
Cherry (wild/gean)	*Prunus avium*	Europe
Chestnut (horse)	*Aesculus hippocastanum*	Asia/SW Europe
Chestnut (sweet/Spanish)	*Castanea sativa*	Europe/Africa/Asia
Cypress (Lawson)	*Chamaecyparis lawsoniana*	America
Deodar	*Cedrus deodara*	Asia
Dogwood (common)	*Cornus sanguinea*	Europe
Elm (Dutch)	*Ulmus hollandica*	Europe
Elm (English)	*Ulmus procera*	Europe
Elm (wych)	*Ulmus glabra*	Europe
Fig	*Ficus carica*	Asia
Fir (Douglas)	*Pseudotsuga menziesii*	America
Fir (red)	*Abies magnifica*	America
Ginkgo	*Ginkgo biloba*	Asia
Grapefruit	*Citrus paradisi*	Asia
Gum (blue)	*Eucalyptus globulus*	Australia
Gum (cider)	*Eucalyptus gunnii*	Australia
Gum (snow)	*Eucalyptus panciflora*	Australia
Gutta-percha	*Eucommia ulmoides*	China
Hawthorn	*Crataegus monogyna*	Europe
Hazel	*Corylus avellana*	Europe/W Asia/N Africa
Hemlock	*Tsuga heterophylla*	America
Holly	*Ilex aquifolium*	Europe/N Africa/W Asia
Hornbeam	*Carpinus betulus*	Europe/Asia
Joshua-tree	*Yucca brevifolia*	America
Judas-tree	*Cercis siliquastrum*	S Europe/Asia
Juniper	*Juniperus communis*	Europe/Asia
Laburnum	*Laburnum anagyroides*	Europe
Larch (European)	*Larix decidua*	Europe
Larch (golden)	*Pseudolarix kaempferi*	E Asia
Leatherwood	*Eucryphia lucida*	Australia
Lemon	*Citrus limon*	Asia
Lime	*Citrus aurantiifolia*	Asia
Lime (small-leafed)	*Tilia cordata*	Europe
Locust	*Robinia pseudoacacia*	America
Magnolia (white laurel)	*Magnolia virginiana*	America
Maple (field/common)	*Acer campestre*	Europe
Maple (sugar)	*Acer saccharum*	America
Medlar	*Mespilus germanica*	Europe
Mimosa	*Acacia dealbata*	Australia/Europe
Mockernut	*Carya tomentosa*	America
Monkey puzzle	*Araucaria araucana*	S America
Mulberry (common)	*Morus nigra*	Asia
Mulberry (white)	*Morus alba*	Asia

Myrtle	*Myrtus apiculata*	S America
Nutmeg	*Torreya californica*	America
Oak (California live)	*Quercus agrifolia*	America
Oak (cork)	*Quercus suber*	S Europe/N Africa
Oak (English/common)	*Quercus robur*	Europe/Asia/Africa
Oak (red)	*Quercus rubra*	America
Olive	*Olea europaea*	S Europe
Orange (sweet)	*Citrus sinensis*	Asia
Pagoda-tree	*Sophora japonica*	China/Japan
Pear	*Pyrus communis*	Europe/W Asia
Pine (Austrian)	*Pinus nigra subsp. nigra*	Europe/Asia
Pine (Corsican)	*Pinus nigra subsp. laricio*	Europe
Pine (Monterey)	*Pinus radiata*	America
Pine (Scots)	*Pinus sylvestris*	Europe
Plane (London)	*Platanus hispanica*	Europe
Plane (Oriental)	*Platanus orientalis*	SE Europe/Asia
Plum	*Prunus domestica*	Europe/Asia
Poplar (balsam)	*Populus balsamifera*	America/Asia
Poplar (black)	*Populus nigra*	Europe/Asia
Poplar (Lombardy)	*Populus nigra 'Italica'*	Europe
Poplar (white)	*Populus alba*	Europe
Quince	*Cydonia oblonga*	Asia
Raoul	*Nothofagus procera*	S America
Rowan (mountain ash)	*Sorbus aucuparia*	Europe
Sassafras	*Sassafras albidum*	America
Service tree	*Sorbus domestica*	Europe
Silver fir	*Abies alba*	Europe
Spruce (Norway)	*Picea abies*	Europe
Spruce (sitka)	*Picea sitchensis*	America/Europe
Strawberry tree	*Arbutus unedo*	Europe
Sycamore (plane)	*Acer pseudoplatanus*	Europe/W Asia
Tamarack	*Larix laricina*	N America
Tree of heaven	*Ailanthus altissima*	China
Tulip tree	*Liriodendron tulipifera*	America
Walnut (black)	*Juglans nigra*	America
Walnut (common)	*Juglans regia*	Europe/Asia
Whitebeam	*Sorbus aria*	Europe
Willow (pussy/goat/sallow)	*Salix caprea*	Europe/Asia
Willow (weeping)	*Salix babylonica*	Asia
Willow (white)	*Salix alba*	Europe
Yew	*Taxus baccata*	N hemisphere

3.3 *Animals*

Classification of animals

Phylum	Number of species	Examples
Acanthocephala	600	Spiny-headed worms
Annelida	8 900	Earthworms, leeches, lugworms
Arthropoda	more than 2 000 000	Ants, beetles, bugs, centipedes, crabs, flies, lobsters, millipedes, ticks, wasps, woodlice
Brachiopoda	335	Lamp shells
Chaetognatha	more than 100	Arrow worms
Chordata	45 000	Birds, bony fish, crocodiles, frogs, lizards, mammals, newts, rays, salamanders, sharks, snakes, toads, turtles
Cnidaria	9 500	Corals, jellyfish, sea anemones
Ctenophora	90	Comb jellies, sea gooseberries
Echinodermata	6 000	Sea cucumbers, sea urchins, starfish
Echiura	140	Spoon worms
Ectoprocta	5 000	Ectoprocts
Entoprocta	150	Entoprocts
Gastrotricha	400	Gastrotrichs
Gnasthostomulida	80	Jaw worms
Hemichordata	90	Hemichordates
Kinorhyncha	150	Kinorhynchs
Loricifera	10	Loriciferans
Mesozoa	50	Mesozoans
Mollusca	110 000	Clams, mussels, octopus, oysters, slugs, snails, squid
Nematoda	more than 80 000	Roundworms
Nematomorpha	240	Hair-worms, horsehair worms
Nemertina	900	Ribbon worms
Onychophora	80	Velvet worms
Pentastoma	70	Tongue worms
Phoronida	10	Horseshoe worms
Placozoa	1	Trichoplax adhaerens
Platyhelminthes	15 000	Flatworms, flukes, roundworms, tapeworms
Pogonophora	100	Beard worms
Porifera	10 000	Sponges
Priapulida	10	Priapulids
Rotifera	2 000	Rotifers
Sipuncula	more than 300	Peanut worms
Tardigrada	380	Water bears

Amphibians

Order	Family	Number of species	Examples
Anura	Brachycephalidae	2	Terrestrial toads
	Bufonidae	235	True toads
	Centrolenidae	60	Leaf frogs
	Dendrobatidae	70	Arrow-poison frogs
	Discoglossidae	8	Fire-bellied toads, midwife toads
	Hylidae	400	Tree frogs
	Leiopelmatidae	4	Primitive frogs
	Leptodactylidae	650	Terrestrial neotropical frogs
	Microhylidae	230	Narrow-mouthed frogs
	Myobatrachidae	95	Aquatic frogs, arboreal frogs, terrestrial frogs
	Pelobatidea	59	Spadefoots
	Pipidae	14	Tongueless frogs
	Pseudidae	5	Fully aquatic frogs
	Ranidae	850	True frogs
	Rhinodermatidae	1	Mouth-breeding frogs
	Rhinophrynidae	1	Burrowing toads
	Sooglossidae	3	Terrestrial frogs
Gymnophiona		160	Caecilians
Trachystomata		3	Sirens
Urodela/Caudata	Ambystomatidae	33	Axolotls, mole salamanders
	Amphiumidae	3	Congo eels
	Cryptobranchidae	3	Giant salamanders
	Hynobiidae	30	Asiatic salamanders
	Necturidae	5	Mud puppies
	Plethodontidae	210	Lungless salamanders
	Proteidae	1	Olms
	Salamandridae	42	Newts, salamanders
	Sirenidae	3	Dwarf sirens, sirens

Birds

Order	Family	Number of species	Examples
Anseriformes	Anatidae	147	Ducks, geese, swans
	Anhimidae	3	Screamers
Apodiformes	Apodidae	80	Swifts
	Hemiprocnidae	3	Crested swifts
	Trochilidae	320	Hummingbirds
Apterygiformes	Apterygidae	3	Kiwis
Caprimulgiformes	Aegothelidae	8	Owlet-nightjars
	Caprimulgidae	70	Nightjars
	Nyctibiidae	5	Potoos
	Podargidae	12	Frogmouths
	Steatornithidae	1	Oilbirds

Order	Family	Number of species	Examples
Casuariiformes	Casuariidae	3	Cassowaries
	Dromaiidae	1	Emus
Charadriiformes	Burhinidae	9	Stonecurlews
	Charadriidae	62	Lapwings, plovers
	Chionididae	2	Sheathbills
	Dromadidae	1	Crab plovers
	Glareolidae	17	Pratincoles
	Haematopodidae	6	Oystercatchers
	Jacanidae	7	Jacanas
	Phalaropodidae	3	Phalaropes
	Recurvirostridae	7	Avocets
	Rostratulidae	2	Painted snipe
	Scolopacidae	81	Sandpipers
	Thinocoridae	4	Seed snipe
Ciconiiformes	Ardeidae	60	Bitterns, herons
	Balaenicipitidae	1	Whale-headed storks
	Ciconiidae	17	Storks
	Phoenicopteridae	5	Flamingos
	Scopidae	1	Hammerheads
	Threskiornithidae	31	Ibises, spoonbills
Coliiformes	Coliidae	6	Mousebirds
Columbiformes	Columbidae	300	Doves, pigeons
	Pteroclididae	16	Sandgrouse
Coraciiformes	Alcedinidae	87	Kingfishers
	Bucerotidae	45	Hornbills
	Coraciidae	16	Rollers
	Leptosomatidae	1	Cuckoo-rollers
	Meropidae	24	Bee-eaters
	Momotidae	8	Motmots
	Phoeniculidae	6	Woodhoopoes
	Todidae	5	Todies
	Upupidae	1	Hoopoes
Cuculiformes	Cuculidae	128	Cuckoos, roadrunners
	Musophagidae	22	Turacos
	Opisthocomidae	1	Hoatzins
Falconiformes	Accipitridae	217	Buzzards, eagles, harriers, hawks, kites, Old World vultures
	Cathartidae	7	New World vultures
	Falconidae	60	Caracaras, falcons
	Pandionidae	1	Ospreys
	Sagittariidae	1	Secretary birds
Galliformes	Cracidae	42	Curassows, guans
	Megapodidae	9	Megapodes
	Meleagrididae	2	Turkeys
	Numididae	7	Guineafowls
	Phasianidae	180	Partridges, pheasants, quails
	Tetraonidae	16	Grouse
Gaviiformes	Gaviidae	4	Divers
Gruiformes	Aramidae	1	Limpkin

	Cariamidae	2	Seriemas
	Eurypygidae	1	Sunbitterns
	Gruidae	15	Cranes
	Heliornithidae	3	Finfoots
	Mesitornithidae	3	Mesites
	Otididae	22	Bustards
	Pedionomidae	1	Plains wanderer
	Psophiidae	3	Trumpeters
	Rallidae	129	Rails
	Rhynochetidae	1	Kagu
	Turnicidae	16	Buttonquails
Passeriformes	Acanthizinae	65	Australian warblers
	Aegithalidae	7	Long-tailed tits
	Alaudidae	75	Larks
	Artamidae	10	Wood swallows
	Atrichornithidae	2	Scrub-birds
	Bombycillidae	8	Waxwings
	Bubalornithinae	3	Buffalo weavers
	Callaeidae	3	New Zealand wattlebirds
	Campephagidae	72	Cuckoo-shrikes
	Cardinalinae	37	Cardinals, grosbeaks
	Carduelinae	122	Cardueline finches
	Catamblyrhynchinae	1	Plush-capped finches
	Certhiidae	5	Holarctic treecreepers
	Cinclidae	5	Dippers
	Climacteridae	8	Australasian treecreepers
	Conopophagidae	9	Gnateaters
	Corcoracidae	2	Australian mudnesters
	Corvidae	113	Crows, jays, magpies
	Cotingidae	65	Cotingas
	Cracticidae	9	Bell magpies
	Dendrocolaptidae	48	Woodcreepers
	Dicaeidae	50	Flowerpeckers
	Dicruridae	20	Drongos
	Drepanidinae	23	Hawaiian honeycreepers
	Dulidae	1	Palmchats
	Emberizinae	281	New World sparrows, Old World buntings
	Ephthianuridae	5	Australian chats
	Estrildidae	124	Waxbills
	Eurylaimidae	14	Broadbills
	Formicariidae	230	Antbirds
	Fringillinae	3	Fringilline finches
	Furnariidae	220	Ovenbirds
	Grallinidae	2	Magpie larks
	Hirundinidae	74	Martins, swallows
	Icteridae	94	American blackbirds
	Irenidae	14	Leafbirds
	Laniidae	69	Shrikes
	Malurinae	26	Fairy-wrens
	Meliphagidae	169	Honeyeaters
	Menuridae	2	Lyrebirds

Order	Family	Number of species	Examples
	Mimidae	30	Mockingbirds
	Monarchinae	133	Monarch flycatchers
	Motacillidae	54	Pipits, wagtails
	Muscicapinae	155	Old World flycatchers
	Nectariniidae	116	Sunbirds
	Oriolidae	28	Orioles
	Orthonychinae	20	Logrunners
	Oxyruncidae	1	Sharpbills
	Pachycephalinae	46	Thickheads
	Paradox-ornithinae	19	Parrotbills
	Paradisaeidae	43	Birds of paradise
	Pardalotidae	5	Pardalotes
	Paridae	46	Tits
	Parulidae	119	Wood warblers
	Passerinae	37	Sparrows
	Philepittidae	4	Sunbird asities
	Phytotomidae	3	Plantcutters
	Pipridae	53	Manakins
	Pittidae	29	Pittas
	Ploceinae	95	True weavers
	Prionopidae	9	Helmet shrikes
	Prunellidae	13	Accentors
	Ptilonorhynchidae	18	Bowerbirds
	Pycnonotidae	120	Bulbuls
	Remizidae	10	Penduline tits
	Rhabdornithidae	2	Philippine treecreepers
	Rhinocryptidae	29	Tapaculos
	Rhipidurinae	39	Fantail flycatchers
	Sittidae	21	Nuthatches
	Sturnidae	106	Starlings
	Sylviidae	350	Old World warblers
	Tersininae	1	Swallow tanager
	Thraupinae	233	Honeycreepers
	Timaliidae	252	Babblers
	Troglodytidae	60	Wrens
	Turdidae	305	Thrushes
	Tyrannidae	375	Tyrant flycatchers
	Vangidae	13	Vanga shrikes
	Viduinae	10	Widow birds
	Vireonidae	43	Pepper shrikes
	Xenicidae	4	New Zealand wrens
	Zosteropidae	85	White-eyes
Pelecaniformes	Anhingidae	4	Darters
	Fregatidae	5	Frigatebirds
	Pelecanidae	7	Pelicans
	Phaethontidae	3	Tropicbirds
	Phalacrocoracidae	29	Cormorants
	Sulidae	9	Gannets
Piciformes	Bucconidae	30	Puffbirds
	Capitonidae	76	Barbets

Galbulidae	15	Jacamars
Indicatoridae	15	Honeyguides
Picidae	200	Woodpeckers
Ramphastidae	40	Toucans

Podicipediformes	Podicipedidae	20	Grebes
Procellariiformes	Diomedeidae	14	Albatrosses
	Hydrobatidae	4	Storm petrels
	Pelecanoididae	55	Diving petrels
	Procellariidae	20	Petrels, fulmars
Psittaciformes	Psittacidae	330	Parrots, cockatoos, macaws
Rheiformes	Rheidae	2	Rheas
Sphenisciformes	Spheniscidae	16	Penguins
Strigiformes	Strigidae	124	Owls
Struthioniformes	Struthionidae	1	Ostriches
Tinamiformes	Tinamidae	45	Tinamous
Trogoniformes	Trogonidae	35	Trogons

Fish

Class	Order	Number of species	Examples
Agnatha	Cyclostomata	60	Hagfishes, lampreys
Chondrichthyes	Batoidei	more than 300	Rays, skates, stingrays
	Selachii	more than 200	Sharks
Osteichthyes	Acipenseriformes	27	Paddlefishes, sturgeons
	Anguilliformes	more than 500	Eels
	Atheriniformes	575	Cyprinodonts, flying fishes, garfishes
	Characiformes	more than 1300	Darters, piranhas
	Clupeiformes	390	Anchovies, herrings
	Dipnoi	6	Lungfishes
	Elopiformes	12	Bonefishes, ladyfish, tarpons
	Gasterosteiformes	36	Sea horses, sticklebacks
	Ostariophysi	6 000	Carps, catfishes, loaches, minnows
	Osteoglossiformes	7	Bony tongues, freshwater butterfly fish
	Paracanthopterygii	853	Codfishes, toadfishes, trout-perches
	Perciformes	173	Marlins, perches, tunas
	Pleuronectiformes	more than 400	Flatfishes, flounders, soles
	Polypteriformes	11	Reedfishes
	Salmoniformes	160	Chars, graylings, pikes, salmon, trout, whitefishes
	Scorpaeniformes	330	Gunards, rockfishes, scorpion fishes
	Tetraodontiformes	35	Box fishes, ocean sunfishes, puffer fishes

Insects

Order	Number of species	Examples
Blattaria	3 700	Cockroaches
Coleoptera	250 000	Beetles, weevils
Collembola	2 000	Springtails
Dermaptera	1 500	Earwigs
Diplura	660	Diplurans
Diptera	150 000	True flies
Embioptera	200	Webspinners
Ephemeroptera	2 000	Mayflies
Hemiptera	35 000	True bugs
Homoptera	45 000	Aphids, cicadas, hoppers, scale insects, whiteflies
Hymenoptera	130 000	Ants, bees, sawflies, wasps
Isoptera	2 000	Termites
Lepidoptera	138 000	Butterflies, moths, skippers
Mantodea	1 800	Mantids, mantises
Mecoptera	450	Scorpion flies
Neuroptera	4 500	Alderflies, lacewings
Odonata	5 000	Damselflies, dragonflies
Orthoptera	24 000	Crickets, grasshoppers, locusts
Phasmida	2 500	Leaf insects, stick insects
Phthiraptera	3 400	Biting lice, booklice
Protura	120	Proturans
Siphonaptera	1 750	Fleas
Strepsiptera	400	Stylopids
Thysanoptera	5 000	Thrips
Thysanura	600	Bristletails, silverfish
Trichoptera	7 000	Caddisflies
Zoraptera	20	Zorapterans

Mammals

Order	Family	Number of species	Examples
Artiodactyla	Antilocapridae	1	Pronghorn
	Bovidae	110	Antelopes, cattle, goats, sheep
	Camelidae	4	Camels, llamas
	Cervidae	35	Deer
	Giraffidae	2	Giraffe, okapi
	Hippopotamidae	2	Hippopotami
	Suidae	8	Pigs
	Tayassuidae	3	Peccaries
	Tragulidae	4	Chevrotains
Carnivora	Canidae	35	Dogs, foxes, jackals, wolves
	Felidae	35	Cats
	Hyaenidae	4	Hyenas

	Mustelidae	65	Badgers, otters, weasels
	Otariidae	15	Walrus
	Phocidae	20	Earless seals
	Procyonidae	15	Coatis, raccoons
	Ursidae	7	Bears, giant pandas
	Viverridae	70	Civets, mongooses
Cetacea	Balaenidae	3	Right whales
	Balaenopteridae	8	Humpback whales
	Delphinidae	30	Dolphins, killer whales
	Eschrichtiidae	1	Grey whales
	Hyperoodontidae	15	Beaked whales
	Monodontidae	2	Narwhals
	Phocoenidae	6	Porpoises
	Physeteridae	3	Sperm whales
	Platanistidae	4	River dolphins
	Stenidae	4	Long-snouted dolphins
Chiroptera	Desmodontidae	3	Vampire bats
	Emballonuridae	50	Sheath-tailed bats
	Furipteridae	2	Smoky bats
	Hipposideridae	60	Old World leaf-nosed bats
	Megadermatidae	5	False vampires
	Molossidae	90	Free-tailed bats
	Mormoopidae	9	Insectivorous bats
	Mystacinidae	1	New Zealand short-tailed bats
	Myzopodidae	1	Old World sucker-footed bats
	Natalidae	4	Funnel-eared bats
	Noctilionidae	2	Bulldog bats
	Nycteridae	13	Slit-faced bats
	Phyllostomatidae	120	American leaf-nosed bats
	Pteropodidae	154	Flying foxes, Old World fruit bats
	Rhinolophidae	70	Horseshoe bats
	Rhinopomatidae	3	Mouse-tailed bats
	Thyropteridae	2	Disk-wing bats
	Vespertilionidae	290	Common bats
Edentata	Bradypodidae	520	Tree sloths
	Dasypodidae	20	Armadillos
	Myrmecophagidae	3	Anteaters
Insectivora	Chrysochloridae	11	Golden moles
	Erinaceidae	14	Hedgehogs
	Macroscelididae	28	Elephant shrews
	Potamogalidae	3	Otter shrews
	Solenodontidae	2	Almiqui, solenodon
	Soricidae	291	Shrews
	Talpidae	22	Moles
	Tenrecidae	20	Tenrecs
	Tupaiidae	15	Tree shrews
Lagomorpha	Leporidae	46	Hares, rabbits
	Ochotonidae	14	Pikas
Marsupialia	Burramyidae	6	Pigmy possums
	Caenolestidae	7	Rat oppossums
	Dasyuridae	48	Marsupial mice, native cats

Order	Family	Number of species	Examples
	Didelphidae	65	Opossums
	Macropodidae	47	Kangaroos, wallabies
	Myrmecobiidae	1	Numbats
	Notoryctidae	2	Marsupial moles
	Peramelidae	22	Bandicoots
	Petauridae	25	Gliding phalangers
	Phalangeridae	15	Phalangers
	Phascolarctidae	1	Koala
	Tarsipedidae	1	Honey possum
	Thylacinidae	1	Tasmanian wolf
	Thylacomyidae	20	Burrowing bandicoots
	Vombatidae	4	Wombats
Monotremes	Ornithorhynchidae	1	Platypus
	Tachyglossidae	2	Echidna
Perissodactyla	Equidae	7	Asses, donkeys, horses, zebras
	Rhinocerotidae	5	Rhinoceri
	Tapiridae	4	Tapirs
Primates	Callitrichidae	15	Marmosets, tamarins
	Cebidae	30	New World monkeys
	Cercopithecidae	72	Old World monkeys
	Cheirogaleidae	4	Dwarf lemurs, mouse lemurs
	Daubentoniidae	1	Aye aye
	Galagidae	7	Galagos
	Hominidae	1	Humans
	Hylobatidae	74	Gibbons
	Indriidae	4	Avahi, indris
	Lemuridae	14	Lemurs
	Lepilmuridae	2	Sportive lemurs
	Lorisidae	12	Bushbabies, lorises
	Pongidae	10	Chimpanzees, gorillas, orang-utans
	Tarsiidae	3	Tarsiers
	Tupaiidae	17	Tree shrews
Proboscidea	Elephantidae	2	African elephants, Asian elephants
Rodentia	Abrocomidae	2	Chinchilla rats
	Anomaluridae	7	Scaly-tailed squirrels
	Aplodontidae	1	Mountain beaver
	Bathyergidae	9	African mole rats
	Capromyidae	10	Coypus
	Castoridae	2	Beavers
	Caviidae	12	Cavies, guinea pigs
	Chinchillidae	6	Chinchillas
	Cricetidae	560	Field mice, lemmings, voles
	Ctenodactylidae	8	Gundis
	Ctenomyidae	26	Tuco-tucos
	Dasyproctidae	13	Agoutis, pacas
	Dinomyidae	1	Pacarana
	Dipodidae	25	Jerboas
	Echimyidae	40	Spiny rats

Erethizontidae	8	New World porcupines
Geomyidae	40	Pocket gophers
Gliridae	20	Dormice
Heteromyidae	75	Kangaroo rats, mice
Hydrochoeridae	2	Capybaras
Hystricidae	15	Old World porcupines
Muridae	450	Old World mice, Old World rats
Octodontidae	7	Octodonts
Pedetidae	1	Springhaas
Petromuridae	1	Rock rats
Rhizomyidae	18	Bamboo rats
Sciuridae	250	Chipmunks, marmots, squirrels
Seleveniidae	1	Jumping dormouse
Spalacidae	3	Mole rats
Thryonomyidae	2	Cane rats
Zapodidae	10	Jumping mice
Sirenia	Dugongidae	1	Dugong
	Trichechidae	3	Manatees

| Reptiles

Order	Family	Number of species	Examples
Chelonia	Carettochelyidae	1	New Guinea plateless turtles
	Cheloniidae	5	Sea turtles
	Chelydridae	2	Alligator snapping turtles, common snapping turtles
	Chelyidae	31	Snake-necked turtles
	Dermatemydidae	1	Central American river turtles
	Dermochelyidae	1	Leatherback turtles
	Emydidae	76	Common turtles
	Kinosternidae	21	Mud turtles, musk turtles
	Pelomedusidae	14	Side-necked turtles
	Platysternidae	1	Big-headed turtles
	Testudinidae	40	Tortoises
	Trionychidae	20	Soft-shell turtles
Crocodilia	Alligatoridae	7	Alligators, caimans
	Crocodilidae	13	True crocodiles
	Gavialidae	1	Gavials
Rhynchocephalia	Sphenodontidae	1	Tuatara
Squamata	Acrochordidae	2	Wart snakes
	Agamidae	300	Agamid lizards
	Amphisbaenidae	100	Worm lizards
	Anguidae	67	Alligator lizards, glass lizards
	Anniellidae	2	California legless lizards
	Boidae	60	Boas, pythons
	Chameleontidae	85	Old World chameleons
	Colubridae	more than 1 500	Aquatic snakes, arborial snakes, terrestrial snakes

Order	Family	Number of species	Examples
	Cordylidae	50	Girdle-tailed lizards
	Dibamidae	3	Burrowers
	Elapidae	170	Cobras, coral snakes, mambas
	Gekkonidae	650	Geckos
	Helodermatidae	2	Bearded lizards, Gila monster lizards
	Hydrophiidae	50	Sea snakes
	Iguanidae	600	Iguanas
	Lacertidae	150	Old World terrestrial lizards
	Lanthanotidae	1	Earless monitor lizards
	Letotyphlopidae	40	Slender blind snakes
	Pygopodidae	15	Flap-footed lizards
	Scincidae	800	Skinks
	Teiidae	200	Whiptail lizards
	Typhlopidae	200	Blind snakes, worm snakes
	Uropeltidae	50	Shieldtail snakes
	Varanidae	30	Monitor lizards
	Viperidae	180	Moccasin snakes, rattlesnakes, vipers
	Xantusiidae	12	Night lizards
	Xenopeltidae	1	Sunbeam snakes
	Xenosauridae	4	Xenosaurs

Animal records

Mammals

Largest animal	Blue whale	Up to 190 tonnes (187 tons)
Largest land mammal	African bush elephant	Up to 12.2 tonnes (12 tons)
Tallest mammal	Giraffe	Up to 5.8 m (19 ft)
Smallest mammal	Bumblebee (or Kitti's) hog-nosed bat	1.7–2 g (0.06–0.07 oz)
Fastest land mammal	Cheetah	Up to 100 kmh (62 mph)
Slowest mammal	Three-toed sloth	1.8–2.4 m (6–8 ft) per minute
Longest pregnancy	Asiatic elephant	650–760 days
Loudest animal call	Blue whale	Up to 188 decibels

Birds

Largest bird	Ostrich	Up to 156.5 kg (345 lb)
Longest wingspan	Wandering albatross	Up to 3.63 m (11 ft 11 in)
Smallest bird	Bee hummingbird (male)	1.6 g (0.056 oz)
Fastest bird	Peregrine falcon	Up to 200 kmh (124 mph)
Highest flight	Ruppell's vulture	Up to 11 300 m (37 000 ft)
Largest egg	Ostrich	Up to 2.35 kg (5 lb 3 oz)

Fish

Largest fish	Whale shark	Up to 15–21 tonnes (14.8–20.7 tons)
Smallest fish	Dwarf goby (male)	8.6 mm (0.339 in)
Fastest fish	Cosmopolitan sailfish	Up to 109 kmh (68 mph)
Slowest fish	Sea horse	0.016 kmh (0.001 mph)
Most poisonous fish	Puffer fish	Contains tetrodotoxin

Reptiles

Largest reptile	Estuarine or saltwater crocodile	Up to 7 m (23 ft)
Largest snake	Anaconda	Up to 8.5 m (27 ft 9 in)
Longest snake	Reticulated python	Up to 10 m (32 ft 10 in)
Longest venomous snake	King cobra	Up to 5.71 m (18 ft 9 in)
Largest lizard	Komodo monitor	Up to 2.25 m (7 ft 5 in)
Smallest lizard	Sphaerodactylus parthenopion gecko	1.8 cm (0.7 in)

Amphibians

Largest amphibian	Giant salamandar	Up to 1.2 m (3.9 ft)

Molluscs

Largest mollusc	Atlantic giant squid	Up to 17 m (56 ft)

Crustaceans

Largest crustacean	Giant spider crab	(claw span) Up to 2.7 m (8 ft 9 in)

Jellyfish

Largest jellyfish	Arctic giant	Up to 2.2 m (7 ft 3 in)

Worms

Longest worm	Bootlace worm	Up to 40 m (131 ft)

Insects

Largest insect	Goliath beetle	Up to 0.11 m (4 in)
Largest butterfly	Queen Alexandra's birdwing	(wingspan) Up to 0.28 m (11 in)
Fastest flying insect	Dragonfly	Up to 75 kmh (45 mph)

Spiders

Largest spider	Goliath bird-eating spider	(leg-span) Up to 0.25 m (10 in)

Periods of gestation or incubation

Species	Average gestation/incubation (days)
African elephant	640
Camel	406
Canary	14
Cat	62
Chicken	21
Chimpanzee	237
Cow	280
Dog	62
Dolphin	276
Duck	28
Ferret	42
Fox	52
Giraffe	395–425
Goat	151
Grey squirrel	44
Guinea pig	68

Species	Average gestation/incubation (days)
Hamster	16
Hedgehog	35–40
Horse	337
Human	266–273
Hyena	110
Kangaroo	40
Lion	108
Mink	50
Mouse	21
Northern fur seal	350
Opossum	13
Orang-utan	245–75
Pig	113
Pigeon	18
Rabbit	32
Rat	21
Reindeer	215–45
Rhesus monkey	164
Sheep	148
Skunk	62
Tiger	105–9
Turkey	28
Whale	365
Zebra	392

Extinct and endangered species

Class	Number of extinct species	Number of species extinct in the wild	Number of endangered species
Actinopterygii	80	11	715
Amphibia (amphibians)	5	0	124
Anthozoa	0	0	2
Arachnida (spiders etc.)	0	0	10
Aves (birds)	104	4	1107
Bivalvia (bivalves)	12	0	114
Cephalaspidomorphi	1	0	3
Chilopoda	0	0	1
Crustacea (crustaceans)	9	1	407
Echinoidea	0	0	0
Elasmobranchii	0	0	15
Enopla	0	0	2
Gastropoda (gastropods)	216	9	806
Hirudinea	0	0	0
Insecta (insects)	72	1	537
Mammalia (mammals)	86	3	1096
Merostomata	0	0	0
Oligochaeta	0	0	5

Onychophora	3	0	6
Polychaeta	0	0	1
Reptilia (reptiles)	20	1	253
Sarcopterygii (coelocanths)	0	0	1
Turbellaria	1	0	0

Endangered birds

Bird	Species	Habitat
Adjutant (greater)	*Leptoptilos dubius*	India
Akialoa (Kauai)	*Hemignathus obscurus*	Kauai (Hawaii, USA)
Akiapola'au	*Hemignathus wilsoni*	Hawaii (USA)
Albatross (Amsterdam Island)	*Diomedea amsterdamensis*	Amsterdam Island (French Southern and Antarctic Territories)
Albatross (short-tailed)	*Diomedea albatrus*	Japan
Alethe (Cholo)	*Alethe choloensis*	Malawi, Mozambique
Antbird (grey-headed)	*Myrmeciza griseiceps*	Ecuador, Peru
Antpitta (brown banded)	*Grallaria milleri*	Colombia
Antpitta (moustached)	*Grallaria alleni*	Colombia
Antpitta (Tachira)	*Grallaris chthonia*	Venezuela
Antwren (Alagoas)	*Myrmotherula snowi (Terenura sicki)*	Brazil
Antwren (ash-throated)	*Herpsilochmus parkeri*	Peru
Antwren (black-hooded)	*Formicivora erythronotos*	Brazil
Antwren (Restinga)	*Formicivora littoralis*	Brazil
Attila (ochraceous)	*Attila torridus*	Colombia, Ecuador, Peru
Becard (slaty)	*Pachyramphus spodiurus*	Ecuador, Peru
Blackbird (Forbes's)	*Curaeus forbesi*	Brazil
Blackbird (yellow-shouldered)	*Agelaius xanthomus*	Puerto Rico
Booby (Abbott's)	*Papasula abbotti (Sula abbotti)*	Christmas Island and Cocos Islands (Australia), Indonesia
Bushbird (recurve-billed)	*Clytoctantes alixii*	Colombia, Venezuela
Calyptura (Kinglet)	*Calyptura cristata*	Brazil
Cockatoo (Philippine)	*Cacatua haematuropygia*	Philippines
Cockatoo (salmon-crested)	*Cacatua moluccensis*	Indonesia
Cockatoo (Tanimbar)	*Cacatua goffini*	Tanimbar Island (Indonesia)
Cockatoo (white)	*Cacatua alba*	Indonesia
Condor (California)	*Gymnogyps californianus*	California (USA)
Coquette (short-crested)	*Lophornis brachylopha*	Mexico
Coucal (green-billed)	*Centropus chlororhynchus*	Sri Lanka
Crane (whooping)	*Grus americana*	Canada
Creeper (oahu)	*Paroreomyza maculata*	Hawaii (USA)
Crow (Hawaiian)	*Corvus hawaiiensis*	Hawaii (USA)
Crow (Mariana)	*Corvus kubaryi*	Guam, Mariana Islands (USA)
Curassow (Alagoas)	*Mitu mitu*	Brazil

Bird	Species	Habitat
Curassow (blue-knobbed)	*Crax alberti*	Colombia
Curassow (helmeted)	*Pauxi pauxi*	Colombia, Venezuela
Curlew (Eskimo)	*Numenius borealis*	Alaska (USA), Canada, S America
Dove (blue-eyed ground)	*Columbina cyanopsis*	Brazil
Dove (Grenada)	*Leptotila wellsi*	Grenada
Dove (ochre-bellied)	*Leptotila ochraceiventris*	Ecuador, Peru
Dove (purple-winged ground)	*Claravis godefrida*	Argentina, Brazil, Paraguay
Dove (Socorro)	*Zeanaida graysoni*	Revillagigedo Island (Mexico)
Eagle (Adalbert's)	*Aquila adalberti*	Portugal, Spain
Eagle (Great Philippine)	*Pithecophaga jefferyi*	Philippines
Eagle (Madagascar fish)	*Haliaeetus vociferoides*	Madagascar
Eagle (Madagascar serpent)	*Eutriorchis astur*	Madagascar
Emerald (Honduran)	*Amazilia luciae*	Honduras
Finch (Cochabamba mountain-)	*Poospiza garleppi*	Bolivia
Finch (Laysan)	*Telespiza cantans*	Hawaii (USA)
Finch (Nihoa)	*Telespiza ultima*	Hawaii (USA)
Finch (pale-headed brush-)	*Atlapetes pallidiceps*	Ecuador
Finch (rufous-breasted warbling-)	*Poospiza rubecula*	Peru
Fire-eye (fringe-backed)	*Pyriglena atra*	Brazil
Florican (Bengal)	*Eupodotis bengalensis (Houbaropsis bengalensis)*	India, Nepal, Vietnam
Florican (lesser)	*Eupoditis indica (Sypheotides indica)*	India, Nepal
Flycatcher (Guam)	*Myiagra freycineti*	Guam, Mariana Islands (USA)
Flycatcher (Tahiti monarch)	*Pomarea nigra*	Tahiti
Fody (Mauritius)	*Foudia rubra*	Mauritius
Fody (yellow)	*Foudia flavicans*	Rodrigues Island (Mauritius)
Foliage-gleaner (Alagoas)	*Philydor novaesi*	Brazil
Foliage-gleaner (rufous-necked)	*Automolus ruficollis*	Ecuador, Peru
Francolin (ochre-breasted)	*Francolinus ochropectus*	Djibouti
Grebe (Alaotra)	*Tachybaptus rufolavatus*	Madagascar
Grebe (Colombian)	*Podiceps andinus*	Colombia
Grebe (Puna)	*Podiceps taczanowskii*	Peru
Guan (Trinidad piping)	*Pipile pipile*	Trinidad
Guan (white-winged)	*Penelope albipennis*	Peru
Guineafowl (white-breasted)	*Agelastes meleagrides*	Côte d'Ivoire, Liberia, Sierra Leone
Hawk (grey-backed)	*Leucopternis occidentalis*	Ecuador, Peru
Heron (white-bellied)	*Ardea insignis (Ardea imperialis)*	Bangladesh, Bhutan, India, Myanmar
Heron (white-eared night)	*Gorsachius magnificus*	China
Honeyeater (Tagula)	*Meliphaga vicina*	Tagula Island (Papua New Guinea)
Ibis (crested)	*Nipponia nippon*	Sado Island (Japan)

Ibis (Waldrapp)	*Geronticus eremita*	Morocco
Jacamar (three-toed)	*Jacamaralcyon tridactyla*	Brazil
Jay (dwarf)	*Cyanolyca nana*	Mexico
Junco (Guadalupe)	*Junco insularis*	Guadalupe Island (Mexico)
Kagu	*Rhynochetos jubatos*	New Caledonia
Kakapo	*Strigops habroptilus*	New Zealand
Kamao	*Myadestes mydestinus*	Hawaii (USA)
Kestrel (Mauritius)	*Falco punctatus*	Mauritius
Kokako	*Callaeas cinerea*	New Zealand
Lark (Raso)	*Alauda razae*	Raso Island (Cape Verde)
Macaw (blue-throated)	*Ara glaucogularis*	Bolivia
Macaw (glaucous)	*Anodorhynchus glaucus*	S America
Macaw (Lear's/indigo)	*Anodorhynchus leari*	S America
Macaw (little blue)	*Cyanopsitta spixii*	Brazil
Malimbe (Ibadan)	*Malimbus ibadanensis*	Nigeria
Merganser (Brazilian)	*Mergus octosetaceus*	Argentina, Brazil, Paraguay
Mockingbird (Charles)	*Nesomimus trifasciatus*	Galapagos Islands (Ecuador)
Mockingbird (Socorro)	*Mimodes graysoni*	Socorro Island (Mexico)
Monal (Chinese)	*Lophophorus lhuysii*	W China
Myna (Bali/Rothschild's starling)	*Leucopsar rothschildi*	Bali (Indonesia)
Nightjar (white winged)	*Caprimulgus candicans*	Brazil
Nukupu'u	*Hemignathus lucidus*	Hawaii (USA)
Olomao	*Myadestes lanaiensis*	Hawaii (USA)
Oo (bishop's)	*Moho bishopi*	Hawaii (USA)
Oo (kauai)	*Moho braccatus*	Hawaii (USA)
Oriole (Martinique)	*Icterus bonana*	Martinique
O'u	*Psittirostra psittacea*	Hawaii (USA)
Owl (Madagascar red)	*Tyto soumagnei*	Madagascar
Owl (Sokeke scops-)	*Otus ireneae*	Kenya
Oystercatcher (Chatham Islands)	*Haematopus unicolor chuthumensis*	Chatham Islands (New Zealand)
Palila	*Loxioidea bailleui*	Hawaii (USA)
Parakeet (Mauritius)	*Psittacula echo*	Mauritius
Parrot (ground)	*Pezoporus wallicus*	SW Australia
Parrot (Imperial)	*Amazona imperialis*	Dominica
Parrot (indigo-winged)	*Hapalopsittaca fuertesi*	Colombia
Parrot (Paradise)	*Psephotus pulcherrimus*	Australia
Parrot (Puerto Rican)	*Amazona vittata*	Puerto Rico
Parrot (red-faced)	*Hapalopsittaca pyrrhops*	Ecuador, Peru
Parrot (red-tailed)	*Amazona brasiliensis*	SE Brazil
Parrot (St Lucia)	*Amazona versicolor*	St Lucia (West Indies)
Parrot (yellow-eared)	*Ognorhynchus icterotis*	Colombia, Ecuador
Partridge (bearded wood-)	*Dendrortyx barbatus*	Mexico
Partridge (Hainan)	*Arborophila ardens*	China
Partridge (Sichuan)	*Arborophila rufipectus*	China
Petrel (Bermuda)	*Pterodroma cahow*	Bermuda
Petrel (black)	*Procellaria parkinsoni*	New Zealand
Petrel (Chatham Islands)	*Pterodroma axillaris*	Chatham Islands (New Zealand)
Petrel (Galapagos)	*Pterodroma phaeopygia*	Galapagos Islands (Ecuador)

Bird	Species	Habitat
Petrel (Guadalupe storm-)	*Oceanodroma macrodactyla*	Guadalupe Island (Mexico)
Petrel (Hawaiian dark-rumped)	*Pterodroma phaeopygia sandwichensis*	Hawaii (USA)
Petrel (Madeira)	*Pterodroma madeira*	Madeira
Petrel (magenta)	*Pterodroma magentae*	New Zealand
Petrel (Mascarene)	*Pterodroma aterrima (Pseudobulweria aterrima)*	Réunion
Pheasant (brown-eared)	*Crossoptilon mantchuricum*	N China
Pheasant (cheer)	*Catreus wallichii*	India, Nepal, Pakistan
Pheasant (Elliot's)	*Syrmaticus ellioti*	E China
Pigeon (Marquesan imperial-)	*Ducula galeata*	Nukuhiva (French Polynesia)
Pigeon (pink)	*Columba mayeri (Nesoenas mayeri)*	Mauritius
Pigeon (plain)	*Columba inornata wetmorei*	Puerto Rico
Pitta (Gurney's)	*Pitta gurneyi*	Thailand
Pitta (Schneider's)	*Pitta schneideri*	Indonesia
Plantcutter (Peruvian)	*Phytotoma raimondii*	Peru
Plover (shore)	*Charadrius novaeseelandiae (Thinornis novaeseelandiae)*	Chatham Islands (New Zealand)
Pochard (Madagascar)	*Aytha innotata*	Madagascar
Poorwill (Jamaican)	*Siphonorhis americanus*	Jamaica
Puaiohi	*Myadestes palmeri*	Hawaii (USA)
Puffleg (black-breasted)	*Eriocnemis nigrivestis*	Ecuador
Puffleg (turquoise-throated)	*Eriocnemis godini*	Colombia, Ecuador
Rail (Austral)	*Rallus antarcticus*	Argentina, Chile
Rail (bar-winged)	*Nesoclopeus poecilopterus*	Fiji
Rail (junin)	*Laterallus tuerosi*	Peru
Rail (Lord Howe)	*Gallirallus sylvestris (Tricholimnas sylvestris)*	Lord Howe Island (Australia)
Rail (plain-flanked)	*Rallus wetmorei*	Venezuela
Recurvebill (Bolivian)	*Simoxenops striatus*	Bolivia
Redstart (yellow-faced)	*Myiobarus pariae*	Venezuela
Robin (Chatham)	*Petroica traversi*	Chatham Islands (New Zealand)
Robin (Seychelles magpie)	*Copsychus sechellarum*	Seychelles
Scrub-bird (noisy)	*Atrichornis clamosus*	SW Australia
Seedeater (hooded)	*Sporophila melanops*	Brazil
Seedeater (Narosky's)	*Sporophila zelichi*	Argentina
Seedeater (Tumaco)	*Sporophila insulata*	Tumaco Island (Colombia)
Shama (black)	*Copsychus cebuensis*	Philippines
Shelduck (crested)	*Tadorna cristata*	China, North Korea, Russia
Siskin (red)	*Carduelis cucullata*	Colombia, Venezuela
Spinetail (blackish-headed)	*Synallaxis tithys*	Ecuador, Peru
Spoonbill (black-faced)	*Platalea minor*	China, North Korea
Starling (Rarotonga)	*Aplonis cinerascens*	Cook Island
Stilt (black)	*Himantopus novaesealandiae*	New Zealand
Stork (Oriental)	*Ciconia boyciana*	China, Russia
Sunbird (Prigogine's double-collared)	*Nectarinia prigoginei*	Congo
Takahe	*Porphyrio mantelli (Notornis mantelli)*	South Island (New Zealand)

Tanager (cherry-throated)	*Nemosia rourei*	SE Brazil
Tanager (cone-billed)	*Conothraupis mesoleuca*	Brazil
Tapaculo (chestnut-sided)	*Scytalopus psychopompus*	Brazil
Thicketbird (long-legged)	*Trichocichla rufa*	Fiji
Thrasher (white-breasted)	*Ramphocinclus brachyurus*	Martinique
Tinamou (Kalinowski's)	*Nothoprocta kalinowskii*	Peru
Tit-spinetail (white-browed)	*Leptasthenura xenothorax*	Peru
Tit-tyrant (ash-breasted)	*Anairetes alpinus*	Bolivia, Peru
Tragopan (Cabot's)	*Tragopan caboti*	SE China
Tragopan (western)	*Tragopan melanocephalus*	India, Pakistan
Turaco (Bannerman's)	*Tauraco bannermani*	Cameroon
Tyrannulet (Alagoas)	*Phylloscartes ceciliae*	Brazil
Viero (black-capped)	*Vireo atricapillus*	Mexico, USA
Warbler (Aldabra bush-)	*Nesillas aldabrana*	Seychelles
Warbler (Bachman's)	*Vermivora bachmanii*	USA
Warbler (Kirtland's)	*Dendroica kirtlandii*	USA
Warbler (Nauru reed-)	*Acrocephalus rehsei*	Nauru
Warbler (Rodrigues brush-)	*Bebrornis rodericanus (Acrocephalus rodericamus)*	Rodrigues Island (Mauritius)
Warbler (Semper's)	*Leucopeza semperi*	St Lucia (West Indies)
Wattle-eye (banded)	*Platysteira laticincta*	Cameroon
Weaver (Clarke's)	*Ploceus golandi*	Kenya
White-eye (Seychelles grey)	*Zosterops modestus*	Seychelles
White-eye (Truk)	*Rukia ruki*	Caroline Islands (Federated States of Micronesia)
White-eye (white-chested)	*Zosterops albogularis*	Norfolk Island
Woodpecker (American ivory-billed)	*Campephilus principalis*	Cuba, SE USA
Woodpecker (Imperial)	*Campephilus imperialis*	Mexico
Woodpecker (ivory-billed)	*Campephilus principalis*	Cuba, USA
Woodpecker (Okinawa)	*Sapheopipo noguchii*	Okinawa (Japan)
Woodpecker (red-cockaded)	*Picoides borealis*	USA
Woodstar (Chilean)	*Eulidua yarrellii*	Chile
Woodstar (Esmeraldas)	*Acestrura berlepschi*	Ecuador
Woodstar (little)	*Acestrura bombus*	Ecuador, Peru
Wren (New Zealand bush)	*Xenicus longipes*	New Zealand

Endangered mammals

Mammal	Species	Habitat
Addax	*Addax nasomaculatus*	Chad, Mali, Mauritania, Niger
Anoa (lowland)	*Bubalus depressicornis (Anoa depressicornis)*	Sulawesi (Indonesia)
Anoa (mountain)	*Bubalus quarlesi (Anoa quarlesi)*	Buton and Sulawesi (Indonesia)
Antelope (giant sable)	*Hippotragus niger variani*	Angola
Armadillo (Brazilian three-banded)	*Tolypeutes tricinctus*	Brazil

Mammal	Species	Habitat
Ass (African wild)	*Equus africanus (Equus asinus)*	Ethiopia, Somalia
Aye-aye	*Daubentonia madagascariensis*	Madagascar
Bandicoot (giant)	*Peroryctes broadbenti*	Papua New Guinea
Bandicoot (golden)	*Isoodon auratus*	Australia
Bandicoot (western barred)	*Perameles bougainville*	Australia
Bat (Bulmer's fruit)	*Aproteles bulmerae*	Papua New Guinea
Bat (cusp-toothed fruit)	*Pteralopex atrata*	Solomon Islands
Bat (golden-capped fruit)	*Acerodon jubatus*	Philippines
Bat (gray)	*Myotis grisescens*	SE USA
Bat (Philippines tube-nosed fruit)	*Nyctimene rabori*	Philippines
Bat (Seychelles sheath-tailed)	*Coleura seychellensis*	Seychelles
Bat	*Pteralopex acrodonta*	Fiji
Bat	*Pteralopex anceps*	Papua New Guinea
Bat	*Pteralopex pulchra*	Solomon Islands
Bear (Baluchistan)	*Selenarctos thibetanus gedrosianus (Ursus thibetanus gedrosianus)*	Iran, Pakistan
Bettong (northern)	*Bettongia tropica*	Australia
Boodie	*Bettongia lesueur*	Australia
Buffalo (wild water)	*Bubalus arnee*	Bhutan, India, Nepal, Thailand
Cat (Iriomote)	*Prionailurus bengalensis iriomotensis (Prionailurus iriomotensis)*	Iriomote Island (Japan)
Cat (Pakistan sand)	*Felis margarita scheffeli*	Pakistan
Cheetah (Asiatic)	*Acinonyx jubatus venaticus*	Iran
Chuditch	*Dasyurus geoffroii*	Australia
Civet (Malabar large spotted)	*Viverra megaspila civettina*	S India
Cougar (Florida)	*Puma concolor coryi (Felis concolor coryi)*	SE USA
Deer (Argentinian pampas)	*Ozotoceros bezoarticus celer*	Argentina
Deer (Calamian hog)	*Axis calamianensis*	Calamian Island (Philippines)
Deer (Key)	*Odocoileus virginianus clavium*	USA
Deer (Kuhl's hog/Bawean)	*Axis kuhlii*	Bawean Island (Indonesia)
Deer (Manipur brow-antlered)	*Cervus eldii eldii*	India
Deer (Père David's)	*Elaphurus davidianus*	China
Deer (Persian fallow)	*Dama mesopotamica*	Iran
Deer (Siberian musk)	*Moschus moschiferus (Moschus sibiricus)*	China, Korea, Mongolia, Russia
Deer (swamp)	*Cervus duvauceli*	India, Nepal
Deer (Thailand brow-antlered)	*Cervus eldi siamensis*	Cambodia, Laos, Thailand, Vietnam
Deer (Visayan spotted)	*Cervus alfredi*	Visayan Island (Philippines)
Deer (Yarkand)	*Cervus elaphus yarkandensis*	China
Dibbler	*Parantechinus apicalis (Antechinus apicalis)*	Australia
Dog (wild)	*Lycaon pictus*	Africa

Dog (Mexican prairie)	*Cynomys mexicanus*	Mexico
Dolphin (Indus River)	*Platanista minor (Platanista indi)*	Indus River (Pakistan)
Dolphin (Yangtse River)	*Lipotes vexillifer*	Chiang Jiang River (China)
Drill	*Mandrillus leucophaeus (Papio leucophaeus)*	Cameroon, Equatorial Guinea, Nigeria
Dulker (Jentink's)	*Cephalophus jentinki*	Côte d'Ivoire, Liberia, Sierra Leone
Dunnart (Julia creek)	*Sminthopsis douglasi*	Australia
Echidna (long-beaked)	*Zaglossus bruijni*	Indonesia, Papua New Guinea
Elephant (Indian)	*Elephas maximus*	Asia
Ferret (black-footed)	*Mustela nigripes*	USA
Flying fox (Chuuk)	*Pteropus insularis*	Federated States of Micronesia
Flying fox (Comoro black)	*Pteropus livingstonei*	Comoros
Flying fox (Guam)	*Pteropus tokudae*	Guam, Mariana Islands (USA)
Flying fox (Mortlock Island)	*Pteropus phaecephalus*	Federated States of Micronesia
Flying fox (Pemba)	*Pteropus voeltzkowi*	Tanzania
Flying fox (pohnpei)	*Pteropus molossinus*	Federated States of Micronesia
Flying fox (Rodrigues)	*Pteropus rodricensis*	Rodrigues Island (Mauritius)
Flying fox (Ryuku)	*Pteropus dasymallus*	Japan, Taiwan
Fox (Simien/Ethiopian wolf)	*Canis simensis*	Ethiopia
Gazelle (Arabian sand)	*Gazella subgutturosa marica*	Arabian peninsula, Jordan
Gazelle (Cuvier's)	*Gazella cuvieri*	Algeria, Morocco, Tunisia
Gazelle (dama)	*Gazella dama*	Burkina Faso, Chad, Mali, Niger, Sudan
Gazelle (slender-horned)	*Gazella leptoceros*	Algeria, Chad, Egypt, Libya, Mali, Niger, Sudan, Tunisia
Genet (crested)	*Genetta cristata*	Cameroon, Nigeria
Gibbon (black)	*Hylobates concolor*	Cambodia, China, Laos, Vietnam
Gibbon (hoolock)	*Hylobates hoolock*	Bangladesh, China, India, Myanmar
Gibbon (Mentawi)	*Hylobates klossi*	Indonesia
Gibbon (pileated)	*Hylobates pileatus*	Cambodia, Laos, Thailand
Gibbon (silvery)	*Hylobates moloch*	Indonesia
Glider (Mahogany)	*Petaurus gracilis*	Australia
Guenon (Preuss's)	*Cercopithecus preussi*	Cameroon, Equatorial Guinea
Guenon (red-bellied)	*Cercopithecus erythrogaster*	Nigeria, Togo
Guenon (sun-tailed)	*Cercopithecus solatus*	Gabon
Guenon (white-throated)	*Cercopithecus sclateri*	Nigeria
Hare (hispid)	*Caprolagus hispidus*	Bangladesh, India, Nepal
Hartebeest (Swayne's)	*Alcelaphus buselaphus swaynei*	Ethiopia
Hartebeest (Tora)	*Alcelaphus buselaphus tora*	Egypt, Ethiopia, Sudan
Hirola	*Damaliscus hunteri*	Kenya, Somalia
Hog (pygmy)	*Sus salvanius*	N India
Horse (Przewalski's)	*Equus ferus przewalskii*	China, Mongolia

Mammal	Species	Habitat
Huemul (South Andean)	*Hippocamelus bisulcus*	Argentina, Chile
Hutia (Cabrera's)	*Capromys angelcabrerai (Mesocapromys angelcabrerai)*	Cuba
Hutia (dwarf)	*Capromys nanus (Mesocapromys nanus)*	Cuba
Hutia (Garrido's)	*Capromys garridoi (Mysateles garridoi)*	Cuba
Hutia (large-eared)	*Capromys auritus (Mesocapromys auritus)*	Cuba
Hutia (little earth)	*Capromys sanfelipensis (Mesocapromys sanfelipensis)*	Cuba
Hyena (Barbary)	*Hyaena hyaena barbara*	N Africa
Ibex (Pyrenean)	*Capra pyrenaica pyrenaica*	Spain
Ibex (Walia)	*Capra walia*	Ethiopia
Impala (black-faced)	*Aepyceros melampus petersi*	Angola, Namibia
Indri	*Indri indri*	Madagascar
Kangaroo rat (Morro Bay)	*Dipodomys heermanni morroensis*	SW USA
Kangaroo rat (Stephens')	*Dipodomys stephensi*	USA
Kangaroo rat (San Quintin)	*Dipodomys elator*	Mexico
Kangaroo (Goodfellow's tree)	*Dendrolagus goodfellowi*	Papua New Guinea
Kangaroo (Scott's tree)	*Dendrolagus scottae*	Papua New Guinea
Kouprey	*Bos sauveli (Novibos sauveli)*	Cambodia, Laos, Thailand, Vietnam
Kowari	*Dasycercus byrnei*	Australia
Lemur (broad-nosed gentle)	*Hapalemur sinus*	Madagascar
Lemur (crowned)	*Eulemur coronatus*	Madagascar
Lemur (golden bamboo)	*Hapalemur aureus*	Madagascar
Lemur (mongoose)	*Eulemur mongoz (Lemur mongoz)*	Comoros, Madagascar
Lemur (ruffed)	*Varecia variegata*	Madagascar
Lemur (hairy-eared dwarf)	*Allocebus trichotis (Cheirogaleus trichotis)*	Madagascar
Leopard (Amur)	*Panthera pardus orientalis*	China, North Korea, Russia
Leopard (South Arabian)	*Panthera pardus nimr*	Oman, Saudi Arabia, Yemen
Leopard (snow)	*Uncia uncia (Panthera uncia)*	Afghanistan, Bhutan, China, India, Nepal, Russia
Leopard (Sri Lankan)	*Panthera pardus kotiya*	Sri Lanka
Lion (Asiatic)	*Panthera leo persica*	India
Lynx (Spanish)	*Lynx pardinus (Felis pardinus)*	Portugal, Spain
Macaque (lion-tailed)	*Macaca silenus*	S India
Mala	*Lagorchestes hirsutus*	Australia
Mangabey (Tana River)	*Cercocebus galeritus galeritus*	Kenya, Tanzania
Markhor	*Capra falconeri*	Afghanistan, India, Pakistan
Marmoset (buffy-headed)	*Callithrix flaviceps*	SE Brazil
Marmoset (buffy-tufted ear)	*Callithrix aurita*	Brazil
Marmot (Vancouver Island)	*Marmota vancouverensis*	Vancouver Island (Canada)

Mink (European)	*Mustela lutreola*	Belarus, Estonia, France, Georgia, Russia, Spain
Mongoose (Liberian)	*Liberiictis kuhni*	Côte d'Ivoire, Guinea, Liberia
Monkey (Central American/red-backed squirrel monkey)	*Saimiri oerstedii*	Costa Rica, Panama
Monkey (Douc)	*Pygaturix nemaeus*	Cambodia, China, Laos
Monkey (François's leaf)	*Trachypithecus francoisi*	China, Laos, Vietnam
Monkey (grizzled leaf)	*Presbytis comata (Presbytis aygula)*	Indonesia
Monkey (Ka'apor capuchin)	*Cebus kaapori*	Brazil
Monkey (mentawai leaf)	*Presbytis potenziani*	Indonesia
Monkey (pig-tailed snub-nosed)	*Nasalis concolor (Simias concolor)*	Indonesia
Monkey (tonkin snub-nosed)	*Pygathrix avunculus (Rhinopithecus avunculus)*	Vietnam
Monkey (woolly spider/ muriqui monkey)	*Brachyteles arachnoides*	Brazil
Monkey (yellow-tailed woolly)	*Lagothrix flavicauda*	Peru
Mouse (saltmarch harvest)	*Reithrodontomys raviventris*	SW USA
Muntjac (Fea's)	*Muntiacus feae*	China, Myanmar
Numbat	*Myrmecobius fasciatus*	Australia
Nyala (mountain)	*Tragelaphus buxtoni*	Ethiopia
Orang-utan	*Pongo pygmaeus*	Indonesia, Malaysia
Oryx (Arabian)	*Oryx leucoryx*	Oman
Oryx (scimitar-horned)	*Oryx damnah (Oryx tao)*	Chad
Otter-civet	*Cynogale bennettii*	Brunei, Indonesia, Malaysia, Thailand
Ox (Vu Quang)	*Pseudoryx nghetinhensis*	Vietnam
Pacarana	*Dinomys branickii*	Bolivia, Brazil, Colombia, Ecuador, Peru, Venezuela
Peccary (Chacoan)	*Catagonus wagneri*	Argentina, Bolivia, Paraguay
Phascogale (red-tailed)	*Phascogale calura*	Australia
Pig (Visayan warty)	*Sus cebifrons*	Philippines
Possum (Fergusson Island striped)	*Dactilopsila tatei*	Papua New Guinea
Possum (Leadbetter's)	*Gymnbelideus leadbeateri*	Australia
Possum (mountain pygmy)	*Burramys parvus*	Australia
Potoroo (long-faced)	*Potorus longipes*	Australia
Pronghorn (Baja Californian)	*Antilocapra americana peninsularis*	Mexico
Pronghorn (Sonoran)	*Antilocapra americana sonoriensis*	Mexico, S USA
Rabbit (Amami)	*Pentalagus furnessi*	Ryukyu Islands (Japan)
Rabbit (Omilteme)	*Sylvilagus insonus*	Mexico
Rabbit (riverine)	*Bunolagus monticularis*	Tres Marias Island (Mexico)
Rabbit (Sumatran)	*Nesolagus netscheri*	Mexico
Rabbit (Tehuantepec jack-)	*Lepus flavigularis*	South Africa
Rabbit (Tres Marias)	*Sylvilagus graysoni*	Indonesia
Rabbit (volcano)	*Romerolagus diazi*	Mexico

Mammal	Species	Habitat
Rat (Anthony's wood)	*Neotoma anthonyi*	Todos Santos Island (Mexico)
Rat (Bunker's wood)	*Neotoma bunkeri*	Mexico
Rat (central rock)	*Zyzomys pedunculatus*	Australia
Rat (Poncelet's giant)	*Solomys ponceleti*	Papua New Guinea
Rat (San Martin Island wood)	*Neotoma martinensis*	San Martin Island (Mexico)
Rat	*Phaenomys ferrugineus*	Brazil
Rat	*Rhagomys rufescens*	Brazil
Rat	*Juscelinomys candango*	Brazil
Rhinoceros (black)	*Diceros bicornis*	Africa
Rhinoceros (great Indian)	*Rhinoceros unicornis*	Bhutan, India, Nepal
Rhinoceros (Javan)	*Rhinoceros sondaicus*	Cambodia, Java, Laos, Vietnam
Rhinoceros (northern white)	*Ceratotherium simum cottoni*	Congo
Rhinoceros (Sumatran)	*Dicerorhincus sumatrensis (Didermocerus sumatrensis)*	SE Asia
Seal (Hawaiian monk)	*Monachus schauinslandi*	Hawaii (USA)
Seal (Mediterranean monk)	*Monachus monachus*	Albania, N Africa, Cyprus, Lebanon, Turkey
Serow (Sumatran)	*Capricornis sumatraensis sumatraensis*	Malaysia, Sumatra
Sheep (dwarf blue)	*Pseudois schaeferi*	China
Shrew (nimba otter)	*Micropotamogale lamottei*	Côte d'Ivoire, Guinea, Liberia
Sifaka (diademed)	*Propithecus diadema*	Madagascar
Sifaka (golden-crowned)	*Propithecus tattersalli*	Madagascar
Sika (Formosan)	*Cervus nippon taiouanus*	Taiwan
Sika (North China)	*Cervus nippon mandarinus*	China
Sika (Ryukyu)	*Cervus nippon keramae*	Ryukyu Islands (Japan)
Sika (Shansi)	*Cervus nippon grassianus*	China
Sika (South China)	*Cervus nippon pseudaxis (Cervus nippon kopschi)*	China, Vietnam
Sloth (maned)	*Bradypus torquatus*	Brazil
Solenodon (Cuban)	*Solenodon cubanus*	Cuba
Solenodon (Haitian)	*Solenodon paradoxus*	Dominica, Haiti
Squirrel (Delmarva fox)	*Sciurus niger cinereus*	USA
Tamaraw	*Bubalus mindorensis*	Philippines
Tamarin (cotton-top)	*Saguinus oedipus oedipus*	NW Colombia
Tamarin (black-faced lion)	*Leontopithecus caissara*	Brazil
Tamarin (golden-headed lion)	*Leontopithecus rosalia chrysomelas*	E Brazil
Tamarin (golden lion)	*Leontopithecus rosalia*	Brazil
Tamarin (golden-rumped lion)	*Leontopithecus rosalia chrysopygus*	Brazil
Tamarin (white-footed)	*Saguinus leucopus*	Colombia
Tapir (Malayan)	*Tapirus indicus*	Indonesia, Malaysia, Myanmar, Thailand, Vietnam
Tapir (mountain)	*Tapirus pinchaque (Tapirus roulini)*	S America
Tiger	*Panthera tigris*	Eurasia
Uakari (bald)	*Cacajao calvus*	Brazil, Peru

Uakari (black)	*Cacajao melanocephalus*	Brazil, Colombia, Venezuela
Vaquita	*Phocoena sinus*	Mexico
Wallaby (Alpine)	*Thylogale calabyi*	Papua New Guinea
Wallaby (banded hare)	*Logostrophus fasciatus*	Australia
Wallaby (bridle nailtail)	*Onychogalea fraenata*	Australia
Wallaby (prosperine rock)	*Petrogale persephone*	Australia
Weasel (Colombian)	*Mustela felipei*	Colombia, Ecuador
Whale (blue)	*Balaenoptera musculus*	Atlantic, Indian and Pacific oceans
Whale (northern right)	*Eubalaena glacialis (Baleana glacialus)*	N Atlantic, N Pacific
Wolf (red)	*Canis rufus (Canis niger)*	S USA
Wombat (northern hairy-nosed)	*Lasiorhinus krefftii*	Australia
Woylie	*Bettongia penicillata*	Australia
Yak (wild)	*Bos mutus (Bos grunniens)*	W China, Kashmir, Tibet
Zebra (Grevy's)	*Equus grevyi*	Ethiopia, Kenya

Endangered reptiles

Reptile	Species	Habitat
Alligator, Chinese	*Alligator sinensis*	E China
Anole (giant/Culebra Island giant)	*Anolis roosevelti*	Puerto Rico
Blue tongue (pygmy)	*Tiliqua adelaidensis*	Australia
Boa (Round Island)	*Bolyeria multocarinata*	Round Island (Mauritius)
Boa (Round Island keel-scaled)	*Casarea dussumieri*	Round Island (Mauritius)
Chamaeleon (Smith's dwarf)	*Bradypodion taeniabronchum*	South Africa
Cobra (Central Asian/Oxus)	*Naja oxiana*	Central Asia
Crocodile (Cuban)	*Crocodylus rhombifer*	Cuba
Crocodile (Mindoro/Philippines)	*Crocodylus mindorensis*	Philippines
Crocodile (Orinoco)	*Crocodylus intermedius*	Colombia, Venezuela
Crocodile (Siamese)	*Crocodylus siamensis*	Cambodia, Indonesia, Malaysia, Thailand
Gecko (Monito)	*Sphaerodactylus micropithecus*	Puerto Rico
Gecko (Round Island day)	*Phelsuma guentheri*	Mauritius
Gharial	*Gavialis gangeticus*	Bangladesh, India, Nepal, Pakistan
Gharial (false)	*Tomistoma schlegelii*	Borneo, Malay Peninsula, Sumatra
Iguana (Acklin's ground)	*Cyclura rileyi*	Bahamas
Iguana (Anegada ground)	*Cyclura pinguis*	Virgin Islands (USA)
Iguana (Jamaica ground)	*Cyclura collei (Cychera lophoma)*	Jamaica
Lerista (Allen's)	*Lerista allanae*	Australia
Lizard (black/Californian legless)	*Anniella pulchra niger*	SW USA

Reptile	Species	Habitat
Lizard (blunt-nosed/San Joaquin leopard lizard)	*Gambelia silus (Crotaphytus wislizenii silus)*	Mexico, USA
Lizard (Hierro ground)	*Gallotia simonyi*	Hierro (Canary Islands)
Lizard (St Croix ground)	*Ameiva polops*	Virgin Islands (USA)
Lizard	*Liolaemus gravenhorstii*	Chile
Racer (Antiguan)	*Alsophis antiguae*	Antigua and Barbuda
Racer (black)	*Alsophis ater*	Jamaica
Skink (Blue Mountain water)	*Eulamprus leuraensis*	Australia
Skink (Chevron)	*Leiolopisma bomalonotum*	New Zealand
Skink (Lancelin Island)	*Ctenotus lancelini*	Australia
Snake (black striped)	*Simoselaps calonotus*	Australia
Snake (Kikuzato's brook)	*Opisthotropis kikuzatoi (Liopeltis kikuzatoi)*	Japan
Snake (San Francisco garter)	*Thamnophis sirtalis tetrataenia*	SW USA
Snake	*Liophis cursor*	Martinique
Snake	*Liophis ornatus*	St Lucia (West Indies)
Terrapin (Batagur)	*Batagur baska*	Bangladesh, India, Indonesia, Malaysia
Terrapin (painted)	*Callagur borneoensis*	Indonesia, Malaysia, Thailand
Tortoise (Bolson)	*Gopherus flavormarginatus*	Mexico
Tortoise (Madagascar)	*Geochelone yniphora*	Madagascar
Tuatara (Brother's Island)	*Sphendon guntheri*	New Zealand
Turtle (green)	*Chelonia mydas*	Indian Ocean, Pacific Ocean
Turtle (hawksbill)	*Eretmochelys imbricata*	Atlantic, Indian and Pacific oceans, Caribbean, Gulf of Mexico
Turtle (Kemp's Ridley)	*Lepidochelys kempii*	Gulf of Mexico, USA
Turtle (leatherback)	*Dermochelys coriacea*	Atlantic, Indian and Pacific oceans
Turtle (Olive Ridley)	*Lepidochelys olivacea*	Atlantic, Indian and Pacific oceans, Costa Rica, India, Mexico
Turtle (South American river)	*Podocnemis expansa*	Boliva, Brazil
Turtle (western swamp)	*Pseudemydura umbrina*	Australia
Viper (Cyclades blunt-nosed)	*Vipera schweizeri (Macrovipera schweizeri)*	Greece
Viper (Latifi's)	*Vipera latifii*	Iran
Woma	*Aspidites ramsayi*	Australia

Close seasons (UK)

Angling

Species	Close season
Salmon	1 November–31 January
Trout	1 October–end of February

Deer

Species	Close season (England and Wales)	Close season (Scotland)
Fallow deer (male)	1 May–31 July	1 May–31 July
Fallow deer (female)	1 March–31 October	16 February–20 October
Red deer (male)	1 May–31 July	21 October–30 June
Red deer (female)	1 March–31 October	16 February–20 October
Roe deer (male)	1 November–31 March	21 October–31 March
Roe deer (female)	1 March–31 October	1 April–20 October
Sika deer (male)	1 May–31 July	21 October–30 June
Sika deer (female)	1 March–31 October	16 February–20 October
Red/sika hybrids (male)	(not applicable)	21 October–30 June
Red/sika hybrids (female)	(not applicable)	16 February–20 October

Game

Species	Close season
Black game	11 December–19 August (31 August in Somerset, Devon and New Forest)
Grouse	11 December–11 August
Partridge	2 February–31 August
Pheasant	2 February–30 September
Ptarmigan	11 December–11 August (Scotland)

3.4 *Human Beings*

Human evolution

Dates	Species	Distribution
4–1.4 million years BC	*Australopithecus*	Africa
2–1.6 million years BC	*Homo habilis (small)*	E Africa
2–1.6 million years BC	*Homo habilis (large)*	E Africa
1.8–0.3 million years BC	*Homo erectus*	Africa, Asia, Indonesia
400 000–100 000 years BC	*Archaic Homo sapiens*	Africa, Asia, Europe
150 000–30 000 years BC	*Neanderthal man*	Europe, W Asia
130 000–60 000 years BC	*Early modern Homo sapiens*	Africa, W Asia

Human skeleton

Bone	Number
Skull	
Occipetal	1
Parietal	2
Sphenoid	1
Ethmoid	1
Inferior nasal conchae	2
Frontal	1
Nasal	2
Lacrimal	2
Temporal	2
Maxilla	2
Zygomatic	2
Vomer	1
Palatine	2
Mandible	1
Ears	
Malleus (hammer)	2
Incus (anvil)	2
Stapes (stirrups)	2
Throat	
Hyoid	1
Arms	
Humerus	2
Radius	2
Ulna	2
Scaphoid	2
Lunate	2
Triquetral	2
Pisiform	2
Trapezium	2
Trapezoid	2
Capitate	2
Hamate	2
Hands	
Metacarpals phalanges	10
First digit	4
Second digit	6
Third digit	6
Fourth digit	6
Fifth digit	6
Pectoral girdle	
Clavicle	2
Scapula	2

Vertebrae

Cervical	7
Thoracic	12
Lumbar	5
Sacral	1
Coccyx	1

Vertebral ribs

'True' ribs	14
'False' ribs	10

Sternum

Manubrium	1
Sternebrae	1
Xiphisternum	1

Pelvic girdle

Hip	2

Legs

Femur (thighbone)	2
Tibia	2
Fibula	2
Patella (kneebone)	2

Ankles

Talus	2
Calcaneus	2
Navicular	2
Cuneiform medial	2
Cuneiform, intermediate	2
Cuneiform, lateral	2
Cuboid	2

Toes

Metatarsals Phalanges	10
First digit	4
Second digit	6
Third digit	6
Fourth digit	6
Fifth digit	6

Note There are 208 bones in the human body

Muscle groups

Muscle group	Location
Abductors	Outer thigh
Adductors	Inner thigh
Anterior tibialis	Shin
Biceps brachii	Upper arm
Biceps femoris	Back of thigh
Deltoideus	Shoulder/upper arm

Muscle group	Location
Erector spinae	Lower back
Gastrocnemius	Calf
Gluteus maximus	Buttocks
Iliopsoas	Hip
Latissimus dorsi	Back
Obliques	Waist
Pectoralis major	Chest
Quadriceps femoris	Thigh
Rectus abdominus	Stomach
Sartorius	Thigh
Soleus	Lower calf
Trapezius	Neck/upper back
Triceps brachii	Upper arm/back

Teeth

Milk teeth

Tooth	Eruption	Shed
Incisor 1	6–10 months	6–7 years
Incisor 2	8–12 months	7–8 years
Canine	16–22 months	10–12 years
Molar 1	13–19 months	9–11 years
Molar 2	25–33 months	10–12 years

Permanent teeth

Tooth	Eruption
Incisor 1	7–8 years
Incisor 2	8–9 years
Canine	10–12 years
Premolar 1	10–11 years
Premolar 2	11–12 years
Molar 1	6–7 years
Molar 2	12 years
Molar 3	17–21 years

4
Human Geography

4.1 *Population*

World population

Date (AD)	Population (millions)
1	200
1000	275
1250	375
1500	420
1700	615
1750	790
1800	900
1850	1 260
1900	1 625
1920	1 860
1930	2 070
1940	2 295
1950	2 500
1960	3 050
1970	3 700
1980	4 450
1985	4 485
1990	5 246
1995	5 734
2000	6 100
2015	7 470
2025	8 290
2050	11 000

Note The figures from 2000 are based on averaged UN estimates

Largest nations by population

Rank	Nation	Population (1998 est)
1	China	1 255 698 000
2	India	982 223 000
3	USA	274 028 000
4	Indonesia	206 338 000
5	Brazil	165 851 000
6	Pakistan	148 166 000
7	Russian Federation	147 434 000
8	Japan	126 281 000
9	Bangladesh	124 774 000
10	Nigeria	106 409 000
11	Mexico	95 831 000
12	Germany	82 133 000
13	Vietnam	77 562 000
14	Philippines	72 944 000
15	Egypt	65 978 000
16	Iran	65 758 000
17	Turkey	64 479 000
18	Thailand	60 300 000
19	Ethiopia	59 649 000
20	France	58 683 000

Note The UK, with a population of 58 649 000, occupies the 21st place in world ranking

Largest cities by population

Rank	City	Population
1	Tokyo (Japan)	28 025 000
2	Mexico City (Mexico)	18 131 000
3	Mumbai (India)	18 042 000
4	São Paulo (Brazil)	17 711 000
5	New York (USA)	16 626 000
6	Shanghai (China)	14 173 000
7	Lagos (Nigeria)	13 488 000
8	Los Angeles (USA)	13 129 000
9	Calcutta (India)	12 900 000
10	Buenos Aires (Argentina)	12 431 000
11	Seoul (South Korea)	12 215 000
12	Beijing (China)	12 033 000
13	Karachi (Pakistan)	11 774 000
14	Delhi (India)	11 680 000
15	Dhaka (Bangladesh)	10 979 000
16	Manila (Philippines)	10 818 000
17	Cairo (Egypt)	10 772 000
18	Osaka (Japan)	10 609 000
19	Rio de Janeiro (Brazil)	10 556 000
20	Tianjin (China)	10 239 000
21	Jakarta (Indonesia)	9 815 000

22	Paris (France)	9 638 000
23	Istanbul (Turkey)	9 413 000
24	Moscow (Russia)	9 299 000
25	London (UK)	7 640 000
26	Lima (Peru)	7 443 000
27	Tehran (Iran)	7 380 000
28	Bangkok (Thailand)	7 221 000
29	Chicago (USA)	6 945 000
30	Bogotá (Colombia)	6 834 000
31	Hyderabad (India)	6 883 000
32	Chennai (India)	6 639 000
33	Essen (Germany)	6 559 000
34	Hangzhou (China)	6 389 000
35	Hong Kong (China)	6 097 000
36	Lahore (Pakistan)	6 030 000
37	Shenyang (China)	5 681 000
38	Changchun (China)	5 566 000
39	Bangalore (India)	5 544 000
40	Harbin (China)	5 475 000

Note Figures relate to urban agglomerations

4.2 *Countries of the World*

Afghanistan, Republic of

Location	SW Asia
Area	652 090 sq km (251 771 sq mi)
Capital	Kabul
Major cities/towns	Herat, Jalalabad, Kandahar, Mazar-i-Sharif
Population	21 354 000 (1998 est)
Language	Dari, Pashtu, Uzbek, Turkoman, Kirgiz
Religion	Muslim
Currency	Afghani (= 100 puls)
GDP	US$12.8 billion (1995 est)
Economy	Chiefly agricultural; exports include fruit and nuts, natural gas, sugar, carpets, textiles
Political system	Transitional
Head of state	Mohammed Rabbani
Head of government	Gulbardin Hekmatyar

Albania, Republic of

Location	SE Europe
Area	28 748 sq km (11 099 sq mi)
Capital	Tirana
Major cities/towns	Durres, Elbasan, Korce, Shkoder, Vlore
Population	3 119 000 (1998 est)
Language	Albanian, Greek

Religion	Muslim, Orthodox, Roman Catholic
Currency	Lek (= 100 qintars)
GDP	US\$ 2.3 billion (1997)
Economy	Mixed agricultural and industrial; exports include chromium and chrome products, foodstuffs, plant and animal products, electricity
Political system	Emergent democracy
Head of state	Rexhep Mejdani
Head of government	Pandeli Majko

Algeria, Democratic and Popular Republic of

Location	NW Africa
Area	2 381 741 sq km (919 590 sq mi)
Capital	Algiers
Major cities/towns	Annaba, Blida, Constantine, Oran, Sétif
Population	30 081 000 (1998 est)
Language	Arabic, Berber, French
Religion	Sunni Muslim
Currency	Algerian dinar (= 100 centimes)
GDP	US\$45.9 billion (1997)
Economy	Agriculture in N; exports include natural gas, petroleum, iron ore and phosphates
Political system	Military rule
Head of state	Abdel Aziz Bouteflika
Head of government	Ahmed Benbitour

Andorra, Principality of

Location	W Europe
Area	468 sq km (181 sq mi)
Capital	Les Escaldes
Major cities/towns	
Population	72 000 (1998 est)
Language	Catalan, Spanish, French
Religion	Roman Catholic
Currency	French franc (= 100 centimes), Spanish peseta (= 100 céntimos)
GDP	US\$960 million (1995)
Economy	Import centre for Europe and Asia; exports include textiles, cigars and cigarettes, electricity; also revenue from winter skiing
Political system	Co-principality
Head of state	Bishop of Urgel (Spain)/President of France
Head of government	Marc Forné Molné

Angola, People's Republic of

Location	W Africa
Area	1 246 700 sq km (481 350 sq mi)
Capital	Luanda
Major cities/towns	Benguela, Huambo, Lobito, Lubango, Malange, Namibe
Population	12 092 000 (1998 est)
Language	Portuguese, Bantu
Religion	Roman Catholic, Protestant, animist
Currency	Kwanza (= 100 lweis)
GDP	US\$7.39 billion (1997)
Economy	Chiefly agricultural and mineral extraction; exports include diamonds, minerals and petroleum.

Political system	Emergent democracy
Head of state	José Eduardo dos Santos
Head of government	José Eduardo dos Santos

Antigua and Barbuda, State of

Location	C America
Area	280 sq km (108 sq mi)
Capital	St John's (Antigua)
Major cities/towns	Codrington (Barbuda)
Population	67 000 (1998 est)
Language	English
Religion	Anglican, Roman Catholic
Currency	Eastern Caribbean dollar (= 100 cents)
GDP	US$446 million (1996 est)
Economy	Chiefly tourism; exports include petroleum products, sugar and cotton
Political system	Liberal democracy
Head of state	Elizabeth II
Head of government	Lester Bird

Argentina, Republic of

Location	S America
Area	2 780 092 sq km (1 073 393 sq mi)
Capital	Buenos Aires
Major cities/towns	Córdoba, La Plata, Mendoza, Rosario, San Miguel de Tucumán, Santa Fé
Population	36 123 000 (1998 est)
Language	Spanish, Italian
Religion	Roman Catholic
Currency	Peso (= 100 centavos)
GDP	US$322.7 billion (1997)
Economy	Chiefly agricultural and exploitation of natural resources; exports include meat, cereals, petroleum, minerals and soya beans.
Political system	Democratic federal republic
Head of state	Carlos Menem
Head of government	Fernando de la Rua

Armenia, Republic of

Location	W Asia
Area	29 800 sq km (11 505 sq mi)
Capital	Yerevan
Major cities/towns	Gyumri, Vanadzor
Population	3 893 000 (1998 est)
Language	Armenian
Religion	Armenian Christian
Currency	Dram (= 100 louma)
GDP	US$1.6 billion (1997 est)
Economy	Predominantly reliant upon mineral resources; exports include chemical and petroleum products and machinery
Political system	Authoritarian nationalist
Head of state	Robert Kocharyan
Head of government	Andrik Markarian

Australia, Commonwealth of

Location	Oceania
Area	7 682 300 sq km (2 966 136 sq mi)
Capital	Canberra
Major cities/towns	Adelaide, Alice Springs, Brisbane, Darwin, Geelong, Hobart, Melbourne, Newcastle, Perth, Sydney, Townsville, Wollongong
Population	18 520 000 (1998 est)
Language	English, Aboriginal languages
Religion	Protestant, Roman Catholic
Currency	Australian dollar (= 100 cents)
GDP	US$394 billion (1997)
Economy	Predominantly natural resources and agricultural; exports include iron ore, aluminium, coal, gold, uranium, wool, meat and cereals as well as engineering products
Political system	Federal constitutional monarchy
Head of state	Elizabeth II
Head of government	John Howard

Austria, Republic of

Location	C Europe
Area	83 500 sq km (32 239 sq mi)
Capital	Vienna
Major cities/towns	Graz, Innsbruck, Klagenfurt, Linz, Salzburg
Population	8 140 000 (1998 est)
Language	German
Religion	Roman Catholic, Protestant
Currency	Schilling (= 100 groschen)
GDP	US$206.2 billion (1997)
Economy	Mixed agricultural and industrial; exports include dairy products, wood and paper, machinery and chemicals; also revenue from tourism
Political system	Democratic federal republic
Head of state	Thomas Klestil
Head of government	Wolfgang Schüssel

Azerbaijan, Republic of

Location	W Asia
Area	86 600 sq km (33 436 sq mi)
Capital	Baku
Major cities/towns	Gyandzha, Nakhichevan, Stepanakert, Sumgait
Population	7 669 000 (1998 est)
Language	Azeri
Religion	Shi'ite Muslim, Sunni Muslim, Orthodox Christian
Currency	Manat (= 100 gopik)
GDP	US$4.39 billion (1997)
Economy	Formerly dependent on oil production; exports include petroleum products, building materials, machinery and textiles
Political system	Authoritarian nationalist
Head of state	Geidar Aliyev
Head of government	Artur Rasizade

Bahamas, Commonwealth of the

Location	C America
Area	13 864 sq km (5 352 sq mi)
Capital	Nassau (New Providence Island)

Major cities/towns	Freeport (Grand Bahama)
Population	296 000 (1998 est)
Language	English, Creole
Religion	Roman Catholic, Protestant
Currency	Bahamian dollar (= 100 cents)
GDP	US$3.7 billion (1997)
Economy	Dominated by tourism and financial services; exports include fish, oil products and rum
Political system	Constitutional monarchy
Head of state	Elizabeth II
Head of government	Hubert Ingraham

Bahrain, State of

Location	SW Asia
Area	688 sq km (266 sq mi)
Capital	Al Manamah
Major cities/towns	Hidd, Isa Town, Jiddhafs, Muharraq, Rifa'a, Sitra
Population	595 000 (1998 est)
Language	Arabic, Farsi, English, Urdu
Religion	Muslim, Christian
Currency	Bahraini dinar (= 1 000 fils)
GDP	US$5.5 billion (1997 est)
Economy	Financial and commercial centre; exports include petroleum, aluminium and chemicals
Political system	Absolute emirate
Head of state	Sheik Hamad II bin Isa al-Khalifa
Head of government	Sheik Khalifa bin Sulman al-Khalifa

Bangladesh, People's Republic of

Location	S Asia
Area	144 000 sq km (55 598 sq mi)
Capital	Dhaka
Major cities/towns	Barisal, Chittagong, Comilla, Khulna, Rajshahi, Sylhet
Population	124 774 000 (1998 est)
Language	Bengali, English
Religion	Sunni Muslim, Hindu
Currency	Taka (= 100 paisa)
GDP	US$32.8 billion (1997)
Economy	Chiefly agricultural; exports include jute, tea, paper and aluminium
Political system	Emergent democracy
Head of state	Shehabuddin Ahmed
Head of government	Shaikh Hasina Wajed

Barbados

Location	C America
Area	430 sq km (166 sq mi)
Capital	Bridgetown
Major cities/towns	Holetown, Oistins, Speightstown
Population	259 000 (1998 est)
Language	English, Bajan
Religion	Anglican, Pentecostalist, Methodist, Roman Catholic
Currency	Barbados dollar (= 100 cents)
GDP	US$2.1 billion (1997 est)

Economy	Largely based on tourism; exports include sugar cane, cotton and bananas
Political system	Constitutional monarchy
Head of state	Elizabeth II
Head of government	Owen Arthur

Belarus, Republic of

Location	W Asia
Area	207 600 sq km (80 154 sq mi)
Capital	Minsk
Major cities/towns	Bobruisk, Brest, Gomel, Hrodna, Mogilev, Vitebsk
Population	10 315 000 (1998 est)
Language	Belarussian, Russian, Polish
Religion	Russian Orthodox, Roman Catholic
Currency	Rouble (= 100 kopec), zaichik
GDP	US$22.4 billion (1997)
Economy	Agricultural and industrial; exports include machinery, chemicals, iron and steel, textiles and timber
Political system	Emergent democracy
Head of state	Alexander Lukashenko
Head of government	Syargey Ling

Belau

Location	W Pacific Ocean
Area	494 sq km (191 sq mi)
Capital	Koror
Major cities/towns	Garusuun, Malakal, Melekeiok
Population	19 000 (1998 est)
Language	Palauan, English
Religion	Christian, local beliefs
Currency	US dollar (= 100 cents)
GDP	US$109 million (1995 est)
Economy	Exports include copra, coconut oil and tuna
Political system	Democracy
Head of state	Kuniwo Nakamura
Head of government	Kuniwo Nakamura

Belgium, Kingdom of

Location	N Europe
Area	30 510 sq km (11 799 sq mi)
Capital	Brussels
Major cities/towns	Antwerp, Bruges, Charleroi, Ghent, Leuven, Liège, Mons, Namur, Ostend, Zeebrugge
Population	10 141 000 (1998 est)
Language	Flemish, Walloon, German, Dutch, French
Religion	Roman Catholic, Protestant
Currency	Belgian franc (= 100 centimes)
GDP	US$242.5 billion (1997)
Economy	Mixed agricultural and industrial; exports include iron and steel, machinery and livestock
Political system	Federal constitutional monarchy
Head of state	King Albert II
Head of government	Guy Verhofstadt

Belize

Location	C America
Area	22 963 sq km (8 866 sq mi)
Capital	Belmopan
Major cities/towns	Belize City, Corozal, Dangriga, Orange Walk, Punta Gorda
Population	230 000 (1998 est)
Language	English, Spanish, Creole
Religion	Roman Catholic, Protestant
Currency	Belize dollar (= 100 cents)
GDP	US$651 million (1997 est)
Economy	Chiefly agricultural; exports include timber, sugar, bananas and clothing
Political system	Constitutional monarchy
Head of state	Elizabeth II
Head of government	Said Musa

Benin, People's Republic of

Location	W Africa
Area	112 622 sq km (43 483 sq mi)
Capital	Porto-Novo (official), Cotonou (political and economic)
Major cities/towns	Abomey, Bouhicou, Djougou, Kandi, Natitingou, Ouidah, Parakou
Population	5 781 000 (1998 est)
Language	French, Fon, Yoruba
Religion	Animist, Muslim, Roman Catholic
Currency	CFA franc (= 100 centimes)
GDP	US$2.13 billion (1997)
Economy	Chiefly agricultural; exports include palm-oil products, cashew nuts, cotton and coffee
Political system	Socialist pluralist republic
Head of state	Ahmed Kérékou
Head of government	Adrien Houngbedji

Bhutan, Kingdom of

Location	S Asia
Area	46 500 sq km (17 953 sq mi)
Capital	Thimphu
Major cities/towns	Bumthang, Mongar, Paro, P'sholing, Punakha, W'phodrang
Population	2 004 000 (1998 est)
Language	Dzongkha, Sharcop, Bumthap, Nepali and English
Religion	Mahayana Buddhist, Hindu
Currency	Ngultrum (= 100 chetrum)
GDP	US$0.3 billion (1995 est)
Economy	Chiefly agricultural
Political system	Absolute monarchy
Head of state	Jigme Singye Wangchuk
Head of government	Lyonpo Jigme Yoser Thinley

Bolivia, Republic of

Location	S America
Area	1 098 581 sq km (424 162 sq mi)
Capital	La Paz (government), Sucre (legal and judiciary)
Major cities/towns	Cochabamba, El Alto, Oruro, Potosí, Santa Cruz
Population	7 957 000 (1998 est)
Language	Spanish, Aymara, Quechua

Religion	Roman Catholic
Currency	Boliviano (= 100 centavos)
GDP	US$8.1 billion (1997)
Economy	Dominated by mineral resources and illegal cocaine production; exports include tin, oil, natural gas and timber
Political system	Emergent democracy
Head of state	Hugo Banzer Suarez
Head of government	Hugo Banzer Suarez

Bosnia-Herzegovina, Republic of

Location	SE Europe
Area	51 129 sq km (19 740 sq mi)
Capital	Sarajevo
Major cities/towns	Banja Luka, Mostar, Prijedor, Tuzla, Zenica
Population	3 675 000 (1998 est)
Language	Serbo-Croat
Religion	Sunni Muslim, Serbian Orthodox, Roman Catholic
Currency	Dinar (= 100 paras)
GDP	US$1 billion (1995 est)
Economy	Largely industrialized; exports include steel, domestic appliances and coal
Political system	Emergent democracy
Head of state	Ante Jelavic/Alija Izetbegovic/Zivko Radišic (rotating)
Head of government	Sparsoe Tusevljak

Botswana, Republic of

Location	S Africa
Area	582 000 sq km (224 710 sq mi)
Capital	Gaborone
Major cities/towns	Francistown, Kange, Lobatse, Mahalapye, Mochudi, Molepolol, Selebi-Phikwe, Serowe, Tutume
Population	1 448 000 (1998 est)
Language	English, Setswana
Religion	Christian, animist, Baha'i, Muslim, Hindu
Currency	CFA franc (= 100 centimes)
GDP	US$4.93 billion (1997 est)
Economy	Chiefly agricultural; exports include diamonds
Political system	Democracy
Head of state	Festus Mogae
Head of government	Festus Mogae

Brazil, Federative Republic of

Location	S America
Area	8 511 965 sq km (3 286 469 sq mi)
Capital	Brasília
Major cities/towns	Belém, Belo Horizonte, Curitiba, Fortaleza, Manaus, Nova Iguaçu, Pôrto Alegre, Recife, Rio de Janeiro, Salvador, São Paulo
Population	165 851 000 (1998 est)
Language	Portuguese, Indian dialects
Religion	Roman Catholic
Currency	Real (= 100 centavos)
GDP	US$786.4 billion (1997)
Economy	Primarily agricultural; exports include coffee, cocoa, soya beans and timber

Political system	Democratic federal republic
Head of state	Fernando Henrique Cardosa
Head of government	Fernando Henrique Cardosa

Brunei, State of

Location	SE Asia
Area	5 765 sq km (2 225 sq mi)
Capital	Bandar Seri Begawan
Major cities/towns	Bangar, Kuala Belait, Seria
Population	315 000 (1998 est)
Language	Malay, Chinese, English
Religion	Muslim, Buddhist, Christian
Currency	Brunei dollar (= 100 sen)
GDP	US$4.9 billion (1995)
Economy	Primarily dependent on crude petroleum and natural gas exports
Political system	Absolute monarchy
Head of state	Sultan Muda Hassan al Bolkiah Mu'izzaddin Waddaulah
Head of government	Sultan Muda Hassan al Bolkiah Mu'izzaddin Waddaulah

Bulgaria, Republic of

Location	SE Europe
Area	110 912 sq km (42 823 sq mi)
Capital	Sofia
Major cities/towns	Burgas, Plovdiv, Ruse, Stara Zagora, Varna
Population	8 336 000 (1998 est)
Language	Bulgarian, Turkish
Religion	Eastern Orthodox Christian, Muslim, Roman Catholic, Protestant
Currency	Lev (= 100 stotinki)
GDP	US$10 billion (1997)
Economy	Chiefly agricultural; exports include coal and wine
Political system	Emergent democracy
Head of state	Petar Stoyanov
Head of government	King Simeon II

Burkina Faso, People's Democratic Republic of

Location	W Africa
Area	274 122 sq km (105 838 sq mi)
Capital	Ouagadougou
Major cities/towns	Bobo-Dioulasso, Koudougou
Population	11 305 000 (1998 est)
Language	French, Sudanic languages
Religion	Animist, Sunni Muslim, Roman Catholic
Currency	CFA franc (= 100 centimes)
GDP	US$2.44 billion (1997)
Economy	Largely agricultural; exports include cotton, gold and livestock
Political system	Emergent democracy
Head of state	Blaise Compaoré
Head of government	Kadre Desire Ouedraogo

Burundi, Republic of

Location	C Africa
Area	27 834 sq km (10 746 sq mi)
Capital	Bujumbura
Major cities/towns	Bururi, Kitega, Muhinga, Muramuya, Ngozi

Population	6 457 000 (1998 est)
Language	Kirundi, French, Kiswahili
Religion	Roman Catholic, Pentecostalist, Anglican, Muslim, animist
Currency	Burundi franc (= 100 centimes)
GDP	US$1.24 billion (1997 est)
Economy	Chiefly agricultural; exports include coffee, tea and cotton
Political system	Authoritarian nationalist
Head of state	Pierre Buyoya
Head of government	Pascal-Firmin Ndimira

Cambodia, State of

Location	SW Asia
Area	181 035 sq km (69 897 sq mi)
Capital	Phnom Penh
Major cities/towns	Battambang, Kompong Cham
Population	10 716 000 (1998 est)
Language	Khmer, French
Religion	Thravada Buddhist, Muslim, Roman Catholic
Currency	Riel (= 100 sen)
GDP	US$3.09 billion (1997)
Economy	Mostly agricultural; exports include timber and rubber
Political system	Constitutional monarchy
Head of state	Prince Norodom Sihanouk
Head of government	Hun Sen

Cameroon, Republic of

Location	W Africa
Area	475 440 sq km (183 567 sq mi)
Capital	Yaoundé
Major cities/towns	Bafoussam, Bamenda, Douala, Garoua, Maroua, Nkongsamba
Population	14 305 000 (1998 est)
Language	French, English, African languages
Religion	Roman Catholic, animist, Muslim, Protestant
Currency	CFA franc (= 100 centimes)
GDP	US$9.1 billion (1997)
Economy	Chiefly agricultural; exports include petroleum, timber, coffee and bananas
Political system	Emergent democracy
Head of state	Paul Biya
Head of government	Peter Mafany Musonge

Canada

Location	N America
Area	9 970 610 sq km (3 849 652 sq mi)
Capital	Ottawa
Major cities/towns	Calgary, Edmonton, Halifax, Hamilton, Kitchener, London, Montréal, Oshawa, Québec, Regina, Saskatoon, Toronto, Vancouver, Windsor, Winnipeg
Population	30 563 000 (1998 est)
Language	English, French, American Indian dialects, Inuit Inuktitut
Religion	Roman Catholic, Protestant
Currency	Canadian dollar (= 100 cents)
GDP	US$603.1 billion (1997)

Economy	Predominantly agricultural and natural resources; exports include wheat, lumber, paper, crude petroleum, natural gas and aluminium
Political system	Federal constitutional monarchy
Head of state	Elizabeth II
Head of government	Jean Chrétien

Cape Verde, Republic of

Location	W Africa
Area	4 033 sq km (1 557 sq mi)
Capital	Praia (on São Tiago)
Major cities/towns	Mindelo
Population	408 000 (1998 est)
Language	Portuguese, Creole
Religion	Roman Catholic, Protestant
Currency	Cape Verde escudo (= 100 centavos)
GDP	US$425 million (1997)
Economy	Chiefly agricultural; exports include fish and bananas
Political system	Emergent democracy
Head of state	Antonio Mascarenhas Monteiro
Head of government	Carlos Veiga

Central African Republic

Location	C Africa
Area	622 436 sq km (240 322 sq mi)
Capital	Bangui
Major cities/towns	Bambari, Berbérati, Bossangoa, Bouar, Carnot
Population	3 485 000 (1998 est)
Language	French, Sangho, Arabic, Hunsa, Swahili
Religion	Protestant, Roman Catholic, Muslim, animist
Currency	CFA franc (= 100 centimes)
GDP	US$978 million (1997 est)
Economy	Chiefly agricultural; exports include diamonds, coffee and timber
Political system	Emergent democracy
Head of state	Ange-Félix Patasse
Head of government	Anicet Georges Dologuélé

Chad, Republic of

Location	C Africa
Area	1 284 000 sq km (495 752 sq mi)
Capital	N'djamena
Major cities/towns	Abéché, Bongor, Doba, Moundou, Sarh
Population	7 270 000 (1998 est)
Language	French, Arabic, African languages
Religion	Muslim, Christian, animist
Currency	CFA franc (= 100 centimes)
GDP	US$1.6 billion (1997 est)
Economy	Chiefly agricultural; exports include meat, cotton, salt and petroleum
Political system	Emergent democracy
Head of state	Idriss Déby
Head of government	Negoum Yamassoum

Chile, Republic of

Location	S America
Area	756 950 sq km (292 258 sq mi)
Capital	Santiago
Major cities/towns	Chillán, Concepción, Puente Alto, Rancagua, San Bernardo, Talca, Talcahuano, Temuco, Valparaiso, Via del Mar
Population	14 824 000 (1998 est)
Language	Spanish
Religion	Roman Catholic
Currency	Chilean peso (= 100 centavos)
GDP	US$77.1 billion (1997)
Economy	Dominated by agriculture and mineral resources; exports include copper, silver, fruit, timber and foodstuffs
Political system	Emergent democracy
Head of state	Ricardo Lagos Escobar
Head of government	Ricardo Lagos Escobar

China, People's Republic of

Location	E Asia
Area	9 572 900 sq km (3 696 000 sq mi)
Capital	Beijing
Major cities/towns	Chengdu, Chongqing, Guangzhou, Harbin, Hong Kong, Nanjing, Qingdao, Shanghai, Shenyang, Tianjin, Wuhan, Xiang, Zibo
Population	1 255 698 000 (1998 est)
Language	Chinese (many dialects)
Religion	Taoist, Confucianist, Buddhist, Muslim, Catholic, Protestant
Currency	Yuan (= 100 fen)
GDP	US$902 billion (1997)
Economy	Increasingly industrialized; exports include crude petroleum, natural gas, iron ore, lead, tin, zinc, clothing, toys, machinery, foodstuffs, tea, silk and cotton
Political system	Communist republic
Head of state	Jiang Zemin
Head of government	Zhu Rongji

Colombia, Republic of

Location	S America
Area	1 141 748 sq km (440 828 sq mi)
Capital	Bogotá
Major cities/towns	Barranquilla, Bucaramanga, Buenaventura, Cali, Cartagena, Medellín
Population	40 803 000 (1998 est)
Language	Spanish
Religion	Roman Catholic
Currency	Colombian peso (= 100 centavos)
GDP	US$96.4 billion (1997)
Economy	Dominated by agriculture and natural resources; exports include coffee, bananas, cotton, gold and oil; also revenue from illegal cocaine production
Political system	Democracy
Head of state	Andrés Pastrana Arango
Head of government	Andrés Pastrana Arango

Comoros, Federal Islamic Republic of

Location	SE Africa
Area	1 862 sq km (718 sq mi)
Capital	Moroni (on Njazidja)
Major cities/towns	Domoni, Dzaoudzi, Fomboni, Mutsamudu
Population	658 000 (1998 est)
Language	Arabic, Comorian, Makua, French
Religion	Muslim
Currency	Comorian franc (= 100 centimes)
GDP	US$231 million (1996 est)
Economy	Chiefly agricultural; exports include vanilla, cloves and copra
Political system	Transitional
Head of state	Azali Assoumani
Head of government	Tarmidi Bianrifi

Congo, Democratic Republic of

Location	C Africa
Area	2 344 900 sq km (905 366 sq mi)
Capital	Kinshasa
Major cities/towns	Bukavu, Kalemie, Kananga, Kikwit, Kisangani, Lubumbashi, Matadi, Mbuji-Mayi
Population	49 139 000 (1998 est)
Language	French, Swahili, Lingala, Kikongo, Tshiluba
Religion	Roman Catholic, Protestant, Kimbanguist, Muslim
Currency	Zaïre (= 100 makuta)
GDP	US$5.4 billion (1996 est)
Economy	Chiefly agricultural; exports include copper, cobalt, industrial diamonds, petroleum and coffee
Political system	Transitional
Head of state	Laurent Kabila
Head of government	Laurent Kabila

Congo

Location	W Africa
Area	342 000 sq km (132 046 sq mi)
Capital	Brazzaville
Major cities/towns	Bouenza, Cuvette, Loubomo, Niari, Nkayi, Plateaux, Pointe-Noire, Pool
Population	2 785 000 (1998 est)
Language	French, Kongo languages
Religion	Animist, Christian, Muslim
Currency	CFA franc (= 100 centimes)
GDP	US$2.29 billion (1997)
Economy	Chiefly agricultural; exports include petroleum, timber and sugar cane
Political system	Emergent democracy
Head of state	Denis Sassou-Nguesso
Head of government	Bernard Kolelas

Costa Rica, Republic of

Location	Central America
Area	51 100 sq km (19 735 sq mi)
Capital	San José
Major cities/towns	Alajuela, Cartago, Limón, Puntarenas

Population	3 383 000 (1995 est)
Language	Spanish
Religion	Roman Catholic
Currency	Colón (= 100 céntimos)
GDP	US$9 233 million (1995)
Economy	Chiefly agricultural; exports include coffee, bananas, sugar, silver, bauxite and livestock
Political system	Liberal democracy
Head of state	Miguel Angel Rodríguez Echeverría
Head of government	Miguel Angel Rodríguez Echeverría

Côte d'Ivoire, Republic of

Location	NW Africa
Area	322 463 sq km (124 471 sq mi)
Capital	Yamoussoukro
Major cities/towns	Abidjan, Bouaké, Daloa, Man, San-Pédro
Population	14 651 000 (1995 est)
Language	French, native languages
Religion	Animist, Muslim, Christian
Currency	CFA franc (= 100 centimes)
GDP	US$10 078 million (1995)
Economy	Chiefly agricultural; exports include cocoa and coffee
Political system	Emergent democracy
Head of state	Henri Konan Bédié
Head of government	Robert Guéi

Croatia, Republic of

Location	SE Europe
Area	56 538 sq km (21 824 sq mi)
Capital	Zagreb
Major cities/towns	Dubrovnik, Osijek, Rijeka, Sibenik, Split, Zadar
Population	4 876 000 (1995 est)
Language	Croatian
Religion	Roman Catholic, Orthodox Christian
Currency	Kuna (= 100 lipa)
GDP	US$18 081 million (1995)
Economy	Mixed economy including agriculture and industry; products include cereals, livestock, machinery, textiles
Political system	Emergent democracy
Head of state	Stipe Mesic
Head of government	Ivica Racan

Cuba, Republic of

Location	Central Caribbean
Area	110 860 sq km (42 820 sq mi)
Capital	Havana
Major cities/towns	Camagüey, Guantánamo, Holguín, Santa Clara, Santiago de Cuba
Population	11 089 000 (1995 est)
Language	Spanish
Religion	Roman Catholic, Episcopalian, Methodist
Currency	Cuban peso (= 100 centavos)
GDP	US$21 737 million (1995)
Economy	Restricted by lack of international trade links; exports include sugar, nickel and tobacco

Political system	Communist republic
Head of state	Fidel Castro Ruz
Head of government	Fidel Castro Ruz

Cyprus

Location	E Mediterranean Sea
Area	9 251 sq km (3 571 sq mi)
Capital	Nicosia
Major cities/towns	Famagusta, Kyrenia, Larnaca, Limassol, Morphou, Paphos
Population	600 000 (1995 est)
Language	Greek, Turkish, English
Religion	Greek Orthodox, Sunni Muslim
Currency	Cyprus pound (= 100 cents)
GDP	US$8 537 million (1995)
Economy	Chiefly agricultural in the N; exports from the S include clothing, grapes, wine and footwear; tourism in the S recovering
Political system	Divided into the Greek Republic of Cyprus (S) and the largely unrecognized Turkish Republic of Northern Cyprus (N); both democratic republics
Head of state	Glafcos Clerides (S); Rauf Denktas (N)
Head of government	Glafcos Clerides (S); Rauf Denktas (N)

Czech Republic

Location	Central Europe
Area	78 864 sq km (30 461 sq mi)
Capital	Prague
Major cities/towns	Brno, Hradec Krlové, Liberec, Olomouc, Ostrava, Plzen, Ustí nad Labem
Population	10 411 000 (1995 est)
Language	Czech
Religion	Roman Catholic, Protestant, Hussite, Orthodox
Currency	Koruna (= 100 halér)
GDP	US$45 667 million (1995)
Economy	Mixed agricultural and industrial; exports include steel, machinery, motor vehicles and raw materials
Political system	Emergent democracy
Head of state	Václav Havel
Head of government	Miloš Zeman

Denmark, Kingdom of

Location	N Europe
Area	43 075 sq km (16 627 sq mi)
Capital	Copenhagen
Major cities/towns	Aalborg, Aarhus, Esbjerg, Odense, Randers
Population	5 188 000 (1995 est)
Language	Danish, German
Religion	Lutheran
Currency	Danish krone (= 100 øre)
GDP	US$173 357 million (1995)
Economy	Highly developed industrial sector and intensive agriculture; exports include machinery, textiles and dairy products
Political system	Liberal democracy
Head of state	Queen Margrethe II
Head of government	Poul Nyrup Rasmussen

Djibouti, Republic of

Location	NE Africa
Area	23 200 sq km (8 955 sq mi)
Capital	Djibouti
Major cities/towns	Dikhil, Obock, Tadjoura
Population	607 000 (1995 est)
Language	French, Somali, Afar, Arabic
Religion	Sunni Muslim
Currency	Djibouti franc (= 100 centimes)
GDP	US$537 million (1995)
Economy	Chiefly agricultural and fishing
Political system	Authoritarian nationalism
Head of state	Ismael Omar Guelleh
Head of government	Barkat Gourad Hamadou

Dominica, Commonwealth of

Location	E Caribbean Sea
Area	751 sq km (290 sq mi)
Capital	Roseau
Major cities/towns	Marigot, Portsmouth
Population	83 900 (1995 est)
Language	English, Dominican patois
Religion	Roman Catholic
Currency	East Caribbean dollar (= 100 cents)
GDP	US$201 million (1995)
Economy	Chiefly agriculture and tourism; exports include coconut, cigars, citrus fruit and bananas
Political system	Liberal democracy
Head of state	Vernon Shaw
Head of government	Rosie Douglas

Dominican Republic

Location	Central Caribbean
Area	48 442 sq km (18 700 sq mi)
Capital	Santo Domingo
Major cities/towns	Duarte, La Vega, Puerto Plata, San Cristóbal, San Juan, San Pedro de Macoris, Santiago de los Caballeros
Population	7 994 000 (1995 est)
Language	Spanish
Religion	Roman Catholic
Currency	Dominican peso (= 100 centavos)
GDP	US$11 801 million (1995)
Economy	Chiefly agriculture and tourism; exports include sugar and cocoa
Political system	Democratic republic
Head of state	Hipolito Mejia
Head of government	Hipolito Mejia

Ecuador

Location	NW South America
Area	270 699 sq km (104 490 sq mi)
Capital	Quito
Major cities/towns	Ambeto, Cuenca, Esmeraldas, Guayaquil, Machala, Manta, Portoviejo
Population	12 175 000 (1998 est)

Language	Spanish, Quechua
Religion	Roman Catholic
Currency	Sucre (= 100 centavos)
GDP	US$18.88 billion (1997)
Economy	Mixed agriculture and heavy industry, exports include bananas, coffee, petrochemicals, steel
Political system	Emergent democracy
Head of state	Jamil Mahuad Witt
Head of government	Gustavo Noboa Bejarano

Egypt

Location	NE Africa
Area	1 001 449 sq km (386 559 sq mi)
Capital	Cairo
Major cities/towns	Alexandria, El Giza, El Mahalla el-Koubra, El-Mansoura, Port Said, Shubra Al Khayma, Tauta
Population	65 978 000 (1998 est)
Language	Arabic
Religion	Sunni Muslim, Coptic Christian
Currency	Egyptian pound (= 100 piastres)
GDP	US$75.5 billion (1997)
Economy	Agriculture and tourism important; exports include petroleum and petroleum products
Political system	Democracy
Head of state	Mohammed Hosni Mubarak
Head of government	Atef Ebeid

El Salvador

Location	Central America
Area	21 476 sq km (8 290 sq mi)
Capital	San Salvador
Major cities/towns	Mejicanos, Nueva San Salvador, San Miguel, Santa Ana, Soyapango
Population	6 032 000 (1998 est)
Language	Spanish
Religion	Roman Catholic
Currency	Colón (= 100 centavos)
GDP	US$11.3 billion (1997 est)
Economy	Primarily agricultural; exports include coffee, cotton and chemicals
Political system	Emergent democracy
Head of state	Francisco Flores
Head of government	Francisco Flores

Equatorial Guinea

Location	W Africa
Area	28 051 sq km (10 828 sq mi)
Capital	Malabo
Major cities/towns	Bata, Ebebiyin, Evinayong, Mongomo
Population	431 000 (1998 est)
Language	Spanish
Religion	Roman Catholic
Currency	CFA franc (= 100 centimes)
GDP	US$392 million (1997 est)

Economy	Chiefly agricultural; exports include cocoa, coffee and timber
Political system	Emergent democracy
Head of state	Teodoro Obiang Nguema Mbasogo
Head of government	Angel Serafin Seriche Dougan

Eritrea

Location	NE Africa
Area	93 700 sq km (36 200 sq mi)
Capital	Asmara
Major cities/towns	Asab, Keren, Massawa
Population	3 577 000 (1998 est)
Language	Tigrinya, Tigray, Amharic
Religion	Islamic, Coptic Christian
Currency	Nafka
GDP	US$714 million (1996)
Economy	Chiefly agricultural; exports include textiles and leather
Political system	Emergent democracy
Head of state	Isaias Afwerki
Head of government	Isaias Afwerki

Estonia

Location	E Baltic Sea
Area	45 100 sq km (17 409 sq mi)
Capital	Tallinn
Major cities/towns	Kohtla-Järve, Narva, Pärnu, Tartu
Population	1 429 000 (1996 est)
Language	Estonian, Russian
Religion	Evangelical Lutheran, Russian Orthodox
Currency	Kroon (= 100 senti)
GDP	US$4.6 billion (1997)
Economy	Heavy industry and agriculture; exports include machinery, grain and livestock
Political system	Emergent democracy
Head of state	Lennart Meri
Head of government	Mart Laar

Ethiopia

Location	E central Africa
Area	1 251 282 sq km (483 123 sq mi)
Capital	Addis Ababa
Major cities/towns	Dessie, Dire Dawa, Gonder, Harar, Jimma, Mek'ele, Nazret
Population	59 649 000 (1998 est)
Language	Amharic
Religion	Muslim, Ethiopian Orthodox, traditional beliefs
Currency	Ethiopian birr (= 100 cents)
GDP	US$6.3 billion (1997)
Economy	Chiefly agricultural; exports include coffee and petroleum products
Political system	Transitional democracy
Head of state	Negaso Gidada
Head of government	Meles Zenawi

Fiji

Location	SW Pacific Ocean
Area	18 333 sq km (7 076 sq mi)
Capital	Suva
Major cities/towns	Ba, Labasa, Lautoka, Levuka, Nadi
Population	796 000 (1998 est)
Language	English
Religion	Methodist, Hindu, Muslim, Sikh
Currency	Fijian dollar (= 100 cents)
GDP	US$1.8 billion (1997 est)
Economy	Chiefly agricultural; exports include sugar cane and bananas
Political system	Democracy
Head of state	Ratu Josefa Iloilovatu
Head of government	Laisenia Qarase

Finland

Location	NW Baltic Sea
Area	338 145 sq km (130 524 sq mi)
Capital	Helsinki
Major cities/towns	Espoo, Oulu, Tampere, Turku, Vantaa
Population	5 154 000 (1998 est)
Language	Finnish, Swedish, Saame
Religion	Lutheran, Finnish/Greek Orthodox
Currency	Markka (= 100 penni)
GDP	US$117.5 billion (1997)
Economy	Forestry, farming and industry; exports include metal and engineering products, wood and pulp, chemicals
Political system	Democracy
Head of state	Tarja Halonen
Head of government	Paavo Lipponen

France

Location	W Europe
Area	551 000 sq km (212 686 sq mi)
Capital	Paris
Major cities/towns	Bordeaux, Grenoble, Le Havre, Lille, Lyon, Marseilles, Montpellier, Nantes, Nice, Reims, Rennes, Saint-Etienne, Strasbourg, Toulouse
Population	58 683 000 (1998 est)
Language	French
Religion	Roman Catholic, Protestant, Muslim, Jewish
Currency	Franc (= 100 centimes)
GDP	US$1 393.8 billion (1997)
Economy	Mixed modern industry and agriculture; exports include machinery, chemicals, textiles, food, wine, perfumes
Political system	Democracy
Head of state	Jacques René Chirac
Head of government	Lionel Jospin

Gabon

Location	W central Africa
Area	267 667 sq km (103 347 sq mi)
Capital	Libreville
Major cities/towns	Lambaréné, Masuku, Mouanda, Owendo, Port-Gentil

Population	1 167 000 (1998 est)
Language	French, Fang, Myene, Bateke and other local dialects
Religion	Roman Catholic, Protestant, traditional beliefs
Currency	CFA franc (= 100 centimes)
GDP	US$5.43 billion (1997)
Economy	Chiefly agricultural; exports include petrol and petroleum products, manganese and wood products
Political system	Emergent democracy
Head of state	Omar Bongo
Head of government	Jean-François Ntoutoume-Emane

Gambia, The

Location	W Africa
Area	11 295 sq km (4 361 sq mi)
Capital	Banjul
Major cities/towns	Bakau, Birkama, Farafenni, Georgetown, Gunjur, Serekunda, Sukuta
Population	1 229 000 (1998 est)
Language	English, Madinka, Wolof, Fula
Religion	Muslim, Christian, traditional local beliefs
Currency	Dalasi (= 100 butut)
GDP	US$385 million (1997 est)
Economy	Chiefly agricultural; exports include groundnuts, fish products, hides and skins
Political system	Transitional
Head of state	Yayeh Jameh
Head of government	Yayeh Jameh

Georgia

Location	W Asia
Area	69 700 sq km (26 900 sq mi)
Capital	Tbilisi
Major cities/towns	Batumi, Kutaisi, Rustavi, Sukhumi
Population	5 059 000 (1998 est)
Language	Georgian, Russian
Religion	Georgian Church
Currency	Lari
GDP	US$4.1 billion (1997 est)
Economy	Tourism, agriculture and heavy industry; exports include metal products, machinery and tea
Political system	Transitional
Head of state	Eduard Shevardnadze
Head of government	Vazha Lortkipanidze

Germany

Location	N Europe
Area	357 868 sq km (138 136 sq mi)
Capital	Berlin
Major cities/towns	Bremen, Cologne, Dortmund, Dresden, Duisberg, Düsseldorf, Essen, Frankfurt am Main, Hamburg, Hannover, Leipzig, Munich, Stuttgart
Population	82 133 000 (1998 est)
Language	German
Religion	Lutheran, Roman Catholic, Muslim

Currency	Deutsche Mark (= 100 Pfennige)
GDP	US$2 115.4 billion (1997)
Economy	Highly developed industrial sector; exports include road vehicles, electrical machinery, metal products, textiles, chemicals
Political system	Democracy
Head of state	Johannes Rau
Head of government	Gerhard Schröder

Ghana

Location	W central Africa
Area	238 537 sq km (92 100 sq mi)
Capital	Accra
Major cities/towns	Bolgatanga, Cape Coast, Ho, Koforidua, Kumasi, Sekondi-Takoradi, Sunyani, Tamale, Tarkwa, Tema, Wa, Yendi
Population	19 162 000 (1998 est)
Language	English, Akan, Ewe, Ga
Religion	Christian, traditional local beliefs, Muslim
Currency	Cedi (= 100 pesewas)
GDP	US$6.76 billion (1997)
Economy	Chiefly agricultural; exports include gold, cocoa, timber
Political system	Emergent democracy
Head of state	John Kufuor
Head of government	John Kufuor

Greece

Location	SE Europe
Area	131 957 sq km (50 935 sq mi)
Capital	Athens
Major cities/towns	Irákleion, Larissa, Patras, Piraeus, Thessaloníki, Volos
Population	10 600 000 (1998 est)
Language	Greek, English, French
Religion	Greek Orthodox, Roman Catholic, Protestant, Muslim, Judaism
Currency	Drachma (= 100 lepta)
GDP	US$119.1 billion (1997)
Economy	Large service sector, agriculture and tourism; exports include fruit and vegetables, textiles, iron and steel
Political system	Democracy
Head of state	Kostas Stephanopoulos
Head of government	Kostas Simitis

Grenada

Location	SW Caribbean Sea
Area	344 sq km (133 sq mi)
Capital	St George's
Major cities/towns	Grenville, Hillsborough, Sauteurs, Victoria
Population	93 000 (1998 est)
Language	English, French patois
Religion	Roman Catholic, Protestant
Currency	East Caribbean dollar (= 100 cents)
GDP	US$310 million (1997 est)
Economy	Chiefly agricultural; exports include cocoa, bananas, fruit
Political system	Emergent democracy
Head of state	Daniel Charles Williams
Head of government	Keith Mitchell

Guatemala

Location	Central America
Area	108 889 sq km (42 031 sq mi)
Capital	Guatemala City
Major cities/towns	Chiquimula, Escuintla, Puerto Barrios, Quezaltenango, Retalhuleu
Population	10 801 000 (1998 est)
Language	Spanish, Indian dialects
Religion	Roman Catholic, Protestant
Currency	Quetzal (= 100 centavos)
GDP	US$17.8 billion (1997)
Economy	Chiefly agricultural; exports include coffee, bananas, sugar and tobacco
Political system	Democracy
Head of state	Alfonso Portillo Cabrera
Head of government	Alfonso Portillo Cabrera

Guinea

Location	W Africa
Area	246 048 sq km (94 974 sq mi)
Capital	Conakry
Major cities/towns	Kankan, Kindia, Labé, Nzérékoré
Population	7 337 000 (1998 est)
Language	French, Fulani, Malinké, Susu, Kissi, Kpelle
Religion	Muslim, traditional local beliefs
Currency	Guinean franc (= 100 cauris)
GDP	US$4 billion (1997)
Economy	Chiefly agricultural and mineral mining; exports include bauxite, alumina, diamonds and coffee
Political system	Emergent democracy
Head of state	Lansana Conté
Head of government	Lamine Sidime

Guinea-Bissau

Location	W Africa
Area	36 125 sq km (13 948 sq mi)
Capital	Bissau
Major cities/towns	Bolama/Bijagós, Buba, Butata, Cacine, Catio, Farim, Mansôa, São Domingos
Population	1 161 000 (1998 est)
Language	Portuguese, Criolo, Balante
Religion	Traditional local beliefs, Muslim, Christian
Currency	CFA franc (= 100 centimes)
GDP	US$265 million (1997)
Economy	Chiefly agricultural; exports include cashew nuts, fish and shrimp and timber
Political system	Emergent democracy
Head of state	Kumba Ialá
Head of government	Caetano N'Tchama

Guyana

Location	N South America
Area	21 496 sq km (82 978 sq mi)
Capital	Georgetown
Major cities/towns	Corriverton, Linden, New Amsterdam, Rose Hall

Population	850 000 (1998 est)
Language	English, Hindi, Urdu, Amerindian dialects
Religion	Christian, Hindu, Muslim
Currency	Guyana dollar (= 100 cents)
GDP	US$740 million (1997)
Economy	Chiefly agricultural; exports include sugar, bauxite, alumina, rice, gold, rum and timber
Political system	Democracy
Head of state	Bharrat Jagdeo
Head of government	Samuel Hinds

Haiti

Location	Central Caribbean Sea
Area	27 750 sq km (10 712 sq mi)
Capital	Port-au-Prince
Major cities/towns	Cap-Haïtien, Gonaïves, Jacmée, Jérémie, Les Cayes, Port-de-Paix, St Marc
Population	7 952 000 (1998 est)
Language	French, Creole French
Religion	Roman Catholic, Voodoo
Currency	Gourde (= 100 centimes)
GDP	US$2.3 billion (1997)
Economy	Chiefly agricultural; exports include coffee, essential oils and sisal
Political system	Transitional
Head of state	Réne Préval
Head of government	Jacques Edouard Aléxis

Honduras

Location	Central America
Area	112 088 sq km (43 266 sq mi)
Capital	Tegucigalpa
Major cities/towns	Choluteca, Danlí, El Progreso, Juticalpa, La Ceiba, San Pedro Sula
Population	6 147 000 (1998 est)
Language	Spanish, Indian dialects
Religion	Roman Catholic, Protestant
Currency	Lempira (= 100 centavos)
GDP	US$4.5 billion (1997)
Economy	Chiefly agricultural; exports include bananas, lobsters and prawns, zinc and meat
Political system	Democracy
Head of state	Carlos Roberto Flores Facussé
Head of government	Carlos Roberto Flores Facussé

Hungary

Location	SE Europe
Area	93 033 sq km (35 912 sq mi)
Capital	Budapest
Major cities/towns	Debrecen, Gyor, Kecskemét, Miskolc, Nyiregyháza, Pécs, Szeged, Székesfehérvár
Population	10 116 000 (1998 est)
Language	Hungarian/Magyar
Religion	Roman Catholic, Calvinist, Lutheran
Currency	Forint (= 100 fillér)
GDP	US$44 billion (1997)

Economy	Mixed agricultural and industrial; exports include consumer goods, raw materials, transport equipment
Political system	Emergent democracy
Head of state	Arpád Göncz
Head of government	Viktor Orban

Iceland

Location	N Atlantic Ocean
Area	103 000 sq km (40 000 sq mi)
Capital	Reykjavik
Major cities/towns	Akranes, Akureyri, Hadnerfjördur, Kópavogur, Vestmannaeyjar
Population	276 000 (1998 est)
Language	Icelandic
Religion	Evangelical Lutheran, Roman Catholic
Currency	Króna (= 100 aurar)
GDP	US$7.4 billion (1997)
Economy	Agriculture, fishing and tourism; exports include fish products, aluminium and animal products
Political system	Democracy
Head of state	Olafur Ragnar Grimsson
Head of government	David Oddsson

India

Location	S central Asia
Area	3 166 829 sq km (1 222 3976 sq mi)
Capital	New Delhi
Major cities/towns	Ahmadabad, Bangalore, Bhopal, Bombay, Calcutta, Chennai (Madras), Hyderabad, Jaipur, Kanpur, Lucknow, Nagpur, Pune, Surat
Population	982 223 000 (1998 est)
Language	Hindi, English, Urud, Panjabi, Gujarati, Marathi, Bengali, Oriya, Kashmiri, Assamese, Kannada, Malayalam, Sindhi, Tamil, Telugu
Religion	Hindu, Muslim, Christian, Sikh, Buddhist
Currency	Indian rupee (= 100 paisa)
GDP	US$378.6 billion (1997)
Economy	Mixed agricultural and industrial; exports include tea, coffee, fish, iron and steel, leather and textiles
Political system	Democracy
Head of state	K. R. Narayan
Head of government	Atal Behari Vajpayee

Indonesia

Location	W Pacific Ocean
Area	1 906 200 sq km (735 800 sq mi)
Capital	Jakarta
Major cities/towns	Banda Aceh, Bandung, Denpasar, Kupang, Malang, Medan, Padang, Palembang, Semarang, Surabaya, Ujung Pandang, Yogyakarta
Population	206 338 000 (1998 est)
Language	Bahasa Indonesia, English, Dutch and Javanese
Religion	Muslim, Roman Catholic, Protestant, Hindu, Buddhist
Currency	Indonesian rupiah (= 100 sen)
GDP	US$214.6 billion (1997)
Economy	Chiefly agricultural; exports include petroleum, gas, textiles, rubber, palm oil and wood

Political system	Authoritarian nationalist republic
Head of state	Abdurraham Wahid
Head of government	Abdurraham Wahid

Iran

Location	SW Asia
Area	1 648 000 sq km (636 128 sq mi)
Capital	Teheran
Major cities/towns	Abadan, Ahvaz, Bakhtaran, Esfahan, Kara, Mashhad, Qom, Shiraz, Tabriz
Population	65 758 000 (1998 est)
Language	Farsi (Persian), Kurdish, Baluchi, Luri, Turkic
Religion	Muslim, Zoroastrian, Jewish, Baha'i, Christian
Currency	Iranian rial (= 100 dinars)
GDP	US$93.1 billion (1997 est)
Economy	Dominated by oil production, agriculture and forestry; exports include crude petroleum and petroleum products, agricultural products and metal ores
Political system	Authoritarian Islamic republic
Head of state	Ayatollah Sayed Ali Khameini
Head of government	Sayed Mohammad Khatami

Iraq

Location	W Asia
Area	434 925 sq km (167 881 sq mi)
Capital	Baghdad
Major cities/towns	Basra, Hilla, Kirkuk, Mosul, Najaf, Nasiriya
Population	21 800 000 (1998 est)
Language	Arabic, English, Kurdish, Persian, Turkish and Assyrian
Religion	Muslim, Christian
Currency	Iraqi dinar (= 1000 fils)
GDP	US$11.5 billion (1996 est)
Economy	Largely dependent on oil production, exports include crude petroleum and fruit
Political system	One-party socialist republic
Head of state	Saddam Hussein at-Takriti
Head of government	Saddam Hussein at-Takriti

Ireland, Republic of

Location	NW Europe
Area	70 282 sq km (27 129 sq mi)
Capital	Dublin
Major cities/towns	Cork, Galway, Limerick, Waterford, Wexford
Population	3 681 000 (1998 est)
Language	Irish Gaelic, English
Religion	Roman Catholic
Currency	Irish pound/punt (= 100 new pence)
GDP	US$72.7 billion (1997)
Economy	Chiefly agricultural; exports include animal products, machinery, electronic goods and chemicals
Political system	Democracy
Head of state	Mary McAleese
Head of government	Bertie Ahern

Israel

Location	E Mediterranean
Area	20 770 sq km (8 017 sq mi)
Capital	Jerusalem
Major cities/towns	Bat-Yam, Beersheba, Haifa, Holon, Petach Tikva, Ramat Gan, Rishon Leziyyon, Tel Aviv-Yafo
Population	5 984 000 (1998 est)
Language	Hebrew, Arabic
Religion	Jewish, Muslim, Christian
Currency	New Israeli shekel (= 100 agorot)
GDP	US$97.9 billion (1997)
Economy	Mixed industrial and agricultural; exports include citrus fruits, worked gold, salt, petroleum and natural gas
Political system	Democracy
Head of state	Ezer Weizmann
Head of government	Ariel Sharon

Italy

Location	S Europe
Area	301 255 sq km (116 314 sq mi)
Capital	Rome
Major cities/towns	Bologna, Genoa, Milan, Naples, Palermo, Turin
Population	57 369 000 (1998 est)
Language	Italian
Religion	Roman Catholic
Currency	Italian lira (= 100 centesimi)
GDP	US$1 146.2 billion (1997)
Economy	Mixed industrial and agricultural; exports include machinery, textiles, footwear, wine, metal products and chemicals
Political system	Democracy
Head of state	Carlo Ciampi
Head of government	Giuliano Amato

Jamaica

Location	Central Caribbean Sea
Area	10 957 sq km (4 229 sq mi)
Capital	Kingston
Major cities/towns	May Pen, Montego Bay, Portmore, St Andrew, Spanish Town
Population	2 538 000 (1998 est)
Language	English, Jamaican Creole
Religion	Protestant, Roman Catholic
Currency	Jamaican dollar (= 100 cents)
GDP	US$5.3 billion (1996)
Economy	Chiefly agricultural; exports include bauxite, marble, gypsum, sugar, bananas, clothing and rum
Political system	Constitutional monarchy
Head of state	Queen Elizabeth II
Head of government	Percival Patterson

Japan

Location	W Pacific Ocean
Area	377 728 sq km (145 803 sq mi)
Capital	Tokyo
Major cities/towns	Fukuoka, Hiroshima, Kawasaki, Kitakyushu, Kobe, Kyoto, Nagoya, Osaka, Sapporo, Yokohama

Population	126 281 000 (1998 est)
Language	Japanese
Religion	Shintoist, Buddhist, Christian
Currency	Yen (= 100 sen)
GDP	US$4 201.6 billion (1997)
Economy	Highly developed industry; exports include motor vehicles, electronic goods, chemicals and metal products
Political system	Democracy
Head of state	Emperor Akihito
Head of government	Junichiro Koizumi

Jordan

Location	E Mediterranean
Area	96 188 sq km (37 129 sq mi)
Capital	Amman
Major cities/towns	Aqaba, Irbid, Ma'an, Saet, Zarqa
Population	6 304 000 (1998 est)
Language	Arabic
Religion	Muslim, Christian
Currency	Jordanian dinar (= 1000 fils)
GDP	US$7.9 billion (1997)
Economy	Dependent on raw materials and agriculture; exports include phosphate, potash, fertilizers and foodstuffs
Political system	Constitutional monarchy
Head of state	King Abdullah II
Head of government	Abdul-Raouf Rawabdeh

Kazakhstan

Location	SW Asia
Area	2 717 300 sq km (1 048 878 sq mi)
Capital	Astana
Major cities/towns	Chimkent, Karaganda, Pavlodar, Petropavlovsk, Semipalatinsk
Population	16 319 000 (1998 est)
Language	Kazakh, Russian, German, Ukrainian
Religion	Muslim, Christian
Currency	Tenge
GDP	US$22.5 billion (1997)
Economy	Raw materials and heavy industry; exports include metals, mineral products and chemicals
Political system	Authoritarian nationalist
Head of state	Nursultan A. Nazarbayev
Head of government	Kasymzhomart Tokayev

Kenya

Location	E Africa
Area	580 367 sq km (224 081 sq mi)
Capital	Nairobi
Major cities/towns	Eldoret, Kisumu, Mombasa, Nakuru, Nyeri
Population	29 008 000 (1998 est)
Language	English, Swahili, local languages
Religion	Roman Catholic, Protestant, local beliefs, Muslim
Currency	Kenyan shilling (= 100 cents)
GDP	US$9.9 billion (1997)

Economy	Chiefly agricultural; exports include coffee, tea and petroleum products
Political system	Authoritarian nationalist
Head of state	Daniel Arap Moi
Head of government	Daniel Arap Moi

Kiribati

Location	W Pacific Ocean
Area	717 sq km (277 sq mi)
Capital	Bairiki
Major cities/towns	Betio
Population	81 700 (1998 est)
Language	English, Gilbertese
Religion	Roman Catholic, Kiribati Protestant, Baha'i, Seventh-Day Adventist
Currency	Australian dollar (= 100 cents)
GDP	US$68 million (1995 est)
Economy	Chiefly agricultural; exports include copra, fish, seaweed, bananas and breadfruit
Political system	Democracy
Head of state	Teburoro Tito
Head of government	Teburoro Tito

Korea, North

Location	SE Asia
Area	122 098 sq km (47 130 sq mi)
Capital	Pyongyang
Major cities/towns	Chongjin, Hamhung, Nampo, Sinuiji, Wonsan
Population	23 348 000 (1998 est)
Language	Korean
Religion	Atheist, with Buddhist and Christian minorities
Currency	Won (= 100 chon)
GDP	US$21.5 billion (1995 est)
Economy	Chiefly agricultural; exports include metals, textiles, vegetable products and machinery
Political system	Communism
Head of state	Kim Jong-il
Head of government	Hong Song-nam

Korea, South

Location	SE Asia
Area	98 913 sq km (38 180 sq mi)
Capital	Seoul
Major cities/towns	Inchon, Kwangju, Pusan, Taegu, Taejon
Population	46 109 000 (1998 est)
Language	Korean
Religion	Buddhist, Protestant, Roman Catholic, Confucianist
Currency	Won (= 100 chon)
GDP	US$438.2 billion (1997)
Economy	Heavy industry and raw materials; exports include electrical machinery, textiles, chemicals and ships.
Political system	Emergent democracy
Head of state	Kim Dae-jung
Head of government	Park Tae-joon

Kuwait

Location	SW Asia
Area	17 818 sq km (6 878 sq mi)
Capital	Kuwait City
Major cities/towns	Abraq Kheetan, Ahmadi, as-Salimiya, Fahaheel, Faranawiya, Hawalli, Jahra
Population	1 811 000 (1998 est)
Language	Arabic
Religion	Muslim, Christian, Hindu
Currency	Kuwaiti dinar (= 1000 fils)
GDP	US$32.1 billion (1997 est)
Economy	Heavily dependent upon oil; exports include petroleum and petroleum products
Political system	Absolute monarchy
Head of state	Emir Jabir al-Ahmad al-Jabir
Head of government	Saad al-Abdallah al-Salim al-Sabah

Kyrgyzstan

Location	Central Asia
Area	198 500 sq km (76 621 sq mi)
Capital	Bishkek
Major cities/towns	Djalal-Abad, Kyzyl-Kiya, Osh, Przhevalsk, Tokmak
Population	4 643 000 (1998 est)
Language	Russian, Kyrgyz
Religion	Sunni Muslim
Currency	Rouble (= 100 kopecks)
GDP	US$1.83 billion (1997)
Economy	Mixed industrial and agricultural; exports include wool, cotton yarn, tobacco, electric and engineering products
Political system	Emergent democracy
Head of state	Askaar Akayev
Head of government	Amangeldy Muraliev

Laos

Location	SE Asia
Area	236 800 sq km (91 405 sq mi)
Capital	Vientiane
Major cities/towns	Louangphrabang, Pakse, Savannakhet
Population	5 163 000 (1998 est)
Language	Lao, French, local languages
Religion	Buddhist, animist, Christian
Currency	Kip (= 100 at)
GDP	US$1.7 billion (1997)
Economy	Chiefly agricultural; exports include timber, textiles, motorcycles, coffee and tin
Political system	Communist one-party state
Head of state	Khamtay Siphandone
Head of government	Sisavath Keobounphan

Latvia

Location	E Baltic Sea
Area	64 600 sq km (24 900 sq mi)
Capital	Riga
Major cities/towns	Daugavpils, Jelgava, Jurmala, Leipaja, Ventspils

Population	2 422 000 (1998 est)
Language	Latvian
Religion	Evangelical Lutheran
Currency	Lat (= 100 santims)
GDP	US$5.4 billion (1997)
Economy	Mixed industrial and agricultural; exports include timber, textiles, food products, machinery and electrical products
Political system	Emergent democracy
Head of state	Vaira Vike-Freiberga
Head of government	Andris Berzins

Lebanon

Location	E Mediterranean
Area	10 452 sq km (4 034 sq mi)
Capital	Beirut
Major cities/towns	Baabda, Baalbek, Jezzine, Tripoli, Tyre, Zahlé
Population	3 191 000 (1998 est)
Language	Arabic, French, English and Armenian
Religion	Muslim, Christian, Armenian, Greek, Roman Catholic, Alawite, Druze and Jewish
Currency	Lebanese pound/livre (= 100 piastres)
GDP	US$14.9 billion (1997)
Economy	Mixed industrial and agricultural; exports include paper products, textiles, fruit and vegetables and jewellery
Political system	Emergent democracy
Head of state	Emile Lahoud
Head of government	Selim al-Hoss

Lesotho

Location	SE Africa
Area	30 355 sq km (11 720 sq mi)
Capital	Maseru
Major cities/towns	Hlotse, Mafeteng, Qach'a Nek, Quthing, Roma, Teyateyaneng
Population	2 062 000 (1998 est)
Language	Lesotho, English, Zulu, Afrikaans, French, Xhosa
Religion	Roman Catholic, Protestant, local beliefs
Currency	Loti (= 100 lisente)
GDP	US$950 million (1997)
Economy	Chiefly agricultural; exports include clothing, footwear, furniture, food and livestock
Political system	Constitutional monarchy
Head of state	King Letsie III
Head of government	Bethuel Pakalitha Mosisili

Liberia

Location	W Africa
Area	111 370 sq km (42 989 sq mi)
Capital	Monrovia
Major cities/towns	Bensonville, Buchanan, Gbarnga, Saniquillie, Voinjama
Population	2 666 000 (1998 est)
Language	English, local dialects
Religion	Animist beliefs, Muslim, Christian
Currency	Liberian dollar (= 100 cents)
GDP	US$2.4 billion (1995)

Economy	Dependent upon mineral resources; exports include iron ore, rubber, timber, coffeel, cocoa and gold
Political system	Emergent democracy
Head of state	Charles Taylor
Head of government	Charles Taylor

Libya

Location	N Africa
Area	1 758 610 sq km (678 823 sq mi)
Capital	Tripoli
Major cities/towns	Ajdabiya, Az-Zaiwa, Benghazi, Derna, Misurata, Tobruk
Population	5 339 000 (1998 est)
Language	Arabic, English, French
Religion	Sunni Muslim, Roman Catholic, Anglican, Coptic Orthodox, Jewish
Currency	Libyan dinar (= 1000 dirhams)
GDP	US$29.7 billion (1995)
Economy	Largely dependent on oil and natural gas; exports include crude petroleum and chemicals
Political system	One-party socialist state
Head of state	Muammar al-Gaddafi
Head of government	Muammar al-Gaddafi

Liechtenstein

Location	Central Europe
Area	160 sq km (62 sq mi)
Capital	Vaduz
Major cities/towns	Balzers, Eschen, Ruggell, Schaan, Triesen
Population	32 000 (1998 est)
Language	German
Religion	Roman Catholic, Protestant
Currency	Swiss franc (= 100 centimes)
GDP	US$1.3 billion (1995)
Economy	Developed industrial sector; exports include machinery, false teeth, stamps, precision instruments and ceramics
Political system	Constitutional monarchy
Head of state	King Hans Adam II
Head of government	Mario Frick

Lithuania

Location	E Baltic Sea
Area	65 200 sq km (25 167 sq mi)
Capital	Vilnius
Major cities/towns	Kaunas, Klaipeda, Panevezys, Siauliai
Population	3 694 000 (1998 est)
Language	Lithuanian
Religion	Roman Catholic
Currency	Litas (= 100 centai)
GDP	US$9.2 billion (1997)
Economy	Mixed heavy industry and agriculture; exports include textiles, machinery, metals, animal products and timber
Political system	Emergent democracy
Head of state	Valdas Adamkus
Head of government	Andrius Kubilius

Luxembourg

Location	N Europe
Area	2 586 sq km (998 sq mi)
Capital	Luxembourg
Major cities/towns	Differdange, Dudelange, Esch-Alzette, Petange
Population	422 000 (1998 est)
Language	French, German, Letzeburgish
Religion	Roman Catholic, Protestant, Jewish
Currency	Luxemburgish franc (= 100 centimes)
GDP	US$15.5 billion (1997)
Economy	Mixed industrial and agricultural; exports include metals, electrical equipment, rubber, plastics and textiles
Political system	Democracy
Head of state	Grand Duke Jean
Head of government	Jean-Claude Juncker

Macedonia, Former Yugoslav Republic of

Location	SE Europe
Area	25 713 sq km (9 925 sq mi)
Capital	Skopje
Major cities/towns	Bitolj, Kumanovo, Prilep, Tetovo
Population	1 999 000 (1998 est)
Language	Macedonian
Religion	Macedonian Orthodox Christian, Muslim
Currency	Denar (= 100 paras)
GDP	US$2.06 billion (1997)
Economy	Chiefly agricultural; exports include machinery, sugar beet, cheese and tobacco
Political system	Emergent democracy
Head of state	Boris Trajkovski
Head of government	Ljubco Georgievski

Madagascar

Location	W Indian Ocean
Area	587 041 sq km (228 658 sq mi)
Capital	Antananarivo
Major cities/towns	Ambatondrazaka, Antsirabe, Fianarantsoa, Mahajanga, Toamasina
Population	15 057 000 (1998 est)
Language	Malagasy, French
Religion	Animist, Roman Catholic, Protestant, Muslim
Currency	Malagasy franc (= 100 centimes)
GDP	US$3.5 billion (1997)
Economy	Chiefly agricultural; exports include coffee, shrimps, petroleum products and cotton fabrics
Political system	Emergent democracy
Head of state	Didier Ratsiraka
Head of government	Tantely Andrianarivo

Malawi

Location	SW Africa
Area	118 484 sq km (47 747 sq mi)
Capital	Lilongwe
Major cities/towns	Blantyre, Lilongwe, Mzuzu, Zomba
Population	10 346 000 (1998 est)

Language	English, Chichewa
Religion	Protestant, Roman Catholic, Muslim, animist
Currency	Kwacha (= 100 tambala)
GDP	US$2.4 billion (1997)
Economy	Chiefly agricultural; exports include tobacco, tea, sugar, cotton and groundnuts
Political system	Emergent democracy
Head of state	Bakili Muluzi
Head of government	Bakili Muluzi

Malaysia

Location	SE Asia
Area	329 749 sq km (127 283 sq mi)
Capital	Kuala Lumpur
Major cities/towns	George Town, Ipoh, Johor Baharu, Kelang, Kota Kinabalu, Kuala Baharu, Kuala Trengganu, Kuching, Petalong Jaya
Population	21 410 000 (1998 est)
Language	Bahasa Malaysia (Malay), Chinese, English, Tamil
Religion	Muslim, Buddhist, Chinese folk religionist, Hindu, Christian
Currency	Malaysian dollar/ringgit (= 100 cents)
GDP	US$97.5 billion (1997)
Economy	Rich mineral resources and some industry; exports include palm oil, rubber, crude petroleum, machinery, timber, tin, textiles and electronic goods
Political system	Democracy
Head of state	Sultan Salehuddin Abdul Aziz Shah
Head of government	Mahathir bin Mohamad

Maldives

Location	N Indian Ocean
Area	300 sq km (116 sq mi)
Capital	Malé
Major cities/towns	Anthimatha, Dhiggiri, Kunfunadhoo, Kurehdhu, Seenu
Population	271 000 (1998 est)
Language	Dhivehi, Arabic, Hindi, English
Religion	Sunni Muslim
Currency	Rufiyaa (= 100 laaris)
GDP	US$274 million (1995)
Economy	Fishing and tourism; exports include marine products and clothing
Political system	Authoritarian nationalist
Head of state	Maumoon Abdul Gayoom
Head of government	Maumoon Abdul Gayoom

Mali

Location	NW Africa
Area	1 240 192 sq km (478 714 sq mi)
Capital	Bamako
Major cities/towns	Kayes, Mopti, Ségou, Sikasso, Timbuktu
Population	10 694 000 (1998 est)
Language	French, local languages
Religion	Muslim, animist beliefs
Currency	CFA franc (= 100 centimes)
GDP	US$2.5 billion (1997)

Economy	Chiefly agricultural; exports include cotton, livestock and gold
Political system	Emergent democracy
Head of state	Alpha Oumar Konaré
Head of government	Mande Sidibe

Malta

Location	Central Mediterranean
Area	316 sq km (122 sq mi)
Capital	Valletta
Major cities/towns	Birkirkara, Qormi, Rabat, Sliema, Zabor, Zetjun
Population	384 000 (1998 est)
Language	English, Maltese
Religion	Roman Catholic Apostolic, Anglican
Currency	Maltese pound (= 100 cents)
GDP	US$3.4 billion (1997 est)
Economy	Revenue from ship repair and tourism; exports include machinery, chemicals and tobacco
Political system	Democracy
Head of state	Guido de Marco
Head of government	Eddie Fenech Adami

Marshall Islands

Location	W Pacific Ocean
Area	c.180 sq km (c.70 sq mi)
Capital	Dalap-Uliga-Darrit
Major cities/towns	Ebeye
Population	60 000 (1998 est)
Language	Marshallese (Kajin-Majol), English, Japanese
Religion	Protestant, Roman Catholic
Currency	US dollar (= 100 cents)
GDP	US$94 million (1995 est)
Economy	Agriculture and fishing; exports include coconut products, copra and fish
Political system	Democracy
Head of state	Imata Kabua
Head of government	Imata Kabua

Mauritania

Location	NW Africa
Area	1 029 920 sq km (397 549 sq mi)
Capital	Nouakchott
Major cities/towns	Atar, Kaédi, Kiffa, Nouâdhibou, Rosso, Zouerate
Population	2 229 000 (1998 est)
Language	Arabic, French, local languages
Religion	Sunni Muslim, Roman Catholic
Currency	Ouguija (= 5 khoums)
GDP	US$1.06 billion (1997)
Economy	Chiefly agricultural; exports include fish and iron ore
Political system	Emergent democracy
Head of state	Moaouia Ould Sidi Mohammed Taya
Head of government	Cheikh el Avia Ould Mohamed Khouna

Mauritius

Location	W Indian Ocean
Area	1 865 sq km (720 sq mi)
Capital	Port Louis
Major cities/towns	Beau Bassin-Rose Hill, Curepipe, Quatre Bornes, Vacoas-Phoenix
Population	1 141 000 (1998 est)
Language	English, French, Hindi, Urdu, Bojpoori, Hakka
Religion	Hindu, Roman Catholic, Muslim, Protestant
Currency	Mauritanian rupee (= 100 cents)
GDP	US$4.1 billion (1997)
Economy	Dominated by production of sugar cane; exports include sugar, clothing, tea, molasses and jewellery
Political system	Democracy
Head of state	Cassum Uteem
Head of government	Navin Ramgoolam

Mexico

Location	Central America
Area	1 978 000 sq km (763 817 sq mi)
Capital	Mexico City
Major cities/towns	Ciudad Juárez, Guadalajara, Monterrey, Netzahualcóyotl, Puebla, Tijuana
Population	95 831 000 (1998 est)
Language	Spanish, local languages
Religion	Roman Catholic, Protestant
Currency	Mexican peso (= 100 centavos)
GDP	US$404.2 billion (1997)
Economy	Revenue from minerals and mixed industry; exports include petroleum, engines, motor vehicles, coffee and cotton
Political system	Democracy
Head of state	Vincente Fox
Head of government	Vincente Fox

Micronesia, Federated States of

Location	W Pacific Ocean
Area	700 sq km (270 sq mi)
Capital	Palikir
Major cities/towns	Lelu, Weno
Population	114 000 (1998 est)
Language	English, local languages
Religion	Roman Catholic, Protestant
Currency	US dollar (= 100 cents)
GDP	US$259 million (1995 est)
Economy	Chiefly agricultural and fishing; exports include copra, pepper and fish
Political system	Democracy
Head of state	Leo Falcam
Head of government	Leo Falcam

Moldova

Location	W Asia
Area	33 700 sq km (13 008 sq mi)
Capital	Chisinau
Major cities/towns	Beltsy, Bendery, Tiraspol

Population	4 378 000 (1998 est)
Language	Moldovan, Ukrainian
Religion	Russian Orthodox, Baptist, Roman Catholic
Currency	Leu
GDP	US$2.1 billion (1997)
Economy	Mixed industrial and agricultural; exports include food products, machinery and textiles
Political system	Emergent democracy
Head of state	Petru Lucinschi
Head of government	Dumitru Barghis

Monaco

Location	S Europe
Area	1.95 sq km (0.75 sq mi)
Capital	Monaco
Major cities/towns	Fontvieille, La Condamine, Monte Carlo
Population	33 000 (1998 est)
Language	French, English, Italian, Monegasque
Religion	Roman Catholic
Currency	French franc (= 100 centimes)
GDP	US$847 million (1995)
Economy	Tourism and mixed industry; exports include chemicals and textiles
Political system	Constitutional monarchy
Head of state	Prince Rainier III
Head of government	Michel Lévêque

Mongolia

Location	E Asia
Area	1 566 500 sq km (604 800 sq mi)
Capital	Ulaanbaatar
Major cities/towns	Choybalsan, Darhan, Erdenet
Population	2 579 000 (1998 est)
Language	Khalka, Russian, Chinese
Religion	Minority Tibetan Buddhist
Currency	Tugrik (= 100 möngö)
GDP	US$862 million (1997)
Economy	Chiefly agricultural; exports include minerals and metals, consumer goods, food products
Political system	Emergent democracy
Head of state	Natsagiyn Bagabandi
Head of government	Nambariin Enkhbayar

Morocco

Location	NW Africa
Area	409 200 sq km (157 951 sq mi)
Capital	Rabat
Major cities/towns	Agadir, Casablanca, Fez, Kenitra, Marrakesh, Meknès, Oujda, Tangier, Tetouan
Population	27 377 000 (1998 est)
Language	Arabic, Berber, Spanish, French
Religion	Sunni Muslim
Currency	Moroccan dirham (= 100 centimes)
GDP	US$33.2 billion (1997)

Economy	Chiefly agricultural; exports include phosphates, mineral products, seafoods and clothing
Political system	Constitutional monarchy
Head of state	King Mohammed VI
Head of government	Abderrahmane el-Yousifi

Mozambique

Location	SE Africa
Area	799 380 sq km (308 641 sq mi)
Capital	Maputo
Major cities/towns	Beira, Chimoio, Nacala, Nampula
Population	18 880 000 (1998 est)
Language	Portuguese, Swahili, Bantu
Religion	Animist beliefs, Christian, Muslim
Currency	Metical (= 100 centavos)
GDP	US$1.9 billion (1997)
Economy	Chiefly agricultural; exports include shrimps, cashew nuts, cotton, sugar and copra
Political system	Emergent democracy
Head of state	Joaquim Alberto Chissanó
Head of government	Pascoal Mocumbi

Myanmar

Location	SE Asia
Area	678 576 sq km (261 930 sq mi)
Capital	Yangon (Rangoon)
Major cities/towns	Bago, Bassein, Mandalay, Manywa, Mawlamyine, Sittwe, Taunggyi
Population	44 497 000 (1998 est)
Language	Burmese, local languages
Religion	Theravada Buddhist, animist, Muslim, Hindu, Christian
Currency	Kyat (= 100 pyas)
GDP	US$133.5 billion (1996)
Economy	Chiefly agricultural; exports include teak, rice, rubber, hardwood and cement
Political system	Military republic
Head of state	Than Shwe
Head of government	Than Shwe

Namibia

Location	SW Africa
Area	824 292 sq km (318 261 sq mi)
Capital	Windhoek
Major cities/towns	Rehoboth, Rundu, Swakopmund
Population	1 660 000 (1998 est)
Language	English, Afrikaans, German, local languages
Religion	Christian, animist beliefs
Currency	Namibian dollar (= 100 cents)
GDP	US$3.4 billion (1997)
Economy	Chiefly agricultural; exports include diamonds, fish, livestock and uranium
Political system	Democracy
Head of state	Sam Daniel Nujoma
Head of government	Hage Geingob

Nauru

Location	W Pacific Ocean
Area	21.3 sq km (8.2 sq mi)
Capital	Yaren District
Major cities/towns	
Population	11 000 (1998 est)
Language	Nauruan, English
Religion	Christian
Currency	Australian dollar (= 100 cents)
GDP	US$368 million (1995)
Economy	Based on phosphate mining and tourism; exports include phosphates and coconuts
Political system	Democracy
Head of state	Bernard Dowiyogo
Head of government	Bernard Dowiyogo

Nepal

Location	Central Asia
Area	145 391 sq km (56 121 sq mi)
Capital	Kathmandu
Major cities/towns	Bhádgáon, Bhaktapur, Biratnagar, Lalitpur, Moráng, Pátan, Pokhara
Population	22 847 000 (1998 est)
Language	Nepali, Maithir, Bhojpuri
Religion	Hindu, Buddhist, Muslim, Christian
Currency	Nepalese rupee (= 100 paise/pice)
GDP	US$4.9 billion (1997)
Economy	Chiefly agricultural; exports include woollen carpets, clothing, timber and vegetables
Political system	Constitutional monarchy
Head of state	King Gyanendra
Head of government	Girija Prasad Koirala

Netherlands, The

Location	N Europe
Area	33 929 sq km (13 097 sq mi)
Capital	Amsterdam
Major cities/towns	Apeldoorn, Eindhoven, Enschede, Groningen, Haarlem, The Hague, Maastricht, Nijmegen, Rotterdam, Tilburg, Utrecht
Population	15 678 000 (1998 est)
Language	Dutch
Religion	Roman Catholic, Protestant
Currency	Guilder/Florin (= 100 cents)
GDP	US$360.5 billion (1997)
Economy	Mixed agriculture and industry; exports include machinery, food products, petroleum, natural gas and cut flowers
Political system	Constitutional monarchy
Head of state	Queen Beatrix
Head of government	Wim Kok

New Zealand

Location	SW Pacific Ocean
Area	268 812 sq km (103 761 sq mi)
Capital	Wellington

Major cities/towns	Auckland, Christchurch, Dunedin, Hamilton, Napier-Hastings, Palmerston North
Population	3 796 000 (1998 est)
Language	English, Maori
Religion	Anglican, Presbyterian, Roman Catholic
Currency	New Zealand dollar (= 100 cents)
GDP	US$64.9 billion (1997)
Economy	Chiefly agricultural; exports include meat, dairy products, wool, fish and timber
Political system	Constitutional monarchy
Head of state	Queen Elizabeth II
Head of government	Helen Clark

Nicaragua

Location	Central America
Area	148 000 sq km (57 128 sq mi)
Capital	Managua
Major cities/towns	Chinandega, Granada, León, Masaya
Population	4 807 000 (1998 est)
Language	Spanish, Indian languages, English
Religion	Roman Catholic, Protestant
Currency	Córdobaoro (= 100 centavos)
GDP	US$2 billion (1997)
Economy	Chiefly agricultural; exports include coffee, meat, cotton, sugar, seafood and bananas
Political system	Emergent democracy
Head of state	Arnoldo Aleman Lacayo
Head of government	Arnoldo Aleman Lacayo

Niger

Location	Central N Africa
Area	1 267 000 sq km (489 191 sq mi)
Capital	Niamey
Major cities/towns	Agadez, Birui N'Konui, Maradi, Tahoua, Zinder
Population	10 078 000 (1998 est)
Language	French, Hausa, Songhai, Fulfulde, Tamashek, Arabic
Religion	Muslim, local beliefs, Roman Catholic
Currency	CFA franc (= 100 cents)
GDP	US$1.8 billion (1997)
Economy	Largely dependent on agriculture and mining; exports include uranium ore, livestock and cotton
Political system	Transitional
Head of state	Tandja Mamadou
Head of government	Hama Amadou

Nigeria

Location	W Africa
Area	923 768 sq km (356 669 sq mi)
Capital	Abuja
Major cities/towns	Abeokuta, Ibadan, Ilorin, Iwo, Kaduna, Kano, Lagos, Ugbomosho, Oshogbo, Ouitsha, Zaria
Population	106 409 000 (1998 est)
Language	English, Hausa, Yoruba, Ibo, Niger-Congo dialects
Religion	Muslim, Christian, animist beliefs

Currency	Naira (= 100 kobos)
GDP	US$36.5 billion (1997)
Economy	Largely dependent upon oil production; exports include petroleum, cocoa beans, rubber and fish
Political system	Military republic
Head of state	Olusegun Obasanjo
Head of government	Olusegun Obasanjo

Norway

Location	NW Europe
Area	323 895 sq km (125 023 sq mi)
Capital	Oslo
Major cities/towns	Bergen, Drammen, Kristiansand, Stavanger, Trondheim
Population	4 419 000 (1998 est)
Language	Norwegian
Religion	Evangelical Lutheran, Baptist, Pentecostalist, Methodist, Roman Catholic
Currency	Norwegian krone (= 100 øre)
GDP	US$153.4 billion (1997)
Economy	Based on extraction of oil and raw materials; exports include petroleum, natural gas, fish products and wood pulp
Political system	Constitutional monarchy
Head of state	King Harald V
Head of government	Jens Stoltenberg

Oman

Location	W Asia
Area	300 000 sq km (115 800 sq mi)
Capital	Muscat
Major cities/towns	Al-Buraimi, Ibri, Nizwa, Salalah, Sohar
Population	2 382 000 (1998 est)
Language	Arabic, English, Baluchi, Urdu, Indian dialects
Religion	Ibadhi Muslim, Sunni Muslim, Shi'a Muslim, Hindu
Currency	Rial Omani (= 1000 baizas)
GDP	US$13.7 billion (1995)
Economy	Dependent upon oil production; exports include petroleum, natural gas, copper, chromite and gold
Political system	Absolute monarchy
Head of state	Sultan Qaboos bin Said
Head of government	Sultan Qaboos bin Said

Pakistan

Location	SW Asia
Area	803 943 sq km (310 322 sq mi)
Capital	Islamabad
Major cities/towns	Faisalabad, Gujranwala, Hyderabad, Islamabad, Karachi, Lahore, Multan, Peshawar, Quetta, Rawalpindi, Sargodha, Sialkot
Population	148 166 000 (1998 est)
Language	Urdu, Punjabi, Sindhi, Pashto, Baluchi, Brahvi
Religion	Sunni Muslim, Shi'a Muslim, Christian, Hindu, Parsee, Buddhist
Currency	Pakistan rupee (= 100 paisa)
GDP	US$64.3 billion (1997)
Economy	Chiefly agricultural; exports include cotton, textiles, petroleum, clothing, leather and livestock

Political system	Emergent democracy
Head of state	Muhammad Rafiq Tarar
Head of government	Pervez Musharraf

Panama

Location	Central America
Area	77 082 sq km (29 753 sq mi)
Capital	Panama City
Major cities/towns	Balboa, Chitré, Colón, David, La Chorrera, San Miguelito, Santiago
Population	2 767 000 (1998 est)
Language	Spanish, English, local languages
Religion	Roman Catholic, Protestant
Currency	Balboa (= 100 cents)
GDP	US$8.7 billion (1997)
Economy	Largely dependent upon revenue raised by Panama Canal; exports include bananas, shrimps, sugar, clothing and coffee
Political system	Emergent democracy
Head of state	Mireya Moscoso
Head of government	Mireya Moscoso

Papua New Guinea

Location	SE Asia
Area	462 840 sq km (178 656 sq mi)
Capital	Port Moresby
Major cities/towns	Arawa, Goroka, Lae, Madang, Mount Hagen, Rabaul, Wewak
Population	4 600 000 (1998 est)
Language	Pidgin English, Motu, Tok Pisin, local languages
Religion	Protestant, Roman Catholic, local beliefs
Currency	Kina (= 100 toea)
GDP	US$5.1 billion (1997)
Economy	Chiefly agriculture, fishing and forestry; exports include gold, copper ore, crude petroleum, timber, coffee beans and coconut
Political system	Democracy
Head of state	Queen Elizabeth II
Head of government	Mekere Morauta

Paraguay

Location	Central S America
Area	406 750 sq km (157 000 sq mi)
Capital	Asunción
Major cities/towns	Ciudad del Este, Concepción, Encaración, Fernando de la Mora, Lambare, Pedro Juan Caballero, San Lorenzo, Villartica
Population	5 222 000 (1998 est)
Language	Spanish, Guaraní
Religion	Roman Catholic
Currency	Guaraní (= 100 céntimos)
GDP	US$10.1 billion (1997)
Economy	Chiefly agricultural; exports include soya beans, cotton, timber and meat
Political system	Emergent democracy
Head of state	Luis Gonzalez Macchi
Head of government	Luis Gonzalez Macchi

Peru

Location	S America
Area	1 284 640 sq km (495 871 sq mi)
Capital	Lima
Major cities/towns	Arequipa, Chiclayo, Chimbote, Cuzco, Iquitos, Piura, Trujillo
Population	24 797 000 (1998 est)
Language	Spanish, Quechua, Aymará
Religion	Roman Catholic, Anglican, Methodist, Peruvian Baha'i
Currency	New sol (= 100 céntimos)
GDP	US$62.4 billion (1997)
Economy	Rich mineral resources; exports include copper, zinc, gold and refined petroleum products
Political system	Democracy
Head of state	Alejandro Toledo
Head of government	Alberto Bustamante Belaúnde

Philippines

Location	W Pacific Ocean
Area	299 679 sq km (115 676 sq mi)
Capital	Manila
Major cities/towns	Caloocan, Cebu, Davao, Quezon City, Zamboanga
Population	72 944 000 (1998 est)
Language	Tagalog (Pilipino), English, local languages
Religion	Roman Catholic, Protestant
Currency	Philippine peso (= 100 centavos)
GDP	US$83.1 billion (1997)
Economy	Chiefly agricultural; exports include electronic products, clothing and agricultural products
Political system	Emergent democracy
Head of state	Joseph Arap Estrada
Head of government	Joseph Arap Estrada

Poland

Location	NE Europe
Area	312 683 sq km (120 695 sq mi)
Capital	Warsaw
Major cities/towns	Bydgoszcz, Gdansk, Katowice, Kraków, Lódz, Lublin, Poznan, Szczecin, Wroclaw
Population	38 718 000 (1998 est)
Language	Polish
Religion	Roman Catholic
Currency	Zloty (= 100 groszy)
GDP	US$135.6 billion (1997)
Economy	Mixed agricultural and heavy industry; exports include machinery, textiles, chemicals, coal, copper, foodstuffs and wood products
Political system	Emergent democracy
Head of state	Alexander Kwasniewski
Head of government	Jerzy Buzek

Portugal

Location	W Europe
Area	91 630 sq km (35 370 sq mi)
Capital	Lisbon

Major cities/towns	Amadora, Coimbra, Guarde, Portalegre, Porto, Setúbal
Population	9 869 000 (1998 est)
Language	Portuguese
Religion	Roman Catholic
Currency	Escudo (= 100 centavos)
GDP	US$97.5 billion (1997)
Economy	Mixed agricultural and industrial; exports include textiles, footwear, pulp, wood products and tinned fish
Political system	Democracy
Head of state	Jorge Sampaio
Head of government	Antonio Guterres

Qatar

Location	W Asia
Area	11 437 sq km (4 415 sq mi)
Capital	Doha
Major cities/towns	Al-Khour, Dukhan, Halul, Ruwais, Umm Said, Wakra
Population	579 000 (1998 est)
Language	Arabic, English
Religion	Sunni Muslim
Currency	Qatar riyal (= 100 dirhams)
GDP	US$9 billion (1996)
Economy	Dependent upon oil production; exports include petroleum
Political system	Absolute monarchy
Head of state	Emir Hamad bin Khalifa
Head of government	Abdulla bin Khalifa

Romania

Location	SE Europe
Area	237 500 sq km (91 675 sq mi)
Capital	Bucharest
Major cities/towns	Brasov, Cluj-Napoca, Constanta, Craiova, Galati, Iasl, Ploiesti, Timisoara
Population	22 474 000 (1998 est)
Language	Romanian, French, Hungarian, German
Religion	Eastern Orthodox Christian, Roman Catholic
Currency	Leu (= 100 bani)
GDP	US$35.2 billion (1997)
Economy	Mixed agricultural and industrial; exports include metals, textiles, machinery and foodstuffs
Political system	Emergent democracy
Head of state	Emil Constantinescu
Head of government	Mugur Isarescu

Russia

Location	N Asia
Area	17 075 400 sq km (6 591 100 sq mi)
Capital	Moscow
Major cities/towns	Chelyabinsk, Kazan, Nizhniy Novgorod, Novosibirsk, Omsk, Perm, Rostov-na-Don, St Petersburg, Samara, Tver, Ufa, Volgograd, Vyatka, Yekaterinburg
Population	147 434 000 (1998 est)
Language	Russian
Religion	Christian, Muslim

Currency	Rouble
GDP	US$449.8 billion (1997)
Economy	Mixed heavy industry and agriculture; exports include mineral fuels, metals, precious stones, chemical products, machinery, weapons, timber and paper
Political system	Emergent democracy
Head of state	Vladimir Putin
Head of government	Mikhail Kasyanov

Rwanda

Location	Central Africa
Area	26 338 sq km (10 169 sq mi)
Capital	Kigali
Major cities/towns	Butare, Gisenyi, Ruhengeri
Population	6 604 000 (1998 est)
Language	French, Kinyarwanda, English, Kiswahili
Religion	Christian, local beliefs, Muslim
Currency	Rwanda franc (= 100 centimes)
GDP	US$1.7 billion (1997)
Economy	Chiefly agricultural; exports include coffee and tin
Political system	Transitional
Head of state	Paul Kagame
Head of government	Bernard Makuza

Saint Kitts and Nevis

Location	E Caribbean Sea
Area	269 sq km (104 sq mi)
Capital	Basseterre
Major cities/towns	Charlestown, Dieppe Bay Town, Newcastle, Sandy Point Town
Population	39 000 (1998 est)
Language	English, creole-English
Religion	Christian
Currency	East Caribbean dollar (= 100 cents)
GDP	US$254 million (1997)
Economy	Largely dependent upon sugar; exports include sugar and sugar products
Political system	Constitutional monarchy
Head of state	Queen Elizabeth II
Head of government	Denzil Douglas

Saint Lucia

Location	E Caribbean Sea
Area	616 sq km (238 sq mi)
Capital	Castries
Major cities/towns	Laborie, Soufrière, Vieux-Fort
Population	150 000 (1998 est)
Language	English, French patois
Religion	Roman Catholic, Protestant, Anglican
Currency	East Caribbean dollar (= 100 cents)
GDP	US$601 million (1996 est)
Economy	Tourism a major factor; exports include bananas, coconut oil and cocoa beans

Political system	Constitutional monarchy
Head of state	Queen Elizabeth II
Head of government	Kenny Anthony

Saint Vincent and the Grenadines

Location	SE Caribbean Sea
Area	390 sq km (150 sq mi)
Capital	Kingstown
Major cities/towns	Baronallie, Châteaubelair, Georgetown, Layon
Population	112 000 (1998 est)
Language	English, French patois
Religion	Anglican, Methodist, Roman Catholic
Currency	East Caribbean dollar (= 100 cents)
GDP	US$277 million (1996 est)
Economy	Chiefly agricultural; exports include bananas, sweet potatoes, ginger and plantains
Political system	Constitutional monarchy
Head of state	Queen Elizabeth II
Head of government	James FitzAllen Mitchell

Samoa

Location	W Pacific Ocean
Area	2 842 sq km (1 097 sq mi)
Capital	Apia
Major cities/towns	Falealup, Falevai, Lalomanu, Tuasivi
Population	174 000 (1998 est)
Language	Samoan, English
Religion	Protestant, Roman Catholic
Currency	Tala (= 100 sene)
GDP	US$187 million (1997 est)
Economy	Chiefly agricultural; exports include coconut cream, beer, cigarettes, copra and cocoa
Political system	Democracy
Head of state	King Malietoa Tanumafili II
Head of government	Tuilaepa Sailele Malielegaoi

San Marino

Location	S Europe (within Italy)
Area	61 sq km (23 sq mi)
Capital	San Marino
Major cities/towns	Faetano, Fiorentino, Monte Giardino, Serravalle
Population	26 000 (1998 est)
Language	Italian
Religion	Roman Catholic
Currency	Lira (= 100 centesimi)
GDP	US$478 million (1995)
Economy	Chiefly agricultural; exports include wood machinery, chemicals, wine, olive oil and textiles
Political system	Democracy
Head of state	(two captains regent, on six-month terms)
Head of government	Gabriele Gatti

São Tomé and Príncipe

Location	Off W Africa
Area	1001 sq km (387 sq mi)
Capital	São Tomé
Major cities/towns	Porto-Alegre, Santana, São António
Population	141 000 (1998 est)
Language	Portuguese, creole languages
Religion	Roman Catholic, Seventh Day Adventist, Evangelical Protestant
Currency	Dobra (= 100 centimos)
GDP	US$34 million (1997 est)
Economy	Chiefly agricultural; exports include cocoa, copra, coffee, bananas and palm oil
Political system	Emergent democracy
Head of state	Miguel dos Anjos da Costa Lisboa Trovoada
Head of government	Guilherme Posser da Costa

Saudi Arabia

Location	W Asia
Area	2 331 000 sq km (899 766 sq mi)
Capital	Riyadh
Major cities/towns	Dammam, Hufuf, Jiddah, Mecca, Medina, Taif
Population	20 181 000 (1998 est)
Language	Arabic
Religion	Sunni Muslim, Shi'ite Muslim
Currency	Saudi Arabian riyal (= 100 halalah)
GDP	US$145.8 billion (1997)
Economy	Based on oil production; exports include crude and refined petroleum and petrochemicals
Political system	Absolute monarchy
Head of state	King Fahd ibn Abdulaziz
Head of government	King Fahd ibn Abdulaziz

Senegal

Location	W Africa
Area	196 790 sq km (75 729 sq mi)
Capital	Dakar
Major cities/towns	Diourbel, Kaolack, Saint-Louis, Thiès, Ziguinchor
Population	9 003 000 (1998 est)
Language	French, local languages
Religion	Sunni Muslim, Roman Catholic, local beliefs
Currency	CFA franc (= 100 centimes)
GDP	US$145.8 billion (1997)
Economy	Chiefly agricultural; exports include fish products, refined petroleum and chemicals
Political system	Emergent socialist democracy
Head of state	Abdoulaye Wade
Head of government	Moustapha Niasse

Seychelles

Location	W Indian Ocean
Area	455 sq km (175 sq mi)
Capital	Victoria
Major cities/towns	Cascade, Misere, Port Glaud

Population	76 100 (1998 est)
Language	Creole French, English
Religion	Roman Catholic
Currency	Seychelles rupee (= 100 cents)
GDP	US$536 million (1997 est)
Economy	Chiefly agricultural; exports include fish, canned tuna and refined petroleum products
Political system	Emergent democracy
Head of state	France-Albert René
Head of government	France-Albert René

Sierra Leone

Location	W Africa
Area	71 740 sq km (27 692 sq mi)
Capital	Freetown
Major cities/towns	Bo, Kenema, Koidu, Makeni
Population	4 568 000 (1998 est)
Language	English, Krio
Religion	Local beliefs, Sunni Muslim, Protestant, Roman Catholic
Currency	Leone (= 100 cents)
GDP	US$941 million (1995)
Economy	Dominated by mining; exports include diamonds, bauxite, gold, coffee and cocoa beans
Political system	Transitional
Head of state	Ahmed Tejan Kabbah
Head of government	Ahmed Tejan Kabbah

Singapore

Location	SE China
Area	618 sq km (238 sq mi)
Capital	Singapore City
Major cities/towns	Changi, Jurong
Population	3 476 000 (1998 est)
Language	English, Malay, Chinese, Tamil
Religion	Buddhist, Muslim, Taoist, Christian, Hindu
Currency	Singapore dollar (= 100 cents)
GDP	US$96.3 billion (1997)
Economy	Shipping and oil industry important; exports include electrical machinery, petroleum products, rubber, foodstuffs, clothing and metals
Political system	Democracy
Head of state	Sellapan Ramanathan Nathan
Head of government	Goh Chok Tong

Slovak Republic

Location	E Europe
Area	49 035 sq km (18 927 sq mi)
Capital	Bratislava
Major cities/towns	Banská Bystrica, Košice, Nitra, Preov, Trnava, Zilina
Population	5 377 000 (1998 est)
Language	Slovak, Czech, Hungarian
Religion	Roman Catholic, Protestant
Currency	Slovak koruna (= 100 halura)
GDP	US$19.5 billion (1997)

Economy	Mixed agriculture and heavy industry; exports include machinery and transport equipment
Political system	Emergent democracy
Head of state	Rudolf Schuster
Head of government	Mikuláš Dzurinda

Slovenia

Location	SE Europe
Area	20 251 sq km (7 817 sq mi)
Capital	Ljubljana
Major cities/towns	Celji, Kranj, Koper, Maribor, Velenje
Population	1 993 000 (1998 est)
Language	Slovene, Croatian
Religion	Roman Catholic, Protestant, Eastern Orthodox
Currency	Slovene tolar (= 100 paras)
GDP	US$17.9 billion (1997)
Economy	Mixed agriculture and industry; exports include raw materials, machinery, electric motors, foodstuffs, clothing and cosmetics
Political system	Emergent democracy
Head of state	Milan Kucan
Head of government	Andrej Bajuk

Solomon Islands

Location	W Pacific Ocean
Area	27 556 sq km (10 637 sq mi)
Capital	Honiara
Major cities/towns	Auki, Gizo, Kieta
Population	417 000 (1998 est)
Language	English, pidgin English, local languages
Religion	Protestant, Anglican, Roman Catholic
Currency	Solomon Islands dollar (= 100 cents)
GDP	US$400 million (1997 est)
Economy	Chiefly agricultural; exports include timber, fish products and oil palm products
Political system	Constitutional monarchy
Head of state	Queen Elizabeth II
Head of government	Bartholomew Ulufa'alu

Somalia

Location	E Africa
Area	637 357 sq km (246 201 sq mi)
Capital	Mogadishu
Major cities/towns	Berbera, Hargeysa, Kismayo, Marka
Population	9 237 000 (1998 est)
Language	Somali, Arabic
Religion	Sunni Muslim
Currency	Somali shilling (= 100 cents)
GDP	US$1.2 billion (1995)
Economy	Chiefly agricultural; exports include livestock, bananas and fish
Political system	Transitional
Head of state	Ali Mahdi Muhammed
Head of government	Hussein Mohamed Aidid

South Africa

Location	S Africa
Area	1 233 404 sq km (476 094 sq mi)
Capital	Cape Town (legislative), Pretoria (administrative), Bloemfontain (judicial)
Major cities/towns	Durban, East London, Johannesburg, Kimberley, Pietermaritzburg, Port Elizabeth, Vereeniging
Population	39 357 000 (1998 est)
Language	English, Afrikaans, Xhosa, Zulu, Sesotho, other local languages
Religion	Christian, local beliefs
Currency	Rand (= 100 cents)
GDP	US$129.1 billion (1997)
Economy	Mixed industry and agriculture; exports include metals, gold, precious stones, mineral products, machinery, wool, fruit and sugar
Political system	Democracy
Head of state	Thabo Mbeki
Head of government	Thabo Mbeki

Spain

Location	W Europe
Area	504 750 sq km (194 833 sq mi)
Capital	Madrid
Major cities/towns	Barcelona, Bilbao, Córdoba, Granada, Las Palmas de Gran Canarias, Málaga, Murcia, Palma de Mallorca, Seville, Valencia, Zaragoza
Population	39 628 000 (1998 est)
Language	Spanish, Catalan, Galician, Basque
Religion	Roman Catholic
Currency	Peseta (= 100 céntimos)
GDP	US$531.3 billion (1997)
Economy	Mixed agriculture and industry; exports include motor vehicles, machinery, vegetable products, metals and foodstuffs
Political system	Constitutional monarchy
Head of state	King Juan Carlos I
Head of government	Jose Maria Aznar

Sri Lanka

Location	N Indian Ocean
Area	65 610 sq km (25 325 sq mi)
Capital	Sri Jayawardenapura
Major cities/towns	Dehiwala-Mount Lavinia, Jaffna, Kandy, Kotte, Moratuwa
Population	18 455 000 (1998 est)
Language	Sinhala, Tamil, English
Religion	Buddhist, Hindu, Christian, Muslim
Currency	Sri Lanka rupee (= 100 cents)
GDP	US$15.1 billion (1997)
Economy	Chiefly agricultural; exports include clothing, textiles, tea, precious stones, coconuts and rubber
Political system	Democracy
Head of state	Chandrika Bandaranaike Kumaratunga
Head of government	Sirimavo R. D. Bandaranaike

Sudan, The

Location	NE Africa
Area	2 505 870 sq km (967 243 sq mi)
Capital	Khartoum
Major cities/towns	al-Obeid, al-Qadarif, Atbara, Juba, Kassala, Kosti, Omdurman, Port Sudan, Wadi Medani
Population	28 292 000 (1998 est)
Language	Arabic, local languages
Religion	Sunni Muslim, animist beliefs, Christian
Currency	Sudanese dinar (= 100 piastres)
GDP	US$7 billion (1997 est)
Economy	Chiefly agricultural; exports include cotton, sesame seed and livestock
Political system	Emergent democracy
Head of state	Omar Hassan Ahmad al-Bashir
Head of government	Omar Hassan Ahmad al-Bashir

Suriname

Location	S America
Area	163 265 sq km (63 020 sq mi)
Capital	Paramaribo
Major cities/towns	Brokopondo, Moengo, Nieuw Amsterdam, Nieuw Nickerie, Pontoetoe
Population	414 000 (1998 est)
Language	Dutch, Hindu, Javanese, Sranan Tongo, Chinese, Spanish
Religion	Hindu, Protestant, Roman Catholic, Muslim, local beliefs
Currency	Suriname guilder/florin (= 100 cents)
GDP	US$555 million (1997 est)
Economy	Based on agriculture and mining; exports include bauxite, iron ore, copper and gold
Political system	Emergent democracy
Head of state	Jules Wijdenbosch
Head of government	Pretaapnarain Radhakishun

Swaziland

Location	SW Africa
Area	17 363 sq km (6 702 sq mi)
Capital	Mbabane
Major cities/towns	Big Bend, Havelock Mine, Manzini, Mhlume, Nhlangano
Population	952 000 (1998 est)
Language	English, Siswati
Religion	Christian, animist beliefs
Currency	Lilangeni (= 100 cents)
GDP	US$1.2 billion (1997 est)
Economy	Chiefly agricultural; exports include sugar, wood pulp, cotton yarn, diamonds and gold
Political system	Transitional absolute monarchy
Head of state	King Mswati III
Head of government	Sibusiso Barnabus Dlamini

Sweden

Location	NW Europe
Area	411 479 sq km (158 830 sq mi)
Capital	Stockholm

Major cities/towns	Borås, Göteborg, Helsingborg, Jönköping, Linköping, Malmö, Norrköping, Orebro, Uppsala, Västerås
Population	8 875 000 (1998 est)
Language	Swedish, Finnish, Lapp
Religion	Lutheran Protestant, Roman Catholic
Currency	Swedish krona (= 100 øre)
GDP	US$227.8 billion (1997)
Economy	Mixed industry, agriculture and forestry; exports include wood, paper, machinery, motor vehicles, chemicals, iron and steel
Political system	Constitutional monarchy
Head of state	King Carl XVI Gustaf
Head of government	Goran Persson

Switzerland

Location	Central Europe
Area	41 228 sq km (15 914 sq mi)
Capital	Bern
Major cities/towns	Basel, Geneva, Lausanne, Luzern, St Gallen, Winterthur, Zürich
Population	7 299 000 (1998 est)
Language	German, French, Italian, Romansch
Religion	Roman Catholic, Protestant
Currency	Swiss franc (= 100 centimes)
GDP	US$252.1 billion (1997)
Economy	Revenue as a centre of international finance and from mixed industry and agriculture; exports include machinery, pharmaceutical products, foodstuffs, clocks and watches
Political system	Democracy
Head of state	Adolf Ogi
Head of government	Adolf Ogi

Syria

Location	E of the Mediterranean
Area	185 180 sq km (71 479 sq mi)
Capital	Damascus
Major cities/towns	Aleppo, Hama, Homs, Latakia
Population	15 333 000 (1998 est)
Language	Arabic, Kurdish, Armenian, Aramaic, Circassian
Religion	Sunni Muslim, Alawite, Druse, Christian
Currency	Syrian pound (= 100 piastres)
GDP	US$18.8 billion (1997 est)
Economy	Dependent upon oil production; exports include crude petroleum, textiles, vegetables and fruit
Political system	Socialist republic
Head of state	Bashar al-Assad
Head of government	Muhammad Mustafa Miro

Taiwan

Location	SE Asia
Area	36 000 sq km (13 896 sq mi)
Capital	Taibei
Major cities/towns	Kaohsiung, Panchiao, Taichung, Tainan, Yunlin
Population	21 843 000 (1998 est)
Language	Mandarin Chinese, Taiwanese, Hakka, local dialects
Religion	Taoist, Buddhist, Christian

Currency	New Taiwan dollar (= 100 cents)
GDP	US$283.4 billion (1997)
Economy	Mixed agriculture and industry; exports include electronic products, metals, textiles, machinery, motor vehicles, plastic and rubber products, toys and games
Political system	Emergent democracy
Head of state	Chen Shui-ban
Head of government	Tang Fei

Tajikistan

Location	SW Asia
Area	143 100 sq km (55 200 sq mi)
Capital	Dushanbe
Major cities/towns	Khodzhent, Kulyab, Kurgan-Tyube
Population	6 015 000 (1998 est)
Language	Tajik, Russian
Religion	Sunni Muslim
Currency	Tajik rouble
GDP	US$1.9 billion (1997 est)
Economy	Mixed agricultural and industry; exports include aluminium and cotton lint
Political system	Authoritarian nationalist
Head of state	Imamoli Rakhmanov
Head of government	Akil Akilov

Tanzania

Location	E Africa
Area	945 087 sq km (364 900 sq mi)
Capital	Dodoma
Major cities/towns	Dar Es Salaam, Mbeya, Mwanza, Tabora, Tanga, Zanzibar Town
Population	32 102 000 (1998 est)
Language	Swahili, English, local languages
Religion	Christian, Muslim, animist beliefs, Hindu
Currency	Tanzanian shilling (= 100 cents)
GDP	US$6.7 billion (1997)
Economy	Chiefly agricultural; exports include coffee beans, raw cotton, tobacco, tea and petroleum products
Political system	Emergent democracy
Head of state	Benjamin Mkapa
Head of government	Frederick Sumaye

Thailand

Location	SE Asia
Area	513 115 sq km (198 062 sq mi)
Capital	Bangkok
Major cities/towns	Chiangmai, Chon Buri, Hat Yai, Khon Kaen, Lampang, Nakhon Si Thammarat, Phitsannlok, Ratchasima, Songkhla
Population	60 300 000 (1998 est)
Language	Thai, Malay, English
Religion	Theravada Buddhist, Muslim, Hindu, Sikh, Christian
Currency	Baht (= 100 satang)
GDP	US$157.2 billion (1997)
Economy	Mixed agriculture and industry; exports include textiles, electronic goods, rice, rubber, gemstones, sugar, fish and chemicals

Political system	Emergent democracy
Head of state	King Bhumibol Adulyadej (Rama IX)
Head of government	Chuan Leekpai

Togo

Location	W Africa
Area	56 790 sq km (21 941 sq mi)
Capital	Lomé
Major cities/towns	Atakpamé, Bassar, Kara, Kpalimé, Sokodé, Tsévié
Population	4 397 000 (1998 est)
Language	French, local languages
Religion	Animist beliefs, Christian, Muslim
Currency	CFA franc (= 100 centimes)
GDP	US$1.3 billion (1997)
Economy	Chiefly agricultural; exports include phosphates, cotton, coffee and cocoa beans
Political system	Emergent democracy
Head of state	Gnassingbé Eyadéma
Head of government	Koffi Eugene Adoboli

Tonga

Location	S Pacific Ocean
Area	646 sq km (249 sq mi)
Capital	Nuku'alofa
Major cities/towns	Neiafu, Pangai
Population	98 000 (1998 est)
Language	Tongan, English
Religion	Free Wesleyan Methodists, Roman Catholic, Mormon
Currency	Pa'anga/Tongan dollar (= 100 senti)
GDP	US$194 million (1996)
Economy	Chiefly agricultural; exports include vanilla beans, pumpkins, coconut oil, clothing and footwear
Political system	Democracy
Head of state	King Taufa'ahau Tupou IV
Head of government	Lavaka ata Ulukalala

Trinidad and Tobago

Location	SE Caribbean Sea
Area	5 128 sq km (1 979 sq mi)
Capital	Port of Spain
Major cities/towns	Arima, Point Fortin, San Fernando
Population	1 283 000 (1998 est)
Language	English, Hindi, French, Spanish
Religion	Roman Catholic, Protestant, Hindu, Muslim
Currency	Trinidad and Tobago dollar (= 100 cents)
GDP	US$5.8 billion (1997)
Economy	Based on natural resources; exports include mineral fuels, chemicals and food
Political system	Democracy
Head of state	Arthur Napoleon Raymond Robinson
Head of government	Basdeo Panday

Tunisia

Location	N Africa
Area	164 150 sq km (63 362 sq mi)
Capital	Tunis
Major cities/towns	Ariana, Bardo, Bizerte, Djerba, Gabès, Kairouan, La Goulette, Sfax, Sousse
Population	9 335 000 (1998 est)
Language	Arabic, French, Berber
Religion	Sunni Muslim
Currency	Tunisian dinar (= 1000 millèmes)
GDP	US$19.06 billion (1997)
Economy	Based on agriculture and mining; exports include textiles, crude petroleum, phosphates, fertilizers, olive oil, fruit, leather and machinery
Political system	Emergent democracy
Head of state	Zine al-Abidine bin Ali
Head of government	Mohammed Ghannouchi

Turkey

Location	W Asia
Area	779 452 sq km (300 868 sq mi)
Capital	Ankara
Major cities/towns	Adana, Antalya, Bursa, Edirne, Gaziantep, Istanbul, Izmir, Kayseri, Konya, Mersin
Population	64 479 000 (1998 est)
Language	Turkish, Kurdish, Arabic, Greek, Armenian, Yiddish
Religion	Sunni Muslim
Currency	Turkish lira (= 100 kurus)
GDP	US$193.8 billion (1997)
Economy	Mixed agriculture and industry; exports include textiles, foodstuffs, tobacco, leather, glass and petroleum products
Political system	Democracy
Head of state	Ahmet Necdet Sezer
Head of government	Bulent Ecevit

Turkmenistan

Location	W Asia
Area	488 100 sq km (188 400 sq mi)
Capital	Ashkhabad
Major cities/towns	Chardzhov, Krasnovodsk, Mary, Nebit-Dag, Turkmenbashi
Population	4 309 000 (1998 est)
Language	Turkmenian, other Turkic languages, Russian
Religion	Sunni Muslim
Currency	Manat (= 100 gapik)
GDP	US$2.3 billion (1997 est)
Economy	Revenue from natural resources and agriculture; exports include natural gas, cotton yarn, electric energy and petroleum
Political system	Authoritarian nationalist
Head of state	Saparmurad Niyazov
Head of government	Saparmurad Niyazov

Tuvalu

Location	W Pacific Ocean
Area	26 sq km (10 sq mi)
Capital	Funafuti

Major cities/towns	Nanumea, Niutao, Vaitupu
Population	11 000 (1998 est)
Language	Tuvaluan, English
Religion	Christian
Currency	Australian dollar (= 100 cents)
GDP	US$8 million (1995 est)
Economy	Chiefly agricultural; exports include foodstuffs, livestock, tobacco and machinery
Political system	Democracy
Head of state	Queen Elizabeth II
Head of government	Ionatana Ionatana

Uganda

Location	Central Africa
Area	241 038 sq km (150 645 sq mi)
Capital	Kampala
Major cities/towns	Bugembet, Entebbe, Jinja, Masaka, Mbale
Population	20 554 000 (1998 est)
Language	English, Swahili, Luganda (Ganda), Ateso, Luo
Religion	Roman Catholic, Protestant, animist beliefs, Muslim
Currency	Uganda shilling (= 100 cents)
GDP	US$6.5 billion (1997)
Economy	Chiefly agricultural; exports include coffee, cotton, tea, tobacco and textiles
Political system	Emergent democracy
Head of state	Yoweri Kaguta Museveni
Head of government	Apolo Nsibambi

Ukraine

Location	W Asia
Area	603 700 sq km (233 028 sq mi)
Capital	Kiev
Major cities/towns	Dnepropetrovsk, Donetsk, Kharkov, Krivoy Rog, Lugansk, Lviv, Mariupol, Odessa, Zaporozhye
Population	50 861 000 (1998 est)
Language	Ukrainian, Russian
Religion	Orthodox, Roman Catholic
Currency	Hryvna (= 100 kopijka)
GDP	US$49.7 billion (1997)
Economy	Mixed agriculture and heavy industry; exports include grain, coal, oil and minerals
Political system	Emergent democracy
Head of state	Leonid Kuchma
Head of government	Viktor Yushchenko

United Arab Emirates

Location	W Asia
Area	83 600 sq km (32 300 sq mi)
Capital	Abu Dhabi
Major cities/towns	Ajman, Dubai, Fujairah, Ras al-Khaimah, Sharjah
Population	2 353 000 (1998 est)
Language	Arabic, English, Farsi, Urdu, Hindi
Religion	Sunni Muslim, Shi'ite Muslim, Christian, Hindu
Currency	United Arab Emirates dirham (= 100 fils)

GDP	US$45.1 billion (1997 est)
Economy	Based on oil and gas extraction; exports include crude petroleum and natural gas
Political system	Absolutism
Head of state	Zayed bin Sultan al-Nahyan
Head of government	Maktoum bin Rashid al-Maktoum

United Kingdom

Location	N Europe
Area	244 755 sq km (94 475 sq mi)
Capital	London
Major cities/towns	Belfast, Birmingham, Bradford, Bristol, Cardiff, Coventry, Edinburgh, Glasgow, Leeds, Liverpool, Manchester, Newcastle-upon-Tyne, Sheffield
Population	58 649 000 (1998 est)
Language	English, Irish Gaelic, Scots Gaelic, Welsh
Religion	Anglican, Roman Catholic, Presbyterian, Methodist, Baptist, Orthodox, Muslim, others
Currency	Pound sterling (= 100 pence)
GDP	US$1 278.4 billion (1997)
Economy	Mixed industry and agriculture and highly developed service sector; exports include industrial and electronic goods, motor vehicles, petroleum, chemicals, manufactured goods and foodstuffs
Political system	Democracy
Head of state	Queen Elizabeth II
Head of government	Tony Blair

United States of America

Location	N America
Area	9 160 454 sq km (3 535 935 sq mi)
Capital	Washington, DC
Major cities/towns	Baltimore, Boston, Chicago, Dallas, Detroit, Honolulu, Houston, Indianapolis, Los Angeles, Memphis, New York, Philadelphia, Phoenix, San Antonio, San Diego, San Francisco, San José, Washington
Population	274 028 000 (1998 est)
Language	English
Religion	Protestant, Roman Catholic, Jewish, others
Currency	Dollar (= 100 cents)
GDP	US$7 819.3 billion (1997)
Economy	Highly diversified; exports include machinery, motor vehicles, foodstuffs, aircraft, weapons, chemicals and electronics
Political system	Federal republic
Head of state	George W. Bush
Head of government	George W. Bush

Uruguay

Location	S America
Area	176 215 sq km (68 018 sq mi)
Capital	Montevideo
Major cities/towns	Las Piedras, Paysandú, Salto
Population	3 289 000 (1998 est)
Language	Spanish
Religion	Roman Catholic
Currency	New Uruguayan peso (= 100 centésimos)

GDP	US$20 billion (1997)
Economy	Chiefly agricultural; exports include textiles, meat, livestock, cereals and footwear
Political system	Democracy
Head of state	Jorge Luis Ibáes
Head of government	Jorge Luis Ibáes

Uzbekistan

Location	W Asia
Area	447 400 sq km (172 696 sq mi)
Capital	Tashkent
Major cities/towns	Andizhan, Bukhara, Namangan, Samarkand
Population	23 574 000 (1998 est)
Language	Uzbek
Religion	Sunni Muslim
Currency	Som
GDP	US$23.8 billion (1997 est)
Economy	Based on agriculture and mineral extraction; exports include cotton fibre, textiles, machinery, foodstuffs and gold
Political system	Authoritarian nationalist
Head of state	Islam A. Karimov
Head of government	Otkir Sultonov

Vanuatu

Location	W Pacific Ocean
Area	14 763 sq km (5 698 sq mi)
Capital	Port Vila
Major cities/towns	Luganville, Santo
Population	182 000 (1998 est)
Language	Bislama, English, French
Religion	Presbyterian, Roman Catholic, Anglican, local beliefs
Currency	Vatu (= 100 centimes)
GDP	US$250 million (1997 est)
Economy	Chiefly agriculture; exports include copra, beef, timber and cocoa
Political system	Democracy
Head of state	John Bani
Head of government	Barak Sope

Vatican City State

Location	W Italy (within Rome)
Area	0.44 sq km (0.17 sq mi)
Capital	The Holy See, Vatican City
Major cities/towns	
Population	1000 (1998 est)
Language	Latin, Italian
Religion	Roman Catholic
Currency	Vatican lira (= 100 centesimi)
GDP	Not applicable
Economy	Not applicable
Political system	Absolute Catholicism
Head of state	Pope John Paul II (Karol Wojtyla)
Head of government	Cardinal Angelo Sodano

Venezuela

Location	S America
Area	912 050 sq km (352 051 sq mi)
Capital	Caracas
Major cities/towns	Barquisimeto, Ciudad Guayana, Maracaibo, Maracay, San Cristobál, Valencia
Population	23 242 000 (1998 est)
Language	Spanish, Italian, Indian languages
Religion	Roman Catholic
Currency	Bolívar (= 100 céntimos)
GDP	US$87.5 billion (1997)
Economy	Based on oil production; exports include petroleum, metals, natural gas, chemicals and motor vehicles
Political system	Federal democracy
Head of state	Hugo Chávez Frías
Head of government	Hugo Chávez Frías

Vietnam

Location	SE Asia
Area	329 566 sq km (127 212 sq mi)
Capital	Hanoi
Major cities/towns	Can Tho, Da Nang, Haiphong, Ho Chi Minh City, Nam Dinh, Nha Trang
Population	77 562 000 (1998 est)
Language	Vietnamese, French, Chinese, English, Khmer
Religion	Buddhist, Taoist, Confucian, Muslim, Roman Catholic, Hoa Hoa, Cao Dai, Protestant, animist beliefs
Currency	Dông (= 10 hao)
GDP	US$24.9 billion (1997)
Economy	Chiefly agriculture; exports include rice, crude petroleum, coal and coffee
Political system	Communism
Head of state	Tran Duc Luong
Head of government	Phan Van Khai

Yemen

Location	W Asia
Area	531 570 sq km (205 186 sq mi)
Capital	Sana (political), Aden (commercial)
Major cities/towns	Aden, Al Mukalla, Dhamar, Hodeida, Ibb, Ta'izz
Population	16 887 000 (1998 est)
Language	Arabic, English
Religion	Sunni Muslim, Shiite Muslim
Currency	Yemeni riyal (= 100 fils)
GDP	US$5.4 billion (1997)
Economy	Chiefly agricultural; exports include petroleum, cotton, clothing, livestock and coffee
Political system	Emergent democracy
Head of state	Ali Abdullah Saleh
Head of government	Abdul Karim al-Iriani

Yugoslavia

Location	SE Europe
Area	102 173 sq km (39 438 sq mi)
Capital	Belgrade

Major cities/towns	Kragujevac, Novi Sad, Niš, Podgorica, Priština, Rijeka, Subotica
Population	10 635 000 (1998 est)
Language	Serbian, Albanian, Hungarian
Religion	Serbian Orthodox, Roman Catholic, Muslim
Currency	Yugoslav dinar (= 100 paras)
GDP	US$17.8 billion (1997)
Economy	Based on agriculture; exports include machinery, clothing, foodstuffs and livestock
Political system	Socialist pluralist republic
Head of state	Vojislav Kostunica
Head of government	Zoran Zizic

Zambia

Location	Central S Africa
Area	752 613 sq km (290 586 sq mi)
Capital	Lusaka
Major cities/towns	Chingola, Kabwe, Kitwe, Livingstone, Luanshya, Mufulira, Ndola
Population	8 781 000 (1998 est)
Language	English, local languages
Religion	Christian, local beliefs
Currency	Kwacha (= 100 ngwee)
GDP	US$4.05 billion (1997)
Economy	Based on mineral extraction; exports include copper, zinc, lead, cobalt and tobacco
Political system	Emergent democracy
Head of state	Frederick Chiluba
Head of government	Godfrey Miyanda

Zimbabwe

Location	SE Africa
Area	390 759 sq km (150 873 sq mi)
Capital	Harare
Major cities/towns	Bulawayo, Chitungwiza, Gweru, Hwange, Kwekwe, Mutare
Population	11 377 000 (1998 est)
Language	English, Ndebele, Shona
Religion	Christian, local beliefs
Currency	Zimbabwe dollar (= 100 cents)
GDP	US$8.8 billion (1997 est)
Economy	Chiefly agriculture; exports include tobacco, metals and textiles
Political system	One-party socialist republic
Head of state	Robert Gabriel Mugabe
Head of government	Robert Gabriel Mugabe

5
Human Society

5.1 Calendar

International time differences

Country	Hours ahead/behind Greenwich Mean Time
Afghanistan	4.0
Albania	1.0
Algeria	1.0
Andorra	1.0
Angola	1.0
Anguilla	−4.0
Antigua and Barbuda	−4.0
Argentina	−3.0
Armenia	3.0
Aruba	−4.0
Ascension Island	0.0
Australia	10.0
Australia (Broken Hill area, NSW)	9.5
Australia (Lord Howe Island)	10.5
Australia (Northern Territory)	9.5
Australia (South Australia)	9.5
Australia (Western Australia)	8.0
Austria	1.0
Azerbaijan	4.0
Azores	−1.0
Bahamas	−5.0
Bahrain	3.0
Bangladesh	6.0
Barbados	−4.0
Belarus	2.0
Belgium	1.0
Belize	−6.0

Benin	1.0
Bermuda	−4.0
Bhutan	6.0
Bolivia	−4.0
Bosnia-Herzegovina	1.0
Botswana	2.0
Brazil (Acre)	−5.0
Brazil (eastern)	−3.0
Brazil (Fernando de Noronha Island)	−2.0
Brazil (southern)	−4.0
Brazil (western)	−4.0
British Antarctic Territory	−3.0
British Indian Ocean Territory	5.0
British Indian Ocean Territory (Diego Garcia)	6.0
British Virgin Islands	−4.0
Brunei	8.0
Bulgaria	2.0
Burkina Faso	0.0
Burundi	2.0
Cambodia	7.0
Cameroon	1.0
Canada (Alberta)	−7.0
Canada (British Columbia)	−8.0
Canada (Labrador)	−4.0
Canada (Manitoba)	−6.0
Canada (New Brunswick)	−4.0
Canada (Newfoundland)	−3.5
Canada (Northwest Territories east of 85°W)	−5.0
Canada (Northwest Territories 85°W–102°W)	−6.0
Canada (Northwest Territories west of 102°W)	−7.0
Canada (Nova Scotia)	−4.0
Canada (Ontario east of 90°W)	−5.0
Canada (Ontario west of 90°W)	6.0
Canada (Prince Edward Island)	−4.0
Canada (Quebec east of 63°W)	−4.0
Canada (Quebec west of 63°W)	−5.0
Canada (Saskatchewan)	−6.0
Canada (Yukon)	−8.0
Canary Islands	0.0
Cape Verde	−1.0
Cayman Islands	−5.0
Central African Republic	1.0
Chad	1.0
Chatham Islands	12.75
Chile	−4.0
China	8.0
Christmas Island	7.0
Cocos Keeling Islands	6.5
Colombia	−5.0
Comoros	3.0
Congo, Democratic Republic of (east)	2.0

Country	Hours ahead/behind Greenwich Mean Time
Congo, Democratic Republic of (west)	1.0
Congo, Republic of	1.0
Cook Islands	−10.0
Costa Rica	−6.0
Côte d'Ivoire	0.0
Croatia	1.0
Cuba	−5.0
Cyprus	2.0
Czech Republic	1.0
Denmark	1.0
Djibouti	3.0
Dominica	−4.0
Dominican Republic	−4.0
Ecuador	−5.0
Ecuador (Galápagos Islands)	−6.0
Egypt	2.0
Equatorial Guinea	1.0
Eritrea	3.0
Estonia	2.0
Ethiopia	3.0
Falkland Islands	−4.0
Faröe Islands	0.0
Fiji	12.0
Finland	2.0
France	1.0
French Guinea	−3.0
French Polynesia	−10.0
French Polynesia (Marquesas Islands)	−9.5
Gabon	1.0
The Gambia	0.0
Georgia	5.0
Germany	1.0
Ghana	0.0
Gibraltar	1.0
Greece	2.0
Greenland	−3.0
Greenland (Danmarkshavn)	0.0
Greenland (Mesters Vig)	0.0
Greenland (Scoresby Sound)	−1.0
Greenland (Thule area)	−4.0
Grenada	−4.0
Guadeloupe	−4.0
Guam	10.0
Guatemala	−6.0
Guinea	0.0
Guinea-Bissau	0.0
Guyana	−4.0
Haiti	−5.0
Honduras	−6.0

Hungary	1.0
Iceland	0.0
India	5.5
Indonesia (Bali)	8.0
Indonesia (Flores)	8.0
Indonesia (Irian Jaya)	9.0
Indonesia (Java)	7.0
Indonesia (south and east Kalimantan)	8.0
Indonesia (west and central Kalimantan)	7.0
Indonesia (Molucca Islands)	9.0
Indonesia (Sulawesi)	8.0
Indonesia (Sumatra)	7.0
Indonesia (Sumbawa)	8.0
Indonesia (Tanimbar)	9.0
Indonesia (Timor)	8.0
Iran	3.5
Iraq	3.0
Ireland, Republic of	0.0
Israel	2.0
Italy	1.0
Jamaica	−5.0
Japan	9.0
Jordan	2.0
Kazakhstan (western)	4.0
Kazakhstan (central)	5.0
Kazakhstan (eastern)	6.0
Kenya	3.0
Kiribati	12.0
Kiribati (Line Islands)	14.0
Kiribati (Phoenix Islands)	13.0
Korea, North	9.0
Korea, South	9.0
Kuwait	3.0
Kyrgyzstan	5.0
Laos	7.0
Latvia	2.0
Lebanon	2.0
Lesotho	2.0
Liberia	0.0
Libya	1.0
Liechtenstein	1.0
Line Islands	−10.0
Lithuania	2.0
Luxembourg	1.0
Macao	8.0
Macedonia	1.0
Madagascar	3.0
Madeira	0.0
Malawi	2.0
Malaysia	8.0

Country	Hours ahead/behind Greenwich Mean Time
Maldives	5.0
Mali	0.0
Malta	1.0
Marshall Islands	12.0
Marshall Islands (Ebon Atoll)	−12.0
Martinique	−4.0
Mauritania	0.0
Mauritius	4.0
Mexico	−6.0
Mexico (central)	−7.0
Mexico (Quintana Roo)	−5.0
Mexico (western)	−8.0
Micronesia (Caroline Islands)	10.0
Micronesia (Kosrae)	11.0
Micronesia (Pingelap)	11.0
Micronesia (Pohnpei)	11.0
Moldova	2.0
Monaco	1.0
Mongolia	8.0
Montserrat	−4.0
Morocco	0.0
Mozambique	2.0
Myanmar	6.5
Namibia	1.0
Nauru	12.0
Nepal	5.75
Netherlands	1.0
Netherlands Antilles	−4.0
New Caledonia	11.0
New Zealand	12.0
Nicaragua	−6.0
Niger	1.0
Nigeria	1.0
Niue	−11.0
Norfolk Island	11.5
Northern Mariana Islands	10.0
Norway	1.0
Oman	4.0
Pakistan	5.0
Palau	9.0
Panama	−5.0
Papua New Guinea	10.0
Paraguay	−4.0
Peru	−5.0
Philippines	8.0
Poland	1.0
Portugal	0.0
Puerto Rico	−4.0
Qatar	3.0

Réunion	4.0
Romania	2.0
Russia (Zone 1)	2.0
Russia (Zone 2)	3.0
Russia (Zone 3)	4.0
Russia (Zone 4)	5.0
Russia (Zone 5)	6.0
Russia (Zone 6)	7.0
Russia (Zone 7)	8.0
Russia (Zone 8)	9.0
Russia (Zone 9)	10.0
Russia (Zone 10)	11.0
Russia (Zone 11)	12.0
Rwanda	2.0
St Helena	0.0
St Christopher and Nevis	−4.0
St Lucia	−4.0
St Pierre and Miquelon	−3.0
St Vincent and the Grenadines	−4.0
El Salvador	−6.0
Samoa	−11.0
Samoa, American	−11.0
San Marino	1.0
São Tomé and Príncipe	0.0
Saudi Arabia	3.0
Senegal	0.0
Seychelles	4.0
Sierra Leone	0.0
Singapore	8.0
Slovakia	1.0
Slovenia	1.0
Solomon Islands	11.0
Somalia	3.0
South Africa	2.0
South Georgia	−2.0
Spain	1.0
Sri Lanka	6.0
Sudan	2.0
Suriname	−3.0
Swaziland	2.0
Sweden	1.0
Switzerland	1.0
Syria	2.0
Taiwan	8.0
Tajikistan	5.0
Tanzania	3.0
Thailand	7.0
Togo	0.0
Tonga	13.0
Trinidad and Tobago	−4.0

Country	Hours ahead/behind Greenwich Mean Time
Tristan da Cunha	0.0
Tunisia	1.0
Turkey	2.0
Turkmenistan	5.0
Turks and Caicos Islands	−5.0
Tuvalu	12.0
Uganda	3.0
Ukraine	2.0
United Arab Emirates	4.0
United Kingdom	0.0
United States (Alaska)	−9.0
United States (Aleutian Islands east of 169°30W)	−9.0
United States (Aleutian Islands west of 169°30W)	−10.0
United States (eastern time)	−5.0
United States (central time)	−6.0
United States (Hawaii)	−10.0
United States (mountain time)	−7.0
United States (Pacific time)	−8.0
Uruguay	−3.0
Uzbekistan	5.0
Vanuatu	11.0
Vatican City State	1.0
Venezuela	−4.0
Vietnam	7.0
Virgin Islands (US)	−4.0
Yemen	3.0
Yugoslavia, Federal Republic of	1.0
Zambia	2.0
Zimbabwe	2.0

Note Figures may vary at certain times of year owing to variance from standard time due to Summer Time, Daylight Saving Time etc.

Perpetual calendar

Year /
Calendar

1780 = N	1833 = E	1886 = K	1939 = A	1992 = H
1781 = C	1834 = G	1887 = M	1940 = D	1993 = K
1782 = E	1835 = I	1888 = B	1941 = G	1994 = M
1783 = G	1836 = L	1889 = E	1942 = I	1995 = A
1784 = J	1837 = A	1890 = G	1943 = K	1996 = D
1785 = M	1838 = C	1891 = I	1944 = N	1997 = G
1786 = A	1839 = E	1892 = L	1945 = C	1998 = I
1787 = C	1840 = H	1893 = A	1946 = E	1999 = K
1788 = F	1841 = K	1894 = C	1947 = G	2000 = N
1789 = I	1842 = M	1895 = E	1948 = J	2001 = C
1790 = K	1843 = A	1896 = H	1949 = M	2002 = E
1791 = M	1844 = D	1897 = K	1950 = A	2003 = G
1792 = B	1845 = G	1898 = M	1951 = C	2004 = J
1793 = E	1846 = L	1899 = A	1952 = F	2005 = M
1794 = G	1847 = K	1900 = C	1953 = I	2006 = A
1795 = I	1848 = N	1901 = E	1954 = K	2007 = C
1796 = L	1849 = C	1902 = G	1955 = M	2008 = F
1797 = A	1850 = E	1903 = I	1956 = B	2009 = I
1798 = C	1851 = G	1904 = L	1957 = E	2010 = K
1799 = E	1852 = J	1905 = A	1958 = G	2011 = M
1800 = G	1853 = M	1906 = C	1959 = I	2012 = B
1801 = I	1854 = A	1907 = E	1960 = L	2013 = E
1802 = K	1855 = C	1908 = H	1961 = A	2014 = G
1803 = M	1856 = F	1909 = K	1962 = C	2015 = I
1804 = B	1857 = I	1910 = M	1963 = E	2016 = L
1805 = E	1858 = K	1911 = A	1964 = H	2017 = A
1806 = G	1859 = M	1912 = D	1965 = K	2018 = C
1807 = I	1860 = B	1913 = G	1966 = M	2019 = E
1808 = L	1861 = E	1914 = I	1967 = A	2020 = H
1809 = A	1862 = G	1915 = K	1968 = D	2021 = K
1810 = C	1863 = I	1916 = N	1969 = G	2022 = M
1811 = E	1864 = L	1917 = C	1970 = I	2023 = A
1812 = H	1865 = A	1918 = E	1971 = K	2024 = D
1813 = K	1866 = C	1919 = G	1972 = N	2025 = G
1814 = M	1867 = E	1920 = J	1973 = C	2026 = I
1815 = A	1868 = H	1921 = M	1974 = E	2027 = K
1816 = D	1869 = K	1922 = A	1975 = G	2028 = N
1817 = G	1870 = M	1923 = C	1976 = J	2029 = C
1818 = I	1871 = A	1924 = F	1977 = M	2030 = E
1819 = K	1872 = D	1925 = I	1978 = A	2031 = G
1820 = N	1873 = G	1926 = K	1979 = C	2032 = J
1821 = C	1874 = I	1927 = M	1980 = F	2033 = M
1822 = E	1875 = K	1928 = B	1981 = I	2034 = A
1823 = G	1876 = N	1929 = E	1982 = K	2035 = C
1824 = J	1877 = C	1930 = G	1983 = M	2036 = F
1825 = M	1878 = E	1931 = I	1984 = B	2037 = I
1826 = A	1879 = G	1932 = L	1985 = E	2038 = K
1827 = C	1880 = J	1933 = A	1986 = G	2039 = M
1828 = F	1881 = M	1934 = C	1987 = I	2040 = B
1829 = I	1882 = A	1935 = E	1988 = L	
1830 = K	1883 = C	1936 = H	1989 = A	
1831 = M	1884 = F	1937 = K	1990 = C	
1832 = B	1885 = I	1938 = M	1991 = E	

A

January

S	1	8	15	22	29
M	2	9	16	23	30
T	3	10	17	24	31
W	4	11	18	25	
T	5	12	19	26	
F	6	13	20	27	
S	7	14	21	28	

February

S		5	12	19	26
M		6	13	20	27
T		7	14	21	28
W	1	8	15	22	
T	2	9	16	23	
F	3	10	17	24	
S	4	11	18	25	

March

S		5	12	19	26
M		6	13	20	27
T		7	14	21	28
W	1	8	15	22	29
T	2	9	16	23	30
F	3	10	17	24	31
S	4	11	18	25	

April

S		2	9	16	23
M		3	10	17	24
T		4	11	18	25
W		5	12	19	26
T		6	13	20	27
F		7	14	21	28
S	1	8	15	22	29

May

S		7	14	21	28
M	1	8	15	22	29
T	2	9	16	23	30
W	3	10	17	24	31
T	4	11	18	25	
F	5	12	19	26	
S	6	13	20	27	

June

S		4	11	18	25
M		5	12	19	26
T		6	13	20	27
W		7	14	21	28
T	1	8	15	22	29
F	2	9	16	23	30
S	3	10	17	24	

July

S		2	9	16	23	30
M		3	10	17	24	31
T		4	11	18	25	
W		5	12	19	26	
T		6	13	20	27	
F		7	14	21	28	
S	1	8	15	22	29	

August

S		6	13	20	27
M		7	14	21	28
T	1	8	15	22	29
W	2	9	16	23	30
T	3	10	17	24	31
F	4	11	18	25	
S	5	12	19	26	

September

S		3	10	17	24
M		4	11	18	25
T		5	12	19	26
W		6	13	20	27
T		7	14	21	28
F	1	8	15	22	29
S	2	9	16	23	30

October

S	1	8	15	22	29
M	2	9	16	23	30
T	3	10	17	24	31
W	4	11	18	25	
T	5	12	19	26	
F	6	13	20	27	
S	7	14	21	28	

November

S		5	12	19	26
M		6	13	20	27
T		7	14	21	28
W	1	8	15	22	29
T	2	9	16	23	30
F	3	10	17	24	
S	4	11	18	25	

December

S		3	10	17	24
M		4	11	18	25
T		5	12	19	26
W		6	13	20	27
T		7	14	21	28
F	1	8	15	22	29
S	2	9	16	23	30

B (leap year)

January

S	1	8	15	22	29
M	2	9	16	23	30
T	3	10	17	24	31
W	4	11	18	25	
T	5	12	19	26	
F	6	13	20	27	
S	7	14	21	28	

February

S		5	12	19	26
M		6	13	20	27
T		7	14	21	28
W	1	8	15	22	29
T	2	9	16	23	
F	3	10	17	24	
S	4	11	18	25	

March

S		4	11	18	25
M		5	12	19	26
T		6	13	20	27
W		7	14	21	28
T	1	8	15	22	29
F	2	9	16	23	30
S	3	10	17	24	31

April

S	1	8	15	22	29
M	2	9	16	23	30
T	3	10	17	24	
W	4	11	18	25	
T	5	12	19	26	
F	6	13	20	27	
S	7	14	21	28	

May

S		6	13	20	27
M		7	14	21	28
T	1	8	15	22	29
W	2	9	16	23	30
T	3	10	17	24	31
F	4	11	18	25	
S	5	12	19	26	

June

S		3	10	17	24
M		4	11	18	25
T		5	12	19	26
W		6	13	20	27
T		7	14	21	28
F	1	8	15	22	29
S	2	9	16	23	30

July

S	1	8	15	22	29
M	2	9	16	23	30
T	3	10	17	24	31
W	4	11	18	25	
T	5	12	19	26	
F	6	13	20	27	
S	7	14	21	28	

August

S		5	12	19	26
M		6	13	20	27
T		7	14	21	28
W	1	8	15	22	29
T	2	9	16	23	30
F	3	10	17	24	31
S	4	11	18	25	

September

S		2	9	16	23	30
M		3	10	17	24	
T		4	11	18	25	
W		5	12	19	26	
T		6	13	20	27	
F		7	14	21	28	
S	1	8	15	22	29	

October

S		7	14	21	28
M	1	8	15	22	29
T	2	9	16	23	30
W	3	10	17	24	31
T	4	11	18	25	
F	5	12	19	26	
S	6	13	20	27	

November

S		4	11	18	25
M		5	12	19	26
T		6	13	20	27
W		7	14	21	28
T	1	8	15	22	29
F	2	9	16	23	30
S	3	10	17	24	

December

S		2	9	16	23	30
M		3	10	17	24	31
T		4	11	18	25	
W		5	12	19	26	
T		6	13	20	27	
F		7	14	21	28	
S	1	8	15	22	29	

C

January

S		7	14	21	28
M	1	8	15	22	29
T	2	9	16	23	30
W	3	10	17	24	31
T	4	11	18	25	
F	5	12	19	26	
S	6	13	20	27	

February

S		4	11	18	25
M		5	12	19	26
T		6	13	20	27
W		7	14	21	28
T	1	8	15	22	
F	2	9	16	23	
S	3	10	17	24	

March

S		4	11	18	25
M		5	12	19	26
T		6	13	20	27
W		7	14	21	28
T	1	8	15	22	29
F	2	9	16	23	30
S	3	10	17	24	31

April

S	1	8	15	22	29
M	2	9	16	23	30
T	3	10	17	24	
W	4	11	18	25	
T	5	12	19	26	
F	6	13	20	27	
S	7	14	21	28	

May

S		6	13	20	27
M		7	14	21	28
T	1	8	15	22	29
W	2	9	16	23	30
T	3	10	17	24	31
F	4	11	18	25	
S	5	12	19	26	

June

S		3	10	17	24
M		4	11	18	25
T		5	12	19	26
W		6	13	20	27
T		7	14	21	28
F	1	8	15	22	29
S	2	9	16	23	30

July

S	1	8	15	22	29
M	2	9	16	23	30
T	3	10	17	24	31
W	4	11	18	25	
T	5	12	19	26	
F	6	13	20	27	
S	7	14	21	28	

August

S		5	12	19	26
M		6	13	20	27
T		7	14	21	28
W	1	8	15	22	29
T	2	9	16	23	30
F	3	10	17	24	31
S	4	11	18	25	

September

S		2	9	16	23	30
M		3	10	17	24	
T		4	11	18	25	
W		5	12	19	26	
T		6	13	20	27	
F		7	14	21	28	
S	1	8	15	22	29	

October

S		7	14	21	28
M	1	8	15	22	29
T	2	9	16	23	30
W	3	10	17	24	31
T	4	11	18	25	
F	5	12	19	26	
S	6	13	20	27	

November

S		4	11	18	25
M		5	12	19	26
T		6	13	20	27
W		7	14	21	28
T	1	8	15	22	29
F	2	9	16	23	30
S	3	10	17	24	

December

S		2	9	16	23	30
M		3	10	17	24	31
T		4	11	18	25	
W		5	12	19	26	
T		6	13	20	27	
F		7	14	21	28	
S	1	8	15	22	29	

D (leap year)

January

S		7	14	21	28
M	1	8	15	22	29
T	2	9	16	23	30
W	3	10	17	24	31
T	4	11	18	25	
F	5	12	19	26	
S	6	13	20	27	

February

S		4	11	18	25
M		5	12	19	26
T		6	13	20	27
W		7	14	21	28
T	1	8	15	22	29
F	2	9	16	23	
S	3	10	17	24	

March

S		3	10	17	24	31
M		4	11	18	25	
T		5	12	19	26	
W		6	13	20	27	
T		7	14	21	28	
F	1	8	15	22	29	
S	2	9	16	23	30	

April

S		7	14	21	28
M	1	8	15	22	29
T	2	9	16	23	30
W	3	10	17	24	31
T	4	11	18	25	
F	5	12	19	26	
S	6	13	20	27	

May

S		5	12	19	26
M		6	13	20	27
T		7	14	21	28
W	1	8	15	22	29
T	2	9	16	23	30
F	3	10	17	24	31
S	4	11	18	25	

June

S		2	9	16	23	30
M		3	10	17	24	
T		4	11	18	25	
W		5	12	19	26	
T		6	13	20	27	
F		7	14	21	28	
S	1	8	15	22	29	

July

S		7	14	21	28
M	1	8	15	22	29
T	2	9	16	23	30
W	3	10	17	24	31
T	4	11	18	25	
F	5	12	19	26	
S	6	13	20	27	

August

S		4	11	18	25
M		5	12	19	26
T		6	13	20	27
W		7	14	21	28
T	1	8	15	22	29
F	2	9	16	23	30
S	3	10	17	24	31

September

S	1	8	15	22	29
M	2	9	16	23	30
T	3	10	17	24	
W	4	11	18	25	
T	5	12	19	26	
F	6	13	20	27	
S	7	14	21	28	

October

S		6	13	20	27
M		7	14	21	28
T	1	8	15	22	29
W	2	9	16	23	30
T	3	10	17	24	31
F	4	11	18	25	
S	5	12	19	26	

November

S		3	10	17	24
M		4	11	18	25
T		5	12	19	26
W		6	13	20	27
T		7	14	21	28
F	1	8	15	22	29
S	2	9	16	23	30

December

S	1	8	15	22	29
M	2	9	16	23	30
T	3	10	17	24	31
W	4	11	18	25	
T	5	12	19	26	
F	6	13	20	27	
S	7	14	21	28	

E

January

S	1	6	13	20	27
M		7	14	21	28
T	1	8	15	22	29
W	2	9	16	23	30
T	3	10	17	24	31
F	4	11	18	25	
S	5	12	19	26	

February

S		3	10	17	24
M		4	11	18	25
T		5	12	19	26
W		6	13	20	27
T		7	14	21	28
F	1	8	15	22	
S	2	9	16	23	

March

S		3	10	17	24	31
M		4	11	18	25	
T		5	12	19	26	
W		6	13	20	27	
T		7	14	21	28	
F	1	8	15	22	29	
S	2	9	16	23	30	

April

S		7	14	21	28
M	1	8	15	22	29
T	2	9	16	23	30
W	3	10	17	24	
T	4	11	18	25	
F	5	12	19	26	
S	6	13	20	27	

May

S		5	12	19	26
M		6	13	20	27
T		7	14	21	28
W	1	8	15	22	29
T	2	9	16	23	30
F	3	10	17	24	31
S	4	11	18	25	

June

S		2	9	16	23	30
M		3	10	17	24	
T		4	11	18	25	
W		5	12	19	26	
T		6	13	20	27	
F		7	14	21	28	
S	1	8	15	22	29	

July

S		7	14	21	28
M	1	8	15	22	29
T	2	9	16	23	30
W	3	10	17	24	31
T	4	11	18	25	
F	5	12	19	26	
S	6	13	20	27	

August

S		4	11	18	25
M		5	12	19	26
T		6	13	20	27
W		7	14	21	28
T	1	8	15	22	29
F	2	9	16	23	30
S	3	10	17	24	31

September

S	1	8	15	22	29
M	2	9	16	23	30
T	3	10	17	24	
W	4	11	18	25	
T	5	12	19	26	
F	6	13	20	27	
S	7	14	21	28	

October

S		6	13	20	27
M		7	14	21	28
T	1	8	15	22	29
W	2	9	16	23	30
T	3	10	17	24	31
F	4	11	18	25	
S	5	12	19	26	

November

S		3	10	17	24
M		4	11	18	25
T		5	12	19	26
W		6	13	20	27
T		7	14	21	28
F	1	8	15	22	29
S	2	9	16	23	30

December

S	1	8	15	22	29
M	2	9	16	23	30
T	3	10	17	24	31
W	4	11	18	25	
T	5	12	19	26	
F	6	13	20	27	
S	7	14	21	28	

F (leap year)

January

S		6	13	20	27
M		7	14	21	28
T	1	8	15	22	29
W	2	9	16	23	30
T	3	10	17	24	31
F	4	11	18	25	
S	5	12	19	26	

February

S		3	10	17	24
M		4	11	18	25
T		5	12	19	26
W		6	13	20	27
T		7	14	21	28
F	1	8	15	22	29
S	2	9	16	23	

March

S		2	9	16	23
M		3	10	17	24
T		4	11	18	25
W		5	12	19	26
T		6	13	20	27
F		7	14	21	28
S	1	8	15	22	29

April

S		6	13	20	27
M		7	14	21	28
T	1	8	15	22	29
W	2	9	16	23	30
T	3	10	17	24	
F	4	11	18	25	
S	5	12	19	26	

May

S		4	11	18	25
M		5	12	19	26
T		6	13	20	27
W		7	14	21	28
T	1	8	15	22	29
F	2	9	16	23	30
S	3	10	17	24	31

June

S	1	8	15	22	29
M	2	9	16	23	30
T	3	10	17	24	
W	4	11	18	25	
T	5	12	19	26	
F	6	13	20	27	
S	7	14	21	28	

July

S		6	13	20	27
M		7	14	21	28
T	1	8	15	22	29
W	2	9	16	23	30
T	3	10	17	24	31
F	4	11	18	25	
S	5	12	19	26	

August

S		3	10	17	24	31
M		4	11	18	25	
T		5	12	19	26	
W		6	13	20	27	
T		7	14	21	28	
F	1	8	15	22	29	
S	2	9	16	23	30	

September

S		7	14	21	28
M	1	8	15	22	29
T	2	9	16	23	30
W	3	10	17	24	
T	4	11	18	25	
F	5	12	19	26	
S	6	13	20	27	

October

S		5	12	19	26
M		6	13	20	27
T		7	14	21	28
W	1	8	15	22	29
T	2	9	16	23	30
F	3	10	17	24	31
S	4	11	18	25	

November

S		2	9	16	23	30
M		3	10	17	24	
T		4	11	18	25	
W		5	12	19	26	
T		6	13	20	27	
F		7	14	21	28	
S	1	8	15	22	29	

December

S		7	14	21	28
M	1	8	15	22	29
T	2	9	16	23	30
W	3	10	17	24	31
T	4	11	18	25	
F	5	12	19	26	
S	6	13	20	27	

G

January

S		5	12	19	26	
M		6	13	20	27	
T		7	14	21	28	
W	1	8	15	22	29	
T	2	9	16	23	30	
F	3	10	17	24	31	
S	4	11	18	25		

February

S		2	9	16	23
M		3	10	17	24
T		4	11	18	25
W		5	12	19	26
T		6	13	20	27
F		7	14	21	28
S	1	8	15	22	

March

S		2	9	16	23	30
M		3	10	17	24	31
T		4	11	18	25	
W		5	12	19	26	
T		6	13	20	27	
F		7	14	21	28	
S	1	8	15	22	29	

April

S		6	13	20	27
M		7	14	21	28
T	1	8	15	22	29
W	2	9	16	23	30
T	3	10	17	24	
F	4	11	18	25	
S	5	12	19	26	

May

S		4	11	18	25
M		5	12	19	26
T		6	13	20	27
W		7	14	21	28
T	1	8	15	22	29
F	2	9	16	23	30
S	3	10	17	24	31

June

S	1	8	15	22	29
M	2	9	16	23	30
T	3	10	17	24	
W	4	11	18	25	
T	5	12	19	26	
F	6	13	20	27	
S	7	14	21	28	

July

S		6	13	20	27
M		7	14	21	28
T	1	8	15	22	29
W	2	9	16	23	30
T	3	10	17	24	31
F	4	11	18	25	
S	5	12	19	26	

August

S		3	10	17	24	31
M		4	11	18	25	
T		5	12	19	26	
W		6	13	20	27	
T		7	14	21	28	
F	1	8	15	22	29	
S	2	9	16	23	30	

September

S		7	14	21	28
M	1	8	15	22	29
T	2	9	16	23	30
W	3	10	17	24	
T	4	11	18	25	
F	5	12	19	26	
S	6	13	20	27	

October

S		5	12	19	26
M		6	13	20	27
T		7	14	21	28
W	1	8	15	22	29
T	2	9	16	23	30
F	3	10	17	24	31
S	4	11	18	25	

November

S		2	9	16	23	30
M		3	10	17	24	
T		4	11	18	25	
W		5	12	19	26	
T		6	13	20	27	
F		7	14	21	28	
S	1	8	15	22	29	

December

S		7	14	21	28
M	1	8	15	22	29
T	2	9	16	23	30
W	3	10	17	24	31
T	4	11	18	25	
F	5	12	19	26	
S	6	13	20	27	

H (leap year)

January

S		5	12	19	26
M		6	13	20	27
T		7	14	21	28
W	1	8	15	22	29
T	2	9	16	23	30
F	3	10	17	24	31
S	4	11	18	25	

February

S		2	9	16	23
M		3	10	17	24
T		4	11	18	25
W		5	12	19	26
T		6	13	20	27
F		7	14	21	28
S	1	8	15	22	29

March

S	1	8	15	22	29
M	2	9	16	23	30
T	3	10	17	24	31
W	4	11	18	25	
T	5	12	19	26	
F	6	13	20	27	
S	7	14	21	28	

April

S		5	12	19	26
M		6	13	20	27
T		7	14	21	28
W	1	8	15	22	29
T	2	9	16	23	30
F	3	10	17	24	
S	4	11	18	25	

May

S		3	10	17	24	31
M		4	11	18	25	
T		5	12	19	26	
W		6	13	20	27	
T		7	14	21	28	
F	1	8	15	22	29	
S	2	9	16	23	30	

June

S		7	14	21	28
M	1	8	15	22	29
T	2	9	16	23	30
W	3	10	17	24	
T	4	11	18	25	
F	5	12	19	26	
S	6	13	20	27	

July

S		5	12	19	26
M		6	13	20	27
T		7	14	21	28
W	1	8	15	22	29
T	2	9	16	23	30
F	3	10	17	24	
S	4	11	18	25	

August

S		2	9	16	23	30
M		3	10	17	24	31
T		4	11	18	25	
W		5	12	19	26	
T		6	13	20	27	
F		7	14	21	28	
S	1	8	15	22	29	

September

S		6	13	20	27
M		7	14	21	28
T	1	8	15	22	29
W	2	9	16	23	30
T	3	10	17	24	
F	4	11	18	25	
S	5	12	19	26	

October

S		4	11	18	25
M		5	12	19	26
T		6	13	20	27
W		7	14	21	28
T	1	8	15	22	29
F	2	9	16	23	30
S	3	10	17	24	31

November

S	1	8	15	22	29
M	2	9	16	23	30
T	3	10	17	24	
W	4	11	18	25	
T	5	12	19	26	
F	6	13	20	27	
S	7	14	21	28	

December

S		6	13	20	27
M		7	14	21	28
T	1	8	15	22	29
W	2	9	16	23	30
T	3	10	17	24	31
F	4	11	18	25	
S	5	12	19	26	

I

January

S		4	11	18	25
M		5	12	19	26
T		6	13	20	27
W		7	14	21	28
T	1	8	15	22	29
F	2	9	16	23	30
S	3	10	17	24	31

February

S	1	8	15	22
M	2	9	16	23
T	3	10	17	24
W	4	11	18	25
T	5	12	19	26
F	6	13	20	27
S	7	14	21	28

March

S	1	8	15	22	29
M	2	9	16	23	30
T	3	10	17	24	31
W	4	11	18	25	
T	5	12	19	26	
F	6	13	20	27	
S	7	14	21	28	

April

S		5	12	19	26
M		6	13	20	27
T		7	14	21	28
W	1	8	15	22	29
T	2	9	16	23	30
F	3	10	17	24	
S	4	11	18	25	

May

S		3	10	17	24	31
M		4	11	18	25	
T		5	12	19	26	
W		6	13	20	27	
T		7	14	21	28	
F	1	8	15	22	29	
S	2	9	16	23	30	

June

S		7	14	21	28
M	1	8	15	22	29
T	2	9	16	23	30
W	3	10	17	24	
T	4	11	18	25	
F	5	12	19	26	
S	6	13	20	27	

July

S		5	12	19	26
M		6	13	20	27
T		7	14	21	28
W	1	8	15	22	29
T	2	9	16	23	30
F	3	10	17	24	31
S	4	11	18	25	

August

S		2	9	16	23	30
M		3	10	17	24	31
T		4	11	18	25	
W		5	12	19	26	
T		6	13	20	27	
F		7	14	21	28	
S	1	8	15	22	29	

September

S		6	13	20	27
M		7	14	21	28
T	1	8	15	22	29
W	2	9	16	23	30
T	3	10	17	24	
F	4	11	18	25	
S	5	12	19	26	

October

S		4	11	18	25
M		5	12	19	26
T		6	13	20	27
W		7	14	21	28
T	1	8	15	22	29
F	2	9	16	23	30
S	3	10	17	24	31

November

S	1	8	15	22	29
M	2	9	16	23	30
T	3	10	17	24	
W	4	11	18	25	
T	5	12	19	26	
F	6	13	20	27	
S	7	14	21	28	

December

S		6	13	20	27
M		7	14	21	28
T	1	8	15	22	29
W	2	9	16	23	30
T	3	10	17	24	31
F	4	11	18	25	
S	5	12	19	26	

J (leap year)

January

S		4	11	18	25	
M		5	12	19	26	
T		6	13	20	27	
W		7	14	21	28	
T	1	8	15	22	29	
F	2	9	16	23	30	
S	3	10	17	24	31	

February

S	1	8	15	22	29
M	2	9	16	23	
T	3	10	17	24	
W	4	11	18	25	
T	5	12	19	26	
F	6	13	20	27	
S	7	14	21	28	

March

S		7	14	21	28	
M	1	8	15	22	29	
T	2	9	16	23	30	
W	3	10	17	24	31	
T	4	11	18	25		
F	5	12	19	26		
S	6	13	20	27		

April

S		4	11	18	25	
M		5	12	19	26	
T		6	13	20	27	
W		7	14	21	28	
T	1	8	15	22	29	
F	2	9	16	23	30	
S	3	10	17	24		

May

S		2	9	16	23	30
M		3	10	17	24	31
T		4	11	18	25	
W		5	12	19	26	
T		6	13	20	27	
F		7	14	21	28	
S	1	8	15	22	29	

June

S		6	13	20	27
M		7	14	21	28
T	1	8	15	22	29
W	2	9	16	23	30
T	3	10	17	24	
F	4	11	18	25	
S	5	12	19	26	

July

S		4	11	18	25	
M		5	12	19	26	
T		6	13	20	27	
W		7	14	21	28	
T	1	8	15	22	29	
F	2	9	16	23	30	
S	3	10	17	24	31	

August

S	1	8	15	22	29
M	2	9	16	23	30
T	3	10	17	24	31
W	4	11	18	25	
T	5	12	19	26	
F	6	13	20	27	
S	7	14	21	28	

September

S		5	12	19	26
M		6	13	20	27
T		7	14	21	28
W	1	8	15	22	29
T	2	9	16	23	30
F	3	10	17	24	
S	4	11	18	25	

October

S		3	10	17	24	31
M		4	11	18	25	
T		5	12	19	26	
W		6	13	20	27	
T		7	14	21	28	
F	1	8	15	22	29	
S	2	9	16	23	30	

November

S		7	14	21	28
M	1	8	15	22	29
T	2	9	16	23	30
W	3	10	17	24	
T	4	11	18	25	
F	5	12	19	26	
S	6	13	20	27	

December

S		5	12	19	26	
M		6	13	20	27	
T		7	14	21	28	
W	1	8	15	22	29	
T	2	9	16	23	30	
F	3	10	17	24	31	
S	4	11	18	25		

K

January

S		3	10	17	24	31
M		4	11	18	25	
T		5	12	19	26	
W		6	13	20	27	
T		7	14	21	28	
F	1	8	15	22	29	
S	2	9	16	23	30	

February

S		7	14	21	28
M	1	8	15	22	
T	2	9	16	23	
W	3	10	17	24	
T	4	11	18	25	
F	5	12	19	26	
S	6	13	20	27	

March

S		7	14	21	28
M	1	8	15	22	29
T	2	9	16	23	30
W	3	10	17	24	31
T	4	11	18	25	
F	5	12	19	26	
S	6	13	20	27	

April

S		4	11	18	25
M		5	12	19	26
T		6	13	20	27
W		7	14	21	28
T	1	8	15	22	29
F	2	9	16	23	30
S	3	10	17	24	

May

S		2	9	16	23	30
M		3	10	17	24	31
T		4	11	18	25	
W		5	12	19	26	
T		6	13	20	27	
F		7	14	21	28	
S	1	8	15	22	29	

June

S		6	13	20	27
M		7	14	21	28
T	1	8	15	22	29
W	2	9	16	23	30
T	3	10	17	24	
F	4	11	18	25	
S	5	12	19	26	

July

S		4	11	18	25
M		5	12	19	26
T		6	13	20	27
W		7	14	21	28
T	1	8	15	22	29
F	2	9	16	23	30
S	3	10	17	24	31

August

S	1	8	15	22	29
M	2	9	16	23	30
T	3	10	17	24	31
W	4	11	18	25	
T	5	12	19	26	
F	6	13	20	27	
S	7	14	21	28	

September

S		5	12	19	26
M		6	13	20	27
T		7	14	21	28
W	1	8	15	22	29
T	2	9	16	23	30
F	3	10	17	24	
S	4	11	18	25	

October

S		3	10	17	24	31
M		4	11	18	25	
T		5	12	19	26	
W		6	13	20	27	
T		7	14	21	28	
F	1	8	15	22	29	
S	2	9	16	23	30	

November

S		7	14	21	28
M	1	8	15	22	29
T	2	9	16	23	30
W	3	10	17	24	
T	4	11	18	25	
F	5	12	19	26	
S	6	13	20	27	

December

S		5	12	19	26
M		6	13	20	27
T		7	14	21	28
W	1	8	15	22	29
T	2	9	16	23	30
F	3	10	17	24	31
S	4	11	18	25	

L (leap year)

January

S		3	10	17	24	31
M		4	11	18	25	
T		5	12	19	26	
W		6	13	20	27	
T		7	14	21	28	
F	1	8	15	22	29	
S	2	9	16	23	30	

February

S		7	14	21	28
M	1	8	15	22	29
T	2	9	16	23	
W	3	10	17	24	
T	4	11	18	25	
F	5	12	19	26	
S	6	13	20	27	

March

S		6	13	20	27	
M		7	14	21	28	
T	1	8	15	22	29	
W	2	9	16	23	30	
T	3	10	17	24	31	
F	4	11	18	25		
S	5	12	19	26		

April

S		3	10	17	24
M		4	11	18	25
T		5	12	19	26
W		6	13	20	27
T		7	14	21	28
F	1	8	15	22	29
S	2	9	16	23	30

May

S	1	8	15	22	29
M	2	9	16	23	30
T	3	10	17	24	31
W	4	11	18	25	
T	5	12	19	26	
F	6	13	20	27	
S	7	14	21	28	

June

S		5	12	19	26
M		6	13	20	27
T		7	14	21	28
W	1	8	15	22	29
T	2	9	16	23	30
F	3	10	17	24	
S	4	11	18	25	

July

S		3	10	17	24	31
M		4	11	18	25	
T		5	12	19	26	
W		6	13	20	27	
T		7	14	21	28	
F	1	8	15	22	29	
S	2	9	16	23	30	

August

S		7	14	21	28	
M	1	8	15	22	29	
T	2	9	16	23	30	
W	3	10	17	24	31	
T	4	11	18	25		
F	5	12	19	26		
S	6	13	20	27		

September

S		4	11	18	25
M		5	12	19	26
T		6	13	20	27
W		7	14	21	28
T	1	8	15	22	29
F	2	9	16	23	30
S	3	10	17	24	

October

S		2	9	16	23	30
M		3	10	17	24	31
T		4	11	18	25	
W		5	12	19	26	
T		6	13	20	27	
F		7	14	21	28	
S	1	8	15	22	29	

November

S		6	13	20	27
M		7	14	21	28
T	1	8	15	22	29
W	2	9	16	23	30
T	3	10	17	24	
F	4	11	18	25	
S	5	12	19	26	

December

S		4	11	18	25	
M		5	12	19	26	
T		6	13	20	27	
W		7	14	21	28	
T	1	8	15	22	29	
F	2	9	16	23	30	
S	3	10	17	24	31	

M

January

S		2	9	16	23	30
M		3	10	17	24	31
T		4	11	18	25	
W		5	12	19	26	
T		6	13	20	27	
F		7	14	21	28	
S	1	8	15	22	29	

February

S		6	13	20	27
M		7	14	21	28
T	1	8	15	22	
W	2	9	16	23	
T	3	10	17	24	
F	4	11	18	25	
S	5	12	19	26	

March

S		6	13	20	27
M		7	14	21	28
T	1	8	15	22	29
W	2	9	16	23	30
T	3	10	17	24	31
F	4	11	18	25	
S	5	12	19	26	

April

S		3	10	17	24
M		4	11	18	25
T		5	12	19	26
W		6	13	20	27
T		7	14	21	28
F	1	8	15	22	29
S	2	9	16	23	30

May

S	1	8	15	22	29
M	2	9	16	23	30
T	3	10	17	24	31
W	4	11	18	25	
T	5	12	19	26	
F	6	13	20	27	
S	7	14	21	28	

June

S		5	12	19	26
M		6	13	20	27
T		7	14	21	28
W	1	8	15	22	29
T	2	9	16	23	30
F	3	10	17	24	
S	4	11	18	25	

July

S		3	10	17	24	31
M		4	11	18	25	
T		5	12	19	26	
W		6	13	20	27	
T		7	14	21	28	
F	1	8	15	22	29	
S	2	9	16	23	30	

August

S		7	14	21	28
M	1	8	15	22	29
T	2	9	16	23	30
W	3	10	17	24	31
T	4	11	18	25	
F	5	12	19	26	
S	6	13	20	27	

September

S		4	11	18	25
M		5	12	19	26
T		6	13	20	27
W		7	14	21	28
T	1	8	15	22	29
F	2	9	16	23	30
S	3	10	17	24	

October

S		2	9	16	23	30
M		3	10	17	24	31
T		4	11	18	25	
W		5	12	19	26	
T		6	13	20	27	
F		7	14	21	28	
S	1	8	15	22	29	

November

S		6	13	20	27
M		7	14	21	28
T	1	8	15	22	29
W	2	9	16	23	30
T	3	10	17	24	
F	4	11	18	25	
S	5	12	19	26	

December

S		4	11	18	25
M		5	12	19	26
T		6	13	20	27
W		7	14	21	28
T	1	8	15	22	29
F	2	9	16	23	30
S	3	10	17	24	31

N (leap year)

January

S		2	9	16	23	30
M		3	10	17	24	31
T		4	11	18	25	
W		5	12	19	26	
T		6	13	20	27	
F		7	14	21	28	
S	1	8	15	22	29	

February

S		6	13	20	27
M		7	14	21	28
T	1	8	15	22	29
W	2	9	16	23	
T	3	10	17	24	
F	4	11	18	25	
S	5	12	19	26	

March

S		5	12	19	26	
M		6	13	20	27	
T		7	14	21	28	
W	1	8	15	22	29	
T	2	9	16	23	30	
F	3	10	17	24	31	
S	4	11	18	25		

April

S		2	9	16	23	30
M		3	10	17	24	
T		4	11	18	25	
W		5	12	19	26	
T		6	13	20	27	
F		7	14	21	28	
S	1	8	15	22	29	

May

S		7	14	21	28
M	1	8	15	22	29
T	2	9	16	23	30
W	3	10	17	24	31
T	4	11	18	25	
F	5	12	19	26	
S	6	13	20	27	

June

S		4	11	18	25
M		5	12	19	26
T		6	13	20	27
W		7	14	21	28
T	1	8	15	22	29
F	2	9	16	23	30
S	3	10	17	24	

July

S		2	9	16	23	30
M		3	10	17	24	31
T		4	11	18	25	
W		5	12	19	26	
T		6	13	20	27	
F		7	14	21	28	
S	1	8	15	22	29	

August

S		6	13	20	27
M		7	14	21	28
T	1	8	15	22	29
W	2	9	16	23	30
T	3	10	17	24	31
F	4	11	18	25	
S	5	12	19	26	

September

S		3	10	17	24
M		4	11	18	25
T		5	12	19	26
W		6	13	20	27
T		7	14	21	28
F	1	8	15	22	29
S	2	9	16	23	30

October

S	1	8	15	22	29
M	2	9	16	23	30
T	3	10	17	24	31
W	4	11	18	25	
T	5	12	19	26	
F	6	13	20	27	
S	7	14	21	28	

November

S		5	12	19	26
M		6	13	20	27
T		7	14	21	28
W	1	8	15	22	29
T	2	9	16	23	30
F	3	10	17	24	
S	4	11	18	25	

December

S		3	10	17	24	31
M		4	11	18	25	
T		5	12	19	26	
W		6	13	20	27	
T		7	14	21	28	
F	1	8	15	22	29	
S	2	9	16	23	30	

Year equivalents

Jewish	Islamic	Hindu (Saka era)
5760 (11 September 1999– 29 September 2000)	1420 (17 April 1999– 5 April 2000)	1921 (22 March 1999– 21 March 2000)
5761 (30 September 2000– 17 September 2001)	1421 (6 April 2000– 25 March 2001)	1922 (21 March 2000– 21 March 2001)
5762 (18 September 2001– 6 September 2002)	1422 (26 March 2001– 14 March 2002)	1923 (21 March 2001– 21 March 2002)
5763 (7 September 2002– 26 September 2003)	1423 (15 March 2002– 4 March 2003)	1924 (22 March 2002– 21 March 2003)
5764 (27 September 2003– 15 September 2004)	1424 (5 March 2003– 21 February 2004)	1925 (22 March 2003– 20 March 2004)
5765 (16 September 2004– 3 October 2005)	1425 (22 February 2004– 9 February 2005)	1926 (21 March 2004– 21 March 2005)
5766 (4 October 2005– 22 September 2006)	1426 (10 February 2005– 30 January 2006)	1927 (22 March 2005– 21 March 2006)

Note The Jewish calendar is calculated from 3761 BC, marking the creation of the world; the Islamic calendar is calculated from AD 622, marking the Prophet's journey from Mecca to Medina; the Hindu calendar is calculated from AD 78, marking the beginning of the Saka era

Month equivalents

Gregorian	Jewish*	Islamic	Hindu
January 31	Tishri 30 (September– October)	Muharram 30 (September–October)	Caitra 29/30 (March– April)
February 28 (29 in leap years)	Heshvan 29/30 (October–November)	Safar 29 (October– November)	Vaisakha 29/30 (April– May)
March 31	Kislev 29/30 (November–December)	Rabi I 30 (November– December)	Jyaistha 29/30 (May– June)
April 30	Tevet 29 (December– January)	Rabi II 29 (December– January)	Asadha 29/30 (June– July)
May 31	Shevat 30 (January– February)	Jumada I 30 (January– February)	Dvitiya Sravana (certain leap years)
June 30	Adar 29/30 (February– March)	Jumada II 29 (February–March)	Bhadrapada 29/30 (August–September)
July 31	Nisan 30 (March– April)	Rajab 30 (March–April)	Asvina 29/30 (September–October)
August 31	Iyar 29 (April–May)	Shaban 29 (April–May)	Karttika 29/30 (October–November)
September 30	Sivan 30 (May–June)	Ramadan 30 (May– June)	Margasirsa 29/30 (November–December)
October 31	Tammuz 29 (June– July)	Shawwal 29 (June– July)	Pausa 29/30 (December–January)
November 30	Av 30 (July–August)	Dhu al-Qadah 30 (July–August)	Magha 29/30 (January–February)
December 31	Elul 29 (August– September)	Dhu al-Hijjah 29/30 (August–September)	Phalguna 29/30 (February–March)

Note Figures refer to the number of solar days in each month
*In leap years only the Jewish calendar includes the extra month of Adar Sheni (equivalent to March)

Chinese calendar

Year	Chinese name	English name
1999	T'u	Year of the Rabbit
2000	Lung	Year of the Dragon
2001	She	Year of the Snake
2002	Ma	Year of the Horse
2003	Yang	Year of the Goat or Sheep
2004	Hou	Year of the Monkey
2005	Chi	Year of the Chicken or Rooster
2006	Kou	Year of the Dog
2007	Chu	Year of the Pig
2008	Shu	Year of the Rat
2009	Niu	Year of the Ox
2010	Hu	Year of the Tiger

Note The Chinese calendar is associated with a cycle of twelve animals, which begins anew every twelve years

French Revolutionary calendar

Month	Dates
Vendémiaire (month of the grape harvest)	23 September–22 October
Brumaire (month of mist)	23 October–21 November
Frimaire (month of frost)	22 November–21 December
Nivôse (month of snow)	22 December–20 January
Pluviôse (month of rain)	21 January–19 February
Ventôse (month of wind)	20 February–21 March
Germinal (month of buds)	22 March–20 April
Floréal (month of flowers)	21 April–20 May
Prairial (month of meadows)	21 May–19 June
Messidor (month of harvest)	20 June–19 July
Thermidor (month of heat)	20 July–18 August
Fructidor (month of fruit)	19 August–22 September

Note The calendar was introduced in 1793, taking the foundation of the first Republic (22 September 1792) as its starting point, but was ultimately abolished by Napoleon in 1806

Seasons of the year

Dates	N hemisphere	S hemisphere
c. 21 March– c. 21 June	Spring (vernal equinox– summer solstice)	Autumn (autumnal equinox– winter solstice)
c. 21 June– c. 23 September	Summer (summer solstice– autumnal equinox)	Winter (winter solstice–spring equinox)
c. 23 September– c. 21 December	Autumn (autumnal equinox– winter solstice)	Spring (spring equinox–summer solstice)
c. 21 December– c. 21 March	Winter (winter solstice–vernal equinox)	Summer (summer solstice– autumnal equinox)

Months of the year

Month	Derivation of name
January (31)	After Janus (two-faced Roman god of gates)
February (28/29)	After Februa (Roman festival of purification, 15 February)
March (31)	After Mars (Roman god of war)
April (30)	After Apru (Etruscan goddess of love) or from Latin *aperire* (to open)
May (31)	After Maia (Roman goddess of spring)
June (30)	After Juno (Roman goddess of marriage)
July (31)	After Julius Caesar (Roman emperor)
August (31)	After Augustus (Roman emperor)
September (30)	From Latin *septem* (seven)
October (31)	From Latin *octo* (eight)
November (30)	From Latin *novem* (nine)
December (31)	From Latin *decem* (ten)

Number of days calendar

	Jan	Feb	Mar	Apr	May	Jun	Jul	Aug	Sep	Oct	Nov	Dec
January	365	31	59	90	120	151	181	212	243	273	304	334
February	334	365	28	59	89	120	150	181	212	242	273	303
March	306	337	365	31	61	92	122	153	184	214	245	275
April	275	306	334	365	30	61	91	122	153	183	214	244
May	245	276	304	335	365	31	61	92	123	153	184	214
June	214	245	273	304	334	365	30	61	92	122	153	183
July	184	215	243	274	304	335	365	31	62	92	123	153
August	153	184	212	243	273	304	334	365	31	61	92	122
September	122	153	181	212	242	273	303	334	365	30	61	91
October	92	123	151	182	212	243	273	304	335	365	31	61
November	61	92	120	151	181	212	242	273	304	334	365	30
December	31	62	90	121	151	182	212	243	274	304	335	365

Note Figures represent the number of days between a given day and the same day in any other month (does not apply to leap years)

Days of the week

Day	Derivation of name
Sunday	Sun day
Monday	Moon day
Tuesday	Tiw's day (after the Anglo-Saxon god of battle)
Wednesday	Woden's day (after the Anglo-Saxon god of victory, from the Norse Odin)
Thursday	Thor's day (after the Norse god of thunder)
Friday	Frigg's day (after the Norse goddess of love)
Saturday	Saeternes' day (after Saturn, the Roman god of fertility and agriculture)

Wedding anniversaries

1st	Cotton
2nd	Paper
3rd	Leather
4th	Fruit and flowers or books
5th	Wood or clocks
6th	Sugar or iron
7th	Copper, bronze, brass or wool
8th	Electrical appliances, bronze or pottery
9th	Pottery or copper
10th	Tin or aluminium
11th	Steel
12th	Silk or linen
13th	Lace
14th	Ivory
15th	Crystal
20th	China
25th	Silver
30th	Pearl
35th	Coral
40th	Ruby
45th	Sapphire
50th	Gold
55th	Emerald
60th	Diamond
70th	Platinum

National days

Country	National day
Afghanistan	19 August
Albania	28 November
Algeria	1 November
Andorra	8 September
Angola	11 November
Antigua and Barbuda	1 November
Argentina	25 May
Armenia	21 September
Australia	26 January
Austria	26 October
Azerbaijan	28 May
Bahamas	10 July
Bahrain	16 December
Bangladesh	26 March, 16 December
Barbados	30 November
Belarus	3 July, 27 July
Belgium	21 July
Belize	21 September

Country	National day
Benin	1 August, 30 November
Bhutan	17 December
Bolivia	6 August
Bosnia-Herzegovina	1 March
Botswana	30 September
Brazil	7 September
Brunei	23 February
Bulgaria	3 March
Burkina Faso	4 August, 11 December
Burundi	1 July
Cambodia	9 November
Cameroon	20 May
Canada	1 July
Cape Verde	5 July
Central African Republic	1 December
Chad	13 April, 11 August
Chile	18 September
China	1–2 October
Colombia	20 July
Comoros	6 July
Congo, Democratic Republic of	24 November
Congo, Republic of the	15 August
Costa Rica	15 September
Côte d'Ivoire	7 August, 7 December
Croatia	30 May
Cuba	1 January
Cyprus	1 October
Czech Republic	8 May, 6 July, 28 October
Denmark	16 April, 5 June
Djibouti	27 June
Dominica	3 November
Dominican Republic	27 February
Ecuador	10 August
Egypt	23 July
El Salvador	15 September
Equatorial Guinea	12 October
Eritrea	24 May
Estonia	24 February
Ethiopia	2 March, 6 April
Fiji	10 October
Finland	6 December
France	14 July
Gabon	17 August
The Gambia	18 February
Georgia	26 May
Germany	3 October
Ghana	6 March
Greece	25 March
Grenada	7 February
Guatemala	15 September
Guinea	2 October

Guinea-Bissau	24 September
Guyana	23 February, 26 May
Haiti	1 January
Honduras	15 September
Hungary	15 March, 20 August, 23 October
Iceland	17 June
India	26 January
Indonesia	17 August
Iran	11 February
Iraq	8 February, 14 July, 17 July, 8 August
Ireland, Republic of	17 March
Israel	14 May
Italy	2 June
Jamaica	First Monday in August
Japan	23 December
Jordan	25 May
Kazakhstan	25 October
Kenya	12 December
Kiribati	12 July
Korea, North	16 February, 9 September
Korea, South	1 March, 15 August
Kuwait	25 February
Kyrgyzstan	31 August
Laos	2 December
Latvia	18 November
Lebanon	22 November
Lesotho	4 October
Liberia	26 July
Libya	1 September
Liechtenstein	15 August
Lithuania	16 February
Luxembourg	23 June
Macedonia	2 August, 8 September
Madagascar	26 June
Malawi	6 July
Malaysia	31 August
Maldives	26 July
Mali	22 September
Malta	31 March, 7 June, 8 September, 21 September, 13 December
Marshall Islands	1 May, 21 October
Mauritania	28 November
Mauritius	12 March
Mexico	16 September
Moldova	27 August
Monaco	19 November
Mongolia	11 July
Morocco	3 March
Mozambique	25 June
Myanmar	4 January
Namibia	21 March
Nauru	31 January
Nepal	18 February, 28 December

Country	National day
Netherlands	30 April
New Zealand	6 February
Nicaragua	15 September
Niger	18 December
Nigeria	1 October
Norway	17 May
Oman	18 November
Pakistan	23 March, 14 August
Palau	1 October
Panama	3 November
Papua New Guinea	16 September
Paraguay	14–15 May
Peru	28–29 July
Philippines	12 June
Poland	3 May
Portugal	10 June
Qatar	3 September
Romania	1 December
Russia	12 June
Rwanda	1 July
St Kitts and Nevis	19 September
St Lucia	22 February
St Vincent and the Grenadines	27 October
Samoa	1–3 June
San Marino	3 September
São Tomé e Príncipe	12 July
Saudi Arabia	23 September
Senegal	4 April
Seychelles	5 June, 18 June, 29 June
Sierra Leone	27 April
Singapore	9 August
Slovakia	1 January, 5 July, 29 August, 1 September
Slovenia	25 June, 26 December
Solomon Islands	7 July
Somalia	1 July
South Africa	27 April
Spain	12 October
Sri Lanka	4 February
Sudan	1 January
Suriname	25 November
Swaziland	6 September
Sweden	6 June
Switzerland	1 August
Syria	17 April
Taiwan	10 October
Tajikistan	9 September
Tanzania	26 April
Thailand	5 December
Togo	13 January
Tonga	4 June
Trinidad and Tobago	31 August, 24 September

Tunisia	20 March
Turkey	29 October
Turkmenistan	27–28 October
Tuvalu	1 October
Uganda	9 October
UK (Wales)	1 March
UK (Northern Ireland)	17 March
UK (England)	23 April
UK (Scotland)	30 November
Ukraine	24 August
United Arab Emirates	2 December
Uruguay	25 August
USA	4 July
Uzbekistan	I September, 8 December
Vanuatu	30 July
Vatican City State	22 October
Venezuela	5 July
Vietnam	1–2 September
Yemen	22 May
Yugoslavia, Federal Republic of	27 April, 29–30 November
Zambia	24 October
Zimbabwe	18 April

Note This list represents a selection of national holidays or celebrations and is not exhaustive

Civil calendar (UK)

Date	Day
6 February	Accession of Queen Elizabeth II
19 February	Birthday of the Duke of York
1 March	St David's Day (Wales only)
Second Monday in March	Commonwealth Day
10 March	Birthday of Prince Edward
17 March	St Patrick's Day
21 April	Birthday of Queen Elizabeth II
23 April	St George's Day
9 May	Europe Day
2 June	Coronation of Queen Elizabeth II
10 June	Birthday of the Duke of Edinburgh
Second Saturday in June	Official birthday of Queen Elizabeth II
4 August	Birthday of Queen Elizabeth, the Queen Mother
15 August	Birthday of the Princess Royal
21 August	Birthday of Princess Margaret
Early November	Remembrance Day
14 November	Birthday of the Prince of Wales
20 November	Wedding day of Queen Elizabeth II
30 November	St Andrew's Day (Scotland only)

Note On these dates the Union flag is flown on government buildings throughout the UK between the hours of 8.00 am and sunset

Public holidays (UK)

Holiday	England and Wales 2000	2001	Scotland 2000	2001	Northern Ireland 2000	2001
New Year	1 Jan	1 Jan	1, 2 Jan	1, 2 Jan	1 Jan	1 Jan
St Patrick's Day					17 Mar	17 Mar
Good Friday	13 Apr	29 Apr	13 Apr	29 Apr	13 Apr	29 Apr
Easter Monday	16 Apr	1 May	16 Apr	1 May	16 Apr	1 May
May Day	7 May	6 May	7 May	6 May	7 May	6 May
Spring	28 May	4 Jun	28 May	4 Jun	28 May	4 Jun
Battle of the Boyne					12 Jul	12 Jul
Summer	27 Aug	26 Aug	27 Aug	26 Aug	27 Aug	26 Aug
Christmas	25, 26 Dec	25, 26 Dec	25, 26 Dec	25, 26 Dec	25, 26 Dec	25, 26 Dec

Quarter days

Day	Date
Lady	25 March
Midsummer	24 June
Michaelmas	29 September
Christmas	25 December

Note Applicable in England, Wales, and Northern Ireland

5.2 *Language*

Language families

Language family	Number of speakers
Indo-European	2 500 000 000
Sino-Tibetan	1 088 000 000
Austronesian	200 000 000
Niger-Congo	206 000 000
Afro-Asiatic	250 000 000
Dravidian	165 000 000
Japanese	126 000 000
Altaic	115 000 000
Austro-Asiatic	75 000 000
Tai	75 000 000
Korean	60 000 000
Nilo-Saharan	28 000 000
Uralic	24 000 000

Amerindian	22 400 000
Caucasian	7 800 000
Miao-Yao	5 600 000
Indo-Pacific	3 500 000
Khoisan	300 000
Australian aborigine	30 000
Palaeosiberian	18 000

Main languages

Language	Language group	Number of speakers (including as a second language)
Putonghua/Mandarin	Chinese	1 000 000 000
English		1 000 000 000
Hindi and Urdu	Indic	900 000 000
Spanish	Romance	450 000 000
Russian	Slavic	320 000 000
Arabic		250 000 000
Bengali	Indic	250 000 000
Portuguese	Romance	200 000 000
Malay and Indonesian	Malayic	160 000 000
Japanese		130 000 000
German	Continental West Germanic	125 000 000
French	Romance	125 000 000
Panjabi	Indic	85 000 000
Wu	Chinese	85 000 000
Javanese		80 000 000
Marathi	Indic	80 000 000
Korean		75 000 000
Vietnamese		75 000 000
Italian	Romance	70 000 000
Yue	Chinese	70 000 000
Tamil	Dravidian	70 000 000
Telugu	Dravidian	70 000 000
Turkish	Turkic	60 000 000
Min-nan	Chinese	55 000 000
Swahili	Bantu	55 000 000
Ukrainian	Slavic	47 000 000
Gujarati	Indic	45 000 000
Thai	Tai	45 000 000
Hausa		42 000 000
Kannada	Dravidian	42 000 000
Persian	West Iranian	40 000 000
Tagalog	Transphilippine	40 000 000
Malayalam	Dravidian	39 000 000
Hakka	Chinese	35 000 000
Burmese		33 000 000
Oriya	Indic	33 000 000
Laotian and Isan	Tai	30 000 000
Sundanese		30 000 000

Language	Language group	Number of speakers (including as a second language)
Dutch, Flemish and Afrikaans	Continental West Germanic	30 000 000
Romanian and Moldavian	Romance	27 000 000
Yoruba		26 000 000
Amharic		25 000 000
Pashto		25 000 000
Kazakh	Turkic	20 000 000
Igbo		19 000 000
Serbian and Croatian	Slavic	19 000 000
Sindhi	Indic	18 000 000
Uzbek	Turkic	18 000 000
Cebuano	Transphilippine	17 000 000
Nepali	Indic	17 000 000
Czech and Slovak	Slavic	16 000 000
Fula/Peul		16 000 000
Hungarian		15 000 000
North and South Kurdish	West Iranian	15 000 000
Huang and Buyi	Tai	15 000 000
Lingala	Bantu	14 000 000
Oromo		14 000 000
Rwanda and Rundi	Bantu	14 000 000
Sinhalese	Indic	14 000 000
Bihari and Bhojpuri	Indic	13 000 000
Madurese	Malayic	13 000 000
Malagasy		13 000 000
Mandinka, Bambara and Jula		13 000 000
Greek		12 000 000
Min-bei	Chinese	12 000 000
Sotho and Tswana	Bantu	12 000 000
Swedish		12 000 000
Assamese	Indic	11 000 000
Catalan	Romance	11 000 000
Zulu, Swazi and Ndebele	Bantu	11 000 000
Bulgarian and Macedonian	Slavic	10 000 000

Speakers of English

Country	Number of speakers (as a first language)	Number of speakers (as a second language)
Antigua and Barbuda	61 000 (c. 95%)	2 000 (4%)
Australia	15 316 000 (85%)	2 084 000 (12%)
Bahamas	250 000 (c. 90%)	25 000 (9%)
Bangladesh	3 200 000 (4%)	c. 3 100 000 (c. 3%)
Barbados	265 000 (c. 100%)	
Belize	135 000 (c. 65%)	c. 30 000 (c. 12%)
Bermuda	60 000 (95%)	not known
Bhutan	not known	c. 60 000 (c. 5%)
Botswana	not known	c. 620 000 (c. 4%)
Brunei	10 0000 (3%)	c. 104 000 (c. 36%)

Cameroon	not known	6 600 000 (c. 50%)
Canada	19 700 000 (63%)	c. 6 000 000 (c. 20%)
Dominica	3 000 (4%)	c. 12 000 (c. 16%)
Fiji	c. 5 000 (c. 1%)	c. 160 000 (c. 20%)
Gambia	not known	c. 33 000 (c. 73%)
Ghana	not known	c. 1 153 000 (c. 7%)
Gibraltar	25 000 (90%)	c. 2 000 (c. 7%)
Grenada	91 000 (c. 99%)	not known
Guyana	700 000 (c. 90%)	c. 30 000 (c. 4%)
India	c. 320 000 (c. 0.0003%)	37 000 000 (c. 4%)
Ireland	3 400 000 (95%)	c. 190 000 (c. 5%)
Jamaica	2 400 000 (95%)	c. 50 000 (c. 2%)
Kenya	not known	2 576 000 (c. 9%)
Kiribati	not known	c. 20 000 (c. 25%)
Lesotho	not known	c. 488 000 (c. 24%)
Liberia	c. 60 000 (c. 2%)	c. 2 000 000 (c. 84%)
Malawi	not known	c. 517 000 (c. 5%)
Malaysia	375 000 (2%)	5 984 000 (30%)
Malta	8 000 (2%)	c. 86 000 (c. 23%)
Mauritius	2 000 (c. 0.002%)	c. 167 000 (c. 15%)
Montserrat	11 000 (c. 100%)	
Namibia	c. 13 000 (c. 0.008 %)	c. 300 000 (c. 18%)
Nauru	800 (8%)	c. 9 400 (c. 90 %)
Nepal	not known	c. 5 927 000 (c. 30%)
New Zealand	3 396 000 (95%)	c. 150 000 (c. 4%)
Nigeria	not known	c. 43 000 000 (c. 45%)
Pakistan	not known	c. 16 000 000 (c. 11%)
Papua New Guinea	120 000 (c. 3%)	c. 2 800 000 (c. 65%)
Philippines	c. 15 000 (c. 0.0002%)	36 400 000 (52%)
Samoa	c. 1 000 (c. 0.006%)	c. 86 000 (c. 52%)
St Kitts	39 000 (c. 100%)	
St Lucia	29 000 (20%)	c. 22 000 (c. 15%)
St Vincent and the Grenadines	111 000 (c. 99%)	not known
Seychelles	2 000 (3%)	c. 11 000 (c. 15%)
Sierra Leone	c. 450 000 (c. 10%)	c. 3 830 000 (c. 85%)
Singapore	c. 300 000 (c. 10%)	c. 1 046 000 (c. 35%)
Solomon Islands	c. 2 000 (c. 0.005%)	135 000 (c. 35%)
South Africa	3 600 000 (9%)	c. 10 000 000 (c. 24%)
Suriname	c. 258 000 (c. 60%)	c. 150 000 (c. 35%)
Swaziland	not known	c. 40 000 (c. 4%)
Tanzania	not known	c. 3 000 000 (c. 11%)
Tonga	not known	c. 30 000 (c. 30%)
Trinidad and Tobago	1 200 000 (c. 95%)	not known
Tuvalu	not known	600 (6%)
Uganda	not known	2 000 000 (c. 11%)
UK	56 990 000 (97%)	1 110 000 (2%)
USA	226 710 000 (86%)	30 000 000 (11%)
US Virgin Islands	79 000 (c. 80%)	c. 10 000 (c. 10%)
Vanuatu	c. 2 000 (c. 2%)	c. 160 000 (c. 95%)
Zambia	c. 50 000 (c. 0.005%)	c. 1 000 000 (c. 11%)
Zimbabwe	c. 250 000 (c. 2%)	c. 3 300 000 (c. 30%)

Note Countries listed include those where English is spoken as an official or first language

Word frequency

Most frequent	English (spoken)	English (written)	French	German
1	the	the	de	der
2	and	of	le	die
3	I	to	la	und
4	to	in	et	in
5	of	and	les	des
6	a	a	des	den
7	you	for	est	zu
8	that	was	un	das
9	in	is	une	von
10	it	that	du	für

Greek alphabet

Upper case	Lower case	Name	Transliteration
Α	α	alpha	a
Β	β	beta	b
Γ	γ	gamma	g
Δ	δ	delta	d
Ε	ε	epsilon	e
Ζ	ζ	zeta	z
Η	η	eta	ē
Θ	θ	theta	th
Ι	ι	iota	i
Κ	κ	kappa	k
Λ	λ	lambda	l
Μ	μ	mu	m
Ν	ν	nu	n
Ξ	ξ	xi	x
Ο	ο	omicron	o
Π	π	pi	p
Ρ	ρ	rho	r
Σ	σ	sigma	s
Τ	τ	tau	t
Υ	υ	upsilon	u
Φ	φ	phi	ph
Χ	χ	chi	ch
Ψ	ψ	psi	ps
Ω	ω	omega	ō/Ω

Russian alphabet

Upper case	Lower case	Transliteration
А	а	a
Б	б	b
В	в	v
Г	г	g
Д	д	d
Е	е	e
Ж	ж	ž/zh
З	з	z
И	и	I
Й	й	j
К	к	k
Л	л	l
М	м	m
Н	н	n
О	о	o
П	п	p
Р	р	r
С	с	s
Т	т	t
У	у	u
Ф	ф	f
Х	х	x/kh
Ц	ц	c/ts
Ч	ч	ch
Ш	ш	sh
Щ	щ	shch
Ъ	ъ	"
Ы	ы	y
Ь	ь	'
Э	э	è/é
Ю	ю	ju/yu
Я	я	ja/ya

Anglo-Saxon runes

Rune	Name	Meaning	Modern letter
ᚠ	feoh	wealth	f
ᚢ	ur	aurochs	u
ᚦ	þorn	thorn	th
ᚩ	os	mouth	o
ᚱ	rad	riding	r
ᚳ	cen	torch	c
ᚷ	gyfu	gift	g
ᚹ	wynn	joy	w

Rune	Name	Meaning	Modern letter
ᚻ	hgl	hail	h
ᚾ	nyd	need	n
ᛁ	is	ice	i
ᛄ	ger	harvest	j
ᛇ	eoh	yew	eo
ᛈ	peorð	hearth	p
ᛉ	eolhxsecg	elksedge	x
ᛋ	sigel	sun	s
ᛏ	Tir	Tiw	t
ᛒ	beorc	birch	b
ᛖ	eh	horse	e
ᛗ	man	man	m
ᛚ	lagu	water	l
ᛝ	Ing	Ing	ng
ᛟ	eþel	homeland	oe
ᛞ	dæg	day	d
ᚪ	ac	oak	a
ᚫ	æsc	ash	æ
ᛦ	yr	weapon	y
ᛡ	ior	beaver	ia
ᛠ	ear	grave	ea

Accents

Name	Symbol
Acute	´
Angstrom	°
Asper	ʼ
Breve	˘
Cedilla	¸
Circumflex	^
Diaeresis	¨
Grave	`
Haček	ˇ
Lenis	ʼ
Macron	¯
Tilde	~
Umlaut	¨

Proof-correcting marks

Instruction	Textual mark	Marginal mark
Correction is concluded	None	/
Leave unchanged	- - - - - (under characters to be retained)	Ⓙ
Remove extraneous marks	Encircle marks to be removed	✕
Refer to appropriate authority anything of doubtful accuracy	Encircle word or words affected	⟮?⟯
Insert in text the matter indicated in the margin	⅄	New matter followed by ⅄
Insert additional matter identified by a letter in a diamond	⅄	◇Ⓐ ⅄ Matter to be inserted can then be written where there is more space, identified by ◇Ⓐ
Delete	/ through character, or ⊢——⊣ through words to be deleted	♪
Delete and close up	⍑ through character or ⊏—⊐ through characters	♫
Substitute character or part of one or more words	/ through character or ⊢——⊣ through words	New character or new word followed by /
Replace wrong fount with character in correct fount	Encircle character to be changed	⊗
Change damaged character	Encircle character to be changed	✕
Set in italic	Underline character to be set or changed	⊔
Set in capital letters	Triple underline character to be set or changed	≡
Set in small capital letters	Double underline character to be set or changed	=
Set in bold type	∿∿∿ under character to be set or changed	∿
Set in bold italic type	∿∿∿ under character to be set or changed	⊔̰

Change capital letters to lower case letters	Encircle character to be set or changed	$\not\equiv$
Change small capital letters to lower case letters	Encircle character to be changed	$\not=$
Change italic to upright type	Encircle character to be changed	
Substitute or insert character in raised position	/ through character or ⅄ where required	⌐ under character e.g. ²⌐/
Substitute or insert character in lowered position	/ through character or ⅄ where required	∟ over character e.g. ∟₂/
Substitute ligature	├────┤ through characters affected	⌒ e.g. ãe /
Substitute separate letters for ligature	/ through characters	Write out separate letters
Substitute or insert full stop or decimal point	/ through character or ⅄ where required	⊙ /
Substitute or insert colon	/ through character or ⅄ where required	⊙ /
Substitute or insert semi-colon	/ through character or ⅄ where required	;/
Substitute or insert comma	/ through character or ⅄ where required	,/
Substitute or insert apostrophe	/ through character or ⅄ where required	,/
Substitute or insert single quotation marks	/ through character or ⅄ where required	,/ ,/
Substitute or insert double quotation marks	/ through character or ⅄ where required	,,/ ,,/
Substitute or insert ellipsis	/ through character or ⅄ where required	⋯/
Substitute or insert leader dots	/ through character or ⅄ where required	⋯⋯⋯/
Substitute or insert hyphen	/ through character or ⅄ where required	⊨⊨/ /
Substitute or insert rule	/ through character or ⅄ where required	— /
Substitute or insert oblique	/ through character or ⅄ where required	⊘

Start new paragraph		
Run on		
Transpose characters or words	between characters or words	
Transpose lines		
Transpose a number of lines	≡ 3 2 1	Rules extend from the margin into the text with each line to be transposed numbered in the correct sequence
Centre	enclosing matter to be centred	
Indent		
Cancel indent		
Set line justified to specified measure	and/or	
Move matter specified distance to the right		
Move matter specified distance to the left		
Take over character, word, or line to next line, column, or page		Extend mark into margin
Take back character, word, or line to previous line, column, or page		Extend mark into margin
Raise matter	over matter to be raised; under matter to be raised	
Lower matter	over matter to be lowered; under matter to be lowered	
Move matter to position indicated	Enclose matter to be moved and indicate new position	

Correct vertical alignment	‖	‖
Correct horizontal alignment	Single line above and below misaligned matter	Enclose matter to be moved and indicate new position
Close up	⌣ (linking characters)	⌣
Insert space between characters	| between characters affected	Y
Insert space between words	Y between words affected	Y
Reduce space between characters	| between characters affected	⌒
Reduce space between words	⌒ between words affected	⌒
Make space appear equal between characters or words	| between characters or words affected	Y̲
Close up to normal interline spacing	( ) (positioned to left and right of the column)	

Common abbreviations

Abbreviation	Meaning
A	Associate of
AA	Alcoholics Anonymous; Automobile Association
AAA	Amateur Athletic Association; American Automobile Association
AA(A)	anti-aircraft (artillery)
AAAS	American Association for the Advancement of Science
AB	Able-bodied seaman
ABA	Amateur Boxing Association; American Bar Association
abbr(ev)	abbreviation
ABC	anti-ballistic missile
ABM	antilock braking system
ABS	Australian Broadcasting Corporation
abr	abridged
ABTA	Association of British Travel Agents
ac	alternating current
a/c	account
AC	Aircraftman; *Ante Christum* (Before Christ); Companion, Order of Australia
ACAD	auto computer aided design
ACAS	Advisory, Conciliation and Arbitration Service
ACT	Australian Capital Territory

ACTH	adrenocorticotrophic hormone
AD	*Anno Domini* (in the year of our Lord)
A-D	analog-to-digital (computing)
ADC	*aide-de-camp*
ADC(P)	Personal ADC to The Queen
ADH	antidiuretic hormone
adj	adjective
Adj	Adjutant
ad lib	*ad libitum* (at pleasure)
Adm	Admiral; admission
ADP	adenosine diphosphate
adv	adverb
AE	Air Efficiency Award
AEA	Atomic Energy Authority (UK)
AEC	Atomic Energy Commission (USA)
AEEU	Amalgamated Engineering and Electrical Union
AEM	Air Efficiency Medal
AFC	Air Force Cross
AFM	Air Force Medal
AFP	Agence France Presse
AFV	armoured fighting vehicle
AG	Adjutant-General; Attorney-General
AGM	air-to-ground missile; annual general meeting
AGR	advanced gas-cooled reactor
AH	Anno Hegirae (in the year of the Hegira)
AI	artifical intelligence
AID	artificial insemination by donor
Aids	acquired immune deficiency syndrome
AIH	artificial insemination by husband
AIM	Alternative Investment Market
aka	also known as
ALCM	air-launched cruise missile
ALGOL	algorithmic language
alt	altitude
am	*ante meridiem* (before noon)
AM	*Anno mundi* (in the year of the world); amplitude modulation; Member of the Welsh Assembly
amp	ampere; amplifier
AMU	atomic mass unit
ANC	African National Congress
anon	anonymous
ANZAC	Australian and New Zealand Army Corps
AO	Air Officer; Officer, Order of Australia
AOB	any other business
AOC	Air Officer Commanding
AONB	Area of Outstanding Natural Beauty
AP	Associated Press
APR	annual percentage rate
APT	Advanced Passenger Train
AR	autonomous republic
ARP	air-raid precautions

Abbreviation	Meaning
AS	Anglo-Saxon
ASA	Advertising Standards Authority; Amateur Swimming Association; American Standards Association
asap	as soon as possible
ASB	Alternative Service Book
ASDIC	Admiralty Submarine Detection Investigation Committee
ASEAN	Association of South East Asian Nations
ASH	Action on Smoking and Health
ASLEF	Associated Society of Locomotive Engineers and Firemen
ASLIB	Association for Information Management
ASM	air-to-surface missile
ATC	Air Training Corps
ATS	Auxiliary Territorial Service
AU	astronomical unit
AUC	*ab urbe condita* (in the year from the foundation of Rome); *anno urbis conditae* (in the year of the founding of the city)
AUT	Association of University Teachers
AV	audio-visual; Authorized Version (Bible)
AVR	Army Volunteer Reserve
AWACS	Airborne Warning and Control System
AWOL	absent without leave
b	born; bowled
BA	Bachelor of Arts
BAA	British Airports Authority; British Astronomical Association
BAF	British Athletics Federation
BAFTA	British Academy of Film and Television Arts
Bart	Baronet
BAS	Bachelor in Agricultural Science; British Antarctic Survey
BBC	British Broadcasting Corporation
BBSRC	Biotechnology and Biological Sciences Research Council
BC	Before Christ; British Columbia
BCG	bacille (bacillus) Calmette Guérin
B Ch(D)	Bachelor of (Dental) Surgery
BCL	Bachelor of Civil Law
B Com	Bachelor of Commerce
BD	Bachelor of Divinity
BDA	British Dental Association
BDS	Bachelor of Dental Surgery
B Ed	Bachelor of Education
BEF	British Expeditionary Force
BEM	British Empire Medal
B Eng	Bachelor of Engineering
BFI	British Film Institute
BFPO	British Forces Post Office
BL	British Library
B Litt	Bachelor of Letters; Bachelor of Literature
BM	Bachelor of Medicine; British Museum
BMA	British Medical Association
B Mus	Bachelor of Music
BOTB	British Overseas Trade Board
BP	blood pressure

Bp	Bishop
B Pharm	Bachelor of Pharmacy
B Phil	Bachelor of Philosophy
Br(it)	Britain; British
BR	British Rail
Brig	Brigadier
BSc	Bachelor of Science
BSE	bovine spongiform encephalopathy
BSI	British Standards Institution
BST	British Summer Time
Bt	Baronet
BTEC	Business and Technology Education Council
B Th	Bachelor of Theology
Btu	British thermal unit
BVM	*Beata Virgo Maria* (Blessed Virgin Mary)
BVMS	Bachelor of Veterinary Medicine and Surgery
c	*circa* (about)
C	Celsius; Centigrade; Conservative
CA	Chartered Accountant (Scotland)
CAA	Civil Aviation Authority
CAB	Citizens' Advice Bureau
CAD	computer-aided design
Cantab	of Cambridge
Cantuar:	of Canterbury (Archbishop)
CAP	Common Agricultural Policy
Capt	Captain
Caricom	Caribbean Community and Common Market
Carliol:	of Carlisle (Bishop)
CAT	computerized axial tomography
CB	citizens' band (radio); Companion, Order of the Bath
CBE	Commander, Order of the British Empire
CBI	Confederation of British Industry
CBS	Columbia Broadcasting System
CC	Chamber of Commerce; Companion, Order of Canada; City Council, County Council, County Court
CCC	Country Cricket Club
CCF	Combined Cadet Force
C Chem	Chartered Chemist
CCTV	closed-circuit television
CD	Civil Defence; compact disc; Corps Diplomatique
Cdr	Commander
Cdre	Commodore
CD-ROM	compact disc read-only memory
CDS	Chief of the Defence Staff
CDU	Christian Democratic Union
CE	Christian Era; Civil Engineer
C Eng	Chartered Engineer
CENTO	Central Treaty Organization
CERN	Organisation Européene pour la Recherche Nucléaire
Cestr:	of Chester (Bishop)
CET	Central European Time; Common External Tariff

Abbreviation	Meaning
cf	confer (compare)
CF	Chaplain to the Forces
CFC	chlorofluorocarbon
CFS	Chronic Fatigue Syndrome
CGC	Conspicuous Gallantry Cross
CGM	Conspicuous Gallantry Medal
CGS	centimetre-gramme-second; Chief of General Staff
CH	Companion of Honour
ChB/M	Bachelor/Master of Surgery
CI	Channel Islands; Imperial Order of the Crown of India
CIA	Central Intelligence Agency
Cicestr:	of Chichester (Bishop)
CID	Criminal Investigation Department
CIE	Companion, Order of the Indian Empire
cif	cost, insurance, and freight
C-in-C	Commander-in-Chief
CIPFA	Chartered Institute of Public Finance and Accountancy
CJD	Creutzfeld-Jakob disease
C Lit	Companion of Literature
CLJ	Commander, Order of St Lazarus of Jerusalem
CM	Chirurgiae Magister (Master of Surgery)
CMG	Companion, Order of St Michael and St George
CND	Campaign for Nuclear Disarmament
CNN	Cable News Network
c/o	care of
CO	Commanding Officer; conscientious objector
COBOL	Common Business Oriented Language
COD	cash on delivery
COED	computer-operated electronic display
C of E	Church of England
COI	Central Office of Information
Col	Colonel
COMECON	Council for Mutual Economic Assistance
Con	Conservative
cons	consecrated
Cpl	Corporal
CPM	Colonial Police Medal
CPR	cardio-pulmonary resuscitation
CPRE	Council for the Protection of Rural England
CPS	characters per second; Crown Prosecution Service
CPU	central processing unit
CPVE	Certificate of Pre-Vocational Education
CRE	Commission for Racial Equality
CSA	Child Support Agency
CSE	Certificate of Secondary Education
CSI	Companion, Order of the Star of India
CV	*curriculum vitae*
CVO	Commander, Royal Victorian Order
CVS	chorionic villus sampling
d	denarius (penny)
DA	District Attorney

DBE	Dame Commander, Order of the British Empire
DBS	direct broadcasting from satellite
dc	direct current
DC	District Council; District of Columbia
D&C	dilation and curettage
DCB	Dame Commander, Order of the Bath
D Ch	Doctor Chirurgiae (Doctor of Surgery)
DCL	Doctor of Civil Law
DCM	Distinguished Conduct Medal
DCMG	Dame Commander, Order of St Michael and St George
DCMS	Department for Culture, Media, and Sport
DCVO	Dame Commander, Royal Victorian Order
DD	Doctor of Divinity
DDS	Doctor of Dental Surgery
DDT	dichloro-diphenyl-trichloroethane
del	*delineavit* (he/she drew it)
DERV	diesel-engined road vehicle
DES	Department of Education and Science
DETR	Department of the Environment, Transport, and the Regions
DFC	Distinguished Flying Cross
DFID	Department for International Development
DFM	Distinguished Flying Medal
DG	*Dei gratia* (by the grace of God)
DH	Department of Health
DHA	District Health Authority
Dip Ed	Diploma in Education
Dip HE	Diploma in Higher Education
Dip Tech	Diploma in Technology
DIY	do-it-yourself
DJ	disc jockey
DL	Deputy Lieutenant
D Litt	Doctor of Letters; Doctor of Literature
DM	Deutsche Mark
D Mus	Doctor of Music
DNA	deoxyribonucleic acid
DNB	Dictionary of National Biography
do	ditto (the same)
DOA	dead on arrival
DoE	Department of the Environment
DOS	disk operating system
DP	data processing
D Phil	Doctor of Philosophy
DPP	Director of Public Prosecutions
Dr	Doctor
D Sc	Doctor of Science
DSC	Distinguished Service Cross
DSM	Distinguished Service Medal
DSO	Companion, Distinguished Service Order
DSS	Department of Social Security
DST	daylight-saving time
DTI	Department of Trade and Industry
DTP	desk-top publishing

Abbreviation	Meaning
Dunelm:	of Durham (Bishop)
DV	*Deo volente* (God willing)
DVD	digital video (versatile) disc
DVLC	Driver and Vehicle Licensing Centre
E	east
EAC	European Atomic Commission
EARM	electrically alterable read-only memory
Ebor:	of York (Archbishop)
EBRD	European Bank for Reconstruction and Development
EC	European Community
ECB	European Central Bank
ECG	electrocardiogram
ECOSOC	Economic and Social Council (of the United Nations)
ECSC	European Coal and Steel Community
ECT	electroconvulsive therapy
ECU	European Currency Unit
EEC	European Economic Community
EEG	electroencephalogram
EFA	European Fighter Aircraft
EFTA	European Free Trade Association
eg	*exempli gratia* (for example)
EIB	European Investment Bank
ELT	English language teaching
E-MAIL	electronic mail
EMF	electromotive force
EMS	European Monetary System
EMU	electromagnetic unit; European Monetary Union
ENIAC	electronic numeral indicator and calculator
EOC	Equal Opportunities Commission
EOKA	Ethniki Organosis Kipriakou Agonos (National Organization of Cypriot Struggle)
EP	European Parliament
EPA	Environmental Protection Agency
EPOS	electronic point of sale
ER	Elizabetha Regina (Queen Elizabeth)
ERM	Exchange Rate Mechanism
ERNIE	electronic random number indicator equipment
ESA	European Space Agency
ESP	extra-sensory perception
ESRC	Economic and Social Research Council
ESRO	European Space Research Organization
ETA	estimated time of arrival; Euzkadi ta Askatasuna (Basque separatist organization)
et al	*et alibi* (and elsewhere)
etc	*et cetera* (and so forth)
et seq	*et sequentia* (and the following)
EU	European Union
Euratom	European Atomic Energy Commission
Exon:	of Exeter (Bishop)
f	*forte* (loud)
F	Fahrenheit; Fellow of

FA	Football Association
FAA	Federal Aviation Administration
FANY	First Aid Nursing Yeomanry
FAO	Food and Agriculture Organization (United Nations)
FBA	Fellow, British Academy
FBAA	Fellow, British Association of Accountants and Auditors
FBI	Federal Bureau of Investigation
FBIM	Fellow, British Institute of Management
FC	Football Club
FCA	Fellow, Institute of Chartered Accountants in England and Wales
FCCA	Fellow, Chartered Association of Certified Accountants
FCIB	Fellow, Chartered Institute of Bankers; Fellow, Corporation of Insurance Brokers
FCII	Fellow, Chartered Insurance Institute
FCO	Foreign and Commonwealth Office
FD	*Fidei Defensor* (Defender of the Faith)
FDA	Food and Drug Administration
FE	Further Education
fec	*fecit* (made this)
ff	*fortissimo* (very loud)
FIFA	Fédération Internationale de Football Association (International Association Football Federation)
FILO	first in, last out
FIMBRA	Financial Intermediaries, Managers and Brokers Regulatory Association
fl	*floruit* (flourished)
FLN	Front de Libération Nationale (National Liberation Front)
FM	frequency modulation
FO	Flying Officer; Foreign Office
fob	free on board
FORTRAN	formula translation
FPS	foot-pound-second
FRELIMO	Frente de Libertação de Moçambique (Liberation Front of Mozambique)
FRS	Fellow, Royal Society
FRSA	Fellow, Royal Society of Arts
FT	*Financial Times*
FWA	Federal Works Agency
G7	Group of Seven (Canada, France, Germany, Italy, Japan, UK, USA)
GATT	General Agreement on Tariffs and Trade
GBE	Knight/Dame Grand Cross, Order of the British Empire
GBH	grievous bodily harm
GC	George Cross
GCE	General Certificate of Education
GCHQ	Government Communications Headquarters
GCMG	Knight/Dame Grand Cross, Order of St Michael and St George
GCSE	General Certificate of Secondary Education
GCVO	Knight/Dame Grand Cross, Royal Victorian Order
GDP	gross domestic product
Gen	General
GHQ	general headquarters
GI	government issue
GIGO	garbage in, garbage out
GLCM	ground launched cruise missile

Abbreviation	Meaning
GM	George Medal
GMC	General Medical Council
GMT	Greenwich Mean Time
GNP	gross national product
GOC	General Officer Commanding
GP	General Practitioner
Gp Capt	Group Captain
GUT	grand unified theory
GW	gigawatt
HAMAS	Harakat al-Muqawamma al-Islamiyya (movement of Islamic Resistance)
HE	His/Her Excellency
HF	high frequency
HGV	heavy goods vehicle
HH	His/Her Highness; His/Her Honour; His Holiness
HIH	His/Her Imperial Highness
HIM	His/Her Imperial Majesty
HJS	*hic jacet sepultus* (here lies buried)
HIV	human immunodeficiency virus
HM	His/Her Majesty
HMG	His/Her Majesty's Government
HMI	His/Her Majesty's Inspectorate
HMO	health maintenance organization
HMS	His/Her Majesty's Ship/Service
HMSO	His/Her Majesty's Stationery Office
HNC	Higher National Certificate
HND	Higher National Diploma
HOLMES	Home Office Large Major Enquiry System
Hon	Honorary; Honorable
HOTOL	horizontal take-off and landing
hp	horsepower
HP	hire purchase
HQ	headquarters
HR	House of Representatives
HRH	His/Her Royal Highness
HRT	hormone replacement therapy
HSBC	Hong Kong and Shanghai Banking Corporation
HTML	hypertext markup language
I	Island
IAEA	International Atomic Energy Agency
IATA	International Air Transport Association
IBA	Independent Broadcasting Authority
ibid	*ibidem* (in the same place)
IBM	International Business Machines
IBRD	International Bank for Reconstruction and Development
ICAO	International Civil Aviation Organization
ICBM	intercontinental ballistic missile
ICFTU	International Confederation of Free Trade Unions
ICI	Imperial Chemical Industries
ID	identification
IDA	International Development Agency
ie	*id est* (that is)

IEA	International Energy Agency
IFC	International Finance Corporation
IHS	*Iesus Hominum Salvator* (Jesus the Saviour of Mankind)
ILO	International Labour Organization
ILR	independent local radio
IMF	International Monetary Fund
Inc	Incorporated
INLA	Irish National Liberation Army
INRI	*Iesus Nazarenus Rex Iudeorum* (Jesus of Nazareth, King of the Jews)
inst	instant (current month)
INTELSAT	International Telecommunications Satellite Organization
Interpol	International Criminal Police Commission
IOC	International Olympic Committee
IOU	I owe you
IPA	International Phonetic Alphabet
IQ	intelligence quotient
IRA	Irish Republican Army
IRB	Irish Republican Brotherhood
IRBM	intermediate-range ballistic missile
IRC	International Red Cross
IRS	Internal Revenue Service
Is	Islands
ISA	Individual Savings Account
ISBN	International Standard Book Number
ISDN	integrated services digital network
ISP	Internet service provider
ISSN	International Standard Serial Number
IT	information technology
ITN	Independent Television News
ITV	Independent Television
IUCN	World Conservation Union
IUD	intra-uterine device
IVF	in vitro fertilization
IVR	International Vehicle Registration
IWW	Industrial Workers of the World
JCB	Joseph Cyril Bamford (earth-movers)
JP	Justice of the Peace
JPL	Jet Propulsion Laboratory
KB	Knight Bachelor; Knight of the Bath
KBE	Knight Commander, Order of the British Empire
KC	King's Counsel
KCB	Knight Commander of the Bath
KCMG	Knight Commander Grand Cross, Order of St Michael and St George
KCVO	Knight Commander, Royal Victorian Order
KG	Knight, Order of the Garter
KGB	Komitet Gosudarstvennoye Bezhopaznosti (Committee of State Security)
kHz	kiloHertz
KKK	Ku Klux Klan
KO	knock-out
kPC	kiloparsec
KT	Knight of the Thistle
kW	kilowatt

Abbreviation	Meaning
kWh	kilowatt hour
LA	Los Angeles
Lab	Labour
LAFTA	Latin American Free Trade Association
Lat	latitude
LAUTRO	Life Assurance and Unit Trust Companies
lbw	leg before wicket
lc	lower case (printing)
LCD	liquid-crystal display
LD	Liberal Democrat
LEA	Local Education Authority
LED	light-emitting diode
LIFFE	London International Financial Futures Exchange
Litt D	Doctor of Letters
LLB	Bachelor of Laws
LLD	Doctor of Laws
LLM	Master of Laws
loc cit	*loco citato* (in the place cited)
Londin:	of London (Bishop)
Long	longitude
LPG	liquefied petroleum gas
LSD	lysergic acid diethylamide; *librae, solidi, denarii* (pounds, shillings, and pence)
LSE	London School of Economics and Political Science
Lt	Lieutenant
Ltd	Limited (liability)
LV	luncheon voucher
LW	long wave
M	Monsieur
MA	Master of Arts
MAFF	Ministry of Agriculture, Fisheries and Food
Maj	Major
MASH	Mobile Army Surgical Hospital
max	maximum
MB	Bachelor of Medicine
MBE	Member, Order of the British Empire
MC	Master of Ceremonies; Military Cross
MCC	Marylebone Cricket Club
MCP	male chauvinist pig
MD	Doctor of Medicine; Managing Director
MDMA	methylenedioxymethamphetamine
ME	myalgic encephalomyelitis
MEP	Member of the European Parliament
Mgr	Monsignor
MH	Medal of Honor
MI	Military Intelligence
MIA	missing in action
min	minimum
MIRV	multiple independently targetted re-entry vehicle
MKSA	metre-kilogram-second-ampere
MLITT	Master of Letters

Mlle	Mademoiselle
MLR	minimum lending rate
MM	Military Medal
Mme	Madame
MMF	magnetomotive force
MO	Medical Officer
MOD	Ministry of Defence
MODEM	modulator/demodulator
MORI	Market and Opinion Research International
MOT	Ministry of Transport (certificate)
MP	Member of Parliament; Military Police
mph	miles per hour
M Phil	Master of Philosophy
MOH	Medal of Honor
MPC	megaparsec
MRA	Moral Rearmament
MS	manuscript; multiple sclerosis
MSC	Manpower Services Commission
MSG	monosodium glutamate
MSP	Member of the Scottish Parliament
Mt	million tonnes; Mount
MV	Merchant Vessel; Motor Vessel
MVO	Member, Royal Victorian Order
MW	medium wave
N	north
n/a	not applicable; not available
NAACP	National Association for the Advancement of Coloured People
NAAFI	Navy, Army and Air Force Institutes
NACRO	National Association for the Care and Resettlement of Offenders
NASA	National Aeronautics and Space Administration
NASDA	National Space Development Agency
NB	*nota bene* (note well)
NATO	North Atlantic Treaty Organization
NBA	National Basketball Association
NBC	National Broadcasting Corporation
NCO	non-commissioned officer
NEP	new economic policy
NF	National Front
NFC	National Football Conference
NFL	National Football League
NFT	National Film Theatre
NFU	National Farmers' Union
NGO	non-governmental organization
NHL	National Hockey League
NHRBC	National Home Builders' Registration Council
NHS	National Health Service
NI	National Insurance; Northern Ireland
NICAM	near instantaneously companded audio multiplex
NIMBY	not in my back yard
NIREX	Nuclear Industry Radioactive Waste Disposal Executive
NKVD	Narodnyi Komissariat Vnutrennikh Del (People's Commissariat of Internal Affairs)

Abbreviation	Meaning
NMR	nuclear magnetic resonance
No	*numero* (number)
Norvic:	of Norwich (Bishop)
NRA	National Recovery Administration; National Rifle Association
NSPCC	National Society for the Prevention of Cruelty to Children
NSW	New South Wales
NT	National Theatre; National Trust; New Testament
NUJ	National Union of Journalists
NUM	National Union of Mineworkers
NUS	National Union of Students
NUT	National Union of Teachers
NVQ	National Vocational Qualification
NY	New York
NYC	New York City
NYPD	New York Police Department
NZ	New Zealand
OAP	old age pensioner
OAPEC	Organization of Arab Petroleum Exporting Countries
OAS	Organisation de l'Armée Secrète (Secret Army Organization); Organization of American States
OAU	Organization of African Unity
OB	Order of the Bath; outside broadcast
obit	died
OBE	Officer, Order of the British Empire
OC	Officer Commanding
OCR	optical character recognition/reader
OECD	Organization for Economic Co-operation and Development
OED	Oxford English Dictionary
Offer	Office of Electricity Regulation
Ofgas	Office of Gas Supply
Ofsted	Office for Standards in Education
OFT	Office of Fair Trading
Oftel	Office of Telecommunications
Ofwat	Office of Water Services
OGPU	Otdelenie Gosudarstvenni Politcheskoi Upravi (Special Government Political Administration)
OHMS	On His/Her Majesty's Service
OHP	overhead projector
OM	Order of Merit
ONO	or near offer
op	*opus* (work)
op cit	*opere citato* (in the work cited)
OPEC	Organization of Petroleum Exporting Countries
OS	Old Style (calendar); Ordnance Survey
OT	Old Testament
OTC	Officers' Training Corps; over-the-counter
OU	Open University
OXFAM	Oxford Committee for Famine Relief
Oxon	of Oxford; Oxfordshire
p	page
p	*piano* (softly)

PA	personal assistant
PAC	Pan-African Congress; political action committee
PAYE	pay as you earn
PC	personal computer; Police Constable; politically correct; Privy Counsellor
PCP	phenylcyclohexylpiperidine
PDR	precision depth recorder
PE	Physical Education
PEP	personal equity plan
PF	Patriotic Front
PG	parental guidance (film)
PGA	Professional Golfers' Association
PH	Purple Heart
PhD	Doctor of Philosophy
PIN	personal identification number
pl	plural
PLA	People's Liberation Army
PLC	public limited company
PLO	Palestine Liberation Organization
pm	*post meridiem* (after noon)
PM	Prime Minister
PMT	pre-menstrual tension
PO	Petty Officer; Pilot Officer; Post Office; postal order
POW	prisoner-of-war
pp	pages
PPP	personal pension plan
PPS	Parliamentary Private Secretary
PR	proportional representation; public relations
PRO	Public Record Office; public relations officer
PROM	programmable read-only memory
PSBR	public sector borrowing requirement
PTA	parent-teacher association
Pte	Private
PTFE	polytetrafluoroethylene
PTO	please turn over
PVA	polyvinyl acetate
PVC	polyvinyl chloride
PWA	Public Works Administration
PWR	pressurized-water reactor
PYO	pick-your-own
QC	Queen's Counsel
QCD	quantum chromodynamics
QED	quantum electrodynamics; *quod erat demonstrandum* (which was to be proved)
quango	quasi-autonomous non-governmental organization
qv	*quod vide* (which see)
RA	Royal Academy
RAAF	Royal Australian Air Force
RAC	Royal Armoured Corps; Royal Automobile Club
RADA	Royal Academy of Dramatic Art
RAF	Royal Air Force
RAM	random access memory; Royal Academy of Music
RAMC	Royal Army Medical Corps

Abbreviation	Meaning
RAN	Royal Australian Navy
RBS	Royal Society of British Sculptors
RC	Red Cross; Roman Catholic
RCM	Royal College of Music
RDA	recommended daily allowance
RE	religious education; Royal Engineers
REM	rapid eye movement
REME	Royal Electrical and Mechanical Engineers
Rep	Representative; Republican
Rev	Reverend
RFU	Rugby Football Union
RGN	Registered General Nurse
RGS	Royal Geographical Society
RHA	Regional Health Authority
RHS	Royal Horticultural Society
RI	Royal Institution
RIP	*requiescat in pace* (rest in peace)
RL	Rugby League
RM	Royal Marines
RMS	root mean square
RN	Royal Navy
RNA	ribonucleic acid
RNIB	Royal National Institute for the Blind
RNID	Royal National Institite for Deaf People
RNLI	Royal National Lifeboat Institution
RNR	Royal Naval Reserve
RNVR	Royal Naval Volunteer Reserve
ROM	read-only memory
RORO	roll-on, roll-off (ferry)
RoSPA	Royal Society for the Prevention of Accidents
RP	received pronunciation
RPG	rocket propelled grenade
RPI	retail price index
RPM	resale price maintenance; revolutions per minute
RRP	recommended retail price
RS	Royal Society
RSA	Royal Society of Arts
RSPB	Royal Society for the Protection of Birds
RSC	Royal Shakespeare Company
RSI	repetitive strain injury
RSM	Regimental Sergeant Major
RSPCA	Royal Society for the Prevention of Cruelty to Animals
RSVP	*répondez s'il vous plaît* (please reply)
RTA	road traffic accident
RU	Rugby Union
RUC	Royal Ulster Constabulary
RVO	Royal Victorian Order
s	second
S	south
SA	Sturm Abteilung (Storm Troopers)
SAE	stamped addressed envelope

SALT	Strategic Arms Limitation Talks
SAM	surface-to-air missile
SAS	Special Air Service
SAT	scholastic aptitude test
SBS	Special Boat Squadron
SDI	strategic defence initiative
SDP	Social Democratic Party
SDR	special drawing rights
SEAQ	Stock Exchange Automated Quotations
SEATO	South-East Asia Treaty Organization
SEN	State Enrolled Nurse
SERPS	state earnings-related pension scheme
SHAEF	Supreme Headquarters Allied Expeditionary Force
SHAPE	Supreme Headquarters Allied Powers, Europe
SHF	super-high frequency
SI	Système International (International System)
SIB	Securities and Investments Board
SLR	single-lens reflex
SNP	Scottish National Party
SOE	Special Operations Executive
SONAR	sound navigation and ranging
SOR	sale or return
SOS	Save Our Souls
SRN	State Registered Nurse
SRO	self-regulatory organization; single room occupancy
SS	Schutzstaffel (Protective Squad)
SSR	Soviet Socialist Republic
SSSI	Site of Special Scientific Interest
START	Strategic Arms Reduction Talks
STB	set top box
STD	sexually transmitted disease; subscriber trunk dialling
STOL	short take-off and landing
Sub Lt	Sub-Lieutenant
SW	short wave
SWAPO	South-West Africa People's Organization
SWF	single white female
TA	Territorial Army
TASS	Telegrafnoe Agentsvo Sovetskovo Soyuza (Telegraph Agency of the Soviet Union)
TB	tuberculosis
TBA	to be announced
TCP	trichlorophenylmethyliodialicyl
TES	Times Educational Supplement
TGV	Transport and General Workers' Union
TGWU	train à grande vitesse (high-speed train)
TLS	Times Literary Supplement
TNT	trinitrotoluene
TSB	Trustee Savings Bank
TT	Tourist Trophy
TUC	Trades Union Congress
TV	television
TVA	Tennessee Valley Authority

Abbreviation	Meaning
TVP	textured vegetable protein
TWOC	taking without owner's consent
TXT	text file
UAE	United Arab Emirates
uc	upper case (printing)
UCCA	University Central Council on Admissions
UDA	Ulster Defence Association
UDI	Unilateral Declaration of Independence
UEFA	Union of European Football Associations
UFO	unidentified flying object
UHF	ultra-high frequency
UHT	ultra-high temperature
UK	United Kingdom
UKAEA	United Kingdom Atomic Energy Authority
UN	United Nations
UNCTAD	United Nations Conference on Trade and Development
UNESCO	United Nations Economic, Scientific and Cultural Organization
UNHCR	United Nations High Commission for Refugees
UNICEF	United Nations Children's Fund
UNO	United Nations Organization
UNRWA	United Nations Relief and Works Agency for Palestine Refugees in the Near East
UNSC	United Nations Security Council
USA	United States of America
USAF	United States Air Force
USS	United States Ship
USSR	Union of Soviet Socialist Republics
UV	ultra-violet
UVF	Ulster Volunteer Force
UBX	unexploded bomb
v	versus
VAT	value-added tax
VC	Victoria Cross
VCR	video cassette recorder
VD	venereal disease
VDU	visual display unit
VHF	very high frequency
VHS	video home system
VIP	very important person
VLF	very low frequency
VSO	Voluntary Service Overseas
VTOL	vertical take-off and landing
VTR	video tape recorder
W	west
WAAC	Women's Auxiliary Army Corps
WAAF	Women's Auxiliary Air Force
WAC	Women's Army Corps
WASP	white Anglo-Saxon protestant
WBA	World Boxing Association
WBC	World Boxing Council
WCC	World Council of Churches

WEA	Workers' Educational Association
WEU	Western European Union
WHO	World Health Organization
WI	Women's Institute
WMO	World Meteorological Organization
WO	Warrant Officer
WRAC	Women's Royal Army Corps
WRAF	Women's Royal Air Force
WRNS	Women's Royal Naval Service
WRVS	Women's Royal Voluntary Service
WTO	World Trade Organization
WVS	Women's Voluntary Service
WWF	World Wildlife Fund
www	world wide web
WYSIWYG	what you see is what you get
YHA	Youth Hostels Association
YMCA	Young Men's Christian Association
YWCA	Young Women's Christian Association
YUPPIE	young upwardly mobile professional

Collective nouns

Subject	Collective noun
Actors	Cast/company/troupe
Aeroplanes	Flight/squadron
Angels	Host
Antelopes	Herd
Arrows	Sheaf
Asses	Herd/pace
Badgers	Cete
Bears	Sloth
Bees	Grist/swarm
Bells	Peal
Birds	Congregation/flock/flight/volery
Bitterns	Sedge/siege
Bishops	Bench
Boars	Singular
Bowls	Set
Bread	Batch
Cards	Deck/pack
Cars	Fleet
Cattle	Drove/herd
Chickens	Brood
Choughs	Chattering
Coots	Covert
Cranes	Herd/sedge/siege
Cricketers	Eleven
Crows	Murder
Cubs	Litter
Curlews	Herd

Subject	Collective noun
Dancers	Troupe
Deer	Herd
Doves	Flight
Ducks	Paddling/team
Eggs	Clutch
Elks	Gang
Ferrets	Fesnyng
Fishes	Catch/draught/haul/run/shoal
Flies	Swarm
Flowers	Bouquet/bunch/nosegay/posy
Foxes	Skulk
Geese	Gaggle/skein
Girls	Bevy
Gnats	Cloud/swarm
Goats	Herd/tribe
Goldfinches	Charm
Golf-clubs	Set
Grapes	Bunch/cluster
Grouse	Covey/pack
Gulls	Colony
Hares	Down/husk
Hawks	Cast
Hens	Brood
Herons	Sedge/siege
Herrings	Glean/shoal
Horses	Drove/herd
Hounds	Mute/pack
Insects	Swarm
Kangaroos	Troop
Kittens	Kindle
Labourers	Gang
Larks	Exaltation
Leopards	Leap
Lions	Pride
Magistrates	Bench
Mares	Stud
Minstrels	Troupe
Moles	Labour
Monkeys	Troop
Musicians	Band/orchestra
Nightingales	Watch
Onions	Rope
Oxen	Drove/herd/team/yoke
Partridges	Covey
Peacocks	Muster
Pearls	Rope/string
Pigs	Litter
Pheasants	Nide/nye
Plovers	Congregation/wing
Porpoises	School
Pups	Litter

Quails	Bevy
Rabbits	Nest
Rags	Bundle
Rooks	Building/clamour
Runners	Field
Sailors	Crew
Sails	Suit
Seals	Herd/pod
Sheep	Flock
Ships	Fleet/flotilla/squadron
Sparrows	Host
Starlings	Murmuration
Stars	Cluster/constellation
Steps	Flight
Swans	Bevy/herd
Swifts	Flock
Swine	Drift/sounder
Teals	Spring
Trees	Clump
Whales	Gam/pod/school
Wolves	Herd/pack/rout
Woodcock	Fall
Worshippers	Congregation

Collectors and enthusiasts

Name	Interest
Aerophilatelist	Airmail stamps
Ailurophile	Cats
Antiquary	Antiquities
Arachnologist	Spiders
Arctophile	Teddy bears
Argyrothecologist	Money boxes
Audiophile	Sound reproduction, recordings and broadcasts
Balletomane	Ballet
Bibliomane	Collecting books
Bibliopegist	Bookbinding
Bibliophile	Books
Cagophilist	Keys
Campanologist	Bell-ringing
Canophilist/cynophilist	Dogs
Cartophilist	Cigarette and chewing-gum cards
Coleopterist	Beetles
Conchologist	Shells
Copoclephilist	Key-rings
Cruciverbamorist	Crossword puzzles
Cumyxaphilist	Matchboxes
Deltiologist	Picture postcards
Ecclesiologist	Churches
Egger	Birds' eggs

Name	Interest
Entomologist	Insects
Ephemerist	Diary or journal keeping
Epicure	Good food and drink
Errinophilist	Stamps (other than postage stamps)
Ex-librist	Bookplates
Fusilatelist	Phonecards
Gastronome	Good eating
Gemmologist	Gems
Gourmet	Good food and drink
Herpetologist	Reptiles
Hippophile	Horses
Hostelaphilist	Pub signs
Iconophilist	Engravings, prints, pictures etc.
Incunabulist	Early printed books
Labeorphilist	Beer bottle labels
Lepidopterist	Butterflies and moths
Medallist	Medals
Monarchist	Monarchy
Myrmecologist	Ants
Notaphilist	Banknotes
Numismatist	Coins and medals
Oenophile	Wine
Omnibologist	Buses
Ophiophilist	Snakes
Orchidophilist	Orchids
Ornithologist	Birds
Paroemographer	Proverbs
Peridromophilist	Transport tickets
Philatelist	Postage stamps
Phillumenist	Matchbox labels
Philologist	Learning and literature
Philometrist	Envelopes with postmarks
Phonophilist	Gramophone records
Plangonologist	Dolls
Pteridophilist	Ferns
Sericulturist	Silkworms
Speleologist	Caves
Steganographist	Cryptography
Stegophilist	Climbing buildings
Tegestologist	Beer-mats
Ufologist	UFOs
Vexillologist	Flags

First name choices

England and Wales

	Boys	Girls
	1700	
1	John	Mary
2	William	Elizabeth
3	Thomas	Ann
4	Richard	Sarah
5	James	Jane
6	Robert	Margaret
7	Joseph	Susan
8	Edward	Martha
9	Henry	Hannah
10	George	Catherine
	1800	
1	William	Mary
2	John	Ann
3	Thomas	Elizabeth
4	James	Sarah
5	George	Jane
6	Joseph	Hannah
7	Richard	Susan
8	Henry	Martha
9	Robert	Margaret
10	Charles	Charlotte
	1900	
1	William	Florence
2	John	Mary
3	George	Alice
4	Thomas	Annie
5	Charles	Elsie
6	Frederick	Edith
7	Arthur	Elizabeth
8	James	Doris
9	Albert	Dorothy
10	Ernest	Ethel
	1920s	
1	John	Joan
2	William	Mary
3	George	Joyce
4	James	Margaret
5	Ronald	Dorothy
6	Robert	Doris
7	Kenneth	Kathleen
8	Frederick	Irene
9	Thomas	Betty
10	Albert	Eileen

	1950s	
1	David	Susan
2	John	Linda
3	Peter	Christine
4	Michael	Margaret
5	Alan	Carol
6	Robert	Jennifer
7	Stephen	Janet
8	Paul	Patricia
9	Brian	Barbara
10	Graham	Ann

	1960s	
1	Paul	Tracey
2	David	Deborah
3	Andrew	Julie
4	Stephen	Karen
5	Mark	Susan
6	Michael	Alison
7	Ian	Jacqueline
8	Gary	Helen
9	Robert	Amanda
10	Richard	Sharon

	1970s	
1	Stephen	Claire
2	Mark	Sarah
3	Paul	Nicola
4	Andrew	Emma
5	David	Joanne
6	Richard	Helen
7	Matthew	Rachel
8	Daniel	Lisa
9	Christopher	Rebecca
10	Darren	Karen Michelle

	1980s	
1	Christopher	Sarah
2	Matthew	Claire
3	David	Emma
4	James	Laura
5	Daniel	Rebecca
6	Andrew	Gemma
7	Steven	Rachel
8	Michael	Kelly
9	Mark	Victoria
10	Paul	Katharine

	1990s	
1	Daniel	Emma
2	Matthew	Sarah
3	James	Laura
4	Christopher	Charlotte
5	Adam	Amy
6	Thomas	Rebecca
7	David	Gemma
8	Luke	Katharine
9	Jamie	Lauren
10	Robert	Hayley

USA

	Boys	Girls
	1900	
1	John	Mary
2	William	Ruth
3	Charles	Helen
4	Robert	Margaret
5	Joseph	Elizabeth
6	James	Dorothy
7	George	Catherine
8	Samuel	Mildred
9	Thomas	Frances
10	Arthur	Alice
		Marion

	1920s	
1	Robert	Mary
2	John	Barbara
3	William	Dorothy
4	James	Betty
5	Charles	Ruth
6	Richard	Margaret
7	George	Helen
8	Donald	Elizabeth
9	Joseph	Jean
10	Edward	Ann

	1950s	
1	Robert	Linda
2	Michael	Mary
3	James	Patricia
4	John	Susan
5	David	Deborah
6	William	Kathleen
7	Thomas	Barbara
8	Richard	Nancy
9	Gary	Sharon
10	Charles	Karen

	1970s	
1	Michael	Michelle
2	Robert	Jennifer
3	David	Kimberly
4	James	Lisa
5	John	Tracy
6	Jeffrey	Kelly
7	Steven	Nicole
8	Christopher	Angela
9	Brian	Pamela
10	Mark	Christine

	1990s (Whites)		**(Non-Whites)**	
1	Michael	Ashley	Michael	Brittany
2	Christopher	Jessica	Christopher	Ashley
3	Matthew	Amanda	Brandon	Jasmine
4	Joshua	Sarah	James	Jessica
5	Andrew	Brittany	Anthony	Tiffany
6	Daniel	Megan	Joshua	Erica
7	Justin	Jennifer	Robert	Crystal
8	David	Nicole	David	Danielle
9	Ryan	Stephanie	Brian	Christina
10	John	Katherine	Jonathan	Alicia

Australia

	Boys	Girls
	1950s	
1	John	Susan
2	Peter	Margaret
3	Michael	Anne
4	David	Elizabeth
5	Robert	Christine
6	Stephen	Jennifer
7	Paul	Judith
8	Philip	Patricia
9	Christopher	Catherine
10	Ian	Helen

	1970s	
1	Matthew	Michelle
2	Andrew	Catherine
3	David	Kylie
4	Michael	Nicole
5	Paul	Rebecca
6	Adam	Melissa
7	Christopher	Lisa
8	Daniel	Belinda
9	Mark	Rachel
10	Scott	Sarah

	1990s	
1	Matthew	Jessica
2	Daniel	Sarah
3	Michael	Emma
4	Thomas	Lauren
5	Benjamin	Rebecca
6	James	Ashleigh
7	Samuel	Amy
8	Nicholas	Emily
9	Joshua	Kate
10	Christopher	Katherine

5.3 *Social Structure*

Ranks of the aristocracy

England	France	Holy Roman Empire (Germany)	Italy	Spain
King	Roi	Kaiser	Re	Rey
Prince	Prince	Herzog	Duca	Duque
Duke	Duc	Pfalzgraf	Principe	Principe
Marquess	Marquis	Markgraf	Marchese	Marques
Earl	Comte	Landgraf	Conde	Conde
Viscount	Vicomte		Visconte	Vizconde
Baron			Barone	
Baronet				
Knight	Chevalier	Ritter	Cavaliere	Caballero

Honours

Honour	Date instituted	Notes
Denmark		
Order of the Dannebrog	1219	For general merit
Order of the Elephant	1462	Premier order of Denmark
France		
Croix de Guerre	1915	Military decoration
Légion d'Honneur	1802	For civil or military service
Germany		
Iron Cross	1813	Military decoration
Pour le Mérite	1740	Divided into eight classes

Honour	Date instituted	Notes
Italy		
Al Merita della Republica Italiana	1952	Divided into five classes
Japan		
Order of the Chrysanthemum	1877	Highest order of Japan (males only)
Order of the Paulownia Sun	1888	For outstanding military and civil merit (males only)
Order of the Rising Sun	1875	For outstanding military or civil merit
Netherlands		
Order of the House of Orange	1905	For service to the Royal House
Military Order of William	1815	Highest military decoration (also awarded to civilians)
Netherlands Lion	1815	For patriotism and outstanding devotion to duty
UK		
Order of the Bath	1725	Three divisions: Knight or Dame Grand Cross (GCB), Knight or Dame Commander (KCB or DCB), and Companion (CB)
Order of the British Empire	1917	Five orders: Knight or Dame Grand Cross (GBE), Knight or Dame Commander (KBE or DBE), Commander (CBE), Officer (OBE), and Member (MBE)
Order of the Companions of Honour (CH)	1917	For services to the nation
Distinguished Service Order (DSO)	1886	Military service order
Order of the Garter	c. 1344–51	The oldest order of chivalry
George Cross (GC)	1940	For acts of great heroism
Imperial Service Order	1902	Awarded to members of the civil service
Order of Merit (OM)	1902	For distinguished military or civil service
Royal Victorian Order (RVO)	1896	For service to the sovereign. Five orders: Knight or Dame Grand Cross (GCVO), Knight or Dame Commander (KCVO or DCVO), Commander (CVO), Lieutenant (LVO), and Member (MVO)
Order of St Michael and St George	1818	For service abroad. Three classes: Knight Grand Cross (GCMG), Knight Commander (KCMG), and Companion (CMG)
Order of the Thistle	c. 1460–88	Scottish order of chivalry
Victoria Cross (VC)	1856	Highest military decoration
USA		
Bronze Star	1944	Military decoration for service beyond the call of duty
Congressional Medal of Honor	1862	Highest military decoration
Distinguished Service Cross	1918	Army decoration for extraordinary heroism
Legion of Merit	1942	For distinguished service in peace and war

Medal for Merit	1942	Awarded to civilians for service in peace or war
Presidential Medal of Freedom	1963	Highest civilian peacetime decoration
Purple Heart	1782	For wounds received in military action
Silver Star	World War I	Military decoration taking precedence over Legion of Merit

Order of postnominal initials

Order	Initials
1	Orders and decorations conferred by the Crown
2	Appointments to the Queen
3	University degrees
4	Religious orders
5	Medical qualifications
6	Fellowships of learned societies
7	Royal academies of art
8	Fellowships of professional institutions, associations
9	Writers to the Signet
10	Appointments
11	Memberships of the armed forces

Forms of address

Rank	Envelope address	Letter opening	Spoken address
Ambassador	His/Her Excellency the Ambassador of — (or 'His/Her Excellency the — Ambassador')	Your Excellency (thereafter, 'Your Excellency' once and then 'you')	Your Excellency (thereafter, 'Sir/Madam' or by name)
Archbishop (Anglican)	The Most Reverend Lord Archbishop of —	My Lord Archbishop (or 'Dear Archbishop')	Your Grace (or 'My Lord Archbishop')
Archbishop (US)	The Most Reverend —, Archbishop of —	Your excellency	Your Grace
Archbishop (Roman Catholic)	His Grace the Archbishop of —	My Lord Archbishop	Your Grace
Archdeacon	The Venerable the Archdeacon of —	Dear Archdeacon (or 'Venerable Sir')	Archdeacon (or 'Venerable Sir')
Baron	The Right Hon. the Lord —	My Lord	My Lord
Baron's wife	The Right Hon. the Lady S—	Dear Madam	Madam
Baroness (in her own right)	The Right Hon. the Lady S— (or 'The Right Hon. the Baroness S—)	Dear Madam	Madam
Baronet	Sir F— S—, Bt	Dear Sir	Sir F—
Baronet's wife	Lady S—	Dear Madam	Madam
Bishop (Anglican)	The Right Reverend the Lord Bishop of —	Dear Bishop (or 'My Lord')	Bishop (or 'My Lord')

Rank	Envelope address	Letter opening	Spoken address
Bishop (Episcopal Church in Scotland)	The Right Reverend F— S—, Bishop of — (or 'The Right Reverend the Lord Bishop of — ')	Dear Bishop (or 'My Lord', or 'Right Reverend Sir')	Bishop (or 'My Lord')
Bishop (Roman Catholic)	His Lordship the Bishop of — (or 'The Right Reverend F— S— Bishop of —')	My Lord (or 'My Lord Bishop')	My Lord (or 'My Lord Bishop')
Bishop (Roman Catholic, US)	The Most Reverend F— S—, Bishop of —	Most Reverend Sir (or 'Your Excellency')	Bishop (or 'My Lord')
Bishop (other, US)	The Reverend F— S—	Reverend Sir	Bishop (or 'My Lord')
Canon (Anglican)	The Reverend Canon F— S—	Dear Canon (or 'Dear Canon S—')	Canon (or 'Canon S—')
Canon (Roman Catholic)	The Very Reverend Canon F— S—	Very Reverend Sir	Canon S—
Cardinal	His Eminence Cardinal S—	Your Eminence (or 'My Lord Cardinal')	Your Eminence
Cardinal (US)	His Eminence F— Cardinal S—	Your Eminence (or 'My Lord Cardinal')	Your Eminence
Clergy (Anglican)	The Reverend F— S—	Dear Sir (or 'Dear Mr S—')	Reverend
Clergy (Roman Catholic)	The Reverend F— S—	Dear Reverend Father	Father
Congressman/woman	The Honorable F— S— (or 'Honorable F— S—')	Dear Sir (or 'Dear Mr S—')	Mr/Mrs/Miss
Countess	The Right Hon. the Countess of —	Dear Madam	Madam
Dean (Anglican)	The Very Reverend the Dean of —	Dear Dean (or 'Very Reverend Sir')	Dean (or 'Very Reverend Sir')
Doctor	Dr S— (or 'Doctor S—')	Dear Doctor	Doctor
Duchess	Her Grace the Duchess of —	Dear Madam	Your Grace
Duke	His Grace the Duke of —	My Lord Duke	Your Grace
Earl	The Right Hon. the Earl of —	My Lord	My Lord
Governor of a colony/Governor-General	His Excellency, Governor of — (or 'His Excellency, Governor-General of —')	Dear Governor (or 'Dear Governor-General')	Your Excellency
Governor (US state)	The Honorable F— S—, Governor of —	Sir/Madam	Governor S—
Judge (High Court)	The Hon. Mr/Mrs Justice S—	Dear Sir/Madam (or 'My Lord/Lady')	Sir/Madam (or, in court, 'My Lord/Lady' or 'Your Lordship/Ladyship')
Judge (Circuit)	His/Her Honour Judge S—	Dear Sir/Madam	Sir/Madam (or, in court, 'Your Honour')
Judge (US, federal)	The Honorable F— S—, Judge of the United States District Court of the — District of —	Sir/Madam	Judge S—
Knight Bachelor	Sir F— S—	Dear Sir	Sir F—
Knight's wife	Lady S—	Dear Madam	Madam
Lady Mayoress	The Lady Mayoress of —	My Lady Mayoress	Lady Mayoress

Lord Mayor	The Right Hon. the Lord Mayor of — (or 'The Right Worshipful the Lord Mayor of —')	My Lord Mayor	Lord Mayor
Marchioness	The Most Hon. the Marchioness of —	Dear Madam	Madam
Marquess	The Most Hon. the Marquess of —	My Lord	My Lord
Mayor	The Worshipful the Mayor of — (or, in some cases, 'The Right Worshipful' or, in the USA, 'The Honorable')	Mr Mayor (or 'Dear Sir')	Mr Mayor
Mayoress	The Mayoress of —	Madam Mayor (or 'Madam Mayoress')	Mayoress (or 'Madam Mayor')
Monsignor	The Reverend Monsignor F— S—	Reverend Sir	Monsignor S—
Pope	His Holiness, the Pope	Your Holiness (or 'Most Holy Father')	Your Holiness
President of the USA	The President	Mr President	Mr President
Prince	His Royal Highness the Prince F— (or, if a Duke, 'His Royal Highness the Duke of —'; otherwise, 'His Royal Highness Prince F— of —')	Sir	Your Royal Highness (thereafter, 'Sir')
Princess	Her Royal Highness the Princess F— (or, if a Duchess, 'Her Royal Highness the Duchess of —'; otherwise, 'Her Royal Highness Princess F— of —')	Madam	Your Royal Highness (thereafter, 'Ma'am')
Privy Counsellor	The Right Hon. F— S— (or, if a peer, 'The Right Hon. the Earl of —, PC')	(According to rank)	(According to rank)
Professor	Professor	Dear Sir/Madam	(According to rank)
Queen	Her Majesty the Queen	Madam, with my humble duty	Your majesty (thereafter, 'Ma'am')
Rabbi	Rabbi (initial of forename) S—	Dear Sir	Rabbi S—
Secretary of State	The Right Hon. F— S—, MP (or 'The Secretary of State for —')	Dear Sir/Madam	Sir/Madam
Senator	The Honorable F— S—	Dear Sir (or 'Dear Senator')	Senator
Viscount	The Right Hon. the Viscount —	My Lord	My Lord
Viscountess	The Right Hon. the Viscountess —	Dear Madam	Madam

Note F = forename; S = surname

Heraldry

Terms

Term	Meaning
Achievement	A complete armorial display, comprising a shield, helmet, crest, torse, mantling, and motto
Base	The lowest part of a shield
Billet	An oblong figure
Billette	A field with an irregular arrangement of ten or more billets
Blazon	To describe the design of arms of a whole achievement
Charges	Heraldic symbols and signs
Chevron	An inverted V-shaped stripe
Chief	The top third of a shield
Compartment	The ground on which supporters stand
Crest	An object placed on top of a helmet and bound to it by a wreath of colours
Dexter side	The right-hand side of a shield
Escutcheon	The shield on which a coat of arms is displayed
Fess point	The central part of a shield
Field	The basic background colour of a shield
Helmet	A helmet placed on top of a shield
Honour point	The part of a shield below the chief
Impalement	The division of a shield by a straight line
Inescutcheon	A smaller shield design placed inside the main shield
Lozenge	A parallelogram
Lozengy	A field divided by diagonal lines
Mascle	A lozenge voided
Mantling or lambrequin	The drapery suspended from the helmet, usually in the main colour of the shield
Nombril point	The part of a shield between the fess point and the base
Ordinaries	Basic charges
Orle	An inner border not touching the edge of a shield
Party per fess	A field divided by a horizontal line
Party per pale	A field divided by a perpendicular line
Pile	An inverted pyramid
Quartering	The division of a shield into four parts
Roundel	A circular symbol
Shield	A coat of arms
Sinister side	The left-hand side of a shield
Supporters	Animals or figures placed on either side of a shield
Tressure	A smaller version of an orle

Tinctures

Colours

Azure	Blue
Gules	Red
Proper	An animal or object displayed in its natural colours
Purpure	Purple
Sable	Black
Vert	Green

Stains

Murrey	Mulberry or maroon
Tenné	Tawny orange
Sanguine	Blood-coloured red

Metals

Or	Gold
Argent	Silver

Furs

Ermine	White field with black spots
Ermines	Black field with white spots
Erminois	Gold field with black spots
Pean	Black field with gold spots
Vair	Blue and white

Heraldic animals

Term	Posture
Addorsed	Animals placed back to back
Affronté	Whole body facing forwards
Close	With wings folded
Combattant	Two animals fighting on their hindlegs
Couchant	Lying down
Displayed	With wings extended
Dormant	Sleeping
At gaze	Looking full face
Passant	Walking, usually with one foot raised
Rampant	On hind legs
Rampant guardant	Full-faced, on hind legs
Reguardant	Looking back
Rising	With wings raised
Salient	Springing up with both feet on the ground
Sejant	Sitting
Statant	Standing
Trippant	At a trot, with one foot raised

Scottish clans

Clan	Clan seat
Brodie	Brodie Castle, Forres
Bruce	Clackmannan Tower, Alloa/Broomhall, Fife
Buchanan	Buchanan Castle, Drymen
Cameron	Achnacarry, Spean Bridge
Campbell of Lochow	Inverary Castle, Argyll/Ardchonnel Castle, Loch Awe
Campbell of Breadalbane	Kilchurn Castle, Loch Awe
Campbell of Cawdor	Cawdor Castle, Nairnshire
Campbell of Loudoun	
Chisholm	Erchless Castle/Comer, Strathglass
Colquhoun	Rossdhu, Luss, Dunbartonshire/Luss Barony, Dunbartonshire
Crawfurd	Auchinames, Lanarkshire
Cumming	Altyre, Forres/Durdargue Castle and Inverallochy, Fraserburgh

Clan	Clan seat
Cunningham	Kilmaurs
Davidson	Tulloch Castle, Dingwall/Cantray, Inverness
Douglas	Douglas Castle, Lanarkshire/Tantallon Castle, East Lothian
Drummond	Castle-Drummond, Crieff/Stobhall, Perthshire
Dundas	Dundas Castle, South Queensferry/Inchgarvie, Firth of Forth
Elliot	Redheugh, Roxburghshire/Larriston Tower
Erskine	Alloa Tower, Clackmannan/Erskine, Renfrewshire
Farquharson	Invercauld Castle and Braemar Castle, Aberdeenshire
Fergusson	Kilkerran Tower, Ayrshire/Glenshellich in Strachur, Argyll
Forbes	Castle-Forbes and Drumminor Castle, Aberdeenshire
Fraser of Lovat	Castle-Fraser, Sauchen/Caernbulg Castle, Philorth, Aberdeenshire/Beaufort Castle, Beauly
Gordon	Huntly Castle, Huntly/Aboyne Castle, Aboyne, Aberdeenshire
Graham of Montrose	Mugdock Castle, Stirlingshire/Dundaff Hills, West Stirlingshire
Graham of Menteith	Inchtalla Castle, Lake of Menteith
Grant	Castle-Grant, Grantown-on-Spey
Gunn	Clyth Castle, Caithness
Hamilton	Cadzow Castle
Hay	Mote of Erroll, Perthshire/Old Slains Castle, Aberdeenshire
Home	Home Castle, Berwickshire
Innes	Innes, Elgin, Moray/Motte of Innes, Moray/Edder-Innes, Garmouth
Johnston	Lochwood Tower, Dumfries
Kennedy	Cassillis House, Maybole/Culzean Castle, Ayrshire
Kerr	Ferniehirst Castle, Jedburgh
Lamont	Ardlamont, Argyll/Castle Toward
Leslie	Leslie Castle, Aberdeenshire/Rothes Castle, Moray/ Ballinbreich Castle and Leslie-on-Leven, Fife
Lindsay	Balcarres, Colinsburgh/Ochterutherstruther Castle, Fife/ Finhaven Castle, Angus
MacAlistair	Menstrie Castle, Stirling
MacAlpine	
MacArthur	Tirracladdich on Loch Awe, Argyll
Macaulay	Ardincaple Castle, Row, Dunbartonshire
MacBain	Kinchyle, Inverness
Macbeth	
Macdonald	Dunscaith Castle, Skye/Armadale Castle, Skye/Ostaig Castle, Skye
Macdonald of Clanranald	Ellan Tirrim Castle, Knoydart, Inverness
Macdonald of Sleat	Duntulm Castle, Skye
MacDougall	Dunollie Castle, Oban/Gylen Castle, Kerrera, Argyll
Macduff	Duff House, Banff/Keithmore, Dufftown, Banffshire
MacEwan	
Macfarlane	Arrochar
Macfie	Isle of Colonsay
MacGillivray	Dunmaghlass, Inverness
MacGregor	Edinchip, Balquhidder/Glenstrae
MacInnes	Kinlochaline Castle, Morvern, Argyll
Macintyre	

Mackay	House of Tongue, Sutherland
MacKenzie	Brahan Castle, Urray, Rosshire/Eilean Donan Castle, Lochalsh
Mackinlay	
Mackinnon	Strathardal, Skye
Mackintosh	Moy Hall, Inverness/Dunauchton
MacLachlan	Castle-Lachlan, Strathlachlan, Argyll
Maclaine	Lochbuie Castle, Mull, Argyll
MacLaren	Auchleskine and Achtow, Balquhidder, Perthshire
Maclean of Duart	Duart Castle, Mull
Maclennan or Logan	Drumderfit, Rosshire
MacLeod of MacLeod	Dunvegan Castle, Skye
MacLeod of Lewis	Stornoway Castle, Lewis/Assynt, Rosshire
Macmillan	Knapdale
Macnab	Kinnell, Killin, Perthshire/Bovain, Perthshire
MacNaughten	Dunderawe, Argyll
MacNeil of Barra	Kismull Castle, Isle of Barra
McNeill of Gigha	Isles of Gigha and Colonsay/Castle-Sweyn, Knapdale
MacNicol or Nicolson	Scorrybreac House, Skye
Macpherson	Cluny-in-Badenoch, Kingussie
Macquarrie	Isle of Ulva
Macqueen	Corrybrough, Strathdearn, Inverness
Macrae	Inverinate, Inverness
MacTavish	Dunardry, Argyll
Malcolm or Maccallum	Poltalloch, Argyll
Matheson	
Maxwell	Caerlaverock Castle, Dumfriesshire
Menzies	Castle-Menzies, Weem, Aberfeldy
Morrison	Duneystein Castle, Isle of Lewis/Dun of Pabbay-of-Tarbert, Harris
Munro	Foulis Castle, Evanton, Rosshire
Murray of Atholl	Blair Castle, Blair Atholl, Perthshire/Tullibardine, Perthshire/ Duffus Castle, Elgin
Ogilvy	Airlie Castle and Cortachy Castle, Angus
Ramsay	Dalhousie Castle, Midlothian
Robertson	Dunalastair, Perthshire/Rannoch Barracks, Perthshire
Rose	Kilravock Castle, Gollanfield
Ross	Balnagowan Castle, Rosshire/Delny, Rosshire/Pitcalnie, Tain
Scott	Branxholm Castle, Hawick
Sinclair	Girnigoe Castle, Wick/Brawl Castle, Caithness/Roslin Castle, Midlothian/Ravensheugh Castle, Dysart, Fife
Skene	Skene House, Aberdeenshire/Hallyards Castle, Fife
Stewart	Castle-Stalcaire, Appin, Argyll
Sutherland	Dunrobin Castle, Sutherland
Urquhart	Castle-Craig, Urquhart, Black Isle

Ranks in the armed forces

	Navy	Army	Air Force
France			
1	Amiral	Général d'Armée	Général d'Armée Aérienne
2	Vice-Amiral d'Escadre	Général de Corps d'Armée	Général de Corps Aérien
3	Vice-Amiral	Général de Division	Général de Division Aérienne
4	Contre-Amiral	Général de Brigade	Général de Brigade Aérienne
5	Capitaine de Vaisseau	Colonel	Colonel
6	Capitaine de Frégate	Lieutenant-Colonel	Lieutenant-Colonel
7	Capitaine de Corvette	Commandant	Commandant
8	Lieutenant de Vaisseau	Capitaine	Capitaine
9	Enseigne de Vaisseau de 1ème classe	Lieutenant	Lieutenant
10	Enseigne de 2ème classe	Sous-Lieutenant	Sous-Lieutenant
Germany			
1	Admiral	General	General
2	Vizeadmiral	Generalleutnant	Generalleutnant
3	Konteradmiral	Generalmajor	Generalmajor
4	Flotillenadmiral	Brigadegeneral	Brigadegeneral
5	Kapitän zur See	Oberst	Oberst
6	Fregattenkapitän	Oberstleutnant	Oberstleutnant
7	Korvettenkapitän	Major	Major
8	Kapitänleutnant	Hauptmann	Hauptmann
9	Oberleutnant zur See	Oberleutnant	Leutnant
10	Leutnant zur See	Leutnant	Oberfähnrich
UK			
1	Admiral of the Fleet	Field Marshal	Marshal of the RAF
2	Admiral (Adm.)	General (Gen.)	Air Chief Marshal
3	Vice-Admiral (Vice-Adm.)	Lieutenant-General (Lt.-Gen.)	Air Marshal
4	Rear-Admiral (Rear-Adm.)	Major-General (Maj.-Gen.)	Air Vice-Marshal
5	Commodore (Cdre)	Brigadier (Brig.)	Air Commodore (Air Cdre)
6	Captain (Capt.)	Colonel (Col.)	Group Captain (Gp Capt)
7	Commander (Cdr.)	Lieutenant-Colonel (Lt.-Col.)	Wing Commander (Wg Cdr.)
8	Lieutenant-Commander (Lt.-Cdr.)	Major (Maj.)	Squadron Leader (Sqn. Ldr.)
9	Lieutenant (Lt.)	Captain (Capt.)	Flight Lieutenant (Flt. Lt.)
10	Sub-Lieutenant (Sub-Lt.)	Lieutenant (Lt.)	Flying Officer (FO)
11	Acting Sub-Lieutenant (Acting Sub-Lt.)	Second Lieutenant (2nd Lt.)	Pilot Officer (PO)
USA			
1	Fleet Admiral	General of the Army	General of the Air Force
2	Admiral	General	General
3	Vice-Admiral	Lieutenant-General	Lieutenant-General

4	Rear-Admiral	Major-General	Major-General
5	Commodore Admiral	Brigadier-General	Brigadier-General
6	Captain	Colonel	Colonel
7	Commander	Lieutenant-Colonel	Lieutenant-Colonel
8	Lieutenant-Commander	Major	Major
9	Lieutenant	Captain	Captain
10	Lieutenant Junior Grade	First-Lieutenant	First-Lieutenant
11	Ensign	Second-Lieutenant	Second-Lieutenant

Ranks in the police (UK)

	Rank
1	Chief Constable
2	Assistant Chief Constable
3	Superintendent
4	Chief Inspector
5	Inspector
6	Sergeant
7	Constable

Metropolitan Police (senior ranks)

1	Metropolitan Commissioner
2	Deputy Commissioner
3	Assistant Commissioner
4	Commander

Marriages and divorces

Country	Marriages per thousand people (1986)	Marriages per thousand people (1996)	Divorces per thousand people (1986)	Divorces per thousand people (1996)
Austria	6.0	5.2	1.9	2.2
Belgium	5.8	5.0	1.9	2.8
Canada	6.7	5.4	3.0	2.6
Denmark	6.0	6.8	2.8	2.4
Finland	5.2	4.8	2.0	2.7
France	4.8	4.8	2.0	2.0
Germany	6.6	5.2	2.3	2.1
Greece	5.8	4.5	0.9	0.9
Iceland	5.1	4.6	2.0	1.9
Ireland	5.2	4.5	not applicable	not applicable
Italy	5.3	4.8	0.3	0.5
Japan	5.9	6.4	1.4	1.6
Luxembourg	5.1	5.1	1.8	2.0
Netherlands	6.0	5.4	2.0	2.3
Norway	4.9	5.0	1.9	2.4
Portugal	6.9	6.4	0.8	1.4

Country	Marriages per thousand people (1986)	Marriages per thousand people (1996)	Divorces per thousand people (1986)	Divorces per thousand people (1996)
Spain	5.4	5.0	0.5	0.8
Sweden	4.6	3.8	2.3	2.4
Switzerland	6.2	5.7	1.8	2.3
UK	6.9	5.5	3.0	2.9
USA	10.0	8.9	4.8	4.4

Note Divorce was illegal in Ireland before 1997

5.4 *Health and Nutrition*

Life expectancy

Country	Males and females	Males	Females
Liechtenstein	81	78	83
Japan	79	76	82
Switzerland	78	74	82
Australia	78	75	80
Netherlands	78	74	81
Sweden	78	74	81
Iceland	77	74	80
Spain	77	74	80
Italy	77	73	80
Jamaica	77	75	78
Norway	77	73	80
Canada	76	72	79
USA	76	72	79
Belgium	75	72	78
Denmark	75	72	78
France	75	71	79
New Zealand	75	72	78
UK	75	72	78
Israel	75	73	76
Luxembourg	75	71	78
Malta	75	72	77
Portugal	75	71	78
Brunei	74	74	74
Kuwait	74	72	76
Singapore	74	71	77
Cyprus	74	72	76
Finland	74	70	78
Greece	74	72	76
Costa Rica	74	71	76
Cuba	74	72	75

San Marino	74	70	77
Austria	74	70	77
Panama	73	71	75
Ireland	73	70	76
Taiwan	73	70	75
Barbados	73	70	75
Yugoslavia (former)	72	69	75
Tonga	72	69	74
Uruguay	72	68	75
Czech Republic	72	68	75
Slovakia	72	68	75
Bulgaria	72	69	74
St Vincent and the Grenadines	72	69	74
Albania	71	69	73
Germany	71	68	74
St Lucia	71	68	73
St Christopher-Nevis	71	69	72
Hungary	71	67	74
United Arab Emirates	70	68	72
Qatar	70	68	72
Venezuela	70	67	73
Mexico	70	67	73
Korea, North	70	67	73
Trinidad and Tobago	70	68	72
Antigua and Barbuda	70	70	70
Poland	70	66	74
Romania	70	67	73
Paraguay	70	67	72
Tunisia	70	68	71
Sri Lanka	70	67	72
Argentina	70	66	73
Korea, South	70	66	73
Bahrain	69	67	71
Jordan	69	67	71
Vanuatu	69	67	71
Fiji	69	67	71
Grenada	69	69	69
Solomon Islands	69	66	71
Guyana	69	66	71
Chile	69	64	73
Suriname	69	66	71
Syria	68	67	69
China	68	67	69
Malaysia	68	65	70
Mauritius	68	64	71
Lebanon	68	65	70
Libya	67	64	69
Samoa, Western	67	64	69
Philippines	66	63	69
Seychelles	66	66	66
Saudi Arabia	66	64	67

Country	Males and females	Males	Females
Mongolia	65	63	67
Thailand	65	62	68
El Salvador	65	63	66
Turkey	65	63	66
Ecuador	64	62	66
Vietnam	64	62	66
Peru	64	61	66
Morocco	64	62	65
Colombia	64	61	66
Brazil	64	61	66
Dominican Republic	63	61	65
Iraq	63	62	63
Nicaragua	62	61	63
São Tomé e Principe	62	62	62
Maldives	62	60	63
Tuvalu	62	60	63
Kenya	61	59	63
Zimbabwe	61	59	63
Algeria	61	59	62
Lesotho	61	59	62
Honduras	60	58	62
Belize	60	60	60
Botswana	59	59	59
Guatemala	59	57	61
Cape Verde	59	57	61
Egypt	59	57	60
Dominica	58	57	59
Iran	57	57	57
Oman	57	55	58
Zambia	56	54	57
India	56	56	55
Togo	55	53	57
Pakistan	55	54	55
Liberia	55	53	56
Myanmar	55	53	56
Ivory Coast	54	52	55
Papua New Guinea	54	53	54
Indonesia	54	52	55
Somalia	53	53	53
Sudan	53	51	55
Senegal	53	51	54
Zaire	53	51	54
Bolivia	53	51	54
Haiti	53	51	54
Ghana	52	50	54
Tanzania	52	49	54
Madagascar	52	50	53
Rwanda	51	49	53
Cameroon	51	49	53
Bangladesh	51	50	52
Swaziland	51	47	54

Djibouti	50	50	50
Uganda	50	49	51
Comoros	50	48	52
Nepal	50	50	49
Laos	50	48	51
Niger	49	48	50
Gabon	49	47	51
Yemen	49	47	50
Nigeria	48	47	49
Malawi	48	46	50
Burundi	47	45	48
Mozambique	47	45	48
Congo	47	45	48
Equatorial Guinea	46	44	48
Mauritania	46	43	48
Mali	46	44	47
Burkina Faso	46	44	47
Benin	44	42	46
Sierra Leone	44	41	47
Chad	44	42	45
Cambodia	44	42	45
Bhutan	44	44	43
Central African Republic	43	41	45
Angola	42	40	44
Guinea-Bissau	42	42	42
Gambia	42	42	42
Afghanistan	42	43	41
Guinea	41	39	42
Ethiopia	38	38	38

Note Figures relate to the early 1990s

Major causes of death

Males and females

Rank	Cause	Deaths worldwide (1998)	Percentage of deaths worldwide
1	Ischaemic heart disease	7 375 000	13.7
2	Cerebrovascular disease	5 106 000	9.5
3	Acute lower respiratory infections	3 452 000	6.4
4	HIV/Aids	2 285 000	4.2
5	Chronic obstructive pulmonary disease	2 249 000	4.2
6	Diarrhoeal diseases	2 219 000	4.1
7	Perinatal conditions	2 155 000	4.0
8	Tuberculosis	1 498 000	2.8
9	Cancer of trachea/bronchus/lung	1 244 000	2.3
10	Road traffic accidents	1 171 000	2.2

Males

Rank	Cause	Deaths worldwide (1998)	Percentage of deaths worldwide
1	Ischaemic heart disease	3 659 000	12.8
2	Cerebrovascular disease	2 340 000	8.2
3	Acute lower respiratory infections	1 753 000	6.1
4	Chronic obstructive pulmonary disease	1 240 000	4.3
5	HIV/Aids	1 164 000	4.1
6	Diarrhoeal diseases	1 149 000	4.0
7	Perinatal conditions	1 121 000	3.9
8	Cancer of trachea/bronchus/ lung	1 911 000	3.2
9	Tuberculosis	1 893 000	3.1
10	Road traffic accidents	1 855 000	3.0

Females

Rank	Cause	Deaths worldwide (1998)	Percentage of deaths worldwide
1	Ischaemic heart disease	3 717 000	14.6
2	Cerebrovascular disease	2 766 000	10.9
3	Acute lower respiratory infections	1 699 000	6.7
4	HIV/Aids	1 121 000	4.4
5	Diarrhoeal diseases	1 070 000	4.2
6	Perinatal conditions	1 034 000	4.1
7	Chronic obstructive pulmonary disease	1 010 000	4.0
8	Tuberculosis	1 605 000	2.4
9	Malaria	1 538 000	2.1
10	Measles	1 432 000	1.7

Communicable diseases

Disease	Cause	Transmission	Incubation
Aids (Acquired Immune Deficiency Syndrome)	Human Immuno-deficiency Virus (HIV)	Sexual intercourse, sharing of syringes, blood transfusion	Several years
Amoebiasis	Entamoeba histolytica	Organisms in contaminated food	Up to several years
Anthrax	Bacillus antracis bacterium	Animal hair	1–3 years
Bilharziasis (schistomiasis)	Schistosoma haematobium (or Bilharzia), Schistosoma mansoni, or Schistosoma japonicum	Certain freshwater snails	Varies with lifespan of parasite
Bronchiolitis (babies only)	Respiratory syncytical virus (RSV)	Droplet infection	1–3 years
Brucellosis	Brucellus abortus or B meliteusis bacteria	Cattle or goats	3–6 years
Bubonic plague	Yersinia pestis bacterium	Fleas	3–6 years
Chickenpox (varicella)/shingles	Varicella zoster virus (US)/ Herpes zoster virus (UK)	Droplet infection	14–21 days

Cholera	Vibrio cholerae bacterium	Contaminated water and seafood	A few hours–5 days
Common cold (coryza)	Numerous rhinoviruses	Droplet infection	1–4 days
Conjunctivitis	Virus, bacterium, or allergy	Variable	Variable
Dengue fever (break-bone fever)	B group of arboviruses	Bite from infected mosquito	5–6 days
Diphtheria	Corynebacterium diphtheriae bacterium	Droplet infection	2–6 days
Dysentery	Shigella genus of bacteria	Contaminated food or water	Variable
Encephalitis	Viruses	Bite from infected mosquito	4–21 days
Gas gangrene	Clostridium welchii bacterium	Soil or soil-contaminated articles	1–4 days
Gastro-enteritis	Bacteria, viruses, and food poisoning	Droplet infection of food	Variable
German measles (rubella)	Togavirus	Droplet infection	18 days
Glandular fever (infectious mononucleosis)	Epstein-Barr virus	Saliva of infected person	1–6 weeks
Gonorrhoea	Neisseria gonorrhoeae bacterium	Usually sexually transmitted	2–10 days
Hepatitis A (infectious)	Hepatitis A virus	Contaminated food and water	15–50 days
Hepatitis B (serum type B)	Hepatitis B virus	Infected blood	6 weeks–6 months
Influenza	Numerous viruses (types A, B, C)	Droplet infection	1–4 days
Kala-azar (leishmaniasis)	Parasites genus leishmania	Sandfly	1–2 months (can be up to 10 years)
Laryngitis	Various adenoviruses and rhinoviruses	Droplet infection	1–3 days
Lassa fever	Arenavirus	Urine	3 weeks
Legionnaires' disease	Legionella pneumophila bacterium	Infected water droplets (in humidifiers, cooling towers, etc)	1–3 days
Leprosy	Mycobacterium leprae bacillus	Droplet infection	Variable
Malaria	Plasmodium protozoa	Bite from infected mosquito	6–37 days
Marburg (Green Monkey)	Unclassified virus	Monkeys, body fluids	5–9 days
Measles (rubeola)	Rubeola virus	Droplet infection	10–15 days
Meningitis	Various bacteria and viruses	Droplet infection	Variable
Mumps	Virus	Droplet infection	14–21 days
Orchitis	Bacterium or virus	Urinary infection etc.	Variable
Osteomyelitis	Usually staphylococci organisms	Infected boil, impetigo, etc.	1–10 days
Parotitis	Salmonella bacteria	Contaminated food and water	1–14 days
Paratyphoid fevers	Bacterium or virus	Following illness or operation	1–10 days

Disease	Cause	Transmission	Incubation
Pericarditis	Bacterium or virus	Following chest disease or heart attack	Variable
Peritonitis	Usually E. Coli organism	Usually following appendicitis	1–10 days
Pharyngitis	Bacteria or virus	Droplet infection	3–5 days
Pneumonia	Streptococcus pneumoniae bacterium	Droplet infection	1–3 weeks
Poliomyelitis	Polio viruses	Droplet infection	7–21 days
Proctitis	Possibly fungal infection	Contact	Variable
Psittacosis	Chlamydis psittaci	Infected birds	1–2 weeks
Puerperal fever	Uterine or vaginal infection	Following childbirth	1–10 days
Pylitis	Bacteria	Kidney infection	1–10 days
Rabies	Virus	Bite or lick from a rabid animal	10 days–6 months
River blindness (onchocerciasis)	Onchocerca volvulus worm	Bite from an infected fly of genus Simulium	Worms mature in 2–4 months (can live 12 years)
Salpingitis	Infection of the Fallopian tubes	Usually gonorrhea	Variable
Scarlet fever	Group A haemolytic Streptococcus bacteria	Direct contact or droplet infection	1–5 days
Sinusitis	Virus or bacteria	Droplet infection, usually accompanying a cold	1–3 days
Sleeping sickness (African trypanosomiasis)	Trypanosoma brucei gambieuse or Trypanosoma rhodesieuse	Bite from infected tsetse fly	1 week–months (T brucei gambieuse) or 2.7–14 days (T rhodesieuse)
Smallpox (variola)	Poxvirus variola	Direct contact or droplet infection	7–14 days
Syphilis	Treponema pallidum bacterium	Sexual relations, contact with open lesions, blood transfusion	10–90 days
Tetanus (lockjaw)	Clostridium tetani bacillus	Animal faeces or soil	3–21 days
Thrush	Candida albicans yeast	When resistance to infection is low	Variable
Tonsillitis	Cold viruses or bacteria	Droplet infection	1–3 days
Trachoma	Chlamydia trachomatis organism	Poor hygiene	5 days
Tuberculosis	Mycobacterium tuberculosis bacillus	Droplet infection, contaminated milk	Variable
Typhoid fever	Salmonella typhi bacillus	Contaminated food or water	7–21 days
Typhus	Rickettsiae parasites	Bite from an infected flea, tick, mite, or louse	7–14 days
Urethritis	Virus or bacteria	May accompany cystitis or venereal infection	Variable
Whooping cough (pertussis)	Bordetella pertussis bacterium	Droplet infection	10–21 days
Yellow fever	Arbovirus	Bite from infected mosquito	3–6 days

Landmarks in medicine

Date	Event
c. 400 BC	Hippocrates lays the foundation of modern scientific medicine
c. AD 200	Galen diagnoses by the pulse and becomes the standard authority on medical matters
1543	Andreas Vesalius conducts studies of human anatomy
1628	William Harvey discovers the circulation of the blood
1768	John Hunter advances the practice of surgery and promotes the science of dentistry
1785	Digitalis used to treat heart disease
1798	Edward Jenner experiments with the first vaccinations
1877	Patrick Manson identifies the mosquito as host of the malaria parasite
1882	Robert Koch isolates the tuberculosis bacillus
1884	Edwin Klebs isolates the diphtheria bacillus
1885	Louis Pasteur develops rabies vaccine
1890	Joseph Lister introduces antiseptic surgery
1895	Wilhelm Röntgen discovers X-rays
1897	Martinus Beijerinck discovers viruses
1899	Felix Hoffman develops aspirin; Sigmund Freud founds modern psychiatry
1900	Karl Landsteiner identifies blood groups
1910	Paul Ehrlich discovers cure for syphilis
1922	Introduction of insulin as a treatment for diabetes
1928	Alexander Fleming discovers penicillin
1937	Development of electro-convulsive therapy (ECT)
1950	Cigarette smoking identified as a cause of lung cancer
1950s	Introduction of anti-depressant drugs and of beta blockers to treat heart disease
1953	Francis Crick and James Watson describe structure of DNA; Jonas Salk introduces polio vaccine
1960s	Introduction of benzodiazepine tranquillizers
1967	Christiaan Barnard conducts first human heart transplant
1972	Introduction of CAT scans
1975	Development of monoclonal antibodies, by César Milstein
1978	Birth of first test-tube baby
1980	Eradication of smallpox virus
1983	Identification of Aids virus HIV
1984	Development of first leprosy vaccine
1991	First successful use of gene therapy
1990s	Analysis of human genetic code completed

Immunizations for travellers

Disease	Immunization	Duration of protection
Cholera	Two injections given at least one week apart, the course to be completed at least one week before departure	6 months
Hepatitis A	One injection of immunoglobulin just before departure, or two injections given one month apart and a third 6–12 months later, the course to be completed two months before departure	3 months (for single injection); 10 years (for course)
Hepatitis B	Two injections given one month apart and a booster four months later, the course to be completed one month before travel	5 years
Malaria	Anti-malarial tablets to be taken between one week before departure and four weeks after return	ends with course of tablets
Polio	Three–four doses of oral vaccine, or 3–4 injections, to be administered up to seven months before departure	10 years
Rabies	Three injections administered over the month before departure	3 months
Tetanus	Usually administered in childhood with 10-yearly boosters	10 years
Typhoid	One or two injections given 4–6 weeks apart administered 5–7 weeks before departure, or four oral doses	1–3 years (for course of injections); 3 years (for single injection)
Yellow fever	One injection given at least 10 days before departure	10 years

Note Travellers should always take proper medical advice before going to parts of the world where there is a risk of infection with any of the above named diseases

Drugs

Drug	Uses
Adrenaline	Used to treat cardiac problems, allergic reactions, and asthma
Anabolic steroids	Used to promote muscle and body growth and to treat anaemia
Aspirin	Relieves pain and reduces fever
AZT (azidothymidine)	Used to suppress the Aids virus
Beta blockers	Used to treat angina, hypertension, heart problems, and migraines
Chloral hydrate	Sleeping drug
Cimetidine	Used to treat stomach and duodenal ulcers
Codeine	Relieves mild pain
Cortisone	Used as an anti-inflammatory drug and to treat rheumatoid arthritis
Co-trimoxazole	Used as an anti-bacterial drug to treat respiratory and other infections
Diazepam	Used as a muscle relaxant and to treat anxiety and insomnia
Digoxin	Reduces heart rate and used to treat breathlessness, tiredness, and fluid retention
Ethambutol	Used to treat tuberculosis
Frusemide	Used to treat liver and kidney problems and fluid retention

Ibuprofen	Relieves headaches, menstrual pain, and symptoms of rheumatoid arthritis
Insulin	Used to treat diabetes
Magnesium hydroxide	Used as a laxative
Morphine	Relieves severe pain
Paracetamol/acetaminophen	Relieves mild pain and fever
Penicillin	Widely used as an antibiotic
Pethidine	Relieves pain in childbirth
Phenylpropanolamine	Relieves symptoms of colds and hay fever
Quinidine	Used to treat irregular heart rhythms
Quinine	Used to treat malaria
Ranitidine	Used to treat gastric and duodenal ulcers
Salbutamol/albuterol	Used to treat asthma, bronchitis, and emphysema
Sodium bicarbonate	Relieves pain and indigestion
Temazepam	Used to treat insomnia
Terfenadine	Used to treat allergic rhinitis (withdrawn)
Testosterone	Used to treat fertility problems in males
Tetracycline	Used to treat bronchitis, pneumonia, and chest infections

Phobias

Fear of	Name
Air	Aerophobia
Animals	Zoophobia
Bacteria	Bacteriophobia (or microphobia)
Beards	Pogonophobia
Bees	Apiphobia (or melissophobia)
Being alone	Monophobia (or autophobia)
Being buried alive	Taphophobia
Birds	Orthinophobia
Blood	Hematophobia
Blushing	Erythrophobia
Books	Bibliophobia
Cancer	Cancerophobia (or carcinophobia)
Carriages	Amakaphobia
Cats	Ailourophobia (or gatophobia)
Chickens	Alektorophobia
Childbirth	Tocophobia
Children	Paediphobia
Closed spaces	Claustrophobia
Clouds	Nephophobia (or nephelophobia)
Cold	Cheimophobia
Colour	Chromophobia
Comets	Cometophobia
Contamination	Misophobia (or mysophobia)
Corpses	Necrophobia
Crossing a bridge	Gephyrophobia
Crossing streets	Dromophobia
Crowds	Demophobia
Crystals	Chrystallophobia

Fear of	Name
Darkness	Achluophobia
Dawn	Eosophobia
Daylight	Phengophobia
Death	Thanatophobia
Deformity	Dysmorphophobia
Demons	Demonophobia
Dirt	Mysophobia
Disease	Nosophobia (or pathophobia)
Disorder	Ataxiophobia
Dogs	Cynophobia
Draughts	Anemophobia
Dreams	Oneirophobia
Drinks	Potophobia
Drugs	Pharmacophobia
Duration	Chronophobia
Dust	Amathophobia
Eating	Phagophobia
Electricity	Elektrophobia
Everything	Panphobia (or pantophobia)
Eyes	Ommatophobia
Faeces	Coprophobia
Failure	Kakorraphiaphobia
Fatigue	Kopophobia
Fears	Phobophobia
Feathers	Pteronophobia
Fire	Pyrophobia
Fish	Ichthyophobia
Flashes	Selaphobia
Flogging	Mastigophobia
Flood	Antlophobia
Flute	Aulophobia
Flying	Aerophobia
Fog	Homichlophobia
Food	Sitophobia
Freedom	Eleutherophobia
Fur	Doraphobia
Germs	Spermaphobia (or spermatophobia)
Ghosts	Phasmophobia
Girls	Parthenophobia
Glass	Nelophobia
God	Theophobia
Going to bed	Clinophobia
Graves	Taphophobia
Gravity	Barophobia
Hair	Chaetophobia
Heart conditions	Cardiophobia
Heat	Thermophobia
Heaven	Ouranophobia
Heights	Acrophobia
Hell	Stygiophobia (or hadephobia)
Heredity	Patroiophobia

Home	Oikophobia (or domatophobia)
Horses	Hippophobia
Human beings	Anthrophobia
Ice	Kristallophobia
Ideas	Ideophobia
Illness	Nosemaphobia
Imperfection	Atelophobia
Infection	Mysophobia
Infinity	Aperiophobia
Injustice	Dikephobia
Inoculations	Trypanophobia
Insanity	Lyssophobia (or maniaphobia)
Insects	Entomophobia
Itching	Acarophobia (or scabiophobia)
Jealousy	Zelophobia
Justice	Dikephobia
Lakes	Limnophobia
Leaves	Phyllophobia
Leprosy	Leprophobia
Lice	Pediculophobia
Light	Photophobia
Lightning	Astraphobia
Machinery	Mechanophobia
Man	Anthropophobia
Many things	Polyphobia
Marriage	Gamophobia
Meat	Carnophobia
Men	Androphobia
Metals	Metallophobia
Skin	Dermatophobia
Sleep	Hypnophobia
Smell	Olfactophobia
Smothering	Pnigerophobia
Snakes	Ophidiophobia
Snow	Chionophobia
Soiling	Rypophobia
Solitude	Eremophobia
Sound	Akousticophobia
Sourness	Acerophobia
Speaking aloud	Phonophobia
Speed	Tachophobia
Spiders	Arachnophobia
Standing	Stasiphobia
Stars	Siderophobia
Stealing	Kleptophobia
Stillness	Eremophobia
Stings	Cnidophobia
Strangers	Xenophobia
String	Linonophobia
Strong light	Photophobia
Stuttering	Laliophobia
Sun	Heliophobia

Fear of	Name
Surgical operations	Ergasiophobia
Syphilis	Syphilophobia
Taste	Geumaphobia (or geumatophobia)
Teeth	Odontophobia
Thinking	Phronemophobia
Thirteen	Triskaidekaphobia
Thunder	Brontophobia (or tonitrophobia)
Touch	Haptophobia
Travel	Hodophobia
Trees	Dendrophobia
Trembling	Tremophobia
Vehicles	Ochophobia
Venereal disease	Cypridophobia
Voids	Kenophobia
Vomiting	Emetophobia
Walking	Basophobia
Wasps	Spheksophobia
Water	Hydrophobia
Weakness	Asthenophobia
Wind	Anemophobia
Women	Gynophobia
Words	Logophobia
Work	Ergophobia
Worms	Helminthophobia
Wounds	Traumatophobia
Writing	Graphophobia

Body weights

Men

Height	Ideal weight
155 cm (61 in)	53.5–63.9 kg (117.9–140.9 lb)
157 cm (62 in)	54.8–65.3 kg (120.8–143.9 lb)
160 cm (63 in)	56.2–67.1 kg (143.7–147.9 lb)
162 cm (64 in)	57.6–68.9 kg (127.0–151.9 lb)
165 cm (65 in)	58.9–70.8 kg (129.9–156.1 lb)
168 cm (66 in)	60.8–73.0 kg (134.0–160.9 lb)
170 cm (67 in)	62.6–75.3 kg (138.0–166.0 lb)
173 cm (68 in)	65.4–77.1 kg (144.2–170.0 lb)
175 cm (69 in)	66.2–78.9 kg (145.9–173.9 lb)
178 cm (70 in)	68.0–81.2 kg (149.9–179.0 lb)
180 cm (71 in)	69.8–83.5 kg (153.9–184.1 lb)
183 cm (72 in)	71.6–86.7 kg (157.8–191.1 lb)
185 cm (73 in)	73.5–87.9 kg (162.0–193.8 lb)
188 cm (74 in)	75.7–90.2 kg (166.9–198.8 lb)
190 cm (75 in)	78.0–92.5 kg (171.9–203.9 lb)
193 cm (76 in)	80.3–94.8 kg (177.0–209.0 lb)

Women

Height	Ideal weight
153 cm (60 in)	46.3–53.9 kg (102.0–118.8 lb)
155 cm (61 in)	47.6–55.3 kg (104.9–121.9 lb)
157 cm (62 in)	48.9–57.1 kg (107.8–125.9 lb)
160 cm (63 in)	50.3–58.9 kg (110.9–129.8 lb)
162 cm (64 in)	51.7–61.2 kg (114.0–134.9 lb)
165 cm (65 in)	53.5–63.0 kg (117.9–138.9 lb)
168 cm (66 in)	55.3–64.8 kg (121.9–142.8 lb)
170 cm (67 in)	57.1–66.7 kg (125.9–147.0 lb)
173 cm (68 in)	58.9–68.5 kg (129.9–151.0 lb)
175 cm (69 in)	60.8–70.3 kg (134.0–155.0 lb)
178 cm (70 in)	62.6–72.1 kg (138.0–158.9 lb)
180 cm (71 in)	64.4–73.9 kg (142.0–162.9 lb)
183 cm (72 in)	66.2–75.7 kg (145.9–166.9 lb)
185 cm (73 in)	68.0–77.6 kg (149.9–171.0 lb)
188 cm (74 in)	69.8–79.3 kg (153.9–174.8 lb)

Pulse rates

Age	Beats per minute
Foetus in utero	150
Newborn	140
First year	120
Second year	110
5 years	100
10 years	90
20 years	71
50 years	72
70 years	75
Over 80	78

Note Refers to the normal resting pulse rate of a healthy person

Energy expenditure

Activity	Energy used per hour
Swimming	720 kcals (3 024 kJ)
Cycling	660 kcals (2 772 kJ)
Jogging	630 kcals (2 646 kJ)
Climbing stairs	620 kcals (2 604 kJ)
Squash	600 kcals (2 520 kJ)
Football	540 kcals (2 268 kJ)
Hockey	540 kcals (2 268 kJ)
Rugby	540 kcals (2 268 kJ)
Tennis	480 kcals (2 016 kJ)
Gardening (heavy)	420 kcals (1 764 kJ)
Gymnastics	420 kcals (1 764 kJ)
Badminton	340 kcals (1 428 kJ)

Activity	Energy used per hour
Walking (brisk)	300 kcals (1 260 kJ)
Gardening (light)	270 kcals (1 134 kJ)
Golf	270 kcals (1 134 kJ)
Housework	270 kcals (1 134 kJ)
Walking (easy)	180 kcals (756 kJ)
Standing	120 kcals (504 kJ)
Staying in bed	60 kcals (252 kJ)

Note Figures are approximate, relating to a person of average size and fitness; kcals = kilocalories, kJ = kilojoules

Recommended daily intake of nutrients

Males

Age	Energy	Pro-tein	Calcium	Iron	Vita-min A	Thiamine (retinol)	Ribo-flavin	Niacin	Vita-min C	Vita-min D
0–1	3.25 MJ (780 kcal)	19 g	600 mg	6 mg	450 µg	0.3 mg	0.4 mg	5 mg	20 mg	7.5 µg
1	5.00 MJ (1 200 kcal)	30 g	600 mg	7 mg	300 µg	0.5 mg	0.6 mg	7 mg	20 mg	10.0 µg
2	5.75 MJ (1 400 kcal)	35 g	600 mg	7 mg	300 µg	0.6 mg	0.7 mg	8 mg	20 mg	10.0 µg
3–4	6.50 MJ (1 560 kcal)	39 g	600 mg	8 mg	300 µg	0.6 mg	0.8 mg	9 mg	20 mg	10.0 µg
5–6	7.25 MJ (1 740 kcal)	43 g	600 mg	10 mg	300 µg	0.7 mg	0.9 mg	10 mg	20 mg	
7–8	8.25 MJ (1 980 kcal)	49 g	600 mg	10 mg	400 µg	0.8 mg	1.0 mg	11 mg	20 mg	
9–11	9.50 MJ (2 280 kcal)	56 g	700 mg	12 mg	575 µg	0.9 mg	1.2 mg	14 mg	25 mg	
12–14	11.00 MJ (2 640 kcal)	66 g	700 mg	12 mg	725 µg	1.1 mg	1.4 mg	16 mg	25 mg	
15–17	12.00 MJ (2 880 kcal)	72 g	600 mg	12 mg	750 µg	1.2 mg	1.7 mg	19 mg	30 mg	
18–34 (sedentary)	10.50 MJ (2 510 kcal)	62 g	500 mg	10 mg	750 µg	1.0 mg	1.6 mg	18 mg	30 mg	
18–34 (moderately active)	12.00 MJ (2 900 kcal)	72 g	500 mg	10 mg	750 µg	1.2 mg	1.6 mg	18 mg	30 mg	
18–34 (very active)	14.00 MJ (3 350 kcal)	84 g	500 mg	10 mg	750 µg	1.3 mg	1.6 mg	18 mg	30 mg	
35–64 (sedentary)	10.00 MJ (2 400 kcal)	60 g	500 mg	10 mg	750 µg	1.0 mg	1.6 mg	18 mg	30 mg	
35–64 (moderately active)	11.50 MJ (2 750 kcal)	69 g	500 mg	10 mg	750 µg	1.1 mg	1.6 mg	18 mg	30 mg	
35–64 (very active)	14.00 MJ (3 350 kcal)	84 g	500 mg	10 mg	750 µg	1.3 mg	1.6 mg	18 mg	30 mg	
65–74	10.00 MJ (2 400 kcal)	60 g	500 mg	10 mg	750 µg	1.0 mg	1.6 mg	18 mg	30 mg	
over 74	9.00 MJ (2 150 kcal)	54 g	500 mg	10 mg	750 µg	0.9 mg	1.6 mg	18 mg	30 mg	

Females

Age	Energy	Pro-tein	Calcium	Iron	Vita-min A	Thiamine (retinol)	Ribo-flavin	Niacin	Vita-min C	Vita-min D
0–1	3.00 MJ (720 kcal)	18 g	600 mg	6 mg	450 µg	0.3 mg	0.4 mg	5 mg	20 mg	7.5 µg
1	4.50 MJ (1 100 kcal)	27 g	600 mg	7 mg	300 µg	0.4 mg	0.6 mg	7 mg	20 mg	10.0 µg
2	5.50 MJ (1 300 kcal)	32 g	600 mg	7 mg	300 µg	0.5 mg	0.7 mg	8 mg	20 mg	10.0 µg
3–4	6.25 MJ (1 500 kcal)	37 g	600 mg	8 mg	300 µg	0.6 mg	0.8 mg	9 mg	20 mg	10.0 µg
5–6	7.00 MJ (1 680 kcal)	42 g	600 mg	10 mg	300 µg	0.7 mg	0.9 mg	10 mg	20 mg	
7–8	8.00 MJ (1 900 kcal)	48 g	600 mg	10 mg	400 µg	0.8 mg	1.0 mg	11 mg	20 mg	
9–11	8.50 MJ (2 050 kcal)	51 g	700 mg	12 mg	575 µg	0.8 mg	1.2 mg	14 mg	25 mg	
12–14	9.00 MJ (2 150 kcal)	53 g	700 mg	12 mg	725 µg	0.9 mg	1.4 mg	16 mg	25 mg	
15–17	9.00 MJ (2 150 kcal)	53 g	600 mg	12 mg	750 µg	0.9 mg	1.7 mg	19 mg	30 mg	
18–54 (averagely active)	9.00 MJ (2 150 kcal)	54 g	500 mg	12 mg	750 µg	0.9 mg	1.3 mg	15 mg	30 mg	
18–54 (very active)	10.50 MJ (2 500 kcal)	62 g	500 mg	12 mg	750 µg	1.0 mg	1.3 mg	15 mg	30 mg	
Pregnant	10.00 MJ (2 400 kcal)	60 g	1 200 mg	13 mg	750 µg	1.0 mg	1.6 mg	18 mg	60 mg	
Lactating	11.50 MJ (2 750 kcal)	69 g	1 200 mg	15 mg	1 200 µg	1.1 mg	1.8 mg	21 mg	60 mg	
55–74	8.00 MJ (1 900 kcal)	47 g	500 mg	10 mg	750 µg	0.8 mg	1.3 mg	15 mg	30 mg	
over 74	7.00 MJ (1 680 kcal)	42 g	500 mg	10 mg	750 µg	0.7 mg	1.3 mg	15 mg	30 mg	

Note The recommended iron intakes for girls and women do not take into account the effect of heavy menstrual loss.

Vitamins

Vitamin	Chemical name	Dietary sources	Symptoms of deficiency
A	Retinol, carotene	(Retinol) whole milk, butter, cheese, egg yolk, liver, fatty fish; (carotene) green, red, and yellow vegetables	Xerophthalmia (eye disease), rough skin
B_1	Thiamine	Seeds and grains	Beri-beri, Korsakov's syndrome
B_2	Riboflavin	Liver, milk, cheese, yeast	Failure to thrive, skin disorders
	Nicotinic acid	Meat, fish, cereals, pulses	Pellagra
B_6	Pyridoxine	Cereals, liver, meat, fruits, leafy vegetables	Dermatitis, neurological disorders
B_{12}	Cyanocobalamin	Meat, milk, liver	Anaemia
	Folic acid	Liver, green vegetables	Anaemia
	Pantothenic acid	Numerous sources	Dermatitis
	Biotin	Liver, kidney, yeast extracts	Dermatitis

Vitamin	Chemical name	Dietary sources	Symptoms of deficiency
C	Ascorbic acid	Citrus fruits, potatoes, leafy green vegetables	Scurvy
D	Cholecalciferol	Fatty fish, margarine, fortified milks	Rickets, osteomalacia
E	Tocopherols	Vegetable oils	Multiple diseases
K	Phytomenadione	Leafy green vegetables, liver, dairy products, fruit	Haemorrhagic problems

Trace minerals

Mineral	Dietary sources	Symptoms of deficiency
Calcium	Milk and dairy products, sardines, leafy green vegetables, citrus fruits	Rickets (children), osteoporosis (adults)
Chromium	Brewer's yeast, black pepper, liver, wholemeal bread, beer	Adult-onset diabetes
Copper	Green vegetables, fish, oysters, liver	Anaemia, Menkes' syndrome
Fluorine	Fluoridated drinking water, seafood, tea	Tooth decay
Iodine	Seafood, salt-water fish, seaweed, iodized salt, table salt	Goitre, cretinism in infants
Iron	Offal, beans, leafy green vegetables, shellfish, egg yolk, dried fruit, potatoes, molasses	Anaemia
Magnesium	Raw leafy green vegetables, nuts, whole grains	Muscular weakness, insomnia, irregular heartbeat
Manganese	Legumes, cereals, leafy green vegetables, tea	Unknown in humans
Molybdenum	Legumes, cereals, offal, some dark-green vegetables	Unknown in humans
Phosphorus	Meat, poultry, fish, eggs, dried beans and peas, milk and dairy products	Muscular weakness, bone pain, loss of appetite
Potassium	Fresh vegetables, meat, milk, orange juice, bananas, bran	Muscular weakness, fatigue, irregular heartbeat, kidney and lung failure
Selenium	Seafood, cereals, meat, fish, egg yolk, garlic	Unknown in humans
Sodium	Table salt, bread, cereal products, meat, milk	Impaired acid-base balance in body fluids (rare)
Zinc	Meat, whole grains, bread, legumes, oysters, milk	Impaired wound healing, loss of appetite, impaired sexual development

Nutritional content of foods

Food	Energy	Protein	Carbohydrate	Fat	Saturated fat
Cereals and cereal products					
Bread (brown)	218 kcal (927 kJ)	8.5	44.3	2.0	2.0
Bread (white)	235 kcal (1 002 kJ)	8.4	49.3	1.9	1.9
Flour (plain white)	341 kcal (1 450 kJ)	9.4	77.7	1.3	1.3
Flour (wholemeal)	310 kcal (1 318 kJ)	12.7	63.9	2.2	2.2

Oats (porridge)	375 kcal (1 587 kJ)	11.2	66.0	9.2	9.2
Rice (brown boiled)	141 kcal (597 kJ)	2.6	32.1	1.1	1.1
Rice (white boiled)	138 kcal (587 kJ)	2.6	30.9	1.3	1.3
Spaghetti (white boiled)	104 kcal (442 kJ)	3.6	22.2	0.7	0.7

Dairy products

Butter	737 kcal (3 031 kJ)	0.5	0.0	81.7	54.0
Cheddar cheese	412 kcal (1 708 kJ)	25.5	0.1	34.4	21.7
Cottage cheese	98 kcal (413 kJ)	13.8	2.1	3.9	2.4
Cream (fresh heavy)	449 kcal (1 849 kJ)	1.7	2.7	48.0	30.0
Cream (fresh)	198 kcal (817 kJ)	2.6	4.1	19.1	11.9
Eggs (boiled)	147 kcal (612 kJ)	12.5	0.0	10.8	3.1
Low-fat spread	390 kcal (1 605 kJ)	5.8	0.5	40.5	11.2
Margarine (polyunsaturated)	739 kcal (3 039 kJ)	0.2	1.0	81.6	16.2
Milk (semi-skimmed)	46 kcal (195 kJ)	3.3	5.0	1.6	1.0
Milk (skimmed)	33 kcal (140 kJ)	3.3	5.0	0.1	0.1
Milk (whole)	66 kcal (275 kJ)	3.2	4.8	3.9	2.4
Yoghurt (whole milk plain)	79 kcal (333 kJ)	5.7	7.8	3.0	1.7

Fish

White fish (steamed)	98 kcal (417 kJ)	22.8	0.0	0.8	0.2
Shrimps (boiled)	107 kcal (451 kJ)	22.6	0.0	1.8	0.4

Fruit

Apples	47 kcal (199 kJ)	0.4	11.8	0.1	0.0
Apricots	158 kcal (674 kJ)	4.0	36.5	0.6	0.0
Avocados	190 kcal (784 kJ)	1.9	1.9	19.5	4.1
Bananas	95 kcal (403 kJ)	1.2	23.2	0.3	0.1
Cherries	48 kcal (203 kJ)	0.9	11.5	0.1	0.0
Grapefruit	30 kcal (126 kJ)	0.8	6.8	0.1	0.0
Grapes	60 kcal (257 kJ)	0.4	15.4	0.1	0.0
Mangoes	57 kcal (245 kJ)	0.7	14.1	0.2	0.1
Melon	28 kcal (119 kJ)	0.6	6.6	0.1	0.0
Oranges	37 kcal (158 kJ)	1.1	8.5	0.1	0.0
Peaches	33 kcal (142 kJ)	1.0	14.0	0.1	0.0
Pears	40 kcal (169 kJ)	0.3	10.0	0.1	0.0
Plums	36 kcal (155 kJ)	0.6	8.8	0.1	0.0
Raspberries	25 kcal (109 kJ)	1.4	4.6	0.3	0.1
Strawberries	27 kcal (113 kJ)	0.8	6.0	0.1	0.0

Meat

Beef (lean)	123 kcal (517 kJ)	20.3	0.0	4.6	1.9
Chicken	230 kcal (954 kJ)	17.6	0.0	17.7	5.9
Lamb (lean)	162 kcal (679 kJ)	20.8	0.0	8.8	4.2
Pork (lean)	147 kcal (615 kJ)	20.7	0.0	7.1	2.5

Vegetables

Aubergine	15 kcal (64 kJ)	0.9	2.2	0.4	0.1
Beetroot	46 kcal (195 kJ)	2.3	9.5	0.0	0.0
Cabbage	26 kcal (109 kJ)	1.7	4.1	0.4	0.1
Celery	7 kcal (32 kJ)	0.5	0.9	0.2	0.0
Courgettes	18 kcal (74 kJ)	1.8	1.8	0.4	0.1

Food	Energy	Protein	Carbohydrate	Fat	Saturated fat
Cucumber	10 kcal (40 kJ)	0.7	1.5	0.1	0.0
Lettuce	14 kcal (59 kJ)	0.8	1.7	0.5	0.1
Mushrooms	13 kcal (55 kJ)	1.8	0.4	0.5	0.1
Onions	36 kcal (150 kJ)	1.2	7.9	0.2	0.0
Parsnips	66 kcal (278 kJ)	1.6	12.9	1.2	0.2
Peas	69 kcal (291 kJ)	6.0	9.7	0.9	0.2
Peppers	15 kcal (65 kJ)	0.8	2.6	0.3	0.1
Potatoes (new)	70 kcal (298 kJ)	1.7	16.1	0.3	0.1
Potatoes (old)	75 kcal (318 kJ)	2.1	17.2	0.2	0.0
Spinach	21 kcal (90 kJ)	301	0.5	0.8	0.1
Sweetcorn kernels	122 kcal (519 kJ)	2.9	26.6	1.2	0.2
Sweet potatoes	84 kcal (358 kJ)	1.1	20.5	0.3	0.1
Tofu (steamed)	73 kcal (304 kJ)	8.1	0.7	4.2	0.5
Watercress	22 kcal (94 kJ)	3.0	0.4	1.0	0.3

Note All values approximate per 100 g of food

Food additives

Colours

Number	Name
E100	Curcumin
E101	Riboflavin
101 (a)	Riboflavin-5'-phosphate
E102	Tartrazine
E104	Quinoline yellow
107	Yellow 2G
E110	Sunset Yellow FCF
E120	Cochineal
E122	Carmoisine
E123	Amaranth
E124	Ponceau 4R
E127	Erythrosine
128	Red 2G
129	Allura red AC
E131	Patent blue V
E132	Indigo carmine
133	Brilliant blue FCF
E140	Chlorophyll
E141	Copper complexes of chlorophyll and chlorophyllins
E142	Green S
E150	Caramel colour
E151	Black PN
E153	Carbon black
154	Brown FK
155	Brown HT
E160 (a)	Alpha-carotene, beta-carotene, gamma-carotene
E160 (b)	Annatto, Bixin, Norbixin
E160 (c)	Capsanthin
E160 (d)	Lycopene

E160 (e)	Beta-apo-8'-carotenal
E160 (f)	Ethyl ester of beta-apo-8'-carotenic acid
E161 (a)	Xanthophylls Flavoxanthin
E161 (b)	Xanthophylls Lutein
E161 (c)	Xanthophylls Cryptoxanthin
E161 (d)	Xanthophylls Rubixanthin
E161 (e)	Xanthophylls Violoxanthin
E161 (f)	Xanthophylls Rhodoxanthin
E161 (g)	Xanthophylls Cathaxanthin
E162	Beetroot red
E163	Anthocyanins
E170	Calcium carbonate
E171	Titanium dioxide
E172	Iron oxides, iron hydroxides
E173	Aluminium
E174	Silver
E175	Gold
E180	Pigment Rubine

Preservatives

E200	Sorbic acid
E201	Sodium sorbate
E202	Potassium sorbate
E203	Calcium sorbate
E210	Benzoic acid
E211	Sodium benzoate
E212	Potassium benzoate
E213	Calcium benzoate
E214	Ethyl 4-hydroxybenzoate
E215	Ethyl 4-hydroxybenzoate, sodium salt
E216	Propyl 4-hydroxybenzoate
E217	Propyl 4-hydroxybenzoate, sodium salt
E218	Methyl 4-hydroxybenzoate
E219	Methyl 4-hydroxybenzoate, sodium salt
E220	Sulphur dioxide
E221	Sodium sulphite
E222	Sodium hydrogen sulphite
E223	Sodium metabisulphite
E224	Potassium metabisulphite
E226	Calcium sulphite
E227	Calcium hydrogen sulphite
E230	Biphenyl
E231	2-Hydroxybiphenyl
E232	Sodium biphenyl-2-yl oxide
E233	2 (Thiazol-4-yl) benzimidazole
234	Nisin
E236	Formic acid
E237	Sodium formate
E238	Calcium formate
E239	Hexamine
E249	Potassium nitrate
E250	Sodium nitrite

Number	Name
E251	Sodium nitrate
E252	Potassium nitrate
E260	Acetic acid
E261	Potassium acetate
E262	Sodium hydrogen diacetate
262	Sodium acetate
E263	Calcium acetate
E270	Lactic acid
E280	Propionic acid
E281	Sodium propionate
E282	Calcium propionate
E283	Potassium propionate
E290	Carbon dioxide
296	Malic acid
297	Fumaric acid

Antioxidants

Number	Name
E300	L-Ascorbic acid
E301	Sodium L-ascorbate
E302	Calcium L-ascorbate
E304	6-o-Palmitoyl-L-ascorbic acid
E306	Extracts of natural tocopherols
E307	Synthetic alpha-tocopherol
E308	Synthetic gamma-tocopherol
E309	Synthetic delta-tocopherol
E310	Propyl gallate
E311	Octyl gallate
E312	Dodecyl gallate
E320	Butylated hydroxyanisole
E321	Butylated hydroxytoluene
E322	Lecithins
E325	Sodium lactate
E326	Potassium lactate
E327	Calcium lactate
E330	Citric acid
E331 (a)	Sodium dihydrogen citrate
E331 (b)	di Sodium citrate
E331 (c)	tri Sodium citrate
E332	Potassium dihydrogen citrate
E332	tri Potassium citrate
E333	mono, di and tri Calcium citrate
E334	L-(+)-Tartaric acid
E335	mono Sodium L-(+)-tartrate and di Sodium L-(+)-tatrate
E336	mono Potassium L-(+)-tartrate (cream of tartar)
E336	di Potassium L-(+)-tartrate
E337	Potassium sodium L-(+)-tartrate
E338	Orthophosphoric acid
E339	Sodium dihydrogen orthophosphate
E340 (a)	Potassium dihydrogen orthophosphate
E340 (b)	di Potassium hydrogen orthophosphate
E340 (c)	tri Potassium orthophosphate

E341 (a)	Calcium tetrahydrogen diorthophosphate
E341 (b)	Calcium hydrogen orthophosphate
E341 (c)	tri Calcium di orthophosphate
350	Sodium malate
350	Sodium hydrogen malate
351	Potassium malate
352	Calcium malate
352	Calcium hydrogen malate
353	Metatartaric acid
355	Adipic acid
363	Succinic acid
370	1,4-Heptonolactone
375	Nicotinic acid
380	tri Ammonium citrate
381	Ammonium ferric citrate
381	Ammonium ferric citrate, green
385	Calcium disodium ethylenediamine-NNN'N' tetra-acetate (EDTA)
E400	Alginic acid
E401	Sodium alginate
E402	Potassium alginate
E403	Ammonium alginate
E404	Calcium alginate
E405	Propane-1,2-diol alginate
E406	Agar
E407	Carrageenan
E410	Locust gum or Carob bean gum
E412	Guar gum
E413	Tragacanth
E414	Gum arabic
E415	Xanthan gum
416	Karaya gum
E420	Sorbitol syrup
E421	Mannitol
E422	Glycerol
430	Polyoxyethylene (8) stearate
431	Polyoxyethylene (40) stearate
432	Polyoxyethylene (20) sorbitan monolaurate
433	Polyoxyethylene (20) sorbitan mono-oleate
434	Polyoxyethylene (20) sorbitan monopalmitate
435	Polyoxyethylene (20) sorbitan monostearate
436	Polyoxyethylene (20) sorbitan tristearate
E440 (a)	Pectin
E440 (b)	Amidated pectin
442	Ammonium phosphatides
E450 (a)	di Sodium dihydrogen diphosphate
E450 (a)	tri Sodium diphosphate
E450 (a)	tetra Sodium diphosphate
E450(a)	tetra Potassium diphosphate
E450 (b)	penta Sodium triphosphate
E450 (b)	penta Potassium triphosphate
E450 (c)	Sodium polyphosphates
E450 (c)	Potassium polyphosphates

Number	Name
E460	Microcrystalline cellulose
E460	Alpha-cellulose
E461	Methylcellulose
E463	Hydroxypropylcellulose
E464	Hydroxyproplymethylcellulose
E465	Ethylmethylcellulose
E466	Carboxymethylcellulose, sodium salt
E470	Sodium, potassium and calcium salts of fatty acids
E471	Mono- and di-glycerides of fatty acids
E472 (a)	Acetic acid esters of mono- and di-glycerides of fatty acids
E472 (b)	Lactic acid esters of mono- and di-glycerides of fatty acids
E472 (c)	Citric acid esters of mono- and di-glycerides of fatty acids
E472 (d)	Tartaric acid esters of mono- and di-glycerides of fatty acids
E472 (e)	Mono- and di-acetyltartaric acid esters of mono- and di-glycerides of fatty acids
E473	Sucrose esters of fatty acids
E474	Sucroglycerides
E475	Polyglycerol esters of fatty acids
476	Polyglycerol esters of polycondensed fatty acids of castor oil
E477	Propane-1,2-diol esters of fatty acids
478	Lactylated fatty acid esters of glycerol and propane-1,2-diol
E481	Sodium stearoyl-2-lactylate
E482	Calcium stearoyl-2-lactylate
E483	Stearyl tartrate
491	Sorbitan monostearate
492	Sorbitan tristearate
493	Sorbitan monolaurate
494	Sorbitan mono-oleate
495	Sorbitan monopalmitate
500	Sodium carbonate
500	Sodium hydrogen carbonate
500	Sodium sesquicarbonate
501	Potassium carbonate and potassium hydrogen carbonate
503	Ammonium carbonate
503	Ammonium hydrogen carbonate
504	Magnesium carbonate
507	Hydrochloric acid
508	Potassium chloride
509	Calcium chloride
510	Ammonium chloride
513	Sulphuric acid
514	Sodium sulphate
515	Potassium sulphate
516	Calcium sulphate
518	Magnesium sulphate
524	Sodium hydroxide
525	Potassium hydroxide
526	Calcium hydroxide
527	Ammonium hydroxide
528	Magnesium hydroxide
529	Calcium oxide

530	Magnesium oxide
535	Sodium ferrocyanide
536	Potassium ferrocyanide
540	di Calcium diphosphate
541	Sodium aluminium phosphate
541	Sodium aluminium phosphate, basic
542	Edible bone phosphate
544	Calcium polyphosphates
545	Ammonium polyphosphates

Anti-caking agents

551	Silicon dioxide
552	Calcium silicate
553 (a)	Magnesium silicate, synthetic and magnesium trisilicate
553 (b)	Talc
554	Aluminium sodium silicate
556	Aluminium calcium silicate
558	Bentonite
559	Kaolin
570	Stearic acid
572	Magnesium stearate
575	D-Glucono-1,5-lactone
576	Sodium gluconate
577	Potassium gluconate
578	Calcium gluconate

Flavour enhancers

620	L-Glutamic acid
621	mono Sodium glutamate
622	Potassium hydrogen L-glutamate
623	Calcium dihydrogen di-L-glutamate
627	Guanosine 5'-(di Sodium phosphate)
631	Inosine 5' (di Sodium phosphate)
635	Sodium 5'-ribonucleotide
636	Maltol
637	Ethyl maltol
900	Dimethylpolysiloxane

Glazing agents

901	Beeswax
903	Carnauba wax
904	Shellac
905	Mineral hydrocarbons
907	Refined microcrystalline wax

Improving agents

920	L-cysteine hydrochloride and L-cysteine hydrochloride monohydrate
924	Potassium bromate
925	Chlorine
926	Chlorine dioxide
927	Azo dicarbonamide

Note Numbers prefixed by the letter E are accepted as safe throughout the European community; others are accepted in the UK but not elsewhere in Europe

6
Politics, Law and Economics

6.1 International Politics

International alliances and organizations

Alliance/Organization	Established	Members
Amazon Pact	1978	Bolivia, Brazil, Colombia, Ecuador, Guyana, Peru, Suriname, Venezuela
Andean League	1969	Bolivia, Chile, Colombia, Ecuador, Peru, Venezuela
Arab League	1945	Egypt, Iraq, Lebanon, Saudi Arabia, Syria, Transjordan, Yemen, Algeria, Bahrain, Comoros, Djibouti, Jordan, Kuwait, Libya, Mauritania, Morocco, Oman, Palestine, Qatar, Somalia, Sudan, Tunisia, United Arab Emirates
Arab Maghreb Union (AMU)	1989	Algeria, Libya, Mauritania, Morocco, Tunisia
Association of Caribbean States (ACS)	1994	Antigua and Barbuda, Bahamas, Barbados, Belize, Colombia, Costa Rica, Cuba, Dominica, Dominican Republic, El Salvador, Grenada, Guatemala, Guyana, Haiti, Honduras, Jamaica, Mexico, Nicaragua, Panama, St Kitts and Nevis, St Lucia, St Vincent and the Grenadines, Suriname, Trinidad and Tobago, Venezuela
Association of South-East Asian Nations (ASEAN)	1967	Indonesia, Malaysia, Philippines, Thailand, Singapore, Brunei, Vietnam, Laos, Myanmar
Caribbean Community and Common Market (CARICOM)	1973	Barbados, Guyana, Jamaica, Trinidad and Tobago, Antigua and Barbuda, Bahamas, Belize, Dominica, Grenada, Haiti, Montserrat, St Kitts and Nevis, St Lucia, St Vincent and the Grenadines, Suriname
Cooperation Council for the Arab States of the Gulf	1982	Bahrain, Kuwait, Oman, Qatar, Saudi Arabia, United Arab Emirates
Council for Mutual Economic Assistance (COMECON)	1949 (disbanded 1991)	Bulgaria, Cuba, Czechoslovakia, East Germany, Hungary, Mongolia, Poland, Romania, USSR, Vietnam

Council of Europe	1949	Albania, Andorra, Austria, Belgium, Bulgaria, Croatia, Cyprus, Czech Republic, Denmark, Estonia, Finland, France, Germany, Greece, Hungary, Iceland, Ireland, Italy, Latvia, Liechtenstein, Lithuania, Luxembourg, Yugoslavia, Malta, Moldova, Netherlands, Norway, Poland, Portugal, Romania, Russia, San Marino, Slovenia, Slovak Republic, Spain, Sweden, Switzerland, Turkey, UK, Ukraine
Council of the Baltic Sea States	1992	Denmark, Estonia, Finland, Iceland, Germany, Latvia, Lithuania, Norway, Poland, Russia, Sweden, the European Union
Council of the Entente (CE)	1959	Benin, Burkina Faso, Côte d'Ivoire, Niger, Togo
Economic Community of West African States (ECOWAS)	1975	Benin, Burkina Faso, Cape Verde, Côte d'Ivoire, the Gambia, Ghana, Guinea, Guinea-Bissau, Liberia, Mali, Mauritania, Niger, Nigeria, Senegal, Sierra Leone, Togo
European Free Trade Organization (EFTA)	1959	Austria (left 1995), Denmark (left 1972), Norway, Portugal (left 1985), Sweden (left 1995), Switzerland, UK (left 1972); Iceland, Finland (left 1995), Liechtenstein
Group of Seven (G7)	1975	Canada, France, Germany, Italy, Japan, UK, USA
International Organization for Migration (IOM)	1951	Australia, Austria, Belgium, Bolivia, Brazil, Canada, West Germany, Greece, Italy, Luxembourg, Netherlands, Switzerland, Turkey, USA
Nordic Council	1952	Denmark, Finland, Iceland, Norway, Sweden
North Atlantic Treaty Organization (NATO)	1949	Belgium, Canada, Denmark, France, Iceland, Italy, Luxembourg, the Netherlands, Norway, Portugal, UK, USA, Greece, Turkey, West Germany, Spain, Germany, Czech Republic, Hungary, Poland
Organization for Economic Cooperation and Development (OECD)	1961	Australia, Austria, Belgium, Canada, Czech Republic, Denmark, Finland, France, Germany, Greece, Iceland, Ireland, Italy, Japan, Luxembourg, Mexico, Netherlands, New Zealand, Norway, Portugal, Spain, Sweden, Switzerland, Turkey, UK, USA; Hungary, Poland, Slovak Republic, South Korea
Organization of African Unity (OAU)	1963	Algeria, Angola, Benin, Botswana, Burkina Faso, Burundi, Cameroon, Cape Verde, Central African Republic, Chad, Comoros, Democratic Republic of Congo, Republic of Congo, Côte d'Ivoire, Djibouti, Egypt, Equatorial Guinea, Eritrea, Ethiopia, Gabon, Gambia, Ghana, Guinea, Guinea-Bissau, Kenya, Lesotho, Liberia, Libya, Madagascar, Malawi, Mali, Mauritania, Mauritius, Mozambique, Namibia, Niger, Nigeria, Rwanda, São Tomé and Principe, Senegal, Seychelles, Sierra Leone, Somalia, South Africa, Sudan, Swaziland, Tanzania, Togo, Tunisia, Uganda, Zambia, Zimbabwe
Organization of American States (OAS)	1951	Antigua and Barbuda, Argentina, Bahamas, Barbados, Belize, Bolivia, Brazil, Canada, Chile, Colombia, Costa Rica, Cuba, Dominica, Dominican Republic, Ecuador, El Salvador, Grenada, Guatemala, Guyana, Haiti, Honduras, Jamaica, Mexico, Nicaragua, Panama, Paraguay, Peru, St Kitts and Nevis, St Lucia, St Vincent and the Grenadines, Suriname, Trinidad and Tobago, Uruguay, USA, Venezuela
Organization of Central American States	1961	Costa Rica, El Salvador, Guatemala, Honduras, Nicaragua
Organization of Arab Petroleum Exporting Countries (OAPEC)	1968	Kuwait, Libya, Saudi Arabia, Algeria, Bahrain, Egypt, Iraq, Qatar, Syria, United Arab Emirates

Alliance/Organization	Established	Members
Organization of the Petroleum Exporting Countries (OPEC)	1960	Algeria, Indonesia, Iran, Iraq, Kuwait, Libya, Nigeria, Qatar, Saudi Arabia, United Arab Emirates, Venezuela
Schengen Group	1995	Austria, Belgium, Germany, Greece, Italy, Luxembourg, Netherlands, Portugal, Spain
Visegrad Group	1991	Czech Republic, Hungary, Poland, Slovak Republic
Warsaw Pact	1955 (dissolved 1991)	Albania, Bulgaria, Czechoslovakia, East Germany, Hungary, Poland, Romania, USSR
Western European Union (WEU)	1954	Belgium, France, Germany, Greece, Italy, Luxembourg, Netherlands, Portugal, Spain, UK
World Trade Organization (WTO)	1995 (replaced GATT)	134 members (1999)

Note See also separate information for United Nations, Commonwealth, European Union and Space Agencies

United Nations members

Year of entry	Country
1945	Argentina, Australia, Belgium, Byelorussian SSR (Belarus from 1991), Bolivia, Brazil, Canada, Chile, China (Taiwan to 1971), Colombia, Costa Rica, Cuba, Czechoslovakia (to 1993), Denmark, Dominican Republic, Ecuador, Egypt, El Salvador, Ethiopia, France, Greece, Guatemala, Haiti, Honduras, India, Iran, Iraq, Lebanon, Liberia, Luxembourg, Mexico, Netherlands, New Zealand, Nicaragua, Norway, Panama, Paraguay, Peru, Philippines, Poland, Saudi Arabia, South Africa, Syria, Turkey, Ukrainian SSR (Ukraine from 1991), USSR (Russia from 1991), UK, USA, Uruguay, Venezuela, Yugoslavia (to 1992)
1946	Afghanistan, Iceland, Sweden, Thailand
1947	Pakistan, Yemen (North Yemen to 1990)
1948	Burma (Myanmar from 1989)
1949	Israel
1950	Indonesia
1955	Albania, Austria, Bulgaria, Kampuchea (Cambodia from 1989), Ceylon (Sri Lanka from 1970), Finland, Hungary, Ireland, Italy, Jordan, Laos, Libya, Nepal, Portugal, Romania, Spain
1956	Japan, Morocco, Sudan, Tunisia
1957	Ghana, Malaya (Malaysia from 1963)
1958	Guinea
1960	Cameroon, Central African Republic, Chad, Congo, Côte d'Ivoire (Ivory Coast), Cyprus, Dahomey (Benin from 1975), Gabon, Madagascar, Mali, Niger, Nigeria, Senegal, Somalia, Togo, Upper Volta (Burkina Faso from 1984), Zaïre (Democratic Republic of Congo from 1997)
1961	Mauritania, Mongolia, Sierra Leone, Tanganyika
1962	Algeria, Burundi, Jamaica, Rwanda, Trinidad and Tobago, Uganda
1963	Kenya, Kuwait, Zanzibar
1964	Malawi, Malta, Zambia, Tanzania
1965	The Gambia, Maldives, Singapore
1966	Barbados, Botswana, Guyana, Lesotho
1966	Yemen (South Yemen to 1990)
1968	Equatorial Guinea, Mauritius, Swaziland
1970	Fiji
1971	Bahrain, Bhutan, China (People's Republic), Oman, Qatar, United Arab Emirates
1973	The Bahamas, German Democratic Republic, German Federal Republic

1974	Bangladesh, Grenada, Guinea-Bissau
1975	Cape Verde, Comoros, Mozambique, Papua New Guinea, São Tomé and Principe, Suriname
1976	Angola, Seychelles, Western Samoa (Samoa from 1997)
1977	Djibouti, Vietnam
1978	Dominica, Solomon Islands
1979	St Lucia
1980	St Vincent and the Grenadines, Zimbabwe
1981	Antigua and Barbuda, Belize, Vanuatu
1983	St Kitts and Nevis
1984	Brunei
1990	Namibia, Yemen
1991	Estonia, Federated States of Micronesia, Latvia, Lithuania, Marshall Islands, North Korea, South Korea
1992	Armenia, Azerbaijan, Bosnia-Herzegovina, Croatia, Georgia, Kazakhstan, Kyrgyzstan, Moldova, San Marino, Slovenia, Tajikistan, Turkmenistan, Uzbekistan
1993	Andorra, Czech Republic, Eritrea, Former Yugoslav Republic of Macedonia, Monaco, Slovakia
1995	Belau
1999	Kiribati, Nauru, Tonga
2000	Tuvalu

United Nations structure

Body	Headquarters	Members	Role
General Assembly	New York	189 (one from each member state)	Directs work of the UN and debates international affairs
Security Council	New York	China, France, Russia, UK, USA plus ten other elected members	Investigates disputes and maintains international peace
Secretariat	New York	66 000 staff under the leadership of the Secretary-General	Undertakes diplomatic work worldwide
International Court of Justice	The Hague	15 independent elected judges	Advises UN organizations and decides disputes between states
Economic and Social Council (ECOSOC)	New York	54 elected members	Directs UN committees, commissions and specialized bodies relating to economics and social affairs
Trusteeship Council	New York	China, France, Russia, UK, USA	Directs the transition of Trust territories to self-government

United Nations specialized agencies and programmes

Agency/Programme	Abbrev.	Headquarters	Responsibility
Food and Agriculture Organization	FAO	Rome	Raising standards of living and improving food production and distribution
General Agreement on Tariffs and Trade	GATT	Geneva	Promotion and protection of international trade
International Atomic Energy Association	IAEA	Vienna	Research into and development of peaceful uses of nuclear energy
International Bank for Reconstruction and Development	IBRD	Washington	Promotion of development through investment
International Civil Aviation Organization	ICAO	Montreal	Promotion of safety in aviation
International Development Association	IDA	Washington	Provision of credit to assist less-developed nations
International Finance Corporation	IFC	Washington	Provision of loans and financial assistance to private companies
International Fund for Agricultural Development Organization	IFAD	Rome	Promotion of food production through grants and loans
International Labour Organization	ILO	Geneva	Improvement of labour conditions and standards of living
International Maritime Organization	IMO	London	Coordination of safety at sea
International Monetary Fund	IMF	Washington	Promotion of international monetary cooperation
International Telecommunication Union	ITU	Geneva	Improvement of telecommunications
Multilateral Investment Guarantee Agency	MIGA	Washington	Promotion of private investment in less-developed nations
United Nations Centre for Human Settlements	UNCHS/ Habitat	New York	Provision of planning, construction, land development and finance
United Nations Children's Fund	UNICEF	New York	Provision of help for children in less-developed countries
United Nations Conference on Trade and Development	UNCTAD	Geneva	Promotion of international trade
United Nations Development Fund for Women	UNIFEM	New York	Promotion of the economic and social development of women
United Nations Development Programme	UNDP	New York	Promotion of standards of living in less-developed nations
United Nations Educational, Scientific and Cultural Organization	UNESCO	Paris	Promotion of peace through education and culture
United Nations Environmental Programme	UNEP	Nairobi	Protection of the environment
United Nations High Commissioner for Refugees	UNHCR	Geneva	Provision of protection for refugees

United Nations Industrial Development Organization	UNIDO	Vienna	Promotion of industrialization in less-developed countries
United Nations Institute for Training and Research	UNITAR	Geneva	Improvement of the UN through training and research
United Nations Population Fund	UNFPA	New York	Assistance in matters of reproductive health and population
United Nations Research Institute for Social Development	UNRISD	New York	Research into social and economic development
Universal Postal Union	UPU	Berne	Improvement of standards in postal services
World Food Programme	WFP	Rome	Improvement of economic and social development through food aid
World Health Organization	WHO	Geneva	Promotion of health
World Meteorological Organization	WMO	Geneva	Promotion of cooperation in relation to study of the weather worldwide
World Intellectual Property Organization	WIPO	Geneva	Protection of patents and trademarks throughout the world

Note The IAEA is linked with the UN but is not strictly a specialized agency of the organization

United Nations secretaries-general

Period in office	Secretary-General
1946–53	Trygve Lie (Norway)
1953–61	Dag Hammarskjöld (Sweden)
1962–71	U Thant (Burma)
1971–81	Kurt Waldheim (Austria)
1982–92	Javier Pérez de Cuéllar (Peru)
1992–96	Boutros Boutros Ghali (Egypt)
1997–	Kofi Annan (Ghana)

Commonwealth members

Year of entry	Country
1931	Australia, Canada, New Zealand, UK; South Africa (left 1961; rejoined 1994)
1947	India, Pakistan (left 1972; rejoined 1989)
1948	Sri Lanka
1957	Ghana, Malaysia
1960	Nigeria (suspended 1995; readmitted 1999)
1961	Cyprus, Sierra Leone (suspended 1997), Tanzania
1962	Jamaica, Trinidad and Tobago, Uganda
1963	Kenya
1964	Malawi, Malta, Zambia
1965	The Gambia, Singapore
1966	Barbados, Botswana, Guyana, Lesotho
1968	Mauritius, Nauru, Swaziland
1970	Tonga, Western Samoa; Fiji (suspended 1987; readmitted 1997)
1972	Bangladesh

Year of entry	Country
1973	The Bahamas
1974	Grenada
1975	Papua New Guinea
1976	Seychelles
1978	Dominica, Solomon Islands, Tuvalu
1979	Kiribati, St Lucia, St Vincent and the Grenadines
1980	Vanuatu, Zimbabwe
1981	Antigua and Barbuda, Belize
1982	Maldives
1983	St Kitts and Nevis
1984	Brunei
1990	Namibia
1995	Cameroon, Mozambique

Commonwealth secretaries-general

Period in office	Secretary-General
1965–75	Arnold Smith (Canada)
1975–90	Shridath S. Ramphal (Guyana)
1990–99	Emeka Anyaoku (Nigeria)
1999–	Don McKinnon (New Zealand)

European Union members

Year of entry	Country
1958	Belgium, France, Germany, Italy, Luxembourg, Netherlands
1973	Denmark, Republic of Ireland, UK
1981	Greece
1986	Portugal, Spain
1995	Austria, Finland, Sweden

Note Cyprus, the Czech Republic, Estonia, Hungary, Poland and Switzerland are currently being considered for membership of the EU

European Union structure

Body	Headquarters	Members	Role
European Commission	Brussels	20 members (two each from France, Germany, Italy, Spain and the UK; one each from Austria, Belgium, Denmark, Finland, Greece, Ireland, Luxembourg, Netherlands, Portugal and Sweden)	Initiation of EU policies
Council of Ministers of the European Union	Brussels	Foreign ministers of member states	Making decisions based on Commission proposals

Committee of the Regions	Brussels		Representation of regions of the EU
Committee of Permanent Representatives (COREPER)	Brussels	Permanent officials representing member states	Undertaking work on behalf of the Commission
Economic and Social Committee	Brussels		Representation of employers, workers, consumers and other interest groups
European Parliament	Strasbourg/ Brussels/ Luxembourg	626 MEPs	Debates legislative proposals of the Commission
European Court of Justice	Luxembourg	15 judges and 9 advocates-general	Hears cases involving member states and interprets Community treaties and legislation

European Union Commission

Period in office	President
1967–70	Jean Rey (Belgium)
1970–72	Franco M. Malfatti (Italy)
1972–73	Sicco L. Mansholt (Netherlands)
1973–77	François-Xavier Ortoli (France)
1977–81	Roy Jenkins (UK)
1981–85	Gaston Thorn (Luxembourg)
1985–95	Jacques Delors (France)
1995–99	Jacques Santer (Luxembourg)
1999–	Romano Prodi (Italy)

European parliament

National composition

Member state	Number of seats (1999)
Austria	21
Belgium	25
Denmark	16
Finland	16
France	87
Germany	99
Greece	25
Ireland	15
Italy	87
Luxembourg	6
Netherlands	31
Portugal	25
Spain	64
Sweden	22
UK	87
TOTAL	626

Political groupings

Party	Number of seats (1999)
European People's Party (PPE)	224
Party of European Socialists (PSE)	180
Liberal, Democrat and Reform Party (ELDR)	43
Greens in the European Parliament (V)	38
European United Left/Nordic Green Left (GUE/NGL)	35
Independents/Europe of Nations (I-EDN)	21
Union for Europe (UPE)	17
European Radical Alliance (ARE)	13
Others	37
Non-attached	18
TOTAL	626

European Union specialized organizations

Organization	Abbreviation	Headquarters	Responsibility
European Atomic Energy Community	EURATOM	Brussels	Promotion of peaceful nuclear research
European Coal and Steel Community	ECSC	Luxembourg	Coordination of European coal and steel industries
European Investment Bank	EIB	Luxembourg	Provision of loans for capital projects
European Monetary System	EMS	Brussels	Promotion of financial cooperation and monetary stability

Nobel Prize for Peace

Year	Winner	Nationality
1901	Jean Henri Dunant and Frédéric Passy	Swiss/French
1902	Elie Ducommun and Charles Albert Gobat	Swiss/Swiss
1903	Sir William Cremer	British
1904	Institute of International Law	
1905	Bertha von Suttner	Austrian
1906	Theodore Roosevelt	US
1907	Ernesto Teodoro Moneta and Louis Renault	Italian/French
1908	Klas Pontus Arnoldson and Fredrik Bajer	Swedish/Danish
1909	Baron d'Estournelles de Constant and Auguste Beernaert	French/Belgian
1910	International Peace Bureau	
1911	Tobias Asser and Alfred Fried	Dutch/Austrian
1912	Elihu Root	US
1913	Henri Lafontaine	Belgian
1914	(No award)	
1915	(No award)	
1916	(No award)	

1917	International Red Cross Committee	
1918	(No award)	
1919	Woodrow Wilson	US
1920	Léon Bourgeois	French
1921	Karl Branting and Christian Louis Lange	Swedish/Norwegian
1922	Fridtjof Nansen	Norwegian
1923	(No award)	
1924	(No award)	
1925	Sir Austen Chamberlain and Charles G. Dawes	British/US
1926	Aristide Briand and Gustav Stresemann	French/German
1927	Ferdinand Buisson and Ludwig Quidde	French/German
1928	(No award)	
1929	Frank B. Kellogg	US
1930	Nathan Söderblom	Swedish
1931	Jane Addams and Nicholas Murray Butler	US/US
1932	(No award)	
1933	Sir Norman Angell	British
1934	Arthur Henderson	British
1935	Carl von Ossietzky	German
1936	Carlos Saavedra Lamas	Argentinian
1937	Viscount Cecil of Chetwood	British
1938	Nansen International Office for Refugees	
1939	(No award)	
1940	(No award)	
1941	(No award)	
1942	(No award)	
1943	(No award)	
1944	International Red Cross Committee	
1945	Cordell Hull	US
1946	Emily Greene Balch and John R. Mott	US/US
1947	American Friends Service Committee and Friends Service Council	US/British
1948	(No award)	
1949	Lord Boyd-Orr	British
1950	Ralph Bunche	US
1951	Léon Jouhaut	French
1952	Albert Schweitzer	German
1953	George C. Marshall	US
1954	Office of the United Nations High Commissioner for Refugees	
1955	(No award)	
1956	(No award)	
1957	Lester B. Pearson	Canadian
1958	Dominique Georges Pire	Belgian
1959	Philip Noel-Baker	British
1960	Albert Lutuli	South African
1961	Dag Hammarskjöld	Swedish
1962	Linus Pauling	US
1963	International Red Cross Committee	
1964	Martin Luther King	US

Year	Winner	Nationality
1965	United Nations Children's Fund	
1966	(No award)	
1967	(No award)	
1968	René Cassin	French
1969	International Labour Organization	
1970	Norman E. Borlaug	US
1971	Willy Brandt	German
1972	(No award)	
1973	Henry Kissinger and Le Duc Tho	US/North Vietnamese
1974	Eisaku Sato and Sean MacBride	Japanese/Irish
1975	Andrei D. Sakharov	Russian
1976	Mairead Corrigan and Betty Williams	British/British
1977	Amnesty International	
1978	Menachem Begin and Anwar el-Sadat	Israeli/Egyptian
1979	Mother Teresa of Calcutta	Yugoslavian
1980	Adolfo Pérez Esquivel	Argentinian
1981	United Nations High Commissioner for Refugees	
1982	Alva Myrdal and Alfonso Garciá Robles	Swedish/Mexican
1983	Lech Walesa	Polish
1984	Desmond Tutu	South African
1985	International Physicists for the Prevention of Nuclear War	
1986	Elie Wiesel	French
1987	Oscar Arias Sánchez	Costa Rican
1988	United Nations peacekeeping forces	
1989	The Dalai Lama	Tibetan
1990	Mikhail Gorbachev	Russian
1991	Aung San Suu Kyi	Burmese
1992	Rigoberta Menchu	Guatemalan
1993	Nelson Mandela and Frederik Willem de Klerk	South African/South African
1994	Yassir Arafat, Yitzhak Rabin and Shimon Perez	Palestinian/Israeli/Israeli
1995	Joseph Roblat and the Pugwash Conferences on Science and World Affairs	Polish-born British
1996	Carlos Filipe Ximenes Belo and José Ramos-Horta	Timorese/Timorese
1997	Jody Williams and the International Campaign to Ban Landmines	US
1998	John Hume and David Trimble	British/British
1999	Médecins Sans Frontières	
2000	Kim Dae Jung	South Korean

6.2 *Administrative Organization*

Local government in England

Counties

County	Area	Administrative centre	Population
Bedfordshire	1 192 sq km (460 sq mi)	Bedford	524 105
Buckinghamshire	1 565 sq km (604 sq mi)	Aylesbury	632 487
Cambridgeshire	3 410 sq km (1 316 sq mi)	Cambridge	645 125
Cheshire	2 320 sq km (896 sq mi)	Chester	956 616
Cornwall	3 550 sq km (1 370 sq mi)	Truro	468 425
Cumbria	6 810 sq km (2 629 sq mi)	Carlisle	483 163
Derbyshire	2 550 sq km (984 sq mi)	Matlock	928 636
Devon	6 720 sq km (2 594 sq mi)	Exeter	1 009 950
Dorset	2 541 sq km (981 sq mi)	Dorchester	645 166
Durham	2 232 sq km (862 sq mi)	Durham	593 430
East Sussex	1 725 sq km (666 sq mi)	Lewes	690 447
Essex	3 670 sq km (1 417 sq mi)	Chelmsford	1 528 577
Gloucestershire	2 640 sq km (1 019 sq mi)	Gloucester	528 370
Hampshire	3 679 sq km (1 420 sq mi)	Winchester	1 541 547
Hertfordshire	1 630 sq km (629 sq mi)	Hertford	975 829
Kent	3 730 sq km (1 440 sq mi)	Maidstone	1 508 873
Lancashire	3 040 sq km (1 173 sq mi)	Preston	1 383 998
Leicestershire	2 084 sq km (804 sq mi)	Leicester	867 521
Lincolnshire	5 890 sq km (2 274 sq mi)	Lincoln	584 534
Norfolk	5 360 sq km (2 069 sq mi)	Norwich	745 613
Northamptonshire	2 370 sq km (915 sq mi)	Northampton	578 807
Northumberland	5 030 sq km (1 942 sq mi)	Morpeth	307 709
North Yorkshire	8 037 sq km (3 102 sq mi)	Northallerton	556 200
Nottinghamshire	2 160 sq km (834 sq mi)	Nottingham	993 872
Oxfordshire	2 610 sq km (1 007 sq mi)	Oxford	547 584
Shropshire	3 490 sq km (1 347 sq mi)	Shrewsbury	406 387
Somerset	3 460 sq km (1 336 sq mi)	Taunton	460 368
Staffordshire	2 720 sq km (1 050 sq mi)	Stafford	1 031 135
Suffolk	3 800 sq km (1 467 sq mi)	Ipswich	636 266
Surrey	1 660 sq km (641 sq mi)	Kingston upon Thames	1 018 003
Warwickshire	1 980 sq km (764 sq mi)	Warwick	484 247
West Sussex	1 990 sq km (768 sq mi)	Chichester	702 290
Wiltshire	3 480 sq km (1 343 sq mi)	Trowbridge	564 471
Worcestershire	1 640 sq km (1 020 sq mi)	Worcester	531 909

Unitary authorities

Authority	Area	Administrative centre	Population
Bath and North East Somerset	351 sq km (136 sq mi)	Bath	158 700
Blackburn with Darwen	136 sq km (53 sq mi)	Blackburn	139 400
Blackpool	35 sq km (14 sq mi)	Blackpool	261 400

Authority	Area	Administrative centre	Population
Bournemouth	46 sq km (18 sq mi)	Bournemouth	161 500
Bracknell Forest	109 sq km (42 sq mi)	Bracknell	109 600
Brighton and Hove	84 sq km (32 sq mi)	Hove	248 000
Bristol	109 sq km (42 sq mi)	Bristol	516 500
Darlington	197 sq km (76 sq mi)	Darlington	100 600
Derby City	200 sq km (124 sq mi)	Derby	218 800
East Riding of Yorkshire	2 416 sq km (933 sq mi)	Beverley	310 000
Halton	74 sq km (29 sq mi)	Widnes	122 300
Hartlepool	94 sq km (36 sq mi)	Hartlepool	90 400
Herefordshire	2 288 sq km (884 sq mi)	Hereford	166 100
Kingston upon Hull	71 sq km (27 sq mi)	Kington upon Hull	265 000
Leicester City	73 sq km (28 sq mi)	Leicester	270 500
Luton	43 sq km (17 sq mi)	Luton	181 400
Medway Towns	194 sq km (75 sq mi)	Strood	240 000
Middlesbrough	54 sq km (21 sq mi)	Middlesbrough	146 000
Milton Keynes	311 sq km (120 sq mi)	Milton Keynes	198 600
North East Lincolnshire	192 sq km (74 sq mi)	Grimsby	164 000
North Lincolnshire	850 sq km (328 sq mi)	Scunthorpe	153 000
North Somerset	372 sq km (144 sq mi)	Weston-Super-Mare	177 000
Nottingham City	74 sq km (29 sq mi)	Nottingham	285 000
Peterborough	334 sq km (129 sq mi)	Peterborough	156 900
Plymouth	79 sq km (31 sq mi)	Plymouth	257 000
Poole	64 sq km (25 sq mi)	Poole	138 100
Portsmouth	42 sq km (16 sq mi)	Portsmouth	189 300
Reading	37 sq km (14 sq mi)	Reading	131 000
Redcar and Cleveland	240 sq km (93 sq mi)	Redcar	144 000
Rutland	394 sq km (152 sq mi)	Oakham	34 600
Slough	28 sq km (11 sq mi)	Slough	105 000
Southampton	52 sq km (20 sq mi)	Southampton	207 100
Southend	42 sq km (16 sq mi)	Southend	171 000
South Gloucestershire	497 sq km (192 sq mi)	Thornbury	220 000
Stockton-on-Tees	200 sq km (77 sq mi)	Stockton-on-Tees	176 600
Stoke-on-Trent	93 sq km (36 sq mi)	Stoke-on-Trent	254 200
Swindon	230 sq km (89 sq mi)	Swindon	170 000
Telford and Wrekin	291 sq km (112 sq mi)	Telford	144 600
Thurrock	163 sq km (63 sq mi)	Grays	130 600
Torbay	627 sq km (242 sq mi)	Torquay	128 000
Warrington	176 sq km (68 sq mi)	Warrington	151 000
West Berkshire	705 sq km (272 sq mi)	Newbury	142 600
Wight, Isle of	380 sq km (147 sq mi)	Newport	130 000
Windsor and Maidenhead	198 sq km (76 sq mi)	Maidenhead	140 200
Wokingham	179 sq km (69 sq mi)	Wokingham	142 000
York	271 sq km (105 sq mi)	York	174 800

Local government in Scotland

Unitary Authority	Area	Administrative centre	Population
Aberdeen City	185 sq km (71 sq mi)	Aberdeen	219 100
Aberdeenshire	6 308 sq km (2 436 sq mi)	Aberdeen	226 500
Angus	2 187 sq km (844 sq mi)	Forfar	111 300
Argyll and Bute	7 016 sq km (2 709 sq mi)	Lochgilphead	89 300
Clackmannanshire	161 sq km (62 sq mi)	Alloa	47 700
Dumfries and Galloway	6 421 sq km (2 479 sq mi)	Dumfries	147 800
Dundee City	62 sq km (24 sq mi)	Dundee	155 000
East Ayrshire	1 269 sq km (490 sq mi)	Kilmarnock	124 000
East Dunbartonshire	175 sq km (67 sq mi)	Kirkintilloch	110 000
East Lothian	677 sq km (261 sq mi)	Haddington	85 500
East Renfrewshire	174 sq km (67 sq mi)	Giffnock	86 800
Edinburgh	263 sq km (122 sq mi)	Edinburgh	477 600
Falkirk	297 sq km (115 sq mi)	Falkirk	142 500
Fife	1 321 sq km (510 sq mi)	Glenrothes	351 200
Glasgow	176 sq km (68 sq mi)	Glasgow	618 400
Highlands	26 157 sq km (10 100 sq mi)	Inverness	207 500
Inverclyde	161 sq km (62 sq mi)	Greenock	90 000
Midlothian	363 sq km (140 sq mi)	Dalkeith	79 900
Moray	2 224 sq km (859 sq mi)	Elgin	85 000
North Ayrshire	889 sq km (343 sq mi)	Irvine	139 200
North Lanarkshire	475 sq km (183 sq mi)	Motherwell	326 700
Orkney Islands	1 014 sq km (391 sq mi)	Kirkwall	19 600
Perth and Kinross	5 388 sq km (2 080 sq mi)	Perth	131 800
Renfrewshire	260 sq km (100 sq mi)	Paisley	178 300
Scottish Borders	4 733 sq km (1 827 sq mi)	Newtown St Boswells	105 300
Shetland Islands	1 452 sq km (560 sq mi)	Lerwick	22 500
South Ayrshire	1 245 sq km (480 sq mi)	Ayr	114 000
South Lanarkshire	1 772 sq km (684 sq mi)	Hamilton	307 100
Stirling	2 196 sq km (848 sq mi)	Stirling	82 000
West Dunbartonshire	177 sq km (68 sq mi)	Dumbarton	97 800
Western Isles	3 057 sq km (1 180 sq mi)	Stornoway	27 800
West Lothian	428 sq km (165 sq mi)	Livingston	147 900

Local government in Wales

Unitary Authority	Area	Administrative centre	Population
Anglesey	720 sq km (278 sq mi)	Llangefni	71 100
Blaenau Gwent	109 sq km (42 sq mi)	Ebbw Vale	73 000
Bridgend	40 sq km (15 sq mi)	Bridgend	128 300
Caerphilly	270 sq km (104 sq mi)	Hengoed	172 000
Cardiff	139 sq km (54 sq mi)	Cardiff	306 500
Carmarthenshire	2 390 sq km (923 sq mi)	Carmarthen	68 900
Ceredigion	1 793 sq km (692 sq mi)	Aberaeron	68 900
Conwy	1 107 sq km (427 sq mi)	Conwy	113 000
Denbighshire	844 sq km (326 sq mi)	Ruthin	91 000

Unitary Authority	Area	Administrative centre	Population
Flintshire	437 sq km (167 sq mi)	Mold	144 000
Gwynedd	2 546 sq km (983 sq mi)	Caernarfon	116 000
Merthyr Tydfil	111 sq km (43 sq mi)	Merthyr Tydfil	60 000
Monmouthshire	851 sq km (328 sq mi)	Cwmbran	80 400
Neath Port Talbot	442 sq km (171 sq mi)	Port Talbot	139 400
Newport	190 sq km (73 sq mi)	Newport	133 300
Pembrokeshire	1 588 sq km (613 sq mi)	Haverfordwest	117 700
Powys	5 179 sq km (1 999 sq mi)	Llandrindod Wells	123 600
Rhondda Cynon Taff	440 sq km (170 sq mi)	Clydach Vale	232 600
Swansea	377 sq km (156 sq mi)	Swansea	232 000
Torfaen	98 sq km (38 sq mi)	Pontypool	90 700
Vale of Glamorgan	337 sq km (130 sq mi)	Barry	119 500
Wrexham	500 sq km (193 sq mi)	Wrexham	123 500

Local government in Northern Ireland

Counties

County	Area	County town
Antrim	2 830 sq km (1 092 sq mi)	Belfast
Armagh	1 250 sq km (483 sq mi)	Armagh
Down	2 470 sq km (953 sq mi)	Downpatrick
Fermanagh	1 680 sq km (648 sq mi)	Enniskillen
Londonderry/Derry	2 070 sq km (799 sq mi)	Londonderry/Derry
Tyrone	3 160 sq km (1 220 sq mi)	Omagh

Note The administrative functions of the six counties of Northern Ireland have been transferred to 26 district councils (*see* below).

Districts

District	Area	Administrative centre	Population
Antrim	563 sq km (217 mi)	Antrim	49 000
Ards	369 sq km (142 sq mi)	Newtownards	68 000
Armagh	672 sq km (259 sq mi)	Armagh	53 000
Ballymena	638 sq km (246 sq mi)	Ballymena	58 000
Ballymoney	419 sq km (162 sq mi)	Ballymoney	25 000
Banbridge	444 sq km (171 sq mi)	Banbridge	37 000
Belfast	140 sq km (54 sq mi)	Belfast	297 000
Carrickfergus	87 sq km (34 sq mi)	Carrickfergus	35 000
Castlereagh	85 sq km (33 sq mi)	Belfast	64 000
Coleraine	485 sq km (187 sq mi)	Coleraine	55 000
Cookstown	623 sq km (240 sq mi)	Cookstown	32 000
Craigavon	383 sq km (147 sq mi)	Craigavon	79 000
Down	646 sq km (249 sq mi)	Downpatrick	61 000
Dungannon	779 sq km (301 sq mi)	Dungannon	47 000
Fermanagh	1 876 sq km (715 sq mi)	Enniskillen	55 000
Larne	338 sq km (131 sq mi)	Larne	30 000
Limavady	587 sq km (227 sq mi)	Limavady	31 000
Lisburn	444 sq km (171 sq mi)	Lisburn	108 000
Londonderry/Derry	382 sq km (147 sq mi)	Londonderry/Derry	104 000
Magherafelt	573 sq km (221 sq mi)	Magherafelt	38 000
Moyle	495 sq km (191 sq mi)	Ballycastle	15 000

Newry and Mourne	895 sq km (346 sq mi)	Newry	85 000
Newtownabbey	152 sq km (59 sq mi)	Newtownabbey	79 000
North Down	73 sq km (28 sq mi)	Bangor	74 000
Omagh	1 129 sq km (436 sq mi)	Omagh	47 000
Strabane	870 sq km (336 sq mi)	Strabane	37 000

UK islands

Island	Area	Administrative centre	Population (1998 est)
Isle of Man	572 sq km (221 sq mi)	Douglas	77 800
Jersey	116 sq km (45 sq mi)	St Helier	89 100
Guernsey	63 sq km (24 sq mi)	St Peter Port	64 500
Alderney	8 sq km (3 sq mi)	St Anne's	2 150
Sark	4 sq km (2 sq mi)		581

Administrative divisions of Europe

Albania

Province	Area	Population (1993 est)
Berat	939 sq km (363 sq mi)	136 939
Bulquize	469 sq km (181 sq mi)	43 363
Delvinë	348 sq km (134 sq mi)	29 926
Devoll	429 sq km (166 sq mi)	37 744
Dibrë	1 088 sq km (420 sq mi)	91 916
Durrës	433 sq km (167 sq mi)	162 846
Elbasan	1 372 sq km (530 sq mi)	215 240
Fier	785 sq km (303 sq mi)	208 646
Gjirokastër	1 752 sq km (676 sq mi)	60 547
Gramsh	695 sq km (268 sq mi)	42 087
Has	393 sq km (152 sq mi)	21 271
Kavajë	414 sq km (160 sq mi)	85 120
Kolonjë	805 sq km (311 sq mi)	25 089
Korçë	1 752 sq km (676 sq mi)	171 205
Krujë	333 sq km (129 sq mi)	59 997
Kucovë	84 sq km (32 sq mi)	40 035
Kukës	938 sq km (362 sq mi)	78 061
Kurbin	273 sq km (105 sq mi)	50 712
Lezhë	479 sq km (185 sq mi)	65 075
Librazhd	1 023 sq km (395 sq mi)	75 300
Lushnjë	712 sq km (275 sq mi)	136 865
Malesia e Madhe	555 sq km (214 sq mi)	43 924
Mallakastër	393 sq km (152 sq mi)	36 287
Mat	1 029 sq km (397 sq mi)	75 436
Mirditë	867 sq km (335 sq mi)	49 900
Peqin	109 sq km (42 sq mi)	29 831
Permet	930 sq km (359 sq mi)	36 979
Pogradec	725 sq km (280 sq mi)	72 203

Province	Area	Population (1993 est)
Pukë	1 034 sq km (399 sq mi)	47 621
Sarandë	749 sq km (289 sq mi)	53 730
Shkodër	1 973 sq km (762 sq mi)	195 424
Skrapar	775 sq km (299 sq mi)	44 339
Tepelenë	817 sq km (315 sq mi)	42 365
Tiranë	1 238 sq km (478 sq mi)	384 010
Tropojë	1 043 sq km (403 sq mi)	44 761
Vlorë	1 609 sq km (621 sq mi)	171 131

Austria

State	Area	Capital	Population (1996 est)
Burgenland	3 966 sq km (1 531 sq mi)	Eisenstadt	275 000
Carinthia (Kärnten)	9 533 sq km (3 681 sq mi)	Klagenfurt	563 000
Lower Austria (Niederösterreich)	19 172 sq km (7 402 sq mi)	Sankt Pölten	1 524 000
Salzburg	7 154 sq km (2 762 sq mi)	Salzburg	509 000
Styria (Steiermark)	16 387 sq km (6 327 sq mi)	Graz	1 207 000
Tyrol (Tirol)	12 647 sq km (4 883 sq mi)	Innsbruck	660 000
Upper Austria (Oberösterreich)	11 980 sq km (4 626 sq mi)	Linz	1 381 000
Vienna (Wien)	415 sq km (160 sq mi)	Vienna	1 595 000
Vorarlberg	2 601 sq km (1 004 sq mi)	Bregenz	344 000

Belgium

Province	Area	Capital	Population (1994 est)
Antwerp	2 867 sq km (1 107 sq mi)	Antwerp	1 628 710
Brabant	3 358 sq km (1 297 sq mi)	Brussels	2 283 351
E Flanders	2 982 sq km (1 151 sq mi)	Ghent	1 349 382
Hainaut	3 787 sq km (1 462 sq mi)	Mons	1 286 649
Liège	3 862 sq km (1 491 sq mi)	Liège	1 015 007
Limburg	2 422 sq km (935 sq mi)	Hasselt	771 613
Luxembourg	4 441 sq km (1 715 sq mi)	Arlon	230 827
Namur	3 665 sq km (1 415 sq mi)	Namur	434 446
W Flanders	3 314 sq km (1 210 sq mi)	Bruges	1 102 501

Bulgaria

Province	Area	Capital	Population (1994 est)
Burgas	14 724 sq km (5 683 sq mi)	Burgas	850 003
Khaskovo	13 824 sq km (5 336 sq mi)	Khashkovo	903 928
Lovech	15 150 sq km (5 848 sq mi)	Lovech	1 009 196
Montana	10 606 sq km (4 098 sq mi)	Montana	626 205
Plovdiv	13 585 sq km (5 244 sq mi)	Plovdiv	1 221 449
Ruse	10 842 sq km (4 185 sq mi)	Ruse	765 719
Sofiya	19 021 sq km (7 342 sq mi)	Sofia	980 588
Varna	11 928 sq km (4 604 sq mi)	Varna	914 079

Cyprus

District	Area	Capital	Population (1989 est)
Famagusta	1 979 sq km (764 sq mi)	Famagusta	29 100
Larnaca	1 126 sq km (435 sq mi)	Larnaca	91 500

Limassol	1 393 sq km (538 sq mi)	Limassol	158 400
Nicosia	2 717 sq km (1 049 sq mi)	Nicosia	234 200
Paphos	1 395 sq km (539 sq mi)	Paphos	49 500

Czech Republic

Region	Area	Capital	Population (1996 est)
C Bohemia (Stredocesky)	11 013 sq km (4 251 sq mi)	Prague	1 106 738
E Bohemia (Východoceský)	11 240 sq km (4 339 sq mi)	Hradec Králové	1 235 641
N Bohemia (Severoceský)	7 799 sq km (3 010 sq mi)	Ústí nad Labem	1 178 208
N Moravia (Severomoravský)	11 067 sq km (4 273 sq mi)	Ostrava	1 972 336
Prague	496 sq km (192 sq mi)	Prague	1 209 855
S Bohemia (Jihoceský)	11 345 sq km (4 380 sq mi)	České Budejovice	700 831
S Moravia (Jihomoravský)	15 028 sq km (5 802 sq mi)	Brno	2 057 239
W Bohemia (Západoceský)	10 875 sq km (4 199 sq mi)	Plzen	860 469

Denmark

County	Area	Capital	Population (1995 est)
Aarhus (Aerhus)	4 561 sq km (1 761 sq mi)	Acerhus	619 232
Bornholm	588 sq km (227 sq mi)	Rønne	44 936
Copenhagen (København)	526 sq km (203 sq mi)	Copenhagen	605 868
Frederiksborg	1 347 sq km (520 sq mi)	Hillerød	350 236
Fyn	3 486 sq km (1 346 sq mi)	Odense	467 695
N Jutland (Nordjylland)	6 173 sq km (2 383 sq mi)	Aalborg (Aelborg)	488 303
Ribe	3 131 sq km (1 209 sq mi)	Ribe	221 750
Ringkøbing	4 853 sq km (1 874 sq mi)	Ringkøbing	270 128
Roskilde	891 sq km (344 sq mi)	Roskilde	224 052
S Jutland (Sønderjylland)	3 938 sq km (1 520 sq mi)	Aebeurace	251 992
Storstrøm	3 398 sq km (1 312 sq mi)	Nykøbing Falster	256 562
Vejle	2 997 sq km (1 157 sq mi)	Vejle	336 663
Viborg	4 122 sq km (1 592 sq mi)	Viborg	230 778
W Zealand (Vestsjaelland)	2 984 sq km (1 152 sq mi)	Sorø	288 221

Finland

Province	Area	Capital	Population (1997est)
Åland	1 527 sq km (590 sq mi)	Mariehamn	25 392
Eastern Finland	48 727 sq km (18 813 sq mi)	Mikkeli	603 724
Lapland	93 057 sq km (35 929 sq mi)	Robaniemi	199 051
Oulu	56 868 sq km (21 957 sq mi)	Oulu	452 942
Southern Finland	30 229 sq km (11 671 sq mi)	Hämeenlinna	2 037 147
Western Finland	74 186 sq km (28 643 sq mi)	Turku	1 829 093

France

Region	Area	Administrative Centre	Population (1996 est)
Alsace	8 280 sq km (3 197 sq mi)	Strasbourg	1 701 000
Aquitaine	41 308 sq km (15 949 sq mi)	Bordeaux	2 880 000
Auvergne	26 013 sq km (10 044 sq mi)	Clermont-Ferrand	1 315 000

Region	Area	Administrative Centre	Population (1996 est)
Basse-Normandie	17 589 sq km (6 791 sq mi)	Caen	1 416 000
Brittany (Bretagne)	27 208 sq km (10 505 sq mi)	Rennes	2 861 000
Burgundy (Bourgogne)	31 582 sq km (12 194 sq mi)	Dijon	1 625 000
Centre	39 151 sq km (15 116 sq mi)	Orléans	2 443 000
Champagne-Ardenne	25 606 sq km (9 886 sq mi)	Châlons-sur-Marne	1 353 000
Corsica (Corse)	8 680 sq km (3 351 sq mi)	Ajaccio	260 000
Franche-Comté	16 202 sq km (6 256 sq mi)	Besançon	1 116 000
Haute-Normandie	12 317 sq km (4 756 sq mi)	Rouen	1 782 000
Ile de France	12 012 sq km (4 638 sq mi)	Paris	11 027 000
Languedoc-Roussillon	27 376 sq km (10 570 sq mi)	Montpellier	2 243 000
Limousin	16 942 sq km (6 541 sq mi)	Limoges	718 000
Lorraine	23 547 sq km (9 091 sq mi)	Metz	2 312 000
Midi-Pyrénées	45 348 sq km (17 509 sq mi)	Toulouse	2 506 000
Nord-Pas-de-Calais	12 414 sq km (4 793 sq mi)	Lille	4 001 000
Pays de la Loire	32 082 sq km (12 387 sq mi)	Nantes	3 154 000
Picardie	19 399 sq km (7 490 sq mi)	Amiens	1 864 000
Poitou-Charentes	25 809 sq km (9 965 sq mi)	Poitiers	1 622 000
Provence-Alpes-Côte d'Azur	31 400 sq km (12 123 sq mi)	Marseille	4 448 000
Rhône-Alpes	43 698 sq km (16 872 sq mi)	Lyon	5 608 000

Germany

State	Area	Capital	Population (1995)
Baden-Württemberg	35 752 sq km (13 804 sq mi)	Stuttgart	10 319 400
Bavaria	70 551 sq km (27 240 sq mi)	Munich	11 993 500
Berlin	889 sq km (343 sq mi)	Berlin	3 471 400
Brandenburg	29 479 sq km (11 382 sq mi)	Potsdam	2 542 000
Bremen	404 sq km (156 sq mi)	Bremen	679 800
Hamburg	755 sq km (292 sq mi)	Hamburg	1 705 900
Hessen	21 114 sq km (8 152 sq mi)	Wiesbaden	6 009 900
Lower Saxony	47 606 sq km (18 381 sq mi)	Hannover	7 780 400
Mecklenburg-West Pomerania	23 170 sq km (8 946 sq mi)	Schwerin	1 823 100
North Rhine-Westphalia	34 077 sq km (13 157 sq mi)	Düsseldorf	17 893 000
Rhineland-Palatinate	19 852 sq km (7 665 sq mi)	Mainz	3 983 300
Saarland	2 570 sq km (992 sq mi)	Saarbrücken	1 084 400
Saxony	18 412 sq km (7 109 sq mi)	Dresden	4 566 600
Saxony-Anhalt	20 446 sq km (7 894 sq mi)	Magdeburg	2 738 900
Schleswig-Holstein	15 770 sq km (6 089 sq mi)	Kiel	2 725 500
Thuringia	16 171 sq km (6 244 sq mi)	Erfurt	2 503 800

Greece

Region	Area	Administrative centre	Population (1991)
Attica (Attikí)	3 808 sq km (1 470 sq mi)	Athens	3 523 407
C Greece (Stereá Ellás)	15 549 sq km (6 004 sq mi)	Lamia	582 280
C Macedonia (Kedrikí Makedhonía)	19 147 sq km (7 393 sq mi)	Thessaloniki	1 710 513
Crete (Kríti)	8 336 sq km (3 218 sq mi)	Heraklion	540 054
E Macedonia and Thrace (Anatolikí Makedhonía kaí Thráki)	14 157 sq km (5 466 sq mi)	Comotini	570 496
Epirus (Ípiros)	9 203 sq km (3 553 sq mi)	Ioannina	339 728

Ionian Islands (Iónioi Nísoi)	2 307 sq km (891 sq mi)	Corfu	193 734
N Aegean (Vóreion Aiyaíon)	3 836 sq km (1 481 sq mi)	Mytilene	199 231
Peleponnese (Pelopónnisos)	15 490 sq km (5 981 sq mi)	Tripolis	607 428
S Aegean (Nótion Aiyaíon)	5 286 sq km (2 041 sq mi)	Hermoupolis	257 481
Thessaly (Thessalía)	14 037 sq km (5 420 sq mi)	Larissa	734 846
W Greece (Dhytikí Ellás)	11 350 sq km (4 382 sq mi)	Patras	707 687
W Macedonia (Dhytikí Makedhonía)	9 451 sq km (3 649 sq mi)	Kozani	293 015

Hungary

County	Area	Capital	Population (1994)
Baranya	4 487 sq km (1 732 sq mi)	Pécs	416 000
Bács-Kiskun	8 362 sq km (3 229 sq mi)	Kecskemét	539 000
Békés	5 632 sq km (2 175 sq mi)	Békéscsaba	401 000
Borsod-Abaúj-Zemplén	7 247 sq km (2 798 sq mi)	Miskolc	744 000
Budapest	525 sq km (203 sq mi)	Budapest	1 996 000
Csongrád	4 263 sq km (1 646 sq mi)	Szeged	437 000
Fejér	4 373 sq km (1 688 sq mi)	Székesfehérvár	422 000
Györ-Moson-Sopron	4 062 sq km (1 568 sq mi)	Györ	427 000
Hajdú-Bihar	6 211 sq km (2 398 sq mi)	Debrecen	549 000
Heves	3 637 sq km (1 404 sq mi)	Eger	329 000
Jász-Nagykun-Szolnok	5 607 sq km (2 165 sq mi)	Szolnok	419 000
Komárom-Esztergom	2 251 sq km (869 sq mi)	Tatabánya	312 000
Nógrád	2 544 sq km (982 sq mi)	Salgótarján	221 000
Pest	6 394 sq km (2 469 sq mi)	Budapest	965 000
Somogy	6 036 sq km (2 331 sq mi)	Kaposvár	338 000
Szabolcs-Szatmár-Bereg	5 938 sq km (2 293 sq mi)	Nyíregyháza	561 000
Tolna	3 704 sq km (1 430 sq mi)	Szekszárd	250 000
Vas	3 337 sq km (1 288 sq mi)	Szombathely	273 000
Veszprém	4 639 sq km (1 791 sq mi)	Veszprém	378 000
Zala	3 784 sq km (1 461 sq mi)	Zalaegerszeg	301 000

Iceland

Region	Area	Administrative centre	Population (1989 est)
Austurland	21 991 sq km (8 491 sq mi)	Egilsstadhir	13 243
Höfudhborgarsvaedhi	1 982 sq km (765 sq mi)	Reykjavik	143 864
Nordhurland eystra	22 368 sq km (8 636 sq mi)	Akureyri	26 107
Nordhurland vestra	13 093 sq km (5 055 sq mi)	Saudhárkrókur	10 450
Sudhurland	25 214 sq km (9 735 sq mi)	Selfoss	20 229
Sudhurnes	(lies within Hofudhborgarsvaedhi)	Keflavik	15 082
Vestfirdhir	9 470 sq km (3 657 sq mi)	Ísafjördhur	9 840
Vesturland	8 701 sq km (3 360 sq mi)	Borgarnes	14 685

Ireland

County	Area	Administrative centre	Population (1996)
Carlow	896 sq km (346 sq mi)	Carlow	41 600
Cavan	1 891 sq km (730 sq mi)	Cavan	52 900
Clare	3 188 sq km (1 231 sq mi)	Ennis	94 000
Cork	7 459 sq km (2 880 sq mi)	Cork	420 300

County	Area	Administrative centre	Population (1996)
Donegal	4 830 sq km (1 865 sq mi)	Lifford	129 900
Dublin	922 sq km (356 sq mi)	Dublin	1 056 700
Galway	5 939 sq km (2 293 sq mi)	Galway	188 600
Kerry	4 701 sq km (1 815 sq mi)	Tralee	126 100
Kildare	1 694 sq km (654 sq mi)	Naas	135 000
Kilkenny	2 062 sq km (796 sq mi)	Kilkenny	75 300
Laoise (Leix)	1 720 sq km (664 sq mi)	Portlaoise	52 900
Leitrim	1 526 sq km (589 sq mi)	Carrick	25 100
Limerick	2 686 sq km (1 037 sq mi)	Limerick	177 902
Longford	1 044 sq km (403 sq mi)	Longford	30 200
Louth	821 sq km (317 sq mi)	Dundalk	92 200
Mayo	5 398 sq km (2 084 sq mi)	Castlebar	111 500
Meath	2 339 sq km (903 sq mi)	Trim	109 700
Monaghan	1 290 sq km (498 sq mi)	Monaghan	51 300
Offaly	1 997 sq km (771 sq mi)	Tullamore	59 100
Roscommon	2 463 sq km (951 sq mi)	Roscommon	52 000
Sligo	1 795 sq km (693 sq mi)	Sligo	55 800
Tipperary	4 254 sq km (1 642 sq mi)	Clonmel	133 500
Waterford	1 869 sq km (710 sq mi)	Waterford	94 600
Westmeath	1 764 sq km (681 sq mi)	Mullingar	63 300
Wexford	2 352 sq km (908 sq mi)	Wexford	104 400
Wicklow	2 025 sq km (782 sq mi)	Wicklow	102 700

Italy

Region	Area	Capital	Population (1995)
Abruzzi	10 794 sq km (4 168 sq mi)	L'Aquila	1 267 700
Basilicata	9 992 sq km (3 858 sq mi)	Potenza	610 700
Calabria	15 080 sq km (5 822 sq mi)	Catanzaro	2 076 100
Campania	13 595 sq km (5 249 sq mi)	Naples	5 745 800
Emilia-Romagna	22 123 sq km (8 542 sq mi)	Bologna	3 922 600
Friuli-Venezia Giulia	7 846 sq km (3 029 sq mi)	Trieste	1 191 200
Lazio	17 203 sq km (6 642 sq mi)	Rome	5 193 200
Liguria	5 416 sq km (2 091 sq mi)	Genoa	1 663 700
Lombardy	23 856 sq km (9 211 sq mi)	Milan	8 910 500
Marche	9 694 sq km (3 743 sq mi)	Ancona	1 441 000
Molise	4 438 sq km (1 714 sq mi)	Campobasso	332 200
Piedmont	25 399 sq km (9 807 sq mi)	Turin	4 298 000
Puglia	19 347 sq km (7 470 sq mi)	Bari	4 075 800
Sardinia	24 090 sq km (9 301 sq mi)	Cagliari	1 659 500
Sicily	25 708 sq km (9 926 sq mi)	Palermo	5 082 700
Trentino-Alto Adige	13 613 sq km (5 256 sq mi)	Trento	908 700
Tuscany	22 992 sq km (8 877 sq mi)	Florence	3 526 000
Umbria	8 456 sq km (3 265 sq mi)	Perugia	822 500
Valle d'Aosta	3 262 sq km (1 259 sq mi)	Aosta	118 500
Veneto	18 364 sq km (7 090 sq mi)	Venice	4 400 000

Liechtenstein

Commune	Area	Population (1990 est)
Balzers	19.6 sq km (7.6 sq mi)	3 668
Eschen	10.3 sq km (4.0 sq mi)	2 964
Gamprin	6.1 sq km (2.4 sq mi)	944

Mauren	7.5 sq km (2.9 sq mi)	2 978
Planken	5.3 sq km (2.0 sq mi)	295
Ruggell	7.4 sq km (2.9 sq mi)	1 454
Schaan	26.8 sq km (10.3 sq mi)	4 930
Schellenberg	3.5 sq km (1.4 sq mi)	769
Triesen	26.4 sq km (10.2 sq mi)	3 377
Triesenberg	29.8 sq km (11.5 sq mi)	2 379
Vaduz	17.3 sq km (6.7 sq mi)	4 874

Luxembourg

District	Area	Population (1989 est)
Diekirch	1 157 sq km (447 sq mi)	55 910
Grevenmacher	525 sq km (203 sq mi)	41 370
Luxembourg	904 sq km (349 sq mi)	277 620

Malta

Region	Area	Population (1990 est)
Gozo and Comino	70 sq km (27 sq mi)	25 775
Inner Harbour	15 sq km (6 sq mi)	101 429
N Malta	78 sq km (30 sq mi)	33 157
Outer Harbour	32 sq km (12 sq mi)	101 759
SE Malta	53 sq km (20 sq mi)	44 404
W Malta	69 sq km (27 sq mi)	45 906

The Netherlands

Province	Area	Capital	Population (1995 est)
Drenthe	2 680 sq km (1 025 sq mi)	Assen	454 864
Flevoland	2 412 sq km (549 sq mi)	Lelijstad	262 325
Friesland	5 741 sq km (1 295 sq mi)	Leeuwarden	609 579
Gelderland	5 143 sq km (1 935 sq mi)	Arnhem	1 864 732
Groningen	2 967 sq km (906 sq mi)	Groningen	557 995
Limburg	2 196 sq km (838 sq mi)	Maastricht	1 130 050
N Brabant (Noord-Brabant)	5 016 sq km (1 910 sq mi)	's-Hertogenbosch	2 276 207
N Holland (Noord-Holland)	4 059 sq km (1 029 sq mi)	Haarlem	2 463 611
Overijssel	3 420 sq km (1 289 sq mi)	Zwolle	1 050 389
S Holland (Zuid-Holland)	3 446 sq km (1 123 sq mi)	The Hague	3 325 064
Utrecht	1 434 sq km (514 sq mi)	Utrecht	1 063 460
Zeeland	2 932 sq km (692 sq mi)	Middelburg	365 846

Norway

County	Area	Capital	Population (1996 est)
Akershus	4 917 sq km (1 898 sq mi)		439 928
Aust-Agder	9 212 sq km (3 557 sq mi)	Arendal	100 211
Buskerud	14 927 sq km (5 763 sq mi)	Drammen	229 366
Finnmark	48 637 sq km (18 779 sq mi)	Vadsø	76 461
Hedmark	27 388 sq km (10 575 sq mi)	Hamar	186 247
Hordaland	15 634 sq km (6 036 sq mi)	Bergen	425 247
Møre og Romsdal	15 104 sq km (5 832 sq mi)	Molde	241 032
Nordland	38 327 sq km (14 798 sq mi)	Bodø	241 147

County	Area	Capital	Population (1996 est)
Nord-Trøndelag	22 463 sq km (8 673 sq mi)	Steinkjer	127 325
Oppland	25 260 sq km (9 753 sq mi)	Lillehammer	182 883
Oslo	454 sq km (175 sq mi)	Oslo	488 659
Østfold	4 183 sq km (1 615 sq mi)	Moss	240 251
Rogaland	9 141 sq km (3 529 sq mi)	Stavanger	357 027
Sogn of Fjordane	18 634 sq km (7 195 sq mi)	Leikanger	107 738
Sør-Trøndelag	18 831 sq km (7 271 sq mi)	Trondheim	257 196
Telemark	15 315 sq km (5 913 sq mi)	Skien	163 213
Troms	25 954 sq km (10 021 sq mi)	Tromsø	151 160
Vest-Agder	7 281 sq km (2 811 sq mi)	Kristiansand	150 426
Vestfold	2 216 sq km (856 sq mi)	Tønsberg	204 440

Poland

Province	Area	Capital	Population (1995 est)
Biala Podlaska	5 348 sq km (2 065 sq mi)	Biala Podlaska	309 500
Bialystok	10 055 sq km (3 882 sq mi)	Bialystok	700 700
Bielsko-Biala	3 704 sq km (1 430 sq mi)	Bielsko-Biala	918 600
Bydogszcz	10 349 sq km (3 996 sq mi)	Bydogszcz	1 131 800
Chelm	3 866 sq km (1 493 sq mi)	Chelm	249 900
Ciechanów	6 362 sq km (2 456 sq mi)	Ciechanów	436 400
Czestochow	6 182 sq km (2 387 sq mi)	Czestochow	782 300
Elblag	6 103 sq km (2 356 sq mi)	Elblag	491 400
Gdansk	7 394 sq km (2 855 sq mi)	Gdansk	1 455 900
Gorzów	8 484 sq km (3 276 sq mi)	Gorzów	510 800
Jelenia Góra	4 378 sq km (1 690 sq mi)	Jelenia Góra	524 500
Kalisz	6 512 sq km (2 514 sq mi)	Kalisz	722 000
Katowice	6 650 sq km (2 568 sq mi)	Katowice	3 924 800
Kielce	9 211 sq km (3 556 sq mi)	Kielce	1 136 600
Konin	5 139 sq km (1 984 sq mi)	Konin	479 700
Koszalin	8 470 sq km (3 270 sq mi)	Koszalin	521 900
Kraków	3 254 sq km (1 256 sq mi)	Kraków	1 241 400
Krosno	5 702 sq km (2 202 sq mi)	Krosno	506 600
Legnica	4 037 sq km (1 559 sq mi)	Legnica	523 600
Leszno	4 154 sq km (1 604 sq mi)	Leszno	397 200
Lódz	1 523 sq km (588 sq mi)	Lódz	1 116 200
Lomzda	6 684 sq km (2 581 sq mi)	Lomzda	353 800
Lublin	6 792 sq km (2 622 sq mi)	Lublin	1 026 800
Nowy Sacz	5 576 sq km (2 153 sq mi)	Nowy Sacz	733 100
Olsztyn	12 327 sq km (4 759 sq mi)	Olsztyn	771 700
Opole	8 535 sq km (3 295 sq mi)	Opole	1 025 200
Ostroleka	6 498 sq km (2 509 sq mi)	Ostroleka	408 400
Pila	8 205 sq km (3 168 sq mi)	Pila	494 000
Piotrków	6 266 sq km (2 419 sq mi)	Piotrków	644 200
Plock	5 117 sq km (1 976 sq mi)	Plock	522 000
Poznan	8 151 sq km (3 147 sq mi)	Poznan	1 353 700
Przemysl	4 437 sq km (1 713 sq mi)	Przemysl	414 600
Radom	7 294 sq km (2 816 sq mi)	Radom	763 800
Rzeszów	4 397 sq km (1 698 sq mi)	Rzeszów	746 300
Siedlce	8 499 sq km (3 281 sq mi)	Siedlce	661 700
Sieradz	4 869 sq km (1 880 sq mi)	Sieradz	412 900

Skierniewice	3 960 sq km (1 529 sq mi)	Skierniewice	424 000
Slupsk	7 453 sq km (2 878 sq mi)	Slupsk	425 900
Suwalki	10 490 sq km (4 050 sq mi)	Suwalki	485 500
Szczecin	9 981 sq km (3 854 sq mi)	Szczecin	990 500
Tarnobrzeg	6 283 sq km (2 426 sq mi)	Tarnobrzeg	609 300
Tarnów	4 151 sq km (1 603 sq mi)	Tarnów	693 500
Torun	5 348 sq km (2 065 sq mi)	Torun	671 100
Walbrzych	4 168 sq km (1 609 sq mi)	Walbrzych	739 400
Warsaw	3 788 sq km (1 463 sq mi)	Warsaw	2 416 600
Wloclawek	4 402 sq km (1 700 sq mi)	Wloclawek	435 000
Wroclaw	6 287 sq km (2 427 sq mi)	Wroclaw	1 137 700
Zamosc	6 980 sq km (2 695 sq mi)	Zamosc	492 800
Zielona Góra	8 868 sq km (3 424 sq mi)	Zielona Góra	674 100

Portugal

Region	Area	Administrative centre	Population (1992 est)
Aveiro	2 808 sq km (1 084 sq mi)	Aveiro	658 400
Beja	10 225 sq km (3 948 sq mi)	Beja	166 500
Braga	2 695 sq km (1 041 sq mi)	Braga	754 700
Bragança	6 597 sq km (2 546 sq mi)	Bragança	154 700
Castelo Branco	6 616 sq km (2 553 sq mi)	Castelo Branco	211 800
Coimbra	3 971 sq km (1 532 sq mi)	Coimbra	425 400
Évora	7 393 sq km (2 854 sq mi)	Évora	172 400
Faro	4 986 sq km (1 924 sq mi)	Faro	342 900
Guarda	5 540 sq km (2 138 sq mi)	Guarda	185 400
Leiria	3 508 sq km (1 354 sq mi)	Leiria	426 200
Lisboa	2 758 sq km (1 064 sq mi)	Lisboa (Lisbon)	2 048 000
Portalegre	6 065 sq km (2 342 sq mi)	Portalegre	132 400
Porto	2 341 sq km (904 sq mi)	Porto	1 652 000
Santarém	6 707 sq km (2 588 sq mi)	Santarém	441 900
Setúbal	5 064 sq km (1 955 sq mi)	Setúbal	716 200
Viana do Castelo	2 210 sq km (853 sq mi)	Viana do Castelo	248 300
Vila Real	4 305 sq km (1 661 sq mi)	Vila Real	233 100
Viseu	5 007 sq km (1 933 sq mi)	Viseu	398 800
The Azores	2 247 sq km (868 sq mi)	Ponta Delgada	237 800
Madeira	794 sq km (306 sq mi)	Funchal	253 800

Romania

County	Area	Capital	Population (1994 est)
Alba	6 242 sq km (2 409 sq mi)	Alba Iulia	408 457
Arad	7 754 sq km (2 993 sq mi)	Arad	482 144
Arges	6 826 sq km (2 634 sq mi)	Pitesti	679 868
Bacau	6 621 sq km (2 555 sq mi)	Bacau	742 901
Bihor	7 544 sq km (2 911 sq mi)	Oradea	633 629
Bistrita-Nasaud	5 355 sq km (2 067 sq mi)	Bistrita	328 786
Botosani	4 986 sq km (1 924 sq mi)	Botosani	462 370
Braila	4 766 sq km (1 840 sq mi)	Braila	391 923
Brasov	5 363 sq km (2 070 sq mi)	Brasov	642 764
Bucharest	1 821 sq km (703 sq mi)	Bucharest	2 343 824
Buzau	6 103 sq km (2 355 sq mi)	Buzau	515 202
Caras-Severin	8 520 sq km (3 288 sq mi)	Resita	370 058

County	Area	Capital	Population (1994 est)
Calarasi	5 088 sq km (1 964 sq mi)	Calarasi	336 657
Cluj	6 674 sq km (2 576 sq mi)	Cluj-Napoka	727 033
Constanta	7 071 sq km (2 729 sq mi)	Constanta	747 441
Covasna	3 795 sq km (1 431 sq mi)	Sfintu Gheorghe	232 951
Dimbovita	4 054 sq km (1 565 sq mi)	Tirgoviste	558 518
Dolj	7 413 sq km (2 862 sq mi)	Craiova	758 895
Galati	4 466 sq km (1 721 sq mi)	Galati	642 983
Giurgiu	3 526 sq km (1 361 sq mi)	Giurgiu	305 661
Gorj	5 602 sq km (2 163 sq mi)	Tirgu Jiu	397 927
Harghita	6 639 sq km (2 562 sq mi)	Miercurea-Ciuc	347 145
Hunedoara	7 063 sq km (2 726 sq mi)	Deva	547 180
Ialomita	4 453 sq km (1 720 sq mi)	Slobozia	305 454
Iasi	5 476 sq km (2 113 sq mi)	Iasi	815 368
Maramures	6 304 sq km (2 433 sq mi)	Baia Mare	539 718
Mehedinti	4 933 sq km (1 904 sq mi)	Drobeta-Turnu-Severin	330 017
Mures	6 714 sq km (2 592 sq mi)	Tirgu Mures	607 355
Neamt	5 896 sq km (2 276 sq mi)	Piatra Neamt	584 364
Olt	5 498 sq km (2 129 sq mi)	Slatina	520 871
Prahova	4 716 sq km 1 819 sq mi)	Ploiesti	874 219
Salaj	3 864 sq km (1 492 sq mi)	Zalau	264 448
Satu Mare	4 418 sq km (1 705 sq mi)	Satu Mare	398 401
Sibiu	5 432 sq km (2 097 sq mi)	Sibiu	448 474
Suceava	8 555 sq km (3 303 sq mi)	Suceava	708 571
Teleorman	5 790 sq km (2 235 sq mi)	Alexandria	477 527
Timis	8 697 sq km (3 358 sq mi)	Timisoara	691 797
Tulcea	8 499 sq km (3 280 sq mi)	Tulcea	269 311
Vaslui	5 318 sq km (2 053 sq mi)	Vaslui	463 832
Valcea	5 765 sq km (2 225 sq mi)	Ramnicu Valcea	436 989
Vrancea	4 857 sq km (1 874 sq mi)	Focsani	394 257

Slovak Republic

Region	Area	Capital	Population (1996 est)
Bratislava	367 sq km (142 sq mi)	Bratislava	450 775
C Slovakia (Stredoslovenský)	17 986 sq km (6 944 sq mi)	Banská Bystrica	1 636 003
E Slovakia (Východoslovenský)	16 191 sq km (6 251 sq mi)	Košice	1 544 077
W Slovakia (Západoslovenský)	14 492 sq km (5 595 sq mi)	Bratislava	1 725 352

Spain

Province	Area	Capital	Population (1995 est)
Álava	3 047 sq km (1 176 sq mi)	Vitoria Gasteiz	282 944
Albacete	14 862 sq km (5 737 sq mi)	Albacete	361 327
Alicante	5 863 sq km (2 263 sq mi)	Alicante	1 363 785
Almería	8 774 sq km (3 387 sq mi)	Almería	493 126
Avila	8 048 sq km (3 106 sq mi)	Avila	176 791
Badajoz	21 657 sq km (8 360 sq mi)	Badajoz	675 592
Baleares (Balearic Islands)	5 014 sq km (1 935 sq mi)	Palma	787 984

Barcelona	7 733 sq km (2 985 sq mi)	Barcelona	4 748 236
Burgos	14 309 sq km (5 523 sq mi)	Burgos	360 377
Cáceres	19 945 sq km (7 699 sq mi)	Cáceres	424 946
Cádiz	7 385 sq km (2 850 sq mi)	Cádiz	1 127 622
Cantabria (Santander)	5 289 sq km (2 041 sq mi)	Santander	541 885
Castellón	6 679 sq km (2 579 sq mi)	Castellón	464 670
Ciudad Real	19 749 sq km (7 519 sq mi)	Ciudad Real	490 573
Córdoba	13 718 sq km (5 295 sq mi)	Córdoba	782 221
La Coruña	7 876 sq km (3 040 sq mi)	La Coruña	1 136 283
Cuenca	17 061 sq km (6 585 sq mi)	Cuenca	207 499
Girona (Gerona)	5 886 sq km (2 272 sq mi)	Girona (Gerona)	541 995
Granada	12 531 sq km (4 387 sq mi)	Granada	841 829
Guadalajara	12 190 sq km (4 705 sq mi)	Guadalajara	155 884
Guipúzcoa	1 997 sq km (771 sq mi)	San Sebastián	684 113
Huelva	10 885 sq km (4 202 sq mi)	Huelva	458 674
Huesca	15 613 sq km (6 027 sq mi)	Huesca	210 276
Jaén	13 498 sq km (5 210 sq mi)	Jaén	666 767
León	15 468 sq km (5 971 sq mi)	León	532 706
Lérida	12 028 sq km (4 642 sq mi)	Lérida	360 407
Lugo	9 803 sq km (3 784 sq mi)	Lugo	386 405
Madrid	7 995 sq km (3 086 sq mi)	Madrid	5 181 659
Málaga	7 276 sq km (2 808 sq mi)	Málaga	1 224 959
Murcia	11 317 sq km (4 368 sq mi)	Murcia	1 109 977
Navarra	10 421 sq km (4 022 sq mi)	Pamplona	536 192
Orense (Asturias)	7 278 sq km (2 809 sq mi)	Orense	364 521
Oviedo	10 565 sq km (4 078 sq mi)	Oviedo	1 117 370
Palencia	8 035 sq km (3 101 sq mi)	Palencia	186 035
Las Palmas	4 072 sq km (1 572 sq mi)	Las Palmas	844 140
Pontevedra	4 477 sq km (1 728 sq mi)	Vigo	937 811
La Rioja	5 034 sq km (1 943 sq mi)	Logrono	268 206
Salamanca	12 336 sq km (4 761 sq mi)	Salamanca	365 293
Santa Cruz de Tenerife	3 170 sq km (1 224 sq mi)	Santa Cruz de Tenerife	787 358
Segovia	6 949 sq km (2 682 sq mi)	Segovia	149 653
Sevilla	14 001 sq km (5 404sq mi)	Sevilla	1 719 446
Soria	10 287 sq km (3 971 sq mi)	Soria	94 396
Tarragona	6 283 sq km (2 425 sq mi)	Tarragona	576 231
Teruel	14 785 sq km (5 707 sq mi)	Teruel	143 055
Toledo	15 368 sq km (5 932 sq mi)	Toledo	515 434
Valencia	10 763 sq km (4 154 sq mi)	Valencia	2 200 319
Valladolid	8 202 sq km (3 166 sq mi)	Valladolid	504 583
Vizcaya	2 217 sq km (856 sq mi)	Bilbao	1 163 726
Zamora	10 559 sq km (4 076 sq mi)	Zamora	214 273
Zaragoza	17 252 sq km (6 659 sq mi)	Zaragoza	852 332

Sweden

County	Area	Capital	Population (1995 est)
Älvsborg	11 395 sq km (4 400 sq mi)	Vänersborg	449 524
Blekinge	2 941 sq km (1 136 sq mi)	Karlskrona	152 737
Dalarnus	28 194 sq km (10 886 sq mi)	Falun	289 956
Gävleborg	18 191 sq km (7 024 sq mi)	Gävle	288 509
Gothenburg (Göteburg)	5 141 sq km (1 985 sq mi)	Gothenburg	770 375

County	Area	Capital	Population (1995 est)
Gotland	3 140 sq km (1 212 sq mi)	Visby	58 120
Halland	5 454 sq km (2 106 sq mi)	Halmstad	269 338
Jämtland	49 443 sq km (19 090 sq mi)	Östersund	135 584
Jönköping	9 944 sq km (3 839 sq mi)	Jönköping	312 686
Kalmar	11 170 sq km (4 313 sq mi)	Kalmar	243 372
Kronoberg	8 458 sq km (3 266 sq mi)	Växjö	180 377
Norrbotten	98 913 sq km (39 191 sq mi)	Lulece	266 011
Örebro	8 519 sq km (3 289 sq mi)	Örebro	276 417
Östergötland	10 562 sq km (4 078 sq mi)	Linköping	416 443
Skane	10 025 sq km (3 870 sq mi)	Malmö	1 111 731
Skaraborg	7 937 sq km (3 065 sq mi)	Mariestad	279 511
Södermanland	6 060 sq km (2 340 sq mi)	Nyköping	258 700
Stockholm	6 488 sq km (2 505 sq mi)	Stockholm	1 725 756
Uppsala	6 989 sq km (2 698 sq mi)	Uppsala	268 475
Värmland	17 584 sq km (6 789 sq mi)	Karlstad	284 011
Västerbotten	55 401 sq km (21 390 sq mi)	Umeå	260 472
Västernorrland	21 678 sq km (8 370 sq mi)	Härnösand	258 290
Västmanland	6 302 sq km (2 433 sq mi)	Västeraces	261 101

Switzerland

Canton	Area	Capital	Population (1995 est)
Aargau	1 395 sq km (540 sq mi)	Aarau	528 887
Appenzell Ausser-Rhoden	243 sq km (94 sq mi)	Herisau	54 104
Appenzell Inner-Rhoden	172 sq km (66 sq mi)	Appenzell	14 750
Basle (Basel-Landschaft)	428 sq km (165 sq mi)	Liestal	252 331
Basle (Basel-Stadt)	37 sq km (14 sq mi)	Basel	195 759
Berne	5 932 sq km (2 290 sq mi)	Berne	941 952
Fribourg	1 591 sq km (614 sq mi)	Fribourg	224 552
Geneva (Genève)	245 sq km (94 sq mi)	Geneva	395 466
Glarus	684 sq km (264 sq mi)	Glarus	39 410
Graubünden	7 106 sq km (2 744 sq mi)	Chur (Coire)	185 063
Jura	837 sq km (323 sq mi)	Delémont	69 188
Lucerne (Luzern)	1 429 sq km (552 sq mi)	Lucerne	340 536
Neuenberg (Neuchâtel)	716 sq km (276 sq mi)	Neuchâtel	165 258
Nidwalden	241 sq km (93 sq mi)	Stans	36 466
Obwalden	480 sq km (186 sq mi)	Sarnen	31 310
St Gall (Sankt Gallen)	1 950 sq km (752 sq mi)	St Gall	422 350
Schaffhausen	298 sq km (115 sq mi)	Schaffhausen	74 035
Schwyz	851 sq km (328 sq mi)	Schwyz	122 409
Solothurn	791 sq km (305 sq mi)	Solothurn	239 264
Thurgau	863 sq km (333 sq mi)	Frauenfeld	223 372
Ticino	2 738 sq km (1 056 sq mi)	Bellinzona	305 199
Uri	1 057 sq km (408 sq mi)	Altdorf	35 876
Valais	5 213 sq km (2 015 sq mi)	Sion	271 291
Vaud	2 822 sq km (1 090 sq mi)	Lausanne	605 677
Zug	207 sq km (80 sq mi)	Zug	92 392
Zürich	1 661 sq km (641 sq mi)	Zürich	1 175 457

Turkey

Region	Area	Population (1990 est)
Black Sea Coast (Karadeniz Kiyisi)	81 295 sq km (31 388 sq mi)	6 900 805
Central Anatolia (İç Anadolu)	236 347 sq km (91 254 sq mi)	13 154 473
East Anatolia (Doğu Anadolu)	176 311 sq km (68 074 sq mi)	6 909 594
Marmara and Aegean coasts (Marmara ve Ege kiyilari)	85 560 sq km (33 035 sq mi)	11 784 535
Mediterranean Coast (Akdeniz kiyisi)	59 395 sq km (22 933 sq mi)	5 497 536
South-East Anatolia (Güneydogu)	39 749 sq km (15 347 sq mi)	2 793 894
Thrace (Trakya)	23 764 sq km (9 175 sq mi)	6 021 591
West Anatolia (Bati Anadolu)	77 031 sq km (29 742 sq mi)	3 906 681

Note Croatia, not listed above, is divided into 21 counties; Macedonia, not listed above, is divided into 34 communes; Slovenia, not listed above, is divided into 148 municipalities; Yugoslavia, not listed above, is divided into 29 districts; see also separate information for administrative divisions of the UK

States of the USA

State	Abbreviation	Area	Capital	Nickname
Alabama	Ala.	133 911 sq km (51 705 sq mi)	Montgomery	Camellia State/ Heart of Dixie
Alaska		1 518 748 sq km (586 412 sq mi)	Juneau	Mainland State/ The Last Frontier
Arizona	Ariz.	295 249 sq km (114 000 sq mi)	Phoenix	Apache State/ Grand Canyon State
Arkansas	Ark.	137 403 sq km (53 187 sq mi)	Little Rock	Bear State/Land of Opportunity
California	Calif.	411 033 sq km (158 706 sq mi)	Sacramento	Golden State
Colorado	Colo.	269 585 sq km (104 091 sq mi)	Denver	Centennial State
Connecticut	Conn.	12 996 sq km (5 018 sq mi)	Hartford	Nutmeg State/ Constitution State
Delaware	Del.	5 296 sq km (2 045 sq mi)	Dover	Diamond State/ First State
Florida	Fla.	151 934 sq km (58 664 sq mi)	Tallahassee	Everglade State/ Sunshine State
Georgia	Ga.	152 571 sq km (58 910 sq mi)	Atlanta	Empire State of the South/Peach State
Hawaii		16 759 sq km (6 471 sq mi)	Honolulu	Aloha State
Idaho		216 422 sq km (83 564 sq mi)	Boise	Gem State
Illinois	Ill.	145 928 sq km (56 345 sq mi)	Springfield	Prairie State/Land of Lincoln
Indiana	Ind.	93 715.5 sq km (36 185 sq mi)	Indianapolis	Hoosier State
Iowa		145 747 sq km (56 275 sq mi)	Des Moines	Hawkeye State/ Corn State

State	Abbreviation	Area	Capital	Nickname
Kansas	Kan.	213 089 sq km (82 277 sq mi)	Topeka	Sunflower State/ Jayhawker State
Kentucky	Ky.	104 658 sq km (40 410 sq mi)	Frankfort	Bluegrass State
Louisiana	La.	123 673 sq km (47 752 sq mi)	Baton Rouge	Pelican State/Sugar State/Creole State
Maine	Me.	86 153 sq km (33 265 sq mi)	Augusta	Pine Tree State
Maryland	Md.	27 090 sq km (10 460 sq mi)	Annapolis	Old Line State/Free State
Massachusetts	Mass.	21 455 sq km (8 284 sq mi)	Boston	Bay State/Old Colony
Michigan	Mich.	151 579 sq km (58 527 sq mi)	Lansing	Wolverine State/ Great Lake State
Minnesota	Minn.	218 593 sq km (84 402 sq mi)	St Paul	Gopher State/ North Star State
Mississippi	Miss.	123 510 sq km (47 689 sq mi)	Jackson	Magnolia State
Missouri	Mo.	180 508 sq km (69 697 sq mi)	Jefferson City	Bullion State/Show Me State
Montana	Mont.	380 834 sq km (147 046 sq mi)	Helena	Treasure State/Big Sky Country
Nebraska	Neb.	200 342 sq km (77 355 sq mi)	Lincoln	Cornhusker State/ Beef State
Nevada	Nev.	286 341 sq km (110 561 sq mi)	Carson City	Silver State/ Sagebrush State
New Hampshire	NH	24 032 sq km (9 279 sq mi)	Concord	Granite State
New Jersey	NJ	20 167 sq km (7 787 sq mi)	Trenton	Garden State
New Mexico	N.Mex./NM	314 914 sq km (121 593 sq mi)	Santa Fé	Sunshine State/ Land of Enchantment
New York	NY	127 185 sq km (49 108 sq mi)	Albany	Empire State
North Carolina	NC	136 407 sq km (52 699 sq mi)	Raleigh	Old North State/ Tar Heel State
North Dakota	N.Dak./ND	180 180 sq km (69 567 sq mi)	Bismarck	Flickertail State/ Sioux State
Ohio		107 040 sq km (41 330 sq mi)	Columbus	Buckeye State
Oklahoma	Okla.	181 083 sq km (69 919 sq mi)	Oklahoma City	Sooner State
Oregon	Ore.	251 409 sq km (97 073 sq mi)	Salem	Sunset State/ Beaver State
Pennsylvania	Pa./Penn./ Penna.	117 343 sq km (45 308 sq mi)	Harrisburg	Keystone State
Rhode Island	RI	3 139 sq km (1 212 sq mi)	Providence	Little Rhody/ Plantation State
South Carolina	SC	80 579 sq km (31 113 sq mi)	Columbia	Palmetto State
South Dakota	S.Dak./SD	199 723 sq km (77 116 sq mi)	Pierre	Sunshine State/ Coyote State
Tennessee	Tenn.	109 149 sq km (42 144 sq mi)	Nashville	Volunteer State

Texas	Tex.	691 003 sq km (266 807 sq mi)	Austin	Lone Star State
Utah		219 880 sq km (84 899 sq mi)	Salt Lake City	Mormon State/ Beehive State
Vermont	Vt.	24 899 sq km (9 614 sq mi)	Montpelier	Green Mountain State
Virginia	Va.	105 582 sq km (40 767 sq mi)	Richmond	Old Dominion State/Mother of Presidents
Washington	Wash.	176 473 sq km (68 139 sq mi)	Olympia	Evergreen State
West Virginia	W.Va.	62 758 sq km (24 232 sq mi)	Charleston	Chinook State
Wisconsin	Wis.	145 431 sq km (56 153 sq mi)	Madison	Panhandle State/ Mountain State
Wyoming	Wyo.	253 315 sq km (97 809 sq mi)	Cheyenne	Badger State/ America's Dairyland
District of Columbia	DC	173.5 sq km (67 sq mi)	Washington	Equality State

Canadian provinces and territories

Province/Territory	Abbreviation	Area	Capital
Alberta	AB	661 190 sq km (255 285 sq mi)	Edmonton
British Columbia	BC	947 800 sq km (365 945 sq mi)	Victoria
Manitoba	MB	649 950 sq km (250 945 sq mi)	Winnipeg
New Brunswick	NB	73 440 sq km (28 355 sq mi)	Fredericton
Newfoundland	NF	405 720 sq km (156 648 sq mi)	St John's
Northwest Territories	NT	3 426 320 sq km (1 322 902 sq mi)	Yellowknife
Nova Scotia	NS	55 490 sq km (21 424 sq mi)	Halifax
Ontario	ON	1 068 580 sq km (412 578 sq mi)	Toronto
Prince Edward Island	PE	5 660 sq km (2 185 sq mi)	Charlottetown
Quebec	QC	1 540 680 sq km (594 856 sq mi)	Quebec City
Saskatchewan	SK	652 380 sq km (251 883 sq mi)	Regina
Yukon	YT	483 450 sq km (186 660 sq mi)	Whitehorse

Australian states and territories

State/Territory	Abbreviation	Area	Capital
Australian Capital Territory	ACT	2 400 sq km (930 sq mi)	Canberra
New South Wales	NSW	801 400 sq km (309 400 sq mi)	Sydney
Northern Territory	NT	1 346 200 sq km (519 800 sq mi)	Darwin
Queensland	Qld	1 727 200 sq km (666 900 sq mi)	Brisbane

State/Territory	Abbreviation	Area	Capital
South Australia	SA	984 000 sq km (379 900 sq mi)	Adelaide
Tasmania	Tas.	67 800 sq km (26 200 sq mi)	Hobart
Victoria	Vic.	227 600 sq km (87 900 sq mi)	Melbourne
Western Australia	WA	2 525 500 sq km (975 000 sq mi)	Perth

6.3 *Law and Legislation*

Legislative systems

Region	Bicameral	Unicameral
Africa	Burkina Faso, Central African Republic, Liberia, Madagascar, Mauritania, South Africa, Swaziland, Zimbabwe	Algeria, Angola, Benin, Botswana, Burundi, Cameroon, Cape Verde, Chad, Comoros, Congo, Côte d'Ivoire, Democratic Republic of Congo, Djibouti, Equatorial Guinea, Ethiopia, Gabon, Gambia, Ghana, Guinea-Bissau, Kenya, Lesotho, Malawi, Mali, Mauritius, Mozambique, Namibia, São Tomé and Principe, Senegal, Seychelles, Sierra Leone, Sudan, Tanzania, Togo, Tunisia, Uganda, Zambia
Asia	India, Japan, Malaysia, Pakistan, Philippines, Thailand	Bangladesh, Bhutan, Brunei, Cambodia, China, Indonesia, Kazakhstan, Laos, Nepal, North Korea, Singapore, South Korea, Sri Lanka, Turkmenistan, Uzbekistan, Vietnam
Australasia	Australia, Fiji	Kiribati, New Zealand, Papua New Guinea, Solomon Islands, Tonga, Tuvalu, Vanuatu, Samoa
Europe	Austria, Belgium, Czech Republic, France, Germany, Ireland, Italy, Netherlands, Poland, Romania, Russia, Spain, Switzerland, UK, Yugoslavia	Albania, Andorra, Belarus, Bulgaria, Croatia, Cyprus, Denmark, Estonia, Finland, Gibraltar, Greece, Greenland, Hungary, Iceland, Liechtenstein, Lithuania, Luxembourg, Macedonia, Malta, Moldova, Norway, Portugal, San Marino, Slovakia, Slovenia, Sweden, Ukraine
Middle East	Afghanistan, Jordan	Armenia, Azerbaijan, Egypt, Iran, Iraq, Israel, Kuwait, Lebanon, Syria, Turkey, United Arab Emirates, Yemen

| North America | Antigua and Barbuda, The Bahamas, Barbados, Belize, Canada, Dominican Republic, Costa Rica, Cuba, El Salvador, Guatemala, Honduras, Nicaragua, Panama, St Kitts and Nevis, Grenada, Haiti, Jamaica, Mexico, Puerto Rico, St Lucia, Trinidad and Tobago, USA | St Vincent and the Grenadines |
| South America | Argentina, Bolivia, Brazil, Chile, Colombia, Paraguay, Peru, Uruguay, Venezuela | Ecuador, Guyana, Suriname |

Note Bicameral = two chamber legislature; Unicameral = single-chamber legislature

Courts of law (UK)

England and Wales

Court (in order of precedence)	Jurisdiction
House of Lords	Civil/Criminal
Court of Appeal	Civil/Criminal
High Court of Justice	Civil
Crown Court	Criminal
County Court	Civil
Magistrates' Court	Civil/Criminal

Scotland

Court (in order of precedence)	Jurisdiction
House of Lords	Civil
Court of Session	Civil
High Court of Justiciary	Criminal
Sheriff's Principal Court	Civil
Sheriff's Court	Civil/Criminal
District Court	Criminal

Northern Ireland

Court (in order of precedence)	Jurisdiction
House of Lords	Civil/Criminal
N Ireland Court of Appeal	Civil/Criminal
High Court of Justice	Civil
Crown Court	Criminal
County Court	Civil
Magistrates' Court	Civil

Crime rates

Country	Homicide	Violent crime	Theft of a motor vehicle	Domestic burglary	Drug trafficking
Australia	360	160 574	130 406	284 974	Not available
Austria	147	46 942	3 848	12 826	16 808
Belgium	145	60 605	35 242	143 769	11 072
Canada	581	296 737	177 286	233 844	16 778

Country	Homicide	Violent crime	Theft of a motor vehicle	Domestic burglary	Drug trafficking
Czech Republic	291	23 223	29 422	13 068	789
Denmark	88	13 963	41 227	111 449	171
England and Wales	739	347 064	407 239	519 265	23 153
Finland	142	27 797	22 015	10 436	8 323
France	963	189 203	417 360	213 561	86 961
Germany	1 178	186 447	190 585	182 009	69 093
Greece	203	10 733	16 555	44 286	5 970
Hungary	289	26 987	14 413	31 269	943
Ireland	38	5 488	13 589	16 970	1 637
Italy	928	64 822	301 233	237 445	41 420
Japan	1 282	40 570	696 370	221 678	2 359
Netherlands	273	66 688	36 772	103 953	6 593
New Zealand	89	42 191	30 776	49 376	14 532
Northern Ireland	42	8 251	8 633	7 435	185
Norway	38	17 396	20 019	16 923	34 705
Poland	807	66 970	56 781	70 187	994
Portugal	131	16 723	22 792	24 202	3 390
Russia	29 285	161 644	41 712	17 490	96 645
Scotland	95	23 656	28 646	36 792	8 180
South Africa	24 588	645 737	100 637	249 375	42 805
Spain	1 032	87 775	133 330	84 430	14 274
Sweden	157	68 310	78 826	18 359	561
Switzerland	87	7 385	21 534	82 559	3 253
USA	19 645	1 682 278	1 395 192	2 501 524	1 506 200

Note Figures relate to 1987.

Prison populations

Country	1997
Australia	17 661
Austria	6 946
Canada	34 166
Czech Republic	21 560
Denmark	3 170
England and Wales	61 940
Finland	2 976
France	54 442
Germany	Not available
Greece	5 577
Hungary	13 405
Ireland	2 424
Italy	50 197
Japan	50 600
Netherlands	11 770
New Zealand	5 152
Northern Ireland	1 581
Norway	Not available

Portugal	14 167
Russia	1 009 863
Scotland	6 082
South Africa	134 202
Spain	42 756
Sweden	5 181
Switzerland	5 980
UK	69 603
USA	1 725 842

6.4 *Economics*

Index of world industrial production

Country	Index (1997)
Australia	112.1
Austria	109.6 (1996)
Belgium	106
Canada	120.1
Czech Republic	80.5
Finland	131.8
France	103.6
Germany	103.3
Greece	100.6
Hungary	100.9
Ireland	197.1
Italy	107.7
Japan	101.9
Korea, South	172.6
Luxembourg	107.4
Mexico	125.9
Netherlands	113.4
Norway	138.6
Poland	139.1
Portugal	103.3
Spain	109.1
Sweden	129.4
Switzerland	109
UK	107.3 (1996)
USA	125.8

Note Figures relate to the position compared with 1990 (= 100)

World agricultural production

Commodity	1992	1997
Coarse grains	871.8	898.9
Fruits	379	429.4
Milk	423.7	381.3
Nuts	5.0	5.2
Oils	61.7	77.2
Poultry	40.6	53.4
Pulses	51	57.7
Rapeseed	25.3	33.7
Red meat	118.6	130.2
Rice	355.7	381.4
Soybeans	117.4	152.2
Vegetables and melons	478.6	595.6
Wheat	562.3	609.8

Note Figures relate to millions of metric tons

World energy production and consumption

Country	Production of dry natural gas (quadrillion Btu)	Production of crude petroleum (1 000 barrels per day)	Production of coal (million short tons)	Total energy consumption (quadrillion Btu)
Algeria	2.56	1 242		1.4
Argentina	1.11	756		2.6
Australia	1.12	570	274	4.1
Austria	0.06	21	1	1.3
Bahrain	0.26	35	Not available	0.3
Bangladesh	0.25	1	Not available	0.4
Belarus	0.01	36	Not available	1.0
Belgium		Not available	1	2.5
Brazil	0.24	795	5	7.2
Bulgaria		1	32	1.0
Canada	5.97	1 837	84	12.2
Chile	0.06	9	1	0.8
China	0.78	3 131	1 550	37.0
Colombia	0.17	623	33	1.3
Congo, Democratic Republic of	Not available	30		Not available
Cuba		30	Not available	0.4
Czech Republic	0.01	4	77	2.3
Denmark	0.25	208	Not available	0.9
Ecuador	0.01	396	Not available	Not available
Egypt	0.50	922	Not available	1.6
Finland	Not available	Not available	Not available	1.1
France	0.10	43	10	9.9
Germany	0.70	60	264	14.4
Greece		8	66	1.2

Hungary	0.16	32	17	1.1
India	0.80	651	311	11.6
Indonesia	2.65	1 547	53	3.5
Iran	1.45	3 686	1	4.0
Iraq	0.12	579	Not available	1.2
Ireland	0.10	Not available		0.5
Israel			Not available	0.6
Italy	0.72	101		7.6
Japan	0.09	12	7	21.4
Korea, North	Not available	Not available	81	2.2
Korea, South	Not available	Not available	5	7.2
Kuwait	0.22	2 062	Not available	0.5
Libya	0.24	1 401	Not available	0.6
Malaysia	1.36	695		1.7
Mexico	1.08	2 855	10	5.6
Morocco			1	0.4
Myanmar	0.06	15		Not available
Netherlands	3.01	56	Not available	3.8
New Zealand	0.20	37	4	0.9
Nigeria	0.19	2 188		0.9
Norway	1.61	3 104		1.7
Pakistan	0.65	55	4	1.7
Peru	0.03	120		Not available
Philippines		2	2	1.0
Poland	0.13	5	219	3.8
Portugal	Not available	Not available		0.9
Romania	0.67	135	45	2.1
Russia	19.35	5 850	302	26
Saudi Arabia	1.53	8 218	Not available	4.0
Serbia	0.02	22	43	0.5
South Africa	0.07	Not available	227	4.3
Spain	0.02	15	33	4.5
Sweden	Not available			2.3
Switzerland		Not available	Not available	1.2
Syria	0.10	604	Not available	0.7
Taiwan	0.04	1		3.1
Tajikistan		2		Not available
Thailand	0.43	61	21	2.3
Trinidad and Tobago	0.32	130	Not available	Not available
Tunisia	0.03	87	Not available	Not available
Turkey	0.01	67	63	2.7
UK	3.34	2 568	56	10.1
Ukraine	0.59	66	77	6.3
United Arab Emirates	1.34	2 278	Not available	1.8
USA	19.54	6 465	1 064	93.4
Venezuela	1.06	3 053	4	2.6
Vietnam	0.03	175	9	0.5
World total	81.9	64 054	5 185	375.1

Note Btu – British thermal unit; figures relate to the year 1996

Inflation rates

Highest

Country	Rate (%)
Angola	1 200.0 (1998)
Congo, Republic of the	659.0 (1996)
Iraq	200.0 (1997)
Chad	152.0 (1997)
Sudan	130.0 (1996)
Belarus	127.0 (1998)
Liberia	100.0 (1996)
Turkmenistan	100.0 (1998)
Turkey	83.1 (1998)
Uzbekistan	57.0 (1998)
Romania	46.0 (1998)
Mongolia	45.8 (1996)
São Tomé and Príncipe	45.0 (1997)
Bosnia-Herzegovina	40.0 (1998)
Guinea-Bissau	40.0 (1996)
Tajikistan	40.0 (1998)
Jamaica	34.7 (1998)
Bulgaria	32.0 (1998)
Libya	30.0 (1998)
Myanmar	29.4 (1997)

Lowest

Country	Rate (%)
Seychelles	0.7 (1997)
Bahrain	0.8 (1998)
Belize	0.8 (1998)
Liechtenstein	0.8 (1998)
Oman	1.0 (1998)
Switzerland	1.0 (1998)
Japan	1.1 (1998)
Dominica	1.5 (1997)
Finland	1.5 (1998)
Panama	1.5 (1998)
Austria	1.6 (1998)
France	1.6 (1998)
Luxembourg	1.6 (1998)
Bahamas	1.7 (1997)
Australia	1.8 (1998)
Argentina	1.9 (1998)
Germany	1.9 (1998)
New Zealand	2.0 (1998)
Senegal	2.0 (1998)
Tonga	2.1 (1997)

Unemployment rates

Country	1998
Australia	8.0
Austria	4.7
Belgium	9.5
Canada	8.3
Czech Republic	6.5
Denmark	5.1
Finland	11.4
France	11.7
Germany	9.4
Hungary	8.0
Ireland	7.8
Italy	11.9
Japan	4.1
Luxembourg	2.8
Netherlands	4.0
New Zealand	7.5
Norway	3.3
Poland	10.6
Portugal	4.9
Spain	18.8
Sweden	8.3
UK	6.3
USA	4.5
European Union	9.9
OECD	7.1

Note Figures relate to percentages of the civilian labour force

British currency

Coins

Pre-decimal

Coin	Metal	Nickname
Farthing (¼d.)	Bronze	
Halfpenny (½d.)	Bronze	
Penny (1d.)	Bronze	Copper
Threepence (3d.)	Nickel-brass (originally cupro-nickel)	Joey
Sixpence (6d.)	Cupro-nickel	Tanner
Shilling (1s.)	Cupro-nickel	Bob
Florin (2s.)	Cupro-nickel	Two bob
Half-Crown (2s. 6d.)	Cupro-nickel	Half a dollar

Decimal

Coin	Metal	Changes
Half-pence (½p)	Bronze	Withdrawn 1984
1 pence (1p)	Copper-plated steel (originally bronze)	
2 pence (2p)	Copper-plated steel (originally bronze)	
5 pence (5p)	Cupro-nickel	Replaced by new coin 1990
10 pence (10p)	Cupro-nickel	Replaced by new coin 1993
20 pence (20p)	Cupro-nickel	
50 pence (50p)	Cupro-nickel	Replaced by new coin 1998
1 pound (£1)	Nickel-brass	Replaced £1 notes in 1983
2 pounds (£2)	Cupro-nickel/nickel-brass	

Banknotes

Banknote	D series (1970–96)	E series (from 1990)
£1	Sir Isaac Newton	
£5	Duke of Wellington	George Stephenson
£10	Florence Nightingale	Charles Dickens (Charles Darwin from 2000)
£20	William Shakespeare	Michael Faraday
£50	Sir Christopher Wren	Sir John Houblon

Nicknames

Amount	Nickname
£1	Quid
£5	Fiver
£10	Tenner
£25	Pony
£500	Monkey
£1,000	Grand
£100 000	Plum

Nobel Prize for Economics

Year	Winner	Nationality
1969	Ragnar Anton Kittil Frisch and Jan Tinbergen	Norwegian/Dutch
1970	Paul Anthony Samuelson	US
1971	Simon Smith Kuznets	US
1972	John Richard Hicks and Kenneth Joseph Arrow	British/US
1973	Wassily Leontief	US
1974	(Karl) Gunnar Myrdal and Friedrich August von Hayek	Swedish/British
1975	Leonid Vitaliyevich Kantorovich and Tjalling Charles Koopmans	Russian/US
1976	Milton Friedman	US
1977	James Edward Meade and Bertil Gotthard Ohlin	British/Swedish
1978	Herbert Alexander Simon	US

1979	(William) Arthur Lewis and Theodore William Schultz	British/US
1980	Lawrence Robert Klein	US
1981	James Tobin	US
1982	George Joseph Stigler	US
1983	Gerard Debreu	US
1984	(John) Richard Nicholas Stone	British
1985	Franco Modigliani	US
1986	James McGill Buchanan	US
1987	Robert Merton Solow	US
1988	Maurice Allais	French
1989	Trygve Haavelmo	Norwegian
1990	Harry M. Markovitz, Merton Miller and William Sharpe	US/US/US
1991	Ronald Coase	US
1992	Gary S. Becker	US
1993	Douglas C. North and Robert W. Fogel	US/US
1994	John Nash, Reinhard Selten and John Harsanyi	US/German/US
1995	Robert E. Lucas Jr	US
1996	James Mirrlees and William Vickrey	British/US
1997	Myron Scholes and Robert Merton	US/US
1998	Amartya Sen	India
1999	Robert A. Mundell	Canadian
2000	James J. Heckman and Daniel L. McFadden	US/US

7
History

7.1 Historical Events

Chronology of world history

Date	Event
2.5 million BC	Homo habilis uses stone tools in Africa
1.7 million BC	Homo habilis erects first simple houses
1 million BC	Homo erectus learns to use fire
800 000 BC	Migration of homo erectus to Asia and Europe
c. 130 000 BC	Emergence of homo sapiens in Africa
c. 50 000 BC	Arrival of modern humans in Asia
c. 35 000 BC	Arrival of modern humans in Europe and Australia
c. 23 000 BC	Arrival of modern humans in the Americas
c. 15 000 BC	Painting of cave wall pictures at Lascaux, France
c. 8500 BC	First development of agriculture in Jordan
c. 3500 BC	Sumerian civilization reaches its peak; construction of megalithic tombs in Europe
c. 3000 BC	Emergence of Minoan civilization in Crete; unification of Egypt under Menes
c. 2850 BC	Flourishing of civilization in China
c. 2600 BC	Emergence of Mayan civilization in the Yucatán Peninsula; semitic tribes settle in Syria and N Africa
c. 2500 BC	Building of the Great Pyramids and first use of papyrus in Egypt; erection of Stonehenge in England; emergence of Indus civilization in India
c. 2350 BC	Foundation of the Akkadian Empire under Sargon
c. 2200 BC	Foundation of the Xia dynasty in China
c. 2200–1450 BC	Minoan civilization reaches its peak
c. 2000	Foundation of Babylon
1991 BC	Start of the Middle Kingdom in Egypt
1925 BC	Hittites invade Babylon
c. 1700 BC	Start of the Bronze Age in Europe
c. 1650 BC	Foundation of Hittite Old Kingdom
c. 1580 BC	Emergence of Mycenean civilization; Egypt reunited under Ahmose

1567 BC	Start of the New Kingdom in Egypt
1500 BC	Emergence of Olmec civilization in central America
c. 1400 BC	Start of the Iron Age in India and W Asia
1400–1200 BC	Hittite New Empire
c. 1300 BC	Emergence of Celtic civilization
c. 1260 BC	Outbreak of Trojan War
c. 1250 BC	Moses leads the Israelites out of Egypt
c. 1175 BC	Egypt divided into Upper and Lower Kingdoms
c. 1122 BC	Foundation of the Zhou dynasty in China
c. 1120 BC	Collapse of Mycenean civilization
c. 1100 BC	Establishment of Assyrian Empire in Mesopotamia
c. 1000 BC	First building of the Temple in Jerusalem
c. 970 BC	Death of King David; coronation of King Solomon
c. 900 BC	Etruscans settle in Italy
c. 800 BC	Building of Carthage
c. 776 BC	First Olympic Games held in Greece
753 BC	Foundation of Rome
750 BC	Foundation of Kushan Kingdom
721 BC	Assyrians invade Israel
689 BC	Assyrians destroy Babylon
660 BC	Jimmu becomes first emperor of Japan
c. 625 BC	Collapse of Assyrian Empire
570 BC	Development of Taoism
560 BC	Birth of the Buddha
551 BC	Birth of Confucius
c. 550 BC	Cyrus the Great expands Persian Empire
529 BC	Persians invade Egypt
510 BC	Foundation of the Roman Republic
c. 500 BC	Emergence of Mayan civilization
499 BC	Outbreak of Greek–Persian wars
431 BC	Outbreak of Peloponnesian wars
406 BC	Death of Sophocles
399 BC	Death of Socrates
c. 370 BC	Foundation of Plato's Academy in Athens
359 BC	Philip becomes king of Macedonia
332 BC	Alexander the Great begins conquest of Asia Minor
321 BC	Foundation of Mauryan dynasty in India
300 BC	Collapse of Olmec civilization
264 BC	Outbreak of First Punic War between Rome and Carthage
238 BC	Hamilcar conquers Spain
221 BC	Foundation of Qin dynasty in China; first building of the Great Wall of China
218 BC	Outbreak of Second Punic War between Rome and Carthage
216 BC	Hannibal invades Italy
206 BC	Foundation of Han dynasty in China
c. 200 BC	Roman invasion of Spain
185 BC	Foundation of Shunga dynasty in India
155 BC	Foundation of Indio-Greek kingdom in Indus valley
149 BC	Outbreak of Third Punic War between Rome and Carthage
133 BC	Rome establishes control over Asia Minor
c. 110 BC	Establishment of Silk Road across Asia
108 BC	China conquers Korea

Date	Event
60 BC	Formation of first triumvirate in Rome
51 BC	Cleopatra becomes Queen of Egypt
50 BC	Roman conquest of Gaul
44 BC	Julius Caesar assassinated
43 BC	Formation of second triumvirate in Rome
31 BC	Foundation of Roman Empire
c. AD 4	Birth of Jesus Christ
30	Crucifixion of Jesus Christ
43	Roman conquest of Britain
54	Nero become emperor of Rome
61	Boudicca leads British revolt against Rome
c. 64	Martyrdom of Saints Peter and Paul
70	Jewish revolt against Rome
79	Pompeii destroyed by eruption of Vesuvius
98	Roman Empire attains its largest size
c. 105	First manufacture of paper in China
122	Work begins on Hadrian's Wall
201	Foundation of Andgra dynasty in India
220	End of Han dynasty in China; Goths invade Asia Minor and Balkans
224	Foundation of Sassanian Empire in Persia
225	End of Andgra dynasty in India
226	Goths sack Athens, Sparta, and Corinth
270	Foundation of Gupta Empire in India
300	Flourishing of Mayan civilization in central America
313	Christianity adopted throughout Roman Empire
330	Roman Empire briefly reunited under Constantine the Great at Constantinople
360	Invasion of Europe by the Huns; Britain attacked by Picts and Scots
395	Roman Empire divided into Eastern (Byzantine) and Western Empires
396	Last Olympic Games of classical era
410	Visigoths sack Rome; Romans evacuate Britain
432	St Patrick begins mission in Ireland
449	Britain invaded by Angles, Saxons, and Jutes
455	Vandals sack Rome
476	Collapse of Western Roman Empire
481	Foundation of Frankish kingdom under Clovis I
539	Outbreak of war between Byzantium and Persia
550	End of Gupta Empire in India
c. 563	St Columba founds monastery at Iona
570	Birth of Muhammad in Mecca
581	Foundation of Sui dynasty in China
597	St Augustine arrives in Britain
600	Foundation of Harsha dynasty in India
602	Foundation of Archbishopric of Canterbury
618	Foundation of Tang dynasty in China; Persian conquest of Egypt
622	Flight of Muhammad to Medina
632	Death of Muhammad
641	Persia conquered by the Arabs
664	Synod of Whitby adopts Roman form of Christianity
697	Arabs sack Carthage
711	Moors invade Spain

732	Moors defeated at Poitiers and driven out of France
735	Death of St Bede
749	Foundation of Abbasid caliphate in Baghdad
771	Accession of Charlemagne as King of the Franks
787	First Viking raids on Britain
800	Charlemagne becomes emperor of the Holy Roman Empire
844	Scotland unified under Kenneth MacAlpin
850	Collapse of Mayan civilization
866	Establishment of Danish kingdom in England
871	Alfred the Great becomes king of England
874	Vikings settle in Iceland
878	Alfred defeats Danes at Edington
900	Christians begin reconquest of Spain
909	Foundation of Fatimid dynasty in N Africa
959	Edgar crowned king of all England
960	Foundation of Song dynasty in China
962	Otto I crowned Holy Roman emperor
985	Vikings settle in Greenland; Toltecs control Mexico
987	Capet crowned king of France
991	Renewal of Viking raids on England
c. 1000	Expansion of Inca Empire in Peru; Vikings under Leif Ericsson discover Vinland (possibly America)
1016	Canute crowned king of England
1054	Schism between Eastern and Western Christianity
1066	Norman Conquest of England
1086	Completion of Domesday Book
1094	El Cid defeats Turks at Valencia
1096	Beginning of First Crusade
1113	Foundation of the Knights Hospitallers of St John of Jerusalem
1122	Concordat of Worms
1127	Foundation of Southern Song dynasty in China; Normans conquer Sicily
1147	Beginning of Second Crusade
1168	Aztecs capture Toltec capital Tula
1170	Murder of Thomas Becket
1174	Saladin begins holy war against Christianity
1187	Saladin captures Jerusalem
1189	Beginning of Third Crusade
1190	Genghis Khan begins to build Mongol Empire
1191	Crusaders capture Acre
c. 1200	Foundation of Inca Empire
1202	Beginning of Fourth Crusade
1204	Normandy reclaimed from England by France; Crusaders sack Constantinople
1212	Children's Crusade
1215	Magna Carta signed at Runymede
1217	Beginning of Fifth Crusade
1228	Beginning of Sixth Crusade
1236	Mongols conquer Russia
1248	Beginning of Seventh Crusade
1250	Foundation of Mameluk dynasty in Egypt
1258	Mongols capture Baghdad
1264	Kublai Khan founds Yuan dynasty in China

Date	Event
1270	Beginning of Eighth Crusade
1271	Marco Polo arrives in China
1276	Edward I begins first Welsh campaign
1279	Mongols control China
1291	End of the Crusades
1294	Death of Kublai Khan
1300	Foundation of Ottoman Empire
1306	Robert the Bruce becomes king of Scotland
1309	Papacy transfers to Avignon
1314	Scottish defeat English at Bannockburn
1337	Beginning of Hundred Years' War between England and France
c. 1344	Aztecs build capital at Tenochtitlan
1346	Edward III defeats French at Crécy
1348	Black Death kills millions in Europe
1368	Foundation of Ming dynasty in China
1369	Timur (Tamerlane) embarks on conquest of Asia
1378	Great Schism of Catholic church between Rome and Avignon
1380	Publication of John Wycliffe's English translation of the Bible
1381	Peasants' Revolt in England
1397	Union of Sweden, Norway, and Denmark
1399	Richard II deposed by Henry IV
c. 1400	Gradual expansion of Aztec Empire through Mexico
1401	Union of Poland and Lithuania
1415	Henry V defeats French at Agincourt
1417	End of Great Schism
1431	Joan of Arc burnt at the stake at Rouen
1440	Montezuma I crowned emperor of the Aztecs
1442	First black slaves arrive in Portugal
c. 1445	Johannes Gutenberg established first printing press
1450	Jack Cade rebellion in England
1453	End of Hundred Years' War between England and France; Turks capture Constantinople
1455	Beginning of the Wars of the Roses
1460	Death of Henry the Navigator
1475	William Caxton prints first book in English
1481	Establishment of Spanish Inquisition
1485	Henry Tudor defeats Richard III at Bosworth Field, ending the Wars of the Roses
1492	Spanish drive Moors out of Granada; Christopher Columbus reaches West Indies
1498	Christopher Columbus reaches South America
1508	Michelangelo Buonnarroti embarks on painting the Sistine Chapel, Rome
1509	Henry VIII becomes king of England
1511	Formation of Holy League
1517	Beginning of Protestant Reformation; Turks conquer Egypt; Martin Luther nails theses to church door at Wittenburg; coffee introduced to Europe
1519	Death of Leonardo da Vinci
1520	Field of the Cloth of Gold meeting between England and France
1521	Cortés completes conquest of Aztec Empire; Diet of Worms
1525	Publication of William Tyndale's English translation of the New Testament

1526	Foundation of Mughal dynasty in India
1531	Francisco Pizarro captures Inca capital
1534	Henry VIII establishes independent Church of England; foundation of Jesuit Order
1535	Publication of first complete English Bible by Miles Coverdale
1536	Union of England and Wales; Henry VIII begins suppression of the monasteries
1541	John Calvin founds church at Geneva
1545	Council of Trent launches Counter-Reformation
1547	Ivan the Terrible becomes Tsar of Russia
1549	Publication of Book of Common Prayer
1555	Accession of Akbar in India
1558	England loses Calais to France; Elizabeth I succeeds to English throne
1559	Acts of Supremacy and Uniformity in England
1562	Beginning of French Wars of Religion; Netherlands revolt against Spain
1563	Outbreak of war between Sweden and Denmark
1564	Birth of William Shakespeare
1571	Turks defeated at Lepanto; adoption of Thirty-Nine Articles in England
1572	St Bartholomew's Day massacre in France
1577	Francis Drake embarks on voyage round globe
1581	Independence of United Provinces (Netherlands) from Spain
1584	Sir Walter Raleigh embarks on first expedition to Virginia
1587	Execution of Mary, Queen of Scots
1588	English defeat Spanish Armada
1589	Foundation of Bourbon dynasty in France
1595	Outbreak of war between France and Spain
1598	Edict of Nantes
1600	Establishment of English East India company
1602	Outbreak of war between Persia and Turkey; establishment of Dutch East India company
1603	James VI of Scotland becomes James I of England; Tokugawa shogunate founded in Japan
1605	Gunpowder Plot against James I of England
1607	Jamestown settlement founded by English in America
1613	Foundation of Romanov dynasty in Russia
1616	Death of William Shakespeare
1618	Outbreak of Thirty Years' War
1620	Puritans sail for America in the Mayflower
1625	New Amsterdam (later New York) founded by the Dutch
1629	English capture Quebec from the French
1632	Shah Jahan starts construction of Taj Mahal
1642	Beginning of the English Civil War; Abel Tasman sights Tasmania
1644	Foundation of Qing (Manchu) dynasty in China
1648	End of Thirty Years' War
1649	Execution of Charles I of England
1652	Outbreak of First Anglo-Dutch War; Dutch found Cape Colony
1653	Oliver Cromwell becomes Lord Protector of England
1658	Foundation of Aurangzeb Empire in India
1660	Restoration of Charles II to English throne; foundation of Royal Society
1665	London ravaged by Great Plague; outbreak of Second Anglo-Dutch War
1666	Great Fire of London
1669	Death of Rembrandt
1670	Foundation of Hudson's Bay Company

Date	Event
1673	Death of Molière
1674	Death of John Milton
1675	Christopher Wren begins new St Paul's Cathedral in London
1678	Popish Plot in England
1685	Revocation of Edict of Nantes
1688	James II flees England; William of Orange invited to accept English throne
1689	Formation of Grand Alliance against Louis XIV of France
1690	William III defeats James II at the Battle of the Boyne in Ireland
1695	Outbreak of Russo-Turkish War
1696	Peter I (the Great) becomes sole Tsar of Russia
1700	Outbreak of Great Northern War
1701	Act of Settlement; outbreak of the War of the Spanish Succession
1704	Marlborough defeats French at Blenheim
1707	Act of Union unites England and Scotland; death of Mogul emperor Aurangzeb
1711	Outbreak of Russo-Turkish War
1713	Treaty of Utrecht
1714	George I founds Hanoverian dynasty in England
1715	Jacobite rising in Scotland; death of Louis XIV
1730	John and Charles Wesley found Methodist Church
1740	Accessions of Frederick the Great and Maria Theresa; outbreak of the War of Austrian Succession
1745	Last Jacobite rising in Scotland
1748	End of the War of Austrian Succession
1750	Death of Johann Sebastian Bach
1752	Adoption of Gregorian calendar in Britain
1756	Outbreak of Seven Years' War in Canada; Black Hole of Calcutta
1757	British defeat French at Plassey
1759	General Wolfe defeats French at Quebec
1762	Accession of Catherine the Great
1768	Captain Cook lands in New Zealand and E Australia
1769	Birth of Napoleon Bonaparte
1773	Boston Tea Party
1775	Outbreak of the American War of Indepence
1776	American Declaration of Independence drawn up
1778	Death of Voltaire
1781	Americans defeat British at Yorktown
1783	British recognize independence of American colonies
1788	British establish colony in Australia
1789	Beginning of French Revolution; George Washington becomes first US President; mutiny on the Bounty
1791	Death of Mozart
1792	Foundation of the French Republic
1793	Outbreak of French Revolutionary Wars; execution of Louis XVI
1794	End of Reign of Terror in France
1795	Establishment of Directory in France
1798	Napoleon invades Egypt
1799	Napoleon assumes power as first consul of France; Beethoven composes first symphony; death of George Washington
1800	Act of Union between England and Ireland
1802	Peace of Amiens between England and France
1803	Outbreak of Napoleonic Wars; Louisiana Purchase in USA

1804	Napoleon becomes emperor of France
1805	Horatio Nelson dies at Trafalgar; Napoleon wins at Austerlitz
1806	End of the Holy Roman Empire
1807	Slavery abolished throughout British Empire
1808	Outbreak of Peninsular War
1810	Chile and Mexico declare independence from Spain
1811	Luddite riots in England
1812	Napoleon retreats from Moscow; outbreak of war between Britain and USA
1814	Restoration of Bourbon monarchy in France; Congress of Vienna
1815	Napoleon returns from exile and is finally defeated at Waterloo
1816	Argentina declares independence from Spain
1819	Peterloo massacre in England
1821	Outbreak of Greek War of Independence; Mexico, Central America, and Peru declare independence
1822	Brazil declares independence
1823	Formulation of Monroe Doctrine; First Ashanti War
1825	Bolivia declares independence; Decembrist uprising; opening of first passenger steam railway in England
1827	Death of Beethoven
1829	Catholic Emancipation Act passed in Britain; George Stephenson builds 'Rocket' locomotive
1830	Revolutions in France, Poland, Belgium, and Italy
1831	Charles Darwin embarks on the Beagle
1832	First Reform Act passed in Britain
1834	German customs union (Zollverein) formed
1836	Boers embark on Great Trek in South Africa; Texas wins independence from Spain after siege of the Alamo
1837	Queen Victoria crowned
1838	Formation of the Anti-Corn Law League in Manchester; First Afghan War
1839	First Opium War between Britain and China
1840	Penny post introduced in Britain
1841	Upper and Lower Canada joined by Act of Union; Britain annexes New Zealand and Hong Kong; beginning of Irish potato famine
1846	Repeal of the Corn Laws; outbreak of Mexican War between Mexico and USA
1848	Revolutions in France and other European countries; publication of Communist manifesto; Californian gold rush
1849	Britain annexes Punjab; death of Frédéric Chopin
1850	Beginning of Taiping Rebellion in China
1851	Great Exhibition in London
1852	Louis Napoleon becomes Emperor of France
1854	Outbreak of the Crimean War; foundation of Orange Free State
1855	David Livingstone reaches Victoria Falls; Second Opium War
1857	Indian Mutiny
1859	Charles Darwin's *The Origin of Species* published
1860	Southern states of America form Confederacy
1861	Outbreak of the American Civil War
1862	Otto von Bismarck becomes prime minister of Prussia
1865	End of the American Civil War; assassination of Abraham Lincoln
1866	Outbreak of Austro-Prussian War
1867	Garibaldi marches on Rome; US purchases Alaska from Russia; dual monarchy established in Austria-Hungary
1868	Restoration of Meiji dynasty in Japan

Date	Event
1869	Suez Canal opened
1870	Outbreak of Franco-Prussian War; death of Charles Dickens
1871	Proclamation of German Empire; establishment of Third Republic in France
1876	Battle of Little Big Horn
1877	Outbreak of Russo-Turkish War; Queen Victoria made empress of India
1879	Outbreak of the War of the Pacific between Chile and Peru and Bolivia; Zulu Wars; Austria and Germany form Dual Alliance
1880	Outbreak of First Boer War
1883	Death of Richard Wagner
1884	Germany acquires SW Africa and other parts of Africa
1885	Death of General Gordon at Khartoum
1886	Statue of Liberty constructed in New York
1887	Establishment of French Indochina
1889	Completion of Eiffel Tower in Paris; construction of first skyscraper in Chicago
1890	Bismarck dismissed; death of Vincent van Gogh
1893	Death of Piotr Ilyich Tchaikovsky
1894	Outbreak of Sino-Japanese War
1896	British win last Ashanti War; Jameson Raid in South Africa
1898	Outbreak of Spanish–American War over Cuba; USA annexes Hawaii; Fashoda Incident
1899	Outbreak of Second Boer War
1900	Boxer Rebellion in China
1901	Russia occupies Manchuria
1902	End of Second Boer War; Cuba gains independence
1903	Panama Canal Zone leased to USA; Wright Brothers make their first powered flight
1904	Entente Cordiale between Britain and France; outbreak of Russo-Japanese War
1905	Revolution in Russia
1906	San Francisco earthquake; Cuba occupied by USA
1907	Triple Entente between Britain, France, and Russia
1908	Young Turks Revolution
1910	Revolutions in Portugal and Mexico; foundation of Union of South Africa; death of Leo Tolstoy
1911	Revolution in China; Agadir crisis between France and Germany over Morocco; outbreak of war between Italy and Turkey
1912	Sinking of SS Titanic; establishment of Chinese Revolution
1914	Opening of Panama Canal; outbreak of First World War
1915	Start of Gallipoli campaign
1916	Battles of Verdun, Jutland, and the Somme; Easter Rising in Ireland; Albert Einstein presents general theory of relativity
1917	Russian Revolution followed by civil war; Balfour Declaration promises Jewish homeland in Palestine; USA enters First World War against Germany
1918	First World War ends with defeat of Germany; outbreak of civil war in Ireland; women over 30 win the right to vote in Britain
1919	Treaty of Versailles; dismantlement of Ottoman Empire; Amritsar massacre in India; foundation of Soviet Republic; Adolf Hitler founds National Socialist German Workers' Party
1920	Establishment of League of Nations; revolution in Turkey; civil war in Mexico; introduction of Prohibition in USA
1921	Establishment of Irish Free State in S Ireland

1922	Formation of USSR; Benito Mussolini becomes prime minister of Italy
1923	French occupy Ruhr; foundation of Turkish republic; Hitler stages Munich putsch
1924	Death of Vladimir Ilyich Lenin
1925	Locarno Conference
1926	General Strike in Britain; Chiang Kai-shek gains control in China
1929	Wall Street Crash leading to Great Depression; establishment of Yugoslavia; Arab–Jewish conflict in Palestine; Lateran Treaty creates Vatican City state
1930	Revolutions in Argentina and Brazil
1931	Japan occupies Manchuria
1932	Establishment of Kingdom of Saudi Arabia; outbreak of war between Bolivia and Paraguay
1933	Franklin Roosevelt introduces New Deal; Hitler becomes Chancellor of Germany; Reichstag Fire in Berlin; end of Prohibition in USA
1934	Chinese Communists begin Long March
1935	Italy invades Abyssinia
1936	Rome–Berlin Axis formed; Germany and Japan sign Anti-Comintern Pact; outbreak of Spanish Civil War; Arab revolt in Palestine; abdication of Edward VIII; first television transmissions in Britain
1937	Outbreak of war between Japan and China; Italy joins Anti-Comintern Pact
1938	Germany occupies Austria; Munich Agreement
1939	Italy invades Albania; USSR signs non-aggression pact with Germany and invades Finland; Germany invades Czechoslovakia and Poland; outbreak of Second World War
1940	Evacuation of Dunkirk; Battle of Britain
1941	Germany attacks Russia; Japanese attack US fleet at Pearl Harbor
1942	Japan invades Singapore; Allies defeat Germany at El Alamein; US forces defeat Japanese at Midway
1943	Germans surrender at Stalingrad; Italy surrenders
1944	Allied landings in Normandy
1945	Germany surrenders; atomic bombs dropped on Hiroshima and Nagasaki; Japan surrenders; Yalta Conference; Nuremberg War Crimes Tribunal opens; foundation of United Nations; Tito establishes Republic of Yugoslavia
1946	Outbreak of civil war in China and Greece
1947	Establishment of Indonesia; India, Pakistan, and Laos achieve independence; introduction of Marshall Plan for European reconstruction
1948	Division of Korea; establishment of state of Israel; introduction of apartheid in South Africa; outbreak of First Arab–Israeli War; Berlin blockade; establishment of Communist state in Czechoslovakia; assassination of Mahatma Gandhi
1949	Establishment of North Atlantic Treaty Organization (NATO); formation of Comecon; Communist victory in China; establishment of East and West Germany; establishment of Communist state in Hungary
1950	Start of McCarthyite anti-communist campaign in USA; outbreak of Korean War
1951	China occupies Tibet; British troops occupy Suez canal zone
1952	Allied occupation of Germany ends; outbreak of Mau Mau rebellion in Kenya; military revolt in Egypt; Elizabeth II accedes to British throne
1953	Death of Josef Stalin; Everest climbed; Egypt becomes a republic
1954	Cambodia and Laos achieve independence; Nasser assumes power in Egypt; outbreak of Algerian War of Independence; Vietnam divided into North and South; formation of Warsaw Pact; formation of SE Asian Treaty Organization (SEATO)
1955	Enosis crisis in Cyprus

Date	Event
1956	Suez Crisis; Morocco, Sudan, and Tunisia achieve independence; Soviet troops quell uprising in Hungary; outbreak of civil war in Cuba; outbreak of Second Arab–Israeli war
1957	Malaya and Ghana achieve independence; reopening of Suez Canal; formation of European Economic Community (EEC); US Civil Rights Act
1958	Establishment of Fifth Republic in France under De Gaulle; Singapore achieves independence; revolution in Iraq; Alaska joins USA
1959	Formation of European Free Trade Association (EFTA); Fidel Castro assumes power in Cuba; Hawaii joins USA
1960	Nigeria and Belgian Congo achieve independence; South Africa becomes a republic; Sharpeville massacre; US invasion of Cuba fails
1961	John F Kennedy becomes US President; Berlin Wall built; Yuri Gagarin becomes first man in space
1962	Algeria, Jamaica, and Trinidad achieve independence; Cuban missile crisis
1963	Assassination of President Kennedy; formation of Organization of African Unity; Kenya achieves independence; nuclear test ban signed; race riots in the USA
1964	US Civil Rights Act; foundation of Tanzania; Malawi and Zambia achieve independence; outbreak of war between Indonesia and Malaysia
1965	Outbreak of war between India and Pakistan; Rhodesia unilaterally declares independence; US forces enter Vietnam
1966	Start of Chinese cultural revolution
1967	Outbreak of Biafran War; Six-Day Arab–Israeli War; military coup in Greece
1968	Soviet invasion of Czechoslovakia; assassination of Martin Luther King
1969	Neil Armstrong becomes first man on the moon; Richard Nixon becomes US President; outbreak of civil conflict in Northern Ireland; revolution in Libya
1971	East Pakistan becomes Bangladesh; decimal currency introduced in Britain
1972	Sri Lanka achieves independence
1973	US troops withdraw from S Vietnam; Yom Kippur Arab–Israeli War; Britain, Ireland, and Denmark join EEC; famine in Ethiopia
1974	Oil crisis; revolution in Portugal; Cyprus partitioned; Watergate affair in USA; Haile Selassie deposed in Ethiopia
1975	Vietnam War ends; death of Francisco Franco followed by restoration of democracy in Spain; outbreak of civil war in Lebanon
1976	Death of Mao Zedong; reunion of North and South Vietnam; outbreak of civil war in Angola; Soweto riots in South Africa
1977	Military coup in Pakistan; Israel occupies West Bank; Jimmy Carter becomes US President
1978	Camp David talks between Egypt and Israel; military coup in Afghanistan
1979	Outbreak of civil war in Afghanistan followed by Russian invasion; Chinese invade Vietnam; Islamic revolution in Iran; Sandinistas stage revolution in Nicaragua; Idi Amin overthrown in Uganda; Margaret Thatcher becomes British prime minister
1980	Rhodesia achieves independence (as Zimbabwe); outbreak of Iran–Iraq War; formation of Solidarity trade union in Poland
1981	Ronald Reagan becomes US President; declaration of martial law in Poland; assassination of President Sadat of Egypt; race riots in British cities; emergence of Aids
1982	Falklands War between Britain and Argentina; Israel invades Lebanon; Palestine Liberation Organization (PLO) expelled from Beirut
1983	US invasion of Grenada
1984	Famine in Ethiopia; assassination of Indian prime minister Indira Gandhi
1985	Mikhail Gorbachev assumes power in USSR

1986	Chernobyl nuclear power disaster; US bombing of Libya; Gorbachev introduces reforms in USSR; President Marcos of Philippines deposed
1987	World population exceeds five thousand million
1989	George Bush becomes US President; USSR withdraws from Afghanistan; communist regimes collapse in Poland, Czechoslovakia, Romania, Hungary, East Germany, and USSR; Berlin Wall breached; USA invades Panama; Chinese crush student protests in Tiananmen Square, Beijing
1990	Reunification of Germany; Margaret Thatcher succeeded by John Major as British prime minister; Nelson Mandela released from prison in South Africa; apartheid policy in South Africa dismantled; Iraq invades Kuwait
1991	Gulf War; outbreak of civil war in Yugoslavia; Croatia, Macedonia, and Slovenia declare independence; USSR is broken up into independent republics and is replaced by Commonwealth of Independent States; Boris Yeltsin replaces Gorbachev as Russian president; end of Warsaw Pact; military coup in Haiti
1992	Bosnia and Herzegovina declare independence; establishment of Muslim regime in Afghanistan; majority rule established in South Africa; US intervention in Somalia, continuing civil war in Yugoslavia; Czechoslovakia divided into Czech and Slovak republics
1993	Bill Clinton becomes US President; introduction of EC single market
1994	Russia invades Chechnya; Nelson Mandela becomes president of South Africa; Israel withdraws from West Bank and Gaza Strip; ceasefire in place in Northern Ireland
1995	Jacques Chirac becomes president of France; assassination of Israeli prime minister Yitzhak Rabin
1996	Peace agreed in Bosnia; foundation of World Trade Organization
1997	Resumption of IRA terrorist campaign in Northern Ireland; Hong Kong returned to China; Zaire renamed Democratic Republic of Congo; Tony Blair elected British prime minister; death of Diana, Princess of Wales
1998	Israel and PLO agree peace accord over future of West Bank; civil war in Congo; peace accord in Northern Ireland; USA resumes air strikes against Iraq
1999	Serbian expulsions of ethnic Albanians from Kosovo provokes NATO bombing campaign against Yugoslavia; conflict in Chechenya intensifies; US President Bill Clinton impeached in Monica Lewinsky scandal; Nelson Mandela steps down as president of South Africa; Scotland and Wales granted their own parliaments, with limited powers; world population passes six billion
2000	Yugoslav president Slobodan Milošević is forced out of office after elections and public protests; renewal of Arab–Israeli conflict in Israel
2001	George W. Bush succeeds Bill Clinton as US president

Major wars and battles

Date	War/campaign	Combatants	Chief battles/sieges
c. 1200 BC	Trojan Wars	Greece v Troy	Siege of Troy (c. 1200)
490–479 BC	Persian Wars	Persia v Greece	Battles of Marathon (490 BC), Thermopylae (480 BC), and Salamis (480 BC)
460–445 BC; 431–404 BC	Peloponnesian Wars	Corinth, Persia, and Sparta v Athens	Siege of Athens (404 BC)
334–323 BC	Conquests of Alexander the Great	Macedonia v Persia and Asia Minor	Battles of Granicus (334 BC), Issus (333 BC), and Guagmela (331 BC)
264–241 BC	First Punic War	Rome v Carthage	Battles of Mylae (260 BC) and Aegates Insulae (241 BC)

Date	War/campaign	Combatants	Chief battles/sieges
218–202 BC	Second Punic War	Rome v Carthage	Battles of Trebia (218 BC), Trasimene (217 BC), Cannae (216 BC), and Zama (202 BC)
149–146 BC	Third Punic War	Rome v Carthage	Sack of Carthage (146 BC)
112–106 BC	Numidian War	Rome v Numidia	
58–51 BC	Gallic Wars	Rome v Gaul	Siege of Alesia (52 BC)
48 BC	Roman Civil War	Julius Caesar v Pompey	Battle of Pharsalus (48 BC)
31 BC	Roman Civil War	Octavian v Antony and Cleopatra	Battle of Actium (31 BC)
AD 84	Invasion of Scotland	Rome v Scottish tribes	Battle of Mons Graupius (84 AD)
375–454	Invasion of the Roman Empire	Huns v Rome	
665	Arab invasion of N Africa	Arabs v Muslims	Battle of Basra (665)
771–814	Conquests of Charlemagne	Holy Roman Empire v Saxons, Italians, and Spanish	Battle of Roncesvalles (778)
800–1016	Viking raids	Vikings v Britain, Normandy, Spain, Italy, Morocco, and Russia	Battles of Edington (878) and Clontarf (1014)
1066	Norman Conquest	Normandy v England	Battle of Hastings (1066)
1089–94	El Cid's conquest of Valencia	Spain v the Moors	Battle of Valencia (1094)
1095–99	First Crusade	Christians v Muslims	
1147–48	Second Crusade	Christians v Muslims	Capture of Jerusalem (1187)
1189–92	Third Crusade	Christians v Muslims	
1190–1227	Conquests of Genghis Khan	Mongols v Tatars, China, Asia Minor, S Russia	
1208–29	Albigensian Crusade	Inquisition v Cathars	
1282–1302	War of the Sicilian Vespers	Sicilian rebels v France	
1297–1305	Revolt of William Wallace	Scotland v England	Battles of Stirling (1297) and Falkirk (1298)
1306–28	Revolt of Robert the Bruce	Scotland v England	Battle of Bannockburn (1314)
1337–1453	Hundred Years' War	England v France	Battles of Sluys (1340), Crécy (1346), Poitiers (1356), and Agincourt (1415)
1360–1405	Conquest of Asia by Timur (Tamerlane)	Mongols v Asia Minor, Turkey, Russia, and India	
1388	Invasion of England	Scotland v England	Battle of Otterburn (1388)
1403	Rebellion of Sir Henry Percy (Hotspur)	Henry IV v Sir Henry Percy	Battle of Shrewsbury (1403)
1453	Turkish conquest of Byzantine Empire	Ottoman Turks v Byzantine Empire	Fall of Constantinople (1453)
1455–85	Wars of the Roses	House of York v House of Lancaster	Battles of St Albans (1455), Towton (1461), Tewkesbury (1471), Bosworth Field (1485), and Stoke (1487)
1491–92	Expulsion of the Moors from Spain	Spain v the Moors	Siege of Granada (1491–92)

1494–1559	Habsburg–Valois Wars	Habsburg v Valois dynasties	
1513	Invasion of England	Scotland v England	Battle of Flodden (1513)
1542	Invasion of Scotland	England v Scotland	Battle of Solway Moss (1542)
1546–47	War of the Schmalkaldic League	France v German Protestant Estates	
1562–98	French Wars of Religion	Catholics v Huguenots	
1568–1648	Dutch Wars of Independence	Netherlands v Spain	
1571	Christians v Ottoman Turks	Spain and Italy v Turks	Battle of Lepanto (1571)
1585–89	War of the Three Henries	Civil war (France)	
1588	Spanish invasion of England	Spain v England	Defeat of the Spanish Armada (1588)
1592–99	Japanese invasion of Korea	Japan v Korea	
1609–14	War of the Julich Succession	German Protestants v Catholics	
1618–48	Thirty Years' War	France v Habsburgs	Battles of White Mountain (1620), Lutter (1626), Breitenfeld (1631), and Lutzen (1632)
1628	War of the Mantuan Succession	France v Spain	
1639	First Bishops' War	Scotland v England	
1640	Second Bishops' War	Scotland v England	
1641–49	Great Irish Rebellion	Ireland v England	
1642–46, 1648–51	English Civil War	Royalists v Parliamentarians	Battles of Edgehill (1642), Marston Moor (1644), Naseby (1645), Dunbar (1650) and Worcester (1651)
1685	Monmouth Rebellion	Protestants v Catholics	Battle of Sedgemoor (1685)
1688–97	War of the League of Augsburg	Grand Alliance v Louis XIV of France	
1689	Scottish rebellion	Scottish Jacobites v England	Battle of Killiecrankie (1689)
1690–91	Irish rebellion	Irish Jacobites v England	Battles of the Boyne (1690) and Aughrim (1691)
1692	Massacre of Glencoe	Campbell clan v McDonald clan	
1701–14	War of the Spanish Succession	Grand Alliance v Louis XIV of France	Battles of Blenheim (1704), Ramillies (1706), Oudenaarde (1708), and Malplaquet (1709)
1702–13	Queen Anne's War	Britain v France	
1715–16	Jacobite Rebellion	Jacobite Scots v Hanoverians	Battle of Sherrifmuir (1715)
1739–43	War of Jenkin's Ear	Britain v Spain	
1740–48	War of the Austrian Succession	Prussia v Austria	Battle of Dettingen (1743)
1745–46	Jacobite Rebellion	Jacobite Scots v Hanoverians	Battles of Prestonpans (1745) and Culloden (1746)
1756–63	Seven Years' War	Austria, France, Russia, Sweden, and Saxony v Prussia, Britain, and Portugal	Battles of Plassey (1757) and Quebec (1759)

Date	War/campaign	Combatants	Chief battles/sieges
1763–66	Pontiac's War	Native Americans v British colonists	
1775–83	US War of Independence	American settlers v Britain	Battles of Bunker Hill (1775), Saratoga (1777), and Yorktown (1781)
1792–1802	French Revolutionary Wars	France v Britain and other European states	Battles of Valmy (1792), Glorious First of June (1794), Cape St Vincent (1797), Camperdown (1797), the Pyramids (1798), the Nile (1798), Hohenlinden (1800), Marengo (1801), and Copenhagen (1801)
1805–15	Napoleonic Wars	France v Britain, Russia, Prussia, and other European states	Battles of Trafalgar (1805), Austerlitz (1805), Jena (1806), Friedland (1806), Borodino (1812), Leipzig (1813), and Waterloo (1815)
1808–14	Peninsular War	France v Britain	Battles of Corunna (1809) and Vitoria (1813)
1814–16	Gurkha War	Gurkhas v Britain	
1821–32	Greek War of Independence	Greek rebels v Turks	Battle of Navarino (1827)
1836	Texan War of Independence	Texas v Mexico	Battle of the Alamo (1836)
1838–39	Boer–Zulu War	Boers v Zulus	
1839–42	First Opium War	Britain v China	
1844–47	First Maori War	Maoris v Britain	
1846–47	Mexican War	USA v Mexico	
1853–56	Crimean War	Britain, France, and the Ottoman Empire v Russia	Battles of Inkerman (1854) and Balaclava (1856)
1856–60	Second Opium War	Britain v China	
1857–58	Mormon Utah War	Mormons v USA	
1857–59	Indian Mutiny	Indian rebels v Britain	Battle of Solferino (1859)
1859–61	Italian War of Unification	Austria v Italy and France	
1860–72	Second Maori War	Maoris v British settlers in New Zealand	Battles of Bull Run (1861), Shiloh (1862), Seven Days' (1862), Antietam (1862), Fredericksburg (1862), Stones River (1862), Chancellorsville (1863), Gettysburg (1863), Vicksburg (1863), Chickamauga (1863), Chatanooga (1863), Cold Harbor (1864), and Petersburg (1864)
1861–65	US Civil War	Union v Confederacy	
1866	Seven Weeks' War/ Austro-Prussian War	Prussia and Italy v Austria and allies	Siege of Lucknow (1857)
1876	Indian Wars	Sioux and Cheyenne tribes v US government	Battle of Little Bighorn (1876)
1879	Zulu War	Britain v Zulus	Battles of Isandhlwana (1879) and Ulundi (1879)
1879–84	War of the Pacific	Chile v Peru and Bolivia	

1880–81	First Boer War	Boers v Britain	Battle of Majuba Hill (1881)
1885	Mahdi Rebellion	Sudanese rebels v Britain	Fall of Khartoum (1885)
1890	Indian War	Sioux v US government	Massacre of Wounded Knee (1890)
1899–1901	Boxer Uprising	Chinese Boxer rebels v Christians	
1899–1902	Second Boer War	Boers v British	Battle of Ladysmith (1900), Siege of Mafeking (1900)
1904–05	Russo-Japanese War	Russia v Japan	Battle of Tsushima Straits (1905)
1911–12	Chinese Revolution	Chinese rebels v Manchu dynasty	
1914–18	First World War	Germany and allies v Britain, France, Russia and allies	Battles of Liège (1914), Marne (1914), Ypres (1914), Tannenberg (1914), Dardanelles and Gallipoli (1915), Loos (1915), Ypres (1915), Jutland (1916), Verdun (1916), Somme (1916), Passchendaele (1917), Amiens (1918), Antwerp (1918), Second Battle of the Somme (1918)
1917–22	Russian Civil War	Communist Red Army v anti-communist Whites	
1935–36	Italian invasion of Abyssinia	Italy v Abyssinia	
1936–39	Spanish Civil War	Spanish Nationalists v Spanish Republicans	Battle of Ebro River (1938)
1939–45	Second World War	Germany, Italy, and Japan v Britain, USA, and allies	Battles of the Atlantic (1939–43), Britain (1940), Pearl Harbor (1941), Stalingrad (1941), Tobruk (1941–42), Coral Sea (1942), Midway Island (1942), Guadalcanal (1942), El Alamein (1942), Singapore (1942), Salerno (1943), Burma (1943–45), Arnhem (1944), Normandy invasion (1944), Anzio (1944), Monte Cassino (1944), Leyte Gulf (1944), the Bulge (1944–45), Iwo Jima (1945), and the Rhine (1945)
1945–49	Chinese Civil War	Communist Chinese v non-Communist Chinese	
1946–54	French War of Indochina	Nationalist rebels v France	Battle of Dien Bhien Phu (1954)
1947–48	Indian Civil War	Pakistan v India	
1950–53	Korean War	Communists v non-Communists	
1952–56	Mau-Mau uprising	Kenyan Mau-Mau rebels v white settlers	
1956	Suez War	Britain, France, and Israel v Egypt	
1956–1975	Vietnam War	North Vietnam v South Vietnam and USA	

Date	War/campaign	Combatants	Chief battles/sieges
1960–68	Civil War in the Congo	Marxist rebels v Republican government	
1961	Invasion of Cuba	USA v Cuba	Bay of Pigs (1961)
1962–74	Mozambique War of Independence	Frelimo guerrillas v Portugal-backed government	
1967	Six-Day War	Israel v Arab states	
1967–70	Nigerian–Biafran War	Nigeria v Biafra	
1968	Soviet invasion of Czechoslovakia	Soviet Union v Czechoslovakia	
1970–71	Jordanian Civil War	Jordan v Palestinian forces	
1970–75	Cambodian War	Cambodia, South Vietnam, and USA v North Vietnam, Viet Cong, and Khmer Rouge	
1971	Pakistan Civil War	East Pakistan v West Pakistan	
1973	Yom Kippur War	Egypt v Israel	
1974	Invasion of Cyprus	Turkey v Greek Cypriots	
1975	Angolan Civil War	Internal factions	
1978–79	Ugandan Civil War	Ugandan exiles and Tanzania v General Idi Amin	
1979	Soviet invasion of Afghanistan	Soviet Union v Afghanistan	
1980–88	Iran–Iraq War	Iran v Iraq	
1982	Lebanese Civil War	Israel v Syria and Palestinian guerillas	
1982	Falklands War	Britain v Argentina	Goose Green (1982)
1982–90	Nicaraguan Civil War	US-backed Contras v socialist Sandinistas	
1983	Invasion of Grenada	USA v Soviet-backed Grenadan forces	
1983–94	Sri Lankan Civil War	Buddhists v Hindus	
1986	Haitian Civil War	Rebels v Duvalier government	
1991	Gulf War	Iraq v Kuwait, USA, Britain, and allies	
1990–96	Rwandan Civil War	Tutsis v Hutus	
1991–99	Civil War in the Balkans	Involving Yugoslavia and emerging states of Slovenia, Macedonia, Croatia, Bosnia-Hercegovina, and Serbia	
1996–99	Civil War in Zaïre	Rebel alliance v Kabila government	
1997–98	Civil War in Sierra Leone	Internal factions	

Voyages of exploration

Date	Event
490 BC	Hanno sails part of the coast of Africa
325 BC	Alexander the Great sails along coasts of N India and Persian Gulf
AD 84	Agricola sails round Britain
985	Eric the Red explores coast of Greenland
1003	Leif Ericsson discovers Vinland (possibly N America)
1275	Marco Polo starts to explore China
1418	João Gonçalves Zarco discovers Madeira
1434	Gil Eanes sails round Cape Bojadar
1446	Dinís Dias discovers Cape Verde and the Senegal River
1469	Diogo Gomes crosses equator
1488	Bartolomeu Dias rounds the Cape of Good Hope
1492	Christopher Columbus discovers the New World
1493	Christopher Columbus discovers Puerto Rico, Antigua, and Jamaica
1497	John Cabot explores the coast of Newfoundland
1497	Vasco da Gama sails round the Cape of Good Hope
1498	Vasco da Gama sails the coast of Mozambique and discovers sea route to India
1498	Christopher Columbus discovers Trinidad and Venezuela
1499	Amerigo Vespucci discovers the mouth of the Amazon
1500	Pedro Alvares Cabral discovers Brazil
1500	Diogo Dias discovers Madagascar
1500	Gaspar Corte Real explores the coast of E Greenland and Labrador
1501	Amerigo Vespucci explores the coast of S America
1502	Christopher Columbus explores Honduras and Panama
1513	Vasco Núñez de Balboa crosses the Panama Isthmus and discovers the Pacific Ocean
1520	Ferdinand Magellan discovers the Straits of Magellan
1521	Ferdinand Magellan discovers the Philippines
1524	Giovanni da Verrazano discovers New York Bay and the Hudson River
1526	Sebastian Cabot explores the Rio de la Plata
1534	Jacques Cartier explores the Gulf of St Lawrence
1535	Jacques Cartier sails up the St Lawrence River
1536	Pedro de Mendoza founds Buenos Aires and sails up the Parana and Paraguay rivers
1539	Hernando de Soto explores Florida
1540	García López de Cárdenas discovers the Grand Canyon
1580	Sir Francis Drake sails round the world
1585	John Davis discovers the Davis Strait
1595	Sir Walter Raleigh explores the Orinoco River
1610	Henry Hudson discovers Hudson's Bay
1616	William Baffin discovers Baffin's Bay
1617	Sir Walter Raleigh sails to Guiana
1642	Abel Janszoon Tasman discovers Tasmania and New Zealand
1678	Robert Cavelier de la Salle explores the Great Lakes of Canada
1683	William Dampier crosses the Pacific Ocean
1692	Ijsbrand Iders explores the Gobi Desert

Date	Event
1736	Anders Celsius leads expedition to Lapland
1761	Carsten Niebuhr leads expedition to Arabia
1766	Louis de Bougainville explores the Pacific
1769	James Cook charts the coasts of New Zealand and E Australia
1770	James Cook lands at Botany Bay, Australia
1772	James Bruce explores Abyssinia
1774	James Cook explores the Pacific
1778	James Cook discovers the Hawaiian islands
1787	Horace Saussure climbs Mont Blanc
1790	George Vancouver explores the coast of NW America
1795	Mungo Park explores the course of the Niger
1803	Matthew Flinders completes first circumnavigation of Australia
1818	John Ross searches for the NW Passage
1823	Walter Oudney discovers Lake Chad
1841	David Livingstone discovers Lake Ngami
1845	John Franklin searches for the NW Passage
1854	Richard Burton and John Speke explore Somaliland
1855	David Livingstone discovers the Victoria Falls
1858	Richard Burton and John Speke discover Lake Tanganyika
1860	Burke and Wills expedition across Australia
1875	Henry Morton Stanley follows the Congo to the Atlantic coast
1888	Fridtjof Nansen crosses Greenland
1893	Fridtjof Nansen tries to reach the North Pole
1905	Roald Amundsen sails through NW Passage
1909	Robert Edwin Peary reaches North Pole
1911	Roald Amundsen reaches South Pole
1912	Robert Falcon Scott reaches South Pole
1914	Ernest Shackleton leads expedition to the Antarctic
1926	Richard Byrd flies over North Pole
1926	Umberto Nobile makes first airship crossing of North Pole
1947	Thor Heyerdahl crosses Atlantic in Kon-Tiki balsa wood craft
1953	Edmund Hillary and Tenzing Norgay climb Everest
1958	Vivian Fuchs makes first land crossing of Antarctica
1966–7	Sir Francis Chichester completes first single-handed non-stop circumnavigation of globe
1993	Ranulph Fiennes makes first unsupported crossing on foot of Antarctica
1999	Brian Jones and Bertrand Piccard complete first non-stop balloon journey round the world

Note See also SPACE EXPLORATION

7.2 Ancient History

Seven wonders of the ancient world

	Date	Location
Pyramids of Egypt	c. 2000 BC	Gizeh, Cairo (Egypt)
Hanging Gardens of Babylon	c. 600 BC	S of Baghdad (Iraq)
Temple of Artemis (Diana)	c. 600 BC	Ephesus (Turkey)
Statue of Zeus at Olympia	c. 500 BC	Olympia (S Greece)
Mausoleum at Halicarnassus	c. 400 BC	Halicarnassus (SE Turkey)
Colossus of Rhodes	c. 300 BC	Rhodes harbour (Rhodes)
Pharos of Alexandria	c. 270 BC	Alexandria (Egypt)

Dynasties of Ancient Egypt

Date	Period	Dynasty	Major rulers
3110–2884 BC	Early Dynastic Period	I	Menes
2884–2780 BC		II	
2780–2680 BC	Old Kingdom	III	Snefru
2680–2565 BC		IV	Khufu (Cheops), Khafre, Menkaure
2565–2420 BC		V	
2420–2258 BC		VI	Pepi I, Pepi II
2258–2225 BC	First Intermediate Period	VII, VIII	
2225–2134 BC		IX, X	
2134–c. 2000 BC		XI	Mentuhotep II
2000–1786 BC	Middle Kingdom	XII	Amenemhet I, Sesostris I, Amenemhet II, Sesostris II, Amenemhet III, Amenemhet IV
1786–1570 BC	Second Intermediate Period	XIII–XVII	Hyksos
1570–c. 1342 BC	New Kingdom	XVIII	Amenhotep I, Thutmose I, Thutmose II, Hatshepsut, Thutmose III, Thutmose IV, Akhenaton, Tutankhamun
c. 1342–1200 BC		XIX	Ramses I, Ramses II
1200–1085 BC		XX	Ramses III
1085–945 BC		XXI	
945–745 BC		XXII	Sheshonk I
745–718 BC		XXIII	
718–712 BC		XXIV	

Date	Period	Dynasty	Major rulers
712–663 BC		XXV	Taharka
663–525 BC		XXVI	Necho
525–405 BC		XXVII	Achaemenids of Persia, Darius II
405–332 BC		XXVIII, XXIX, XXX	Nekhtnebf I

Roman kings

Reign	King
753–715 BC	Romulus
715–673 BC	Numa Pompilius
673–642 BC	Tullus Hostilius
642–616 BC	Ancus Marcius
616–578 BC	Tarquinius Priscus
578–534 BC	Servius Tullius
534–509 BC	Tarquinius Superbus

Roman emperors

Reign	Emperor
27 BC–AD 14	Augustus
14–37	Tiberius
37–41	Gaius Caesar (Caligula)
41–54	Claudius I
54–68	Nero
68–69	Galba
69	Otho
69–79	Vespasian
79–81	Titus
81–96	Domitian
96–98	Nerva
98–117	Trajan
117–138	Hadrian
138–161	Antoninus Pius
161–180	Marcus Aurelius
161–169	Lucius Verus
180–92	Commodus
193	Pertinax
193	Didius Julianus
193–211	Septimius Severus
211–17	Caracalla
211–12	Geta
217–18	Macrinus
218–22	Heliogabalus (Elagabalus)
222–35	Alexander Severus
235–38	Maximin

238	Gordian I and Gordian II, Balbinus, Pupienus
238–44	Gordian III
244–49	Philip
249–51	Decius
251	Hostilianus
251–53	Gallus
253	Aemilianus
253–60	Valerian
253–68	Gallienus
268–70	Claudius II
270–75	Aurelian
275–76	Tacitus
276	Florianus
276–82	Probus
282–83	Carus
283–85	Carinus
283–84	Numerianus
284–305	Diocletian
286–305	Maximian
305–06	Constantius I
305–10	Galerius
308–13	Maximin
308–24	Licinius
306–12	Maxentius
306–37	Constantine I (the Great)
337–40	Constantine II
337–50	Constans
337–61	Constantius II
350–53	Magnentius
361–63	Julian
363–64	Jovian
364–75	Valentinian I
364–78	Valens
375–83	Gratian
383–88	Maximus
375–92	Valentinian II
392–94	Eugenius
375–95	Theodosius I (the Great)
395–408	Arcadius
408–50	Theodosius II
450–57	Marcian
457–74	Leo I
474	Leo II
395–423	Honorius
409–11	Maximus
421	Constantius III
425–55	Valentinian III
455	Petronius Maximus
455–56	Avitus
457–61	Majorian
461–65	Libius Severus

Reign	Emperor
467–72	Anthemius
472	Olybrius
473–74	Glycerius
474–75	Julius Nepos
475–76	Romulus Augustus

Note Overlapping dates indicate periods of joint rule or the division of the empire into east and west

Roman placenames

Modern name	Roman name
Continents	
Africa	Libya, Africa
Europe	Europa
Seas/rivers	
Atlantic Ocean	Mare Atlanticum
Black Sea	Pontus (Euxinus)
Caspian Sea	Mare Caspium
Dardanelles	Hellespontus
Gibraltar, Straits of	Fretum Gaditanum
Marmora, Sea of	Propontis
Mediterranean	Mare internum
Nile, River	Nilus
Persian Gulf	Mare Rubrum
Red Sea	Sinus Arabicus
Rhine, River	Rhenus
Tyrrhenian Sea	Mare Inferum
Country/region	
Belgium	Belgae
Britain	Britannia
Brittany	Armoricae
China	Seres
Denmark	Dania
Egypt	Aegyptus
England	Anglia
Flanders	Menapii
France	Gallia
Gaul	Gallia
Germany	Germania
Gibraltar	Calpe
Greece	Graecia
Holland	Batavi
Ireland	Hibernia
Italy	Italia
Lebanon	Libanus
Malta	Melita
Morocco	Mauretania
Portugal	Lusitania

Scotland	Caledonia
Spain	Hispania
Switzerland	Helvetia
Tuscany	Etruria
Wales	Cambria

Cities

Berlin	Berolinum
Berne	Verona
Cadiz	Gades
Constantinople/Istanbul	Byzantium
Jerusalem	Hierosolyma
Lisbon	Olisipo
Paris	Lutetia

British Isles

Abergavenny	Gobannium
Aldborough	Isurium Brigantum
Ambleside	Galava
Ancaster	Causennae
Anglesey	Mona
Armagh	Armacha
Avon, River	Auvona
Bath	Aquae Sulis
Brancaster	Branodunum
Caerleon	Isca
Caerwent	Venta Silurum
Canterbury	Durovernum Cantiacorum
Cardigan	Ceretica
Carlisle	Luguvalium
Carmarthen	Maridunum
Carnarvon	Segontium
Chelmsford	Caesaromagus
Chester	Deva
Chichester	Noviomagus Regnensium
Cirencester	Corinium Dobunnorum
Clyde, River	Clota
Colchester	Camulodunum
Corbridge	Corstopitum
Dee, River	Deva
Doncaster	Danum
Dorchester	Durnovaria
Dover	Dubris
Dover, Straits of	Fretum Gallicum
Dunstable	Durocobrivae
Eden, River	Ituna
Exeter	Isca Dumnoniorum
Forth, River	Bodotria
Gloucester	Glevum
Hebrides	Ebudae Insulae
Hexham	Axelodunum
Ilkley	Olicana
Jersey	Caesarea

Modern name	Roman name
Kent	Cantium
Lanchester	Longovicium
Land's End	Bolerium Promunturium
Leicester	Ratae Corieltauvorum
Lincoln	Lindum
Lizard Point	Damnonium Promunturium
London	Londinium
Manchester	Mamucium
Man, Isle of	Monapia
Newcastle upon Tyne	Pons Aelius
Orkneys	Orcades
Pevensey	Anderetium
Portsmouth	Magnus Portus
Richborough	Rutupiae
Rochester	Durobrivae
St Albans	Verulamium
Salisbury	Sorviodunum
Scilly Isles	Cassiterides
Severn, River	Sabrina
Silchester	Calleva Atrebatum
Solway Firth	Ituna aestuarium
Thames, River	Tamesis
Wallsend	Segedunum
Wash, The	Metaris aestuarium
Wear, River	Vedra
Wight, Isle of	Vectis
Winchester	Venta Belgarum
Worcester	Vigornia
Wroxeter	Viroconium Cornoviorum
York	Eburacum

7.3 *Monarchs and Emperors*

Austria

Reign	Monarch
1440–93	Frederick III
1493–1519	Maximilian I
1519–58	Karl V
1558–64	Ferdinand I
1564–76	Maximilian II
1576–1612	Rudolf II

1612–19	Matthias
1619–37	Ferdinand II
1637–57	Ferdinand III
1658–1705	Leopold I
1705–11	Josef I
1711–40	Karl VI
1742–45	Karl VII
1745–65	Franz I
1765–90	Josef II
1790–92	Leopold III
1792–1835	Franz II
1835–48	Ferdinand I
1848–1916	Franz Josef
1916–18	Karl I

Note There was an interregnum in the years 1740–42

Belgium

Reign	Monarch
1831–65	Leopold I
1865–1909	Leopold II
1909–34	Albert I
1934–51	Leopold III
1951–93	Baudouin
1993–	Albert II

China

Date	Dynasty
c. 2200–c. 1523 BC	Xia
c. 1480–1050 BC	Shang or Yin
c. 1066–221 BC	Zhou
221–206 BC	Qin (Ch'in)
206 BC–AD 220	Han
AD 220–65	Three Kingdoms (San-kuo)
265–420	Tsin
581–618	Sui
618–907	Tang
907–60	Five Dynasties and Ten Kingdoms
960–1279	Song (Sung)
1279–1368	Yuan
1368–1644	Ming
1644–1912	Ch'ing (Manchu)

Denmark

Reign	Monarch
1448–81	Kristian I
1481–1513	Johan
1513–23	Kristian II
1523–34	Frederik I
1534–59	Kristian III
1559–88	Frederik II
1588–1648	Kristian IV
1648–70	Frederik III
1670–99	Kristian V
1699–1730	Frederik IV
1730–46	Kristian VI
1746–66	Frederik V
1766–1808	Kristian VII
1808–39	Frederik VI
1839–48	Kristian VIII
1848–63	Frederik VII
1863–1906	Kristian IX
1906–12	Frederik VIII
1912–47	Kristian X
1947–72	Frederik IX
1972–	Margrethe II

England

Reign	Monarch
802–39	Egbert
839–58	Æthelwulf
858–60	Æthelbald
860–65	Æthelbert
866–71	Æthelred
871–99	Alfred
899–924	Edward (the Elder)
939–46	Edmund
946–55	Edred
955–59	Edwy
959–75	Edgar
975–78	Edward (the Martyr)
978–1016	Æthelred (the Unready)
1016	Edmund (Ironside)
1016–35	Knut (Canute)
1035–37	Harold
1037–40	Harold I (Harefoot)
1040–42	Hardaknut
1042–66	Edward (the Confessor)
1066	Harold II

1066–87	William I (the Conqueror)
1087–1100	William II (Rufus)
1100–35	Henry I
1135–54	Stephen
1154–89	Henry II
1189–99	Richard I (Coeur de Lion)
1199–1216	John
1216–72	Henry III
1272–1307	Edward I
1307–27	Edward II
1327-77	Edward III
1377–99	Richard II
1399–1413	Henry IV
1413–22	Henry V
1422–61	Henry VI
1461–70	Edward IV
1470–71	Henry VI
1471–83	Edward IV
1483	Edward V
1483–85	Richard III
1485–1509	Henry VII
1509–47	Henry VIII
1547–53	Edward VI
1553–58	Mary I
1558–1603	Elizabeth I

Note For subsequent monarchs see United Kingdom

France

Reign	Monarch
987–996	Hugh Capet
996–1031	Robert II
1031–60	Henry I
1060–1108	Philip I
1108–37	Louis VI
1137–80	Louis VII
1180–1223	Philip II Augustus
1223–6	Louis VIII
1226–70	Louis IX
1270–85	Philip III
1285–1314	Philip IV
1314–16	Louis X
1316	John I
1316–22	Philip V
1322–8	Charles IV
1328–50	Philip VI
1350–64	John II
1364–80	Charles V
1380–1422	Charles VI
1422–61	Charles VII

Reign	Monarch
1461–83	Louis XI
1483–98	Charles VIII
1498–1515	Louis XII
1515–47	Francis I
1547–59	Henry II
1559–60	Francis II
1560–74	Charles IX
1574–89	Henry III
1589–1610	Henry IV (of Navarre)
1610–43	Louis XIII
1643–1715	Louis XIV
1715–74	Louis XV
1774–92	Louis XVI
1814–24	Louis XVIII
1824–30	Charles X
1830–48	Louis-Philippe

Germany

Reign	Monarch
1871–88	William I
1888	Frederick
1888–1918	William II

Greece

Reign	Monarch
1832–62	Otto of Bavaria
1863–1913	George I (of Denmark)
1913–17	Constantine I
1917–20	Alexander
1920–22	Constantine I
1922–23	George II
1935–47	George II
1947–64	Paul
1964–67	Constantine II

Note The monarchy was abolished in 1923, restored in 1935, and abolished once more in 1967

Holy Roman Empire

Reign	Emperor
800–814	Charlemagne (Charles I)
814–840	Louis I (the Pious)
843–855	Lothair
855–875	Louis II

875–877	Charles II (the Bald)
881–887	Charles III (the Fat)
891–894	Guido of Spoleto
892–898	Lambert of Spoleto
896–899	Arnulf
901–905	Louis III
905–924	Berengar
911–918	Conrad I
919–936	Henry I
936–973	Otto I (the Great)
973–983	Otto II
983–1002	Otto III
1002–24	Henry II (the Saint)
1024–39	Conrad II
1039–56	Henry III (the Black)
1056–1106	Henry IV
1077–80	Rudolf
1081–93	Hermann
1093–1101	Conrad
1106–25	Henry V
1125–37	Lothair II
1138–52	Conrad III
1152–90	Frederick I (Barbarossa)
1190–97	Henry VI
1198–1208	Philip
1198–1214	Otto IV
1215–50	Frederick II
1246–47	Henry Raspe
1247–56	William of Holland
1250–54	Conrad IV
1257–72	Richard
1257–75	Alfonso (Alfonso X of Castile)
1273–91	Rudolf I
1292–98	Adolf
1298–1308	Albert I
1308–13	Henry VII
1314–26	Frederick (III)
1314–46	Louis IV
1346–78	Charles IV
1378–1400	Wenceslas
1400–10	Rupert
1410–37	Sigismund
1438–39	Albert II
1440–93	Frederick III
1493–1519	Maximilian I
1519–56	Charles V
1556–64	Ferdinand I
1564–76	Maximilian II
1576–1612	Rudolf II
1612–19	Matthias
1619–37	Ferdinand II
1637–57	Ferdinand III

Reign	Emperor
1658–1705	Leopold I
1705–11	Joseph I
1711–40	Charles VI
1742–45	Charles VII
1745–65	Francis I
1765–90	Joseph II
1790–92	Leopold II
1792–1806	Francis II

Note The succession was disrupted by civil war in the years 840–43, and there were interregnums in the years 877–81, 887–91, 1254–73, and 1740–42

Italy

Reign	Monarch
1861–78	Victor-Emanuel II
1878–1900	Humbert I
1900–1946	Victor-Emanuel III
1946	Humbert II

Note Italy became a republic in 1946

Japan

Reign	Emperor
660–585 BC	Jimmu
581–549 BC	Suizei
549–511 BC	Annei
510–477 BC	Itoku
475–393 BC	Kosho
392–291 BC	Koan
290–215 BC	Korei
214–158 BC	Kogen
158–98 BC	Kaika
97–30 BC	Sujin
29 BC–AD 70	Suinin
71–130	Keiko
131–190	Selmu
192–200	Chuai
270–310	Ojin
313–399	Nintoku
400–405	Richu
406–10	Hanzel
412–53	Ingyo
453–6	Anko
456–79	Yuryaku
480–4	Seinei
485–7	Kenzo
488–98	Ninken

498–506	Buretsu
507–31	Keitai
531–5	Ankan
535–9	Senka
539–71	Kimmei
572–85	Bidatsu
585–7	Yomei
587–92	Sushun
592–628	Suiko
629–41	Jomei
642–5	Kogyoku
645–54	Kotuko
655–61	Saimei
662–71	Tenji
671–2	Kobun
673–86	Temmu
686–97	Jito
697–707	Mommu
707–15	Gemmei
715–24	Gensho
724–49	Shomu
749–58	Koken
758–64	Junnin
764–70	Shotoku
770–81	Konin
781–806	Kammu
806–809	Heizei
809–23	Saga
823–33	Junna
833–50	Nimmyo
850–8	Montoku
858–76	Seiwa
876–84	Yozei
884–7	Koko
887–97	Uda
897–930	Daigo
930–46	Suzaku
946–67	Murakami
967–9	Reizei
969–84	En'yu
984–6	Kazan
986–1011	Ichijo
1011–16	Sanjo
1016–36	Go-Ichijo
1036–45	Go-Suzako
1045–68	Go-Reizei
1068–72	Go-Sanyo
1072–86	Shirakawa
1086–1107	Horikawa
1107–23	Toba
1123–41	Sutoku
1141–55	Konoe

Reign	Emperor
1155–58	Goshirakawa
1158–65	Nijo
1165–68	Rokujo
1168–80	Takakura
1180–83	Antoku
1183–98	Go-Toba
1198–1210	Tsuchimikado
1210–21	Juntoku
1221	Chukyo
1221–32	Goshirakawa
1232–42	Shijo
1242–46	Go-Saga
1246–59	Go-Fukakusa
1259–74	Kameyama
1274–87	Go-Uda
1287–98	Fushimi
1298–1301	Go-Fushimi
1301–08	Go-Nijo
1308–18	Hanazono
1318–39	Go-Daigo
1339–68	Go-Murakami
1368–83	Chokei
1383–92	Go-Kameyama

Northern Court

Reign	Emperor
1331–33	Kogon
1336–48	Komyo
1348–51	Suko
1352–71	Go-Kogon
1371–82	Go-Enyu
1382–1412	Go-Komatsu
1412–28	Shoko
1428–64	Go-Hanazono
1464–1500	Go-Tsuchimikado
1500–26	Go-Kashiwabara
1526–57	Go-Nara
1557–86	Ogimachi
1586–1611	Go-Yozei
1611–29	Go-Mizunoo
1629–43	Meisho
1643–54	Go-Komyo
1654–63	Go-Sai
1663–87	Reigen
1687–1709	Higashiyama
1709–35	Nakamikado
1735–47	Sakuramachi
1747–62	Momozono
1762–70	Go-Sakuramachi
1770–79	Go-Momozono
1779–1817	Kokaku
1817–46	Ninko
1846–66	Komei

1867–1912	Meiji
1912–26	Taisho
1926–89	Hirohito
1989–	Akihito

Note Dates for the first 28 emperors are considered speculative

Luxembourg

Reign	Monarch
1890–1905	Adolf of Nassau
1905–12	William
1912–19	Marie Adélaïde
1919–64	Charlotte
1964–	Jean

Mughal Empire

Reign	Emperor
1526–30	Babur
1530–56	Humayun
1556–1605	Akbar
1605–27	Jahangir
1627–58	Shah Jahan
1658–1707	Aurangzeb (Alamgir)
1707–12	Bahadur Shah I (of Shah Alam I)
1712–13	Jahandar Shah
1713–19	Farruksiyar
1719	Rafid-ud-Darajat
1719	Rafi-ud-Daulat
1719	Nekusiyar
1719	Ibrahim
1719–48	Muhammad Shah
1748–54	Ahmad Shah
1754–59	Alamgir II
1759–1806	Shah Alam II
1806–37	Akbar II
1837–57	Bahadur Shah II

The Netherlands

Reign	Monarch
1572–84	William the Silent
1584–1625	Maurice
1625–47	Frederick Henry
1647–50	William II
1672–1702	William III

Reign	Monarch
1747–51	William IV
1751–95	William V
1806–10	Louis Bonaparte
1813–40	William I
1840–49	William II
1849–90	William III
1890–1948	Wilhelmina
1948–80	Juliana
1980–	Beatrix

Portugal

Reign	Monarch
1095–1112	Henry of Burgundy
1112–85	Alfonso I
1185–1211	Sancho I
1211–23	Alfonso II
1223–45	Sancho II
1245–79	Alfonso III
1279–1325	Diniz
1325–57	Alfonso IV
1357–67	Peter I
1367–83	Ferdinand
1385–1433	John I of Aviz
1433–38	Edward
1438–81	Alfonso V
1481–95	John II
1495–1521	Manuel I
1521–57	John III
1557–78	Sebastian
1578–80	Henry
1580–98	Philip I (II of Spain)
1598–1621	Philip II (III of Spain)
1621–40	Philip III (IV of Spain)
1640–56	John IV of Braganza
1656–83	Alfonso VI
1683–1706	Peter II
1706–50	John V
1750–77	Joseph
1777–1816	Maria I
1777–86	Peter III (King Consort)
1816–26	John VI
1826	Peter IV (I of Brazil)
1826–28	Maria II
1828–34	Miguel
1834–53	Maria II
1853–61	Peter V
1861–89	Luis

| 1889–1908 | Charles |
| 1908–10 | Manuel II |

Note The monarchy was abolished in 1910

Russia

Reign	Monarch
1283–1303	Daniel
1303–25	Yuri
1325–41	Ivan I
1341–53	Semeon
1353–59	Ivan II
1359–89	Dimitri Donskoy
1389–1425	Vasili I
1425–62	Vasili II
1462–1505	Ivan III (the Great)
1505–33	Vasili III
1533–84	Ivan IV (the Terrible)
1584–98	Feodor I
1598–1605	Boris Godunov
1605	Feodor II
1605–6	Dimitri II
1606–10	Vasili IV Shuisky
1613–45	Michael Romanov
1645–76	Alexei
1676–82	Feodor III
1682–96	Ivan V
1682–1725	Peter I (the Great)
1725–27	Catherine I
1727–30	Peter II
1730–40	Anne
1740–41	Ivan VI
1741–62	Elizabeth
1762	Peter III
1762–96	Catherine II (the Great)
1796–1801	Paul
1801–25	Alexander I
1825–55	Nicholas I
1855–81	Alexander II
1881–94	Alexander III
1894–1917	Nicholas II

Scotland

Reign	Monarch
1005–34	Malcolm II
1034–40	Duncan I
1040–57	Macbeth

Reign	Monarch
1057–58	Lulach
1058–93	Malcolm III
1093–94	Donald Bane
1094	Duncan II
1097–1107	Edgar
1107–24	Alexander I
1124–53	David I
1153–65	Malcolm IV
1165–1214	William I
1214–49	Alexander II
1249–86	Alexander III
1286–90	Margaret
1292–96	John Balliol
1306–29	Robert I (the Bruce)
1329–71	David II
1371–90	Robert II
1390–1406	Robert III
1406–37	James I
1437–60	James II
1460–88	James III
1488–1513	James IV
1513–42	James V
1542–67	Mary Queen of Scots
1567–1625	James VI

Note There was an interregnum in the years 1290–92 and 1296–1306; for subsequent monarchs see United Kingdom

Spain

Reign	Monarch
1516–56	Charles I (Emperor Charles V)
1556–98	Philip II
1598–1621	Philip III
1621–65	Philip IV
1665–1700	Charles II
1700–24	Philip V
1724	Luis
1724–46	Philip V
1746–59	Ferdinand VI
1759–88	Charles III
1788–1808	Charles IV
1808	Ferdinand VII
1808–14	Joseph Bonaparte
1814–33	Ferdinand VII
1833–68	Isabella II
1870–73	Amadeus of Savoy
1874–85	Alfonso XII
1886–1931	Alfonso XIII
1975–	Juan Carlos

Note The monarchy was deposed in the years 1868–70 and under Franco in the years 1931–75

Sweden

Reign	Monarch
1523–60	Gustav I
1560–68	Erik XIV
1568–92	Johan III
1592–59	Sigismund
1599–1611	Karl IX
1611–32	Gustav II Adolf
1632–54	Kristina
1654–60	Karl X Gustav
1660–97	Karl XI
1697–1718	Karl XII
1718–20	Ulrika Eleonora
1720–51	Fredrik
1751–71	Adolf Fredrik
1771–92	Gustav III
1792–1809	Gustav IV Adolf
1809–18	Karl XIII
1818–44	Karl XIV Johan
1844–59	Oskar I
1859–72	Karl XV
1872–1907	Oskar II
1907–50	Gustav V
1950–73	Gustav VI Adolf
1973–	Karl XVI Gustav

United Kingdom

Reign	Monarch
1603–25	James I (VI of Scotland)
1625–49	Charles I
1660–85	Charles II
1685–88	James II
1689–94	William III (jointly with Mary II)
1694–1702	William III (alone)
1702–14	Anne
1714–27	George I
1727–60	George II
1760–1820	George III
1820–30	George IV
1830–37	William IV
1837–1901	Victoria
1901–10	Edward VII
1910–36	George V
1936	Edward VIII
1936–52	George VI
1952–	Elizabeth II

Note There was an interregnum in the years 1649–60; for earlier monarchs see under England and Scotland

British royal family

Family of George VI

Name	Date of birth	Married
Queen Elizabeth, the Queen Mother	4 August 1900	Prince Albert, Duke of York/later George VI (26 April 1923)
Queen Elizabeth II	21 April 1926	Prince Philip, Duke of Edinburgh (20 November 1947)
Princess Margaret, Countess of Snowdon	21 August 1930	Antony Armstrong-Jones/later Earl of Snowdon (6 May 1960); marriage dissolved (1978)
Prince Philip	10 June 1921	Princess Elizabeth/later Queen Elizabeth II (20 November 1947)
Charles, Prince of Wales	14 November 1948	Lady Diana Spencer/later Diana, Princess of Wales (29 July 1981); marriage dissolved (1996)
Princess Anne, Princess Royal	15 August 1950	Captain Mark Phillips (14 November 1973); marriage dissolved (1992); Captain Timothy Laurence (12 December 1992)
Prince Andrew, Duke of York	19 February 1960	Sarah Ferguson/later Sarah, Duchess of York (23 July 1986); marriage dissolved (1996)
Prince Edward, Earl of Wessex	10 March 1964	Sophie Rhys-Jones/later Countess of Wessex (19 June 1999)

Children	Grandchildren	Official residence
Queen Elizabeth II; Princess Margaret	Prince Charles; Princess Anne; Prince Andrew; Prince Edward; David, Viscount Linley (born 3 November 1961); Lady Sarah Chatto (born 1 May 1964)	Clarence House; Royal Lodge, Windsor; Castle of Mey
Prince Charles; Princess Anne; Prince Andrew; Prince Edward	Prince William of Wales (born 21 June 1982); Prince Henry of Wales (born 15 September 1984); Peter Phillips (born 15 November 1977); Zara Phillips (born 15 May 1981); Princess Beatrice (born 8 August 1988); Princess Eugenie (born 23 March 1990)	Buckingham Palace; Windsor Castle; Palace of Holyrood House
David, Viscount Linley (born 3 November 1961); Lady Sarah Chatto (born 1 May 1964)	Charles Patrick Inigo Armstrong-Jones (born 2 July 1999); Samuel Chatto (born 28 July 1996); Arthur Chatto (born 5 February 1999)	Kensington Palace
Prince Charles; Princess Anne; Prince Andrew; Prince Edward	Prince William of Wales (born 21 June 1982); Prince Henry of Wales (born 15 September 1984); Peter Phillips (born 15 November 1977); Zara Phillips (born 15 May 1981); Princess Beatrice (born 8 August 1988); Princess Eugenie (born 23 March 1990)	(As Elizabeth II)
Prince William of Wales (born 21 June 1982); Prince Henry of Wales (born 15 September 1984)	None	St James' Palace; Highgrove, Tetbury
Peter Phillips (born 15 November 1977); Zara Phillips (born 15 May 1981)	None	Gatcombe Park, Minchinhampton
Princess Beatrice (born 8 August 1988); Princess Eugenie (born 23 March 1990)	None	Buckingham Palace; Sunninghill Park, Ascot
None	None	Windsor Castle

Family of Henry, Duke of Gloucester

Name	Date of birth	Married
Prince Richard, Duke of Gloucester	26 August 1944	Birgitte Eva van Deurs/later Duchess of Gloucester (8 July 1972)

Family of George, Duke of Kent

Prince Edward, Duke of Kent	9 October 1935	Katherine Worsley/later Duchess of Kent (8 June 1961)
Princess Alexandra, Lady Ogilvy	25 December 1936	Sir Angus Ogilvy (24 April 1963)
Prince Michael of Kent	4 July 1942	Baroness Marie-Christine von Reibnitz/later Princess Michael of Kent (30 June 1978)

Children	Grandchildren	Official residence
Alexander, Earl of Ulster (born 24 October 1974); Lady Davina Windsor (born 19 November 1977); Lady Rose Windsor (born 1 March 1980)	None	Kensington Palace
George, Earl of St Andrews (born 26 June 1962); Lady Helen Taylor (born 28 April 1964); Lord Nicholas Windsor (born 25 July 1970)	Lady Marina Windsor (born 30 September 1982); Edward, Baron Downpatrick (born 2 December 1988); Lady Amelia Windsor (born 24 August 1995); Columbus Taylor (born 6 August 1994); Cassius Taylor (born 26 December 1996)	Wren House, London
James Ogilvy (born 29 February 1964); Marina Mowatt (born 31 July 1966)	Flora Ogilvy (born 15 December 1994); Alexander Ogilvy (born 12 November 1996); Zenouska Mowatt (born 26 May 1990); Christian Mowatt (born 4 June 1993)	Thatched House Lodge, Richmond Park, Surrey
Lord Frederick Windsor (born 6 April 1979); Lady Gabriella Windsor (born 23 April 1981)	None	Kensington Palace; Nether Lypiatt Manor, Stroud

Order of succession

1	The Prince of Wales
2	Prince William of Wales
3	Prince Henry of Wales
4	The Duke of York
5	Princess Beatrice of York
6	Princess Eugenie of York
7	The Earl of Wessex
8	The Princess Royal
9	Peter Phillips
10	Zara Phillips
11	Princess Margaret, Countess of Snowdon
12	Viscount Linley
13	Charles Patrick Inigo Armstrong-Jones
14	Lady Sarah Chatto
15	Samuel Chatto
16	Arthur Chatto
17	The Duke of Gloucester
18	The Earl of Ulster
19	Lady Davina Windsor
20	Lady Rose Windsor
21	The Duke of Kent
22	Baron Downpatrick
23	Lady Marina Charlotte Windsor
24	Lady Amelia Windsor
25	Lord Nicholas Windsor
26	Lady Helen Taylor
27	Columbus Taylor
28	Cassius Taylor
29	Lord Frederick Windsor
30	Lady Gabriella Windsor
31	Princess Alexandra
32	James Ogilvy
33	Alexander Ogilvy
34	Flora Ogilvy
35	Marina, Mrs Paul Mowatt
36	Christian Mowatt
37	Zenouska Mowatt
38	The Earl of Harewood

7.4 **Political Leaders**

Australia (since 1901)

Year appointed	Prime minister	Party
1901	Sir Edmund Barton	Protectionist
1903	Alfred Deacon	Protectionist
1904	John Watson	Labor
1904	Sir G. Reid	Protectionist–Free Trade coalition
1905	Alfred Deakin	Protectionist
1908	Andrew Fisher	Labor
1909	Alfred Deakin	Protectionist–Free Trade coalition
1910	Andrew Fisher	Labor
1913	Sir Joseph Cook	Liberal
1914	Andrew Fisher	Labor
1915	William Morris Hughes	Labor (National Labor from 1917)
1923	James Henry Scullin	Labor
1932	Joseph Aloysius Lyons	United Australia–Country coalition
1939	Robert Gordon Menzies	United Australia
1941	Arthur William Fadden	Country–United Australia coalition
1941	John Joseph Curtin	Labor
1945	Francis Michael Forde	Labor
1945	Joseph Benedict Chifley	Labor
1949	Robert Gordon Menzies	Liberal–Country coalition
1966	Harold Edward Holt	Liberal–Country coalition
1967	John McEwen	Liberal–Country coalition
1968	John Grey Gorton	Liberal–Country coalition
1971	William McMahon	Liberal–Country coalition
1972	Edward Gough Whitlam	Labor
1975	John Malcolm Fraser	Liberal–National coalition
1983	Robert James Lee Hawke	Labor
1991	Paul Keating	Labor
1996	John Howard	Liberal–National coalition

Austria

President

Year appointed	
1918	Karl Sätz
1920	Michael Hainisch
1928	Wilhelm Miklas
1945	Karl Renner
1950	Theodor Körner
1957	Adolf Scharf

Year appointed	
1965	Franz Jonas
1974	Rudolf Kirchsläger
1986	Kurt Waldheim
1992	Thomas Klestil

Chancellor

Year appointed	
1918	Karl Renner
1920	Michael Mayr
1921	Johann Schober
1922	Walter Breisky
1922	Johann Schober
1922	Ignaz Seipel
1924	Rudolph Ramek
1926	Ignaz Seipel
1929	Ernst Streeruwitz
1930	Johann Schober
1930	Carl Vaugoin
1930	Otto Ender
1931	Karl Buresch
1932	Engelbert Dollfus
1934	Kurt von Schuschnigg
1945	Karl Renner
1945	Leopold Figl
1953	Julius Raab
1961	Alfons Gorbach
1964	Josef Klaus
1970	Bruno Kreisky
1983	Fred Sinowatz
1986	Franz Vranitzky
1997	Viktor Klima
2000	Wolfgang Schüssel

Note Austria was under German rule in the years 1938–45

Belgium

Prime minister

Year appointed	
1899	Paul de Smet de Nayer
1907	Jules de Trooz
1908	Frans Schollaert
1911	Charles de Broqueville
1918	Gerhard Cooreman
1918	Léon Delacroix
1920	Henri Carton de Wiart
1921	Georges Theunis
1925	Alois van de Vyvere
1925	Prosper Poullet
1926	Henri Jaspar
1931	Jules Renkin

1932	Charles de Broqueville
1934	Georges Theunis
1935	Paul van Zeeland
1937	Paul Émile Janson
1938	Paul Spaak
1939	Hubert Pierlot
1945	Achille van Acker
1946	Camille Huysmans
1947	Paul Spaak
1949	Gaston Eyskens
1950	Jean Pierre Duvieusart
1950	Joseph Pholien
1952	Jean van Houttc
1954	Achille van Acker
1958	Gaston Eyskens
1961	Théodore Lefèvre
1965	Pierre Harmel
1966	Paul Vanden Boeynants
1968	Gaston Eyskens
1973	Edmond Leburton
1974	Léo Tindemans
1978	Paul Vanden Boeynants
1979	Wilfried Martens
1981	Marc Eyskens
1981	Wilfried Martens
1992	Jean-Luc Dehaene
1999	Guy Verhofstadt

Canada (since 1867)

Year appointed	Prime minister	Party
1867	John A. Macdonald	Conservative
1873	Alexander Mackenzie	Liberal
1878	John A. Macdonald	Conservative
1891	John J. C. Abbott	Conservative
1892	John S. D. Thompson	Conservative
1894	Mackenzie Bowell	Conservative
1896	Charles Tupper	Conservative
1896	Wilfred Laurier	Liberal
1911	Robert L. Borden	Conservative
1920	Arthur Meighen	Conservative
1921	William Lyon Mackenzie King	Liberal
1926	Arthur Meighen	Conservative
1926	William Lyon Mackenzie. King	Liberal
1930	Richard Bedford Bennett	Conservative
1935	William Lyon Mackenzie King	Liberal
1948	Louis S. St Laurent	Liberal
1957	John George Diefenbaker	Conservative
1963	Lester Bowles Pearson	Liberal
1968	Pierre Elliott Trudeau	Liberal

Year appointed	Prime minister	Party
1979	Joseph Clark	Progressive Conservative
1980	Pierre Elliott Trudeau	Liberal
1984	John Turner	Liberal
1984	Brian Mulroney	Progressive Conservative
1993	Kim Campbell	Progressive Conservative
1993	Jean Chrétien	Liberal

China

Leader of the Communist Party

Year appointed	
1935	Mao Zedong
1976	Hua Guofeng
1981	Hu Yaobang
1987	Zhao Ziyang
1989	Jiang Zemin

President

Year appointed	
1949	Mao Zedong
1959	Liu Shaoqi
1968	Dong Biwu
1975	Zhu De
1976	Sung Qingling
1978	Ye Jianying
1983	Li Xiannian
1988	Yang Shangkin
1993	Jiang Zemin

Prime minister

Year appointed	
1949	Zhou Enlai
1976	Hua Guofeng
1980	Zhao Ziyang
1988	Li Peng
1998	Zhu Rongji

Denmark

Prime minister

Year appointed	
1900	H. Sehested
1901	J. H. Deuntzer
1905	J. C. Christensen
1908	N. Neergaard
1909	L. Holstein-Ledreborg
1909	C. Th. Zahle
1910	Klaus Berntsen
1913	C. Th. Zahle

1920	Otto Liebe
1920	M. P. Frlls
1920	N. Neergaard
1924	Thorvald Stauning
1926	Th. Madsen-Mygdal
1929	Thorvald Stauning
1942	Wilhelm Buhl
1942	Erik Scavenius
1945	Wilhelm Buhl
1945	Knud Kristensen
1947	Hans Hedtoft
1950	Erik Eriksen
1953	Hans Hedtoft
1955	Hans Christian Hansen
1960	Viggo Kampmann
1962	Jens Otto Krag
1968	Hilmar Baunsgaard
1971	Jens Otto Krag
1972	Anker Jorgensen
1973	Poul Hartling
1975	Anker Jorgensen
1982	Poul Schlüter
1993	Poul Nyrup Rasmussen

Note There was no prime minister in the years 1943–45

Finland

President

Year appointed

1919	Kaarlo Juho Ståhlberg
1925	Lauri Kristian Relander
1931	Pehr Evind Svinhufvud
1937	Kyösti Kallio
1940	Risto Ryti
1944	Carl Gustaf Mannerheim
1946	Juho Kusti Paasikivi
1956	Urho Kekkonen
1982	Mauno Koivisto
1994	Martti Ahtisaari

Prime minister

Year appointed

1917	Pehr Evind Svinhufvud
1918	Juho Kusti Paasikivi
1918	Lauri Johannes Ingman
1919	Kaarlo Castrén
1919	Juho Vennola
1920	Rafael Erich
1921	Juho Vennola
1922	Aino Kaarlo Cajander
1922	Kyösti Kallio

Year appointed	
1924	Aino Kaarlo Cajander
1924	Lauri Johannes Ingman
1925	Antti Agaton Tulenheimo
1925	Kyösti Kallio
1926	Väinö Tanner
1927	Juho Emil Sunila
1928	Oskari Mantere
1929	Kyösti Kallio
1930	Pehr Evind Svinhufvud
1931	Juho Emil Sunila
1932	Toivo Kivimäki
1936	Kyösti Kallio
1937	Aino Kaarlo Cajander
1939	Risto Ryti
1941	Johann Rangell
1943	Edwin Linkomies
1944	Andreas Hackzell
1944	Urho Jonas Castrén
1944	Juho Kusti Paasikivi
1946	Mauno Pekkala
1948	Karl August Fagerhelm
1950	Urho Kekkonen
1953	Sakari Tuomioja
1954	Ralf Törngren
1954	Urho Kekkonen
1956	Karl August Fagerhelm
1957	Väinö Johannes Sukselainen
1957	Rainer von Fieandt
1958	Reino Ilsakki Kuuskoski
1958	Karl August Fagerhelm
1959	Väinö Johannes Sukselainen
1961	Martti Miettunen
1962	Ahti Karjalainen
1963	Reino Ragnar Lehto
1964	Johannes Virolainen
1966	Rafael Paasio
1968	Mauno Koivisto
1970	Teuvo Ensio Aura
1970	Ahti Karjalainen
1971	Teuvo Ensio Aura
1972	Rafael Paasio
1972	Kalevi Sorsa
1975	Keijo Antero Lllnamaa
1975	Martti Miettunen
1977	Kalevi Sorsa
1979	Mauno Koivisto
1982	Kalevi Sorsa
1987	Harri Holkeri
1991	Esko Aho
1995	Paavo Lipponen

France

President

Year appointed	
1871	Louis Adolphe Thiers
1873	Marie Edmé de MacMahon
1879	Jules Grévy
1887	Sadi Carnot
1894	Jean Paul Pierre Casimir-Périer
1895	François Félix Faure
1899	Émile Loubet
1906	Armand Fallières
1913	Raymond Poincaré
1920	Paul Deschanel
1920	Alexandre Millerand
1924	Gaston Doumergue
1931	Paul Doumer
1932	Albert Lebrun
1947	Vincent Auriol
1954	René Coty
1958	Charles de Gaulle
1969	Georges Pompidou
1974	Valéry Giscard d'Estaing
1981	François Mitterand
1995	Jacques René Chirac

Prime minister

Year appointed	
1815	Charles-Maurice, Prince de Talleyrand-Perigord
1815	Armand-Emmanuel Vignerot Duplessis, Duc de Richelieu
1818	Jean Joseph, Marquis Dessolle
1819	Duc Élie Decazes
1820	Armand-Emmanuel Vignerot-Duplessis, Duc de Richelieu
1821	Guillaume-Aubin, Comte de Villèle
1829	Auguste, Prince de Polignac
1830	Jacques Lafitte
1831	Casimir Périer
1832	Nicolas Soult
1834	Etienne, Comte Gérard
1834	Napoléon Joseph Maret, Duc de Bassano
1834	Étienne Mortier, Duc de Trévise
1835	Achille, Duc de Broglie
1836	Adolphe Thiers
1836	Louis, Comte Molé
1839	Nicolas Soult
1840	Adophe Theirs
1840	Nicolas Soult
1847	François Guyzot
1848	Jacques Charles Dupont de l'Eure
1848	Louis-Eugène Cavaignac
1848	Odilon Barrot
1870	Jules Favre

Year appointed	
1871	Jules Dufaure
1873	Albert, Duc de Broglie
1874	Ernest Louis Cortot de Cissey
1875	Louis Buffet
1876	Jules Dufaure
1876	Jules Simon
1877	Albert, Duc de Broglie
1877	Gaetan de Grimaudet de Rochebouét
1877	Jules Dufaure
1879	William H. Waddington
1879	Louis de Freycinet
1880	Jules Ferry
1881	Léon Gambetta
1882	Louis de Freycinet
1882	Eugène Duclerc
1883	Armand Fallières
1883	Jules Ferry
1885	Henri Brisson
1886	Louis de Freycinet
1886	René Goblet
1887	Maurice Rouvier
1887	Pierre Tirard
1888	Charles Floquet
1889	Pierre Tirard
1890	Louis de Freycinet
1892	Émile Loubet
1892	Alexandre Ribot
1893	Charles Dupuy
1893	Jean Casimir-Périer
1894	Charles Dupuy
1895	Alexandre Ribot
1895	Léon Bourgeois
1896	Jules Méline
1898	Henri Brisson
1898	Charles Dupuy
1899	Pierre Waldeck-Rousseau
1902	Emile Combes
1905	Maurice Rouvier
1906	Jean Sarrien
1906	Georges Clemenceau
1909	Aristide Briand
1911	Ernest Monis
1911	Joseph Caillaux
1912	Raymond Poincaré
1913	Aristide Briand
1913	Jean Louis Barthou
1913	Gaston Doumerge
1914	Alexandre Ribot
1914	René Viviani
1915	Aristide Briand
1917	Alexandre Ribot

1917	Paul Painlevé
1917	Georges Clemenceau
1920	Alexandre Millerand
1920	Georges Leygues
1921	Aristide Briand
1922	Raymond Poincaré
1924	Frédéric François-Marsal
1924	Édouard Herriot
1925	Paul Painlevé
1925	Aristide Briand
1926	Édouard Herriot
1926	Raymond Poincaré
1929	Aristide Briand
1929	André Tardieu
1930	Camille Chautemps
1930	André Tardieu
1930	Théodore Steeg
1931	Pierre Laval
1932	André Tardieu
1932	Édouard Herriot
1932	Joseph Paul-Boncour
1933	Édouard Daladier
1933	Albert Sarrault
1933	Camille Chautemps
1934	Édouard Daladier
1934	Gaston Doumerge
1934	Pierre Étienne Flandin
1935	Fernand Bouisson
1935	Pierre Laval
1936	Albert Sarrault
1936	Léon Blum
1937	Camille Chautemps
1938	Léon Blum
1938	Édouard Daladier
1940	Paul Reynaud
1940	Philippe Pétain
1944	Charles de Gaulle
1946	Félix Gouin
1946	Georges Bidault
1946	Léon Blum
1947	Paul Ramadier
1947	Robert Schuman
1948	André Marie
1948	Robert Schuman
1948	Henri Queuille
1949	Georges Bidault
1950	Henri Oueuille
1950	René Pleven
1951	Henri Queuille
1951	René Pleven
1952	Edgar Faure
1952	Antoine Pinay

Year appointed

1953	René Mayer
1953	Joseph Laniel
1954	Pierre Mendès-France
1955	Edgar Faure
1956	Guy Alcide Mollet
1957	Maurice Bourgès-Maunoury
1957	Félix Gaillard
1958	Pierre Pflimin
1958	Charles de Gaulle
1959	Michel Debré
1962	Georges Pompidou
1968	Maurice Couve de Murville
1969	Jacques Chaban Delmas
1972	Pierre Mesmer
1974	Jacques René Chirac
1976	Raymond Barre
1981	Pierre Mauroy
1984	Laurent Fabius
1986	Jacques René Chirac
1988	Michael Rocard
1991	Edith Cresson
1992	Pierre Bérégovoy
1993	Édouard Balladur
1995	Alain Juppé
1997	Lionel Jospin

Note There was no prime minister in the years 1849–70

Germany

Chancellor

Year appointed

1871	Otto von Bismarck
1890	Georg Leo, Graf von Caprivi
1894	Chlodwic, Fürst zu Hohenlohe-Schillingfürst
1900	Bernard Heinrich, Prince von Bülow
1909	Theobald von Bethmann Hollweg
1917	Georg von Herfling
1918	Prince Max of Baden
1918	Friedrich Ebert
1919	Philipp Scheidemann
1920	Hermann Müller
1920	Konstantin Fehrenbach
1921	Karl Joseph Wirth
1922	Wilhelm Cuno
1923	Gustav Stresemann
1923	Wilhelm Marx
1925	Hans Luther
1926	Wilhelm Marx
1928	Hermann Müller
1929	Heinrich Brüning

1932	Franz van Papen
1932	Kurt von Schleicher
1933	Adolf Hitler
1945	Karl Dönitz

German Democratic Republic (East Germany)

President

Year appointed	
1949	Wilhelm Pieck

Chairman of the Council of State

Year appointed	
1960	Walter Ernst Karl Ulbricht
1973	Willi Stoph
1976	Erich Honecker
1989	Egon Krenz
1989	Gregor Gysi

Premier

Year appointed	
1949	Otto Grotewohl
1964	Willi Stoph
1973	Horst Sindermann
1976	Willi Stoph
1989	Hans Modrow
1990	Lothar de Maizière

German Federal Republic (West Germany)

President

Year appointed	
1949	Theodor Heuss
1959	Heinrich Lübke
1969	Gustav Heinemann
1974	Walter Scheel
1979	Karl Carstens
1984	Richard von Weizsäcker

Chancellor

Year appointed	
1949	Konrad Adenauer
1963	Ludwig Erhard
1966	Kurt Georg Kiesinger
1969	Willy Brandt
1974	Helmut Schmidt
1982	Helmut Kohl

Germany

President

Year appointed	
1990	Richard von Weizsäcker
1994	Roman Herzog
1999	Johannes Rau

Chancellor

Year appointed	
1990	Helmut Kohl
1998	Gerhard Schröder

Greece

President

Year appointed	
1924	Paul Koundouriotis
1926	Theodore Pangalos
1926	Paul Koundouriotis
1929	Alexander T. Zaïmis
1973	George Papadopoulos
1973	Phaedon Gizikis
1974	Michael Stasinopoulos
1975	Constantine Tsatsos
1980	Constantine Karamanlis
1985	Christos Sartzetakis
1990	Constantine Karamanlis
1995	Constantine Stephanopoulos

Note Greece was under the rule of a monarch in the years 1935–67 and under a military junta in the years 1967–73

Prime minister

Year appointed	
1899	George Theotokis
1901	Alexander T. Zaïmis
1902	Theodore Deligiannis
1903	George Theotokis
1903	Demetrius G. Rallis
1903	George Theotokis
1904	Theodore Deligiannis
1905	Demetrius G. Rallis
1905	George Theotokis
1909	Demetrius G. Rallis
1909	Kyriakoulis P. Mavromichalis
1910	Stephen N. Dragoumis
1910	Eleftherios K. Venizelos
1915	Demetrius P. Gounaris
1915	Eleftherios K. Venizelos
1915	Alexander T. Zaïmis
1915	Stephen Skouloudis
1916	Alexander T. Zaïmis
1916	Nicholas P. Kalogeropoulos
1916	Spyridon Lambros
1917	Alexander T. Zaïmis
1917	Eleftherios K. Venizelos
1920	Demetrius G. Rallis
1921	Nicholas P. Kalogeropoulos

1921	Demetrius P. Gounaris
1922	Nicholas Stratos
1922	Peter E. Protopapadakis
1922	Nicholas Triandaphyllakos
1922	Sortirios Krokidas
1922	Alexander T. Zaïmis
1922	Stylianos Gonatas
1924	Eleftherios K. Venizelos
1924	George Kaphandaris
1924	Alexander Papanastasiou
1924	Themistocles Sophoulis
1924	Andreas Michalakopoulos
1925	Alexander N. Chatzikyriakos
1926	Theodore Pangalos
1926	Athanasius Eftaxias
1926	George Kondylis
1926	Alexander T. Zaïmis
1928	Eleftherios K. Venizelos
1932	Alexander Papanastasiou
1932	Eleftherios K. Venizelos
1932	Panagiotis Tsaldaris
1933	Eleftherios K. Venizelos
1933	Nicholas Plastiras
1933	Alexander Othonaos
1933	Panagiotis Tsaldaris
1935	George Kondylis
1935	Constantine Demertzis
1936	John Metaxas
1941	Alexander Koryzis
1941	George II
1941	Emmanuel Tsouderos
1941	George Tsolakoglou
1942	Constantine Logothetopoulos
1943	John Rallis
1945	Nicholas Plastiras
1945	Peter Voulgaris
1945	Damaskinos, Archbishop of Athens
1945	Panagiotis Kanellopoulos
1945	Themistocles Sophoulis
1946	Panagiotis Politzas
1946	Constantine Tsaldaris
1947	Demetrius Maximos
1947	Constantine Tsaldaris
1947	Themistocles Sophoulis
1949	Alexander Diomedes
1950	John Theotokis
1950	Sophocles Venizelos
1950	Nicholas Plastiras
1950	Sophocles Venizelos
1951	Nicholas Plastiras
1952	Demetrius Kiusopoulos

Year appointed	
1952	Alexander Papagos
1955	Stephen C. Stefanopoulos
1955	Constantine Karamanlis
1958	Constantine Georgakopoulos
1958	Constantine Karamanlis
1961	Constantine Dovas
1961	Constantine Karamanlis
1963	Panagiotis Pipinellis
1963	Stylianos Mavromichalis
1963	George Papandreou
1963	John Parskevopoulos
1964	George Papandreou
1965	George Athanasiadis-Novas
1965	Elias Tsirimokos
1965	Stephen C. Stefanopoulos
1966	John Paraskevopoulos
1967	Panagiotis Kanellopoulos
1967	Constantine Kollias
1967	George Papadopoulos
1973	Spyridon Markezinis
1973	Adamantios Androutsopoulos
1974	Constantine Karamanlis
1980	George Rallis
1981	Andreas Papandreou
1989	Tzannia Tzannetakis
1989	Xenofon Zolotas
1993	Andreas Papandreou
1996	Kostas Simitis

Government in exile

Year appointed	Prime minister
1941	Emmanuel Tsouderos
1944	Sophocles Venizelos
1944	George Papandreou

India (since 1949)

President

Year appointed	
1950	Rajendra Prasad
1962	Sarvapalli Radhakrishnan
1967	Zakir Husain
1969	Varahagiri Venkata Giri
1969	Muhammad Hidayat Ullah
1974	Varahagiri Venkata Giri
1977	Fakhruddin Ali Ahmed
1977	Basappa Danappa Jatti
1982	N. Sanjiva Reddy
1987	Zail Singh

1992	Ramaswamy Venkataraman	
1992	Shankar Dayal Sharma	
1997	K. R. Narayanan	

Prime minister

Year appointed		Party
1949	Jawaharlal Nehru	Congress
1964	Lal Bahadur Shastri	Congress
1966	Indira Gandhi	Congress (1)
1977	Morarji Desai	Janata
1979	Charan Singh	Janata/Lok Dal
1980	Indira Gandhi	Congress (1)
1984	Rajiv Gandhi	Congress (1)
1989	Viswanath Pratap Singh	Janata Dal
1990	Chandra Shekha	Janata Dal (Socialist)
1991	P. V. Narasimha Rao	Congress (1)
1996	Atal Bihari Vajpayee	Bharatiya Janata
1996	H. D. Deve Gowda	Janata Dal
1997	Inder Kumar Gujral	Janata Dal
1998	Atal Bihari Vajpayee	Bharatiya Janata

Ireland

Governor General

Year appointed	
1922	Timothy Michael Healy
1927	James McNeill
1932	Donald Buckley

President

Year appointed	
1938	Douglas Hyde
1945	Sean Thomas O'Kelly
1959	Eamon de Valera
1973	Erskine H. Childers
1974	Carroll Daly
1976	Patrick J. Hillery
1990	Mary Robinson
1997	Mary McAleese

Prime minister

Year appointed	
1919	Eamon de Valera
1922	Arthur Griffiths
1922	William Cosgrave
1932	Eamon de Valera
1948	John Aloysius Costello
1951	Eamon de Valera
1954	John Aloysius Costello
1957	Eamon de Valera
1959	Sean Lemass

Year appointed	
1966	John Lynch
1973	Liam Cosgrave
1977	John Lynch
1979	Charles Haughey
1982	Garrett Fitzgerald
1987	Charles Haughey
1992	Albert Reynolds
1994	John Bruton
1997	Bertie Ahern

Israel

President

Year appointed	
1948	Chaim Weizmann
1952	Itzhak Ben-Zvi
1963	Zalman Shazar
1973	Ephraim Katzair
1978	Yitzhak Navon
1983	Chaim Herzog
1993	Ezer Weizman

Prime minister

Year appointed	
1948	David Ben-Gurion
1954	Moshe Sharett
1955	David Ben-Gurion
1963	Levi Eshkol
1969	Golda Meir
1974	Yitzhak Rabin
1977	Menachem Begin
1983	Yitzhak Shamir
1984	Shimon Peres
1988	Yitzhak Shamir
1992	Yitzhak Rabin
1995	Shimon Peres
1996	Binyamin Netanyahu
1999	Ehud Barak
2001	Itzhak Sharon

Italy

President

Year appointed	
1946	Enrico de Nicola
1948	Luigi Einaudi
1955	Giovanni Gronchi
1962	Antonio Segni

1964	Giuseppe Saragat
1971	Giovanni Leone
1978	Alessandro Pertini
1985	Francesco Cossiga
1992	Oscar Luigi Scalfaro
1999	Carlo Azeglio Ciampi

Prime minister

Year appointed	
1900	Giuseppe Saracco
1901	Giuseppe Zanardelli
1903	Giovanni Giolitti
1905	Alessandro Fortis
1906	Sydney Sonnino
1906	Giovanni Giolitti
1909	Sydney Sonnino
1910	Luigi Luzzatti
1911	Giovanni Giolitti
1914	Antonio Salandra
1916	Paolo Boselli
1917	Vittorio Emmanuele Orlando
1919	Francesco Saverio Nitti
1920	Giovanni Giolitti
1921	Ivanoe Bonomi
1922	Luigi Facta
1922	Benito Mussolini
1943	Pietro Badoglio
1944	Ivanoe Bonomi
1945	Ferrucio Parri
1945	Alcide de Gasperi
1953	Giuseppe Pella
1954	Amintore Fanfani
1954	Mario Scelba
1955	Antonio Segni
1957	Adone Zoli
1958	Amintore Fanfani
1959	Antonio Segni
1960	Fernando Tambroni
1960	Amintore Fanfani
1963	Giovanni Leone
1963	Aldo Moro
1968	Giovanni Leone
1968	Mariano Rumor
1970	Emilio Colombo
1972	Giulio Andreotti
1974	Aldo Moro
1976	Giulio Andreotti
1979	Francisco Cossiga
1980	Arnaldo Forlani
1981	Giovanni Spadolini
1982	Amintore Fanfani
1983	Bettino Craxi

Year appointed	
1987	Amintore Fanfani
1987	Giovanni Goria
1988	Ciriaco de Mita
1989	Giulio Andreotti
1992	Giuliano Amato
1993	Carlo Azeglio Ciampi
1994	Silvio Berlusconi
1995	Lamberto Dini
1996	Romano Prodi
1999	Massimo D'Alema
2001	Silvio Berlusconi

Japan (since 1945)

Year appointed	Prime minister	Party
1945	Kijuro Shidehara	coalition
1946	Shigeru Yoshida	Liberal
1947	Tetsu Katayama	coalition
1948	Hitoshi Ashida	Democratic
1948	Shigeru Yoshida	Liberal
1954	Ichiro Hatoyama	Liberal
1956	Tanzan Ishibashi	Liberal Democratic Party
1957	Nobusuke Kishi	Liberal Democratic Party
1960	Hayato Ikeda	Liberal Democratic Party
1964	Eisaku Sato	Liberal Democratic Party
1972	Kakuei Tanaka	Liberal Democratic Party
1974	Takeo Miki	Liberal Democratic Party
1976	Takeo Fukuda	Liberal Democratic Party
1978	Masayoshi Ohira	Liberal Democratic Party
1980	Zenko Suzuki	Liberal Democratic Party
1982	Yasuhiro Nakasone	Liberal Democratic Party
1987	Noboru Takeshita	Liberal Democratic Party
1989	Sosuke Uno	Liberal Democratic Party
1989	Toshiki Kaifu	Liberal Democratic Party
1991	Kiichi Miyazawa	Liberal Democratic Party
1993	Morohiro Hosokawa	coalition
1994	Tsutoma Hata	coalition
1994	Tomiichi Murayama	coalition
1996	Ryutaro Hashimoto	coalition
1998	Keizo Obuchi	coalition
2000	Yoshiro Mori	Liberal Democratic Party
2001	Junichiro Koizumi	Liberal Democratic Party

Luxembourg

Prime minister

Year appointed	
1889	Paul Eyschen
1915	Mathias Mongenast
1915	Hubert Loutsch
1916	Victor Thorn
1917	Léon Kaufmann
1918	Emil Reuter
1925	Pierre Prum
1926	Joseph Bech
1937	Pierre Dupong
1953	Joseph Bech
1958	Pierre Frieden
1959	Pierre Werner
1969	Gaston Thorn
1979	Pierre Werner
1984	Jacques Santer
1995	Jean-Claude Juncker

The Netherlands

Prime minister

Year appointed	
1897	Nicholas G. Pierson
1901	Abraham Kuyper
1905	Theodoor H. de Meester
1908	Theodorus Heemskerk
1913	Pieter W. A. Cort van der Linden
1918	Charles J. M. Ruys de Beerenbrouck
1925	Hendrikus Colijn
1926	Dirk J. de Geer
1926	Charles J. M. Ruys de Beerenbrouck
1933	Hendrikus Colijn
1939	Dirk J. de Geer
1940	Pieter S. Gerbrandy
1945	Willem Schemerhorn/Willem Drees
1946	Louis J. M. Beel
1948	Willem Drees/Josephus R. H. van Schaik
1951	Willem Drees
1958	Louis J. M. Beel
1959	Jan E. de Quay
1963	Victor G. M. Marijnen
1965	Joseph M. L. T. Cals
1966	Jelle Zijlstra
1967	Petrus J. S. de Jong
1971	Barend W. Biesheuvel

Year appointed		
1973	Joop M. Den Uyl	
1977	Andreas A. M. van Agt	
1982	Ruud F. M. Lubbers	
1994	Wim Kok	

Note Pieter S. Gerbrandy led a government in exile in the years 1940–45

New Zealand (since 1891)

Year appointed	Prime minister	Party
1891	J. Ballance	Liberal
1893	Richard John Seddon	Liberal
1906	William Hall-Jones	Liberal
1906	Joseph George Ward	Liberal
1912	Thomas Mackenzie	Liberal
1912	William Ferguson Massey	Reform
1925	Francis Henry Dillon Bell	Reform
1925	Joseph Gordon Coates	Reform
1928	Joseph George Ward	United
1930	George William Forbes	United
1935	Michael Joseph Savage	Labour
1940	Peter Fraser	Labour
1949	Sidney George Holland	National
1957	Keith Jacka Holyoake	National
1957	Walter Nash	Labour
1960	Keith Jacka Holyoake	National
1972	John Ross Marshall	National
1972	Norman Eric Kirk	Labour
1974	Wallace Edward Rowling	Labour
1975	Robert David Muldoon	National
1984	David Russell Lange	Labour
1989	Geoffrey Palmer	Labour
1990	Mike Moore	Labour
1990	Jim Bolger	National
1997	Jenny Shipley	National
1999	Helen Clark	Labour

Norway

Prime minister

Year appointed	
1898	Johannes Steen
1902	Otto Albert Blehr
1903	George Francis Hagerup
1905	Christian Michelsen
1907	Jørgen Løvland
1908	Gunnar Knudsen
1910	Wollert Konow
1912	Jens Bratlie

1913	Gunnar Knudsen
1920	Otto Bahr Halvorsen
1921	Otto Albert Blehr
1923	Otto Bahr Halvorsen
1923	Abraham Berge
1924	Johan Ludwig Mowinckel
1926	Ivar Lykke
1928	Christopher Hornsrud
1928	Johan Ludwig Mowinckel
1931	Peder L. Kolstad
1932	Jens Hundseid
1933	Johan Ludwig Mowinckel
1935	Johan Nygaardsvold
1945	Einar Gerhardsen
1951	Oscar Torp
1955	Einar Gerhardsen
1963	John Lyng
1963	Einar Gerhardsen
1965	Per Borten
1971	Trygve Bratteli
1972	Lars Korvald
1973	Trygve Bratteli
1976	Odvar Nordli
1981	Gro Harlem Brundtland
1981	Kåre Willoch
1986	Gro Harlem Brundtland
1989	Jan P. Syse
1990	Gro Harlem Brundtland
1996	Thorbjørn Jagland
1997	Kjell Magne Bondevik

Portugal

President

Year appointed

1910	Teófilo Braga
1911	Manuel José de Arriaga
1915	Teófilo Braga
1915	Bernardino Machado
1917	Sidónio Pais
1918	João do Canto e Castro
1919	António José de Almeida
1923	Manuel Teixeira Gomes
1925	Bernardino Machado
1926	José Mendes Cabeçadas
1926	Manuel de Oliveira Gomes da Costa
1926	António Oscar Fragoso Carmona
1951	Francisco Craveiro Lopes
1958	Américo de Deus Tomás
1974	António Spínola

Year appointed	
1974	Francisco da Costa Gomes
1976	António does Santos Ramalho Eanes
1986	Mario Soares
1996	Jorge Sampaio

Prime minister

Year appointed	
1932	António de Oliveira Salazar
1968	Marcelo Caetano
1974	Adelino da Palma Carlos
1974	Vasco Gonçalves
1975	José Pinheiro de Azevedo
1976	Mário Soares
1978	Alfredo Nobre da Costa
1978	Carlos Alberto de Mota Pinto
1979	Maria de Lurdes Pintasilgo
1980	Francisco de Sá Carneiro
1981	Francisco Pinto Balsemão
1983	Mário Soares
1985	Aníbal Cavaço Silva
1995	António Guterres

Russia

USSR

Leader of the Communist Party

Year appointed	
1917	Vladimir Ilyich Lenin
1922	Josef Stalin
1953	Nikita Khrushchev
1964	Leonid Brezhnev
1982	Yuri Andropov
1984	Konstantin Chernenko
1985	Mikhail Gorbachev

President

Year appointed	
1917	Lev Borisovich Kamenev
1917	Yakov Mikhailovich Sverlov
1919	Mikhail Ivanovich Kalinin
1946	Nikolai Mikhailovich Shvernik
1953	Klimenti Efremovich Voroshilov
1960	Leonid Ilyich Brezhnev
1964	Anastas Ivanovich Mikoyan
1965	Nikolai Viktorovich Podgorny
1977	Leonid Ilyich Brezhnev
1982	Vasily Vasiliyevich Kuznetsov
1983	Yuri Vladimirovich Andropov
1984	Vasily Vasiliyevich Kuznetsov

1984	Konstantin Ustinovich Chernenko
1985	Vasily Vasiliyevich Kuznetsov
1985	Andrei Andreevich Gromyko
1989	Mikhail Sergeevich Gorbachev

Russian Federation

President
Year appointed

| 1991 | Boris Nikolayevich Yeltsin |
| 1999 | Vladimir Putin |

Prime minister

1991	Boris Yeltsin
1992	Yegor Gaidar
1992	Viktor Chernomyrdin
1998	Yevgeny Primakov
1999	Sergey Stepashin
1999	Vladimir Putin
2000	Mikhail Kasyanov

South Africa

President
Year appointed

1961	Charles Robberts Swart
1967	Theophilus Ebenhaezer Dönges
1967	Jozua François Nandé
1968	Jacobus Johannes Fouché
1975	Nicolaas Diederichs
1978	Balthazar Johannes Vorster
1979	Marais Viljoen
1984	Pieter Willem Botha
1989	Frederick Willem de Klerk
1994	Nelson Rolihlahla Mandela
1999	Thabo Mbeki

Prime minister
Year appointed

1910	Louis Botha
1919	Jan Christiaan Smuts
1924	James Barry Munnick Hertzog
1939	Jan Christiaan Smuts
1948	Daniel François Malan
1954	Johannes Gerardus Strijdom
1958	Hendrik Frensch Verwoerd
1966	Balthazar Johannes Vorster
1978	Pieter Willem Botha

Note The post of prime minister was combined with that of president in 1984

Spain

President

Year appointed	
1931	Niceto Alcalá Zamora y Torres
1936	Diego Martínez Barrio
1936	Manuel Azaña y Díez
1936	Miguel Cabanellas Ferrer
1936	Francisco Franco Bahamonde

Note The monarchy was restored in 1975 after Franco's death

Prime minister

Year appointed	
1900	Marcelo de Azcárraga y Palmero
1901	Práxedes Mateo Sagasta
1902	Francisco Silvela y Le-Vielleuze
1903	Raimundo Fernández Villaverde
1903	Antonio Maura y Montaner
1904	Marcelo de Azcárraga y Palmero
1905	Raimundo Fernández Villaverde
1905	Eugenio Montero Ríos
1905	Segismundo Moret y Prendergast
1906	José López Domínguez
1906	Segismundo Moret y Prendergast
1906	Antonio Aguilar y Correa
1907	Antonio Maura y Montaner
1909	Segismundo Moret y Prendergast
1910	José Canalejas y Méndez
1912	Alvaro Figueroa y Torres
1912	Manuel García Prieto
1913	Eduardo Dato y Iradier
1915	Alvaro Figueroa y Torres
1917	Manuel García Prieto
1917	Eduardo Dato y Iradier
1917	Manuel García Prieto
1918	Antonio Maura y Montaner
1918	Manuel García Prieto
1918	Alvaro Figueroa y Torres
1919	Antonio Maura y Montaner
1919	Joaquín Sánchez de Toca
1919	Manuel Allendesalazar
1920	Eduardo Dato y Iradier
1921	Gabino Bugallal Araujo
1921	Manuel Allendesalazar
1921	Antonio Maura y Montaner
1922	José Sánchez Guerra y Martínez
1922	Manuel García Prieto
1923	Miguel Primo de Rivera y Oraneja
1930	Dámaso Berenguer y Fusté
1931	Juan Bautista Aznar-Cabañas
1931	Niceto Alcalá Zamora y Torres
1931	Manuel Azaña y Díez

1933	Alejandro Lerroux y García
1933	Diego Martínez Barrio
1933	Alejandro Lerroux y García
1934	Ricardo Samper Ibáñez
1934	Alejandro Lerroux y García
1935	Joaquín Chapaprieta y Terragosa
1935	Manuel Portela Valladares
1936	Manuel Azaña y Díez
1936	Santiago Casares Quiroga
1936	Diego Martínez Barrio
1936	José Giral y Pereyra
1936	Francisco Largo Caballero
1937	Juan Negrín
1973	Torcuato Fernández Miranda y Hevia
1973	Carlos Arias Navarro
1976	Adolfo Suárez
1981	Calvo Sotelo
1982	Felipe González
1996	José María Aznar López

Sweden

Prime minister

Year appointed

1900	Fredrik von Otter
1902	Erik Gustaf Boström
1905	Johan Ramstedt
1905	Christian Lundeberg
1905	Karl Staaf
1906	Arvid Lindman
1911	Karl Staaf
1914	Hjalmar Hammarskjöld
1917	Carl Swartz
1917	Nils Edén
1920	Hjalmar Branting
1920	Louis De Geer
1921	Oscar von Sydow
1921	Hjalmar Branting
1923	Ernst Trygger
1924	Hjalmar Branting
1925	Rickard Sandler
1926	Carl Gustaf Ekman
1928	Arvid Lindman
1930	Carl Gustaf Ekman
1932	Felix Hamrin
1932	Per Albin Hansson
1936	Axel Pehrsson-Branstorp
1936	Per Albin Hansson
1946	Tage Erlander
1969	Olof Palme

Year appointed	
1976	Thorbjörn Fälldin
1978	Ola Ullsten
1979	Thorbjörn Fälldin
1982	Olof Palme
1986	Ingvar Carlsson
1991	Carl Bildt
1994	Ingvar Carlsson
1996	Göran Persson

UK

Year appointed	Prime minister	Party
1721	Sir Robert Walpole	Whig
1742	Earl of Wilmington	Whig
1743	Henry Pelham	Whig
1754	Duke of Newcastle	Whig
1756	Duke of Devonshire	Whig
1757	Duke of Newcastle	Whig
1762	Earl of Bute	Tory
1763	George Grenville	Whig
1765	Marquess of Rockingham	Whig
1766	Earl of Chatham	Whig
1767	Duke of Grafton	Whig
1770	Lord North	Tory
1782 (March)	Marquess of Rockingham	Whig
1782 (July)	Earl of Shelburne	Whig
1783 (April)	Duke of Portland	Coalition
1783 (December)	William Pitt	Tory
1801	Henry Addington	Tory
1804	William Pitt	Tory
1806	Lord Grenville	Whig
1807	Duke of Portland	Tory
1809	Spencer Perceval	Tory
1812	Earl of Liverpool	Tory
1827 (April)	George Canning	Tory
1827 (August)	Viscount Goderich	Tory
1828	Duke of Wellington	Tory
1830	Earl Grey	Whig
1834 (July)	Viscount Melbourne	Whig
1834 (November)	Robert Peel	Conservative
1835	Viscount Melbourne	Whig
1841	Robert Peel	Conservative
1846	Lord John Russell	Liberal
1852 (February)	Earl of Derby	Conservative
1852 (December)	Earl of Aberdeen	Peelite
1855	Viscount Palmerston	Liberal
1858	Earl of Derby	Conservative
1859	Viscount Palmerston	Liberal
1865	Earl Russell	Liberal

1866	Earl of Derby	Conservative
1868 (February)	Benjamin Disraeli	Conservative
1868 (December)	William Gladstone	Liberal
1874	Benjamin Disraeli	Conservative
1880	William Gladstone	Liberal
1885	Marquess of Salisbury	Liberal
1886 (February)	William Gladstone	Conservative
1886 (July)	Marquess of Salisbury	Liberal
1892	William Gladstone	Liberal
1894	Earl of Rosebery	Liberal
1895	Marquess of Salisbury	Conservative
1902	Arthur Balfour	Conservative
1905	Sir Henry Campbell-Bannerman	Liberal
1908	Herbert Asquith	Liberal
1915	Herbert Asquith	Coalition
1916	David Lloyd-George	Coalition
1922	Andrew Bonar Law	Conservative
1923	Stanley Baldwin	Conservative
1924 (January)	Ramsay MacDonald	Labour
1924 (November)	Stanley Baldwin	Conservative
1929	Ramsay MacDonald	Labour
1931	Ramsay MacDonald	Coalition
1935	Stanley Baldwin	Coalition
1937	Neville Chamberlain	Coalition
1940	Winston Churchill	Coalition
1945 (May)	Winston Churchill	Conservative
1945 (July)	Clement Attlee	Labour
1951	Sir Winston Churchill	Conservative
1955	Sir Anthony Eden	Conservative
1957	Harold Macmillan	Conservative
1963	Sir Alec Douglas-Home	Conservative
1964	Harold Wilson	Labour
1970	Edward Heath	Conservative
1974	Harold Wilson	Labour
1976	James Callaghan	Labour
1979	Margaret Thatcher	Conservative
1990	John Major	Conservative
1997	Tony Blair	Labour

USA

Year inaugurated	President	Party
1789	George Washington	Federation
1797	John Adams	Federation
1801	Thomas Jefferson	Republican
1809	James Madison	Republican
1817	James Monroe	Republican
1825	John Quincy Adams	Republican
1829	Andrew Jackson	Democrat
1837	Martin Van Buren	Democrat

Year inaugurated	President	Party
1841	William Harrison (died in office)	Whig
1841	John Tyler	Whig
1845	James Polk	Democrat
1849	Zachary Taylor (died in office)	Whig
1850	Millard Fillmore	Whig
1853	Franklin Pierce	Democrat
1857	James Buchanan	Democrat
1861	Abraham Lincoln (assassinated)	Republican
1865	Andrew Johnson	Republican
1869	Ulysses Grant	Republican
1877	Rutherford Hayes	Republican
1881	James Garfield (assassinated)	Republican
1881	Chester Arthur	Republican
1885	Grover Cleveland	Democrat
1889	Benjamin Harrison	Republican
1893	Grover Cleveland	Democrat
1897	William McKinley (assassinated)	Republican
1901	Theodore Roosevelt	Republican
1909	William Taft	Republican
1913	Woodrow Wilson	Democrat
1921	Warren Harding (died in office)	Republican
1923	Calvin Coolidge	Republican
1929	Herbert Hoover	Republican
1933	Franklin D. Roosevelt (died in office)	Democrat
1945	Harry S. Truman	Democrat
1953	Dwight D. Eisenhower	Republican
1961	John F. Kennedy (assassinated)	Democrat
1963	Lyndon Johnson	Democrat
1969	Richard Nixon	Republican
1974	Gerald Ford	Republican
1977	Jimmy Carter	Democrat
1981	Ronald Reagan	Republican
1989	George Bush	Republican
1993	Bill Clinton	Democrat
2001	George W. Bush	Republican

8
Mythology, Religion and Folklore

8.1 *Classical Mythology*

Egyptian gods

Amun/Amon/Ammon/Amen	King of the gods
Anubis/Anpu	God of the dead
Apis/Hapi/Hap/Hep	God of fertility, god of the Nile
Aten/Aton	Sun god, briefly the one and only god
Atum/Tem/Tom	Creator god and god of men
Bast/Bastet/Ubasti	Goddess of music and dance
Bes/Bisu	Protector of the royal house and god of recreation
Buto/Edjo/Udjo/Wadjet/Wadjit	Goddess of Lower Egypt and defender of the king
Geb/Keb/Seb	God of the earth
Hathor/Athyr	Goddess of the sky, love and festivity
Horus/Hor	God of Lower Egypt, also god of the present king
Isis/Aset/Eset	Queen of the gods
Khenty-Imentiu/Khenti-Amentiu	Warrior god and god of the underworld
Khnum/Khnemu	Creator god of the underworld
Khons/Khensu/Khonsu/Chons	God of the moon
Maat/Mayet	Goddess of law, truth and justice
Min	God of fertility and the harvest
Mont	War god of Upper Egypt and lord of the sky
Nefertum/Nefertem/Nefertemu	God of the lotus
Neith/Neit	Goddess of the loom and of war
Nekhbet/Nekhebet	Protectress of childbirth
Nephthys	Goddess of funerals
Nut/Neuth/Nuit	Goddess of the sky
Osiris/Usire	Fertility god, later ruler of the gods and king of the underworld
Ptah/Phtah	Creator of the universe
Re/Ra/Phra	King of the gods
Sati/Satet/Satis	Goddess of fertility
Seker/Sokar/Sokaris	God of darkness and decay

Sekmet	Goddess of might
Seshat/Sesheta	Goddess of writing and history
Set	God of evil
Shu	God of light and supporter of the sky
Taurt/Apet/Opet/Tawaret/Thoueris	Goddess of maternity
Thoth/Djhowtey	God of the moon

Greek gods

Adonis	God of vegetation
Aeolus	God of the winds
Alphito	Goddess of Argos
Aphrodite	Goddess of love, beauty and procreation
Apollo	God of prophecy, poetry, music, archery and healing
Ares	God of war
Arethusa	Goddess of springs and fountains
Artemis	Goddess of the moon, hunting and fertility
Asclepius	God of healing
Athene	Goddess of wisdom and protectress of Athens
Atlas	Titan who carries the earth on his shoulders
Attis	God of vegetation
Boreas	God of the north wind
Cronus	Father of Zeus
Cybele	Goddess of fertility and the mountains
Demeter	Goddess of fruit, crops and vegetation
Dionysus	God of wine
Eos	Goddess of the dawn
Eros	God of love
Gaia	Goddess of the earth
Ganymede	God of rain
Hades	God of the underworld
Hebe	Goddess of youth
Hecate	Goddess of magic, ghosts and witchcraft
Helios	God of the sun
Hephaestus	God of fire
Hera	Goddess of marriage and women and queen of heaven
Hermes	God of science and commerce and messenger of the gods
Hestia	Goddess of the hearth
Hypnos	God of sleep
Iris	Goddess of the rainbow and messenger of the gods
Morpheus	God of dreams
Nemesis	Goddess of vengeance
Nereus	God of the sea
Nike	Goddess of victory
Oceanus	God of the sea
Pan	God of the pastures, forests, flocks and herds
Persephone	Goddess of the underworld
Poseidon	God of the sea

Rhea	Mother of the gods
Selene	Goddess of the moon
Thanatos	God of death
Zeus	Overlord of the gods and goddesses on Olympus, lord of heaven

The Fates (Greek mythology)

Clotho

Lachesis

Atropos

The Furies (Greek mythology)

Alecto

Tisiphone

Megaera

The Three Graces (Greek mythology)

Aglaia

Euphrosyne

Thalia

The Nine Muses (Greek mythology)

Name	Muse of
Calliope	Epic poetry
Clio	History
Erato	Love poetry
Euterpe	Music and lyric poetry
Melpomene	Tragedy
Polyhmnia	Singing, sacred dance and mime
Terpsichore	Dance and choral song
Thalia	Comedy and pastoral poetry
Urania	Astronomy

The Labours of Hercules

1	Killing and skinning the Nemean lion
2	Killing the monster Hydra
3	Capturing the Hind of Ceryneia
4	Capturing the Boar of Erymanthus
5	Cleaning out the stables of Augeas, King of Elis
6	Removing the man-eating birds of the Stymphalian Lake
7	Capturing the Cretan Bull
8	Capturing the four man-eating mares of the Thracian king Diomedes
9	Stealing the golden girdle of the Amazonian queen Hippolyte
10	Capturing the oxen of the giant Geryon
11	Fetching the golden apples of the Hesperides
12	Capturing the three-headed Cerberus, guardian of Hades

Roman gods

Apollo	God of the sun, music, poetry, prophecy and healing
Bacchus	God of wine
Bellona	Goddess of war
Ceres	Goddess of corn
Consus	God of seed sowing
Cupid	God of love
Diana	Goddess of fertility, hunting and the moon
Egeria	Goddess of fountains and childbirth
Epona	Goddess of horses
Fauna	Goddess of fertility
Faunus	God of prophecy
Feronia	Goddess of spring flowers
Fides	God of honesty
Flora	Goddess of flowers
Fortuna	Goddess of chance and fate
Genius	God of individuals, groups and the state
Janus	God of gates and doors
Juno	Goddess of marriage and women
Jupiter	Ruler of the gods, god of the sky and lord of heaven
Lares	Gods of the household and state
Liber Pater	God of agricultural and human fertility
Libitina	Goddess of funerals
Maia	Goddess of growth and increase
Mars	God of war
Mercury	Messenger god and god of commerce
Minerva	Goddess of wisdom, the arts and trade
Mithras	God of the sun and god of light
Neptune	God of the sea
Ops	Goddess of fertility
Orcus	God of death
Pales	Goddess of flocks

Penates	Gods of the household stores
Picus	God of the woods
Pluto	God of the underworld
Pomona	Goddess of fruit trees and fruit
Portunus	God of husbands
Prosperina/Proserpine	Goddess of the underworld
Rumina	Goddess of nursing mothers
Saturn	God of the harvest
Silvanus	God of agriculture and woods
Venus	Goddess of beauty and love
Vertumnus	God of the seasons
Vesta	Goddess of the hearth
Victoria	Goddess of victory
Vulcan	God of fire

The Seven Virtues

1	Faith
2	Hope
3	Charity
4	Prudence
5	Justice
6	Fortitude
7	Temperance

Norse gods

Aegir	God of the sea
Aesir	Race of warrior gods, including Odin and Thor
Alcis	Twin gods of the sky
Baldur	Son of Odin
Bor	Father of Odin
Bragi	God of poetry
Eir	Goddess of medicine
Fafnir	Dragon god
Fjorgynn	Mother of Thor
Freyja	Goddess of love and fertility
Frey	God of fertility, sun and rain
Frigg	Goddess of married love, the wife of Odin
Gefion	Goddess of dead virgins
Heimdall	Warden of the gods
Hel	Goddess of death and queen of Niflheim
Hermod	Son of Odin
Hoenir	Companion of Odin and Loki
Hoder	Blind god who killed Baldur
Idunn	Guardian of the golden apples of youth, wife of Bragi
Kvasir	God of wise utterances

Logi	God of fire
Loki	God of mischief
Mimir	God of wisdom
Nanna	Wife of Baldur
Nehallenia	Goddess of plenty
Nerthus	Goddess of earth
Njord	God of ships and the sea
Norns	Goddesses of destiny
Odin/Woden/Wotan	Ruler of the gods, also the god of war, learning and poetry
Otr	Otter god
Ran	Goddess of the sea
Sif	Wife of Thor
Sigyn	Wife of Loki
Thor/Donar	God of thunder and the sky, also the god of crops
Tyr	God of battle and victory
Ull	God of the hunt
Valkyries	Female attendants of the gods of war
Vanir	Race of benevolent gods, including Njord and Freya
Vidar	Slayer of the wolf Fenir
Vor	Goddess of truth
Weland/Volundr/Weiland/Wayland	Craftsman god

The Four temperaments or humours

Humour	Temperament
Blood	Sanguine
Black bile	Melancholic
Yellow bile/choler	Choleric
Phlegm	Lethargic/Phlegmatic

8.2 Religion

Major religions of the world

Baha'ism

Founder	Mirza Husayn Ali (Baha'u'llah; 1817–92)
Date of foundation	1863 (Iran)
Sacred texts	Kitabal-Aqdas, Haft Wadi, Bayan, al-Kalimat al-Maknnah
Branches/denominations	
State religion in	
Adherents (1998 est)	5 750 000

Buddhism

Founder	Prince Siddharta Gautama (Buddha; c. 563–483 BC)
Date of foundation	c. 500 BC (India)
Sacred texts	Tripitaka
Branches/denominations	Therevada, Mahayana, Tantrism
State religion in	Bhutan, Cambodia, Thailand
Adherents (1998 est)	330 000 000

Christianity

Founder	Jesus Christ (c. 4 BC – AD 30)
Date of foundation	1st century AD
Sacred texts	Bible
Branches/denominations	Anglican, Baptist, Church of Christ, Lutheran, Methodist, Mormon, Orthodox, Pentecostal, Presbyterian, Roman Catholic, Unitarian
State religion in	Argentina, Bolivia, Costa Rica, Denmark, Dominican Republic, Greece, Iceland, Malta, Norway, Paraguay, Peru, Sweden, UK
Adherents (1998 est)	1 760 000 000

Confucianism

Founder	K'ung Fu-tzu (551–479 BC)
Date of foundation	6th century BC (China)
Sacred texts	The Analects, Su Ching, Shi Ching, Li Chi, I Ching, Lu
Branches/denominations	
State religion in	
Adherents (1994 est)	6 334 000

Hinduism

Founder	
Date of foundation	c. 1500 BC (India)
Sacred texts	Rigveda, Yajurveda, Samaveda, Atharveda
Branches/denominations	Vishnu, Shiva, Shakti
State religion in	Nepal
Adherents (1998 est)	750 000 000

Islam (Muslim)

Founder	Mohammed (AD c. 570–632)
Date of foundation	7th century AD (Arabian peninsula)
Sacred texts	Koran, Hadith
Branches/denominations	Sunni, Shi'a, Sufi, Ismaili
State religion in	Afghanistan, Algeria, Bahrain, Bangladesh, Comoros, Egypt, Iran, Iraq, Jordan, Kuwait, Libya, Malaysia, Maldives, Mauritania, Morocco, Oman, Pakistan, Qatar, Saudi Arabia, Somalia, Sudan, Tunisia, United Arab Emirates, Yemen
Adherents (1998 est)	1 000 000 000

Jainism

Founder	Vardhamana Mahavira (599–527 BC)
Date of foundation	c. 600 BC (India)
Sacred texts	Siddhanta, Pakrit
Branches/denominations	Digambara, Swetambara
State religion in	
Adherents (1998 est)	3 900 000

Judaism

Founder	Abraham (c. 2000 BC) and Moses (c. 1200 BC)
Date of foundation	c. 2000 BC
Sacred texts	Torah, Talmud
Branches/denominations	
State religion in	
Adherents (1998 est)	12 500 000

Shintoism

Founder	
Date of foundation	6th century AD (Japan)
Sacred texts	Kojiki, Nohon Shoki
Branches/denominations	
State religion in	
Adherents (1994 est)	3 387 000

Sikhism

Founder	Guru Nanak (AD 1469–1539)
Date of foundation	c. 15th century AD (India)
Sacred texts	Guru Granth Sahib (Adi Granth)
Branches/denominations	
State religion in	
Adherents (1998 est)	20 000 000

Taoism

Founder	Lao Zi (6th century BC)
Date of foundation	600 BC (China)
Sacred texts	Chuang-tzu, Lao-tzu (Tao-te-ching)
Branches/denominations	Tao Te Ching
State religion in	
Adherents (1994 est)	149 336 000

Christian denominations, movements and sects

Baptist Church

Founder	John Smyth (c. 1554–1612)
Date of foundation	1609 (Amsterdam)
Adherents (2000 est)	40 000 000

Church of Christ, Scientist/Christian Science

Founder	Mary Baker Eddy (1821–1910)
Date of foundation	1879 (USA)
Adherents	Not published

Church of England

Founder	Henry VIII (1491–1547)
Date of foundation	1534 (England)
Adherents (2000 est)	70 000 000

Jehovah's Witnesses

Founder	Charles Taze Russell (1852–1916)
Date of foundation	1872 (USA)
Adherents (2000 est)	5 000 000

Lutheranism

Founder	Martin Luther (1483–1546)
Date of foundation	1517–19 (Wittenberg, Germany)
Adherents (2000 est)	70 000 000

Methodism

Founder	John Wesley (1703–91)
Date of foundation	1738
Adherents (1998 est)	60 000 000

Mormon Church/Church of Jesus Christ of Latter-day Saints

Founder	Joseph Smith (1805–44)
Date of foundation	1830 (New York)
Adherents (2000 est)	10 000 000

Orthodox Church

Founder	
Date of foundation	1054
Adherents (2000 est)	300 000 000

Pentecostalism

Founder	
Date of foundation	1906 (USA)
Adherents (2000 est)	105 000 000

Presbyterianism

Founder	John Knox (c. 1513–72)
Date of foundation	1560
Adherents (2000 est)	700 000

Quakers/Religious Society of Friends

Founder	George Fox (1624–91)
Date of foundation	Mid 17th century (England)
Adherents (2000 est)	213 800

Rastafarianism

Founder	
Date of foundation	1930 (Ethiopia)
Adherents (1990 est)	1 000 000

Roman Catholicism

Founder	St Peter (traditionally)
Date of foundation	1st century AD (historically, 4th century AD)
Adherents (2000 est)	890 900 000

Scientology

Founder	L. Ron Hubbard (1911–86)
Date of foundation	1954 (USA)
Adherents	

Seventh-Day Adventist

Founder	William Miller (1782–1849)
Date of foundation	1863 (USA)
Adherents (2000 est)	9 000 000

Unification Church/Moonies

Founder	Sun Myung Moon (1920–)
Date of foundation	1954 (Korea)
Adherents (2000 est)	200 000

Unitarianism

Founder	
Date of foundation	16th century (Poland and Transylvania)
Adherents (1990 est)	750 000

Books of the Bible

Old Testament

Book	Chapters	Date
Genesis	50	mid 8th century BC
Exodus	40	950–586 BC
Leviticus	27	mid 7th century BC
Numbers	36	850–650 BC
Deuteronomy	34	mid 7th century BC
Joshua	24	mid 6th century BC
Judges	21	mid 6th century BC
Ruth	4	late 3rd century BC
1 Samuel	31	900 BC
2 Samuel	24	900 BC
1 Kings	22	550–600 BC
2 Kings	25	550–600 BC
1 Chronicles	29	300 BC
2 Chronicles	36	300 BC
Ezra	10	450 BC
Nehemiah	13	450 BC
Esther	10	200 BC
Job	42	600–400 BC
Psalms	150	6th–2nd century BC
Proverbs	31	350–150 BC
Ecclesiastes	12	200 BC
Song of Solomon	8	3rd century BC
Isaiah	66	late 3rd century BC
Jeremiah	52	604 BC
Lamentations	5	586–536 BC
Ezekiel	48	6th century BC
Daniel	12	c. 166 BC
Hosea	14	c. 732 BC
Joel	3	500 BC
Amos	9	775–750 BC
Obadiah	1	6th–3rd century BC
Jonah	4	600–200 BC
Micah	7	late 3rd century BC
Nahum	3	c. 626 BC
Habakkuk	3	600 BC

Zephaniah	3	3rd century BC
Haggai	2	c. 520 BC
Zechariah	14	c. 520 BC
Malachi	4	c. 430 BC

New Testament

Book	Chapters	Date
Matthew	28	before AD 70
Mark	16	before AD 70
Luke	24	AD 70–80
John	21	AD 90–100
The Acts	28	AD 70–80
Romans	16	AD 120
1 Corinthians	16	AD 57
2 Corinthians	13	AD 57
Galatians	6	AD 53
Ephesians	6	AD 140
Philippians	4	AD 63
Colossians	4	AD 140
1 Thessalonians	5	AD 50–54
2 Thessalonians	3	AD 50–54
1 Timothy	6	before AD 64
2 Timothy	4	before AD 64
Titus	3	before AD 64
Philemon	1	AD 60–62
Hebrews	13	AD 80–90
James	5	before AD 52
1 Peter	5	before AD 64
2 Peter	3	before AD 64
1 John	5	AD 90–100
2 John	1	AD 90–100
3 John	1	AD 90–100
Jude	1	AD 75–80
Revelation	22	AD 81–96

Apocrypha

Baruch

Additions to the Book of Daniel

Book of Ecclesiasticus

Additions to the Book of Esther

Books of Esdras

Letter of Jeremiah

Book of Judith

Books of the Maccabees

Book of Tobit (Tobias)

Wisdom of Solomon

Ten Commandments

1	Thou shalt have no other gods before me.
2	Thou shalt not make unto thee any graven image.
3	Thou shalt not take the name of the Lord thy God in vain.
4	Remember the sabbath day, to keep it holy.
5	Honour thy father and thy mother.
7	Thou shalt not commit adultery.
8	Thou shalt not steal.
9	Thou shalt not bear false witness against thy neighbour.
10	Thou shalt not covet thy neighbour's house, thou shalt not covet thy neighbour's wife, nor his manservant, nor his maidservant, nor his ox, not his ass, nor any thing that is thy neighbour's.

Note Listed at Exodus 20:2–17 and Deuteronomy 5:6–21

Beatitudes

Blessed are the poor in spirit: for theirs is the kingdom of heaven.

Blessed are they that mourn: for they shall be comforted.

Blessed are the meek: for they shall inherit the earth.

Blessed are they which do hunger and thirst after righteousness: for they shall be filled.

Blessed are the merciful: for they shall obtain mercy.

Blessed are the pure in heart: for they shall see God.

Blessed are the peacemakers: for they shall be called the children of God.

Blessed are they which are persecuted for righteousness' sake: for theirs is the kingdom of heaven.

Blessed are ye, when men shall revile you, and persecute you, and shall say all manner of evil against you falsely, for my sake.

Rejoice, and be exceeding glad: for great is your reward in heaven: for so persecuted they the prophets which were before you.

Note Listed at Matthew 5:3–12

Seven Deadly Sins

1	Pride
2	Covetousness
3	Lust
4	Envy
5	Gluttony
6	Anger
7	Sloth

Stations of the Cross

1	Jesus is condemned to death
2	Jesus is made to bear his cross
3	Jesus falls for the first time under his cross
4	Jesus meets his mother
5	Simon the Cyrenean helps to carry the cross
6	Veronica wipes the face of Jesus
7	Jesus falls a second time
8	Jesus addresses the women of Jerusalem
9	Jesus falls a third time
10	Jesus is stripped of his garments
11	Jesus is nailed to the cross
12	Jesus dies on the cross
13	Jesus is taken down from the cross
14	Jesus is laid in the tomb

Seven Sacraments

Baptism
Confirmation
Eucharist
Penance
Ordination
Matrimony
Anointing of the Sick/Extreme unction

Twelve Tribes of Israel

Tribe	Named after and descended from	Borne by
Reuben	Jacob's first son	Leah
Simeon	Jacob's second son	Leah
Levi	Jacob's third son	Leah
Judah	Jacob's fourth son	Leah
Dan	Jacob's fifth son	Bilhah
Naphtali	Jacob's sixth son	Bilhah
Gad	Jacob's seventh son	Zilpah
Asher	Jacob's eighth son	Zilpah
Issachar	Jacob's ninth son	Leah
Zebulun	Jacob's tenth son	Leah
Joseph	Jacob's eleventh son	Rachel
Benjamin	Jacob's twelfth son	Rachel

Note Listed at Genesis 29–30, 35

Ten Plagues of Egypt

1	Water turns to blood
2	Frogs
3	Lice, sand flies, or fleas
4	Swarms of flies
5	Cattle die from disease
6	Boils and sores
7	Hail
8	Locusts
9	Darkness
10	Death of the first-born

Note Listed at Exodus 7–11

Four Horsemen of the Apocalypse

Horseman	Represents
Rider of the White Horse	Victory of God over evil
Rider of the Red Horse	Bloodshed and war
Rider of the Black Horse	Famine
Rider of the Pale Horse	Disease and Death

Note Listed at Revelation 6

Four Last Things

Death
Judgment
Heaven
Hell

Movable Christian feasts 2001–2025

Year	Ash Wednesday	Easter	Ascension	Whit Sunday (Pentecost)	First Sunday in Advent
2000	8 March	23 April	1 June	11 June	3 December
2001	28 February	15 April	24 May	3 June	2 December
2002	13 February	31 March	9 May	19-May	1 December
2003	5 March	20 April	29 May	8 June	30 November
2004	25 February	11 April	20 May	30 May	28 November
2005	9 February	27 March	5 May	15 May	27 November
2006	1 March	16 April	25 May	4 June	3 December
2007	21 February	8 April	17 May	27 May	2 December
2008	6 February	23 March	1 May	11 May	30 November
2009	25 February	12 April	21 May	31 May	29 November
2010	17 February	4 April	13 May	23 May	28 November

2011	9 March	24 April	2 June	12 June	27 November
2012	22 February	8 April	17 May	27 May	2 December
2013	13 February	31 March	9 May	19 May	1 December
2014	5 March	20 April	29 May	8 June	30 November
2015	18 February	5 April	14 May	24 May	29 November
2016	10 March	27 March	5 May	15 May	27 November
2017	1 March	16 April	25 May	4 June	3 December
2018	14 February	1 April	10 May	20 May	2 December
2019	6 March	21 April	30 May	9 June	1 December
2020	26 February	12 April	21 May	31 May	29 November
2021	17 February	4 April	13 May	23 May	28 November
2022	2 March	17 April	26 May	5 June	27 November
2023	22 February	9 April	18 May	28 May	3 December
2024	14 February	31 March	9 May	19 May	1 December
2025	5 March	20 April	29 May	8 June	30 November

Note Palm (or Passion) Sunday falls on the Sunday before Easter; Good Friday falls on the Friday before Easter; Holy (or Easter) Saturday falls on the Saturday before Easter

Immovable Christian feasts

1 January	The naming of Jesus
	The Circumcision of Christ
	The Solemnity of Mary, Mother of God
6 January	Epiphany
7 January	Christmas Day (Eastern Orthodox)
11 January	Baptism of Jesus
25 January	Conversion of Apostle Paul
2 February	Presentation of Jesus in the Temple (Candlemas)
22 February	The Chair of Peter, Apostle
19 March	St Joseph of Nazareth
25 March	Annunciation of the Virgin Mary
25 April	St Mark the Evangelist
1 May	St Philip and St James, Apostles
14 May	St Matthias the Apostle
31 May	The Visitation of the Blessed Virgin Mary
11 June	St Barnabas the Apostle
24 June	The Birth of John the Baptist
29 June	St Peter and St Paul, Apostles
3 July	St Thomas the Apostle
22 July	St Mary Magdalen
25 July	St James the Apostle
6 August	The Transfiguration of our Lord
15 August	Assumption of the Virgin Mary
22 August	Queenship of Mary
24 August	St Bartholomew the Apostle
1 September	New Year (Eastern Orthodox)
8 September	Nativity of the Virgin Mary
14 September	Exaltation of the Holy Cross
21 September	St Matthew the Apostle
29 September	St Michael and All Angels

2 October	Guardian Angels
18 October	St Luke the Evangelist
28 October	St Simon and St Jude, Apostles
1 November	All Saints
2 November	All Souls
9 November	Dedication of the Lateran Basilica
21 November	Presentation of the Blessed Virgin Mary
30 November	St Andrew the Apostle
8 December	Immaculate Conception of the Blessed Virgin Mary
25 December	Christmas Day
26 December	St Stephen the first Martyr
27 December	St John the Evangelist
28 December	Holy Innocents

Saints' days

January

1	Abbot Clarus, Basil (E), Fulgentius, Justin, Telemachus
2	Abel, Basil and Gregory of Nazianzus (W), Caspar, Macarius of Alexandria, Seraphim of Sarov
3	Daniel, Frances, Geneviève
4	Angela of Foligno, Benedicta, Elizabeth Seton, Roger of Eliant
5	Paula, Simeon Stylites (W)
6	Balthasar, Caspar and Melchior, Melanius, Raphaela
7	Cedda, Crispin, Lucian of Antioch (W), Raymond of Peñafort, Reynold, Valentine
8	Atticus (E), Gudule, Lucian, Nathalan, Severinus
9	Adrian of Canterbury, Alix, Basilissa, Hadrian the African, Peter
10	Agatho, Marcian, Peter Orseolo, William
11	Alexander, Brandan, Theodosius the Cenobiarch
12	Ailred, Arcadius, Benedict Biscop, Tatiana
13	Godfrey, Hilary of Poitiers
14	Felix of Nola, Hilary, Kentigern, Malachi, Sava
15	Isidore, Ita, Macarius of Egypt, Maurus, Micah, Paul of Thebes
16	Bernard and his companions, Henry, Honoratus, Juliana, Marcellus, Otto, Priscilla
17	Antony of Egypt, Roseline
18	Dermot, Faustina, Prisca, Susanna
19	Canute IV, Gerontius, Henry, Marius, Martha, Pia, Wulfstan
20	Euthymius, Fabian, Sebastian
21	Agnes, Fructuosus, Josepha, Maximus (E), Meinrad
22	Dominic, Timothy (G), Vincent of Saragossa
23	Aquila, Bernard, Emerentiana, Ildefonsus, Raymond
24	Babylas (W), Francis de Sales, Timothy
25	Artemas, Dwyn, Gregory of Nazianzus (E), Joel, Paul, Praejectus
26	Aubrey, Conan, Paula, Timothy and Titus, Xenophon (E)
27	Angela Merici, Candida, John Chrysostom, Julian, Marius, Theodoric
28	Ephraem Syrus (E), Paulinus of Nola, Peter, Thomas Aquinas
29	Francis, Gildas
30	Aidan, Bathildis, Hyacintha, Martina, Matthias
31	Adamnan, Aidan, Cyrus, John Bosco, Julius, Marcella, Tryphena

February

1	Bridget (or Bride), Ignatius, Pionius
2	Joan de Lestonnac, Theodoric
3	Anskar, Blaise (W), Ives, Laurence, Margaret, Oliver, Simeon (E), Werburga
4	Andrew Corsini, Gilbert of Sempringham, Isidore of Pelusium, Joan, John de Britto, Joseph, Nicholas, Phileas, Theophilus
5	Adelaide, Agatha, Avitus, Caius, Joachim, Matthias
6	Amand, Dorothy, Gerald, Luke, Mel, Paul Miki and companions, Silvanus, Titus, Vedast
7	Juliana, Luke, Moses, Richard, Theodore the General
8	Isaiah, Jerome Emiliani, Sebastian, Stephen, Theodore (G)
9	Apollonia, Cyril, Teilo
10	Hyacinth, Scholastica, Silvanus
11	Benedict of Aniane, Blaise (E), Caedmon, Finnian, Gregory II, Jonas, Lazarus, Lucius, Theodore, Victoria
12	Alexis, Eulalia, Julian the Hospitaller, Marina, Meletius, Seven Servite Founders
13	Agabus (W), Beatrice, Catherine dei Ricci, Huna, Priscilla (E)
14	Abraham, Adolf, Cyril and Methodius (W), Valentine (W)
15	Claud, Georgia, Jordan, Sigfrid
16	Elias, Flavian (E), Gilbert, Jeremy, Juliana, Pamphilus (E), Philippa, Samuel, Valentine (F)
17	Fintan, Reginald
18	Bernadette, Colman of Lindisfarne, Flavian (W), Leo I (E), Simeon
19	Boniface, Conrad, Mesrop
20	Amata, Ulric of Haselbury, Wulfric
21	George, Peter Damian
22	Margaret of Cortona
23	Lazarus, Martha, Mildburga, Milo, Polycarp
24	Adela, Ethelbert, Matthias, Montanus and Lucius
25	Tarasius, Walburga
26	Alexander (W), Isabel, Porphyrius of Gaza, Victor
27	Gabriel Possenti, Leander
28	Antonia, Hedwig, Hilary, Louisa, Oswald of York

March

1	Albinus, David, Felix, Roger
2	Agnes, Chad, Simplicius
3	Ailred, Anselm, Camilla, Cunegund, Marcia, Owen
4	Adrian of Nicomedia, Casimir, Humbert, Lucius, Peter
5	Eusebius of Cremona, Kieran, Piran, Virgil
6	Baldred, Chrodegang, Colette, Cyril, Felicity, Jordan, Perpetua
7	Paul, Perpetua and Felicity, Thomas
8	Beata, Felix, Humphrey, John of God, Julian, Philemon, Pontius, Stephen
9	Catherine, Dominic Savio, Frances of Rome, Gregory of Nyssa, Pacian
10	Anastasia, Caius, John Ogilvie, Macarius of Jerusalem, Simplicius
11	Alberta, Aurea, Constantine, Eulogius of Cordoba, Oengus, Sophronius, Teresa
12	Bernard, Gregory (the Great), Maximilian, Paul, Seraphina
13	Gerald of Mayo, Nicephorus, Patricia, Roderick, Solomon
14	Benedict (E), Eustace, Matilda
15	Clement Hofbauer, Louise de Marillac, Lucretia, Zachary
16	Abraham, Boniface of Ross, Heribert, Julian, René
17	Gertrude, Joseph of Arimathea (W), Patrick, Paul

18	Alexander, Anselm of Lucca, Christian, Cyril of Jerusalem, Edward, Egbert, Fra Angelico, Narcissus, Salvator
19	Joseph
20	Alexandra, Claudia, Cuthbert, Euphemia, Herbert, Hippolytus, John of Parma, Martin of Braga, Sebastian, Theodosia
21	Abbot Benedict, Clementia, Serapion of Thmuis
22	Basil, Catherine of Sweden, Nicholas of Flué, Octavian, Zachary
23	Aquila, Gwinear, Theodosia, Turibius de Mongrovejo
24	Catherine of Sweden, Gabriel, Simon
25	Alfwold, Dismas, Harold, Humbert, Lucy, Richard
26	Basil, Emmanuel, Ludger
27	Augusta, John, Lydia, Matthew, Rupert of Salzburg
28	Guntramnus, Gwendoline, John
29	Berthold, Gwladys, Jonas, Mark, Rupert
30	John Climacus
31	Acacius, Aldo, Amos, Benjamin, Cornelia, Guy

April

1	Gilbert, Hugh of Grenoble, Ludovic, Mary of Egypt (E), Melito
2	Constantine, Drogo, Francis of Paola, Leopold, Mary of Egypt (W), Theodosia, Urban
3	Alexandrina, Irene, Richard of Chichester
4	Benedict the Black, Isidore of Seville
5	Gerald, Juliana of Liège, Vincent Ferrer
6	Celestine, William of Eskill
7	George, Hegesippus, Herman, John Baptist de la Salle, Llewellyn
8	Agabus (E), Dionysius, Perpetuus, Walter of Pontoise
9	Hugh, Madrun, Mary, Reginald, Waudru
10	Ezekiel, Fulbert, Hedda, Michael de Sanctis, Terence
11	Gemma Galgani, Guthlac, Hildebrand, Isaac, Leo, Stanislaus
12	Damian, Julius I, Martin I, Zeno
13	Guinoch, Ida, Martin I
14	Bernard, Caradoc, Eustace, Justin, Lambert, Tibertius and Valerian
15	Anastasia, Aristarchus, Paternus of Wales, Pudus (E), Ruadhan, Silvester, Trophimus of Ephesus
16	Benedict, Bernadette of Lourdes, Drogo, Hervé, Lambert, Magnus of Orkney
17	Agapetus (E), Donnan, Elias, Robert, Stephen Harding
18	Mme Acarie, Andrew, Apollonius the Apologist, James
19	Alphege, Expeditus, Leo IX
20	Agnes of Montepulciano, Caedwalla
21	Anastasius (E), Anselm, Beuno, Conrad, Januarius (E), Simeon
22	Alexander and Epipodius (C), Caius, Theodore of Sykean
23	Fortunatus, George, Gerard, Giles, Helen
24	Egbert, Fidelis of Sigmaringen, Ivo, Mellitus
25	Mark, Phaebadius
26	Alda, Cletus, Franca, Stephen of Perm
27	Zita
28	Louis, Patrick, Paul, Peter Mary Chanel, Theodora, Vitalis and Valeria
29	Antonia, Ava, Catherine of Siena, Hugh of Cluny, Peter Martyr, Robert, Wilfrid
30	Adjutor, Catherine, Hildegard, James (the Great) (E), Miles, Pius V, Sophia

May

1	Asaph, Bertha, Isidora, Joseph the Worker, Peregrine Laziosi, Sigismund, Walburga
2	Athanasius, Zoë
3	Alexander and Eventius, Antonina, Maura, Philip and James (the Less) (W), Timothy
4	Ethelrad, Florian, Gotthard, Monica, Pelagia, Silvanus
5	Angelo, Asaph, Hilary of Arles
6	Adbert, Benedicta, Prudence
7	Augustus, Flavia, Gisela, John of Beverley, Stanislas
8	Benedict, Boniface, John (E), Michael, Peter of Tarantaise, Victor Maurus
9	Gerontius, Pachomius
10	Antoninus, Aurelian, Beatrice, Cathal, Comgall, Job, John of Avila, Simon (E)
11	Aloysius, Cyril and Methodius (E), Gengulf, Ignatius, James, Mamertus, Philip, Walter
12	Dominic, Epiphanius, Gemma, Nereus and Achilleus, Pancras
13	Andrew Fournet, Caradoc, Robert
14	Carthage, Giles, Mary, Matthias (W), Michael, Petronilla
15	Bertha, Dionysia, Dympna, Hilary, Isidore the Farmer, Magdalen, Rupert, Silvanus
16	Brendan, Honoratus, John of Nepomuk, Peregrine, Simon Stock, Ubald
17	Basilla, Paschal Baylon, Robert Bellarmine
18	Alexandra, Camilla, Claudia, Eric, John I, Julitta, Venantius
19	Celestine V, Dunstan, Ivo of Kermatin, Pudens (W), Pudentiana (W)
20	Aquila, Basilissa, Bernardino of Siena, Ethelbert, Orlando
21	Andrew Bobola, Collen, Godric, Helena (E), Theobald, Theophilus
22	Julia, Rita of Cascia
23	Ivo of Chartres, Desiderius, William of Rochester
24	David I of Scotland, Joanna, Patrick, Susanna, Vincent of Lérins
25	Aldhelm, Bede, Dionysius, Gregory VII, Madeleine, Mary Magdalene de Pazzi, Urban
26	Augustine, Lambert, Philip Neri, Quadratus, Zachary
27	Augustine of Canterbury, Frederick, John, Julius
28	Augustine, Bernard of Montjoux, Germain of Paris
29	Bona, Theodosia, William
30	Felix, Ferdinand III of Castile, Hubert, Isaac, Joan of Arc
31	Camilla, Petronilla

June

1	Angela, Justin Martyr, Nicomede, Pamphilus, Simeon, Theobald
2	Erasmus, Eugene, Marcellinus and Peter, Nicephorus (G), Nicholas, Pothinus
3	Charles Lwanga and companions, Clotilde, Isaac, Kevin, Matthias, Paula
4	Cornelius, Francis, Joan of Arc, Optatus, Petrock, Vincentia, Walter
5	Boniface, Ferdinand, Franco, Marcia, Valeria
6	Claud, Felicia, Martha (E), Norbert, Philip
7	Colman of Dromore, Meriadoc, Paul of Constantinople (W), Robert, Willibald
8	Melania, William of York
9	Amata, Cecilia, Columba of Iona, Cyril of Alexandria (E), Diana, Ephraem (W), Richard
10	Landerious of Paris, Margaret, Olive, Zachary
11	Barnabas, Bartholomew (E), Fortunatus
12	Antonia, Christian, Humphrey, Leo III, Ternan
13	Anthony of Padua, Lucian
14	Basil the Great, Dogmael, Methodius

15	Alice, Germaine, Guy, Orsisius, Vitus, Yolanda
16	Aurelian, John Francis Regis, Cyricus and Julitta
17	Alban, Botulph, Emily, Harvey, Manuel, Rainerius, Sanchia, Teresa
18	Elizabeth, Fortunatus, Gregory Barbarigo, Guy, Marina, Mark and Marcellian
19	Bruno, Gervasius and Protasius, Jude (E), Juliana, Odo, Romuald
20	Adalert of Magdeburg, Alban, John, Mary
21	Alban of Mainz, Aloysius Gonzaga, Lazarus, Ralph, Terence
22	Alban, Ederhard, John Fisher and Thomas More, Nicetas, Pantaenus (C), Paulinus of Nola
23	Agrippina, Etheldreda
24	Birth of John the Baptist, Bartholomew, Ivan
25	Febronia, Prosper of Aquitaine, Prosper of Reggio, Solomon, William
26	Anthelm, John and Paul
27	Cyril of Alexandria (W), Ferdinand, Kyned, Ladislaus, Madeleine, Samson
28	Austell, Irenaeus, Marcella, Paul
29	Emma, Judith, Peter and Paul, Salome
30	Bertrand, Erentrude, First Martyrs of the Church of Rome, Lucina, Martial, Theobald of Provins

July

1	Aaron, Cosmas and Damian (E), Oliver Plunket, Serf, Simeon, Theodoric
2	Marcia, Martinian, Otto, Processus, Reginald
3	Aaron, Anatolius, Julius, Leo, Thomas
4	Andrew of Crete (E), Aurelian, Bertha, Elizabeth of Portugal, Odo, Ulrich
5	Anthony Zaccaria, Blanche, Grace, Gwen, Modwenna, Philomena, Zoë
6	Isaiah, Maria Goretti
7	Cyril, Hedda of Winchester, Palladius, Pantaenus
8	Adrian, Aquila and Prisca (W), Arnold, Edgar, Elizabeth, Kilian, Morwenna, Procopius, Raymund
9	Alberic, Barnabas, Cornelius, Everild, Godfrey, Jerome, Nicholas, Thomas, Veronica Giuliani, Virgin Mary
10	Amelia, Emmanuel, Maurice, Rufina and Secunda, Seven Brothers
11	Benedict (W), Drostan, Olga, Oliver, Pius I
12	Fortunatus, Jason, John Gualbert, Monica, Veronica
13	Eugene, Henry II, Joel, Mildred, Silas
14	Camillus de Lellis, Deusdedit, Humbert, Nicholas of the Holy Mountain (E), Ulric
15	Baldwin, Bonaventure, David, Donald, Edith, Henry, Jacob of Nisibis, Swithin, Vladimir
16	Eustathius, Helier, Milo, Our Lady of Mt Carmel, Valentine
17	Alexis, Antoinette, Ennodius, Kenelm, Leo IV, Marcellina, Margaret (E), Nahum, Scillitan Martyrs
18	Arnulf, Bruno, Camillus, Edburga of Winchester, Edith, Frederick, Philastrius
19	Ambrose, Arsenius, Aurea, Gervase, Jerome, Macrina, Protase, Symmachus, Vincent
20	Aurelius, Elias, Elijah, Jerome, Margaret (W)
21	Angelina, Constantine, Daniel, Julia, Lawrence of Brindisi, Praxedes, Victor
22	Joseph, Mary Magdalene, Theophilus
23	Anne, Apollinaris, Balthasar, Bridget of Sweden, Gaspar, Susanna
24	Boris, Christina, Declan, Felicia, Gleb
25	Anne and Joachim (E), Christopher, James (the Great) (W), Margaret, Thea, Valentina
26	Anne and Joachim (W)
27	Berthold, Celestine, Natalia, Pantaleon, Rudolph, Seven Sleepers of Ephesus, Theobald

28	Innocent I, Samson, Victor I
29	Beatrice, Felix, Flora, Lucilla, Lupus, Martha, Olaf, Urban
30	Abdon, Everard, Julitta, Peter Chrysologus, Sennen, Silas (G)
31	Giovanni Colombini, Germanus, Helen, Ignatius of Loyola, Joseph of Arimathea (E)

August

1	Alphonsus Liguori, Charity, Eiluned, Ethelwold, Faith, Hope, Justin, Kenneth
2	Alphonsus, Eusebius of Vercelli, Stephen I, Theodota of Nicaea
3	Gamaliel, Germanus of Auxerre, Lydia, Nicodemus, Waldef
4	Dominic, Jean-Baptiste Vianney, Perpetua
5	Afra, Oswald
6	Hormisdas, Justus and Pastor, Octavian
7	Albert, Cajetan, Claudia, Sixtus II and companions
8	Cyriacus, Dominic, Myron
9	Emygdius, Matthias (G), Oswald, Romanus, Samuel
10	Geraint, Laurence, Oswald of Northumbria, Philomena
11	Alexander, Blane, Clare, Lelia, Susanna
12	Attracta, Clare, Euplius, Murtagh
13	Cassian of Imola, Maximus (W), Pontian and Hippolytus, Radegunde
14	Athanasia of Aegina, Marcellus, Maximilian Kolbe
15	Arnulf, Mary the Virgin, Napoleon, Stanislaus, Tarsicius
16	Joachim, Roch, Serena, Simplicianus, Stephen of Hungary, Titus
17	Benedicta, Cecilia, Clare, Hyacinth, Myron, Septimus
18	Agapitus, Evan, Helena, Milo
19	John Eudes, Louis, Magnus, Sebaldus, Thecla, Timothy
20	Bernard of Clairvaux, Herbert, Oswin, Philibert, Ronald, Samuel
21	Abraham, Jane Frances de Chantal, Pius X
22	Andrew, Hippolytus, Sigfrid, Symphorian, Timothy
23	Claudius, Eleazar, Eugene, Philip, Rose of Lima, Sidonius Apollinaris, Zacchaeus
24	Alice, Bartholomew (W), Emily, Jane, Joan, Nathanael, Ouen
25	Genesius the Comedian, Joseph Calasanctius, Louis IX, Lucilla, Menas of Constantinople, Patricia
26	Blessed Dominic of the Mother of God, Elias, Elizabeth, Ninian, Zephyrinus
27	Caesarius, Gabriel, Hugh, Margaret, Monica, Rufus
28	Adelina, Alexander, Augustine of Hippo, Julian, Moses, Vivian
29	Basilla, Beheading of John the Baptist, Sabina
30	Adauctus, Felix, Pammachius, Rose
31	Aidan of Lindisfarne, Paulinus of Trier, Raymund Nonnatus

September

1	Anna, Augustus, Fiacre, Gideon, Giles, Joshua, Simeon Stylites (E), Verena
2	Brocard, John the Faster (E), René, Stephen, William of Roskilde
3	Basilissa, Dorothy, Euphemia, Gabriel, Gregory (the Great), Phoebe, Simeon
4	Babylas (E), Boniface I, Candida, Hermione, Ida, Macnissi, Marcellus, Moses, Rosalia, Rose
5	Bertin, Laurence Giustiniani, Urban, Vitus, Zacharias (E)
6	Beata, Cagnoald, Magnus of Fussen, Zechariah
7	Eustace, Evurtius, Regina, Sozon
8	Adrian, Natalia, Sergius
9	Isaac, Kieran of Clonmacnoise, Louise, Peter Claver, Seraphina, Sergius, Wilfrida
10	Aubert, Candida, Finnian, Isabel, Nicholas of Tolentino, Pulcheria
11	Deiniol, Ethelburga, Hyacinth, Paphnutius, Theodora

12	Ailbe, Enswida, Guy of Anderlecht
13	Amatus, John Chrysostom (W), Venerius
14	Cormac, Notburga
15	Albinus, Catherine of Genoa, Nicomedes, Our Lady of Sorrows, Roland
16	Cornelius, Cyprian of Carthage, Edith, Eugenia, Euphemia, Lucy, Ninian, Victor
17	Ariadne, Columba, Hildegard, Justin, Lambert, Narcissus, Robert Bellarmine, Satyrus, Theodora
18	Irene, Joseph of Cupertino, Sophia
19	Constantia, Emily, Januarius (W), Susanna, Theodore of Tarsus
20	Agapetus or Eustace (W), Candida, Philippa, Vincent
21	Jonah, Matthew (W), Maura
22	Felix, Jonas, Maurice, Thomas
23	Adamnan, Eunan, Helen, Linus, Thecla
24	Gerard of Csanad, Pacificus
25	Albert, Aurelia, Finbarr, Herman, Sergius of Rostov
26	Cosmas and Damian (W), Cyprian of Carthage, John of Meda (E), Justina, René
27	Adolphus, Caius, Cosmas, Damian, Frumentius (W), Terence, Vincent de Paul
28	Bernard of Feltre, Exuperius, Solomon, Wenceslas
29	Gabriel and Raphael, Michael
30	Jerome, Otto, Simon, Sophia

October

1	Francis, Nicholas, Remigius, Romanos, Teresa of Lisieux
2	Leodegar, Theophilus
3	Gerard, Hewald, Thomas de Cantilupe
4	Ammon, Aurea, Berenice, Francis of Assisi, Petronius
5	Flavia, Flora, Maurus, Placid
6	Aurea, Bruno, Faith, Magnus, Mary, Thomas (G)
7	Augustus, Julia, Justina, Mark, Osith
8	Bridget, Laurentia, Pelagia the Penitent, Sergius, Simeon, Triduana
9	Abraham, Demetrius of Alexandria (W), Denis and companions, Dionysius of Paris, Gunther, James (the Less) (E), John Leonardi, Louis
10	Daniel, Francis Borgia, Paulinus of York, Samuel
11	Atticus (E), Bruno, Juliana, Kenneth, Nectarius
12	Cyprian, Edwin, Ethelburga of Barking, Maximilian, Wilfrid
13	Edward the Confessor, Gerald, Magdalen, Maurice, Theophilus
14	Callistus I, Cosmas Melodus (E), Dominic
15	Aurelia, Leonard, Lucian of Antioch (E), Teresa of Avila, Thecla, Willa
16	Baldwin, Bertrand, Gall, Gerard, Hedwig, Lullus, Margaret Mary Alacoque
17	Etheldreda, Ignatius of Antioch, Margaret, Rudolph, Victor
18	Blanche, Candida, Gwen, Gwendoline, Luke
19	Cleopatra, John de Brébeuf and Isaac Jogues and companions, Laura, Lucius, Paul of the Cross, Peter of Alcántara
20	Acca, Adelina, Andrew of Crete, Irene, Martha
21	Fintan Munnu, Hilarion, Ursula
22	Abercius, Donatus of Fiesole, Philip
23	Bartholomew, Ignatius, James, John of Capistrano, Josephine
24	Anthony Claret, Martin, Raphael, Septimus
25	Balthasar, Crispin and Crispinian, Dorcas, Forty Martyrs of England and Wales, Gaudentius, George, Margaret Clitherow, Marnock, Tabitha, Thaddeus, Theodoric
26	Albinus, Bean, Cedd, Cuthbert, Damian, Demetrius (E), Eata, Lucian
27	Antonia, Frumentius, Sabina
28	Anastasias, Firmilian (E), Godwin, Simon and Jude, Thaddaeus

29	Colman of Kilmacduagh, Narcissus of Jerusalem, Terence
30	Alphonsus, Artemas, Dorothy, Marcellus the Centurion, Serapion of Antioch, Zenobia
31	Bega, Quentin, Wolfgang

November

1	All Saints, Benignus, Cledwyn, Cosmas and Damian (E), Marcel of Paris
2	Eustace (E), Marcian, Maura, Tobias, Victorinus
3	Hubert, Malachy, Martin de Porres, Pirminius, Sylvia, Valentine, Winifred
4	Charles Borromeo, Emeric, Frances, Vitalis and Agricola
5	Cosmo, Elizabeth (W), Martin, Zacharias
6	Illtyd, Leonard of Noblac, Paul of Constantinople (E), Winnoc
7	Carina, Florentius, Gertrude, Rufus, Willibrord
8	Elizabeth (E), Four Crowned Martyrs, Godfrey, Willehad
9	Benignus, Simeon Metaphrastes (E), Theodore the Recruit
10	Andrew Avellino, Florence, Justus, Leo I (W), Tryphena
11	Bartholomew, Martin of Tours (W), Menas of Egypt, Theodore of Studios
12	Josaphat, Martin of Tours (E), Matthew, Nilus the Ascetic, René
13	Abbo, Brice, Eugene, Francis Xavier Cabrini, John Chrysostom (E), Nicholas I, Stanislaus
14	Dubricius, Gregory Palamas (E), Laurence O'Toole
15	Albert the Great, Fintan of Rheinau, Leopold, Machutus
16	Agnes, Edmund of Abingdon, Eucherius, Gertrude (the Great), Margaret of Scotland, Matthew (E)
17	Dionysius, Elizabeth of Hungary, Gregory Thaumaturgus, Gregory of Tours, Hilda, Hugh of Lincoln, Victoria, Zacchaeus
18	Constant, Mawes, Odo, Romanus
19	Crispin, Elizabeth, Mechtild, Nerses I
20	Edmund the Martyr, Octavius, Silvester
21	Albert of Louvain, Gelasius, Rufus
22	Cecilia, Philemon
23	Amphilochius, Clement I (W), Columban, Felicity, Gregory of Agrigentum, Lucretia
24	Chrysogonus, Flora, John, Thaddeus
25	Catherine of Alexandria, Clement I (E), Mercurius, Mesrob, Moses
26	Conrad, John Berchmans, Leonard, Peter, Silvester, Siricius
27	Barlam and Josaphat, Catherine Laboure, Fergus, James, Maximus, Virgil
28	Catherine Labouré, James of the March, Simeon Metaphrastes, Stephen
29	Blaise, Brendan of Birr, Cuthbert Mayne, Frederick, Saturninus
30	Andrew, Frumentius (G), Maura

December

1	Eligius, Nahum, Natalia, Ralph
2	Aurelia, Chromatius, Viviana
3	Claudius, Francis Xavier, Jason, Lucius
4	Ada, Barbara, Bernard, John Damascene, Osmond
5	Bartholomew, Birinus, Clement of Alexandria, Crispina, Sabas
6	Abraham, Dionysia, Gertrude, Nicholas of Bari, Tertius
7	Ambrose, Josepha
8	Budoc, Mary, Romaric
9	Peter Fourier, Leocadia
10	Brian, Eulalia, Gregory, Julia, Miltiades, Sidney
11	Corentin, Damasus, Daniel, Franco, Gentian
12	Agatha, Cormac, Dionysia, Jane Frances de Chantal, Spyridon (E), Vicelin

13	Aubert, Judoc, Lucy, Odilia
14	Conrad, John of the Cross, Spyridon (W)
15	Christiana, Mary di Rosa, Nino, Valerian
16	Adelaide, Albina, Azariah, Eusebius
17	Begga, Florian, Lazarus, Olympias
18	Flannan, Frumentius (C), Rufus, Winebald
19	Anastasius I, Thea, Urban
20	Dominic of Silos, Ignatius of Antioch (G)
21	Peter Canisius, Thomas
22	Adam, Anastasia (E), Chaeremon, Chrysogonus (E)
23	John of Kanty, Thorlac, Victoria
24	Adam, Adela, Charbel Makhlouf, Delphinus, Eve
25	Anastasia, Eugenia
26	Christina, Dionysius, Stephen (W), Vincentia
27	Fabiola, John the Divine (W), Stephen (E), Theodore
28	Holy Innocents, Theophila
29	David, Marcellus, Thomas Becket, Trophimus of Arles
30	Anysia, Egwin, Sabinus
31	Columba, Cornelius, Fabian, Melania, Sextus, Sylvester I

Note (C) = Coptic; (E) = Eastern; (G) = Greek; (W) = Western

Patron saints and intercessors

Country, Profession, etc.	Saint
Accountants	Matthew
Actors	Genesius
Advertisers	Bernardino of Siena
Airmen	Our Lady of Loreto, Thérèse of Lisieux, Joseph of Cupertino
Air stewards	Bona
Animals (danger from)	Vitus
Apprentices	John Bosco
Archaeologists	Damasus
Archers	Sebastian
Architects	Thomas the Apostle
Armies	Maurice
Artists	Luke
Astronauts	Joseph of Cupertino
Astronomers	Dominic
Athletes	Sebastian
Australia	Our Lady Help of Christians
Authors	Francis de Sales
Babies	Maximus
Bakers	Honoratus
Bankers	Matthew
Barbers	Cosmas and Damian
Beekeepers	Bernard of Clairvaux
Belgium	Joseph
Birds	Gall
Blacksmiths	Eligius (Eloi)
Blind people	Thomas the Apostle

Book-keepers	Matthew
Booksellers	John of God
Boys	Dominic Savio
Breast-feeding	Basilissa
Brewers	Amand
Bricklayers	Stephen
Brides	Nicholas of Bari
Bridges	John Nepomucen
Broadcasters	Gabriel the Archangel
Builders	Thomas the Apostle
Businessmen and women	Homobonus
Butchers	Luke
Cabinet makers	Joseph
Cake makers	Honoratus
Canada	Joseph, Anne
Cancer sufferers	Peregrine Laziosi
Cemetary caretakers	Joseph of Arimathea
Charities	Vincent de Paul
Chemists	Cosmas and Damian
Childbirth	Raymond Nonnatus
Childless women	Anne
Children	Nicholas of Bari
Children (desire for)	Rita of Cascia
Christian people (young)	Aloysius
Clergy	Gabriell Possenti
Clothworkers	Homobonus
Coffin-bearers	Joseph of Arimathea
Colic	Erasmus (Elmo)
Colleges	Thomas Aquinas
Comedians	Vitus
Construction workers	Thomas the Apostle
Contagious diseases	Roch
Cooks	Lawrence
Craftsmen and women	Eligius (Eloi)
Criminals, condemned	Dismas
Crops (protection of)	Magnus of Fussen
Customs officers	Matthew
Dancers	Vitus
Deaf people	Francis de Sales
Death	Michael the Archangel
Death (happy)	Joseph
Death (sudden)	Andrew Avellino
Degree candidates	Joseph of Cupertino
Denmark	Asgar, Canute
Dentists	Apollonia
Dieticians (medical)	Martha
Difficult situations	Eustace
Diplomatic services	Gabriel the Archangel
Disasters	Geneviève
Doctors	Luke
Dog bites	Ubald
Domestic animals	Antony the Abbot

Country, Profession, etc.	Saint
Domestic servants	Zita
Doubters	Joseph
Drought	Geneviève
Drowning (protection from)	Adjutor
Dying (the)	Benedict
Earthquakes	Emygdius
Ecologists	Francis of Assisi
Eczema	Antony the Abbot
Editors	John Bosco
Education	Martin de Porres
Embroiderers	Clare
Emigrants	Francis Xavier Cabrini
Engineers	Ferdinand III of Castile
England	George
Epilepsy	Dympna
Examination candidates	Joseph of Cupertino
Eye diseases	Raphael the Archangel
Falsely accused people	Raymond Nonnatus
Farmers	Isidore the Farmer
Farm workers	Benedict
Fathers	Joseph
Fever	Geneviève
Fire (danger from)	Agatha
Firemen	Florian
Fishermen	Peter
Floods	Gregory the Wonderworker
Florists	Rose of Lima
Flying	Joseph of Cupertino
Foresters	John Gualbert
France (unofficial)	Our Lady of the Assumption, Joan of Arc, Denys, Louis, Thérèse
Garage workers	Eligius (Eloi)
Gardeners	Fiacre
Germany	Boniface, Michael
Girls (teenage)	Maria Goretti
Glaziers	Lucy
Goldsmiths	Eligius (Eloi)
Gravediggers	Joseph of Arimathea
Greece	Nicholas, Andrew
Grocers	Michael the Archangel
Haemorrhages	Lucy
Hairdressers	Cosmas and Damian
Harvests	Antony of Padua
Headaches	Denis, Bishop of Paris
Health inspectors	Raphael the Archangel
Hernia sufferers	Cathal
Hoarseness	Bernardino of Siena
Hopeless causes	Jude
Horses	Eligius (Eloi)
Horse-riders	Martin of Tours
Horticulturalists	Fiacre

Hospitals	John of God
Housewives	Martha
Hungary	Our Lady, Stephen
Hunters	Hubert
Illegitimate children	John Francis Regis
India	Our Lady of the Assumption
Infertility	Rita of Cascia
Innkeepers	Gentian
Insanity	Dympna
Invalids	Roch
Ireland	Patrick
Italy	Francis of Assisi, Catherine of Siena
Jewellers	Eligius (Eloi)
Joiners	Joseph
Journalists	Francis de Sales
Judges	Ivo of Kermartin
Juvenile offenders	Dominic Savio
Lame people	Giles
Lawyers	Raymond of Peñafort
Learning	Catherine of Alexandria
Librarians	Jerome
Lighthouse-keepers	Venerius
Lightning (protection against)	Magnus of Fussen
Lost articles	Antony of Padua
Lovers	Valentine
Magistrates	Ferdinand III of Castile
Maritime pilots	Nicholas of Bari
Married women	Monica
Medical profession	Cosmas and Damian
Mental asylums	Dympna
Merchants	Homobonus
Metalworkers	Eligius (Eloi)
Midwives	Raymond Nonnatus
Migrants	Francis Xavier Cabrini
Military signals	Gabriel the Archangel
Miners	Barbara
Missions	Francis Xavier Cabrini
Mothers	Monica
Motorcyclists	Mary, Our Lady of Castellazzo
Motorists	Frances of Rome
Mountaineers	Bernard of Montjoux
Music	Cecilia
Naval officers	Francis of Paola
Navigators	Francis of Paola
Neighbourhood watch schemes	Sebastian
Nervous diseases	Vitus
Netherlands	Willibrord
New Zealand	Our Lady Help of Christians
Norway	Olaf
Notaries	Luke
Nurses	Camillus de Lellis

Country, Profession, etc.	Saint
Old people	Mary, Our Lady of Consolation
Painters	Fra Angelico
Paratroopers	Michael the Archangel
Parenthood	Rita of Cascia
Park-keepers	John Gualbert
Pawnbrokers	Bernard of Feltre
People in authority	Ferdinand III of Castile
Pets	Antony the Abbot
Philatelists	Gabriel the Archangel
Philosophers	Catherine of Alexandria
Physically disabled	Giles
Pilgrims	Nicholas of Bari
Poets	Columba of Iona
Poland	Our Lady of Czestochowa, Casimir, Stanislaus
Policemen and women	Michael the Archangel
Poor people	Antony of Padua
Portugal	Cyriacus
Possession by devils	Immaculate Conception, Francis Borgia, Anthony of Padua, George, Vincent
Postal workers	Gabriel the Archangel
Preachers	John Chrysostom
Pregnant women	Margaret (Marina)
Priests	John Mary Vianney
Printers	John of God
Prison officers	Hippolytus
Prisoners	Leonard of Noblac
Procrastination (protection from)	Expeditus
Publishers	John the Divine
Quantity surveyors	Thomas the Apostle
Radio	Gabriel the Archangel
Radiologists	Michael the Archangel
Rain (excessive)	Geneviève
Rheumatism sufferers	James the Great
Russia	Andrew, Nicholas, Thérèse of Lisieux
Sailors	Erasmus (Elmo)
Scholars	Thomas Aquinas
Scientists	Albert the Great
Scotland	Andrew, Columba
Sculptors	Luke
Secretaries	Genesius the Comedian
Security forces	Michael the Archangel
Security guards	Matthew
Shortsightedness	Clarus
Shorthand writers	Cassian of Imola
Sick animals	Nicholas of Tolentino
Sick people	John of God
Silversmiths	Eligius (Eloi)
Singers	Cecilia
Skiers	Bernard of Montjoux
Skin diseases	Antony the Abbot

Slander	John Nepomucen
Sleepwalkers	Dympna
Snakebites	Pirminus
Social justice	Martin de Porres
Social workers	John Francis Regis
Soldiers	Martin of Tours
Souls in purgatory	Nicholas of Tolentino
South Africa	Our Lady of the Assumption
Spain	James, Teresa
Stomach pains	Erasmus (Elmo)
Stonemasons	Four Crowned Martyrs
Storms (protection against)	Vitus
Students	Thomas Aquinas
Students (female)	Catherine of Alexandria
Students (young)	John Berchmans
Sweden	Bridget, Eric
Swimmers	Adjutor
Tailors	Homobonus
Tax officials	Matthew
Taxi drivers	Fiacre
Teachers	John Baptist de la Salle
Telecommunications	Gabriel the Archangel
Television	Clare
Theatre	Genesius the Comedian
Theft (protection against)	Dismas
Thieves (danger from)	Leonard of Noblac
Throat infections	Blaise
Toothache	Apollonia
Tradesman and women	Homobonus
Travellers	Christopher
Undertakers	Dismas
Unhappy marriages	Gengulf
Unmarried women	Nicholas of Bari
Urgent situations	Expeditus
Vermin (protection against)	Magnus of Fussen
Veterinary surgeons	Eligius (Eloi)
Waiters and waitresses	Martha
Wales	David
War victims (non-combatant)	Mary, Queen of Peace
Water (danger from)	Florian
West Indies	Gertrude
Widows	Paula
Wine merchants	Amand
Workers	Joseph
Writers	Francis de Sales
Yachtsmen	Adjutor
Young people	Raphael the Archangel

Iconographical emblems

Emblem	Saint
Alms	John of God, Matilda
Altar	Philip Neri
Anchor	Clement, Felix, Nicholas of Bari, Rose of Lima
Angel	Bernard, Bertold, Boniface, Cecilia, Congal, Dorothea, Francis of Assisi, Hugh of Lincoln, Isidore of Madrid, Leontius, Pachomius, Paphnutius, Roch
Animal skins	John the Baptist
Anvil	Adrian, Eloi
Apple	Malachy, Nicholas
Arrow	Edmund, Giles, Teresa of Avila
Arrows	Augustine, Christina, Otto, Sebastian
Ass	Antony of Padua, Geriach, Germanus, Philibert
Axe	Anastasius, Barnabas, Boniface, John the Baptist, Josophat, Magnus of Fussen, Malchus, Martian, Matthew, Matthias, Proculus, Rufus, Thomas the Apostle
Balls	Nicholas of Bari
Banner	George, Maurice, Michael the Archangel
Barge	Bertulphus
Barn	Ansovinus, Bridget of Kildare
Barrell	Antonia, Bercher, Willibrord
Basket	Frances, Joanna, John Damascene
Basket of bread	Agatha, Nicholas of Tolentino, Philip, Romanus
Basket of flowers	Dorothea
Basket of fruit	Ann, Dorothea, Sitha
Basket of roses	Elizabeth of Hungary
Bear	Columba, Corbinian, Edmund, Florentius, Gallus, Humbert, James, Maximinus
Beard	Galla, Paula Barbata, Wilgefortis
Bed of iron	Faith
Bees	Ambrose, Bernard of Clairvaux, Isidore the Farmer, John Chrysostom
Bell	Abbot Benedict, Anthony the Great, Francis Xavier, Gildas, Kenan, Paul de Leon, Winwaloc
Bellows	Geneviève
Birds	Francis of Assisi
Boar	Emilion
Boat	Bertin, Jude, Mary Magdalene, Nicholas of Bari, Peter, Simon, Vincent of Saragossa
Boathook	Jude
Bodkin	Leger, Simon of Trent
Book	Antony of Padua, Antoninus, Augustine of Hippo, Bernard of Clairvaux, Boniface, Hubert, Ignatius of Loyola, Luke, Mark, Paul, Samson, Sitha, Teresa of Avila, Urban
Boys in a tub	Nicholas of Bari
Bread	Antony of Padua, Geneviève, Roch
Broken cup	Abbot Benedict
Broom	Gisella, Martha, Martin of Siguenza, Petronilla
Brush	Luke
Bull	Adolphus, Blandina, Marciana, Regnier, Saturninus, Sylvester
Bush	Abbot Benedict

Calves	Walstan
Camel	Aphrodicius, Hormisdas, Julian of Cilicia
Candle	Beatrix, Blaise, Brigid of Ireland, Geneviève
Cannon	Barbara
Captives	Vincent Ferrer
Cardinal's hat	Jerome, Vincent Ferrer
Carpenter's square	Joseph
Carrying the heads of dead nephews	Sigfrid
Cauldron	Boniface, Cecilia, Emilian, Erasmus, Felicity, John the Evangelist, Lucy, Vitus
Chafing dish	Agatha
Chalice	Barbara, Bruno, Josephat, Thomas Aquinas
Chasuble	Ignatius of Loyola, Philip Neri
Children	Vincent de Paul
Chrism	Bernardino of Siena
Christ child	Antony of Padua, Christopher
City	Rose of Lima
Cloak	Martin of Tours
Club	Boniface, Eusebius, Ewald the White, Fabian, Gervase and Protase, James the Less, Jude, Lambert, Magnus, Nicomedes, Panteleon, Valentine, Vitalis
Cock	Peter, Vitus
Colt	Medard
Column	Philip
Comb	Blaise
Companion	Gabriel the Archangel
Cord	Lucy
Cow	Berlinda, Bridget, Modwena, Perpetua
Crocodile	Helenus, Theodore
Cross	Brigid of Ireland, Catherine of Siena, Francis Xavier, John Berchmans, Patrick, Rita of Cascia, Samson, Simon
Crow	Vincent
Crown	Josephat, Sebastian, Wenceslas
Crown of thorns	John of God, Louis of France, Rose of Lima
Crozier	Abbot Benedict, Giles, Pope Gregory the Great
Cruets	Joseph of Arimathea
Crutch	Maurus
Cup and serpent	Benedict, James of Marchia, John a Facundo, John the Evangelist
Dagger	Agnes, Canute, Edward the Confessor, Irene, Kilian, Olave, Solange, Wenceslas
Deer	Francis of Assisi, Henry
Devil	Geneviève, Juliana
Distaff	Geneviève, Rosalie
Doe	Fructuosus, Mammas, Maximus of Turin
Dog	Benignus, Bernard, Dominic, Eustace, Hubert, Roch, Vitus
Dolphin	Adrian, Calistratus, Martianus
Door	Anne
Dove	Ambrose, Basile, Bridget of Sweden, Catherine, Catherine of Siena, Cunibert, David, Dunstan, Pope Gregory the Great, Hilary of Arles, John Chrysostom, John Columbini, Lo, Louis, Medard, Oswald, Peter of Alcantara, Peter Celistin, Sampson, Thomas Aquinas

Emblem	Saint
Dragon	George, Juliana, Margaret, Martha, Michael the Archangel, Sylvester
Eagle	Augustine, Pope Gregory the Great, John the Evangelist, Prisca
Ear of corn	Bridget, Fara, Walburge
Eucharist	Ignatius of Loyola
Eyes in dish	Lucy
Falcon or hawk	Bavo, Edward, Julian Hospitator, Otto
Feather	Barbara
Firebrand	Anthony the Great
Fish	Andrew, Antony of Padua, Eanswide, Francis of Assisi, Gabriel the Archangel, Gregory of Tours, John of Burlington, Raphael, Simon
Fish hooks	Zeno
Flail	·Varus
Flame over head	Brigid of Ireland
Flower	Dorothea, Hugh of Lincoln, Louis of Toulouse, Zita
Fountain	Alton, Antoninus of Toulouse, Apollinaris, Augustine of Canterbury, Boniface, Clement, Egwin, Eric, Guntilda, Humbert, Isidore of Madrid, Julian of Mans, Leonard, Nicholas of Tolentino, Omer, Philip Beniti, Riquier, Servatius, Trond, Venantius, Wolfgang
Fox	Boniface
Frog	Huvas, Rieul, Sinorina, Ulphia
Girdle	Monica
Globe	Henry
Globe of fire	Martin of Tours, Michäel the Archangel
Goose	Martin of Tours
Gosling	Pharaildis
Greyhound	Ferdinand III of Castile
Gridiron	Cyprian, Donatilla, Erasmus, Faith, Lawrence, Vincent of Saragossa
Hair	Patrick
Halberd	James the Less
Hammer	Adrian, Bernward, Eloi, Reinoldus
Hare	Albert of Siena
Harp	Cecilia, Dunstan
Hatchet	Adjutus, Matthew, Matthias
Head held in hands	Denis of Paris
Head on platter	John the Baptist
Heart	Augustine, Catherine of Siena, Francis de Sales, Ignatius, Jane Frances, John of God, Teresa of Avila
Hen	Pharaildis
Herd	Geneviève
Hermitage	Giles
Hind	Bassian, Catherine of Sweden, Geneviève of Brabant, Giles, Lupus of Sens
Hive	Bernard of Clairvaux
Hoe	Isidore of Madrid
Hook	Agatha, Eulalia, Felician, Vincent
Hops	Arnold of Soissons
Horse	Barochus, Irene, Severus of Avranches
Hourglass	Hilarion, Theodosius
Infant Jesus	Joseph

Ink-bottle	Jerome
Intestines	Erasmus (Elmo)
Jug or pitcher	Agatha, Bede, Benedict, Elizabeth of Portugal, Vincent
Key	Egwin, Ferdinand, Germanus of Paris, Hubert, James the Great, Peter, Petronilla, Raymond of Pannafort, Sitha
Keys	Geneviève, Hippolytus, James the Great, Martha, Mary, Maurilius, Nothburge, Peter, Petronilla, Riquier, Zita
Knife	Agatha, Bartholomew, Christina, Ebba, Peter Martyr
Ladder	Emmeran, John Climacus
Ladle	Martha
Lamb	Agnes, Catherine of Alexandria, Francis, Hiltrudis, John the Baptist, Lucy
Lance	Barnabas, Barbara, Canute, Dominic of Silos, Emmeran, Gerhard, Germanus, Hippolytus, John of Goto, Jude, Lambert, Longinus, Matthew, Matthias, Maurice, Oswin, Thomas
Lantern	Gudule, Hugh, Mary of Cabeza
Last	Crispin and Crispinian
Leopard	Marciana
Lily	Antony of Padua, Cajetan, Casimir, Catherine of Sweden, Clare, Dominic, Joseph, Kenelm, Peter Mary Chanel, Philip Neri, Sebastian, Vincent Ferrer
Lion	Adrian, Dorothea, Euphemia, Germanus, Ignatius, Jerome, Mark, Prisca
Loaves of bread	Philip
Loom	Anastasia, Gudule
Lute	Cecilia
Mason's tools	Marinus
Millstone	Christina
Monstrance	Clare, Norbert, Paschal Baylon, Thomas Aquinas
Nails	Alexander, Denys, Fausta, Gemellus, Joseph of Arimathea, Julian of Emesa, Louis of France, Pantaleon, Quintin, Severus of Rome, William of Norwich
Necklace	Etheldreda (Audrey)
Net	Andrew
Oak	Boniface
Oar	Jude
Oil in phial	Remigius, Walburga
Organ	Cecilia
Ox	Blandina, Frideswide, Fursey, Julitta, Leonard, Lucy, Luke, Medard, Otto
Padlock	John of Nepomuk
Phial	Cosmas and Damian, Philip Neri
Pickaxe	Leger
Pig	Anthony the Great
Pilgrim's staff	Dominic, James the Great, Louis
Pincers	Agatha, Apollonia, Christina, Eligius (Eloi), Lucy
Plane	Joseph
Plough	Exuperius, Richard
Pulpit	Vincent Ferrer
Purse	Brieruc, Cyril of Jerusalem, Matilda, Matthew, Nicholas
Rain	Swithin
Rats	Gertrude of Nivelles
Raven	Benedict, Boniface, Erasmus, Ida, Oswald, Paul the Hermit
Razor	Pamphilius

Emblem	Saint
Ring	Barbara, Catherine of Alexandria, Catherine of Siena, Damascus, Edward the Confessor
Rod	Joseph
Rosary	Dominic, John Berchmans
Rose	Rita of Cascia
Saltire	Andrew
Saw	James the Less, Simon
Scales	Athanasia of Aegina, Maurus, Michael the Archangel
Scourge	Ambrose, Boniface, Dorotheus, Gervase and Protase, Guthlac, Peter Damian
Scroll	Paul
Scythe	Guntilda, Nothburge, Sidwell, Walstan
Shamrock	Patrick
Shears	Agatha, Cosmas and Damian, Fortunatus, Marca
Shell	James the Great
Ship	Francis Xavier
Shoe	Crispin and Crispinian
Shovel	Aubert, Honorius
Sieve	Benedict, Hippolytus
Skull	Francis of Assisi
Snakes	Patrick
Spade	Fiacre, Maurus
Sparrow	Dominic
Spit	Gengulph, Quentin
Square rule	James the Less, Jude
Staff	Samson
Stag	Aidan, Eustace, Hubert, Julian Hospitator, Kenan, Kentigern, Osyth, Rieul
Stage (miniature)	Hubert
Star	Anastasia, Bernardin, Bruno, Dominic, Humbert, Nicholas of Tolentino, Thomas Aquinas
Stigmata	Catherine of Siena, Francis of Assisi
Stone	Stephen
Stones	Barnabas
Sun inscribed IHS	Bernardino of Siena
Surgical instruments	Cosmas and Damian
Swan	Cuthbert, Hugh of Grenoble, Hugh of Lincoln, Kentigern
Sword	Adrian, Agnes, Aquila, Arcadius, Beziert, Boniface, Catherine of Alexandria, Euphemia, Ewald the Black, Gervase and Protase, Irene, James the Great, Kilian, Lucy, Michael the Archangel, Pancras, Pantaleon, Paul, Prisca, Thomas of Canterbury
Tablet	Bernardino of Siena
Taper	Gudule
Tears	Monica
Thistle	Caroline, Narcissus
Thorn	Rita of Cascia
Tiara	Pope Gregory the Great, Sylvester
Tongs	Agatha, Apollonia, Christina, Felician, Martina
Torch	Aidan, Barbara, Dorothea, Eutropia, Irenaeus, Medard
Torrent	Christopher
Tower	Barbara, Praxedes

Tree	Christopher
Trowel	William of Montevergine, Winibald
Trumpet	Vincent Ferrer
Veil	Agatha
Vine	Elpidius, Urban, Urban of Langres
Wax	Blaise
Wheel	Catherine of Alexandria, Christina, Euphenia, Quentin
Windlass	Erasmus (Elmo)
Winged man	Matthew
Wolf	Blaise, Francis of Assisi, Simpertus, Vedast, William of Montevergine
Wolfdog	Donatus
Woolcomb	Blaise

Twelve Apostles

Apostle	Symbol
Andrew	X-shaped cross
James	scallop shell, pilgrim's staff, gourd bottle
Philip	staff surmounted by a cross
Matthew (Levi)	hatchet, halberd
James (son of Alphaeus)	fuller's pole
Judas Iscariot	bag
Peter (Simon)	bunch of keys
John	cup and winged serpent
Nathanael (Bartholomew)	knife
Thomas	lance
Judas (son of James)	club
Simon the Zealot	saw

Note After the death of Judas Iscariot Matthias was elected in his place

Seven Champions of Christendom

Champion	Emblem
St Andrew of Scotland	cross saltire gold on blue ground
St Antony of Padua (Italy)	lily, flowered cross, and book
St David of Wales	dove
St Denis of France	carrying his own severed head
St George of England	red cross on white ground
St James of Spain	scallop shell
St Patrick of Ireland	shamrock and snakes

Seven Fathers of the Church

St Athanasius
St Gregory of Nazianzen
St John Chrysostom
St John of Damascus
St Basil of Caesarea
St Gregory of Nyssa
St Cyril of Alexandria

Popes

Reign	Pope
until c. 64	Peter
c. 64–c. 76	Linus
c. 76–c. 90	Anacletus
c. 90–c. 99	Clement I
c. 99–c. 105	Evaristus
c. 105–c. 117	Alexander I
c. 117–c. 127	Sixtus I
c. 127–c. 137	Telesphorus
c. 137–c. 140	Hyginus
c. 140–c. 154	Pius I
c. 154–c. 166	Anicetus
c. 166–c. 175	Soter
175–89	Eleutherius
189–98	Victor I
198–217	Zephyrinus
217–22	Callistus I
217–c. 235	Hippolytus (Antipope)
222–30	Urban I
230–35	Pontian
235–6	Anterus
236–50	Fabian
251–3	Cornelius
251–c. 258	Novatian (Antipope)
253–4	Lucius I
254–7	Stephen I
257–8	Sixtus II
259–68	Dionysius
269–74	Felix I
275–83	Eutychianus
283–96	Caius
296–304	Marcellinus
308–9	Marcellus I
310	Eusebius
311–14	Miltiades

314–35	Sylvester I
336	Mark
337–52	Julius I
352–66	Liberius
355–65	Felix II (Antipope)
366–84	Damasus I
366–7	Ursinus
384–99	Siricius
399–401	Anastasius I
402–17	Innocent I
417–18	Zosimus
418–22	Boniface I
418–19	Eulalius (Antipope)
422–32	Celestine I
432–40	Sixtus III
440–61	Leo I
461–8	Hilarus
468–83	Simplicius
483–92	Felix III (II)
492–6	Gelasius I
496–8	Anastasius II
498–514	Symmachus
498, 501–5	Laurentius (Antipope)
514–23	Hormisdas
523–6	John I
526–30	Felix IV (III)
530–2	Boniface II
530	Dioscorus (Antipope)
533–5	John II
535–6	Agapetus I
536–7	Silverius
537–55	Vigilius
556–61	Pelagius I
561–74	John III
575–9	Benedict I
579–90	Pelagius II
590–604	Gregory I
604–6	Sabinianus
607	Boniface III
608–15	Boniface IV
615–18	Deusdedit/Adeodatus I
619–25	Boniface V
625–38	Honorius I
640	Severinus
640–2	John IV
642–9	Theodore I
649–55	Martin I
654–7	Eugenius I
657–72	Vitalian
672–6	Adeodatus II
676–8	Donus

Reign	Pope
678–81	Agatho
682–3	Leo II
684–5	Benedict II
685–6	John V
686–7	Cono
687	Theodore (Antipope)
687–92	Paschal (Antipope)
687–701	Sergius I
701–5	John VI
706–7	John VII
708	Sisinnius
708–15	Constantine
715–31	Gregory II
731–41	Gregory III
741–52	Zacharias
752	Stephen II (unconsecrated)
752–7	Stephen II (III)
757–67	Paul I
767–9	Constantine II (Antipope)
768	Philip (Antipope)
768–72	Stephen III (IV)
772–95	Hadrian I
795–816	Leo III
816–17	Stephen IV (V)
817–24	Paschal I
824–7	Eugenius II
827	Valentine
827–44	Gregory IV
844	John (Antipope)
844–7	Sergius II
847–55	Leo IV
855–8	Benedict III
855	Anastasius Bibliothecarius (Antipope)
858–67	Nicholas I
867–72	Hadrian II
872–82	John VIII
882–4	Marinus I
884–5	Hadrian III
885–91	Stephen V (VI)
891–6	Formosus
896	Boniface VI
896–7	Stephen VI (VII)
897	Romanus
897	Theodore II
898–900	John IX
900–3	Benedict IV
903	Leo V
903–4	Christopher (Antipope)
904–11	Sergius III
911–13	Anastasius III

913–14	Lando
914–28	John X
928	Leo VI
928–31	Stephen VII (VIII)
931–5	John XI
936–9	Leo VII
939–42	Stephen IX
942–6	Marinus II
946–55	Agapetus II
955–64	John XII
963–5	Leo VIII
964–6	Benedict V
965–72	John XIII
973–4	Benedict VI
974, 984–5	Boniface VII (Antipope)
974–83	Benedict VII
983–4	John XIV
985–96	John XV
996–9	Gregory V
997–8	John XVI (Antipope)
999–1003	Sylvester II
1003	John XVII
1004–9	John XVIII
1009–12	Sergius IV
1012–24	Benedict VIII
1012	Gregory (Antipope)
1024–32	John XIX
1032–44	Benedict IX
1045	Sylvester III
1045	Benedict IX
1045–6	Gregory VI
1046–7	Clement II
1047–8	Benedict IX
1048	Damasus II
1048–54	Leo IX
1055–7	Victor II
1057–8	Stephen IX (X)
1058–9	Benedict X (Antipope)
1059–61	Nicholas II
1061–73	Alexander II
1061–72	Honorius II (Antipope)
1073–85	Gregory VII
1080, 1084–1100	Clement VII (Antipope)
1086–7	Victor III
1088–99	Urban II
1099–1118	Paschal II
1100–2	Theodoric (Antipope)
1102	Albert (Antipope)
1105–11	Sylvester IV (Antipope)
1118–19	Gelasius II
1118–21	Gregory VIII (Antipope)

Reign	Pope
1119–24	Callistus II
1124–30	Honorius II
1124	Celestine II (Antipope)
1130–43	Innocent II
1130–8	Anacletus II (Antipope)
1138	Victor IV (Antipope)
1143–4	Celestine II
1144–5	Lucius II
1145–53	Eugenius III
1153–4	Anastasius IV
1154–9	Hadrian IV
1159–81	Alexander III
1159–64	Victor IV (Antipope)
1164–8	Paschal III (Antipope)
1168–78	Callistus III (Antipope)
1179–80	Innocent III (Antipope)
1181–5	Lucius III
1185–7	Urban III
1187	Gregory VIII
1187–91	Clement III
1191–8	Celestine III
1198–1216	Innocent III
1216–27	Honorius III
1227–41	Gregory IX
1241	Celestine IV
1243–54	Innocent IV
1254–61	Alexander IV
1261–4	Urban IV
1265–8	Clement IV
1271–6	Gregory X
1276	Innocent V
1276	Hadrian V
1276–7	John XXI
1277–80	Nicholas III
1281–5	Martin IV
1285–7	Honorius IV
1288–92	Nicholas IV
1294	Celestine V
1294–1303	Boniface VIII
1303–4	Benedict XI
1305–14	Clement V
1316–34	John XXII
1328–30	Nicholas V (Antipope)
1334–42	Benedict XII
1342–52	Clement VI
1352–62	Innocent VI
1352–70	Urban V
1370–8	Gregory XI
1378–89	Urban VI
1378–94	Clement VII (Antipope)

1389–1404	Boniface IX
1394–1423	Benedict XIII (Antipope)
1404–6	Innocent VII
1406–15	Gregory XII
1409–10	Alexander V (Antipope)
1410–15	John XXIII (Antipope)
1417–31	Martin V
1423–9	Clement VIII (Antipope)
1425–30	Benedict XIV (Antipope)
1431–47	Eugenius IV
1439–49	Felix V (Antipope)
1447–55	Nicholas V
1455–8	Callistus III
1458–64	Pius II
1464–71	Paul II
1471–84	Sixtus IV
1484–92	Innocent VIII
1492–1503	Alexander VI
1503	Pius III
1503–13	Julius II
1513–21	Leo X
1522–3	Hadrian VI
1523–34	Clement VII
1534–49	Paul III
1550–5	Julius III
1555	Marcellus II
1555–9	Paul IV
1559–65	Pius IV
1566–72	Pius V
1572–85	Gregory XIII
1585–90	Sixtus V
1590	Urban VII
1590–1	Gregory XIV
1591	Innocent IX
1592–1605	Clement VIII
1605	Leo XI
1605–21	Paul V
1621–3	Gregory XV
1623–44	Urban VIII
1644–55	Innocent X
1655–67	Alexander VII
1667–9	Clement IX
1670–6	Clement X
1676–89	Innocent XI
1689–91	Alexander VIII
1691–1700	Innocent XII
1700–21	Clement XI
1721–4	Innocent XIII
1724–30	Benedict XIII
1730–40	Clement XII
1740–58	Benedict XIV

Reign	Pope
1758–69	Clement XIII
1769–74	Clement XIV
1775–99	Pius VI
1800–23	Pius VII
1823–9	Leo XII
1829–30	Pius VIII
1831–46	Gregory XVI
1846–78	Pius IX
1878–1903	Leo XIII
1903–14	Pius X
1914–22	Benedict XV
1922–39	Pius XI
1939–58	Pius XII
1958–63	John XXIII
1963–78	Paul VI
1978	John Paul I
1978–	John Paul II

Note The term Antipope denotes a pontiff in rivalry with a canomically chosen pope; the two popes called Victor IV were different people; there was no Pope John XX

Archbishops of Canterbury

Period in office	Archbishop
597–604	St Augustine
604–19	Laurentius
619–24	Mellitus
624–7	Justus
627–53	Honorius
655–64	Deusdedit (Frithona)
668–90	Theodore
693–731	Beorhtweald
731–4	Tatwine
735–9	Nothelm
740–60	Cuthbert
761–4	Breguwine
765–92	Jaenbeorht
793–805	Ethelheard
805–32	Wulfred
832	Feologild
833–70	Ceolnoth
870–89	Aethelred
890–914	Plegmund
914–23	Aethelhelm
923–42	Wulfhelm
942–58	Oda
959	Aelfsige
959	Beorhthelm
960–88	St Dunstan

988–90	Aethelgar
990–4	Sigeric Serio
995–1005	Aelfric
1005–12	Aelfheah
1013–20	Lyfing
1020–38	Aethelnoth
1038–50	Eadsige
1051–2	Robert of Jumiges
1052–70	Stigand
1070–89	Lanfranc
1093–1109	Anselm
1114–22	Ralph d'Escures
1123–36	William of Corbeil
1138–61	Theobald (Tebaldus)
1162–70	Thomas Becket
1174–84	Richard of Dover
1184–90	Baldwin
1193–1205	Hubert Walter
1206–28	Stephen Langton
1229–31	Richard Le Grant
1233–40	St Edmund (Rich)
1241–70	Boniface of Savoy
1272–8	Robert Kilwardby
1279–92	John Pecham
1293–1313	Robert Winchelsey
1313–27	Walter Reynolds
1327–33	Simon Mepham
1333–48	John de Stratford
1348–9	Thomas Bradwardine
1349–66	Simon Islip
1366–8	Simon Langham
1368–74	William Whittlesey
1375–81	Simon Sudbury
1381–96	William Courtenay
1396–7	Thomas Arundel
1397–9	Roger Walden
1399–1414	Thomas Arundel
1414–43	Henry Chichele
1443–52	John Stafford
1452–4	John Kemp
1454–86	Thomas Bourgchier
1486–1500	John Morton
1501–3	Henry Deane
1504–32	William Warham
1532–55	Thomas Cranmer
1555–8	Reginald Pole
1559–75	Matthew Parker
1575–83	Edmund Grindal
1583–1604	John Whitgift
1604–10	Richard Bancroft

Period in office	Archbishop
1611–33	George Abbot
1633–45	William Laud
1645–60	(Vacant)
1660–3	William Juxon
1663–77	Gilbert Sheldon
1677–90	William Sancroft
1691–4	John Tillotson
1694–1715	Thomas Tenison
1715–37	William Wake
1737–47	John Potter
1747–57	Thomas Herring
1757–8	Matthew Hutton
1758–68	Thomas Secker
1768–83	Frederick Cornwallis
1783–1805	John Moore
1805–28	Charles Manners-Sutton
1828–48	William Howley
1848–62	John Bird Sumner
1862–8	Charles Longley
1868–82	Archibald Campbell Tait
1883–96	Edward White Benson
1896–1902	Frederick Temple
1903–28	Randall Davidson
1928–42	Cosmo Lang
1942–4	William Temple
1945–61	Geoffrey Fisher
1961–74	Michael Ramsey
1974–80	Donald Coggan
1980–91	Robert Runcie
1991–	George Carey

Archbishops of York (since the English Reformation)

Period in office	Archbishop
1531	Edward Lee
1545	Robert Holgate
1555	Nicholas Heath
1561	Thomas Young
1570	Edmund Grindal
1577	Edwin Sandys
1589	John Piers
1595	Matthew Hutton
1606	Tobias Matthew
1628	George Montaigne
1629	Samuel Harsnett
1632	Richard Neile
1641	John Williams

1660	Accepted Frewen
1664	Richard Sterne
1683	John Dolben
1688	Thomas Lamplugh
1691	John Sharp
1714	William Dawes
1724	Launcelot Blackburn
1743	Thomas Herring
1747	Matthew Hutton
1757	John Gilbert
1761	Robert Hay Drummond
1777	William Markham
1808	Edward Vernon Harcourt
1847	Thomas Musgrave
1860	Charles Longley
1862	William Thomson
1891	William Connor Magee
1891	William Maclagan
1909	Cosmo Lang
1929	William Temple
1942	Cyril Garbett
1956	Michael Ramsey
1961	Donald Coggan
1975	Stuart Blanch
1983	John Habgood
1995	David Hope

Holy orders

Major orders
Bishop

Priest

Deacon

Sub-deacon (Roman Catholic only)

Minor orders (Roman Catholic only)
Porter/Doorkeeper

Lector/Reader

Exorcist

Acolyte

Templeton Prize for Progress in Religion

Year	Recipient
1973	Mother Teresa of Calcutta (India)
1974	Brother Roger of Taizé (France)
1975	Dr Sarvepalli Radhakrishnan (India)
1976	Cardinal Leon Joseph Suenens (Belgium)
1977	Chiara Lubich (Italy)
1978	Rev Prof Thomas F. Torrance (UK)
1979	Nikkyo Niwano (Japan)
1980	Prof Ralph Wendell Burhoe (USA)
1981	Dame Cecily Saunders (UK)
1982	Rev Dr Billy Graham (USA)
1983	Alexander Solzhenitsyn (USSR)
1984	Rev Michael Bourdeaux (UK)
1985	Sir Alister Hardy (UK)
1986	Rev Dr James I. McCord (USA)
1987	Rev Prof Stanley L. Jaki (Hungary/USA)
1988	Dr Inamullah Khan (Pakistan)
1989	Very Rev Lord Macleod of Fiunary (UK) Prof Carl Friedrich von Weizsäcker (Germany)
1990	Baba Amte (India) Prof L. Charles Birch (Australia)
1991	Rt Hon Lord Jakobovits (UK)
1992	Dr Kyung-Chik Han (South Korea)
1993	Charles W. Colson (USA)
1994	Michael Novak (USA)
1995	Paul Davies (UK)
1996	William Rohl Bright (USA)
1997	Pandurang Shastri Athavale (India)
1998	Sir Sigmund Sternberg (Hungary/UK)
1999	Ian Barbour (USA)
2000	Freeman J. Dyson (USA)
2001	Arthur Peacock (UK)

Eightfold Path (Buddhism)

1	Right views
2	Right thoughts
3	Right speech
4	Right action
5	Right livelihood
6	Right effort
7	Right mindfulness
8	Right concentration

Note According to Buddhist belief, it is through following the Eightfold Path that the faithful will break free of the endless cycle of birth and death

Buddhist festivals

China

June–August	Summer Retreat
August	Festival of Hungry Ghosts
	Gautama Buddha's Birth
	Kuan-Yin

Myanmar

16–17 April	New Year
May–June	The Buddha's Birth, Enlightenment, and Death
July	The Buddha's First Sermon
	Beginning of the Rains Retreat
October	End of the Rains Retreat
November	Kathina Ceremony

Sri Lanka

13 Apr	New Year
May–June	The Buddha's Birth, Enlightenment, and Death
June–July	Establishment of Buddhism in Sri Lanka
July	The Buddha's First Sermon
July–August	Procession of the Month of Asala
September	The Buddha's First Visit to Sri Lanka
December–January	Arrival of Sanghamitta

Thailand

13–16 April	New Year
May	The Buddha's Enlightenment
May–June	The Buddha's Cremation
July–October	Rains Retreat
October	End of the Rains Retreat
November	Kathina Ceremony
	Festival of Lights
February	All Saints' Day

Tibet

February	New Year
May	The Buddha's Birth, Enlightenment, and Death
June	Dzamling Chisang
June–July	The Buddha's First Sermon
October	The Buddha's Descent from Tushita
November	Death of Tsongkhapa
January	The Conjunction of Nine Evils and the Conjunction of Ten Virtues

Dalai Lamas

1391–1475	Gedun Truppa
1475–1542	Gedun Gyatso
1543–88	Sonam Gyatso
1589–1617	Yonten Gyatso
1617–82	Ngawang Lobzang Gyatso
1683–1706	Tsang-yang Gyatso
1708–57	Kezang Gyatso
1758–1804	Jampel Gyatso
1806–15	Luntok Gyatso
1816–37	Tshultrim Gyatso
1838–56	Khedrup Gyatso
1856–75	Trinle Gyatso
1876–1933	Thupten Gyatso
1935–	Tenzin Gyatso (in exile since 1959)

Chinese festivals

Date	Festival
January/February	Chinese New Year
February/March	Lantern Festival
March/April	Ching Ming (Festival of Pure Brightness)
May/June	Dragon Boat Festival
July/August	Herd Boy and Weaving Maid
August	All Souls' Festival
September	Mid-Autumn Festival
September/October	Double Ninth Festival
November/December	Winter Solstice

Hindu gods

Agni	God of fire
Balarama	Brother of Krishna
Bhairava	Incarnation of Krishna
Brahma	God of creation
Durga	Wife of Shiva
Ganesh	Elephant-headed son of Shiva
Garuda	Bird on which Shiva flies
Hanuman	Monkey god
Indra	Storm god
Iswara	God of nature and the human soul
Kali	Goddess of destruction and evil wife of Shiva
Kalkin	Horse-headed incarnation of Vishnu
Kama	God of desire and lust

Karaiffal-Ammaiyar	Mother goddess and teacher
Karrtikeya	Six-headed god mounted on a peacock
Krishna	Incarnation of Vishnu
Kurma	Incarnation of Vishnu as a tortoise
Lakshmana	Half-brother of Rama
Lakshmi	Goddess of wealth and good fortune
Mahadevi Shakti	Supreme goddess
Mahishasuramardini	Consort of Shiva
Matsya	Incarnation of Vishnu as a fish
Nandin	Bull on which Vishnu rides
Narada	Incarnation of Vishnu
Narasimha	Incarnation of Vishnu as a man-lion
Nataraja	Aspect of Shiva as lord of dance and rhythm
Parashurama	Incarnation of Vishnu
Parvati	Good wife of Shiva
Pidari	Consort of Shiva
Pushan	God of enlightenment
Radha	Goddess of romantic love and consort of Krishna
Rama	Incarnation of Vishnu
Rudra	Terrifying aspect of Shiva
Sarasvati	Mother goddess of art, music and learning
Savitri	Creator of the true and the just
Shakti	Female symbol of power or energy
Shani	Bringer of misfortune
Shiva	God of creation and destruction
Shatrughna	Half-brother of Rama
Sita	Wife of Rama
Skanda	Created from the spilled seed of Shiva
Surya	Sun god
Uma	Gracious goddess
Vamana	Incarnation of Vishnu as a dwarf
Varaha	Incarnation of Vishnu as a boar
Virabhadra	Incarnation of Shiva
Vishnu	God of creation
Yashoda	Foster-mother of Krishna

Hindu festivals

Date	Festival
January	Makar Sankranti/Til Sankranti/Lohri, Pongal, Kumbha Mela at Prayag (every 12th year)
January–February	Vasanta Panchami/Shri Panchami/Saraswati Puja, Bhogali Bihu, Mahashivratri
20 February	Ramakrishna Utsav
February–March	Holi
March–April	Ugadi, Basoral, Rama Navami, Hanuman Jayanti
April	Vaisakhi
April–May	Akshaya Tritiya, Chittrai
May–June	Ganga Dasa-hara, Nirjala, Ekadashi, Snan-yatra

Date	Festival
June–July	Ratha-yatra/Jagannatha, Ashadhi Ekadashi/Toli Ekadashi
July–August	Teej, Naga Panchami, Raksha Bandhan/Shravana Purnima/Salono/Rakhi Purnima
August–September	Onam, Ganesha Chaturthi, Janamashtami/Krishna Jayanti
September–October	Mahalaya/Shraddha/Pitri Paksha/Kanagat, Navaratri/Durga Puja/Dassehra, Lakshmi Puja
02 October	Gandhi Jayanti
October–November	Divali/Deepavali Chhath, Karttika Ekadashi Karttika Purnima/Tripuri Purnima, Hoi, Skanda Shasti
November–December	Vaikuntha Ekadashi, Lakshmi Puja (Orissa)

Five Pillars of Islam

1	Repeating the creed
2	Daily prayer or salat
3	Giving alms
4	Fasting during the month of Ramadan
5	Completing the hajj (pilgrimage to Mecca) once in a lifetime

Note The responsibilities of the faithful under the rule of Islam

Islamic festivals

Date	Festival
1 Muharram	New Year's Day
12 Rabi I	Mawlid al-Nabi (birthday of Mohammed)
27 Rajab	Laylat al-Mi'raj (ascent of Mohammed to Heaven)
1 Ramadan	Beginning of month of daylight fasting
27 Ramadan	Laylat al-Qadr (sending of Koran to Mohammed)
1 Shawwal	'Id al-Fitr (end of Ramadan)
8–13 Dhu-I-Hijja	Annual pilgrimage ceremonies
10 Dhu-I-Hijja	'Id al-Adha (Feast of the Sacrifice)

Jewish festivals

Date	Festival
1–2 Tishri	Rosh Hashana (New Year)
3 Tishri	Tzom Gedaliahu (Fast of Gedaliah)
10 Tishri	Yom Kippur (Day of Atonement)
15–21 Tishri	Sukkot (Feast of Tabernacles)
22 Tishri	Shemini Atzeret (8th Day of the Solemn Assembly)
23 Tishri	Simchat Torah (Rejoicing of the Law)
25 Kislev–2–3 Tevet	Hanukkah (Feast of Dedication)
10 Tevet	Asara be-Tevet (Fast of 10th Tevet)
13 Adar	Taanit Esther (Fast of Esther)
14–15 Adar	Purim (Feast of Lots)

15–22 Nisan	Pesach (Passover)
5 Iyar	Israel Independence Day
6–7 Sivan	Shavuot (Feast of Weeks)
17 Tammuz	Shiva Asar be-Tammuz (Fast of 17th Tammuz)
9 Av	Tisha be-Av (Fast of 9th Av)

Chief Rabbis

1709–56	Aaron Hart
1756–64	Hart Lyon
1765–92	David Tevele Schiff
1802–42	Solomon Herschell
1845–90	Nathan Marcus Adler
1891–1911	Hermann Adler
1913–46	Joseph Herman Hertz
1948–65	Israel Brodie
1967–91	Immanuel Jakobovits
1991–	Jonathan Sacks

Five Ks (Sikhism)

1	Kesh (prohibition against cutting of the hair or beard)
2	Kanga (comb to keep the hair tidy)
3	Kara (steel bangle symbolizing one God and one truth)
4	Kirpan (dagger to fight injustice)
5	Kacchera (short trousers or breeches, symbolizing the wearer's readiness to ride into battle)

Sikh festivals

Date	Festival
March–April	Holi Mohalla
13 April	Baisakhi (founding of the Kalsa)
May–June	Martyrdom of Guru Arjan
October–November	Divali
November	Guru Nanak's Birthday
December–January	Birthday of Guru Gobind Sind, Martyrdom of Guru Tegh Bahadur

Japanese festivals

Date	Festival
1–3 January	Oshogatsu (New Year)
03 February	Setsubun
03 March	Ohinamatsuri (Doll or Girls' Festival)
05 May	Tango no Sekku (Boys' Festival)
07 July	Hoshi matsuri/Tanabata (Star Festival)
13–15 July	Obon (Buddhist All Souls)
15 November	Shichi-go-San (children's festivals)

8.3 *Folklore*

Principal knights of the Round Table

Sir Kay	Foster-brother of King Arthur
Sir Gareth	Hero who died in the rescue of Queen Guinevere
Sir Lancelot du Lac	Lover of Queen Guinevere
Sir Galahad	Son of Lancelot and purest of the knights
Sir Bors	Cousin of Lancelot and seeker of the Holy Grail
Sir Mordred	Nephew of King Arthur and the cause of his downfall
Sir Bedivere	Attendant to whom King Arthur entrusted his sword Excalibur
Sir Gawain	Nephew of King Arthur and seeker of the Holy Grail
Sir Tristan de Lyonnais	Hero whose love for Isolt ended in tragedy
Sir Perceval	Seeker of the Holy Grail
Sir Ector	Brother of Lancelot
Sir Lionel	Cousin of Lancelot and brother of Bors

Note Tradition claims that King Arthur's Round Table seated 13, in imitation of the Last Supper, but some accounts claim it could seat as many as 150

Birthstones

Month	Gemstone	Representing
January	Garnet	Constancy
February	Amethyst	Sincerity
March	Aquamarine, bloodstone	Courage
April	Diamond	Innocence, lasting love
May	Emerald	Success, hope
June	Alexandrite, moonstone, pearl	Health, purity
July	Ruby	Love, contentment
August	Peridot, sardonyx	Marital happiness
September	Sapphire	Wisdom
October	Opal, tourmaline	Hope
November	Topaz	Fidelity
December	Turquoise, zircon	Harmony

Language of flowers

Flower	Representing
Almond blossom	Sweetness, delicacy
Anemone	Withered hopes
Asphodel	Lasting regret
Aster	Afterthought
Bayleaf	Loyalty
Bluebell	Constancy
Buttercup	Ingratitude
Carnation	Marriage, eternal love
Carnation (striped)	Refusal
Chrysanthemum (red)	Declaration of love
Chrysanthemum (white)	Truth
Chrysanthemum (yellow)	Rejected love
Columbine	Deserted lovers, folly
Cornflower	Delicacy
Daffodil	Regard
Forget me not	True love
Foxglove	Insincerity
Geranium	Recalling a meeting
Heliotrope	Love and devotion
Honeysuckle	Generous and devoted affection
Hyacinth	Playfulness
Jasmine	Amiability
Lavender	Distrust
Lily (white)	Purity
Lily (yellow)	Falsehood
Marigold (French)	Jealousy
Nasturtium	Patriotism

Flower	Representing
Peony	Bashfulness, shame
Periwinkle (blue)	Recent friendship
Periwinkle (white)	Pleasant memories
Phlox	Agreement
Pink	You are always lovely
Poppy (red)	Consolation
Rose (red)	Declaration of love
Rose (white)	Unrequited love, pure love
Rose (yellow)	Jealousy
Rosemary	Remembering good times together
Sage	Domestic virtue
Snapdragon	Presumption
Snowdrop	Lasting beauty
Stocks	Hope
Sweet pea	Delicate pleasure
Tulip (red)	Declaration of love
Tulip (yellow)	Hopeless love
Veronica	Fidelity

Note The language of flowers was codified during the Victorian era, but many attributes are centuries older

Lore of numbers

Number	Represents	Attribute
One	Unity of God	Good luck
Two	Union of God and man in Christ	Harmony, balance
Three	The Trinity	Good luck (third time lucky)
Four	Number of the Evangelists	The material world (four seasons etc.)
Five	Wounds of Christ	Magic (used in spells and charms)
Six	The creative week	Creation and powers of prophecy
Seven	Gifts of the Holy Ghost/number of times Christ spoke on the Cross	Good luck and the supernatural
Eight	Number of the Beatitudes	The material aspects of existence
Nine	Number of orders of angels	Good luck and healing
Ten	Number of the Commandments	Good luck
Eleven	Number of faithful Apostles	Bad luck
Twelve	The 12 Apostles	Good luck
Thirteen	The number of Apostles after the conversion of Paul	The unluckiest number of all

Note Since ancient times odd numbers have been thought to be luckier than even numbers

Signs of the zodiac

Sign	Symbol	Season	Dates
Aries	The Ram	Spring	21 March–19 April
Taurus	The Bull		20 April–20 May
Gemini	The Twins		21 May–21 June
Cancer	The Crab	Summer	22 June–22 July
Leo	The Lion		23 July–22 August
Virgo	The Virgin		23 August–22 September
Libra	The Balance	Autumn	23 September–23 October
Scorpio	The Scorpion		24 October–21 November
Sagittarius	The Archer		22 November–21 December
Capricorn	The Goat	Winter	22 December–19 January
Aquarius	The Water Bearer		20 January–18 February
Pisces	The Fishes		19 February–20 March

9
Science and Technology

9.1 Science

Landmarks in science

Year	Discovery	Discoverer
550 BC	Pythagoras' theorem	Pythagoras
450 BC	Irrational numbers	Hipparcos
300 BC	Euclidean geometry	Euclid
1039	Operation of lenses	Ibn al-Haytham Alhazen
1543	Orbit of planets around the sun	Copernicus
1546	Earth's magnetic pole	Gerardus Mercator
1552	Eustachian tube	Bartolomeo Eustachio
1561	Fallopian tubes	Gabriello Fallopius
1576	Decimal fractions	François Viète
1581	Pendulum principle	Galileo
1610	Jupiter's satellites	Galileo
1611	Sunspots	Galileo and Christoph Scheiner
1619	Circulation of the blood	William Harvey
1621	Laws of refraction	Willibrord Snell
1642	Principles of hydraulics	Blaise Pascal
1654	Probability theory	Blaise Pascal and Pierre de Fermat
1656	Saturn's satellites	Christiaan Huygens
1662	Boyle's law	Robert Boyle
1665	Binomial theorem	Isaac Newton
1669	Phosphorus	Hennig Brand
1679	Binary mathematics	Gottfried Leibniz
1683	Bacteria	Anton van Leeuwenhoek
1687	Laws of gravity	Isaac Newton
1687	Laws of motion	Isaac Newton
1735	Linnaean classification system	Linnaeus
1746	Theory of complex numbers	Jean d'Alembert
1755	Carbon dioxide	Joseph Black
1766	Hydrogen	Henry Cavendish

1771	Electrical nerve impulses	Luigi Galvani
1772	Nitrogen	Daniel Rutherford
1774	Oxygen	Joseph Priestley
1774	Chlorine	Karl Scheele
1781	Uranus	William Herschel
1787	Charles' law	Jacques Charles
1790	Planetary nebulae	William Herschel
1796	Smallpox inoculation	Edward Jenner
1801	Infrared solar rays	William Herschel
1802	Binary stars	William Herschel
1803	Atomic theory	John Dalton
1803	Palladium	William Hyde Wollaston
1806	Potassium, sodium	Humphry Davy
1808	Gay-Lussac's law	Joseph-Louis Gay-Lussac
1811	Avogadro's hypothesis	Amedeo Avogadro
1817	Cadmium	Friedrich Strohmeyer
1819	Electromagnetism	Hans Christian Oersted
1821	Thermoelectricity	Thomas Seebeck
1822	Dinosaur fossils	Mary Ann Mantell
1825	Isolation of benzene	Michael Faraday
1827	Brownian motion	Robert Brown
1827	Ohm's law	Georg Ohm
1828	Synthesis of urea	Friedrich Wöhler
1829	Group theory	Evariste Galois
c. 1830	Proteins	Johannes Müller
1831	Electromagnetic induction	Michael Faraday
1831	Transformer	Michael Faraday
1833	Laws of electrolysis	Michael Faraday
1833	Enzymes	Anselme Payen
1834	Coriolis effect	Gustave-Gaspard Coriolis
1834	Second law of thermodynamics	Benoit-Pierre Clapeyron
1836	Pepsin	Theodor Schwann
1839	Lanthanum	Carl Mosander
1842	Anaesthetic	Crawford Long
1842	Doppler effect	Christian Doppler
1846	Neptune	Johann Galle
1846	Protoplasm	Hugo von Mohl
1846	Circulation of sap	Giovanni Battista Amici
1848	Stereochemistry	Louis Pasteur
1850	Kinetic theory of gases	Rudolf Clausius
1851	Demonstration of earth's rotation	Léon Foucault
1854	Boolean algebra	George Boole
1856	Role of microorganisms in fermentation	Louis Pasteur
1858	Evolution by natural selection	Charles Darwin
1861	Caesium	Robert Bunsen
1861	Germ theory	Louis Pasteur
1861	Rubidium	Robert Bunsen
1865	Antiseptic surgery	Joseph Lister
1866	Mendelian laws of inheritance	Gregor Mendel
1869	Periodic law for elements	Dmitri Mendeleyev
1869	DNA	Friedrich Miescher
1877	Moons of Mars	Asaph Hall

Year	Discovery	Discoverer
1880	Observation of malarial parasite	Alphonse Laveran
1880	Piezoelectric effect	Pierre Curie
1883	Isolation of diphtheria bacillus	Edwin Krebs
1883	Isolation of tuberculosis bacillus	Robert Koch
1885	Rabies vaccine	Louis Pasteur
1886	Preparation of fluorine	Henri Moissan
1886	Germanium	Clemens Winkler
1887	Production of radio waves	Heinrich Hertz
1892	Argon	William Ramsay
1894	Liquefaction of oxygen	James Dewar
1895	X-rays	Wilhelm Röntgen
1896	Radioactivity	Henri Becquerel
1897	Electromagnetism	J. J. Thomson
1898	Krypton	William Ramsay and Morris Travers
1898	Neon	William Ramsay and Morris Travers
1898	Polonium	Marie and Pierre Curie
1898	Radium	Marie and Pierre Curie
1898	First identification of a virus	Martinus Beijerinck
1898	Xenon	William Ramsay and Morris Travers
1899	Alpha particles, Beta rays	Ernest Rutherford
1900	Radon	Friedrich Dorn
1900	Blood groups	Karl Landsteiner
1902	Conditioning	Ivan Pavlov
1902	Hormones	William Bayliss and Ernest Starling
1902	Stratosphere	Léon Teisserenc
1902	Troposphere	Léon Teisserenc
1905	Special theory of relativity	Albert Einstein
1906	Third law of thermodynamics	Hermann Nernst
1909	DNA and RNA	Phoebus Levene
1910	Isolation of adrenalin	Jokichi Takamine
1911	Cosmic radiation	Victor Hess
1911	Concept of the nuclear atom	Ernest Rutherford
1911	Superconductivity	Heike Kamerlingh-Onnes
1912	Continental drift	Alfred Wegener
1912	X-ray crystallography	Max von Laue
1913	Ozone layer	Charles Fabry
1913	Isolation of Vitamin A	Elmer McCollum
1913	First antibacterial agent	Paul Ehrlich
1913	Bohr atomic model	Niels Bohr
1914	Gutenberg discontinuity	Beno Gutenberg
1914	Proton	Ernest Rutherford
1915	General theory of relativity	Albert Einstein
1916	Bacteriophages	Felix D'Herelle
1920	Growth hormone	Herbert McLean Evans and J. A. Long
1921	Isolation of insulin	Frederick Banting and J. A. Long
1923	Tuberculosis vaccine	Albert Calmette and Camille Guérin
1925	Isolation of Vitamin B	Joseph Goldberger
1925	Exclusion principle	Wolfgang Pauli
1926	Wave mechanics	Erwin Schrödinger
1928	Vitamin C	Charles Glen King and Albert Szent-Györgi

1928	Penicillin	Alexander Fleming
1929	Hubble's law	Edwin Hubble
1930	Pluto	Clyde Tombaugh
1931	Radio emissions from Milky Way	Karl Jansky
1931	Structure of Vitamin A	Paul Karrer
1932	Neutron	James Chadwick
1932	Positron	Carl Anderson
1932	Urea cycle	Hans Kreb
1932	Isolation of Vitamin C	Charles Glen King
1933	Synthesis of Vitamin C	Tadeus Reichstein
1938	Nuclear fission	Otto Han and Fritz Strassman
1940	Neptunium	Edwin McMillan and Philip Abelson
1940	Preparation of penicillin	Ernst Chain and Howard Florey
1940	Rhesus factor	Karl Landsteiner and Alexander Wiener
1947	Pi meson particle	Cecil Powell and Giuseppe Occhialini
1948	Quantum electrodynamics	Richard Feynman, Seymour Schwinger and Shin'chiro Tomonaga
1948	Big Bang theory	Ralph Alpher and George Gamow
1952	Polio vaccine	Jonas Salk
1953	Structure of DNA	Francis Crick and James Watson
1955	Composition of Vitamin B	Dorothy Hodgkin
1956	First tranquillizer	Robert Woodward
1957	Theory of superconductivity	John Bardeen, Leon Cooper and John Schrieffer
1958	Van Allen radiation belts	James Van Allen
1960	Messenger RNA	Sydney Brenner and François Jacob
1963	Quark	Murray Gell-Mann and George Zweig
1963	Quasar	Maarten Schmidt
1967	Electroweak unification theory	Sheldon Lee Glashow, Abdus Salam and Steven Weinberg
1967	Pulsar	Jocelyn Bell Burnell
1969	Structure of insulin	Dorothy Hodgkin
1972	Quantum chromodynamics	Murray Gell-Mann
1975	Endorphins	John Hughes
1975	Monoclonal antibodies	César Milstein and George Köhler
1985	Fullerines	Harold Kroto and David Walton
1990	18th moon of Saturn	Mark Showalter
1997	Cloning of 'Dolly' the sheep	Roslin Institute
2000	Completion of mapping of human genetic code	Human Genome Project and Celera Genomics

Fields of scientific study

Field	Subject
Acoustics	Sound and sound waves
Actinobiology	The effects of radiation upon living organisms
Aerodynamics	The dynamics of gases
Aerology	The atmosphere
Aeronautics	Aerial locomotion
Aerothermodynamics	The exchange of heat between solids and gases

Field	Subject
Aetiology	Causes of disease
Algology	Algae
Angiology	Blood and lymph vascular systems
Astronautics	Space flight
Astronomy	Celestial objects and the universe
Astrophysics	The physical and chemical properties of celestial bodies
Autoecology	The ecology of species
Autonomics	Self-regulating systems
Autoradiography	The distribution of radioactivity in living substances
Bacteriology	Bacteria
Ballistics	The flight dynamics of projectiles
Balneology	The therapeutic value of baths and bathing
Biolclimatology	The effects of climate upon living organisms
Biology	Living organisms
Biometeorology	The effects of atmospheric conditions on living organisms
Biophysics	The physics of biological processes
Biosystematics	The evolution of organisms in relation to their taxonomic classification
Biotechnology	The use of living organisms in industrial or commercial processes
Botany	Plants
Bronchography	Radiological examination of the bronchial tubes
Cardiology	The heart
Chemistry	The composition and properties of substances
Chromatics	Colours
Cladistics	The classification of organisms through shared characteristics
Climatology	Climate
Cosmology	The universe
Cryogenics	The effect of low temperatures upon materials
Crystallography	Crystals
Cybernetics	Control and communications in electronic and mechanical systems
Cytogenetics	The relationship between the structure of chromosomes and heredity
Cytology	The structure and function of cells
Dendrochronology	The use of tree rings for dating purposes
Dermatology	The skin and skin diseases
Dynamics	The relationship between force and motion
Ecology	The relationship between living organisms and the environment
Econometrics	Statistics relating to economics
Ecophysiology	The adaptation of living organisms to the environment
Electrocardiography	Electric currents produced by cardiac muscular activity
Electrokinetics	Electric charges in motion
Electromagnetics	Magnetism and electric currents
Electromyography	Electric currents produced by bodily movement
Electronics	The development, behaviour and applications of electronic devices and circuits
Electrophysiology	Electrical phenomena associated with living organisms
Electrostatics	Static electricity
Embryology	The formation and development of embryos

Endocrinology	Internal secretory glands
Energetics	Energy produced by physical and chemical changes
Entomology	Insects
Epidemiology	Epidemic diseases
Epistemics	Knowledge and information processing in humans
Ergonomics	The relationship between workers and their environment
Ethology	Animal behaviour
Eugenics	The application of genetics to human populations
Exobiology	The possibility of life elsewhere in the universe
Fluidics	Liquid flow
Fractography	Fractures in metal surfaces
Genecology	Genetic explanations of plant and animal distribution
Genetics	Heredity
Geochronology	The dating of events in the earth's history through geology
Geology	The physical properties of the earth
Geophysics	Physical properties of the earth
Gerontology	The processes of ageing
Gynaecology	Diseases of women's reproductive organs
Histology	Structure of tissues in organisms
Horology	Time measurement and timepieces
Hydraulics	The flow of fluids
Hydrodynamics	Motion in fluids
Hydrogeology	Geological study of water on earth
Hydrography	The study of seas, rivers and lakes
Hydrology	The study of water on the earth's surface
Hydroponics	Growing plants without soil
Hydrostatics	The mechanical properties and behaviour of static fluids
Immunology	Study of the body's immunity
Kinematics	The motion of bodies
Kinetics	The rates of chemical and biological reactions
Laryngology	Diseases of the larynx and the upper respiratory tract
Limnology	The study of lakes
Lithology	The systematic description of rocks
Magnetohydrodynamics	The behaviour of conducting fluids in magnetic fields
Magnetostatics	Steady-state magnetic fields
Malacology	Molluscs
Mathematics	The study of number, quantity, shape and space and their interrelationships through specialized notation
Mechanics	The study of forces associated with the equilibrium or motion of bodies
Metallography	The study of metals and their alloys
Meteorology	Study of the weather and climate
Metrology	Weights and measures
Micropalaeontology	Microfossils
Mineralogy	Minerals
Morphology	The structure and forms of organisms
Mycology	Fungi
Muscles	Muscles
Neuroendocrinology	Neuroendocrine systems and neurohormones
Neurology	The nervous system
Neuropathology	Pathology of diseases of the nervous system

Field	Subject
Nosology	The classification of diseases
Nucleonics	Nuclear studies
Obstetrics	Pregnancy, labour and childbirth
Oceanography	Oceans of the world
Odontology	Teeth
Oncology	Tumours
Oölogy	Ova
Ophthalmology	The eye and eye diseases
Optics	Light
Organography	The external form of plants
Ornithology	Birds
Orthopaedics	Deformities arising from injury or disease of bones or of the joints
Osteology	Bones
Otology	The ear and diseases of the ear
Otorhinolaryngology	Diseases of the ear, nose and throat
Palaeoclimatology	Climates of the geological past
Palaeoecology	Fossil animals and plants within their environment
Palaeogeography	Geographical features of the geological past
Palaeontology	Fossil animals and plants
Palaeopathology	Disease of ancient man
Palaeozoology	Fossil animals
Palynology	Fossil spores and pollen
Parapsychology	Paranormal phenomena
Parasitology	Parasites
Pathology	The causes and nature of disease
Pedology	Soil
Petrology	Rocks
Pharmacodynamics	Drugs
Pharmacology	The action of chemicals on living systems
Phenology	Plant and animal responses to climatic conditions
Phenomenology	Psychic awareness
Phonetics	Speech and vocal acoustics
Photobiology	The effect of light upon living organisms
Phycology	Algae
Physics	The properties of matter and energy and the relationships between them
Physiography	The surface of the earth
Phytopathology	Plant diseases and parasites
Phytosociology	The association of plant species
Planetology	Planets of the solar system
Prosthetics	Artifical body parts
Proxemics	Spatial features of human social interaction
Psychodynamics	The workings of the mind
Psychometrics	The application of statistical and mathematical techniques to psychological testing
Psychopathology	Psychological disorders
Psychopharmacology	Drugs that act upon the central nervous system
Psychophysics	The psychology concerned with the relationship between physical stimuli and the psychological effects they produce

Radiobiology	The effect of radiation and radioactive materials on living matter
Radiology	The use of x-rays and radioactive substances in the diagnosis and treatment of disease
Rheology	The flow of matter
Robotics	The design and use of robots
Seismology	Earthquakes
Semeiology	Symptoms of disease
Semiotics	Communication
Serology	Serums
Sonics	Mechanical vibrations in matter
Spelaeology	The fauna and flora of caves
Statics	The forces that produce equilibrium in a system of bodies
Statistics	The collection and analysis of numerical data
Stratigraphy	The composition of rock strata
Superaerodynamics	The study of aerodynamics at very high altitudes
Symptomatology	Symptoms of disease
Synecology	Relationships between communities of plants and animals and their environment
Systematics	Biological classification and nomenclature
Tectonics	Structural features of the earth's crust
Teleology	Animal or plant structures
Teratology	Monstrosities
Thermionics	The emission of electrons from hot bodies
Thermodynamics	Heat
Topology	The properties of shapes and space that are unaffected by distortion or distance
Toxicology	The nature and effects of poisons
Urodynamics	Urine flow
Urology	Diseases and abnormalities of the urinary tract
Virology	Viruses
Zoogeography	Animal distribution
Zoology	Animals
Zootaxy	Classification of animals

9.2 *Physics*

Physical constants

Constant	Symbol	Value in SI units
Acceleration of free fall	g	9.80665 m s^{-2}
Avogadro's constant	N_A	$6.02252 \times 10^{23} \text{ mol}^{-1}$
Boltzmann's constant	$k=R/N_A$	$1.380622 \times 10^{-23} \text{ J K}^{-1}$
Electronic charge	e	$1.602192 \times 10^{-19} \text{ C}$
Electronic rest mass	m_e	$9.109558 \times 10^{-31} \text{ kg}$
Faraday's constant	F	$9.648670 \times 10^4 \text{ C mol}^{-1}$
Gas constant	R	$8.314334 \text{ J K}^{-1} \text{ mol}^{-1}$
Gravitational constant	G	$6.664 \times 10^{-11} \text{ N m}^2 \text{ kg}^{-2}$
Loschmidt's number	N_L	$2.68719 \times 10^{-25} \text{ m}^{-3}$
Neutron rest mass	m_n	$1.67492 \times 10^{-27} \text{ kg}$
Planck's constant	h	$6.626196 \times 10^{-34} \text{ J s}$
Proton rest mass	m_p	$1.672614 \times 10^{-27} \text{ kg}$
Speed of light	c	$2.99792458 \times 10^8 \text{ m s}^{-1}$
Standard atmospheric pressure	P	$1.01325 \times 10^5 \text{ Pa}$
Stefan–Boltzmann constant	S	$5.6697 \times 10^{-8} \text{ W m}^{-2} \text{ K}^{-4}$

Elementary particles

Fundamental particles

Electrons

Muons

Neutrinos

Quarks

Taus

Force particles

Gluons

Gravitons

Photons

W and Z bosons

Radiation

Radiation	Wavelength	Year discovered	Use
Gamma rays	$<3 \times 10^{-11}$ m	1902	Medical diagnosis
Infrared	$10^{-3} - 7.8 \times 10^{-7}$ m	1800	Night vision systems; intruder alarms
Microwaves	1 mm – 10 cm	1886	Microwave cooking; communications
Radio waves	>10 cm	1888	Communications
Ultraviolet	$3 \times 10^{-7} - 10^{-8}$ m	1801	Forensic science; medical treatment
Visible	$7.8 \times 10^{-7} - 3 \times 10^{-7}$ m		Eyesight
X-rays	$10^{-8} - 3 \times 10^{-11}$ m	1895	X-ray photography

Sound intensity level

Decibels	Example
0	Faintest noises
10	Quiet whisper
20	Loud whisper
40	Background conversation
50	Conversation
65	Loud conversation
70	Busy street
80	Train
90	Heavy machinery
90–100	Thunder
110–140	Jet aircraft launch
140–190	Rocket launch

Note Sounds above 130 decibels may cause pain

Nobel Prize for Physics

Year	Winner	Nationality
1901	Wilhelm Röntgen	German
1902	Hendrik Lorentz and Pieter Zeeman	Dutch/Dutch
1903	Antoine Becquerel, Pierre Curie and Marie Curie	French/French/Polish
1904	John Strutt	British
1905	Philipp von Lenard	German
1906	Joseph J. Thomson	British
1907	Albert Michelson	US
1908	Gabriel Lippmann	French
1909	Guglielmo Marconi and Karl Braun	Italian/German
1910	Johannes van der Waals	Dutch
1911	Wilhelm Wien	German

Year	Winner	Nationality
1912	Nils Dalen	Swedish
1913	Heike Kamerlingh-Onnes	Dutch
1914	Max von Laue	German
1915	William Bragg and Lawrence Bragg	British/British
1916	(No award)	
1917	Charles Barkla	British
1918	Max Planck	German
1919	Johannes Stark	German
1920	Charles Guillaume	Swiss
1921	Albert Einstein	Swiss
1922	Niels Bohr	Danish
1923	Robert Millikan	US
1924	Karl Siegbahn	Swedish
1925	James Franck and Gustav Hertz	US/German
1926	Jean Perrin	French
1927	Arthur Compton and Charles Wilson	US/British
1928	Owen Richardson	British
1929	Louis-Victor de Broglie	French
1930	Venkata Raman	Indian
1931	(No award)	
1932	Werner Heisenberg	German
1933	Erwin Schrödinger and Paul Dirac	Austrian/British
1934	(No award)	
1935	James Chadwick	British
1936	Victor Hess and Carl Anderson	Austrian/US
1937	Clinton Davisson and George Thomson	US/British
1938	Enrico Fermi	US
1939	Ernest O. Lawrence	US
1940	(No award)	
1941	(No award)	
1942	(No award)	
1943	Otto Stern	German
1944	Isidor Isaac Rabi	US
1945	Wolfgang Pauli	Austrian
1946	Percy Bridgman	US
1947	Edward Appleton	British
1948	Patrick Blackett	British
1949	Yukawa Hideki	Japanese
1950	Cecil Powell	British
1951	John Cockcroft and Ernest Walton	British/Irish
1952	Felix Bloch and Edward Purcell	US/US
1953	Frits Zernike	Dutch
1954	Max Born and Walther Bothe	German/German
1955	Willis Lamb and Polykarp Kusch	US/US
1956	William Shockley, John Bardeen and Walter Houser Brattain	US/US/US
1957	Yang Chen Ning and Lee Tsung-Dao	US/China
1958	Pavel Cherenkov, Ilya Frank and Igor Tamm	USSR/USSR/US
1959	Emilio Segrè and Owen Chamberlain	Italian/US
1960	Donald Glaser	US

1961	Robert Hofstadter and Rudolf Mössbauer	US/German
1962	Lev Landau	USSR
1963	Eugene Wigner, Maria Goeppert-Mayer and Hans Jensen	US/US/German
1964	Charles Townes, Nickolai Basov and Aleksandr Prokhorov	US/USSR/USSR
1965	Sin-Itiro Tomonaga, Julian Schwinger and Richard Feynman	Japanese/US/US
1966	Alfred Kastler	French
1967	Hans Bethe	US
1968	Luis Alvarez	US
1969	Murray Gell-Mann	US
1970	Hannes Alfvén and Louis Néel	Swedish/French
1971	Dennis Gabor	British
1972	John Bardeen, Leon Cooper and John Robert Schrieffer	US/US/US
1973	Leo Eskai, Ivar Giaver and Brian Josephson	Japanese/US/British
1974	Martin Ryle and Antony Hewish	British/British
1975	Aage Bohr, Ben Mottelson and James Rainwater	Danish/Danish/US
1976	Burton Richter and Samuel Ting	US/US
1977	Philip Anderson, Nevill Mott and John Van Vleck	US/British/US
1978	Pyotr Kapitza, Arno Penzias and Robert Wilson	USSR/German/US
1979	Sheldon Glashow, Abdus Salam and Steven Weinberg	US/Pakistani/US
1980	James W. Cronin and Val Fitch	US/US
1981	Nicolaas Bloemergen, Arthur Schawlow and Kai Siegbahn	US/US/Swedish
1982	Kenneth Wilson	US
1983	Subrahmanyan Chandrasekhar and William Fowler	US/US
1984	Carlo Rubbia and Simon van der Meer	Italian/Dutch
1985	Klaus von Klitzing	German
1986	Erns Ruska, Gerd Binnig and Heinrich Rohrer	German/German/Swiss
1987	Georg Bednorz and Alex Müller	German/Swiss
1988	Leon M. Lederman, Melvin Schwartz and Jack Steinberger	US/US/German
1989	Norman Ramsey, Hans Dehmelt and Wolfgang Paul	US/US/German
1990	Jerome Friedman, Henry Kendall and Richard Taylor	US/US/Canada
1991	Pierre-Gilles de Gennes	French
1992	Georges Charpak	Polish
1993	Joseph Taylor and Russell Hulse	US/US
1994	Bertram N. Brockhouse and Clifford G. Shull	Canada/US
1995	Frederick Reines	US
1996	Douglas Osheroff, David Lee and Robert Richardson	US/US/US
1997	Claude Cohen-Tannoudji, Steven Chu and William Phillips	French/US/US
1998	Robert B. Laughlin and Horst L. Stormer	US/US/US
1999	Gerardhus'T Hooft and Martinus J. G. Veltman	Dutch/Dutch
2000	Zhores I. Alferov, Herbert Kroemer and Jack S. Kilby	Russian/US/US

9.3 *Chemistry*

Periodic table

PERIODIC TABLE OF THE ELEMENTS

Key to Chart:
Atomic Number →
Symbol → **B**
Atomic Weight → 10.811

GROUP	1A Alkali Metals	2A Alkaline earth Metals	3B	4B	5B	6B	7B	8	8	8	1B Noble metals	2B	3A	4A	5A	6A	7A	0 Inert gases
Period 1	1 **H** 1.00797																	2 **He** 4.0026
2	3 Li 6.941	4 Be 9.0122											5 **B** 10.811	6 **C** 12.0111	7 **N** 14.0067	8 **O** 15.9994	9 **F** 18.9984	10 **Ne** 20.179
3	11 Na 22.9898	12 Mg 24.305											13 Al 26.9815	14 *Si* 28.086	15 **P** 30.9738	16 **S** 32.064	17 **Cl** 35.453	18 **Ar** 39.948
4	19 K 39.103	20 Ca 40.08	21 Sc 44.9559	22 Ti 47.90	23 V 50.942	24 Cr 51.996	25 Mn 54.938	26 Fe 55.847	27 Co 58.933	28 Ni 58.71	29 Cu 63.546	30 Zn 65.37	31 Ga 69.72	32 *Ge* 72.59	33 *As* 74.9216	34 Se 78.96	35 **Br** 79.904	36 **Kr** 83.80
5	37 Rb 85.4678	38 Sr 87.62	39 Y 88.9059	40 Zr 91.22	41 Nb 92.9064	42 Mo 95.94	43 Tc 99	44 Ru 101.07	45 Rh 102.905	46 Pd 106.4	47 Ag 107.870	48 Cd 112.40	49 In 114.82	50 Sn 118.69	51 *Sb* 121.75	52 *Te* 127.60	53 **I** 126.904	54 **Xe** 131.30
6	55 Cs 132.905	56 Ba 137.34	57 La* 138.91	72 Hf 178.49	73 Ta 180.947	74 W 183.85	75 Re 186.2	76 Os 190.09	77 Ir 192.2	78 Pt 195.09	79 Au 196.967	80 Hg 200.59	81 Tl 204.37	82 Pb 207.19	83 Bi 208.980	84 Po 210	85 **At** 210	86 **Rn** 222
7	87 Fr 223	88 Ra 226	89 Act 227															

← Transition metals →

*Lanthanides (*see* L72)

58 Ce 140.12	59 *Pr* 140.907	60 *Nd* 144.24	61 Pm 145	62 Sm 150.96	63 Eu 151.96	64 Gd 157.25	65 Tb 158.925	66 Dy 162.50	67 Ho 164.930	68 Er 167.26	69 Tm 168.934	70 Yb 173.04	71 Lu 174.97

† Actinides (*see* L3)

90 Th 232.038	91 *Pa* 231	92 *U* 238.03	93 Np 237	94 Pu 244	95 Am 243	96 Cm 247	97 Bk 247	98 Cf 251	99 Es 254	100 Fm 253	101 Md 256	102 No 254	103 Lr 257

Roman type — metals
Italic type — semiconductors
Bold type — non-metals

These designations refer to the normal materials usually at room temperature. Processes like heating or compressing can turn metals into insulators and vice versa.

Note: It may be possible by artificial methods such as bombardment by other nuclei to produce elements with atomic numbers greater than 103. However all the very heavy elements are unstable and decay spontaneously into lighter elements. Because the lifetime of such elements is short no element with an atomic number greater than Uranium (92) occurs naturally on earth.

Chemical elements

Element	Symbol	Atomic number	Atomic weight
Actinium	Ac	89	(227)
Aluminium	Al	13	26.98154
Americium	Am	95	(243)
Antimony	Sb	51	121.75
Argon	Ar	18	39.948
Arsenic	As	33	74.9216
Astatine	At	85	(210)
Barium	Ba	56	137.33
Berkelium	Bk	97	(247)
Beryllium	Be	4	9.01218
Bismuth	Bi	83	208.9804
Bohrium	Bh	107	(262)
Boron	B	5	10.811
Bromine	Br	35	79.904
Cadmium	Cd	48	112.41
Caesium	Cs	55	132.9054
Calcium	Ca	20	40.078
Californium	Cf	98	(251)
Carbon	C	6	12.011
Cerium	Ce	58	140.12
Chlorine	Cl	17	35.453
Chromium	Cr	24	51.9961
Cobalt	Co	27	58.9332
Copper	Cu	29	63.546
Curium	Cm	96	(249)
Dubnium	Db	104	(261)
Dysprosium	Dy	66	162.5
Einsteinium	Es	99	(252)
Erbium	Er	68	167.26
Europium	Eu	63	151.96
Fermium	Fm	100	(257)
Fluorine	F	9	18.998403
Francium	Fr	87	(223)
Gadolinium	Gd	64	157.25
Gallium	Ga	31	69.723
Germanium	Ge	32	72.59
Gold	Au	79	196.9665
Hafnium	Hf	72	178.49
Hahnium	Hn	108	(266)
Helium	He	2	4.002602
Holmium	Ho	67	164.9304
Hydrogen	H	1	1.00794
Indium	In	49	114.82
Iodine	I	53	126.9045
Iridium	Ir	77	192.22
Iron	Fe	26	55.847
Joliotium	Jl	105	(262)

Element	Symbol	Atomic number	Atomic weight
Krypton	Kr	36	83.8
Lanthanum	La	57	138.9055
Lawrencium	Lr	103	(260)
Lead	Pb	82	207.2
Lithium	Li	3	6.941
Lutetium	Lu	71	174.967
Magnesium	Mg	12	24.305
Manganese	Mn	25	54.938
Meitnerium	Mt	109	(268)
Mendelevium	Md	101	(258)
Mercury	Hg	80	200.59
Molybdenum	Mo	42	95.94
Neodymium	Nd	60	144.24
Neon	Ne	10	20.179
Neptunium	Np	93	(237)
Nickel	Ni	28	58.69
Niobium	Nb	41	92.9064
Nitrogen	N	7	14.0067
Nobelium	No	102	(259)
Osmium	Os	76	190.2
Oxygen	O	8	15.9994
Palladium	Pd	46	106.42
Phosphorus	P	15	30.97376
Platinum	Pt	78	195.08
Plutonium	Pu	94	(244)
Polonium	Po	84	(209)
Potassium	K	19	39.0983
Praseodymium	Pr	59	140.9077
Promethium	Pm	61	(145)
Protactinium	Pa	91	(231)
Radium	Ra	88	(226)
Radon	Rn	86	(222)
Rhenium	Re	75	186.207
Rhodium	Rh	45	102.9055
Rubidium	Rb	37	85.4678
Ruthenium	Ru	44	101.07
Rutherfordium	Rf	106	(263)
Samarium	Sm	62	150.36
Scandium	Sc	21	44.95591
Selenium	Se	34	78.96
Silicon	Si	14	28.0855
Silver	Ag	47	107.8682
Sodium	Na	11	22.98977
Strontium	Sr	38	87.62
Sulphur	S	16	32.066
Tantalum	Ta	73	180.9479
Technetium	Tc	43	(99)
Tellurium	Te	52	127.6
Terbium	Tb	65	158.9254
Thallium	Tl	81	204.383

Thorium	Th	90	232.0381
Thulium	Tm	69	168.9342
Tin	Sn	50	118.71
Titanium	Ti	22	47.88
Tungsten	W	74	183.85
Unilennium	Une	109	(266)
Unilhexium	Unh	106	(263)
Unnilpentium	Unp	105	(262)
Unnilquadium	Unq	104	(261)
Unnilseptium	Uns	107	(262)
Ununnilium	Uun	110	(271)
Unununium	Uuu	111	(272)
Uranium	U	92	238.0289
Vanadium	V	23	50.9415
Xenon	Xe	54	131.29
Ytterbium	Yb	70	173.04
Yttrium	Y	39	88.9059
Zinc	Zn	30	65.39
Zirconium	Zr	40	91.224

Note Figures in brackets indicate the most stable isotope of radioactive elements

Properties of metals

Metal	Electronegativity	Melting point (°C)	Boiling point (°C)
Aluminium	1.5	659	2 447
Barium	0.9	710	1 637
Beryllium	1.5	1 283	2 477
Caesium	0.7	29	685
Calcium	1.0	850	1 492
Chromium	1.6	2 176	2 915
Cobalt	1.8	1 768	3 150
Copper	1.9	1 356	2 855
Iron	1.8	1 812	3 160
Lead	1.8	328	1 751
Lithium	1.0	181	1 331
Magnesium	1.2	650	117
Manganese	1.5	1 517	2 314
Nickel	1.8	1 728	3 110
Potassium	0.8	63	766
Rubidium	0.8	39	701
Sodium	0.9	98	890
Strontium	1.0	770	1 367
Tin	1.8	232	2 690
Titanium	1.5	1 673	2 750
Vanadium	1.6	2 190	3 650
Zinc	1.6	693	1 181

Metals and alloys

Alloy	Constituent elements
Brass	Copper and zinc
Bronze	Copper and tin
Duralumin	Aluminium, magnesium, copper, and manganese
Solder	Tin and lead
Steel	Iron and carbon

Properties of polymers

Polymer	Uses
Polyamides	
Nylon-6,6	Ropes, electrical insulation
Nylon-6,10	Bristles for brushes, sports equipment
Nomex	Space suits, parachute cords
Polyesters and polycarbonates	
Terylene, Dacron	Photographic film, textile fibre
Lexan	Safety glass, food containers, car components
Polyethers	
Polyglycol 166	Oil-well equipment, oil and fuel hoses, urethanes and elastomers
Delrin, Celcon	Gears, pipes, pens
Phenol-based	
Bakelite	Elecrical insulators, telephones, buttons
Polymelamine formaldehyde	Laminated surfaces
Polyurethanes	
Polyurethane	Foam rubber, synthetic leather
Lycra	Clothing, expanded foam rubber, carpet underlay
Alkenes	
ABS (acrylonitrile-butadiene-styrene) polymers	Moulded articles, pipes, telephones
Polybutadiene	Footwear, toys, tyres
Neoprene	Liquid seals
Polythene	Fibres, moulded articles, toys, bottles
Butyl rubber	Waterproof clothing, tyre inner tubes
Natural rubber	Tyres
PTFE (polytetra-fluoroethene)	Nonstick kitchen utensils
Polystyrene	Moulded articles, insulation, packing material
Perspex (polymethyl methacrylate)	Windows, fibre optics
PVC (polyvinyl chloride)	Floor tiles, car-seat covers, tubing
Alkynes	
Polyethyne (polyacetylene)	Electrically conducting polymer

Inorganic

Silicone rubber	Waterproofing, seals, hoses
Carbon fibres	Canoes, aircraft, sports equipment
Polythiazyl	Semiconductors

States of matter

Property	State
Solid	
Volume	Definite
Shape	Definite
Density	High
Expansion when heated	Low
Effect of applied pressure	Very slight
Movement of particles	Very slow
Liquid	
Volume	Definite
Shape	Settles at bottom of container
Density	Medium
Expansion when heated	Medium
Effect of applied pressure	Slight decrease in volume
Movement of particles	Medium
Gas	
Volume	Variable (expands or contracts to fill container)
Shape	Takes up shape of whole container
Density	Low
Expansion when heated	High
Effect of applied pressure	Large decrease in volume
Movement of particles	Fast

pH scale

0	Acid
1	
2	
3	
4	
5	
6	
7	Neutral
8	
9	
10	
11	
12	
13	
14	Alkaline

Nobel Prize for Chemistry

Year	Winner	Nationality
1901	Jacobus van't Hoff	Dutch
1902	Emil Fischer	German
1903	Svante Arrhenius	Swedish
1904	William Ramsay	British
1905	Adolf von Baeyer	German
1906	Henri Moissan	French
1907	Eduard Buchner	German
1908	Ernest Rutherford	New Zealand
1909	Wilhelm Ostwald	German
1910	Otto Wallach	German
1911	Marie Curie	Polish
1912	Victor Grignard and Paul Sabatier	French/French
1913	Alfred Werner	Swiss
1914	Theodore Richards	US
1915	Richard Willstäter	German
1916	(No award)	
1917	(No award)	
1918	Fritz Haber	German
1919	(No award)	
1920	Walther Nernst	German
1921	Frederick Soddy	British
1922	Francis Aston	British
1923	Fritz Pregl	Austrian
1924	(No award)	
1925	Richard Zsigmondy	Austrian
1926	Theodor Svedberg	Swedish
1927	Heinrich Wieland	German
1928	Adolf Windaus	German
1929	Arthur Harden and Hans von Euler-Chelpin	British/German
1930	Hans Fischer	German
1931	Carl Bosch and Friedrich Bergius	German/German
1932	Irving Langmuir	US
1933	(No award)	
1934	Harold Urey	US
1935	Irène and Frédéric Joliot-Curie	French
1936	Peter Debye	Dutch
1937	Norman Haworth and Paul Karrer	British/Swiss
1938	Richard Kuhn	Austrian
1939	Adolf Butenandt and Leopold Ruzicka	German/Swiss
1940	(No award)	
1941	(No award)	
1942	(No award)	
1943	Georg von Hevesy	Swedish
1944	Otto Hahn	German
1945	Artturi Virtanen	Finnish
1946	James Sumner, John Northrop and Wendell Stanley	US/US/US
1947	Robert Robinson	British

1948	Arne Tiselius	Swedish
1949	William Giauque	US
1950	Otto Diels and Kurt Alder	German/German
1951	Edwin McMillan and Glenn Seaborg	US/US
1952	Archer Martin and Richard Synge	British/British
1953	Hermann Staudinger	German
1954	Linus Pauling	US
1955	Vincent Du Vigneaud	US
1956	Cyril Hinshelwood and Nikoly Semenov	British/USSR
1957	Alexander Todd	British
1958	Frederick Sanger	British
1959	Jaroslav Heyrovský	Czech
1960	Willard Libby	US
1961	Melvin Calvin	US
1962	Max Perutz and John Kendrew	British/British
1963	Karl Ziegler and Giulio Natta	German/Italian
1964	Dorothy Crowfoot Hodgkin	British
1965	Robert Woodward	US
1966	Robert Mulliken	US
1967	Manfred Eigen, Ronald Norrish and George Porter	German/British/British
1968	Lars Onsager	US
1969	Derek Barton and Odd Hassel	British/Norwegian
1970	Luis Federico Leloir	Argentinian
1971	Gerhard Herzberg	Canadian
1972	Christian Anfinsen, Stanford Moore and William Stein	US/US/US
1973	Ernst Fischer and Geoffrey Wilkinson	German/British
1974	Paul Flory	US
1975	John Cornforth and Vladimir Prelog	Australian/Yugoslavian
1976	William N. Lipscomb	US
1977	Ilya Prigogine	USSR
1978	Peter Mitchell	British
1979	Herbert Brown and Georg Wittig	US/German
1980	Paul Berg, Walter Gilbert and Frederick Sanger	US/US/British
1981	Kenichi Fukui and Roald Hoffmann	Japanese/US
1982	Aaron Klug	British
1983	Henry Taube	US
1984	Bruce Merrifield	US
1985	Herbert A. Hauptmann and Jerome Karle	US/US
1986	Dudley Herschbach, Yuan Lee and John Polanyi	US/US/Canadian
1987	Donald Cram, Jean-Marie Lehn and Charles Pedersen	US/French/US
1988	Johann Deisenhofer, Robert Huber and Hartmut Michel	German/German/German
1989	Sydney Altman and Thomas Cech	US/US
1990	Elias James Corey	US
1991	Richard R. Ernst	Swiss
1992	Rudolph A. Marcus	US
1993	Kary Mullis and Michael Smith	US/Canadian
1994	George A. Olah	US
1995	Paul Crutzen, Mario Molina and Sherwood Rowland	Dutch/US/US
1996	Harold Croto, Robert Curl and Richard Smalley	British/US/US

Year	Winner	Nationality
1997	Paul Boyer, Jens Skou and John Walker	British/Danish/British
1998	Walter Kohn and John A. Pople	Austrian/British
1999	Ahmed Zewail	Egyptian
2000	Alan J. Heyer, Alan G. MacDiarmid and Hideki Shirakawa	US/US/Japanese

9.4 *Life Sciences*

Nobel Prize for Physiology/Medicine

Year	Winner	Nationality
1901	Emil von Behring	German
1902	Ronald Ross	British
1903	Niels Finsen	Danish
1904	Ivan Pavlov	Russian
1905	Robert Koch	German
1906	Camillo Golgi and Santiago Ramón y Cajal	Italian/Spanish
1907	Charles Laveran	French
1908	Ilya Mechnikov and Paul Ehrlich	Russian/German
1909	Emil Kocher	Swiss
1910	Albrecht Kossel	German
1911	Allvar Gullstrand	Swedish
1912	Alexis Carrel	US
1913	Charles Richet	French
1914	Robert Bárány	Austrian
1915	(No award)	
1916	(No award)	
1917	(No award)	
1918	(No award)	
1919	Jules Bordet	Belgian
1920	August Krogh	Danish
1921	(No award)	
1922	Archibald Hill and Otto Meyerhof	British/German
1923	Frederick Banting and John Macleod	Canadian/British
1924	Willem Einthoven	Dutch
1925	(No award)	
1926	Johannes Fibiger	Danish
1927	Julius Wagner-Jauregg	Austrian
1928	Charles Nicolle	French
1929	Christiaan Eijkman and Frederick Hopkins	Dutch/British
1930	Karl Landsteiner	US
1931	Otto Warburg	German
1932	Charles Sherrington and Edgar Adrian	British/British

1933	Thomas Morgan	US
1934	George Whippe, George Minot and William Murphy	US/US/US
1935	Hans Spemann	German
1936	Henry Dale and Otto Leowi	British/German
1937	Albert Szent-Györgi	Hungarian
1938	Corneille Heymans	Belgian
1939	Gerhard Domagk	German
1940	(No award)	
1941	(No award)	
1942	(No award)	
1943	Carl Dam and Edward Doisy	Danish/US
1944	Joseph Erlanger and Herbert Gasser	US/US
1945	Alexander Fleming, Ernst Chain and Howard Florey	British/British/Australian
1946	Hermann Muller	US
1947	Carl Cori, Gerty Cori and Bernardo Houssay	US/US/Argentinian
1948	Paul Müller	Swiss
1949	Walter Hess and Antonio Egas Moniz	Swiss/Portuguese
1950	Edward Kendall, Tadeus Reichstein and Philip Hench	US/Polish/US
1951	Max Theiler	South African
1952	Selman Waksman	US
1953	Hans Krebs and Fritz Lipmann	British/US
1954	John Enders, Thomas Weller and Frederick Robbins	US/US/US
1955	Hugo Theorell	Swedish
1956	André Cournand, Werner Forssmann and Dickinson Richards Jr	US/German/US
1957	Daniel Bovet	Swiss
1958	George Beadle, Edward Tatum and Joshua Lederberg	US/US/US
1959	Severo Ochoa and Arthur Kornberg	US/US
1960	Macfarlane Burnet and Peter Medawar	Australia/British
1961	Georg von Békésy	US
1962	Francis Crick, James Watson and Maurice Wilkins	British/US/British
1963	John Eccles, Alan Hodgkin and Andrew Huxley	Australian/British/British
1964	Konrad Bloch and Feodor Lynen	US/German
1965	François Jacob, André Lwoff and Jacques Monod	French/French/French
1966	Peyton Rous and Charles Huggins	US/US
1967	Ragnar Granit, Haldan Hartline and George Wald	Swedish/US/US
1968	Robert Holley, Har Gobind Khorana and Marshall Nirenberg	US/US/US
1969	Max Delbruck, Alfred Hershey and Salvador Luria	US/US/US
1970	Bernard Katz, Ulf von Euler and Julius Axelrod	British/Austrian/US
1971	Earl Sutherland	US
1972	Gerald Edelman and Rodney Porter	US/British
1973	Karl von Frisch, Konrad Lorenz and Nikolaas Tinbergen	Austrian/Austrian/Dutch
1974	Albert Claude, Christian de Duve and George Palade	US/Belgian/US
1975	David Baltimore, Renato Dulbecco and Howard Temin	US/US/US
1976	Baruch Blumberg and Carleton Gajdusek	US/US
1977	Roger Guillemin, Andrew Schally and Rosalyn Yalow	US/US/US
1978	Werner Arber, Daniel Nathans and Hamilton Smith	US/US
1979	Allan Cormack and Godfrey Hounsfield	US/British
1980	Baruj Benacerraf, Jean Dausset and George Snell	US/French/US

Year	Winner	Nationality
1981	Roger Sperry, David Hubel and Torsten Wiesel	US/US/Swedish
1982	Sune Bergström, Bengt Samuelson and John Vane	Swedish/Swedish/British
1983	Barbara McClintock	US
1984	Niels Jerne, Georges Köhler and César Milstein	Danish/German/British
1985	Michael Brown and Joseph L. Goldstein	US/US
1986	Stanley Cohen and Rita Levi-Montalcini	US/Italian
1987	Susumu Tonegawa	Japanese
1988	James Black, Gertrude Elion and George Hitchings	British/US/US
1989	Michael Bishop and Harold Varmus	US/US
1990	Joseph Murray and Donnall Thomas	US/US
1991	Erwin Neher and Bert Sakmann	German/German
1992	Edmond Fisher and Edwin Krebs	US/US
1993	Phillip Sharp and Richard Roberts	US/British
1994	Alfred G. Gilman and Martin Rodbell	US/US
1995	Edward B. Lewis, Christiane Nüesslein-Volhard and Eric F. Wieschaus	US/German/US
1996	Peter Doherty and Rolf Zinkernagel	Australian/Swiss
1997	Stanley Prusiner	US
1998	Robert Furchgott, Louis J. Ignarro and Ferid Murad	US/US/US
1999	Gunter Blobel	US
2000	Arvrå Carlsson, Paul Greengard and Eric Kandel	Swedish/US/US

9.5 *Geology*

Mineral composition of rocks

Rock	Mineral component	Percentage
Amphibolite	Amphibole	50
	Biotite	5
	Magnetite	3
	Plagioclase	42
Basalt	Alkali feldspar	5
	Magnetite	5
	Olivine	5
	Plagioclase	45
	Pyroxene	40
Granite	Alkali feldspar	60
	Biotite	4
	Magnetite	1
	Plagioclase	5
	Quartz	30
Limestone	Alkali feldspar	1
	Calcite	94

	Clay minerals	1
	Magnetite	1
	Quartz	3
Sandstone	Alkali feldspar	1
	Magnetite	1
	Muscovite	1
	Quartz	97
Schist	Biotite	7
	Magnetite	3
	Muscovite	38
	Plagioclase	18
	Quartz	32
	Staurolite	2
Shale	Calcite	1
	Clay minerals	80
	Magnetite	1
	Muscovite	1
	Quartz	17

Mohs' hardness scale

Hardness	Mineral	Hardness test
1	Talc	Can be crushed by a fingernail
2	Gypsum	Can be scratched by a fingernail
3	Calcite	Can be scratched by a copper coin
4	Fluorite	Can be scratched by glass
5	Apatite	Can be scratched by a penknife
6	Orthoclase (feldspar)	Can be scratched by quartz
7	Quartz	Can be scratched by a steel file
8	Topaz	Can be scratched by corundum
9	Corundum	Can be scratched by diamond
10	Diamond	

Note Named after the German mineralogist Friedrich Mohs (1773–1839)

9.6 *Mathematics*

Fractions, decimals and percentages

Fraction	Decimal	Percentage
3/4	0.75	75
2/3	0.66667 (recurring)	66.66
1/2	0.5	50

Fraction	Decimal	Percentage
1/3	0.33333 (recurring)	33.33
1/4	0.25	25
1/5	0.2	20
1/6	0.16667 (recurring)	16.67
1/7	0.14286	14.28
1/8	0.125	12.5
1/9	0.11111 (recurring)	11.11
1/10	0.1	10
1/20	0.05	5

Multiplication table

	2	3	4	5	6	7	8	9	10	11	12	13	14	15	16	17	18	19	20
1	2	3	4	5	6	7	8	9	10	11	12	13	14	15	16	17	18	19	20
2	4	6	8	10	12	14	16	18	20	22	24	26	28	30	32	34	36	38	40
3	6	9	12	15	18	21	24	27	30	33	36	39	42	45	48	51	54	57	60
4	8	12	16	20	24	28	32	36	40	44	48	52	56	60	64	68	72	76	80
5	10	15	20	25	30	35	40	45	50	55	60	65	70	75	80	85	90	95	100
6	12	18	24	30	36	42	48	54	60	66	72	78	84	90	96	102	108	114	120
7	14	21	28	35	42	49	56	63	70	77	84	91	98	105	112	119	126	133	140
8	16	24	32	40	48	56	64	72	80	88	96	104	112	120	128	136	144	152	160
9	18	27	36	45	54	63	72	81	90	99	108	117	126	135	144	153	162	171	180
10	20	30	40	50	60	70	80	90	100	110	120	130	140	150	160	170	180	190	200
11	22	33	44	55	66	77	88	99	110	121	132	143	154	165	176	187	198	209	220
12	24	36	48	60	72	84	96	108	120	132	144	156	168	180	192	204	216	228	240
13	26	39	52	65	78	91	104	117	130	143	156	169	182	195	208	221	234	247	260
14	28	42	56	70	84	98	112	126	140	154	168	182	196	210	224	238	252	266	280
15	30	45	60	75	90	105	120	135	150	165	180	195	210	225	240	255	270	285	300
16	32	48	64	80	96	112	128	144	160	176	192	208	224	240	256	272	288	304	320
17	34	51	68	85	102	119	136	153	170	187	204	221	238	255	272	289	306	323	340
18	36	54	72	90	108	126	144	162	180	198	216	234	252	270	288	306	324	342	360
19	38	57	76	95	114	133	152	171	190	209	228	247	266	285	304	323	342	361	380
20	40	60	80	100	120	140	160	180	200	220	240	260	280	300	320	340	360	380	400

Roman numerals

Roman numeral	Number
I	1
II	2
III	3
IV/IIII	4
V	5
VI	6
VII	7
VIII	8
IX	9
X	10

XI	11
XII	12
XIII	13
XIV	14
XV	15
XVI	16
XVII	17
XVIII	18
XIX	19
XX	20
XXI	21
XXII	22
XXIII	23
XXIV	24
XXV	25
XXVI	26
XXVII	27
XXVIII	28
XXIX	29
XXX	30
XL	40
L	50
LX	60
LXX	70
LXXX	80
XC/LXXXX	90
C	100
CL	150
CC	200
CCC	300
CD/CCCC	400
D	500
DC	600
DCC	700
DCCC	800
CM	900
M	1 000
MM	2 000

Note For higher numbers, a bar over a number indicates multiplication by 1 000

Large numbers

Number	UK and Germany	USA and France
Million	1×10^6 (1 000 000)	1×10^6 (1 000 000)
Billion	1×10^{12} (1 000 000 000 000)	1×10^9 (1 000 000 000)
Trillion	1×10^{18} (1 000 000 000 000 000 000)	1×10^{12} (1 000 000 000 000)
Quadrillion	1×10^{24}	1×10^{15}
Quintillion	1×10^{30}	1×10^{18}
Sextillion	1×10^{36}	1×10^{21}
Septillion	1×10^{42}	1×10^{24}

Number	UK and Germany	USA and France
Octillion	1×10^{48}	1×10^{27}
Nonillion	1×10^{54}	1×10^{30}
Decillion	1×10^{60}	1×10^{33}
Vigintillion	1×10^{120}	1×10^{63}
Centillion	1×10^{600}	1×10^{303}

Note The US and French system is in increasing use around the world, including the UK and Germany, especially as used by statisticians and economists

Prime numbers (1–1000)

2	3	5	7	11	13	17	19	23
29	31	37	41	43	47	53	59	61
67	71	73	79	83	89	97	101	103
107	109	113	127	131	137	139	149	151
157	163	167	173	179	181	191	193	197
199	211	223	227	229	233	239	241	251
257	263	269	271	277	281	283	293	307
311	313	317	331	337	347	349	353	359
367	373	379	383	389	397	401	409	419
421	431	433	439	443	449	457	461	463
467	479	487	491	499	503	509	521	523
541	547	557	563	569	571	577	587	593
599	601	607	613	617	619	631	641	643
647	653	659	661	673	677	683	691	701
709	719	727	733	739	743	751	757	761
769	773	787	797	809	811	821	823	827
829	839	853	857	859	863	877	881	883
887	907	911	919	929	937	941	947	953
967	971	977	983	991	997			

Note A prime number is a number that is divisible only by itself or by 1

Binary numbers

Decimal number	Binary equivalent
1	1
2	10
3	11
4	100
5	101
6	110
7	111
8	1 000
9	1 001
10	1 010
11	1 011
12	1 100
13	1 101

14	1 110
15	1 111
16	10 000
17	10 001
18	10010
19	10 011
20	10 100

Squares, cubes and roots

Number	Square	Cube	Square root	Cube root
1	1	1	1	1
2	4	8	1.26	1.26
3	9	27	1.442	1.442
4	16	64	1.587	1.587
5	25	125	1.71	1.71
6	36	216	1.817	1.817
7	49	343	1.913	1.913
8	64	512	2	2
9	81	729	2.08	2.08
10	100	1 000	2.154	2.154
11	121	1 331	2.224	2.224
12	144	1 728	2.289	2.289
13	169	2 197	3.606	2.351
14	196	2 744	3.742	2.41
15	225	3 375	3.873	2.466
16	256	4 096	4	2.52
17	289	4 913	4.123	2.571
18	324	5 832	4.243	2.621
19	361	6 859	4.359	2.668
20	400	8 000	4.472	2.714

Polygons

Number of sides	Polygon
3	Triangle
4	Quadrilateral
5	Pentagon
6	Hexagon
7	Heptagon
8	Octagon
9	Nonagon
10	Decagon
12	Dodecagon

Note A polygon is a closed plane figure with three or more straight sides

Angular and circular measures

Angles

Measure	Symbol	Equivalent to
60 seconds	"	1 minute
60 minutes	'	1 degree
90 degrees	°	1 quadrant/right angle

Circles

Measure	Method of calculation
Circumference	Diameter × 3.1416
Radius	1 degree of circumference × 57.3
Area	Radius squared × 3.1416
Surface of sphere	4 × radius squared × 3.1416
Volume of sphere	4/3 × radius cubed × 0.523

Mathematical signs and symbols

Symbol	Meaning
+	Plus/positive
−	Minus/negative
±	Plus or minus
×	Multiplied by/times
÷	Divided by
=	Equals
‡, ≠	Not equal to
≡	Identical with
≢ ≢	Not identical with
≈	Approximately equal to
~	Corresponds to
:	Ratio of
<	Less than
≪	Much less than
≤	Equal to or less than
≮	Not equal to or less than
>	Greater than
≫	Much greater than
≥	Equal to or greater than
≯	Not equal to or greater than
≶	Less than or greater than
≷	Greater than or less than
∝	Proportional to
∥	Parallel to
∞	Infinity
∫	Integral sign
√	Square root
∛	Cube root
ⁿ√	n-th root
∂	Partial differentiation

Σ	Sum of
∴	Therefore
∵	Because
⇒	Implies
⇐	Implied by
⇔	Implies and is implied by
%	Per cent
°	Degree
( )	Parentheses
[ ]	Brackets
{ }	Braces

9.7 *Weights and Measures*

Metric units

Unit	Abbreviation	Equivalent to
Length		
Millimetre	mm	1/1000 metre
Centimetre	cm	10 mm
Decimetre	dm	10 cm
Metre	m	100 cm
Kilometre	km	1 000 m
Area		
Square millimetre	mm^2	1/100 cm^2
Square centimetre	cm^2	100 mm^2
Square decimetre	dm^2	100 cm^2
Square metre	m^2	10 000 cm^2
Hectare	ha	10 000 m^2
Volume		
Cubic centimetre	cm^3	1 000 mm^3
Cubic decimetre	dm^3	1 000 cm^3
Cubic metre	m^3	1 000 dm^3
Liquid volume		
Millilitre	ml	1/1 000 litre
Centilitre	cl	10 ml
Decilitre	dl	10 cl
Litre	l	1 000 ml
Hectolitre	hl	100 l
Kilolitre	kl	1 000 l

Unit	Abbreviation	Equivalent to
Weight		
Milligram	mg	1/1000 g
Centigram	cg	10 mg
Decigram	dg	10 cg
Gram	g	1 000 mg
Kilogram	kg	1 000 g
Tonne	t	1 000 kg

Imperial units

Unit	Abbreviation	Equivalent to
Length		
Inch	in	1/12 ft
Foot	ft	12 in
Yard	yd	3 ft
Mile	mi	1 760 yds
Area		
Square inch	sq in	
Square foot	sq ft	144 sq in
Square yard	sq yd	9 sq ft
Acre	acre	4 840 sq yd
Square mile	sq mi	640 acres
Volume		
Cubic inch	cu in	
Cubic foot	cu ft	1 728 cu in
Cubic yard	cu yd	27 cu ft
Liquid volume		
Pint	pt	
Quart	qt	2 pt
Gallon	gal	4 qt
Weight		
Ounce	oz	
Pound	lb	16 oz
Stone	st	14 lb
Hundredweight	cwt	8 st
Ton	t	20 cwt

SI units

Base units

Quantity	SI unit	Symbol
Amount of substance	Mole	mol
Electric current	Ampere	A
Length	Metre	m

Luminous intensity	Candela	cd
Mass	Kilogram	kg
Temperature, thermodynamic	Kelvin	K
Time	Second	s

Other units

Quantity	SI unit	Symbol
Absorbed radiation dose	Gray	Gy
Electric capacitance	Farad	F
Electric charge	Coulomb	C
Electric conductance	Siemens	S
Energy or work	Joule	J
Force	Newton	N
Frequency	Hertz	Hz
Illuminance	Lux	lx
Inductance	Henry	H
Luminous flux	Lumen	lm
Magnetic flux	Weber	Wb
Magnetic flux density	Tesla	T
Plane angle	Radian	rad
Potential difference	Volt	V
Power	Watt	W
Pressure	Pascal	Pa
Radiation dose equivalent	Sievert	Sv
Radiation exposure	Roentgen	R
Radioactivity	Becquerel	Bq
Resistance	Ohm	O
Solid angle	Steradian	sr
Sound intensity	Decibel	dB
Temperature	°Celsius	°C

SI prefixes

Factor	Prefix	Symbol
10^{18}	Exa-	E
10^{15}	Peta-	P
10^{12}	Tera-	T
10^{9}	Gig-	G
10^{6}	Mega-	M
10^{3}	Kilo-	k
10^{2}	Hecto-	h
10^{1}	Deca-	da
10^{-1}	Deci-	d
10^{-2}	Centi-	c
10^{-3}	Milli-	m
10^{-6}	Micro-	μ
10^{-9}	Nano-	n
10^{-12}	Pico-	p
10^{-15}	Femto-	f
10^{-18}	Atto-	a

Conversion factors

	Multiply by
Imperial to metric	
Length	
Inches to millimetres	25.4
Inches to centimetres	2.54
Feet to metres	0.3048
Yards to metres	0.9144
Statute miles to kilometres	1.6093
Nautical miles to kilometres	1.852
Area	
Square inches to square centimetres	6.4516
Square feet to square metres	0.0929
Square yards to square metres	0.8361
Acres to hectares	0.4047
Square miles to square kilometres	2.5899
Volume	
Cubic inches to cubic centimetres	16.3871
Cubic feet to cubic metres	0.0283
Cubic yards to cubic metres	0.7646
Capacity	
UK fluid ounces to litres	0.0284
US fluid ounces to litres	0.0296
UK pints to litres	0.5682
US pints to litres	0.4732
UK gallons to litres	4.546
US gallons to litres	3.7854
Weight	
Ounces (avoirdupois) to grams	28.3495
Ounces (troy) to grams	31.1035
Pounds to kilograms	0.4536
Tons to tonnes	1.016
Speed	
Miles per hour to kilometres per hour	1.609344
Feet per second to metres per second	0.3048
Force	
Pound-force to newton	4.44822
Kilogram-force to newton	9.80665
Pressure	
Pound-force per square inch to kilopascals	6.89476
Tons-force per square inch to megapascals	15.4443
Atmospheres to Newtons per square centimetre	10.1325
Atmospheres to pound-force per square inch	14.695942

Energy

| Calories to joules | 4.1868 |
| Watt hours to joules | 3 600 |

Power

| Horsepower to kilowatts | 0.7457 |

Metric to imperial

Length

Millimetres to inches	0.0394
Centimetres to inches	0.3937
Metres to feet	3.2806
Metres to yards	1.9036
Kilometres to statute miles	0.6214
Kilometres to nautical miles	0.54

Area

Square centimetres to square inches	0.155
Square metres to square feet	10.764
Square metres to square yards	1.196
Hectares to acres	2.471
Square kilometres to square miles	0.386

Volume

Cubic centimetres to cubic inches	0.061
Cubic metres to cubic feet	35.315
Cubic metres to cubic yards	1.308

Capacity

Litres to UK fluid ounces	35.1961
Litres to US fluid ounces	33.815
Litres to UK pints	1.7598
Litres to US pints	2.1134
Litres to UK gallons	0.2199
Litres to US gallons	0.2542

Weight

Grams to ounces (avoirdupois)	0.0353
Grams to ounces (troy)	0.0322
Kilograms to pounds	2.2046
Tonnes to tons	0.9842

Speed

| Kilometres per hour to miles per hour | 0.621371 |
| Metres per second to feet per second | 3.28084 |

Force

| Newton to pound-force | 0.224809 |
| Newton to kilogram-force | 0.101972 |

Pressure

Kilopascals to pound-force per square inch	0.145038
Megapascals to tons-force per square inch	0.064779
Newtons per square centimetre to atmospheres	0.098692
Pound-force per square inch to atmospheres	0.068948

	Multiply by
Energy	
Joules to calories	0.238846
Joules to watt hours	0.000278
Power	
Kilowatts to horsepower	1.34102

SI conversion factors

Absorbed dose

Unit	Symbol	SI equivalent
Rad	rad	0.01 Gy

Area

Unit	Symbol	SI equivalent
Acre		0.405 hm^2
Barn	b	100 fm^2
Hectare	ha	1 hm^2
Square foot	sq ft	9.290 dm^2
Square inch	sq in	6.452 cm^2
Square mile	sq mi	2.590 km^2
Square yard	sq yd	0.836 m^2

Consumption

Unit	Symbol	SI equivalent
Gallon (UK) per mile		2.825 dm^{3}km^{-1}

Dose equivalent

Unit	Symbol	SI equivalent
Rem	rem	0.01 Sv

Energy

Unit	Symbol	SI equivalent
British thermal unit	btu	1.055 kJ
Calorie	cal	4.187 J
Electronvolt	eV	0.160 aJ
Erg	erg	0.1 µJ
Therm		0.105 GJ

Exposure

Unit	Symbol	SI equivalent
Röntgen	R	0.258 mC kg^{-1}

Force

Unit	Symbol	SI equivalent
Dyne	dyn	10 µN
Kilogram-force	kgf	9.807 N
Pound force	lbf	4.448 N
Poundal	pdl	0.138 N
Ton-force	tonf	9.964 kN

Illuminance

Unit	Symbol	SI equivalent
Phot	ph	10 klx

Length

Unit	Symbol	SI equivalent
Ångstrom	Å	0.1 nm
Astronomical unit	AU	0.150 Tm
Fathom (6 ft)		1.829 m
Fermi	fm	1 fm
Foot	ft	30.48 cm
Inch	in	2.54 cm
Light year	ly	9.461×10^{15}
Micron	μ	1 μm
Mile (nautical)		1.852 km
Mile (statute)		1.609 km
Parsec	pc	30 857 Tm
X unit		0.100 pm
Yard	yd	0.914 m

Luminance

Unit	Symbol	SI equivalent
Stilb	sb	10 kcd m^{-2}

Magnetic field strength

Unit	Symbol	SI equivalent
Oersted	Oe	1/(4p) kA m^{-1}

Magnetic flux

Unit	Symbol	SI equivalent
Maxwell	Mx	10 nWb

Magnetic flux density

Unit	Symbol	SI equivalent
Gauss	Gs (or G)	100 μT

Mass

Unit	Symbol	SI equivalent
Atomic mass unit	amu	1.661×10^{-27} kg
Grain	gr	0.065 g
Metric carat		0.2 g
Ounce (avoirdupois)	oz	28.349 g
Ounce (troy)		31.103 g
Pound	lb	0.454 kg
Slug		14.594 kg
Solar mass	M	1.989×10^{30}
Ton (2240 lbs)		1.016 Mg
Tonne	t	1 Mg

Plane angle

Unit	Symbol	SI equivalent
Degree	°	p/180 rad
Grade	rt angle	p/200 rad
Minute	′	p/10 800 rad
Second	″	p/648 mrad

Power

Unit	Symbol	SI equivalent
Horsepower	hp	0.746 kW

Pressure

Unit	Symbol	SI equivalent
Bar	bar	0.1 Mpa
Pound force/in		6.895 kPa
Pounds per square inch	psi	6.895×10^3 kPa
Standard atmosphere	atm	0.101 Mpa
Ton-force/sq in		15.444 Mpa
Torr, or mmHg	torr	0.133 kPa

Radioactivity

Unit	Symbol	SI equivalent
Curie	Ci	37 GBq

Temperature

Unit	Symbol	SI equivalent
Degree Celsius	°C	1 K
Degree Centigrade	°C	1 K
Degree Fahrenheit	°F	5/9 K
Degree Rankine	°R	5/9 K

Velocity

Unit	Symbol	SI equivalent
Foot per second	ft s^{-1}	0.305 m s^{-1}/1.097 km h^{-1}
Knot		1.852 km h^{-1}
Mach number	Ma	1193.3 km h^{-1}
Miles per hour	mph (or mile h^{-1})	1.609 km h^{-1}

Viscosity

Unit	Symbol	SI equivalent
Poise	P	0.1 Pa s
Stokes	St	1 cm^2 s^{-1}

Volume

Unit	Symbol	SI equivalent
Barrel (US)	bbl	0.159 m^3
Cubic foot	cu ft	0.028 m^3
Cubic inch	cu in	16.387 cm^3
Cubic yard	cu yd	0.765 m^3
Gallon (UK)	gal	4.546 dm^3
Gallon (US)	gal	3.785 dm^3
Litre	l	1 dm^3
Pint (UK)	pt	0.568 dm^3
Stere	st	1 m^3

Temperature scales

Celsius (°C)	Fahrenheit (°F)
−15	5
−10	14
−5	23
zero	32
5	41
10	50
15	59
20	68
25	77
30	86
35	95
40	104
45	113
50	122
55	131
60	140
65	149
70	158
75	167
80	176
85	185
90	194
95	203
100	212

Note Temperature °F = temperature °C × 1.8 + 32; temperature °C = temperature °F −32 ÷ 1.8

Oven temperatures

Gas mark	Electricity (°Celsius)	Electricity (°Fahrenheit)
½	120	250
1	140	275
2	150	300
3	170	325
4	180	350
5	190	375
6	200	400
7	220	425
8	230	450
9	260	500

Nautical measures

Knots	Miles per hour
1	1.1515
2	2.3030
3	3.4545
4	4.6060
5	5.7575
6	6.9090
7	8.0606
8	9.2121
9	10.3636
10	11.5151
15	17.2727
20	23.0303
25	28.7878
30	34.5454
35	40.3030
40	46.0606

Bottle sizes

Bottle	Capacity
Standard wine bottle	75 cl (27 fl oz)
Flagon	1.13 l (2 pints)
Magnum	1.5 l (2 standard bottles)
Jeroboam	3 l (4 standard bottles)
Rehoboam	4.5 l (6 standard bottles)
Methuselah	6 l (8 standard bottles)
Salmanazar	9 l (16 standard bottles)
Balthazar	12 l (16 standard bottles)
Nebuchadnezzar	15 l (20 standard bottles)

International paper sizes

Classic series

Large post	419 × 533 mm (16½ × 21 in)
Demy	444 × 572 mm (17½ × 22½ in)
Medium	457 × 584 mm (18 × 23 in)
Royal	508 × 635 mm (20 × 25 in)
Double crown	508 × 762 mm (20 × 30 in)

A series (books, magazines, stationery)

A0	841 × 1189 mm (33⅛ × 46¾ in)
A1	594 × 841 mm (23⅜ × 33⅛ in)
A2	420 × 594 mm (16½ × 23⅜ in)
A3	297 × 420 mm (11¾ × 16½ in)

A4	210 × 297 mm (8¼ × 11¾ in)
A5	148 × 210 mm (5⅞ × 8¼ in)

B series (posters etc.)

B0	1 414 × 1 000 mm (55⅝ × 39⅜ in)
B1	1 000 × 707 mm (39⅜ × 27⅞ in)
B2	707 × 500 mm (27⅞ × 19⅝ in)
B3	500 × 353 mm (19⅝ × 13⅞ in)
B4	353 × 250 mm (13⅞ × 9⅞ in)
B5	250 × 176 mm (9⅞ × 7 in)

C series (envelopes)

C4	324 × 229 mm (12¾ × 9 in)
C5	229 × 162 mm (9 × 6⅜ in)
C6	162 × 114 mm (6⅜ × 3¼ in)
DL	220 × 110 mm (8⅝ × 4⅜ in)

International clothing sizes

Men

Shirts

UK	Europe	USA
12	30–31	12
12½	32	12½
13	33	13
13½	34–35	13½
14	36	14
14½	37	14½
15	38	15
15½	39–40	15½
16	41	16
16½	42	16½
17	43	17
17½	44–45	17½

Shoes

6½	39	7
7	40	7½
7½	41	8
8	42	8½
8½	43	9
9	43	9½
9½	44	10
10	44	10½
10½	45	11

Socks

9	38–39	9
10	39–40	10
10½	40–41	10½
11	41–42	11
11½	42–43	11½

Suits

36	46	36
38	48	38
40	50	40
42	52	42
44	54	44
46	56	46

Women

Clothing

8	36	6
10	38	8
12	40	10
14	42	12
16	44	14
18	46	16
20	48	18
22	50	20
24	52	22

Shoes

4	37	5½
4½	37	6
5	38	6½
5½	38	7
6	39	7½
6½	39	8
7	40	8½
7½	40	9
8	41	9½

9.8 *Engineering and Invention*

Major inventions

Year	Invention	Inventor/Place of invention
c. 3500 BC	Writing	Ancient Sumeria
2500 BC	Ink	China
1500 BC	Glassmaking	Mesopotamia
650 BC	Coinage	Asia Minor
600 BC	Sewers	Rome
400 BC	Kite	China
285 BC	Lighthouse	Pharos, Alexandria

Year	Invention	Inventor/Place of invention
221 BC	Gunpowder	China
133 BC	Concrete	Rome
644	Windmill	Persians
800	Printing	China/Japan
1250	Magnifying glass	Roger Bacon
1269	Compass	Petrus Peregrinus de Maricourt
1281	Spectacles	Salvino degli Armati and Alessandro della Spina
1447	Printing (moveable type)	Johannes Gensfleisch zur Laden zum Gutenberg
1498	Toothbrush	China
1520	Rifle barrel	August Kotter
1540	Pistol	Camillo Vettelli
1560	Camera obscura	Giovanna Battista della Porta
1589	Flush toilet	Sir John Harington
1590	Compound microscope	Hans and Zacharias Janssen
1608	Telescope	Hans Lippershey
1638	Micrometer	William Gascoigne
1643	Barometer	Evangelista Torricelli
1644	Anemometer	Robert Hooke
1662	Spirit level	Jean de Melchisedech Thevenot
1672	Reflecting telescope	Isaac Newton
1680	Pressure cooker	Denis Papin
1698	Steam pump	Thomas Savery
1714	Mercury thermometer	Gabriel Fahrenheit
c. 1741	Centigrade scale	Anders Celsius
1752	Lightning conductor	Benjamin Franklin
1757	Sextant	Captain John Campbell
1764	Spinning jenny	Thomas Higgs and James Hargreaves
1768	Spinning frame	Richard Arkwright
1774	Electric telegraph	Georges Louis Lesage
1775	Tram	John Outram
1776	Submarine	David Bushnell
1779	Spinning mule	Samuel Crompton
1783	Balloon	Joseph and Etienne Montgolfier
1787	Theodolite	Jesse Ramsden
1790	Wristwatch	Henri-Louis Jaquet Droz and Leschot
1792	Cotton gin	Eli Whitney
1797	Parachute	André Jacques Garnerin
c. 1799	Electric battery	Alessandro Volta and Luigi Galvani
1804	Steam railway locomotive	Richard Trevithick
1808	Typewriter	Pelegrino Turri
1816	Canning	Nicolas Appert
1823	Miners' safey lamp	Sir Humphry Davy
1826	Waterproof rubber	Charles Macintosh
1828	Photography (on metal)	Joseph Niepce
1831	Microphone	Charles Wheatstone
1835	Electric generator	Michael Faraday
1835	Revolver	Samuel Colt
1838	Computer	Charles Babbage
1839	Photography (on paper)	William Henry Fox Talbot

Year	Invention	Inventor/Place of invention
1845	Bicycle	Kirkpatrick Macmillan
1846	Hydraulic crane	W. G. Armstrong
1855	Sewing machine	Elias Howe
1861	Steel production	Henry Bessemer
1862	Colour photography	James Clerk Maxwell
1866	Refrigerator	James Harrison
1867	Dynamite	Alfred Nobel
1868	Pasteurization	Louis Pasteur
1869	Traffic lights	J. P. Knight
1871	Vacuum cleaner	Ives W. McGaffey
1872	Pneumatic drill	Samuel Ingersoll
1873	Electric typewriter	Thomas Edison
1876	Barbed wire	Joseph Glidden
1877	Telephone	Alexander Graham Bell
1879	Gramophone	Thomas Edison
1882	Electric lamp	Thomas Edison
1883	Electric iron	Harry W. Seeley
1884	Automatic machine gun	Hiram Maxim
1885	Internal combustion engine	Gottlieb Daimler
1886	Petrol engine	Gottlieb Daimler
1886	Car	Karl Benz
1888	Coca-Cola	John Pemberton
1892	Pneumatic tyre	John Boyd Dunlop
1893	Escalator	Jesse Reno
1894	Zip fastener	Whitcombe L. Judson
1895	Cinematograph	Auguste and Louis Lumière
1895	X-rays	Wilhelm Konrad von Röntgen
1898	Safety razor	King C. Gillette
1900	Motor car (diesel)	Rudolf Diesel
1901	Airship	Graf Ferdinand von Zeppelin
1903	Radio	Guglielmo Marconi
1907	Aeroplane	Wilbur and Orville Wright
1911	Helicopter	Louis and Jacques Breguet
1913	Neon lighting	Georges Claude
1922	Stainless steel	Harry Brearley
1926	Radar	A. Taylor and L. Young
1933	Television	John Logie Baird
1934	Electron microscope	Max Knoll and Ernst Ruska
1937	Cat's eyes	Percy Shaw
1937	Nylon	Wallace Carruthers
1938	Jet engine	Frank Whittle
1941	Ballpoint pen	Laszlo and Georg Biro
1942	Terylene	J. R. Whinfield and J. T. Dickson
1944	Turbo-prop engine	Max Mueller
1945	Digital computer	Harvard University
1945	Microwave oven	Percy Le Baron Spencer
1947	Atom bomb	O. Frisch, N. Bohr and R. Peierls
1948	Transistor	William Shockley, John Bardeen and Walter Brattain
1954	Velcro	George de Mestral
1956	Non-stick pan	Marc Gregoire

1956	Oral contraceptive	Gregory Pincus
1959	Video recorder	Ampex Corporation
1959	Hovercraft	Christopher Cockerell
1960	Microchip	Kilby and Robert Noyce
1965	Laser	Charles Townes
1969	Word processor	IBM
1971	Concorde supersonic aircraft	Britain/France
1971	Pocket calculator	Jack St Clair Kilby, James van Tassell and Jerry D. Merryman
1976	Microprocessor	Intel Corporation
1978	Space shuttle	NASA
1979	TGV high-speed train	France
1981	Compact disc	Sony (Japan) and Philips (Netherlands)
1985	Personal computer	IBM
1986	Genetic fingerprinting	Alec Jeffreys
1987	Pocket telephone	
1992	Superconducting ceramic microchip	Sanyo Electric
1993	Pentium 64-bit processor	Intel Corporation
1998	Digital television broadcasting	

Longest bridges

Suspension spans	Location	Date completed	Length
Akashi-Kaikyo	Shikoku (Japan)	1998	1 990 m (6 529 ft)
Store Baelt East Bridge	Halsskov–Kudshoved (Denmark)	1998	1 624 m (5 328 ft)
Humber Estuary	Humberside (England)	1981	1 410 m (4 626 ft)
Jiangyin (Yangtze)	Jiangsu Province (China)	1999	1 385 m (4 544 ft)
Tsing Ma	Hong Kong (China)	1997	1 377 m (4 518 ft)
Verrazano Narrows	Brooklyn–Staten Island (USA)	1964	1 298 m (4 260 ft)
Golden Gate	San Francisco Bay (USA)	1937	1 280 m (4 200 ft)
Höga Kustan	Västernorrland (Sweden)	1997	1 210 m (3 970 ft)
Mackinac Straits	Michigan (USA)	1957	1 158 m (3 800 ft)
Minami Bisan-Seto	Honshu–Shikoku (Japan)	1988	1 100 m (3 609 ft)
Bosporus II	Istanbul (Turkey)	1988	1 089 m (3 576 ft)
Bosporus I	Istanbul (Turkey)	1973	1 074 m (3 524 ft)
George Washington	Hudson River, New York City (USA)	1973	1 067 m (3 500 ft)
Kurushima III	Japan	1931	1 030 m (3 379 ft)
Rio Niteroi	Guanabara Bay (Brazil)	1999	1 025 m (3 363 ft)
Kurushima II	Japan	1972	1 020 m (3 346 ft)
Ponte 25 de Abril (Salazar)	Lisbon (Portugal)	1999	1 013 m (3 323 ft)
Firth of Forth (road)	Edinburgh (Scotland)	1966	1 006 m (3 300 ft)
Kita Bisan-Seto	Japan	1964	990 m (3 248 ft)
Severn River	Severn Estuary (England)	1966	988 m (3 240 ft)

Note Figures refer to main spans

Longest tunnels

Tunnel	Location	Date completed	Length
Seikan	Japan	1985	54 km (33.5 mi)
Channel Tunnel	UK–France	1994	50 km (31 mi)
Moscow subway	Russia	1990	37.9 km (23.5 mi)
Chesapeake Bay	USA	1964	28 km (17.65 mi)
Dai-shimizu	Japan	1979	23 km (14 mi)
Simplon I and II	Switzerland–Italy	1906, 1922	19 km (12 mi)
Kanmon	Japan	1975	19 km (12 mi)
Apennine	Italy	1934	18 km (11 mi)
Rokko	Japan	1972	16 km (10 mi)
Mt MacDonald	Canada	1989	15 km (9.1 mi)
St Gotthard	Switzerland	1882	14 km (9 mi)
Lotschberg	Switzerland	1913	14 km (9 mi)
Hokuriku	Japan	1962	14 km (9 mi)
Mont Canis (Fréjus)	France–Italy	1871	13 km (8 mi)
Shin-Shimizu	Japan	1961	13 km (8 mi)
Aki	Japan	1975	13 km (8 mi)
Cascade	USA	1929	13 km (8 mi)
Flathead	USA	1970	13 km (8 mi)
Mont Blanc	France–Italy	1962	12 km (7.5 mi)
Keijo	Japan	1970	11 km (7 mi)

Highest dams

Dam	Location	Date completed	Length
Rogun	Tajikistan	1985	335 m (1 099 ft)
Nurek	Tajikistan	1980	300 m (984 ft)
Grand Dixence	Switzerland	1962	285 m (935 ft)
Longtan	China	under construction	285 m (935 ft)
Inguri	Georgia	1984	272 m (892 ft)
Boruca	Costa Rica	under construction	267 m (875 ft)
Vaiont	Italy	1961	265 m (869 ft)
Chicoasen	Mexico	1981	261 m (856 ft)
Tehri	India	under construction	261 m (856 ft)
Kambaratinsk	Kyrgyzstan	under construction	255 m (836 ft)
Kinshau	India	1985	253 m (830 ft)
Sayano-Shushensl	Russia	1980	245 m (804 ft)
Guavio	Colombia	1989	243 m (797 ft)
Mica	Canada	1972	242 m (794 ft)
Mihoesti	Romania	1983	242 m (794 ft)

Ertan	China	under construction	240 m (787 ft)
Mauvoisin	Switzerland	1957	237 m (778 ft)
Chivor	Colombia	1975	237 m (778 ft)
El Cajon	Honduras	1984	234 m (768 ft)
Chirkey	Russia	1977	233 m (765 ft)

Tallest structures

Tallest structures

Structure	Location	Date completed	Height
Warszawa Radio Mast	Konstantynow (Poland)	1974 (collapsed 1991)	646 m (2 120 ft)
KTHI-TV Mast	Blanchard, North Dakota (USA)	1963	629 m (2 063 ft)
CN Tower	Metro Center, Toronto (Canada)	1975	555 m (1 822 ft)
Ostankino TV Tower	Moscow (Russia)	1967	537 m (1 762 ft)

Tallest inhabited buildings

Structure	Location	Date completed	Height
Chongqing Tower	Chongqing (China)	1997	457 m (1 499 ft)
Petronas Towers I and II	Kuala Lumpur (Malaysia)	1996	451.9 m (1 482 ft)
Sears Tower	Chicago (USA)	1974	443 m (1 454 ft)
Jin Mao	Shanghai (China)	1998	420 m (1 378 ft)
World Trade Centre	New York (USA)	1972	417 m (1 368 ft)
Plaza Rakyat	Kuala Lumpur (Malaysia)	1988	382 m (1 254 ft)
Empire State Building	New York (USA)	1931	381 m (1 250 ft)
Central Plaza	Hong Kong (China)	1992	373 m (1 227 ft)
Bank of China Tower	Hong Kong (China)	1989	368 m (1 209 ft)
T and C Tower	Kaohsiung (Taiwan)	1997	347 m (1 140 ft)
Amoco Building	Chicago (USA)	1971	346 m (1 136 ft)
John Hancock Centre	Chicago (USA)	1967	343 m (1 127 ft)
Shun Hing Square	Shenzhen (China)	1996	325 m (1 066 ft)
Sky Central Plaza	Guangzhou (China)	1996	321 m (1 056 ft)
Chicago Beach Tower	Dubai	1998	321 m (1 056 ft)
Baiyoke Tower	Bangkok (Thailand)	1998	320 m (1 050 ft)

9.9 *Computers*

Programming languages

Popular name	Full name	Uses
Ada	(Named after computer pioneer Ada, Lady Lovelace)	Complex real-time applications, including control of military devices
AED	Algol Extended for Design	Computer-aided design
ALGOL	Algorithmic Language	Mathematical and scientific
APL	A Programming Language	Educational and mathematical
APT	Automatically Programmed Tools	Operation of machine tools
Assembly language		Rendering of machine code in readable form
BASIC	Beginners All-purpose Symbolic Instruction Code	Educational and microcomputers
BCPL	B Combined Programming Language	Mathematical and scientific
C		Operating systems, business, science, games
CHILL		Telecommunications
COBOL	Common Business Oriented Language	Business data processing
COGO	Co-ordinate Geometry	Geometry, civil engineering
COMAL	Common Algorithmic Language	Education
CORAL	Computer On-line Real-time Application Language	Military
FORTH		Astronomical, robotics
FORTRAN	Formula Translation	Mathematical, scientific, engineering
GPSS	General Purpose Systems Simulation	Simulation programs
Hypertalk		Web page construction
HTML	Hypertext Markup Language	Scripting language
JAVA		Internet applications
LISP	List Processing	Manipulation of mathematical and arithmetic logic, artificial intelligence
LOGO		Education for small children
Machine code		Base for running of high-level languages
ML	Meta Language	Research
MO2		Parallel computations
OCCAM		Artificial intelligence
Pascal		Education
PL1	Programming Language 1	Educational, commercial, scientific
PL/M	Programming Language for Microcomputers	Educational, commercial, scientific
PROLOG	Programming in Logic	Artificial intelligence

SIMULA	Simulation Language	Simulation programs
Smalltalk		Object-orientated language
SNOBOL	String Oriented Symbolic Language	Manipulation of textual data
SQL	Structured Query Language	Database querying

Internet abbreviations and acronyms

Abbreviation/acronym	Meaning
AFAICR	As far as I can recall
AFAICT	As far as I can tell
AIUI	As I understand it
ATM	At the moment
BBL	Be back later
BD	Big deal
BFN	Bye for now
BOHICA	Bend over here it comes again
BRB	Be right back
BTDT	Been there done that
BTW	By the way
CUL	See you later
CYA	See ya
DQM	Don't quote me
DWIM	Do what I mean
FAQ	Frequently asked question
FB	Furrowed brow
FOAF	Friend of a friend
FOC	Free of charge
FOCL	Falls off chair laughing
FUD	Fear, uncertainty and doubt
FWIW	For what it's worth
FYI	For your information
GDM8	G'day mate
GRD	Grinning, running and ducking
GR8	Great
HTH	Hope this helps
IAE	In any event
IIRC	If I recall/remember correctly
IKWYM	I know what you mean
IMHO	In my humble opinion
IMO	In my opinion
IOW	In other words
IRL	In real life
ISTM	It seems to me
ISTR	I seem to recall/remember
IYKWIM	If you know what I mean
IYSWIM	If you see what I mean
LCW	Loud, confident and wrong
LOL	Lots of luck/Laughing out loud
NAFAIK	Not as far as I know

Abbreviation/acronym	Meaning
NALOPKT	Not a lot of people know that
NIMBY	Not in my back yard
NRN	No reply necessary
NW	No way
OIC	Oh I see
OLR	Off line reader
OTOH	On the other hand
OTT	Over the top
OTTH	On the third hand
PBT	Pay back time
PIM	Personal information manager
PMFJI	Pardon me for jumping in
PMJI	Pardon me jumping in
POV	Point of view
ROTFL	Rolling on the floor laughing
RSN	Real soon now
RTM	Read the manual
SO	Significant other
SOL	Sooner or later
SOTA	State of the art
TIA	Thanks in anticipation
TIC	Tongue in cheek
TLA	Three letter abbreviation/acronym
TPTB	The powers that be
TTBOMK	To the best of my knowledge
TTFN	Ta ta for now
TTYL	Talk to you later
TYVM	Thank you very much
UKP	United Kingdom pounds
WRT	With respect to
WYSIWYG	What you see is what you get
YHM	You have mail
YKWIM	You know what I mean
YL	Young lady
YM	Young man
YMMV	Your mileage may vary

Internet smileys and emoticons

Smiley/emoticon	Meaning
:-)	Smiling
:-D	Laughing
:-o	Shock
:-(	Frowning
:'-(	Crying
;-)	Winking
X=	Fingers crossed
{}	Hugging
:*	Kissing

$-)	Greedy
:-L	Drooling
:-P	Sticking out tongue
(hmm)Ooo..:-)	Thinking happy thoughts
(hmm)Ooo..:-(	Thinking sad thoughts
X-)	I see nothing
:-X	I'll say nothing
o:-)	Angel
}:>	Devil
:=)	Little Hitler
@}-'-,-	A rose
8:)3)=	Happy girl

10
Transport, Communication and Media

10.1 Transport

Air distances between major cities

	Bangkok	Beijing	Berlin
Bangkok		2 046	5 352
Beijing	2 046		4 584
Berlin	5 352	4 584	
Cairo	4 523	4 698	1 797
Cape Town	6 300	8 044	5 961
Caracas	10 555	8 950	5 238
Chicago	8 570	6 604	4 414
Hong Kong	1 077	1 217	5 443
Honolulu	6 609	5 077	7 320
London	5 944	5 074	583
Los Angeles	7 637	6 250	5 782
Madrid	6 337	5 745	1 165
Melbourne	4 568	5 643	9 918
Mexico City	9 793	7 753	6 056
Montreal	8 338	6 519	3 740
Moscow	4 389	3 607	1 006
New York	8 669	6 844	3 979
Paris	5 877	5 120	548
Rio de Janeiro	9 994	10 768	6 209
Rome	5 494	5 063	737
San Francisco	7 931	5 918	5 672
Singapore	883	2 771	6 164
Stockholm	5 089	4 133	528
Tokyo	2 865	1 307	5 557
Vienna	5 252	4 468	326
Warsaw	5 033	4 325	322
Washington DC	18 807	6 942	4 181

Note Distances are given in statute miles

Cairo	Cape Town	Caracas	Chicago
4 523	6 300	10 555	8 570
4 698	8 044	8 950	6 604
1 797	5 961	5 238	4 414
	4 480	6 342	6 141
4 480		6 366	8 491
6 342	6 366		2 495
6 141	8 491	2 495	
5 066	7 376	10 165	7 797
8 848	11 535	6 021	4 256
2 185	5 989	4 655	3 958
7 520	9 969	3 632	1 745
2 087	5 308	4 346	4 189
8 675	6 425	9 717	9 673
7 700	8 519	2 234	1 690
5 427	7 922	2 438	745
1 803	6 279	6 177	4 987
5 619	7 803	2 120	714
1 998	5 786	4 732	4 143
6 143	3 781	2 804	5 282
1 326	5 231	5 195	4 824
7 466	10 248	3 902	1 859
5 137	6 008	11 402	9 372
2 096	6 423	5 471	4 331
5 958	9 154	8 808	6 314
1 481	5 656	5 372	4 698
1 619	5 935	5 559	4 679
5 822	7 895	2 047	596

	Hong Kong	Honolulu	London
Bangkok	1 077	6 609	5 944
Beijing	1 217	5 077	5 074
Berlin	5 443	7 320	583
Cairo	5 066	8 848	2 185
Cape Town	7 376	11 535	5 989
Caracas	10 165	6 021	4 655
Chicago	7 797	4 256	3 958
Hong Kong		5 556	5 990
Honolulu	5 556		7 240
London	5 990	7 240	
Los Angeles	7 240	2 557	5 439
Madrid	6 558	7 872	785
Melbourne	4 595	5 505	10 500
Mexico City	8 788	3 789	5 558
Montreal	7 736	4 918	3 254
Moscow	4 437	7 047	1 564
New York	8 060	4 969	3 469
Paris	5 990	7 449	214
Rio de Janeiro	11 009	8 288	5 750
Rome	5 774	8 040	895
San Francisco	6 905	2 398	5 367
Singapore	1 605	6 726	6 747
Stockholm	5 063	6 875	942
Tokyo	1 791	3 859	5 959
Vienna	5 431	7 632	771
Warsaw	5 147	7 366	905
Washington DC	8 155	4 838	3 674

Los Angeles	Madrid	Melbourne	Mexico City
7 637	6 337	4 568	9 793
6 250	5 745	5 643	7 753
5 782	1 165	9 918	6 056
7 520	2 087	8 675	7 700
9 969	5 308	6 425	8 519
3 632	4 346	9 717	2 234
1 745	4 189	9 673	1 690
7 240	6 558	4 595	8 788
2 557	7 872	5 505	3 789
5 439	785	10 500	5 558
	5 848	7 931	1 542
5 848		10 758	5 643
7 931	10 758		8 426
1 542	5 643	8 426	
2 427	3 448	10 395	2 317
6 068	2 147	8 950	6 676
2 451	3 593	10 359	2 090
5 601	655	10 430	5 725
6 330	5 045	8 226	4 764
6 326	851	9 929	6 377
347	5 803	7 856	1 887
8 767	7 080	3 759	10 327
5 454	1 653	9 630	6 012
5 470	6 706	5 062	7 035
6 108	1 128	9 790	6 320
5 922	1 427	9 598	6 337
2 300	3 792	10 180	1 885

	Montreal	Moscow	New York
Bangkok	8 338	4 389	8 669
Beijing	6 519	3 607	6 844
Berlin	3 740	1 006	3 979
Cairo	5 427	1 803	5 619
Cape Town	7 922	6 279	7 803
Caracas	2 438	6 177	2 120
Chicago	745	4 987	714
Hong Kong	7 736	4 437	8 060
Honolulu	4 918	7 047	4 969
London	3 254	1 564	3 469
Los Angeles	2 427	6 068	2 451
Madrid	3 448	2 147	3 593
Melbourne	10 395	8 950	10 359
Mexico City	2 317	6 676	2 090
Montreal		4 401	331
Moscow	4 401		4 683
New York	331	4 683	
Paris	3 432	1 554	3 636
Rio de Janeiro	5 078	7 170	4 801
Rome	4 104	1 483	4 293
San Francisco	2 543	5 885	2 572
Singapore	9 203	5 228	9 534
Stockholm	3 714	716	3 986
Tokyo	6 471	4 660	6 757
Vienna	4 009	1 043	4 234
Warsaw	4 022	721	4 270
Washington DC	489	4 876	205

Paris	Rio de Janeiro	Rome	San Francisco
5 877	9 994	5 494	7 931
5 120	10 768	5 063	5 918
548	6 209	737	5 672
1 998	6 143	1 326	7 466
5 786	3 781	5 231	10 248
4 732	2 804	5 195	3 902
4 143	5 282	4 824	1 859
5 990	11 009	5 774	6 905
7 449	8 288	8 040	2 398
214	5 750	895	5 367
5 601	6 330	6 326	347
655	5 045	851	5 803
10 430	8 226	9 929	7 856
5 725	4 764	6 377	1 887
3 432	5 078	4 104	2 543
1 554	7 170	1 483	5 885
3 636	4 801	4 293	2 572
	5 684	690	5 577
5 684		5 707	6 613
690	5 707		6 259
5 577	6 613	6 259	
6 673	9 785	6 229	8 448
1 003	6 683	1 245	5 399
6 053	11 532	6 142	5 150
645	6 127	477	5 994
852	6 455	820	5 854
3 840	4 779	4 497	2 441

	Singapore	Stockholm	Tokyo
Bangkok	883	5 089	2 865
Beijing	2 771	4 133	1 307
Berlin	6 164	528	5 557
Cairo	5 137	2 096	5 958
Cape Town	6 008	6 423	9 154
Caracas	11 402	5 471	8 808
Chicago	9 372	4 331	6 314
Hong Kong	1 605	5 063	1 791
Honolulu	6 726	6 875	3 859
London	6 747	942	5 959
Los Angeles	8 767	5 454	5 470
Madrid	7 080	1 653	6 706
Melbourne	3 759	9 630	5 062
Mexico City	10 327	6 012	7 035
Montreal	9 203	3 714	6 471
Moscow	5 228	716	4 660
New York	9 534	3 986	6 757
Paris	6 673	1 003	6 053
Rio de Janeiro	9 785	6 683	11 532
Rome	6 229	1 245	6 142
San Francisco	8 448	5 339	5 150
Singapore		5 936	3 300
Stockholm	5 936		5 053
Tokyo	3 300	5 053	
Vienna	6 035	780	5 589
Warsaw	5 843	494	5 689
Washington DC	9 662	4 183	6 791

Vienna	Warsaw	Washington DC
5 252	5 033	8 807
4 648	4 325	6 942
326	322	4 181
1 481	1 619	5 822
5 656	5 935	7 895
5 372	5 559	2 047
4 698	4 679	596
5 431	5 147	8 155
7 632	7 366	4 838
771	905	3 674
6 108	5 922	2 300
1 128	1 427	3 792
9 790	9 598	10 180
6 320	6 337	1 885
4 009	4 022	489
1 043	721	4 876
4 234	4 270	205
645	852	3 840
6 127	6 455	4 779
477	820	4 497
5 994	5 854	2 441
6 035	5 843	9 662
780	494	4 183
5 589	5 347	6 791
	347	4 438
347		4 472
4 438	4 472	

Airline designators

Code	Airline	Country
AA	American Airlines	USA
AC	Air Canada	Canada
AF	Air France	France
AH	Air Algerie	Algeria
AI	Air India	India
AJ	Air Belgium	Belgium
AK	Island Air	Belize
AM	Aeromexico	Mexico
AN	Ansett Australia	Australia
AQ	Aloha Airlines	USA
AR	Aerolineas Argentinas	Argentina
AS	Alaska Airlines	USA
AT	Royal Air Maroc	Morocco
AV	Avianca	Colombia
AY	Finnair	Finland
AZ	Al Italia	Italy
BA	British Airways	UK
BB	Sansa	Costa Rica
BD	British Midland	UK
BG	Biman Bangladesh Airlines	Bangladesh
BH	Augusta Airways	Australia
BI	Royal Brunei Airways	Brunei
BJ	Safe Air	New Zealand
BL	Pacific Airways	Vietnam
BM	Belize Air International	Belize
BO	Bouraq Indonesia Airlines	Indonesia
BP	Air Botswana	Botswana
BT	Air Baltic	Latvia
BU	Braathens SAFE	Norway
BW	BWIA International Trinidad and Tobago Airways	Trinidad and Tobago
BY	Britannia Airways	UK
CA	Air China	China
CB	Suckling Airways	UK
CI	China Airlines	Taiwan
CJ	China Northern Airlines	China
CK	Gambia Airways	Gambia
CM	COPA (Compania Panamena de Aviación)	Panama
CO	Continental Airlines	USA
CP	Canadian Airlines International	Canada
CS	Continental Micronesia	Mariana Islands
CU	Cubana	Cuba
CW	Air Marshall Islands	Marshall Islands
CX	Cathay Pacific Airways	Hong Kong
CY	Cyprus Airways	Cyprus
CZ	China Southern Airlines	China
DI	Deutsche BA	Germany
DL	Delta Airlines	USA
DO	Dominicana de Aviación	Dominican Republic

DS	Air Senegal	Senegal
DT	TAAG Angola Airways	Angola
DU	Hemus Air	Bulgaria
DX	Danair	Denmark
DY	Alymda-Democratic Yemen Airlines	Yemen Republic
EI	Aer Lingus	Ireland
EK	Emirates	United Arab Emirates
ET	Ethiopian Airlines	Ethiopia
EU	Ecuatoriana	Ecuador
EW	Eastwest Airlines	Australia
FC	Tower Air	USA
FF	Berliner Speziel Flug	Germany
FG	Ariana Afghan Airlines	Afghanistan
FI	Icelandair	Iceland
FJ	Air Pacific	Fiji
FO	Western New South Wales Airlines	Australia
FQ	Air Aruba	Aruba
FR	Ryanair (Dublin)	Ireland
FU	Air Littoral	France
GA	Garuda Indonesia	Indonesia
GC	Lina Congo	Congo
GF	Gulf Air Company	Bahrain
GH	Ghana Airlines	Ghana
GI	Air Guinée	Guinea
GL	Gronlandsfly	Greenland
GM	Air Slovakia	Slovakia
GN	Air Gabon	Gabon
GR	Aurigny Air Services	Channel Islands
GT	GB Airways	UK
GV	Riga Airlines	Latvia
GY	Guyana Airways Corporation	Guyana
HA	Hawaiian Airlines	USA
HM	Air Seychelles	Seychelles
HP	America West Airlines	USA
HV	Transavis Airlines	Netherlands
HY	Uzbekistan Airways	Uzbekistan
IB	Iberia	Spain
IC	Indian Airlines	India
IE	Solomon Airlines	Solomon Islands
IF	Great China Airlines	China
IL	Istanbul Airways	Turkey
IP	Airlines of Tasmania	Australia
IR	Iranair	Iran
IV	Air Gambia	Gambia
IY	Yemenia-Yemen Airways	Yemen
JE	Manx Airlines	Isle of Man
JG	Swedair	Sweden
JL	Japan Airlines	Japan
JM	Air Jamaica	Jamaica
JP	Adria Airways	Macedonia
JQ	Trans Jamaica Airlines	Jamaica
JU	JAT Jugoslovenski Aerotransport	Yugoslavia

Code	Airline	Country
JY	Jersey European Airways	Channel Islands
KA	Dragonair	Hong Kong
KE	Korean Air	Republic of Korea
KL	KLM Royal Dutch Airlines	Netherlands
KM	Air Malta	Malta
KP	Kiwi International Airlines	USA
KQ	Kenya Airways	Kenya
KU	Kuwait Airways	Kuwait
KV	Transkei Airways	South Africa
KX	Cayman Airways	Grand Cayman
KY	Waterwings Airways	New Zealand
LA	Lan-Chile	Chile
LC	Loganair	UK
LF	Linjeflyg	Sweden
LG	Luxair	Luxembourg
LH	Lufthansa	Germany
LJ	Sierra National Airlines	Sierra Leone
LM	ALM (Antillean Airlines)	Netherlands Antilles
LN	Jamahiriya Libyan Arab Airlines	Libya
LO	LOT Polish Airlines	Poland
LR	LACSA	Costa Rica
LT	LTU International Airways	Germany
LU	Theron Airways	South Africa
LV	Albanian Airlines	Albania
LX	Crossair	Switzerland
LY	El Al Israel Airlines	Israel
LZ	Balkan-Bulgarian Airlines	Bulgaria
MA	Malev Hungarian Airlines	Hungary
MD	Air Madagascar	Madagascar
MH	Malaysia Airlines	Malaysia
MK	Air Mauritius	Mauritius
MN	Commercial Airways	South Africa
MR	Air Mauritania	Mauritania
MS	Egyptair	Egypt
MV	Ansett WA	Australia
MX	Mexicana	Mexico
NF	Air Vanuatu	Vanuatu
NG	Lauda Air	Austria
NH	All Nippon Airways	Japan
NM	Mount Cook Airlines	New Zealand
NN	Air Martinique	Martinique
NO	Aus-Air	Australia
NQ	Orbi Georgian Airways	Georgia
NR	Norontair	Canada
NU	Southwest Airlines	Japan
NV	Northwest Territorial Airways	Canada
NW	Northwest Airlines	USA
NZ	Air New Zealand	New Zealand
OA	Olympic Airways	Greece
OB	Monarch Air	Australia
OG	Air Guadeloupe	Guadeloupe

OK	Czechoslovak Airlines	Czech Republic
OM	Air Mongol	Mongolian People's Republic
ON	Air Nauru	Republic of Nauru
OO	Sky West Airlines	USA
OR	Air Comores	Comoros
OS	Austrian Airlines	Austria
OU	Croatia Airlines	Republic of Croatia
OV	Estonian Air	Estonia
PB	Air Burundi	Burundi
PC	Fiji Air	Fiji
PH	Polynesian Airlines	Samoa
PK	Pakistan International Airlines	Pakistan
PL	Aeroperu	Peru
PR	Philippine Airlines	Philippines
PS	Ukraine International Airlines	Ukraine
PU	PLUNA (Primeras Lineas Uruguayas de Navigación Aero)	Uruguay
PV	Latvian Airlines	Latvia
PX	Air Niugini	Papua New Guinea
PY	Surinam Airways	Suriname
PZ	LAP (Lineas Aereas Paraguayas)	Paraguay
QC	Air Zaïre	Zaïre
QF	Qantas Airways	Australia
QL	Lesotho Airways	Lesotho
QM	Air Malawi	Malawi
QS	Tatra Air	Slovakia
QU	Uganda Airlines	Uganda
QV	Lao Aviation	Laos PDR
QX	Horizon Airlines	USA
QZ	Zambia Airways	Zambia
RA	Royal Nepal Airlines	Nepal
RB	Syrian Arab Airlines	Syria
RG	Varig Brazilian Airlines	Brazil
RJ	Royal Jordanian	Jordan
RK	Air Afrique	Côte d'Ivoire
RO	Tarom	Romania
RR	Royal Air Force	UK
RY	Air Rwanda	Rwanda
SA	South African Airways	South Africa
SB	Air Caledonie International	New Caledonia
SD	Sudan Airways	Sudan
SH	SAHSA (Servicio Aero de Honduras)	Honduras
SJ	SJ Southern Air	New Zealand
SK	SK SAS (Scandinavian Air)	Sweden
SN	Sabena	Belgium
SQ	Singapore Airlines	Singapore
SR	Swissair	Switzerland
SU	Aeroflot	Russia
SV	Saudia	Saudi Arabia
SW	Air Namibia	Namibia
TC	Air Tanzania	Tanzania
TE	Lithuanian Airlines	Lithuania

Code	Airline	Country
TG	Thai Airways International	Thailand
TI	Baltic International Airlines	Latvia
TK	Turkish Airlines	Turkey
TM	LAM Linhas Aereas de Moçambique	Mozambique
TN	Australian Airlines	Australia
TP	TAP Air Portugal	Portugal
TR	Transbrasil SA Linhas Aereas	Brazil
TT	Air Lithuania	Lithuania
TU	Tunis Air	Tunisia
TV	Virgin Express	Belgium
TW	TWA (Trans World Airlines)	USA
UA	United Airlines	USA
UB	Myanmar Airlines	Myanmar (Burma)
UC	Norlandair	Chile
UI	Ladeco	Iceland
UK	Air UK	UK
UL	Air Lanka	Sri Lanka
UM	Air Zimbabwe	Zimbabwe
UN	Transaero Airlines	Russia
UP	Bahamasair	Bahamas
US	US Air	USA
UY	Cameroon Airlines	Cameroon
VA	VIASA (Venezolana Internacional de Aviación)	Venezuela
VE	Avensa	Venezuela
VH	Air Burkina	Burkina Faso
VJ	Cambodia Airlines	Cambodia
VN	Vietnam Airlines	Vietnam
VO	Tyrolean Airlines	Austria
VP	VASP (Viacão Aèrea São Paulo)	Brazil
VR	Transportes Aereos de Cabo Verde	Cape Verde
VS	Virgin Atlantic Airways	UK
VT	Air Tahiti	Tahiti
VU	Air Ivoire	Côte d'Ivoire
VX	ACES (Aerlineas Centrales de Colombia)	Colombia
WG	Taiwan Airlines	Taiwan
WI	Rottnest Airbus	Australia
WJ	Labrador Airways	Canada
WN	Southwest Airways	USA
WR	Royal Tongan Airlines	Tonga
WT	Nigeria Airways	Nigeria
WX	Cityjet	Ireland
WY	Oman Air	Oman
XE	Cambodia International Airlines	Cambodia
XX	Aeronaves del Peru	Peru
YJ	National Airlines	South Africa
YK	Cyprus Turkish Airlines	Cyprus
YN	Air Creebec	Canada
YP	Aero Lloyd	Germany
YU	Dominair	Dominican Republic
YZ	Transportes Aereos da Guiné Bissau	Guinea Bissau
ZB	Monarch Airlines	UK

ZC	Royal Swazi National Airways	Swaziland
ZP	Virgin Air	Virgin Islands
ZQ	Ansett New Zealand	New Zealand
ZX	Air BC	Canada
2E	Ireland Airways	Ireland
2G	Moldavian Airways	Moldova
2J	Azerbaijan Hava Yollari	Azerbaijan
3D	Palair Macedonia	Macedonia
7E	Nepal Airways	Nepal
7Y	Albanian Airlines	Albania
8Y	Ecuato Guineana de Aviación	Equatorial Guinea
9U	Air Moldova	Republic of Moldova

Aircraft registration codes

Code	Country
AP	Pakistan
A2	Botswana
A3	Tonga
A40	Oman
A5	Bhutan
A6	United Arab Emirates
A7	Qatar
A9C	Bahrain
B	China, People's Republic of
B	China/Taiwan
C, CF	Canada
CC	Chile
CCCP	Former USSR
CN	Morocco
CP	Bolivia
CS	Portugal
CU	Cuba
CX	Uruguay
C2	Nauru
C3	Andorra
C5	The Gambia
C6	The Bahamas
C9	Mozambique
D	Germany
DQ	Fiji
D2	Angola
D4	Cape Verde Islands
D6	Comoros Islands
EC	Spain
EI	Eire
EL	Liberia
EP	Iran
ER	Moldova

Code	Country
ES	Estonia
ET	Ethiopia
EW	Belarus
EY	Tajikistan
EZ	Turkmenistan
F	France
G	Great Britain
HA	Hungary
HB	Switzerland and Lichtenstein
HC	Ecuador
HH	Haiti
HI	Dominican Republic
HK	Colombia
HL	Republic of Korea
HP	Panama
HR	Honduras
HS	Thailand
HV	The Vatican
HZ	Saudi Arabia
H4	Solomon Islands
I	Italy
JA	Japan
JY	Jordan
J2	Djibouti
J3	Grenada
J5	Guinea Bissau
J6	St Lucia
J7	Dominica
J8	St Vincent and the Grenadines
LN	Norway
LV	Argentina
LX	Luxembourg
LY	Lithuania
LZ	Bulgaria
MT	Mongolia
N	USA
OB	Peru
OD	Lebanon
OE	Austria
OH	Finland
OK	Czech Republic
OO	Belgium
OY	Denmark
P	Korea (PDR)
PH	Netherlands
PJ	Netherlands Antilles
PK	Indonesia
PP, PT	Brazil
PZ	Suriname
P2	Papua New Guinea
P4	Aruba

RA	Russia
RDPL	Laos, People's Democratic Republic
RP	Philippines
SE	Sweden
SP	Poland
ST	Sudan
SU	Egypt
SX	Greece
S2	Bangladesh
S5	Slovenia
S7	Seychelles
S9	São Tomé
TC	Turkey
TF	Iceland
TG	Guatemala
TI	Costa Rica
TJ	Cameroon
TL	Central African Republic
TN	Congo, Republic of the
TR	Gabon
TS	Tunisia
TT	Chad
TU	Côte d'Ivoire
TY	Benin
TZ	Mali
T2	Tuvalu
T3	Kiribati
T7	San Marino
UK	Uzbekistan
UR	Ukraine
VH	Australia
VN	Vietnam
VP-F	Falkland Islands
VP-LA	Anguilla
VP-LM	Montserrat
VP-LV	British Virgin Islands
VQ-T	Turks and Caicos Islands
VR-B	Bermuda
VR-C	Cayman Islands
VR-G	Gibraltar
VR-H	Hong Kong
VT	India
V2	Antigua and Barbuda
V3	Belize
V4	St Kitts and Nevis
V5	Namibia
V7	Marshall Islands
V8	Brunei
XA, XB, XC	Mexico
XT	Burkina Faso
XU	Cambodia
XV	Vietnam

Code	Country
XY	Myanmar (Burma)
YA	Afghanistan
YJ	Vanuatu
YK	Syria
YL	Latvia
YN	Nicaragua
YR	Romania
YS	El Salvador
YU	Yugoslavia
YV	Venezuela
Z	Zimbabwe
ZA	Albania
ZK	New Zealand
ZP	Paraguay
ZS	South Africa
3A	Monaco
3B	Mauritius
3C	Equatorial Guinea
3D	Swaziland
3X	Guinea
4K	Azerbaijan
4R	Sri Lanka
4U	United Nations Organization
4X	Israel
5A	Libya
5B	Cyprus
5H	Tanzania
5N	Nigeria
5R	Madagascar
5T	Mauritania
5U	Niger
5V	Togo
5W	Western Samoa
5X	Uganda
5Y	Kenya
6O	Somalia
6V	Senegal
6Y	Jamaica
7O	Yemen
7P	Lesotho
7Q	Malawi
7T	Algeria
8P	Barbados
8Q	Maldives
8R	Guyana
9A	Croatia
9G	Ghana
9H	Malta
9J	Zambia
9K	Kuwait
9L	Sierra Leone

9M	Malaysia
9N	Nepal
9Q, 9T	Zaire
9U	Burundi
9V	Singapore
9XR	Rwanda
9Y	Trinidad and Tobago

Note Aircraft registration codes indicate the country in which an aircraft is registered and are painted on the aircraft's fuselage

Fastest aircraft

Category	Aircraft	Speed	Mach number
Reconnaissance jet	USAF Lockheed SR-71A (Blackbird)	3 529.5 kmh (2 193.17 mph)	3.0
Combat jet	USSR Mikoyan MiG-25 Foxbat-B	3 395 kmh (2 110 mph)	3.0
Bomber	General Dynamics FB-111; Tupolev Tu-22M (Backfire)	3 065 kmh (1 905 mph)	2.5
Airliner	Aérospatiale/BAe Concorde	2 333 kmh (1 450 mph)	2.0
Flying boat	Martin XP6M-1 Seamaster	911.98 kmh (566.69 mph)	0.8
Propeller-driven	USSR Tu-95/142 (Bear)	925 kmh (575 mph)	0.8
Piston-engine	Grumman F8F Bearcat (modified) (Rare Bear)	850.24 kmh (528.33 mph)	0.7
Biplane	Italian Fiat CR42B	520 kmh (323 mph)	0.4
Helicopter	Westland Lynx	400.87 kmh (249.09 mph)	0.3
Autogyro/gyroplane	WA-116F	193.9 kmh (120.3 mph)	0.2
Ultralight	Gypsy Skycycle	104.6 kmh (65 mph)	0.1

Busiest international airports

Airport	Number of passengers (1997)
O'Hare (Chicago, USA)	70 385 073
Atlanta (Atlanta, USA)	68 205 769
Fort Worth (Dallas, USA)	60 488 713
Los Angeles (Los Angeles, USA)	60 142 588
Heathrow (London, UK)	58 142 836
Haneda (Tokyo, Japan)	49 302 268
San Francisco (San Francisco, USA)	40 493 959
Main (Frankfurt, Germany)	40 262 691
Kimpo (Seoul, South Korea)	36 757 716
Charles de Gaulle (Paris, France)	35 293 378
Denver (Denver, USA)	34 969 021
Miami (Florida, USA)	34 533 268
Schiphol (Amsterdam, Netherlands)	31 569 977
Detroit (Detroit, USA)	31 541 650
JFK (New York, USA)	31 355 268

Airport	Number of passengers (1997)
Newark (New Jersey, USA)	30 915 857
Phoenix (Arizona, USA)	30 659 143
Las Vegas (Las Vegas, USA)	30 305 822
St Paul (Minneapolis, USA)	30 208 256
Kai Tak (Hong Kong, China)	29 006 565
Houston (Houston, USA)	28 705 213
St Louis (St Louis, USA)	27 661 144
Orlando (Orlando, USA)	27 305 149
Gatwick (London, UK)	26 961 453
Toronto (Toronto, Canada)	26 094 527
Narita (Tokyo, Japan)	25 667 577
Boston (Boston, USA)	25 567 888
Singapore (Singapore)	25 174 344
Bangkok (Bangkok, Thailand)	25 124 843
Orly (Paris, France)	25 056 321

Shipping

Country of register	Container ships	Bulk carriers	Tankers	Cruise/ passenger ships	Other vessels	Total
Bahamas	43	142	241	47	481	954
China	97	345	233	33	805	1 513
Cyprus	108	555	166	18	629	1 476
Germany	180	1	31	11	181	404
Greece	35	406	266	19	148	874
Indonesia	5	18	118	9	294	444
Japan	37	182	299	15	211	744
Korea, South	65	124	105	0	155	449
Liberia	153	461	642	38	293	1 587
Malta	28	337	265	9	474	1 113
Netherlands	40	8	71	9	317	445
Norway	5	102	285	14	220	626
Panama	329	1 086	893	54	1 636	3 998
Philippines	14	232	65	6	217	534
Russia	27	129	271	10	1 218	1 655
Saint Vincent	17	121	99	1	445	683
Singapore	114	126	331	1	181	753
Turkey	4	177	74	7	254	516
UK	21	6	60	20	33	140
Ukraine	11	21	29	8	346	415
USA	83	15	173	15	209	495
TOTAL	1 936	5 694	6 384	427	12 417	26 858

Longest ship canals

Canal	Length	Date of construction
St Lawrence Canal (Canada/USA)	293 km (182 mi)	1959
Baltic–White Sea (formerly Stalin)	227 km (141 mi)	1933
Suez (Egypt)	162 km (101 mi)	1869
Volga–Don (Russia)	100 km (62 mi)	1952
Kiel/North Sea (Germany)	98 km (61 mi)	1895
Houston (USA)	91 km (57 mi)	1940
Alphonse XIII (Spain)	85 km (53 mi)	1926
Panama (Panama)	82 km (51 mi)	1914
Manchester Ship (UK)	64 km (40 mi)	1894
Welland (Canada/USA)	43.5 km (27 mi)	1932
Brussels (Belgium)	32 km (20 mi)	1922

Rail networks

Country	Track (km)	Electrified track (km)
Austria	5700	3300
Belgium	3400	2400
Croatia	2700	1000
Czech Republic	9400	2600
Denmark	2300	400
Finland	5900	2000
France	31900	13700
Germany	41700	17700
Greece	2500	0
Hungary	7800	2300
Ireland	1900	0
Italy	16000	9900
Japan	20300	11900
Luxembourg	300	300
Netherlands	2700	2000
Norway	3800	2400
Portugal	2900	500
Slovak Republic	3700	1400
Spain	12300	6900
Sweden	9800	7200
Switzerland	5100	5100
UK	16900	5100
USA	174200	1700

Note Figures relate to 1995

Fastest trains

Category	Train	Speed	Date
Fastest railed vehicle	Mach 8 unmanned rocket sled (USA)	9 851 kmh (6 121 mph)	1982
Maglev (Magnetically levitated vehicle)	MLX01 (Japan)	552 kmh (343 mph)	1999
Fastest train on a national rail system	SNCF TGV (Train à Grande Vitesse) (France)	515.3 kmh (320 mph)	1990
Fastest British locomotive	Class 91 25kV Electric	260 kmh (162 mph)	1989
British Rail scheduled train	Edinburgh–London Scottish Pullman	158.9 kmh (98.7 mph) (average)	
Fastest steam locomotive	LNER 4-6-2 No.4468 (Mallard) (UK)	201.16 kmh (126 mph)	1938

Road vehicles

Country	Cars	Cars per 1 000 people	Trucks	Buses	Motorcycles and mopeds
Canada	14 280 000	495.5	7 250 000	65 600	30 600
France	25 100 000	430.4	5 116 000	79 000	2 990 000
Germany	40 499 442	484.8	4 153 086	85 434	2 304 253
Japan	45 000 000	358.7	22 111 000	245 000	15 340 000
Mexico	8 330 000	87	3 501 043	131 000	268 000
Sweden	3 630 760	407.9	307 709	14 577	117 387
UK	20 780 000	355.3	2 624 000	107 000	601 000
USA	136 066 045	517	64 778 472	685 504	3 767 029

Euroroutes (E-routes)

Number	Route
E01	Larne–Dublin–Rosslare–La Coruña–Lisbon–Seville
E03	Cherbourg–La Rochelle
E05	Greenock–Birmingham–Southampton–Le Havre–Paris–Bordeaux–Madrid–Algeciras
E06	Olderfjord–Kirkenes
E07	Pau–Zaragoza
E09	Orléans–Barcelona
E10	Narvik–Kiruna–Luleå
E11	Vierzon–Montpellier
E12	Moi Rana–Umeå–Vaasa–Helsinki
E13	Doncaster–London
E14	Trondheim–Sundsvall
E15	Inverness–Edinburgh–London–Dover–Calais–Paris–Lyon–Barcelona–Algeciras
E16	Londonderry–Belfast–Glasgow–Edinburgh
E17	Antwerp–Beaune
E18	Craigavon–Larne–Stranraer–Newcastle–Stavanger–Oslo–Stockholm–Kappelskär–Mariehamn–Turku–Helsinki–St Petersburg

E19	Amsterdam–Brussels–Paris
E20	Shannon–Dublin–Liverpool–Hull–Esjberg–Nyborg–Korsør–Køge–Copenhagen–Malmö–Stockholm–Tallin–St Petersburg
E21	Metz–Geneva
E22	Holyhead–Manchester–Immingham–Amsterdam–Hamburg–Sassnitz–Trelleborg–Norrköping
E23	Metz–Lausanne
E24	Birmingham–Ipswich
E25	Hook of Holland–Luxembourg–Strasbourg–Basle–Geneva–Turin–Genoa
E26	Hamburg–Berlin
E27	Belfort–Aosta
E28	Berlin–Gdansk
E29	Cologne–Sarreguemines
E30	Cork–Rosslare–Fishguard–London–Felixstowe–Hook of Holland–Utrecht–Hanover–Berlin–Warsaw–Smolensk–Moscow
E31	Rotterdam–Ludwigshafen
E32	Colchester–Harwich
E33	Parma–La Spezia
E34	Antwerp–Bad Oeynhausen
E35	Amsterdam–Cologne–Basle–Milan–Rome
E36	Berlin–Legnica
E37	Bremen–Cologne
E39	Kristiansand–Aalborg
E40	Calais–Brussels–Aachen–Cologne–Dresden–Krakow–Kiev–Rostov na Donu
E41	Dortmund–Altdorf
E42	Dunkirk–Aschaffenburg
E43	Würzburg–Bellinzona
E44	Le Havre–Luxembourg–Giessen
E45	Gothenburg–Frederikshavn–Hamburg–Munich–Innsbruck–Bologna–Rome–Naples–Villa S Giovanni–Messina–Gela
E46	Cherbourg–Liège
E47	Nordkap–Oslo–Copenhagen–Rødby–Puttgarden–Lübeck
E48	Schweinfurt–Prague
E49	Magdeburg–Vienna
E50	Brest–Paris–Metz–Nuremberg–Prague–Mukacevo
E51	Berlin–Nuremberg
E52	Strasbourg–Salzburg
E53	Plzen–Munich
E54	Paris–Basle–Munich
E55	Kemi-Tornio–Stockholm–Helsingborg–Helsinger–Copenhagen–Gedser–Rostock–Berlin–Prague–Salzburg–Rimini–Brindisi–Igoumenitsa–Kalamata
E56	Nuremberg–Sattledt
E57	Sattledt–Ljubljana
E58	Vienna–Bratislava
E59	Prague–Zagreb
E60	Brest–Tours–Besançon–Basle–Innsbruck–Vienna–Budapest–Bucharest–Constantă
E61	Klagenfurt–Rijeka
E62	Nantes–Geneva–Tortona
E63	Sodankylä–Naantali–Stockholm–Gothenburg
E64	Turin–Brescia
E65	Malmö–Ystrad–Swinoujscie–Prague–Zagreb–Dubrovnik–Bitolj–Antirrion–Rion–Kalamata–Kissamos–Chania

Number	Route
E66	Fortezza–Székesfehérvár
E67	Warsaw–Prague
E68	Szeged–Brasov
E69	Tromsø–Tornio
E70	La Coruña–Bilbao–Bordeaux–Lyon–Torino–Verona–Trieste–Zagreb–Belgrade–Bucharest–Varna
E71	Košice–Budapest–Split
E72	Bordeaux–Toulouse
E73	Budapest–Metkovic
E74	Nice–Alessandria
E75	Karasjok–Helsinki–Gdansk–Budapest–Belgrade–Athens–Chania–Sitia
E76	Migliarino–Florence
E77	Gdansk–Budapest
E78	Grosseto–Fano
E79	Oradea–Calafat–Vidin–Thessaloniki
E80	Lisbon–Madrid–Barcelona–Mazara del Vallo–Messina–Reggio di Calabria–Brindisi–Igoumenitsa–Thessaloniki–Gelibolu–Lapseki–Ankara–Iraq
E81	Halmeu–Pitesti
E82	Porto–Tordesillas
E83	Bjala–Sofia
E84	Kesan–Silivri
E85	Cernovy–Bucharest–Alexandropouli
E86	Krystalopigi–Yefira
E87	Tulcea–Eceabat–Canakkale–Antalya
E88	Ankara–Refahiye
E89	Gerede–Ankara
E90	Lisbon–Madrid–Barcelona–Macara del Vallo–Messina–Reggio di Calabria–Brindisi–Igoumenitsa–Thessaloniki–Gelibolu–Lapseki–Ankara–Iraq
E91	Toprakkale–Syria
E92	Igoumenitsa–Volos
E93	Orel–Odessa
E94	Corinth–Athens
E95	St Petersburg–Moscow–Yalta
E96	Izmir–Sivrihisar
E97	Trabzon–Askale
E98	Topbogazi–Syria
E99	Dogubeyazit–S Urfa

Note Roads identified by odd numbers run in a north–south direction, while those with even numbers run east–west

British motorways

Mainland Britain

Number	Route
M1	London–Northampton–Leicester–Nottingham–Sheffield–Leeds
M2	Strood–Faversham
M3	London–Basingstoke–Winchester
M4	London–Reading–Newport–Cardiff–Swansea
M5	Birmingham–Bristol–Exeter
M6	Birmingham–Wolverhampton–Stoke-on-Trent–Preston–Lancaster–Carlisle

M8	Edinburgh–Glasgow–Langbank
M9	Edinburgh–Stirling
M10	M1–St Albans spur
M11	London–Cambridge
M18	Rotherham–M62
M20	Swanley–Folkestone
M23	Redhill–Crawley
M25	London orbital motorway
M26	Chipstead–M20
M27	Portsmouth–Southampton–Cadnam
M32	M4–Bristol spur
M40	London–West Cross
M41	London–Oxford–Birmingham
M42	Birmingham–Solihull–Tamworth–Appleby Magna
M45	Watford–Dunchurch
M50	Ross-on-Wye–M5
M53	Chester–Wallasey
M54	Telford–M6
M55	Fulwood–Blackpool
M56	Chester–Altringham
M57	Liverpool–Aintree
M58	Aintree–Wigan
M61	Manchester–Preston
M62	Liverpool–Manchester–Leeds–North Cave
M63	Salford–Stockport
M65	Blackburn–Burnley–Colne
M66	Middleton–Ramsbottom
M67	Denton–Mottram
M69	Leicester–Coventry
M73	M74–Glasgow spur
M74	Millbank–Maryville
M74	Carlisle–Gretna Green
M77	Ayr Road Route
M80	Longcroft–M9
M85	M90–Perth spur
M90	Perth–Inverkeithing
M180	Stainforth–Elsham
M181	M180–Scunthorpe spur
M271	M27–Totton spur
M275	M27–Portsmouth spur
M606	M62–Bradford spur
M621	M62–Leeds spur
M876	M80–Kincardine Bridge

Northern Ireland

M1	Belfast–Dungannon
M2	Belfast–Antrim
M2	Ballymena bypass
M3	Belfast Cross Harbour Bridge
M5	M2–Greencastle
M12	M1–Craigavon
M22	Antrim–Randalstown

US Interstate highways

Number	Route
I5	San Diego–Los Angeles–Sacramento–Seattle–Vancouver (Canada)
I8	San Diego Tucson
I10	Los Angeles–Phoenix–San Antonio–Houston–New Orleans–Jacksonville
I15	San Diego–Las Vegas–Salt Lake City–Great Falls
I20	Fort Worth–Dallas–Jackson–Birmingham–Atlanta–Columbia
I25	Albuquerque–Colorado Springs–Denver–Buffalo
I30	Dallas–Little Rock
I35	San Antonio–Austin–Fort Worth–Oklahoma City–Wichita–Kansas City–Des Moines–Minneapolis/St Paul–Duluth
I40	Flagstaff–Albuquerque–Oklahoma City–Little Rock–Memphis–Nashville–Greensboro
I45	Dallas–Houston
I55	New Orleans–Jackson–Memphis–St Louis–Chicago
I59	New Orleans–Birmingham–Chattanooga
I64	St Louis–Louisville–Lexington–Charleston
I65	Mobile–Birmingham–Nashville–Louisville–Indianapolis–Chicago
I70	Denver–Kansas City–St Louis–Indianapolis–Columbus–Philadelphia–Baltimore
I71	Louisville–Cincinnati–Columbus
I74	Davenport–Indianapolis–Cincinnati
I75	Tampa–Atlanta–Cincinnati–Toledo–Detroit
I78	Harrisburg–New York
I80	San Francisco–Salt Lake City–Des Moines–Cleveland–New York
I81	Knoxville–Roanoke–Syracuse
I85	Montgomery–Atlanta–Greensboro–Petersburg
I90	Seattle–Billings–Sioux Falls–Chicago–Cleveland–Boston
I94	Billings–Bismarck–Minneapolis/St Paul–Madison–Milwaukee–Chicago–Detroit
I95	Miami–Jacksonville–Richmond–Washington DC–Baltimore–New York–Boston–Augusta

Note Roads identified by odd numbers run in a north–south direction, while those with even numbers run east–west

International vehicle index marks

Index mark	Country
A	Austria
ADN	former Yemen PDR
AFG	Afghanistan
AL	Albania
AND	Andorra
AUS	Australia*
B	Belgium
BD	Bangladesh*
BDS	Barbados*
BG	Bulgaria
BH	Belize
BIH	Bosnia-Herzegovina
BR	Brazil

BRN	Bahrain
BRU	Brunei*
BS	Bahamas*
BUR	Myanmar (Burma)
C	Cuba
CDN	Canada
CH	Switzerland
CI	Côte d'Ivoire
CL	Sri Lanka*
CO	Colombia
CR	Costa Rica
CY	Cyprus*
CZ	Czechoslovakia
D	Germany
DK	Denmark
DOK	Dominican Republic
DY	Benin
DZ	Algeria
E	Spain
EAK	Kenya*
EAT	Tanzania*
EAU	Uganda*
EC	Ecuador
ES	El Salvador
EST	Estonia
ET	Egypt
ETH	Ethiopia
F	France
FIN	Finland
FJI	Fiji*
FL	Liechtenstein
FR	Faroe Islands
GB	UK*
GBA	Alderney*
GBG	Guernsey*
GBJ	Jersey*
GBM	Isle of Man*
GBZ	Gibraltar
GCA	Guatemala
GE	Georgia
GH	Ghana
GR	Greece
GUY	Guyana*
H	Hungary
HK	Hong Kong*
HKJ	Jordan
HR	Croatia
I	Italy
IL	Israel
IND	India*
IR	Iran
IRL	Ireland*

Index mark	Country
IRQ	Iraq
IS	Iceland
J	Japan*
JA	Jamaica*
K	Cambodia
KS	Kyrgyzstan
KWT	Kuwait
KZ	Kazakhstan
L	Luxembourg
LAO	Laos PDR
LAR	Libya
LB	Liberia
LS	Lesotho*
LT	Lithuania
LV	Latvia
M	Malta*
MA	Morocco
MAL	Malaysia*
MC	Monaco
MEX	Mexico
MK	Macedonia
MS	Mauritius*
MW	Malawi*
N	Norway
NA	Netherlands Antilles
NAM	Namibia*
NIC	Nicaragua
NL	Netherlands
NZ	New Zealand*
P	Portugal
PA	Panama
PE	Peru
PK	Pakistan*
PL	Poland
PNG	Papua New Guinea*
PY	Paraguay
RA	Argentina
RB	Botswana*
RC	Taiwan
RCA	Central African Republic
RCB	Congo
RCH	Chile
RH	Haiti
RI	Indonesia*
RIM	Mauritania
RL	Lebanon
RM	Madagascar
RMM	Mali
RN	Niger
RO	Romania
ROK	Korea, Republic of (South Korea)

ROU	Uruguay
RP	Philippines
RSM	San Marino
RU	Burundi
RUS	Russia
RWA	Rwanda
S	Sweden
SD	Swaziland*
SGP	Singapore*
SK	Slovakia
SLO	Slovenia
SME	Suriname*
SN	Senegal
SU	Belarus
SY	Seychelles*
SYR	Syria
T	Thailand*
TG	Togo
TJ	Tajikistan
TM	Turkmenistan
TN	Tunisia
TR	Turkey
TT	Trinidad and Tobago*
UA	Ukraine
USA	USA
V	Vatican City
VN	Vietnam
WAG	Gambia
WAL	Sierra Leone
WAN	Nigeria
WD	Dominica*
WG	Grenada*
WL	St Lucia*
WS	W Samoa
WV	St Vincent and the Grenadines*
YU	Yugoslavia
YV	Venezuela
Z	Zambia*
ZA	South Africa*
ZRE	Congo, Democratic Republic of
ZW	Zimbabwe*

Note *Drivers drive on the left in these countries

British vehicle index marks

Index mark	Issuing office
AA	Bournemouth
AB	Worcester
AC	Coventry
AD	Gloucester

Index mark	Issuing office
AE	Bristol
AF	Truro
AG	Hull
AH	Norwich
AJ	Middlesbrough
AK	Sheffield
AL	Nottingham
AM	Swindon
AN	Reading
AO	Carlisle
AP	Brighton
AR	Chelmsford
AS	Inverness
AT	Hull
AU	Nottingham
AV	Peterborough
AW	Shrewsbury
AX	Cardiff
AY	Leicester
BA	Manchester
BB	Newcastle upon Tyne
BC	Leicester
BD	Northampton
BE	Lincoln
BF	Stoke-on-Trent
BG	Liverpool
BH	Luton
BJ	Ipswich
BK	Portsmouth
BL	Reading
BM	Luton
BN	Manchester
BO	Cardiff
BP	Portsmouth
BR	Newcastle upon Tyne
BS	Inverness
BT	Leeds
BU	Manchester
BV	Preston
BW	Oxford
BX	Haverfordwest
BY	London NW
CA	Chester
CB	Manchester
CC	Bangor
CD	Brighton
CE	Peterborough
CF	Reading
CG	Bournemouth
CH	Nottingham
CJ	Gloucester

CK	Preston
CL	Norwich
CM	Liverpool
CN	Newcastle upon Tyne
CO	Exeter
CP	Huddersfield
CR	Portsmouth
CS	Glasgow
CT	Lincoln
CU	Newcastle upon Tyne
CV	Truro
CW	Preston
CX	Huddersfield
CY	Swansea
DA	Birmingham
DB	Manchester
DC	Middlesbrough
DD	Gloucester
DE	Haverfordwest
DF	Gloucester
DG	Gloucester
DH	Dudley
DJ	Liverpool
DK	Manchester
DL	Portsmouth
DM	Chester
DN	Leeds
DO	Lincoln
DP	Reading
DR	Exeter
DS	Glasgow
DT	Sheffield
DU	Coventry
DV	Exeter
DW	Cardiff
DX	Ipswich
DY	Brighton
EA	Dudley
EB	Peterborough
EC	Preston
ED	Liverpool
EE	Lincoln
EF	Middlesbrough
EG	Peterborough
EH	Stoke-on-Trent
EJ	Haverfordwest
EK	Liverpool
EL	Bournemouth
EM	Liverpool
EN	Manchester
EO	Preston
EP	Swansea

Index mark	Issuing office
ER	Peterborough
ES	Dundee
ET	Sheffield
EU	Bristol
EV	Chelmsford
EW	Peterborough
EX	Norwich
EY	Bangor
FA	Stoke-on-Trent
FB	Bristol
FC	Oxford
FD	Dudley
FE	Lincoln
FF	Bangor
FG	Brighton
FH	Gloucester
FJ	Exeter
FK	Dudley
FL	Peterborough
FM	Chester
FN	Maidstone
FO	Gloucester
FP	Leicester
FR	Preston
FS	Edinburgh
FT	Newcastle upon Tyne
FU	Lincoln
FV	Preston
FW	Lincoln
FX	Bournemouth
FY	Liverpool
GA	Glasgow
GB	Glasgow
GC	London SW
GD	Glasgow
GE	Glasgow
GF	London SW
GG	Glasgow
GH	London SW
GJ	London SW
GK	London SW
GL	Truro
GM	Reading
GN	London SW
GO	London SW
GP	London SW
GR	Newcastle upon Tyne
GS	Luton
GT	London SW
GU	London SE
GV	Ipswich

GW	London SE
GX	London SE
GY	London SE
HA	Dudley
HB	Cardiff
HC	Brighton
HD	Huddersfield
HE	Sheffield
HF	Liverpool
HG	Preston
HH	Carlisle
HJ	Chelmsford
HK	Chelmsford
HL	Sheffield
HM	London C
HN	Middlesbrough
HO	Bournemouth
HP	Coventry
HR	Swindon
HS	Glasgow
HT	Bristol
HU	Bristol
HV	London C
HW	Bristol
HX	London C
HY	Bristol
JA	Manchester
JB	Reading
JC	Bangor
JD	London C
JE	Peterborough
JF	Leicester
JG	Maidstone
JH	Reading
JJ	Maidstone
JK	Brighton
JL	Lincoln
JM	Reading
JN	Chelmsford
JO	Oxford
JP	Liverpool
JR	Newcastle upon Tyne
JS	Inverness
JT	Bournemouth
JU	Leicester
JV	Lincoln
JW	Birmingham
JX	Huddersfield
JY	Exeter
KA	Liverpool
KB	Liverpool
KC	Liverpool

Index mark	Issuing office
KD	Liverpool
KE	Maidstone
KF	Liverpool
KG	Cardiff
KH	Hull
KJ	Maidstone
KK	Maidstone
KL	Maidstone
KM	Maidstone
KN	Maidstone
KO	Maidstone
KP	Maidstone
KR	Maidstone
KS	Edinburgh
KT	Maidstone
KU	Sheffield
KV	Coventry
KW	Sheffield
KX	Luton
KY	Sheffield
LA	London NW
LB	London NW
LC	London NW
LD	London NW
LE	London NW
LF	London NW
LG	Chester
LH	London NW
LJ	Bournemouth
LK	London NW
LL	London NW
LM	London NW
LN	London NW
LO	London NW
LP	London NW
LR	London NW
LS	Edinburgh
LT	London NW
LU	London NW
LV	Liverpool
LW	London NW
LX	London NW
LY	London NW
MA	Chester
MB	Chester
MC	London NE
MD	London NE
ME	London NE
MF	London NE
MG	London NE
MH	London NE

MJ	Luton
MK	London NE
ML	London NE
MM	London NE
MO	Reading
MP	London NE
MR	Swindon
MS	Edinburgh
MT	London NE
MU	London NE
MV	London SE
MW	Swindon
MX	London SE
MY	London SE
NA	Manchester
NB	Manchester
NC	Manchester
ND	Manchester
NE	Manchester
NF	Manchester
NG	Norwich
NH	Northampton
NJ	Brighton
NK	Luton
NL	Newcastle upon Tyne
NM	Luton
NN	Nottingham
NO	Chelmsford
NP	Worcester
NR	Leicester
NS	Glasgow
NT	Shrewsbury
NU	Nottingham
NV	Northampton
NW	Leeds
NX	Dudley
NY	Cardiff
OA	Birmingham
OB	Birmingham
OC	Birmingham
OD	Exeter
OE	Birmingham
OF	Birmingham
OG	Birmingham
OH	Birmingham
OJ	Birmingham
OK	Birmingham
OL	Birmingham
OM	Birmingham
ON	Birmingham
OO	Chelmsford
OP	Birmingham

Index mark	Issuing office
OR	Portsmouth
OS	Glasgow
OT	Portsmouth
OU	Bristol
OV	Birmingham
OW	Portsmouth
OX	Birmingham
OY	London NW
PA	Guildford
PB	Guildford
PC	Guildford
PD	Guildford
PE	Guildford
PF	Guildford
PG	Guildford
PH	Guildford
PJ	Guildford
PK	Guildford
PL	Guildford
PM	Guildford
PN	Brighton
PO	Portsmouth
PP	Luton
PR	Bournemouth
PS	Aberdeen
PT	Newcastle upon Tyne
PU	Chelmsford
PV	Ipswich
PW	Norwich
PX	Portsmouth
PY	Middlesbrough
RA	Nottingham
RB	Nottingham
RC	Nottingham
RD	Reading
RE	Stoke-on-Trent
RF	Stoke-on-Trent
RG	Newcastle upon Tyne
RH	Hull
RJ	Manchester
RK	London NW
RL	Truro
RM	Carlisle
RN	Preston
RO	Luton
RP	Northampton
RR	Nottingham
RS	Aberdeen
RT	Ipswich
RU	Bournemouth
RV	Portsmouth

RW	Coventry
RX	Reading
RY	Leicester
SA	Aberdeen
SB	Glasgow
SC	Edinburgh
SCY	Truro (Isles of Scilly)
SD	Glasgow
SE	Aberdeen
SF	Edinburgh
SG	Edinburgh
SH	Edinburgh
SJ	Glasgow
SK	Inverness
SL	Dundee
SM	Glasgow
SN	Dundee
SO	Aberdeen
SP	Dundee
SR	Dundee
SS	Aberdeen
ST	Inverness
SU	Glasgow
SW	Glasgow
SX	Edinburgh
TA	Exeter
TB	Liverpool
TC	Bristol
TD	Manchester
TE	Manchester
TF	Reading
TG	Cardiff
TH	Swansea
TJ	Liverpool
TK	Exeter
TL	Lincoln
TM	Luton
TN	Newcastle upon Tyne
TO	Nottingham
TP	Portsmouth
TR	Portsmouth
TS	Dundee
TT	Exeter
TU	Chester
TV	Nottingham
TW	Chelmsford
TX	Cardiff
TY	Newcastle upon Tyne
UA	Leeds
UB	Leeds
UC	London C
UD	Oxford

Index mark	Issuing office
UE	Dudley
UF	Brighton
UG	Leeds
UH	Cardiff
UJ	Shrewsbury
UK	Birmingham
UL	London C
UM	Leeds
UN	Exeter
UO	Exeter
UP	Newcastle upon Tyne
UR	Luton
US	Glasgow
UT	Leicester
UU	London C
UV	London C
UW	London C
UX	Shrewsbury
UY	Worcester
VA	Peterborough
VB	Maidstone
VC	Coventry
VE	Peterborough
VF	Norwich
VG	Norwich
VH	Huddersfield
VJ	Gloucester
VK	Newcastle upon Tyne
VL	Lincoln
VM	Manchester
VN	Middlesbrough
VO	Nottingham
VP	Birmingham
VR	Manchester
VS	Luton
VT	Stoke-on-Trent
VU	Manchester
VV	Northampton
VW	Chelmsford
VX	Chelmsford
VY	Leeds
WA	Sheffield
WB	Sheffield
WC	Chelmsford
WD	Dudley
WE	Sheffield
WF	Sheffield
WG	Sheffield
WH	Manchester
WJ	Sheffield
WK	Coventry

WL	Oxford
WM	Liverpool
WN	Swansea
WO	Cardiff
WP	Worcester
WR	Leeds
WS	Bristol
WT	Leeds
WU	Leeds
WV	Brighton
WW	Leeds
WX	Leeds
WY	Leeds
YA	Taunton
YB	Taunton
YC	Taunton
YD	Taunton
YE	London C
YF	London C
YG	Leeds
YH	London C
YJ	Brighton
YK	London C
YL	London C
YM	London C
YN	London C
YO	London C
YP	London C
YR	London C
YS	Glasgow
YT	London C
YU	London C
YV	London C
YW	London C
YX	London C
YY	London C

Fastest cars

Category	Car	Speed	Date
Jet engine	Thrust SSC	1 227.885 kmh (763.055 mph)	1997
Single-piston engine	Speed-O-Motive/Spirit 76	696.331 kmh (432.692 mph)	1991
Gas-turbine engine	Bluebird	690.909 kmh (429.054 mph)	1964
Piston engine	MacLaren F1	386.7 kmh (240.3 mph)	1998
Diesel engine	Mercedes C III/3	327.3 kmh (203.3 mph)	1978
Steam engine	No. 744 Steamin' Demon	234.33 kmh (145.607 mph)	1985
Electric engine	White Lightning Electric Streamliner	395.821 kmh (245.951 mph)	1999

10.2 *Communication*

International direct-dialling codes

Country	Code
Afghanistan	00 93
Albania	00 355
Algeria	00 213
Andorra	00 376
Angola	00 244
Anguilla	00 1 264
Antarctic Australian Territory	00 672
Antigua and Barbuda	00 1 268
Argentina	00 54
Armenia	00 374
Aruba	00 297
Ascension Island	00 247
Australia	00 61
Austria	00 43
Azerbaijan	00 994
Azores	00 351
Bahamas	00 1 242
Bahrain	00 973
Bangladesh	00 880
Barbados	00 1 246
Belarus	00 375
Belgium	00 32
Belize	00 501
Benin	00 229
Bermuda	00 1 441
Bhutan	00 975
Bolivia	00 591
Bosnia-Herzegovina	00 387
Botswana	00 267
Brazil	00 55
Brunei	00 673
Bulgaria	00 359
Burkina Faso	00 226
Burundi	00 257
Cambodia	00 855
Cameroon	00 237
Canada	00 1
Cape Verde	00 238
Cayman Islands	00 1 345
Central African Republic	00 236
Chad	00 235

Chile	00 56
China	00 86
Colombia	00 57
Comoros	00 269
Congo	00 242
Congo, Democratic Republic of	00 243
Cook Islands	00 682
Costa Rica	00 506
Côte d'Ivoire	00 225
Croatia	00 385
Cuba	00 53
Cyprus	00 357
Czech Republic	00 420
Denmark	00 45
Diego Garcia	00 246
Djibouti	00 253
Dominica	00 1 767
Dominican Republic	00 1 809
Ecuador	00 593
Egypt	00 20
El Salvador	00 503
Equatorial Guinea	00 240
Eritrea	00 291
Estonia	00 372
Ethiopia	00 251
Falkland Islands	00 500
Faroe Islands	00 298
Fiji	00 679
Finland	00 358
France	00 33
French Guiana	00 594
French Polynesia	00 689
Gabon	00 241
Gambia	00 220
Georgia	00 995
Germany	00 49
Ghana	00 233
Gibraltar	00 350
Greece	00 30
Greenland	00 299
Grenada	00 1 473
Guadaloupe	00 590
Guam	00 1 671
Guatemala	00 502
Guinea	00 224
Guinea-Bissau	00 245
Guyana	00 592
Haiti	00 509
Honduras	00 504
Hong Kong	00 852
Hungary	00 36
Iceland	00 354

Country	Code
India	00 91
Indonesia	00 62
Iran	00 98
Iraq	00 964
Ireland, Republic of	00 353
Israel	00 972
Italy	00 39
Jamaica	00 1 876
Japan	00 81
Jordan	00 962
Kazakhstan	00 7
Kenya	00 254
Kiribati	00 686
Kuwait	00 965
Kyrgyzstan	00 996
Laos	00 856
Latvia	00 371
Lebanon	00 961
Lesotho	00 266
Liberia	00 231
Libya	00 218
Liechtenstein	00 423
Lithuania	00 370
Luxembourg	00 352
Macau	00 853
Macedonia	00 389
Madagascar	00 261
Malawi	00 265
Malaysia	00 60
Maldives	00 960
Mali	00 223
Malta	00 356
Marshall Islands	00 692
Martinique	00 596
Mauritania	00 222
Mauritius	00 230
Mayotte	00 269
Mexico	00 52
Micronesia	00 691
Moldova	00 373
Monaco	00 377
Mongolia	00 976
Montserrat	00 1 664
Morocco	00 212
Mozambique	00 258
Myanmar	00 95
Namibia	00 264
Nauru	00 674
Nepal	00 977
Netherlands	00 31
Netherlands Antilles	00 599

New Caledonia	00 687
New Zealand	00 64
Nicaragua	00 505
Niger	00 227
Nigeria	00 234
Niue	00 683
Norfolk Island	00 6 72
North Korea	00 850
Northern Marianas	00 1 670
Norway	00 47
Oman	00 968
Pakistan	00 92
Palau	00 680
Panama	00 507
Papua New Guinea	00 675
Paraguay	00 595
Peru	00 51
Philippines	00 63
Poland	00 48
Portugal	00 351
Puerto Rico	00 1 787
Qatar	00 974
Réunion	00 262
Romania	00 40
Russian Federation	00 7
Rwanda	00 250
St Helena	00 290
St Kitts and Nevis	00 1 869
St Lucia	00 1 758
St Pierre and Miquelon	00 508
St Vincent and the Grenadines	00 1 784
Samoa	00 684
Samoa, Western	00 685
San Marino	00 378
São Tomé and Príncipe	00 239
Saudi Arabia	00 966
Senegal	00 221
Seychelles	00 248
Sierra Leone	00 232
Singapore	00 65
Slovakia	00 421
Slovenia	00 386
Solomon Islands	00 677
Somalia	00 252
South Africa	00 27
South Korea	00 82
Spain	00 34
Sri Lanka	00 94
Sudan	00 249
Suriname	00 597
Swaziland	00 268
Sweden	00 46

Country	Code
Switzerland	00 41
Syria	00 963
Taiwan	00 886
Tajikistan	00 7
Tanzania	00 255
Thailand	00 66
Togo	00 228
Tokelau	00 690
Tonga	00 676
Trinidad and Tobago	00 1 868
Tunisia	00 216
Turkey	00 90
Turkmenistan	00 993
Turks and Caicos Islands	00 1 649
Tuvalu	00 688
Uganda	00 256
UK	00 44
Ukraine	00 380
United Arab Emirates	00 971
Uruguay	00 598
USA	00 1
Uzbekistan	00 7
Vanuatu	00 678
Venezuela	00 58
Vietnam	00 84
Virgin Islands (UK)	00 1 284
Virgin Islands (US)	00 1 340
Yemen	00 967
Yugoslavia	00 381
Zambia	00 260
Zimbabwe	00 263

Morse code

A	. —
B	— . . .
C	— . — .
D	— . .
E	.
F	. . — .
G	— — .
H	. . . .
I	. .
J	. — — —
K	— . —
L	. — . .
M	— —
N	— .

O	– – –
P	. – – .
Q	– – . –
R	. – .
S	. . .
T	–
U	. . –
V	. . . –
W	. – –
X	– . . –
Y	– . – –
Z	– – . .

Note The International Morse Code was introduced by Samuel Morse in 1852 but is now no longer officially recognized

International phonetic alphabet

A	Alfa
B	Bravo
C	Charlie
D	Delta
E	Echo
F	Foxtrot
G	Golf
H	Hotel
I	India
J	Juliet
K	Kilo
L	Lima
M	Mike
N	November
O	Oscar
P	Papa
Q	Quebec
R	Romeo
S	Sierra
T	Tango
U	Uniform
V	Victor
W	Whiskey
X	X-Ray
Y	Yankee
Z	Zulu

Braille alphabet

Letter	Symbol	Letter	Symbol
A		B	
C		D	
E		F	
G		H	
I		J	
K		L	
M		N	
O		P	
Q		R	
S		T	

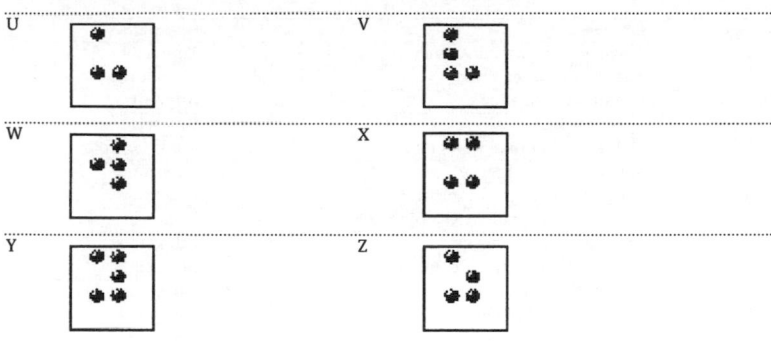

10.3 *Media*

News agencies

Agency	Full name	Headquarters
AA	Anadol Ajansi	Ankara
AAP	Australian Associated Press	Sydney
AASA	Agence Arabe Syrienne d'Information	Damascus
AND	Allgemeiner Deutscher Nachrichtendienst	Berlin
AE	Agence Europe	Brussels
AFP	Agence France Presse	Paris
AIO	Agencia Informativa Orbe de Chile	Santiago
AIP	Agence Ivoirienne de Presse	Abidjan
ALD	Agence Los Diarios	Buenos Aires
ALI	Agencia Lusa de Informacao	Lisbon
AM	Agencia Meridional	Rio de Janeiro
AN	Agencia Nacional	Brasilia
ANA	Athenagence	Athens
ANGOP	Angola Agêcia Naticiosa N'gola Press	Luanda
ANP	Algemeen Nederlands Persbureau	The Hague
ANSA	Agenzia Nazionale Stampa Associate	Rome
ANTARA	Indonesian National News Agency	Jakarta
AP	Associated Press	New York
APA	Austria Presse Agentur	Vienna
APP	Agence Parisienne de Presse	Paris
APP	Associated Press of Pakistan	Islamabad
APS	Agence de Presse Senegalaise	Dakar
APS	Algeria Presse Service	Algiers

Agency	Full name	Headquarters
ATA	Albanian Telegraphic Agency	Tirana
AUP	Australian United Press	Melbourne
BATRA	Jordan News Agency	Amman
BELGA	Agence Belga	Brussels
BERNAMA	Malaysian National News Agency	Kuala Lumpur
BOPA	Botswana Press Agency	Gaborone
BSS	Bangladesh Sangbad Sangstha	Dhaka
BTA	Bulgarska Telegrafitscheka Agentzia	Sofia
CANA	Caribbean News Agency	Bridgetown
CIP	Centre d'Information de Presse	Brussels
CNA	Central News Agency	Taipei
CNA	Cyprus News Agency	Nicosia
CNS	China News Service	Beijing
COLPRENSA	Colprensa	Bogota
CP	Canadian Press	Toronto
CSTK	Ceskoslovenska Tiskova Kancelar	Prague
DPA	Deutsche Presse Agentur	Hamburg
EFE	Agencia EFE	Madrid
ENA	Eastern News Agency	Dhaka
ETA	Eesti Teadate Agentuur	Tallinn
EXTEL	Exchange and Telegraph Company	London
FIDES	Agenzia Internazionale Fides	Vatican City
GNA	Agence Guinéenne de Presse	Conakry
GNA	Ghana News Agency	Accra
GNA	Guyana News Agency	Georgetown
HHA	Hurriyet Haber Ajasi	Istanbul
HINA	Hrvatska Izvjestajna Novinska Agencija	Zagreb
IC	Inforpress Centroamericana	Guatemala
INA	Iraqi News Agency	Baghdad
IPS	Inter Press Service	Rome
IRNA	Islamic Republic News Agency	Tehran
ITIM	Associated Israel Press	Tel Aviv
JAMPRESS	Jampress	Kingston
JANA	Jamahiriya News Agency	Tripoli
JIJI	Jiji Tsushin-Sha	Tokyo
JTA	Jewish Telegraphic Agency	Jerusalem
KCNA	Korean Central News Agency	Pyongyang
KNA	Kenya News Agency	Nairobi
KPL	Khao San Pathet Lao	Vientiane
KUNA	Kuwait News Agency	Kuwait City
KYODO	Kyodo Tsushin	Tokyo
LAI	Logos Agencia de Informacion	Madrid
LETA	Latvijas Telegrafa Agentura	Riga
MENA	Middle East News Agency	Cairo
MTI	Magyar Tavariti Iroda	Budapest
NA	Noticias Argentinas	Buenos Aires
NAEWOE	Naewoe Press	Seoul
NAN	News Agency of Nigeria	Lagos
NOTIMEX	Noticias Mexicanas	Mexico City
NOVOSTI	Agentstvo Pechati Novosti	Moscow
NPS	Norsk Presse Service	Oslo

NTB	Norsk Telegrambyra	Oslo
NZPA	New Zealand Press Agency	Wellington
OPA	Orbis Press Agency	Prague
OTTFNB	Oy Suomen Tietoimisto Notisbyrån Ab	Helsinki
PA	Press Association	London
PANA	Pan-African News Agency	Dakar
PAP	Polska Agencija Prasowa	Warsaw
PNA	Philippines News Agency	Manila
PPI	Pakistan Press International	Karachi
PRELA	Prensa Latina	Havana
PS	Presse Services	Paris
PTI	Press Trust of India	Bombay
RB	Ritzaus Bureau	Copenhagen
REUTERS	Reuters	London
ROMPRESS	Romanian News Agency	Bucharest
SAPA	South African Press Association	Johannesburg
SDA	Schweizerische Depeschenagentur	Berne
SIP	Svensk Internationella Pressbyrån	Stockholm
SLENA	Sierra Leone News Agency	Freetown
SOFIAPRES	Sofia Press Agency	Sofia
SOPAC-NEWS	South Pacific News Service	Wellington
SPA	Saudi Press Agency	Riyadh
SPK	Saporamean Kampuchea	Phnom Penh
STA	Slovenska Tiskovna Agencija	Ljubljana
TANJUG	Novinska Agencija Tanjug	Belgrade
TAP	Tunis Afrique Presse	Tunis
TASS	Telegraph Agency of the Sovereign States	Moscow
TT	Tidningarnes Telegrambyra	Stockholm
UNI	United News of India	New Delhi
UPI	United Press International	New York
UPP	United Press of Pakistan	Karachi
VNA	Vietnam News Agency	Hanoi
XINHUA	Xinhua	Beijing
YONHAP	Yonhap (United) Press Agency	Seoul
ZIANA	Zimbabwe Inter-Africa News Agency	Harare

Newspapers (Europe)

Title	Headquarters	Issue	Circulation
Austria			
Die Ganze Woche	Vienna	Twice-weekly	850 000
Kleine Zeitung	Graz	Weekly	275 000
Kurier	Vienna	Daily and Sunday	620 000
Neue Kronenzeitung	Vienna	Daily	1 000 000
Belgium			
Antwerpse Post	Antwerp	Weekly	313 327
Belgique No 1	Brussels	Weekly	530 000
L'Echo	Brussels	Weekly	380 000
De Gentenaar	Ghent	Daily	326 000

Title	Headquarters	Issue	Circulation
Groupe AZ	Brussels	Weekly	1 625 000
Groep AZ	Brussels	Weekly	2 800 000
Hier Groep	Hasselt	Weekly	350 000
Die Nieuwe Gazet Antwerp	Antwerp	Daily	298 882
Het Nieuwsblad	Groot-Bijgaarden	Daily	382 397
Publi-Hebdo	Liège	Weekly	382 000
De Standaard	Groot-Bijgaarden	Daily	382 397
Visite	Berchem	Monthly	574 355
Vlan	Brussels	Weekly	425 000
Deze Week in	Roeselare	Weekly	840 000

Bulgaria

Duma	Sofia	Daily	300 000
Otechestven Front	Sofia	Daily	280 000

Czech Republic

Práce	Prague	Daily	350 000
Rudé Právo	Prague	Daily	340 000

France

Le Dauphiné Libéré	Veurey-Voroize	Daily	813 209
L'Est Républicain	Heillecourt	Daily	251 236
Le Figaro	Paris	Daily	428 700
France-Dimanche	Paris	Weekly	706 338
France-Soir	Paris	Daily	334 035
Ici Paris	Paris	Weekly	422 796
Le Journal Dimanche	Paris	Weekly	360 029
Le Monde	Paris	Daily	381 549
La Montagne	Clermont Ferrand	Daily	250 288
Nice Matin	Nice	Daily	258 205
La Nouvelle République du Centre-Ouest	Tours	Daily	271 504
Ouest-France	Rennes	Daily	739 047
Le Parisien	Paris	Daily	365 661
Le Progrès	Lyons	Daily	353 608
Sud-Ouest	Bordeaux	Daily	367 860
VSD	Paris	Weekly	261 612

Germany

Augsburger Allgemeine	Augsburg	Daily	362 000
Berliner Zeitung	Berlin	Daily	425 000
Bild	Hamburg	Daily	4 416 240
Bild Berlin	Berlin	Daily	250 000
BZ-Berlin	Berlin	Daily	279 269
Express Köln	Cologne	Daily	437 104
Frankfurter Allgemeine Zeitung	Frankfurt am Main	Daily	366 703
Hannoversche Allgemaine Zeitung	Hannover	Daily	511 027
HNA Hessische/Niedersäch Allgemeine	Kassel	Daily	272 249
Junge Welt	Berlin	Daily	330 000
Lausitzer Rundschau	Cottbus	Daily	291 000

Leipziger Volkszeitung	Leipzig	Daily	484 000
Neue Osnabrücker Zeitung	Osnabruck	Daily	299 572
Nordwest Zeitung	Oldenburg	Daily	317 077
Nürnberger Nachrichten	Nuremburg	Daily	325 000
Ostee Zeitung	Rostock	Daily	293 000
Rheinische Post	Düsseldorf	Daily	391 489
Sächsische Zeitung	Dresden	Daily	513 000
Sonntag Aktuell	Stuttgart	Weekly	877 140
Stuttgarter Zeitung	Stuttgart	Daily	509 710
Süddeutsche Zeitung	Magdeburg	Daily	386 287
Südwest Presse	Ulm	Daily	367 129
Super Zeitung	Munich	Daily	600 000
Das Volk	Erfurt	Daily	401 000
Volksstimme	Magdeburg	Daily	379 407
Westdeutsche Allgemeine Zeitung	Essen	Daily	1 236 304
Die Zeit	Hamburg	Weekly	488 212

Hungary

Népsport	Budapest	Daily	250 000
Népszabadsag	Budapest	Daily	450 000
Reform	Budapest	Weekly	385 000
Vasárnapi Hirek	Budapest	Weekly	270 595

Ireland

| Sunday World | Dublin | Weekly | 263 088 |

Italy

Corriere Della Sera	Milan	Daily	644 856
Corriere Dello Sport-Stadio	Rome	Daily	542 275
La Gazzetta Dello Sport	Milan	Daily	814 889
Il Messaggero	Rome	Daily	400 000
La Repubblica	Rome	Daily	826 224
Il Sole 24 Ore	Milan	Daily	258 771
La Stampa	Turin	Daily	406 951

Netherlands

Algemeen Dagblad	Rotterdam	Daily	417 000
De Telegraaf	Amsterdam	Daily	725 700
De Volkskrant	Amsterdam	Daily	340 038

Norway

| Aftenposten | Oslo | Daily | 262 982 |

Poland

| Gazeta Wyborcza | Warsaw | Daily | 550 000 |
| Zycie Warszawy | Warsaw | Daily | 250 000 |

Romania

| Ardevarul | Bucharest | Daily | 250 000 |
| România Liberia | Bucharest | Daily | 400 000 |

Russia

Izvestiya	Moscow	Daily	10 130 000
Komsomolskaya Pravda	Moscow	Daily	20 354 000
Moskovskaya Pravda	Moscow	Daily	725 000

Title	Headquarters	Issue	Circulation
Pravda	Moscow	Daily	7 700 000
Rabochaya Tribuna	Moscow	Daily	1 405 000
Selskaya Zhizn	Moscow	Daily	5 772 000
Sotsialisticheskaya Industriya	Moscow	Daily	1 500 000
Sovetski Sport	Moscow	Daily	4 863 000
Trud	Moscow	Daily	21 429 000
Vechernyaya Moskva	Moscow	Daily	650 000
Slovakia			
Práca	Bratislava	Daily	260 300
Pravda	Bratislava	Daily	260 000
Spain			
ABC	Madrid	Daily	280 356
El Pais	Madrid	Daily	377 528
Sweden			
Aftonbladet	Stockholm	Daily	480 000
Dagens Nyheter	Stockholm	Daily	519 000
Expressen	Stockholm	Daily	575 000
Göteborg-Posten	Gothenburg	Daily	281 000
Turkey			
Milliyet	Istanbul	Daily	250 000
Sabah	Istanbul	Daily	506 671

Note See separate table for British newspapers

Newspapers (UK)

Title	Headquarters	Issue	Circulation (1999)
Daily Mail	London	Daily	2 350 241
Daily Record	Glasgow	Daily	665 313
Daily Star	London	Daily	525 734
Daily Telegraph	London	Daily	1 044 740
Evening Standard	London	Daily	448 059
Express	London	Daily	1 095 716
Mail on Sunday	London	Daily	2 279 430
Mirror	London	Daily	2 313 063
Financial Times	London	Daily	385 025
Guardian	London	Daily	398 721
Independent	London	Daily	223 304
Independent on Sunday	London	Sunday	250 034
News of the World	London	Weekly	209 173
Observer	London	Sunday	404 859
Racing Post	London	Daily	78 240
Scotland on Sunday	Edinburgh	Sunday	120 644
Scotsman	Edinburgh	Daily	79 925
Sun	London	Daily	3 730 466
Sunday Express	London	Sunday	1 003 287
Sunday Mail	Glasgow	Sunday	779 572
Sunday Mirror	London	Sunday	1 981 059

Sunday People	London	Sunday	1 643 000
Sunday Sport	London	Sunday	214 450
Sunday Telegraph	London	Sunday	816 653
Sunday Times	London	Sunday	1 374 436
The Times	London	Daily	740 883

Newspapers (US)

Title	Headquarters	Issue	Circulation
Alabama			
News	Birmingham	Daily	159 823
Arizona			
New Times	Phoenix	Weekly	135 000
Republic	Phoenix	Daily	362 199
Star	Tucson	Daily	159 698
Arkansas			
Democrat-Gazette	Little Rock	Daily	174 883
California			
Bee	Fresno	Daily	150 438
Central News	Los Angeles	Weekly	210 000
Daily Breeze	Torrance	Daily and Sunday	100 000
Daily News	Los Angeles	Daily and Sunday	207 011
Daily News (Japanese)	Los Angeles	Daily	215 586
Herald-Examiner	Los Angeles	Daily and Sunday	303 320
Investors Daily	Los Angeles	Daily	176 740
L.A. Times	Los Angeles	Daily and Sunday	1 062 202
Mercury News	San José	Daily and Sunday	283 590
La Opinion	Los Angeles	Daily and Sunday	105 918
Press-Enterprise	Riverside	Daily and Sunday	161 659
Press-Telegram	Long Beach	Daily	128 750
Register	Santa Ana	Daily and Sunday	350 387
Sacramento Bee	Sacramento	Daily and Sunday	275 696
San Francisco Chronicle	San Francisco	Daily	509 548
San Francisco Examiner	San Francisco	Daily	136 346
Sun	San Bernadino	Daily and Sunday	100 688
Sun Examiner/Chronicle	San Francisco	Weekly	716 339
Tribune	Oakland	Daily and Sunday	121 537
Union-Tribune	San Diego	Daily and Sunday	372 466
Wall Street Journal (western edition)	San Francisco	Daily	388 013
Colorado			
Gazette Telegraph	Colorado Springs	Daily	115 883
Post	Denver	Daily and Sunday	287 213
Rocky Mountain News	Denver	Daily and Sunday	344 585
Connecticut			
Hartford Courant	Hartford	Daily and Sunday	226 533
Register	New Haven	Daily and Sunday	135 569

Title	Headquarters	Issue	Circulation
Delaware			
News Journal	Wilmington	Daily	125 742
District of Columbia			
Washington Post	Washington	Daily and Sunday	810 675
Washington Times	Washington	Weekly	100 000
Florida			
Florida Times-Union	Jacksonville	Daily and Sunday	181 841
Florida Today	Melbourne	Daily	106 878
Herald-Tribune	Sarasota	Daily	130 872
Miami Herald	Miami	Daily and Sunday	393 791
News Journal	Daytona Beach	Daily and Sunday	106 169
News Press	Fort Myers	Daily and Sunday	102 016
Palm Beach Post	West Palm Beach	Daily	172 744
Sentinel	Orlando	Daily	270 970
State Paper	Miami	Daily	140 000
Suncoast News	New Port Richey	Twice-weekly	172 000
Sun-Sentinel	Fort Lauderdale	Daily	263 256
Times	St Petersburg	Daily and Sunday	354 164
Tribune and Times	Tampa	Daily and Sunday	264 400
Georgia			
Atlanta Constitution	Atlanta	Monday to Friday	309 906
Dekalb News/Sun	Decatur	Weekly	104 000
Journal	Atlanta	Daily	140 473
Macon Telegraph and News	Macon	Daily and Sunday	100 488
Illinois			
Chicago Sun Times	Chicago	Daily	518 094
Chicago Tribune	Chicago	Daily and Sunday	678 085
Daily Herald	Chicago	Daily	124 595
Journal Star	Peoria	Daily and Sunday	110 115
Wall Street Herald (midwest edition)	Chicago	Daily	513 653
Indiana			
Courier	Evansville	Daily and Sunday	116 962
Journal-Gazette	Fort Wayne	Daily and Sunday	139 275
News	Indianapolis	Daily	101 091
Star	Indianapolis	Daily and Sunday	231 423
Iowa			
Register	Des Moines	Daily and Sunday	184 591
Kansas			
Wichita Eagle	Wichita	Daily and Sunday	198 906
Kentucky			
Courier Journal	Louisville	Daily and Sunday	239 595
Herald Leader	Lexington	Daily and Sunday	157 908
Louisiana			
Times Picayune	New Orleans	Daily and Sunday	267 938

Maryland

| Sun | Baltimore | Daily | 248 520 |

Massachusetts

Boston Globe	Boston	Daily and Sunday	506 545
Boston Herald	Boston	Daily and Sunday	309 935
Christian Science Monitor	Boston	Monday to Friday	104 314
Patriot Ledger	Quincy	Daily	101 639
Phoenix	Boston	Weekly	134 000
Union	Springfield	Daily	156 880
Telegram and Gazette	Worcester	Daily	135 891

Michigan

Free Press	Detroit	Daily and Sunday	554 606
Journal	Flint	Daily	107 940
News	Detroit	Daily and Sunday	355 970
Press	Grand Rapids	Daily and Sunday	147 530

Minnesota

| Pioneer Press Dispatch | St Paul | Daily | 207 802 |
| Star Tribune | Minneapolis | Daily and Sunday | 407 504 |

Mississippi

| Clarion Ledger | Jackson | Daily | 123 052 |

Missouri

| Post Dispatch | St Louis | Daily and Sunday | 333 968 |
| Star | Kansas City | Monday to Friday | 290 650 |

Nebraska

| World Herald | Omaha | Daily and Sunday | 233 035 |

Nevada

| Las Vegas Review Journal | Las Vegas | Daily and Sunday | 137 153 |

New Jersey

Asbury Park Press	Asbury Park	Daily	228 140
Courier-Post	Camden-Cherry Hill	Monday to Friday and Sunday	101 803
North Jersey Herald News	Passaic	Daily and Sunday	140 260
Press	Pleasantville	Daily and Sunday	163 282
Record	Hackensack	Daily and Sunday	159 545
Star-Ledger	Newark	Daily and Sunday	455 919

New Mexico

| Journal | Albuquerque | Daily and Sunday | 158 078 |

New York

Daily News	New York	Daily and Sunday	753 024
Democrat and Chronicle	Rochester	Daily and Sunday	143 392
News	Buffalo	Daily and Sunday	296 820
Newsday	Long Island	Daily and Sunday	693 550
New York Post	New York	Daily	405 318
New York Times	New York	Daily and Sunday	1 114 905
Suffolk Life	Riverhead	Weekly	468 000
Times-Herald Record	Middletown	Daily and Sunday	101 097
Times-Union	Albany	Daily and Sunday	173 944

Title	Headquarters	Issue	Circulation
Village Voice	New York	Weekly	147 000
Wall Street Journal	New York	Monday to Friday	1 780 442

North Carolina

Journal	Winston-Salem	Daily and Sunday	107 331
News and Observer	Raleigh	Daily and Sunday	148 618
News and Record	Greensboro	Daily and Sunday	130 977
Observer	Charlotte	Daily and Sunday	236 579

Ohio

Beacon Journal	Akron	Daily and Sunday	155 812
Blade	Toledo	Daily and Sunday	149 760
Cincinnati Post	Cincinnati	Daily	104 264
Dispatch	Columbus	Daily and Sunday	260 355
Enquirer	Cincinnati	Daily and Sunday	203 118
News	Dayton	Daily	162 039
Plain Dealer	Cleveland	Daily	394 692
Vindicator	Youngstown	Daily and Sunday	134 931

Oklahoma

Oklahoman	Oklahoma City	Daily and Sunday	207 759
World	Tulsa	Daily	170 208

Oregon

Oregonian	Portland	Daily and Sunday	334 744
This Week	Portland	Weekly	442 000

Pennsylvania

Daily News	Philadelphia	Daily	196 239
Morning Call	Allentown	Daily and Sunday	136 645
News Gleaner	Philadelphia	Weekly	109 000
Philadelphia Inquirer	Philadelphia	Daily and Sunday	478 999
Post-Gazette	Pittsburgh	Daily	248 183
Times-Northeast	Philadelphia	Weekly	137 000

Rhode Island

Bulletin	Providence	Monday to Friday	265 210
Journal	Providence	Daily	190 876

South Carolina

News and Courier	Charleston	Daily	125 714
State	Columbia	Daily and Sunday	130 649

Tennessee

Commercial Appeal	Memphis	Daily and Sunday	185 834
News-Free Press	Chattanooga	Daily and Sunday	107 373
Tennessean	Nashville	Daily and Sunday	144 331

Texas

American Statesman	Dallas	Daily and Sunday	176 696
Dallas Morning News	Dallas	Daily and Sunday	491 480
Dallas Times Herald	Dallas	Daily and Sunday	340 297
Express-News	San Antonio	Daily and Sunday	232 037
Houston Chronicle	Houston	Daily and Sunday	409 340

Houston Post	Houston	Daily and Sunday	281 628
Light	San Antonio	Daily and Sunday	234 011
Star-Telegram	Fort Worth	Daily and Sunday	237 031
Wall Street Journal (southwest edition)	Dallas	Daily	187 177

Utah

Tribune	Salt Lake City	Daily and Sunday	125 037

Virginia

News Leader	Richmond	Daily	259 093
Times and World News	Roanoke	Daily and Sunday	126 795
Times-Dispatch	Richmond	Daily	211 227
USA Today	Arlington	Monday to Friday	1 456 926
Virginian-Pilot	Norfolk	Daily	165 940

Washington

Chronicle	Spokane	Daily	145 507
News-Tribune	Tacoma	Daily and Sunday	128 932
Post-Intelligencer	Seattle	Daily	203 679
Times	Seattle	Daily	230 286

Wisconsin

Journal	Milwaukee	Daily and Sunday	214 243
Sentinel	Milwaukee	Daily	175 330

11
Art and Culture

11.1 *Literature*

Nobel Prize for Literature

Year	Winner	Nationality
1901	René François Armand Sully-Prudhomme	French
1902	Theodor Mommsen	German
1903	Bjørnstjerne Martinius Bjørnson	Norwegian
1904	Frédéric Mistral and José Echegaray y Eizaguirre	French
1905	Henryk Sienkiewicz	Polish
1906	Giosuè Carducci	Italian
1907	Rudyard Kipling	British
1908	Rudolf Christoph Eucken	German
1909	Selma Ottiliana Lovisa Lagerlöf	Swedish
1910	Paul Johann von Heyse	German
1911	Count Maurice Maeterlinck	Belgian
1912	Gerhart Hauptmann	German
1913	Rabindranath Tagore	Indian
1914	(No award)	
1915	Romain Rolland	French
1916	Karl Gustav Verner von Heidenstam	Swedish
1917	Karl Gjellerup and Henrik Pontoppidan	Danish
1918	(No award)	
1919	Carl Friedrich George Spitteler	Swiss
1920	Knut Hamsun	Norwegian
1921	Anatole France	French
1922	Jacinto Benavente	Spanish
1923	William Butler Yeats	Irish
1924	Wladyslaw Stanislaw Reymont	Polish
1925	George Bernard Shaw	Irish
1926	Grazia Deledda	Italian
1927	Henri Bergson	French
1928	Sigrid Undset	Norwegian

1929	Thomas Mann	German
1930	Harry Sinclair Lewis	US
1931	Erik Axel Karlfeldt	Swedish
1932	John Galsworthy	British
1933	Ivan Alexeievich Bunin	Russian
1934	Luigi Pirandello	Italian
1935	(No award)	
1936	Eugene Gladstone O'Neill	US
1937	Roger Martin du Gard	French
1938	Pearl Buck	US
1939	Frans Eemil Sillanpää	Finnish
1940–1943	(No award)	
1944	Johannes Vilhelm Jensen	Danish
1945	Gabriela Mistral	Chilean
1946	Hermann Hesse	German-born Swiss
1947	André Gide	French
1948	T. S. Eliot	Anglo-US
1949	William Faulkner	US
1950	Bertrand Russell	British
1951	Pär Lagerkvist	Swedish
1952	François Mauriac	French
1953	Winston Churchill	British
1954	Ernest Hemingway	US
1955	Halldór Laxness	Icelandic
1956	Juan Ramón Jiménez	Spanish
1957	Albert Camus	French
1958	Boris Pasternak	Russian
1959	Salvatore Quasimodo	Italian
1960	Saint-John Perse	French
1961	Ivo Andric	Yugoslav
1962	John Steinbeck	US
1963	George Seferis	Greek
1964	Jean Paul Sartre (declined)	French
1965	Mikhail Sholokhov	Russian
1966	Shmuel Yosef Agnon and Nelly Sachs	Israeli/Swedish
1967	Miguel Angel Asturias	Guatemalan
1968	Kawabata Yasunari	Japanese
1969	Samuel Beckett	Irish
1970	Alexander Solzhenitsyn	Russian
1971	Pablo Neruda	Chilean
1972	Heinrich Böll	German
1973	Patrick White	Australian
1974	Eyvind Johnson and Harry Martinson	Swedish
1975	Eugenio Montale	Italian
1976	Saul Bellow	US
1977	Vicente Aleixandre	Spanish
1978	Isaac Bashevis Singer	US
1979	Odysseus Elytis	Greek
1980	Czeslaw Milosz	Polish-US
1981	Elias Canetti	Bulgarian-born German
1982	Gabriel Garcia Márquez	Colombian

Year	Winner	Nationality
1983	William Golding	British
1984	Jaroslav Seifert	Czech
1985	Claude Simon	French
1986	Wole Soyinka	Nigerian
1987	Joseph Brodsky	Russian-US
1988	Naguib Mahfouz	Egyptian
1989	Camilo José Cela	Spanish
1990	Octavio Paz	Mexican
1991	Nadine Gordimer	South African
1992	Derek Walcott	St Lucian
1993	Toni Morrison	US
1994	Kenzaburo Oë	Japanese
1995	Seamus Heaney	Irish
1996	Wislawa Szymborska	Polish
1997	Dario Fo	Italian
1998	José Saramago	Portuguese
1999	Günter Grass	German
2000	Gao Xingjian	Chinese

Pulitzer Prize for Fiction

Year	Winner	Book
1918	Ernest Poole	His Family
1919	Booth Tarkington	The Magnificent Ambersons
1920	(No award)	
1921	Edith Wharton	The Age of Innocence
1922	Booth Tarkington	Alice Adams
1923	Willa Cather	One of Ours
1924	Margaret Wilson	The Able McLaughlins
1925	Edna Ferber	So Big
1926	Sinclair Lewis	Arrowsmith
1927	Louis Bromfield	Early Autumn
1928	Thornton Wilder	The Bridge of San Luis Rey
1929	Julia Peterkin	Scarlet Sister Mary
1930	Oliver LaFarge	Laughing Boy
1931	Margaret Ayer Barnes	Years of Grace
1932	Pearl S. Buck	The Good Earth
1933	T. S. Stribling	The Store
1934	Caroline Miller	Lamb in His Bosom
1935	Josephine Winslow Johnson	Now in November
1936	Harold L. Davis	Honey in the Horn
1937	Margaret Mitchell	Gone With the Wind
1938	John Phillips Marquand	The Late George Apley
1939	Marjorie Kinnan Rawlings	The Yearling
1940	John Steinbeck	The Grapes of Wrath
1941	(No award)	
1942	Ellen Glasgow	In This Our Life
1943	Upton Sinclair	Dragon's Teeth
1944	Martin Flavin	Journey in the Dark

1945	John Hersey	A Bell for Adamo
1946	(No award)	
1947	Robert Penn Warren	All the King's Men
1948	James A. Michener	Tales of the South Pacific
1949	James Gould Cozzens	Guard of Honour
1950	A. B. Guthrie Jr	The Way West
1951	Conrad Richter	The Town
1952	Herman Wouk	The Caine Mutiny
1953	Ernest Hemingway	The Old Man and the Sea
1954	(No award)	
1955	William Faulkner	A Fable
1956	Mackinley Kanter	Andersonville
1957	(No award)	
1958	James Agee	A Death in the Family
1959	Robert Lewis Taylor	The Travels of Jamie McPheeters
1960	Allen Drury	Advise and Consent
1961	Harper Lee	To Kill a Mockingbird
1962	Edwin O'Connor	The Edge of Sadness
1963	William Faulkner	The Reivers
1964	(No award)	
1965	Shirley Ann Grau	The Keepers of the House
1966	Katherine Anne Porter	The Collected Stories of Katherine Anne Porter
1967	Bernard Malamud	The Fixer
1968	William Styron	The Confessions of Nat Turner
1969	N. Scott Momaday	House Made of Dawn
1970	Jean Stafford	Collected Stories
1971	(No award)	
1972	Wallace Stegner	Angle of Repose
1973	Eudora Welty	The Optimist's Daughter
1974	(No award)	
1975	Michael Shaara	The Killer Angels
1976	Saul Bellow	Humboldt's Gift
1977	(No award)	
1978	James Alan McPherson	Elbow Room
1979	John Cheever	The Stories of John Cheever
1980	Norman Mailer	The Executioner's Song
1981	John Kennedy Toole	A Confederacy of Dunces
1982	John Updike	Rabbit is Rich
1983	Alice Walker	The Color Purple
1984	William Kennedy	Ironweed
1985	Alison Lurie	Foreign Affairs
1986	Larry McMurty	Lonesome Dove
1987	Peter Taylor	A Summons to Memphis
1988	Toni Morrison	Beloved
1989	Anne Tyler	Breathing Lessons
1990	Oscar Hijuelos	The Mambo Kings Play Songs of Love
1991	John Updike	Rabbit at Rest
1992	Jane Smiley	A Thousand Acres
1993	Robert Olen Butler	A Good Scent From a Strange Mountain

Year	Winner	Book
1994	E. Annie Proulx	The Shipping News
1995	Carol Shields	The Stone Diaries
1996	Richard Ford	Independence Day
1997	Steven Millhauser	Martin Dressler: The Tale of an American Dreamer
1998	Philip Roth	American Pastoral
1999	Michael Cunningham	The Hours
2000	Jhumpa Lahiri	Interpretation of Maladies

Prix Goncourt

Year	Winner	Book
1903	John-Antoine Nau	Force ennemie
1904	Léon Frapié	La Maternelle
1905	Claude Farrère	Les Civilisés
1906	Jérôme and Jean Tharaud	Dingley, l'illustre écrivain
1907	Émile Moselly	Terres lorraines
1908	Francis de Miomandre	Écrit sur de l'eau
1909	Marius and Ary Leblond	En France
1910	Louis Pergaud	De Goupil Margot
1911	Alphonse de Chateaubriant	Monsieur des Lourdines
1912	André Savignon	Les Filles de la pluie
1913	Marc Elder	Le Peuple de la mer
1914 (awarded 1916)	(Award postponed)	
1915	René Benjamin	Gaspard
1916	Henri Babusse	Le Feu
1916	Adrien Bertrand	L'Appel du sol
1917	Henri Malherbe	La Flamme au poing
1918	Georges Duhamel	Civilisation
1919	Marcel Proust	A l'ombre des jeunes filles en fleur
1920	Ernest Pérochon	Nêne
1921	René Maran	Batouala
1922	Henri Béraud	Le Vitriol de lune et Le Martyre de l'obèse
1923	Lucien Fabre	Rabevel ou Le Mal des ardents
1924	Thierry Sandre	Le Chèvrefeuille; Le Purgatoire; Le Chapitre XIII d'Athénée
1925	Maurice Genevoix	Raboliot
1926	Henri Deberly	Le Supplice de Phèdre
1927	Maurice Bedel	Jérôme 60° latitude Nord
1928	Maurice Constantin-Weyer	Un homme se penche sur son passé
1929	Marcel Arland	L'Ordre
1930	Henri Fauconnier	Malaisie
1931	Jean Fayard	Mal d'amour
1932	Guy Mazeline	Les Loups
1933	André Malraux	La Condition humaine
1934	Roger Vercel	Capitaine Conan

1935	Joseph Peyré	Sang et lumières
1936	Maxence Van der Meersch	L'Empreinte du dieu
1937	Charles Plisnier	Faux Passeports
1938	Henri Troyat	L'Araigne
1939	Philippe Hériat	Les Enfants gatés
1940	Francois Ambrière	Les Grandes Vacances
1941 (awarded 1946)	Henri Pourrat	Vent de mars
1942	Marc Bernard	Pareils des enfants
1943	Marius Grout	Passage de l'homme
1944	Elsa Triolet	Le premier accroc coûte deux cents francs
1945	Jean-Louis Bory	Mon village a l'heure allemande
1946	Jean-Jacques Gautier	Histoire d'un faite divers
1947	Jean-Louis Curtis	Les Fortês de la nuit
1948	Maurice Druon	Les Grandes Familles
1949	Robert Merle	Week-End à Zuydcoote
1950	Paul Colin	Les Jeux sauvages
1951	Julien Gracq	Le Rivage des Syrtes (declined)
1952	Béatrice Beck	Léon Morin, prêtre
1953	Pierre Gascar	Les Temps des morts; Les Bêtes
1954	Simone de Beauvoir	Les Mandarins
1955	Roger Ikor	Les Eaux melées
1956	Romain Gary	Les Racines du ciel
1957	Roger Vailland	La Loi
1958	Francis Walder	Saint-Germain ou La Négociation
1959	André Schwarz-Bart	Le Dernier des justes
1960	Vintila Horia	Dieu est né en exil (declined)
1961	Jean Cau	La Pitié de Dieu
1962	Anne Langfus	Les Bagages de sable
1963	Armand Lanoux	Quand la mer se retire
1964	Georges Conchon	L'État sauvage
1965	Jacques Borel	L'Adoration
1966	Edmonde Charles-Roux	Oublier Palerme
1967	André Pieyre de Mandiargues	La Marge
1968	Bernard Clavel	Les Fruits de l'hiver
1969	Félicien Marceau	Creezy
1970	Michel Tournier	Le Roi des Aulnes
1971	Jacques Laurent	Les Bêtises
1972	Jean Carrière	L'Epervier de Maheux
1973	Jacques Chessex	L'Orgre
1974	Pascal Lainé	La Dentellière
1975	Émile Ajar	La Vie devant soi
1976	Patrick Grainville	Les Flamboyants
1977	Didier Decoin	John L'Enfer
1978	Patrick Modiano	Rue des boutiques obscures
1979	Antonine Maillet	Pélagie la Charrette
1980	Yves Navarre	Le Jardin d'acclimatation
1981	Lucien Bodard	Anne Marie
1982	Dominique Fernandez	Dans la main de l'ange
1983	Frédérick Tristan	Les Égarés

Year	Winner	Book
1984	Marguerite Duras	L'Amant
1985	Yann Queffelec	Les Noces barbares
1986	Michel Host	Valet de nuit
1987	Tahar ben Jalloun	La Nuit sacrée
1988	Erik Orsenna	L'Exposition coloniale
1989	Jean Vautrin	Un Grand Pas vers le bon Dieu
1990	Jean Rouaud	Les Champs d'honneur
1991	Pierre Combescot	Les Filles du Calvaire
1992	Patrick Chamoiseau	Texaco
1993	Amin Maalouf	Le Rocher de Tanois
1994	Didier van Cauwelaert	Un Aller simple
1995	Andrei Makine	Le Testament français
1996	Pascale Roze	Le Chasseur Zéro
1997	Patrick Rambaud	La Bataille
1998	Paule Constant	Confidence pour confidence
1999	Jean Echenoz	Je m'en vais
2000	Jean-Jacques Shuhl	Ingrid Caven

Booker Prize

Year	Winner	Book
1969	P. H. Newby	Something to Answer For
1970	Bernice Rubens	The Elected Member
1971	V. S. Naipaul	In a Free State
1972	John Berger	G
1973	J. G. Farrell	The Siege of Krishnapur
1974	Nadine Gordimer	The Conservationist
	Stanley Middleton	Holiday
1975	Ruth Prawer Jhabvala	Heat and Dust
1976	David Storey	Saville
1977	Paul Scott	Staying On
1978	Iris Murdoch	The Sea, The Sea
1979	Penelope Fitzgerald	Offshore
1980	William Golding	Rites of Passage
1981	Salman Rushdie	Midnight's Children
1982	Thomas Keneally	Schindler's Ark
1983	J. M. Coetzee	Life and Times of Michael K
1984	Anita Brookner	Hotel du Lac
1985	Keri Hulme	The Bone People
1986	Kingsley Amis	The Old Devils
1987	Penelope Lively	Moon Tiger
1988	Peter Carey	Oscar and Lucinda
1989	Kazuo Ishiguro	The Remains of the Day
1990	A. S. Byatt	Possession
1991	Ben Okri	The Famished Road
1992	Barry Unsworth	Sacred Hunger
	Michael Ondaatje	The English Patient
1993	Roddy Doyle	Paddy Clark – Ha ha ha
1994	James Kelman	How late it was, how late

1995	Pat Barker	The Ghost Road
1996	Graham Swift	Last Orders
1997	Arundhati Roy	The God of Small Things
1998	Ian McEwan	Amsterdam
1999	J. M. Coetzee	Disgrace
2000	Margaret Atwood	The Blind Assassin

Whitbread Book of the Year

Year	Winner	Book
1971	Gerda Charles	The Destiny Waltz
1972	Susan Hill	The Bird of Night
1973	Shiva Naipaul	The Chip Chip Gatherers
1974	Iris Murdoch	The Sacred and Profane Love Machine
1975	William McIlvanney	Docherty
1976	William Trevor	The Children of Dynmouth
1977	Beryl Bainbridge	Injury Time
1978	Paul Theroux	Picture Palace
1979	Jennifer Johnston	The Old Jest
1980	David Lodge	How Far Can You Go?
1981	William Boyd	A Good Man in Africa
1982	Bruce Chatwin	On the Black Hill
1983	John Fuller	Flying to Nowhere
1984	James Buchan	A Parish of Rich Women
1985	Douglas Dunn	Elegies
1986	Kazuo Ishiguro	An Artist of the Floating World
1987	Christopher Nolan	Under the Eye of the Clock
1988	Paul Sayer	The Comforts of Madness
1989	Richard Holmes	Coleridge: Early Visions
1990	Nicholas Mosley	Hopeful Monsters
1991	John Richardson	A Life of Picasso
1992	Jeff Torrington	Swing Hammer Swing!
1993	Joan Brady	Theory of War
1994	William Trevor	Felicia's Journey
1995	Kate Atkinson	Behind the Scenes at the Museum
1996	Seamus Heaney	The Spirit Level
1997	Ted Hughes	Tales from Ovid
1998	Ted Hughes	Birthday Letters
1999	Seamus Heaney	Beowulf
2000	Matthew Kneale	The English Passengers

Orange Award (Women Writers)

Year	Winner	Book
1997	Helen Dunmore	A Spell of Winter
1998	Anne Michaels	Fugitive Pieces
1999	Suzanne Berne	A Crime in the Neighbourhood
2000	Linda Grant	When I Lived in Modern Times

Poets Laureate

Year appointed	
1617	Ben Jonson
1638	Sir William Davenant
1668	John Dryden
1689	Thomas Shadwell
1692	Nahum Tate
1715	Nicholas Rowe
1718	Laurence Eusden
1730	Colley Cibber
1757	William Whitehead
1785	Thomas Warton
1790	Henry Pye
1813	Robert Southey
1843	William Wordsworth
1850	Alfred, Lord Tennyson
1896	Alfred Austin
1913	Robert Bridges
1930	John Masefield
1968	Cecil Day Lewis
1972	Sir John Betjeman
1984	Ted Hughes
1999	Andrew Motion

11.2 *Drama*

Plays of William Shakespeare

Title	Category	Performed
Henry VI Part I	History	1589–91
Henry VI Part II	History	1590–92
Henry VI Part III	History	1590–92
Romeo and Juliet	Tragedy	1591–96
The Comedy of Errors	Comedy	1591–94
Richard III	History	1592
The Two Gentlemen of Verona	Comedy	1592–98
Titus Andronicus	Tragedy	1592–94
The Taming of the Shrew	Comedy	1592
King John	History	1594–96
Love's Labour's Lost	Comedy	1594
Richard II	History	1595

A Midsummer Night's Dream	Comedy	1596
Henry IV Part I	History	1596–98
The Merchant of Venice	Comedy	1596–97
Henry IV Part II	History	1597–98
The Merry Wives of Windsor	Comedy	1598–99
Much Ado About Nothing	Comedy	1598–99
Henry V	History	1598–99
Julius Caesar	Roman	1599
As You Like It	Comedy	1599
Hamlet	Tragedy	1599–1601
Twelfth Night	Comedy	1601–2
Troilus and Cressida	Tragedy	1602–3
All's Well That Ends Well	Comedy	1602
Othello	Tragedy	1602–3
Macbeth	Tragedy	1602–6
Measure for Measure	Comedy	1603–4
King Lear	Tragedy	1605
Antony and Cleopatra	Tragedy	1606
Coriolanus	Roman	1607–10
Timon of Athens	Romance	1607
Pericles	Comedy	1608
Cymbeline	Comedy	1610
The Tempest	Comedy	1610–11
The Winter's Tale	Comedy	1611
Henry VIII	History	1612–13
The Two Noble Kinsmen	Romance	1613–14

11.3 *Cinema*

International film festivals

Festival	Location	Date
AFI/European Community Film Festival	Los Angeles (USA)	June
AFI/LA Film Festival	Los Angeles (USA)	April
American Film Market	Los Angeles (USA)	February–March
Amiens	Amiens (France)	November
Annecy	Annecy (France)	May–June (alternate years)
Antwerp	Antwerp (Belgium)	March
Australian International Film Festival	Australia	September
Austrian Film Days	Austria	September
Avoriaz	Avoriaz (France)	January

Festival	Location	Date
Banff TV Festival	Banff (Canada)	June
Barcelona	Barcelona (Spain)	November
Belgian Film Festival	Brussels (Belgium)	January
Belgrade	Belgrade (Yugoslavia)	January–February
Bergamo	Bergamo (Italy)	July
Berlin	Berlin (Germany)	February
Biarritz	Biarritz (France)	September
Birmingham Film and Television Festival	Birmingham (UK)	October–November
Boston	Boston (USA)	September
Bristol Film and Television Festival	Bristol (UK)	September
Cairo	Cairo (Egypt)	December
Cambridge	Cambridge (UK)	July
Cannes	Cannes (France)	May
Cartagena	Cartagena (Colombia)	April
Cherbourg	Cherbourg (France)	October
Chicago	Chicago (USA)	October
Cinetex	Las Vegas (USA)	September
Clermont-Ferrand	Clermont-Ferrand (France)	February
Cognac	Cognac (France)	April
Cork	Cork (Ireland)	September–October
Deauville	Deauville (France)	September
Dublin	Dublin (Ireland)	October
Dutch Film Days and Film Market	Netherlands	September
Edinburgh	Edinburgh (Scotland)	August–September
Festival dei Popoli	Florence (Italy)	November–December
Filmfest DC	Washington (USA)	April–May
Flanders	Ghent (Belgium)	October
Gdansk	Gdansk (Poland)	September
Gothenburg	Gothenburg (Sweden)	January–February
Grenoble	Grenoble (France)	October
Hawaii	Honolulu (Hawaii)	November
Hof	Hof (Germany)	October
Indian International Film Festival	India	January
Jerusalem	Jerusalem (Israel)	June–July
Karlovy Vary	Karlovy Vary (Czech Republic)	July
Katowice	Katowice (Poland)	November
Krakow	Krakow (Poland)	June
Locarno	Locarno (Switzerland)	August
London Film Festival	London (UK)	November–December
Madrid/Imagfic	Madrid (Spain)	March–April
Malmo	Malmo (Sweden)	September
Melbourne	Melbourne (Australia)	June
Miami	Miami (USA)	February
Midnight Sun	Finland	June
Mill Valley Film and Video Festival	Mill Valley (USA)	October
Monte Carlo Film Festival	Monte Carlo (Monaco)	January–February
Montreal World Film Festival	Montreal (Canada)	August

Moscow	Moscow (Russia)	July
Munich	Munich (Germany)	June
NATPE	New Orleans (USA)	January
New Latin American Cinema	Cuba	December
New York	New York (USA)	September–October
Nyon	Switzerland	October
Palm Springs	Palm Springs (USA)	January
Pan African Film Festival	Burkina Faso	February–March
Paris	Paris (France)	March–April
Pesaro International Festival of New Cinema	Pesaro (Italy)	June
Pordenone	Pordenone (Italy)	October
Portland	Portland (USA)	February
Porto Fantasy Film Festival	Porto (Portugal)	February
Prague Television Festival	Prague (Czech Republic)	June
Pula	Pula (Yugoslavia)	July
Rio de Janeiro	Rio de Janeiro (Brazil)	November
Rotterdam Film International	Rotterdam (Netherlands)	March
Rouen	Rouen (France)	March
San Remo	San Remo (Italy)	March
San Sebastian	San Sebastian (Spain)	September
Santa Barbara International Film Festival	Santa Barbara (USA)	March
San Francisco International Film Festival	San Francisco (USA)	April–May
São Paulo	São Paulo (Brazil)	October
Seattle International Film Festival	Seattle (USA)	May–June
Sitges	Sitges (Spain)	September–October
Strasbourg	Strasbourg (France)	March
Sundance Film Festival	Park City, Utah (USA)	January
Sydney	Sydney (Australia)	June
Taipei	Taipei (Taiwan)	October
Tampere Film Festival	Tampere (Finland)	February
Teleforum	Moscow (Russia)	September
Thessaloniki	Thessaloniki (Greece)	October
Tokyo	Tokyo (Japan)	September
Toronto	Toronto (Canada)	September
Trieste Science-Fiction Festival	Trieste (Italy)	July
Vancouver	Vancouver (Canada)	September–October
Varna	Varna (Bulgaria)	June
Venice Film Festival	Venice (Italy)	September
Vevey	Vevey (Switzerland)	August
Viennale	Vienna (Austria)	March
Wellington	Wellington (New Zealand)	July
Women in Film	Los Angeles (USA)	October
Zagreb	Zagreb (Croatia)	June

Motion Picture Academy awards (Oscars)

Year	Best Picture	Best Director
1928	Wings	Frank Borzage (Seventh Heaven)
1929	The Broadway Melody	Frank Lloyd (The Divine Lady)
1930	All Quiet on the Western Front	Lewis Milestone (All Quiet on the Western Front)
1931	Cimarron	Norman Taurog (Skippy)
1932	Grand Hotel	Frank Borzage (Bad Girl)
1933	Cavalcade	Frank Lloyd (Cavalcade)
1934	It Happened One Night	Frank Capra (It Happened One Night)
1935	Mutiny on the Bounty	John Ford (The Informer)
1936	The Great Ziegfeld	Frank Capra (Mr Deeds Goes to Town)
1937	The Life of Emile Zola	Leo McCarey (The Awful Truth)
1938	You Can't Take It with You	Frank Capra (You Can't Take It with You)
1939	Gone with the Wind	Victor Fleming (Gone with the Wind)
1940	Rebecca	John Ford (The Grapes of Wrath)
1941	How Green was My Valley	John Ford (How Green was My Valley)
1942	Mrs Miniver	William Wyler (Mrs Miniver)
1943	Casablanca	Michael Curtiz (Casablanca)
1944	Going My Way	Leo McCarey (Going My Way)
1945	The Lost Weekend	Billy Wilder (The Lost Weekend)
1946	The Best Years of Our Lives	William Wyler (The Best Years of Our Lives)
1947	Gentleman's Agreement	Elia Kazan (Gentleman's Agreement)
1948	Hamlet	John Huston (Treasure of the Sierra Madre)
1949	All the King's Men	Joseph L. Mankiewicz (A Letter to Three Wives)
1950	All about Eve	Joseph L. Mankiewicz (All about Eve)
1951	An American in Paris	George Stevens (A Place in the Sun)
1952	The Greatest Show on Earth	John Ford (The Quiet Man)
1953	From Here to Eternity	Fred Zinnemann (From Here to Eternity)
1954	On the Waterfront	Elia Kazan (On the Waterfront)
1955	Marty	Delbert Mann (Marty)
1956	Around the World in 80 Days	George Stevens (Giant)
1957	The Bridge on the River Kwai	David Lean (The Bridge on the River Kwai)
1958	Gigi	Vincente Minnelli (Gigi)
1959	Ben Hur	William Wyler (Ben Hur)
1960	The Apartment	Billy Wilder (The Apartment)
1961	West Side Story	Robert Wise and Jerome Robbins (West Side Story)
1962	Lawrence of Arabia	David Lean (Lawrence of Arabia)
1963	Tom Jones	Tony Richardson (Tom Jones)
1964	My Fair Lady	George Cukor (My Fair Lady)
1965	The Sound of Music	Robert Wise (The Sound of Music)

Best Actor	Best Actress
Emil Jannings (The Last Command/The Way of All Flesh)	Janet Gaynor (Seventh Heaven, Street Angel, Sunrise)
Warner Baxter (In Old Arizona)	Mary Pickford (Coquette)
George Arliss (Disraeli)	Norma Shearer (The Divorcee)
Lionel Barrymore (A Free Soul)	Marie Dressler (Min and Bill)
Fredric March (Dr Jekyll and Mr Hyde), Wallace Beery (The Champ)	Helen Hayes (The Sin of Madelon Claudet)
Charles Laughton (The Private Life Of Henry VIII)	Katharine Hepburn (Morning Glory)
Clark Gable (It Happened One Night)	Claudette Colbert (It Happened One Night)
Victor McLaglen (The Informer)	Bette Davis (Dangerous)
Paul Muni (The Story of Louis Pasteur)	Luise Rainer (The Great Ziegfeld)
Spencer Tracy (Captains Courageous)	Luise Rainer (The Good Earth)
Spencer Tracy (Boys' Town)	Bette Davis (Jezebel)
Robert Donat (Goodbye, Mr Chips)	Vivien Leigh (Gone with the Wind)
James Stewart (The Philadelphia Story)	Ginger Rogers (Kitty Foyle)
Gary Cooper (Sergeant York)	Joan Fontaine (Suspicion)
James Cagney (Yankee Doodle Dandy)	Greer Garson (Mrs Miniver)
Paul Lukas (Watch on the Rhine)	Jennifer Jones (The Song of Bernadette)
Bing Crosby (Going My Way)	Ingrid Bergman (Gaslight)
Ray Milland (The Lost Weekend)	Joan Crawford (Mildred Pierce)
Fredric March (The Best Years of Our Lives)	Olivia de Havilland (To Each His Own)
Ronald Colman (A Double Life)	Loretta Young (The Farmer's Daughter)
Laurence Olivier (Hamlet)	Jane Wyman (Johnny Belinda)
Broderick Crawford (All the King's Men)	Olivia de Havilland (The Heiress)
Jose Ferrer (Cyrano de Bergerac)	Judy Holliday (Born Yesterday)
Humphrey Bogart (The African Queen)	Vivien Leigh (A Streetcar Named Desire)
Gary Cooper (High Noon)	Shirley Booth (Come Back Little Sheba)
William Holden (Stalag 17)	Audrey Hepburn (Roman Holiday)
Marlon Brando (On the Waterfront)	Grace Kelly (The Country Girl)
Ernest Borgnine (Marty)	Anna Magnani (The Rose Tattoo)
Yul Brynner (The King and I)	Ingrid Bergman (Anastasia)
Alec Guinness (The Bridge on the River Kwai)	Joanne Woodward (The Three Faces of Eve)
David Niven (Separate Tables)	Susan Hayward (I Want to Live!)
Charlton Heston (Ben Hur)	Simone Signoret (Room at the Top)
Burt Lancaster (Elmer Gantry)	Elizabeth Taylor (Butterfield 8)
Maximilian Schell (Judgment at Nuremberg)	Sophia Loren (Two Women)
Gregory Peck (To Kill a Mockingbird)	Anne Bancroft (The Miracle Worker)
Sidney Poitier (Lilies of the Field)	Patricia Neal (Hud)
Rex Harrison (My Fair Lady)	Julie Andrews (Mary Poppins)
Lee Marvin (Cat Ballou)	Julie Christie (Darling)

Year	Best Picture	Best Director
1966	A Man for All Seasons	Fred Zinnemann (A Man for All Seasons)
1967	In the Heat of the Night	Mike Nicholls (The Graduate)
1968	Oliver!	Sir Carol Reed (Oliver!)
1969	Midnight Cowboy	John Schlesinger (Midnight Cowboy)
1970	Patton	Franklin J. Schaffner (Patton)
1971	The French Connection	William Friedkin (The French Connection)
1972	The Godfather	Bob Fosse (Cabaret)
1973	The Sting	George Roy Hill (The Sting)
1974	The Godfather Part II	Francis Ford Coppola (The Godfather Part II)
1975	One Flew Over the Cuckoo's Nest	Milos Forman (One Flew Over the Cuckoo's Nest)
1976	Rocky	John G. Avildsen (Rocky)
1977	Annie Hall	Woody Allen (Annie Hall)
1978	The Deer Hunter	Michael Cimino (The Deer Hunter)
1979	Kramer vs Kramer	Robert Benton (Kramer vs Kramer)
1980	Ordinary People	Robert Redford (Ordinary People)
1981	Chariots of Fire	Warren Beatty (Reds)
1982	Gandhi	Richard Attenborough (Gandhi)
1983	Terms of Endearment	James L. Brooks (Terms of Endearment)
1984	Amadeus	Milos Forman (Amadeus)
1985	Out of Africa	Sydney Pollack (Out of Africa)
1986	Platoon	Oliver Stone (Platoon)
1987	The Last Emperor	Bernardo Bertolucci (The Last Emperor)
1988	Rain Man	Barry Levington (Rain Man)
1989	Driving Miss Daisy	Oliver Stone (Born on the Fourth of July)
1990	Dances with Wolves	Kevin Costner (Dances with Wolves)
1991	The Silence of the Lambs	Jonathan Demme (The Silence of the Lambs)
1992	Unforgiven	Clint Eastwood (Unforgiven)
1993	Schindler's List	Steven Spielberg (Schindler's List)
1994	Forrest Gump	Robert Zemeckis (Forrest Gump)
1995	Braveheart	Mel Gibson (Braveheart)
1996	The English Patient	Anthony Minghella (The English Patient)
1997	Titanic	James Cameron (Titanic)
1998	Shakespeare in Love	Steven Spielberg (Saving Private Ryan)
1999	American Beauty	Sam Mendes (American Beauty)
2000	Gladiator	Steven Soderbergh (Traffic)

Best Actor	Best Actress
Paul Scofield (A Man for All Seasons)	Elizabeth Taylor (Who's Afraid of Virginia Woolf ?)
Rod Steiger (In the Heat of the Night)	Katharine Hepburn (Guess Who's Coming to Dinner)
Cliff Robertson (Charly)	Katharine Hepburn (The Lion in Winter), Barbra Streisand (Funny Girl)
John Wayne (True Grit)	Maggie Smith (The Prime of Miss Jean Brodie)
George C. Scott (Patton)	Glenda Jackson (Women in Love)
Gene Hackman (The French Connection)	Jane Fonda (Klute)
Marlon Brando (The Godfather)	Liza Minnelli (Cabaret)
Jack Lemmon (Save the Tiger)	Glenda Jackson (A Touch of Class)
Art Carney (Harry and Tonto)	Ellen Burstyn (Alice Doesn't Live Here Anymore)
Jack Nicholson (One Flew Over the Cuckoo's Nest)	Louise Fletcher (One Flew Over the Cuckoo's Nest)
Peter Finch (Network)	Faye Dunaway (Network)
Richard Dreyfuss (The Goodbye Girl)	Diane Keaton (Annie Hall)
Jon Voight (Coming Home)	Jane Fonda (Coming Home)
Dustin Hoffman (Kramer vs Kramer)	Sally Field (Norma Rae)
Robert De Niro (Raging Bull)	Sissy Spacek (Coal Miner's Daughter)
Henry Fonda (On Golden Pond)	Katharine Hepburn (On Golden Pond)
Ben Kingsley (Gandhi)	Meryl Streep (Sophie's Choice)
Robert Duvall (Tender Mercies)	Shirley Maclaine (Terms of Endearment)
F. Murray Abraham (Amadeus)	Sally Field (Places in the Heart)
William Hurt (Kiss of the Spider Woman)	Geraldine Page (The Trip to Bountiful)
Paul Newman (The Color of Money)	Marlee Matlin (Children of a Lesser God)
Michael Douglas (Wall Street)	Cher (Moonstruck)
Dustin Hoffman (Rain Man)	Jodie Foster (The Accused)
Daniel Day-Lewis (My Left Foot)	Jessica Tandy (Driving Miss Daisy)
Jeremy Irons (Reversal of Fortune)	Kathy Bates (Misery)
Anthony Hopkins (The Silence of the Lambs)	Jodie Foster (The Silence of the Lambs)
Al Pacino (Scent of a Woman)	Emma Thompson (Howard's End)
Tom Hanks (Philadelphia)	Holly Hunter (The Piano)
Tom Hanks (Forrest Gump)	Jessica Lange (Blue Sky)
Nicolas Cage (Leaving Las Vegas)	Susan Sarandon (Dead Man Walking)
Geoffrey Rush (Shine)	Frances McDormand (Fargo)
Jack Nicholson (As Good As It Gets)	Helen Hunt (As Good As It Gets)
Roberto Benigni (Life is Beautiful)	Gwyneth Paltrow (Shakespeare in Love)
Kevin Spacey (American Beauty)	Hilary Swank (Boys Don't Cry)
Russell Crowe (Gladiator)	Julia Roberts (Erin Brockovich)

BAFTA awards

Year	Best Film	Best Director
1947	The Best Years of Our Lifes	
1948	Hamlet	
1949	The Bicycle Thief	
1950	All About Eve	
1951	La Ronde	
1952	The Sound Barrier	
1953	Forbidden Games	
1954	The Wages of Fear	
1955	Richard III	
1956	Gervaise	
1957	The Bridge on the River Kwai	
1958	Room at the Top	
1959	Ben-Hur	
1960	The Apartment	
1961	Ballad of a Soldier	
1962	Lawrence of Arabia	
1963	Tom Jones	
1964	Dr Strangelove	
1965	My Fair Lady	
1966	Who's Afraid of Virginia Woolf?	
1967	A Man for All Seasons	
1968	The Graduate	Mike Nichols (The Graduate)
1969	Midnight Cowboy	John Schlesinger (Midnight Cowboy)
1970	Butch Cassidy and the Sundance Kid	George Roy Hill (Butch Cassidy and the Sundance Kid)
1971	Sunday, Bloody Sunday	John Schlesinger (Sunday, Bloody Sunday)
1972	Cabaret	Bob Fosse (Cabaret)
1973	Day for Night	François Truffaut (Day for Night)
1974	Lacombe Lucien	Roman Polanski (Chinatown)
1975	Alice Doesn't Live Here Any More	Stanley Kubrick (Barry Lyndon)
1976	One Flew Over the Cuckoo's Nest	Milos Forman (One Flew Over the Cuckoo's Nest)
1977	Annie Hall	Woody Allen (Annie Hall)
1978	Julia	Alan Parker (Midnight Express)
1979	Manhattan	Francis Ford Coppola (Apocalypse Now)
1980	The Elephant Man	Akira Kurosawa (Kagemusha)
1981	Chariots of Fire	Louis Malle (Atlantic City)
1982	Gandhi	Richard Attenborough (Gandhi)
1983	Educating Rita	Bill Forsyth (Local Hero)

Best Actor	Best Actress
Ralph Richardson (The Sound Barrier)	Vivien Leigh (A Streetcar Named Desire)
John Gielgud (Julius Caesar)	Audrey Hepburn (Roman Holiday)
Kenneth More (Doctor in the House)	Yvonne Mitchell (The Divided Heart)
Laurence Olivier (Richard III)	Katie Johnson (The Ladykillers)
Peter Finch (A Town Like Alice)	Virginia McKenna (A Town Like Alice)
Alec Guinness (The Bridge on the River Kwai)	Heather Sears (The Story of Esther Costello)
Trevor Howard (The Key)	Irene Worth (Orders to Kill)
Peter Sellers (I'm All Right Jack)	Audrey Hepburn (The Nun's Story)
Peter Finch (The Trials of Oscar Wilde)	Rachel Roberts (Saturday Night and Sunday Morning)
Peter Finch (No Love for Johnnie)	Dora Bryan (A Taste of Honey)
Peter O'Toole (Lawrence of Arabia)	Leslie Caron (The L-Shaped Room)
Dirk Bogarde (The Servant)	Rachel Roberts (This Sporting Life)
Richard Attenborough (Séance on a Wet Afternoon; Guns at Batasi)	Audrey Hepburn (Charade)
Dirk Bogarde (Darling)	Julie Christie (Darling)
Richard Burton (Who's Afraid of Virginia Woolf?; The Spy Who Came in from the Cold)	Elizabeth Taylor (Who's Afraid of Virginia Woolf?)
Paul Scofield (A Man for All Seasons)	Edith Evans (The Whisperers)
Spencer Tracy (Guess Who's Coming to Dinner?)	Katharine Hepburn (Guess Who's Coming to Dinner?)
Dustin Hoffman (Midnight Cowboy; John and Mary)	Maggie Smith (The Prime of Miss Jean Brodie)
Robert Redford (Butch Cassidy and the Sundance Kid; Tell Them Willie Boy Is Here; Downhill Racers)	Katharine Ross (Butch Cassidy and the Sundance Kid; Tell Them Willie Boy Is Here)
Peter Finch (Sunday, Bloody Sunday)	Glenda Jackson (Sunday, Bloody Sunday)
Gene Hackman (The French Connection; The Poseidon Adventure)	Liza Minnelli (Cabaret)
Walter Matthau (Pete 'n' Tillie; Charley Varrick)	Stéphane Audran (The Discreet Charm of the Bourgeoisie; Just before Nightfall)
Jack Nicholson (Chinatown; The Last Detail)	Joanne Woodward (Summer Wishes; Winter Dreams)
Al Pacino (The Godfather Part II; Dog Day Afternoon)	Ellen Burstyn (Alice Doesn't Live Here Any More)
Jack Nicholson (One Flew Over the Cuckoo's Nest)	Louise Fletcher (One Flew Over the Cuckoo's Nest)
Peter Finch (Network)	Diane Keaton (Annie Hall)
Richard Dreyfuss (The Goodbye Girl)	Jane Fonda (Julia)
Jack Lemmon (The China Syndrome)	Jane Fonda (The China Syndrome)
John Hurt (The Elephant Man)	Judy Davis (My Brilliant Career)
Burt Lancaster (Atlantic City)	Meryl Streep (The French Lieutenant's Woman)
Ben Kingsley (Gandhi)	Katharine Hepburn (On Golden Pond)
Michael Caine (Educating Rita)	Julia Walters (Educating Rita)

Year	Best Film	Best Director
1984	The Killing Fields	Wim Wenders (Paris, Texas)
1985	The Purple Rose of Cairo	Woody Allen (Hannah and Her Sisters)
1986	A Room with a View	Oliver Stone (Platoon)
1987	Jean de Florette	Louis Malle (Au Revoir les Enfants)
1988	The Last Emperor	Kenneth Branagh (Henry V)
1989	Dead Poets Society	Kenneth Branagh (Henry V)
1990	Goodfellas	Martin Scorsese (GoodFellas)
1991	The Commitments	Alan Parker (The Commitments)
1992	Howard's End	Robert Altman (The Player)
1993	Schindler's List	Steven Spielberg (Schindler's List)
1994	Four Weddings and a Funeral	Mike Newell (Four Weddings and a Funeral)
1995	Sense and Sensibility	Michael Radford (The Postman/Il Postino)
1996	The English Patient	Joel Coen (Fargo)
1997	The Full Monty	Baz Luhrmann (William Shakespeare's Romeo and Juliet)
1998	Shakespeare in Love	Peter Weir (The Truman Show)
1999	American Beauty	Pedro Almodovar (All About My Mother)
2000	Gladiator	Ang Lee (Crouching Tiger, Hidden Dragon)

Cannes Film Festival awards

Year	Grand Prix/Palme d'Or	Best Director
1949	The Third Man	René Clément (The Walls of Malapaga)
1951	Miracle in Milan	Louis Buñuel
1952	Two Pennyworth of Hope/Othello	Christian-Jaque (Fanfan la Tulipe)
1953	The Wages of Fear	
1954	Gate of Hell	
1955	Marty	Sergei Vasiliev (The Heroes of Shipka/Jules Dassin (Rififi)
1956	The Silent World	Sergei Yutkevich (Othello)
1957	Friendly Persuasion	Robert Bresson (A Man Escaped)
1958	The Cranes Are Flying	Ingmar Bergman (So Close to Life)
1959	Black Orpheus	François Truffaut (The 400 Blows)
1960	La Dolce Vita	
1961	Viridiana	Julia Sointseva (The Flaming Years)
1962	The Given Word	
1963	The Leopard	
1964	The Umbrellas of Cherbourg	
1965	The Knack . . . and How to Get It	Liviu Ciulei (The Forest of the Hanged)
1966	A Man and a Woman/The Birds, the Bees, and the Italian	Sergei Yutkevich (Lenin in Poland)
1967	Blow Up	Ferenc Kósa (Ten Thousand Suns)

Best Actor	Best Actress
Haing S. Ngor (The Killing Fields)	Maggie Smith (A Private Function)
William Hurt (Kiss of the Spider Woman)	Peggy Ashcroft (A Passage to India)
Bob Hoskins (Mona Lisa)	Maggie Smith (A Room with a View)
Sean Connery (The Name of the Rose)	Anne Bancroft (84 Charing Cross Road)
John Cleese (A Fish Called Wanda)	Maggie Smith (The Lonely Passion of Judith Hearne)
Daniel Day-Lewis (My Left Foot)	Pauline Collins (Shirley Valentine)
Philippe Noiret (Nuovo Cinema Paradiso)	Jessica Tandy (Driving Miss Daisy)
Anthony Hopkins (The Silence of the Lambs)	Jodie Foster (The Silence of the Lambs)
Robert Downey Jr (Chaplin)	Emma Thompson (Howard's End)
Anthony Hopkins (The Remains of the Day)	Holly Hunter (The Piano)
Hugh Grant (Four Weddings and a Funeral)	Susan Sarandon (The Client)
Nigel Hawthorn (The Madness of King George)	Emma Thompson (Sense and Sensibility)
Geoffrey Rush (Shine)	Brenda Blethyn (Secrets and Lies)
Robert Carlyle (The Full Monty)	Judi Dench (Mrs Brown)
Roberto Benigni (Life is Beautiful)	Cate Blanchett (Elizabeth)
Kevin Spacey (American Beauty)	Annette Bening (American Beauty)
Jamie Bell (Billy Elliot)	Julia Roberts (Erin Brockovich)

Best Actor	Best Actress
Edward G. Robinson (House of Strangers)	Isa Miranda (The Walls of Malapaga)
Michael Redgrave (The Browning Version)	Bette Davis (All About Eve)
Marlon Brando (Viva Zapata)	Lee Grant (Detective Story)
Charles Vanel (The Wages of Fear)	
Spencer Tracy*	
	Susan Hayward (I'll Cry Tomorrow)
John Kitzmiller (Valley of Peace)	Giulietta Masina (Nights of Cabiria)
Paul Newman (The Long Hot Summer)	Bibi Andersson, Eva Dahlbeck, Barbro Hiortas-Ornas, Ingrid Thulin (So Close to Life)
Dean Stockwell, Bradford Dillman, Orson Welles (Compulsion)	Simone Signoret (Room at the Top)
	Melina Mercouri (Never on Sunday)/ Jeanne Moreau (Moderate Cantabile)
Anthony Perkins (Goodbye Again)	Sophia Loren (Two Women)
Ralph Richardson, Jason Robards Jr, Dean Stockwell (Long Day's Journey into Night)/ Murray Melvin (A Taste of Honey)	Katharine Hepburn (Long Day's Journey into Night)/Rita Tushingham (A Taste of Honey)
Richard Harris (This Sporting Life)	Marina Vlady (Queen Bee)
Saro Urzi (Seduced and Abandoned)/Antal Pager (The Lark)	(Anne Bancroft (The Pumpkin Eater)/ Barbra Barrie (One Potato, Two Potato)
Terence Stamp (The Collector)	Samantha Eggar (The Collector)
Per Oscarsson (Hunger)	Vanessa Redgrave (Morgan!)
Odded Kotier (Three Days and a Child)	Pia Degermark (Elvira Madigan)

Year	Grand Prix/Palme d'Or	Best Director
1969	If...	Glauber Rocha (Antonio das Mortes)/Vojtech Jasn (All My Good Countrymen)
1970	M*A*S*H	John Boorman (Leo the Last)
1971	The Go-Between	Joseph Losey (The Go-Between)
1972	The Mattei Affair/The Working Class Go to Heaven	Miklós Jancsó (Red Psalm)
1973	Scarecrow/The Hireling	
1974	The Conversation	
1975	Chronicle of the Burning Years	Michel Brault (The Orders)/Costa-Gavras (Special Section)
1976	Taxi Driver	Ettore Scola (Down and Dirty)
1977	Padre Padrone	
1978	The Tree of Wooden Clogs	Nagisa Oshima (Ai No Corrida)
1979	The Tin Drum/Apocalypse Now	Terrence Malick (Days of Heaven)
1980	Kagemusha/All That Jazz	
1981	Man of Iron	
1982	Missing/Yol	Werner Herzog (Fitzcarraldo)
1983	The Ballad of Narayama	
1984	Paris, Texas	Bertrand Tavernier (A Sunday in the Country)
1985	When Father was Away on Business	André Téchiné (Rendezvous)
1986	The Mission	Martin Scorsese (After Hours)
1987	Under Satan's Sun	Wim Wenders (Wings of Desire)
1988	Pelle the Conqueror	Fernando E. Solanas (South)
1989	sex, lies and videotape	Emir Kusturica (The Time of the Gypsies)
1990	Wild at Heart	Pavel Lounguine (Taxi Blues)
1991	Barton Fink	Joel Coen (Barton Fink)
1992	Best Intentions	Robert Altman (The Player)
1993	Farewell My Concubine/The Piano	Mike Leigh (Naked)
1994	Pulp Fiction	Nanni Moretti (Dear Diary)
1995	Underground	Mathieu Kassovitz (La Haine)
1996	Secrets and Lies	Joel Coen (Fargo)
1997	The Eel/Taste of Cherries	Wong Kar-Wai (Happy Together)
1998	Eternity and a Day	John Boorman (The General)
1999	Rosetta	Pedro Almodovar (All About My Mother)
2000	Dancer in the Dark	Edward Yang (Yi Yi)
2001	The Son's Room	Joel Coen (The Man Who Wasn't There)/David Lynch (Mulholland Drive)

Best Actor	Best Actress
Jean-Louis Trintignant (Z)	Vanessa Redgrave (Isadora)
Marcello Mastroianni (Jealousy, Italian Style)	Ottavia Piccolo (Metello)
Riccardo Cucciolla (Sacco e Vanzetti)	Kitty Winn (Panic in Needle Park)
Jean Yanne (We Will Not Grow Old Together)	Susannah York (Images)
Giancarlo Giannini (Love and Anarchy)	Joanne Woodward (The Effect of Gamma Rays on Man-in-the-Moon Marigolds)
Jack Nicholson (The Last Detail)	Marie-José Nat (Les Violons du Bal)
Vittorio Gassman (Scent of a Woman)	Valerie Perrine (Lenny)
José Luis Gomez (Pascual Duarte)	Mari Töröcsic (Where Are You, Mrs Dery?)/ Dominique Sands (The Inheritance)
Fernando Rey (Elisa, My Life)	Shelley Duvall (Three Women)/Monique Mercure (J. A. Martin Photographe)
Jon Voight (Coming Home)	Jill Clauburgh (An Unmarried Woman)/ Isabelle Huppert (Violette)
Jack Lemmon (The China Syndrome)	Sally Field (Norma Rae)
Michel Piccoli (Leap into the Void)	Anouk Aimée (Leap into the Void)
Ugo Tognazzi (Tragedy of a Ridiculous Man)	Isabelle Adjani (Quartet/Possession)
Jack Lemmon (Missing)	Jadwiga Jankowska-Cieslak (Another Way)
Gian Maria Volonte (The Death of Mario Ricci)	Hanna Schygulla (Story of Piera)
Alfredo Landa, Francisco Rabal (The Holy Innocents)	Helen Mirren (Cal)
Wiliam Hurt (Kiss of the Spider Woman)	Cher (Mask)/Norma Aleandro (The Official Story)
Michel Blanc (Menage)/Bob Hoskins (Mona Lisa)	Barbara Sukowa (Rosa Luxemburg)/ Fernanda Torres (I Love You)
Marcello Mastroianni (Dark Eyes)	Barbara Hershey (Shy People)
Forest Whitaker (Bird)	Barbara Hershey, Johdi May, Linda Mvusi (A World Apart)
James Spader (sex, lies and videotape)	Meryl Streep (A Cry in the Dark)
Gérard Depardieu (Cyrano de Bergerac)	Krystyna Janda (Interrogation)
John Turturro (Barton Fink)	Irene Jacob (The Double Life of Veronique)
Tim Robbins (The Player)	Pernilla August (Best Intentions)
David Thewlis (Naked)	Holly Hunter (The Piano)
Ge Yu (To Live)	Virna Lisi (Queen Margaret)
Jonathan Pryce (Carrington)	Helen Mirren (The Madness of King George)
Daniel Auteuil, Pascal Duquenne (The Eighth Day)	Brenda Blethyn (Secrets and Lies)
Sean Penn (She's So Lovely)	Kathy Burke (Nil by Mouth)
Peter Mullen (My Name is Joe)	Elodie Bouchez, Natacha Régnier (Dream Life of Angels)
Emmanuel Schotte (Humanity)	Emillie Dequenne (Rosetta)/Severine Caneele (Humanity)
Tony Leung Chiu-Wai (In the Mood for Love)	Bjork (Dancer in the Dark)
Benoit Magimel (The Piano Teacher)	Isabel Huppert (The Piano Teacher)

Note *Award given for best performance by an actor or actress

11.4 *Art and Sculpture*

Presidents of the Royal Academy

Year appointed	
1768	Sir Joshua Reynolds
1792	Benjamin West
1805	James Wyatt
1806	Benjamin West
1820	Sir Thomas Lawrence
1830	Sir Martin Shee
1850	Sir Charles Eastlake
1866	Sir Francis Grant
1878	Lord Leighton
1896	Sir John Millais
1896	Sir Edward Poynter
1919	Sir Aston Webb
1924	Sir Francis Dicksee
1928	Sir William Llewellyn
1938	Sir Edwin Lutyens
1944	Sir Alfred Munnings
1949	Sir Gerald Kelly
1954	Sir Albert Richardson
1956	Sir Charles Wheeler
1966	Sir Thomas Monnington
1976	Sir Hugh Casson
1984	Sir Roger de Grey
1993	Sir Philip Dowson
1999	Phillip King

Turner Prize

Year	Winner
1984	Malcolm Morley
1985	Howard Hodgkin
1986	Gilbert and George
1987	Richard Deacon
1988	Tony Cragg
1989	Richard Long
1990	(No award)
1991	Anish Kapoor
1992	Grenville Davey
1993	Rachel Whiteread
1994	Anthony Gormley

1995	Damien Hirst
1996	Douglas Gordon
1997	Gillian Wearing
1998	Chris Ofili
1999	Steve McQueen
2000	Wolfgang Tillmans

11.5 *Music*

Musical notation

Symbol	Name	Meaning
𝄞	Treble clef/G clef	Upper stave
𝄢	Bass clef/F clef	Lower stave
𝄡	C clef	
♭	Flat	Lower note by a semi-tone
♯	Sharp	Raise note by a semi-tone
♮	Natural	Return note to its original pitch
𝅝	Semibreve	Whole note
𝅗𝅥	Minim	Half note
♩	Crotchet	Quarter note
♪	Quaver	Eighth note
𝅘𝅥𝅯	Semi-quaver	Sixteenth note

Orchestras of the world

Country	Orchestra
Argentina	National Sinfonia Orchestra
	Philharmonic Orchestra of Buenos Aires
Armenia	Armenian Philharmonia Orchestra
	Armenian State Symphony Orchestra
Australia	Adelaide Symphony Orchestra
	Canberra Symphony Orchestra
	Melbourne Philharmonic Orchestra
	Melbourne Symphony Orchestra
	Queensland Symphony Orchestra
	State Orchestra of Victoria
	Sydney Symphony Orchestra
	Symphony Australia
	Tasmanian Symphony Orchestra
	West Australian Symphony Orchestra

Country	Orchestra
Austria	Austrian Hungarian Haydn Orchestra
	Bruckner Orchestra Linz
	The Haydn Academy
	Mozarteum Orchester
	Symphony Orchestra Vorarlberg/Camerata
	Vienna Chamber Orchestra
	Vienna Mozart Orchestra
	Vienna Philharmonic
Belarus	State Academic Symphony Orchestra of Byelorussia
Belgium	BRTN-Philharmonic Orchestra
	Collegium Instrumentale Brugense
	Orchestra National de Belgique
	Orchestre Philharmonique de Liege et de la Communate Française
	Royal Philharmonic Orchestra of Flanders
	Symphony Orchestra of Minnaie
Brazil	Brazil Sinfonia Orchestra
	Philharmonic Orchestra of Rio de Janeiro
Bulgaria	Bulgarian National Radio Symphony Orchestra
	Sofia Philharmonic Orchestra
	Vratza State Philharmonic Orchestra
Canada	Calgary Philharmonic Orchestra
	Edmonton Symphony Orchestra
	International Symphony Orchestra
	Kingston Symphony
	Kitchener-Waterloo Symphony
	Montreal Chamber Orchestra
	Montreal Symphony Orchestra
	National Arts Centre Orchestra of Canada
	Newfoundland Symphony Orchestra
	Niagara Symphony
	Orchestra London Canada Inc
	Ottawa Symphony Orchestra
	Quebec Symphony Orchestra
	Toronto Symphony Orchestra
	Vancouver Symphony
	Victoria Symphony
	Winnipeg Symphony Orchestra
Chile	Santiago Philharmonic Orchestra
	Sinfonia Orchestra of Concepción
China	Beijing Central Ensemble of National Radio
	Hong Kong Philharmonic Orchestra
	Pan Asia Symphony Orchestra
	Shanghai Symphony Orchestra
Colombia	Bogota Philharmonic Orchestra
	Sinfonia Orchestra of Colombia
Croatia	Dubrovnik Symphony Orchestra
	Zagreb Philharmonic
Czech Republic	Bohemia Symphony Orchestra
	Brno Philharmonic Orchestra
	Czech Philharmonic Orchestra
	Czech Symphony Orchestra FISYO

	Janacek Philharmonic Orchestra
	Moravian Philharmonic Orchestra
	North Bohemian Philharmonic
	Prague Symphony Orchestra
	Radio Symphony Orchestra
	West Bohemian Symphony Orchestra
Denmark	Aalborg Symphony Orchestra
	Aarhus Symphony Orchestra
	Copenhagen Philharmonic Orchestra
	Danish National Radio Symphony Orchestra
	De Unges Symfoniorkester Dusika
	Det Kongelige Kapel
	Foroya Symphony Orchestra
	Odense Symphony Orchestra
	Randers Byorkester
	Royal Danish Orchestra
	Sonderjyllands Symphony Orchestra
	Vestjsk Symphony Orchestra
Estonia	Estonian National Opera Symphony Orchestra
	Estonian National Symphony Orchestra
Finland	Finnish Radio Symphony Orchestra
	Helsinki Philharmonic Orchestra
	Orchestra of the Finnish National Opera
	Symphony Orchestra Vivo
	Tampere Philharmonic Orchestra
	Vaasa City Orchestra
France	The Chapel Royal/Orchestra of the Champs Elysées
	Lorraine Philharmonic
	National Orchestra of Bordeaux-Aquitaine
	National Orchestra of France
	National Orchestra of Lille
	National Orchestra of Lyon
	Orchestra of Paris
	Orchestra of the Concerts Lamoureux
	Orchestre National du Capitole de Toulouse
	Orchestre Philharmonique de Pays de Loire
	Orchestre Symphonique et Lyrique de Nancy
	Philharmonic Orchestra of Montpellier
	Philharmonic Orchestra of Nice
	Philharmonic Orchestra of Radio-France
	Philharmonic Orchestra of Strasbourg
Georgia	Chamber Orchestra
Germany	Bamberger Symphonic
	Bayerische Staatsorchester
	Berlin Philharmonic Orchestra
	Berlin Symphonic Orchestra
	Dresden Philharmonic
	Dusseldorf Symphonic Orchestra
	Essen Philharmonic Orchestra
	Hamburg Symphony Orchestra
	Handelfestspiel Orchestra
	Kolner Rundfunk-Sinfonia-Orchestra

Country	Orchestra
	Leipziger Gewandhausorchester
	MDR Sinfonia Orchestra
	Munich Philharmonic
	Orchestra of the German Opera Berlin
	Philharmonic Orchestra of the Landeschauptstadt Kiel
	Philharmonisches Staatsorchester Halle
	Philharmonisches Staatsorchester Hamburg
	Radio-Sinfonie-Orchester Frankfurt
	Radio-Sinfonia Orchester Suddeutscher Rundfunk Stuttgart
	Robert Schumann Philharmonic
	Staats Philharmonic Ludwigshafen Rheinland-Pfalz
	Stadt Augsburg Philharmonic Orchestra
	Westphalian Symphony Orchestra
Greece	Athens Broadcasting Symphony Orchestra
	La Camerata-Orchestra of the Friends of Music
	Orchestra of the National Opera of Greece
	Thessaloniki State Orchestra
Hungary	Budapest Concert Orchestra MAV
	Budapest Philharmonic Orchestra
	Budapest Symphony Orchestra
	Gyor Philharmonic Orchestra
	Hungarian National Philharmonic Orchestra
	Hungarian Symphony Orchestra
Ireland	National Symphony Orchestra of Ireland
	RTE Concert Orchestra
Israel	Haifa Symphony Orchestra
	Israel Chamber Orchestra
	Israel Chamber Orchestra of Ramat Gam
	Israel Philharmonic Orchestra
	The Israel Symphony Orchestra Rishon Le-Zion
	Jerusalem Symphony Orchestra
Italy	Orchestra of Arena
	Orchestra of Tuscany
	Orchestra Sinfonica Nazionale della RAI
	Orchestra Teatro Regio di Torino
	Philharmonic Orchestra of La Scala
	Philharmonic Orchestra of Marchigiana
	Rome Sinfonia Orchestra for Italian Radio and Television
	Sinfonia Orchestra of Sicily
	Toscanini Symphony Orchestra
Japan	Gunma Symphony Orchestra
	Hiroshima Symphony Orchestra
	Kangawa Philharmonic Orchestra
	Kyoto City Symphony Orchestra
	Kyushu Symphony Orchestra
	Nagoya Philharmonic Orchestra
	New Japan Philharmonic
	NHK Symphony Orchestra
	Osaka Philharmonic Orchestra
	Tokyo Metropolitan Symphony Orchestra
	Tokyo Philharmonic Orchestra

Korea	Korean Symphony Orchestra
	Pusan Philharmonic Orchestra
	Seoul Philharmonic Orchestra
Latvia	Latvian National Orchestra
	Latvian Philharmonic Chamber Orchestra
	Liepaja Symphony Orchestra
Lithuania	Lithuanian National Symphony Orchestra
	Lithuanian State Symphony Orchestra
Luxembourg	Orchestre Philharmonique du Luxembourg
Malaysia	Malaysian Philharmonic Orchestra
Mexico	Estado de Mexico
	National Symphony Orchestra of Mexico
	Philharmonic Orchestra of Jalisco
	Philharmonic of Mexico City
	Philharmonic of Queretaro
	State of Mexico Symphony Orchestra
Moldova	National Orchestra for Radio and Television
	Symphony Orchestra of the National Philharmonic of Moldova
Monaco	Orchestre Philharmonique de Monte-Carlo
Netherlands	Arnhem Philharmonic Orchestra
	Barokrkest van De Nederlands Bachvereniging
	Brabant Philharmonic Orchestra
	The Gelders Orchestra
	Limburgs Symphony Orchestra/Symphony Orchestra of Maastricht
	Netherlands Ballet Orchestra
	Netherlands Philharmonic Orchestra
	Netherlands Radio Philharmonic
	Noordhollands Philharmonic Orchestra
	Radio Symphony Orchestra
	Resident Orchestra of The Hague
	Rotterdam Philharmonic Orchestra
	Royal Concertgebouw Orchestra
Norway	Bergen Philharmonic Orchestra
	Kristiansand Symphony Orchestra
	Norwegian Baroque Orchestra
	Norwegian Chamber Orchestra
	Oslo Philharmonic Orchestra
	Stavanger Symphony Orchestra
	Trondheim Symphony Orchestra
Peru	National Sinfonia Orchestra
Philippines	Manila Symphony Orchestra
	National Philharmonic Orchestra
	Philippine Philharmonic Orchestra
Poland	Kielce Philharmonic
	Krakow Philharmonic
	Lublin Philharmonic
	Orchestra of the National Theatre
	Philharmonic Orchestra
	Polish Chamber Orchestra
	Polish Radio National Symphony Orchestra
	Poznan Philharmonic
	Silesian State Philharmonic in Katowice

Country	Orchestra
	State Philharmonic Orchestra
	Szymanowski Philharmonic Orchestra
	Warsaw Philharmonic
Portugal	Gulbenkian Orchestra
	Lisbon Metropolitan Orchestra
	Oporto Classical Orchestra
	Portuguese Symphony Orchestra
Romania	Arad State Philharmonic
	Brasov State Philharmonic
	Iasi Philharmonic
	Sibiu State Philharmonic
Russia	Bolshoi Symphony Orchestra
	Russian National Symphony Orchestra
	Russian State Philharmonic Orchestra
	St Petersburg Philharmonic
Singapore	Singapore Symphony Orchestra
Slovak Republic	Kosice State Philharmonic
	Slovak Radio Symphony Orchestra
Slovenia	Slovenian Philharmonic
	Slovenian Radio and Television Symphony Orchestra
South Africa	Cape Town Philharmonic Orchestra
	Natal Philharmonic Orchestra
	New Arts Philharmonic Orchestra Pretoria
Spain	Bilbao Symphony Orchestra
	City of Palma Symphony Orchestra, Baleares
	De Catalunya Philharmonic Orchestra of Gran Canaria
	Gran Teatre de Liceu Symphony Orchestra
	La Capella Reial de Catalunya
	Le Concert des Nations
	National Orchestra and Chorus of Spain
	Orchestra of Cadaques
	Orchestra of Valencia
	Orquesta Sinfónica de Barcelona i Nacional de Catalunya
	Real Sinfonia Orchestra of Seville
	Sinfonia Orchestra of Euskadi
	Sinfonia Orchestra of Galicia
	Symphony Orchestra of Castille and Leon
	Tenerife Symphony Orchestra
Sweden	Goteborgs Opera Orchestra
	Royal Stockholm Philharmonic Orchestra
	Royal Swedish Opera Orchestra
	Swedish National Orchestra
	Swedish Radio Symphony Orchestra
Switzerland	Basel Sinfonia Orchestra
	Basel Sionfonietta
	Berner Symphonie-Orchester
	Orchestra of Opera Zürich
	Orchestra de la Suisse Romande
	Tonhalle-Orchester Zürich
Taiwan	Taipei Symphony Orchestra
Thailand	Bangkok Symphony Orchestra

Turkey	Istanbul State Symphony Orchestra
	Izmir State Symphony Orchestra
	Presidential Symphony Orchestra
Ukraine	Crimea State Symphony Orchestra
	Kharkov Philharmonic Orchestra
	National Symphony Orchestra of Ukraine
	Odessa Philharmonic Orchestra
	Ukrainian Chamber Orchestra
	Ukrainian Television and Radio Symphony Orchestra
United Kingdom	Academy of Ancient Music
	Academy of London
	Academy of St Martin-in-the-Fields
	Ambache Chamber Orchestra
	BBC Concert Orchestra
	BBC National Orchestra of Wales
	BBC Philharmonic
	BBC Scottish Symphony Orchestra
	BBC Symphony Orchestra
	Birmingham Contemporary Music Group
	Bournemouth Sinfonietta
	Bournemouth Symphony Orchestra
	The Brandenburg Consort
	Britten Sinfonia
	BT Scottish Ensemble
	Charivari Agréable Simfonie
	City of Birmingham Symphony Orchestra
	City of London Sinfonia
	City of Oxford Orchestra
	Croydon Orchestra
	East of England Orchestra
	English Camerata
	English Classical Players
	English Northern Philharmonia
	English Sinfonia
	English String Orchestra
	English Symphony Orchestra
	Fiori Musicali
	Guildford Philharmonic Orchestra
	Guildhall String Ensemble
	Hallé Orchestra
	The Hanover Band
	The King's Consort
	London Chamber Orchestra
	London Festival Orchestra
	London Handel Orchestra
	London Jupiter Orchestra
	London Mozart Players
	London Philharmonic Orchestra
	London Pro Arte Orchestra
	London Sinfonietta
	London Soloists Chamber Orchestra
	London Symphony Orchestra

Country	Orchestra
	Manchester Camerata
	Milton Keynes City Orchestra
	Mozart Orchestra
	New London Orchestra
	New Queen's Hall Orchestra
	Northern Ballet Theatre Orchestra
	Northern Sinfonia
	Orchestra da Camera
	Orchestra of St John's Smith Square
	Orchestra of the Age of Enlightenment
	Orchestra of the Golden Age
	Orchestra of the Royal Opera House
	Orchestre Révolutionnaire et Romantique
	Oxford Orchestre da Camera
	Performing Arts Symphony Orchestra
	Philharmonia Orchestra
	Philomusica of London
	Royal Liverpool Philharmonic Society
	Royal Philharmonic Concert Orchestra
	Royal Scottish National Orchestra
	Scottish Chamber Orchestra
	Sinfonia 21
	Taverner Players
	Ulster Orchestra
	Welsh Chamber Orchestra
	Welsh National Opera Orchestra
	Welsh Philharmonic Orchestra
United States	Albany Symphony Orchestra
	Amarillo Symphony Orchestra
	American Jazz Philharmonic
	Anchorage Symphony
	Arkansas Symphony Orchestra
	Arlington Philharmonic Orchestra
	Arlington Symphony
	Asia America Symphony
	Atlanta Symphony Orchestra
	Augusta Symphony Orchestra
	Austin Symphony Orchestra
	Baltimore Symphony Orchestra
	Bangor Symphony Orchestra
	Bear Valley Music Festival
	Berkeley Symphony Orchestra
	Billings Symphony Orchestra
	Bismarck-Mandan Symphony Orchestra
	Boca Pops
	Boise Philharmonic Association
	Boston Chamber Ensemble
	Boston Modern Orchestra Project
	Boston Symphony Orchestra
	Boulder Philharmonic Orchestra
	Britt Festival

Buffalo Philharmonic Orchestra
Chamber Orchestra of South Bay
Charlotte Philharmonic Orchestra
Charlotte Symphony Orchestra
Chautauqua Symphony Orchestra
Chicago Symphony Orchestra
Claremont Symphony Orchestra
Clear Lake Symphony Orchestra
The Cleveland Orchestra
Coastside Community Orchestra
Colorado Springs Symphony Orchestra
Colorado Symphony Orchestra
Columbus Symphony Orchestra
Dallas Symphony
Delaware Symphony Orchestra
Detroit Symphony
Evansville Philharmonic Orchestra
Fairfax Symphony Orchestra
Flagstaff Symphony Orchestra
The Florida Orchestra
The Florida Philharmonic
Florida West Coast Symphony Orchestra
Fort Collins Symphony Orchestra
Fort Worth Symphony
Fresno Philharmonic
Galveston Symphony Orchestra
Green Bay Symphony Orchestra
Greensboro Symphony Orchestra
Hollywood Bowl Orchestra
The Houston Symphony
Huntsville Symphony Orchestra
The Indianapolis Symphony Orchestra
Indianapolis Symphony Orchestra
Irving Symphony Orchestra Association
Jackson Symphony Orchestra (Michigan)
Jackson Symphony Orchestra (Tennessee)
Kalamazoo Symphony Orchestra
Livermore-Amador Symphony
Long Beach Symphony Orchestra
Long Island Philharmonic
Los Angeles Philharmonic
Louisiana Philharmonic Orchestra
Manhattan Philharmonic
Maryland Symphony Orchestra
Merced Symphony
Milwaukee Symphony Orchestra
The Minnesota Orchestra
Mississippi Symphony Orchestra
Modesto Symphony
Monterey County Symphony
Muncie Symphony Orchestra
Naples Philharmonic

Country	Orchestra
	Nashua Symphony
	Nassau Pops Symphony Orchestra
	National Symphony Orchestra
	New Hampshire Philharmonic
	New Jersey Symphony
	New World Symphony
	New York Philharmonic
	North Arkansas Symphony Orchestra
	Northeastern Pennsylvania Philharmonic
	Oakland East Bay Symphony
	Oklahoma City Philharmonic Orchestra
	Omaha Symphony
	Oregon Symphony
	Owensboro Symphony Orchestra
	Paducah Symphony Orchestra
	Pasadena Pops
	Peninsula Symphony North
	The Philadelphia Orchestra
	Philharmonic Society of Orange County
	Phoenix Symphony Orchestra
	Pittsburg Symphony Orchestra
	Portland Symphony
	Pro Arte Chamber Orchestra of Boston
	Providence Mandolin Orchestra
	Quad City Symphony
	The Redwood Symphony
	Reno Philharmonic
	Richmond Symphony
	Roanoke Symphony
	Rochester Philharmonic Orchestra
	Roswell Symphony Orchestra
	Saint Louis Symphony Orchestra
	San Antonio Symphony
	San Diego Youth Symphony
	San Francisco Symphony Orchestra
	San José Symphony
	San Luis Obispo Symphony
	Santa Barbara Chamber Orchestra
	Santa Barbara Symphony
	Santa Cruz County Symphony
	Santa Monica Symphony
	Santa Rosa Symphony
	Savannah Symphony Orchestra
	Seattle Symphony
	South Carolina Philharmonic
	South Dakota Symphony Orchestra
	Southwest Chamber Music Society
	Stockton Symphony
	Toledo Symphony Orchestra
	Traverse Symphony Orchestra
	Tulsa Philharmonic Orchestra

Utah Symphony Orchestra
Vermont Symphony Orchestra
Washington Symphony Orchestra
West Virginia Symphony
Wheeling Symphony Orchestra
The Wichita Symphony Orchestra
Wyoming Symphony Orchestra

International music festivals

Festival	Location	Date
Aldeburgh Festival	Aldeburgh, Suffolk (England)	June
Arundel Festival	Arundel, West Sussex (England)	August–September
Aspen Music Festival	Aspen, Colorado (USA)	Summer
Bath International Music Festival	Bath (England)	Summer
Bayreuth Festival/Richard Wagner Festival	Bayreuth, Bavaria (Germany)	May–June
BBC Proms	London (England)	July–September
Buxton Festival	Buxton, Derbyshire (England)	July
Berkshire Festival	Stockbridge, Massachusetts (USA)	Summer
Cheltenham International Festival of Music	Cheltenham, Gloucestershire (England)	July
Dartington International Summer School	Dartington Hall, Totnes (England)	July–August
Edinburgh International Festival	Edinburgh (Scotland)	August–September
Glyndebourne Festival	Lewes, East Sussex (England)	Summer
Harrogate International Festival	Harrogate, North Yorkshire (England)	July–August
Llangollen International Music Eisteddfod	Llangollen, Clwyd (Wales)	July
Marlboro Music Festival	Marlboro, Vermont (USA)	Summer
Montreux Music Festival	Montreux (Switzerland)	Summer
Newport Jazz Festival	Newport (USA)	Summer
Salzburg Festival	Salzburg (Austria)	Summer
Santa Fe Opera	Santa Fe, New Mexico (USA)	Summer
Spoleto Festival/Festival of the Two Worlds	Spoleto (Italy)	Summer
Three Choirs Festival	Worcester (England)	August

Masters of the Queen's (King's) Music

Year appointed	
1626	Nicholas Lanier
1666	Louis Grabu
1674	Nicholas Staggins
1700	John Eccles
1735	Maurice Greene

Year appointed	
1755	William Boyce
1779	John Stanley
1786	Sir William Parsons
1817	William Shield
1829	Christian Kramer
1834	François (Franz) Cramer
1848	George Anderson
1870	Sir William Cusins
1893	Sir Walter Parratt
1924	Sir Edward Elgar
1934	Sir Henry Walford Davies
1941	Sir Arnold Bax
1953	Sir Arthur Bliss
1975	Malcolm Williamson

Pulitzer Prize in Music

Year	Winner	Composer
1943	Secular Cantata No 2, A Free Song	William Schuman
1944	Symphony No 4 (Op. 34)	Howard Hanson
1945	Appalachian Spring	Aaron Copland
1946	The Canticle of the Sun	Leo Sowerby
1947	Symphony No 3	Charles Ives
1948	Symphony No 3	Walter Piston
1949	Louisiana Story	Virgil Thomson
1950	The Consul	Gian Carlo Menotti
1951	Giants in the Earth	Douglas Stuart Moore
1953	Symphony Concertante	Gail Kubik
1954	Concerto for Two Pianos and Orchestra	Quincy Porter
1955	The Saint of Bleecker Street	Gian Carlo Menotti
1956	Symphony No 3	Ernest Toch
1957	Meditations on Ecclesiastes	Norman Dello Joio
1958	Vanessa	Samuel Barber
1959	Concerto for Piano and Orchestra	John La Montaine
1960	Second String Quartet	Elliott Carter
1961	Symphony No 7	Walter Piston
1962	The Crucible	Robert Ward
1963	Piano Concerto No 1	Samuel Barber
1966	Variations for Orchestra	Leslie Bassett
1967	Quartet No 3	Leon Kirchner
1968	Echoes of Time and the River	George Crumb
1969	String Quartet No 3	Karel Husa
1970	Time's Encomium	Charles Wuorinen
1971	Synchronisms No 6 for Piano and Electronic Sound	Mairo Davidowsky
1972	Windows	Jacob Druckman
1973	String Quartet No 3	Elliott Carter
1974	Notturno	Donald Martino
1975	From the Diary of Virginia Woolf	Dominick Argento
1976	Air Music	Ned Rorem

1977	Visions of Terror and Wonder	Richard Wernick
1978	Déjà Vu for Percussion Quartet and Orchestra	Michael Colgrass
1979	Aftertones of Infinity	Joseph Schwantner
1980	In Memory of a Summer Day	David Del Tredici
1981	(No award)	
1982	Concerto for Orchestra	Roger Sessions
1983	Three Movements for Orchestra	Ellen T. Zwilich
1984	Canti del Sole	Bernard Rands
1985	Symphony River Run	Stephen Albert
1986	Wind Quintet IV	George Perle
1987	The Flight into Egypt	John Harbison
1988	12 New Etudes for Piano	William Bolcom
1989	Whispers Out of Time	Roger Reynolds
1990	Duplicates: A Concerto for Two Pianos and Orchestra	Mel Powell
1991	Symphony	Shulamit Ran
1992	The Face of the Night, The Heart of the Dark	Wayne Peterson
1993	Trombone Concerto	Christopher Rouse
1994	Of Remembrances and Reflections	Gunther Schuller
1995	Stringmusic	Morton Gould
1996	Lilacs	George Walker
1997	Blood on the Fields	Wynton Marsalis
1998	String Quartet No 2, Musica Instrumentalis	Aaron J. Kernis
1999	Concerto for Flute, Strings and Percussion	Melinda Wagner
2000	Life Is a Dream, Opera in Three Acts: Act II, Concert Version	Lewis Spratlan

National anthems and songs

Country	Anthem/song
Afghanistan	Soroud-e-Melli
Algeria	Qassaman
Angola	Angola Avante
Antigua and Barbuda	Fair Antigua and Barbuda
Argentina	Oíd, mortales (Hear, oh mortals)
Australia	Advance Australia Fair
Austria	Land der Berge, Land am Strome (Land of Mountains, Land on the River)
Bahamas	March on, Bahamaland
Bangladesh	Amar Sonar Bangla
Barbados	In Plenty and in Time of Need
Belgium	La Brabançonne
Belize	Land of the Free
Bolivia	Bolivianos, El Hado Propicio (Oh Bolivia, Our Long-felt Desires)
Botswana	Fatshe La Rona
Brazil	Ouviram do Ipirangas às Margens Placidas (From Peaceful Ypiranga's Banks)
Brunei	Allah Peliharakan Sultan (God Bless His Majesty)
Burkina Faso	Ditanyé
Burundi	Uburundi Bwacu
Cambodia	Nokoreach

Country	Anthem/song
Cameroon	O Cameroun, Berceau de Nos Ancêtres (O Cameroon, Thou Cradle of Our Forefathers)
Canada	O Canada
Chile	Dulce patria, recibe los votos
China	March of the Volunteers
Colombia	Oh Gloria Inmarcesible
Costa Rica	Himno Nacional de Costa Rica
Côte d'Ivoire	L'Abidjanaise
Croatia	Lijepa naša domovina (Our Beautiful Homeland)
Cuba	Al Combate, Corred Bayameses (To Battle, Men of Bayamo)
Cyprus	Ode to Freedom
Czech Republic	Kde Domov Müj (Where is my Motherland)
Denmark	Kong Kristian
Dominica	Isle of Beauty
Dominican Republic	Quisqueyanos Valientes, Alcemos (Brave Men of Quisqueya, Let's Raise our Song)
El Salvador	Saludemos La Patria Orgullosos (Let us proudly hail the Fatherland)
England	Land of Hope and Glory
Estonia	Mu Isamaa, mu onn ja room (My Native Land, My Joy, Delight)
Ethiopia	Ityopya, Ityopya Kidemi
Fiji	God Bless Fiji
France	La Marseillaise
Gabon	La Concorde
Gambia	For the Gambia, Our Homeland
Germany	Einigkeit und Recht und Freiheit (Unity and Right and Freedom)
Ghana	God Bless our Homeland Ghana
Greece	Imnos Eis Tin Eleftherian (Hymn to Freedom)
Guatemala	Guatemala Feliz (Guatemala be praised)
Guyana	Dear Land of Guyana
Haiti	La Dessalinienne
Honduras	Tu Bandera Es Un Lampo De Cielo (Your Flag is a Heavenly Light)
Hungary	Isten Aldd Meg A Magyart (God Bless the Hungarians)
Iceland	O Gud Vors Lands (Our Country's Good)
India	Jana Gana Mana
Indonesia	Indonesia Raya (Great Indonesia)
Iran	Sorood-e Jomhoori-e Eslami
Ireland	Amhrán Na BhFiann (The Soldier's Song)
Israel	Hatikvah (The Hope)
Italy	Fratelli d'Italia
Jamaica	Jamaica, Land We Love
Japan	Kimigayo
Jordan	Long Live the King
Kiribati	Teirake Kain Kiribati (Stand Kiribati)
Korea, People's Republic of	A Chi Mun Bin No Ra I Gang San (Shine Bright, O Dawn, on this Land so Fair)
Korea, Republic of	Aegukka (Love for the Mother Country)
Latvia	Dievs, sveti Latviju (God Bless Latvia)
Lebanon	Kulluna Lil Watan Lil'ula Lil'alam (We all belong to the homeland)

Lesotho	Pina ea Sechaba
Liberia	All Hail, Liberia, Hail
Liechtenstein	Oben am Jungen Rhein (Up on the young Rhine)
Lithuania	Tautiška Giesme
Luxembourg	Oms Hémécht (Our Homeland)
Macedonia	Denes nad Makedonija se radja novo sonce na slobodata (Today a new sun of liberty appears over Macedonia)
Malawi	O God Bless Our Land of Malawi
Malaysia	Negara-Ku
Mali	A ton appel, Mali (At your call, Mali)
Malta	L-Innu Malti
Mauritius	Glory to thee, Motherland
Mexico	Mexicanos, al grito de guerra (Mexicans, to the war cry)
Monaco	Hymne Monégasque
Nepal	May Glory Crown Our Illustrious Sovereign
Netherlands	Wilhelmus van Nassouwe
New Zealand	God Defend New Zealand
Nicaragua	Salve A Tí Nicaragua (Hail, Nicaragua)
Nigeria	Arise, O Compatriots
Norway	Ja, vi elsker dette Landet (Yes, we love this country)
Pakistan	Quami Tarana
Panama	Alcanzamos Por Fin La Victoria (Victory is ours at last)
Papua New Guinea	Arise All You Sons
Paraguay	Paraguayos, República O Muerte (Paraguayans, republic or death)
Peru	Somos libres, seámos lo siempre
Philippines	Lupang Hinirang
Poland	Jeszcze Polska Nie Zginela (Poland has not yet been destroyed)
Portugal	A Portuguesa
Romania	Desteaptăte, române, din somnul cel de moarte (Awake ye, Romanians, from your deadly slumber)
Russian Federation	The Patriotic Song
St Christopher and Nevis	Oh Land of Beauty
St Lucia	Sons and Daughters of Saint Lucia
St Vincent and the Grenadines	St Vincent, Land So Beautiful
Samoa	The Banner of Freedom
Saudi Arabia	Long live our beloved King
Scotland	Flower of Scotland
Seychelles	Koste Seselwa (Seychellois Unite)
Sierra Leone	High We Exalt Thee, Realm of the Free
Singapore	Majulah Singapura
Slovakia	Nad Tatrou sa blýska (Storm over the Tatras)
Slovenia	Zdravljica (A Toast)
Solomon Islands	God Bless our Solomon Islands
South Africa	Die Stem Van Suid-Afrika (The Call of South Africa)/Nkosi Sikelel'iAfrika (God Bless Africa)
Spain	Marcha Real Española
Sri Lanka	Namo Namo Matha (We all stand together)
Sudan	Nahnu Djundullah (We are the army of God)
Swaziland	Ingoma Yesive
Sweden	Du gamla, duu fria (Thou ancient, thou freeborn)
Switzerland	Trittst im Morgenrot daher (Radiant in the morning sky)

Country	Anthem/song
Tanzania	Mungu Ibariki Afrika (God Bless Africa)
Thailand	Pleng Chart
Tonga	E, 'Otua Mafimafi (Oh, Almighty God Above)
Tunisia	Himat Al Hima
Turkey	Istiklal Marsi (The Independence March)
Tuvalu	Tuvalu Mo Te Atua (Tuvalu for the Almighty)
Uganda	Oh Uganda
UK	God Save the Queen/King
Uruguay	Orientales, La Patria O La Tumba (Uruguayans, the fatherland or death)
USA	The Star Spangled Banner
Vanuatu	Nasonal sing sing blong Vanuatu
Venezuela	Gloria Al Bravo Pueblo (Glory to the brave people)
Vietnam	Tien Quan Ca (The Troops are advancing)
Wales	Hen Wlad fy Nhadau (Land of My Fathers)
Yugoslavia	Nej, Slaveni, Jošte Zivi Rec Naših Dedova (O Slavs, our ancestors' words still live)
Zambia	Stand and Sing of Zambia, Proud and Free
Zimbabwe	Ngaikomberarwe Nyika Ye Zimbabwe (Blessed be the country of Zimbabwe)

11.6 *Dance*

Dance companies

Company	Location	Date founded
Alvin Ailey American Dance Theater	New York (USA)	1958
American Ballet	New York (USA)	1933
American Ballet Theatre	New York (USA)	1940
Australian Ballet Company	Melbourne (Australia)	1962
Australian Dance Theatre	Adelaide (Australia)	1965
Ballet Gulbenkian	Lisbon (Portugal)	1965
Ballet Jooss	Cambridge (UK)	1933
Ballets de Paris	France	1948
Rambert Dance Company	London (UK)	1926
Ballet Russe de Monte Carlo	Monte Carlo (Monaco)	1938
Ballets des Champs-Elysées	Paris (France)	1944
Ballets Russes de Sergei Diaghilev	St Petersburg (Russia)	1909–29
Ballets Suedois	France	1920
Ballet Théâtre Contemporain	Amiens (France)	1968
Les Ballet Trockadero de Monte Carlo	New York (USA)	1974

Ballet West	Salt Lake City, Utah (USA)	1968
Béjart Ballet Lausanne	Lausanne (Switzerland)	1987
Birmingham Royal Ballet	Birmingham (UK)	1946
Bolshoi Ballet	Moscow (Russia)	1776
Borovansky Ballet	Melbourne (Australia)	1942
Boston Ballet	Boston (USA)	1964
Central Ballet of China	Beijing (China)	1959
The Cholmondeleys	London (UK)	1984
Dance Bites	London (UK)	1994
Dance Theater of Harlem	New York (USA)	1971
Dutch National Ballet	Amsterdam (Netherlands)	1961
DV8 Physical Theatre	London (UK)	1986
English National Ballet	London (UK)	1950
Extemporary Dance Theatre	London (UK)	1975
Feld Ballet NY	New York (USA)	1974
Les Grands Ballets Canadiens	Montreal (Canada)	1956
Houston Ballet	Houston (USA)	1968
Joffrey Ballet of Chicago	New York (USA)	1954
José Limon Dance Company	New York (USA)	1946
Kirov-Marinsky Ballet	St Petersburg (Russia)	1935
Lar Lubovitch Dance Company	New York (USA)	1968
London City Ballet	London (UK)	1978
London Contemporary Dance Theatre	London (UK)	1967–95
London Festival Ballet	London (UK)	1950–88
Maly Ballet	St Petersburg (Russia)	1915
Martha Graham Dance Company	New York (USA)	1927
Miami City Ballet	Miami (USA)	1986
National Ballet	Washington (USA)	1962
National Ballet of Canada	Toronto (Canada)	1951
National Ballet of Cuba	Havana (Cuba)	1948
National Ballet of Mexico	Mexico City (Mexico)	1949
Netherlands Dance Theatre	The Hague (Netherlands)	1959
New York City Ballet	New York (USA)	1948
Nikolais Dance Theatre	New York (USA)	1951
Northern Ballet	Manchester (UK)	1969
Paris Opéra Ballet	Paris (France)	1661
Pennsylvania Ballet	Philadelphia (USA)	1963
Pilobolus Dance Theatre	Vermont (USA)	1971
Pittsburgh Ballet Theatre	Pittsburgh (USA)	1970
Richard Alston Dance Company	London (UK)	1994
Royal Ballet	Covent Garden, London (UK)	1931
Royal Danish Ballet	Copenhagen (Denmark)	16th century
Royal New Zealand Ballet Company	Wellington (New Zealand)	1961
Royal Swedish Ballet	Stockholm (Sweden)	1609
Royal Winnipeg Ballet	Winnipeg (Canada)	1938
San Francisco Ballet	San Francisco (USA)	1933
Scottish Ballet	Glasgow (UK)	1956
Stanislavsky Ballet	Moscow (Russia)	1929
Stuttgart Ballet	Stuttgart (Germany)	1609

Company	Location	Date founded
Sydney Dance Company	Sydney (Australia)	1971
Washington Ballet	Washington (USA)	1962
Western Theatre Ballet	Bristol (UK)	1957

11.7 *Education and Knowledge*

The Seven Liberal Arts

The Trivium	The Quadrivium
Logic	Arithmetic
Grammar	Geometry
Rhetoric	Astronomy
	Music

Presidents of the Royal Society

Year appointed	
1662	Viscount Brouncker
1677	Sir Joseph Williamson
1680	Sir Christopher Wren
1682	Sir John Hoskins
1683	Sir Cyril Wyche
1684	Samuel Pepys
1686	Earl of Carbery
1689	Earl of Pembroke
1690	Sir Robert Southwell
1695	Earl of Halifax
1698	Lord Somers
1703	Sir Isaac Newton
1727	Sir Hans Sloane
1741	Martin Folkes
1752	Earl of Macclesfield
1764	Earl of Morton
1768	Sir James Burrow
1768	James West
1772	Sir John Pringle
1778	Sir Joseph Banks
1820	William Hyde Wollaston
1820	Sir Humphrey Davy

1827	Davies Gilbert
1830	Duke of Sussex
1838	Marquess of Northampton
1848	Earl of Rosse
1854	Lord Wrottesley
1858	Sir Benjamin Brodie
1861	Sir Edward Sabine
1871	Sir George Biddell Airy
1873	Sir Joseph Dalton Hooker
1878	William Spottiswoode
1883	Thomas Henry Huxley
1885	Sir George Stokes
1890	Lord Kelvin
1895	Lord Lister
1900	Sir William Huggins
1905	Lord Rayleigh
1908	Sir Archibald Geikie
1913	Sir William Crookes
1915	Sir Joseph John Thomson
1920	Sir Charles Scott Sherrington
1925	Lord Rutherford
1930	Sir Frederick Gowland Hopkins
1935	Sir William Henry Bragg
1940	Sir Henry Dale
1945	Sir Robert Robinson
1950	Lord Adrian
1955	Sir Cyril Hinshelwood
1960	Lord Florey
1965	Lord Blackett
1970	Sir Alan Hodgkin
1975	Lord Todd
1980	Sir Andrew Huxley
1985	Lord Porter of Luddenham
1990	Sir Michael Atiyah
1996	Sir Aaron Klug

Museums and art galleries

Country	Location	Museum/gallery
Afghanistan	Kabul	Kabul Museum
Albania	Tiranë	Albanian National Culture Museum
Algeria	Algiers	National Museum of Algiers
Argentina	Buenos Aires	National History Museum
Armenia	Yerevan	Armenian State Historical Museum
		Armenian State Picture Gallery
Australia	Adelaide	Art Gallery of South Australia
		South Australian Museum
	Brisbane	Queensland Art Gallery
		Queensland Museum
	Canberra	National Gallery of Australia

Country	Location	Museum/gallery
		National Museum of Australia
	Hobart	Tasmanian Museum and Art Gallery
	Launceston	Queen Victoria Museum and Art Gallery
	Melbourne	Museum of Victoria
		National Gallery of Victoria
	Perth	Art Gallery of Western Australia
		Western Australian Museum
	Sydney	Art Gallery of New South Wales
		Australian Museum
		Australian National Maritime Museum
		Powerhouse Musuem, Museum of Applied Arts and Sciences
Austria	Salzburg	Mozart's Birthplace
		Residence Gallery
	Vienna	Belvedere Gallery
		Kunsthistorisches Museum
		Museum of Lower Austria
		Schönbrunn Palace
		Treasury of the Holy Roman Empire
Bahamas	Nassau	Bahamia Museum
Bahrain	Manama	Bahrain Museum
Bangladesh	Dhaka	Bangladesh National Museum
Barbados	St Ann's Garrison	Barbados Museum and Historical Society
Belarus	Minsk	Belarussian State Art Museum
Belgium	Antwerp	Folklore Museum
		Maritime Museum
		Royal Museum of Fine Art
		Rubens's House
	Bruges	Folklore Museum
	Brussels	Erasmus House
		Museum of Brussels
		Museum of Modern Art
		Railway Museum
		Royal Museum of the Army
	Liège	Museum of Firearms
		Museum of Modern Art
		Museum of Walloon Life
Bhutan	Paro	National Museum
Bolivia	La Paz	National Museum
Brazil	Rio de Janeiro	National Museum
Brunei	Kota Batu	Brunei Museum
Bulgaria	Sofia	National Art Gallery
Canada	Edmonton	Provincial Museum of Alberta
	Halifax	Nova Scotia Museum
	Montreal	Montreal Museum of Fine Arts
	Ottawa	Canadian Museum of Nature
		Museum of Civilization
		National Gallery of Canada
		National Museum of Science and Technology
	Quebec	McCord Museum of Canadian History
		Musée du Québec

	Regina	Saskatchewan Museum of Natural History
	Saint John	New Brunswick Museum
	St John's	Newfoundland Museum
	Toronto	Art Gallery of Ontario
		Royal Ontario Museum
	Vancouver	Vancouver Art Gallery
	Victoria	British Columbia Provincial Museum
	Winnipeg	Manitoba Museum of Man and Nature
		Winnipeg Art Gallery
Chile	Santiago	National Historical Museum
China	Beijing	Museum of Chinese History
	Tsimshatsui	Hong Kong Museum of History
Colombia	Carrera	National Museum
Costa Rica	San José	National Museum of Costa Rica
Croatia	Zagreb	Croatian Historical Museum
Cuba	Havana	National Museum
Cyprus	Nicosia	Cyprus Museum
Czech Republic	Prague	National Gallery
		National Museum
		State Jewish Museum
Denmark	Copenhagen	Copenhagen Museum
		National Museum
		State Museum of Art
		Theatre Museum
Dominican Republic	Santo Domingo	National Fine Arts Gallery
Ecuador	Quito	Civic Museum of Arts and History
Egypt	Cairo	Egyptian Museum
El Salvador	San Salvador	National Museum
Estonia	Tallinn	Art Museum of Estonia
		Estonian History Museum
Ethiopia	Addis Ababa	Museum of the Institute of Ethiopian Studies
Finland	Helsinki	Helsinki City Museum
		Museum of Applied Arts
		Museum of Finnish Architecture
		Sports Museum of Finland
France	Beauvais	National Tapestry Gallery
	Fontainebleau	Royal Palace of Fontainebleau
	Paris	Auguste Rodin Museum
		Carnavalet Museum
		The Louvre
		Musée d'Orsay
		Museum of Modern Art at the Pompidou Centre
		Museum of Technology
		Picasso Museum
	Saint-Germain-en-Laye	Museum of National Antiquities
	Versailles	Château de Versailles
		Lambinet Museum
Georgia	Tbilisi	Georgian State Museum
Germany	Berlin	Bauhaus Archives and Museum of Design
		Berlin Museum

Country	Location	Museum/gallery
		Deutsches Historisches Museum
		Haus der Wannsee-Konferenz
		Memorial Museum of the German Resistance
		Museum of German Ethnology
		Museum of Transport and Technology
		New National Gallery
		Old National Gallery
	Brunswick	Museum of Brunswick
	Cologne	Cologne Art Collective
		Diocesan Museum
		Museum of the City of Cologne
		Schnütgen Museum
	Dresden	Grünes Gewölbe
		Semper Gallery
		State Gallery of Art
	Essen	Folkwang Museum
	Frankfurt-am-Main	Goethe Museum
		Historical Museum
		Modern Art Gallery
	Freiburg im Breisgau	Augustiner Museum
		Museum of Modern Art
		Museum of Natural History
	Hamburg	Altona Museum
		Hamburg Art Gallery
		Museum of Art and History
	Leipzig	Museum of Art
	Mainz	Roman-Germanic Central Museum
	Munich	Bavarian National Museum
		City Museum
		Deutsches Museum
		Folklore Museum
		Residence Museum
		State Collection of Minerals
Greece	Athens	Acropolis Museum
		Byzantine Museum
		Goulandris Natural History Museum
		Museum of Cycladic Art
		Museum of Modern Art
		National Archaeological Museum
	Heraklion (Crete)	Archaeological Museum
	Olympia	Museum of Ancient Olympia
	Thessaloniki	Archaeological Museum
		Macedonian Folk Art Museum
Grenada	St George's	Grenada National Museum
Guatemala	Guatemala City	National Museum of History
Guyana	Georgetown	Guyana Museum
Haiti	Port-au-Prince	National Museum
Hungary	Budapest	Hungarian National Museum
Iceland	Reykjavik	National Museum
India	New Delhi	National Museum of India
Indonesia	Jakarta	National Museum

Iran	Tehran	Iran Bastan Museum
Iraq	Baghdad	Archaeological Museum of Iraq
Ireland	Dublin	Dublin Civic Museum
		Guinness Museum
		National Gallery of Ireland
		National Museum of Ireland
		National Transport Museum
Israel	Jerusalem	Israel Museum
	Tel Aviv	Eretz-Israel Museum
Italy	Bologna	Archaeological Museum
		Museum of the Middle Ages and Renaissance
		National Art Gallery
	Florence	Accademia Gallery
		Bardini Museum
		Bargello Museum
		Museum of the History of Science
		Uffizi Gallery
	Genoa	Gallery of Modern Art
		Palazzo Bianco
		Palazzo Rosso
	Milan	Brera Art Gallery
		Castle of the Sforzas
		La Scala Museum of Theatre History
		Leonardo da Vinci Museum of Science and Technology
	Naples	National Archaeological Museum
		Palazzo Capodimonte
	Rome	Borghese Gallery
		National Gallery of Ancient Art
		National Museum of Popular Art
		Vatican Museums
	Siena	Siena Art Gallery
		Siena Museum
	Turin	Sabauda Gallery
	Venice	Accademia Gallery
		Correr Museum
		Peggy Guggenheim Collection
		Treasury of St Mark's
Japan	Tokyo	National Museum
Jordan	Amman	Folklore Museum
		Popular Life Museum
Kazakhstan	Alma Ata	Central State Museum of Kazakhstan
Korea, North	Pyongyang	Korean Central Historical Museum
Korea, South	Seoul	National Museum of Korea
Kuwait	Kuwait City	Kuwait National Museum
Kyrgyzstan	Bishkek	State Historical Museum of Kyrgyzstan
Laos	Vientiane	National Museum
Latvia	Riga	Latvian Historical Museum
		State Museum of Latvian and Russian Art
Lebanon	Beirut	National Museum of Lebanon
Liechtenstein	Vaduz	Liechtenstein Museum
Lithuania	Vilnius	Art Museum of Lithuania

Country	Location	Museum/gallery
		Museum of History and Ethnography of Lithuania
Luxembourg	Luxembourg-Ville	Luxembourg Museum
Malaysia	Kuala Lumpur	National Museum of Malaysia
Maldives	Dhivehi	National Museum
Mexico	Mexico City	National Muscum of Anthropology
Monaco	Monaco-Ville	Oceanographic Museum
Morocco	Rabat	Museum of Antiquities
Nepal	Kathmandu	National Museum of Nepal
Netherlands	Amsterdam	Anne Frank's House
		Museum of Amsterdam
		Rijksmuseum
		Rijksmuseum Vincent Van Gogh
		Stedelijk Museum
	The Hague	Netherlands Costume Museum
		Sikkens Museum of Signs
	Utrecht	Catherine Convent State Museum
		Netherlands Railway Museum
New Zealand	Auckland	Auckland City Art Gallery
		Auckland Institute and Museum
	Wellington	Museum of New Zealand Te Papa Tongarewa
Nicaragua	Managua	National Museum of Nicaragua
Norway	Bergen	Bergen Art Gallery
	Oslo	Edvard Munch Museum
		National Gallery
		National Museum of Contemporary Art
		Norwegian Folk Museum
		Ski Museum
Oman	Muscat	Oman Natural History Museum
Pakistan	Islamabad	National Museum of Pakistan
Panama	Apdo	Museum of the History of Panama
Paraguay	Asunción	National Museum of Fine Arts
Peru	Lima	National Museum of History
Philippines	Manila	National Museum of the Philippines
Poland	Warsaw	National Museum
Portugal	Lisbon	Calouste Gulbenkian Museum
		Museum of Archaeology and Ethnology
		Museum of Art
		Museum of Decorative Art
		Museum of Popular Art
		National Museum of Natural History
Qatar	Doha	Qatar National Museum
Romania	Bucharest	National History Museum of Romania
		National Museum of Art
Russia	Moscow	Armory Museum
		Pushkin Museum of Fine Arts
		Tretyakov Art Gallery
	St Petersburg	Hermitage Museum
		State Russian Museum
Saudi Arabia	Riyadh	Museum of Archaeology and Ethnography
Singapore	Singapore City	National Museum

Spain	Barcelona	Catalan Museum of Art
		Ethnological Museum
		Joán Miró Foundation
		Museum of Costume
		Picasso Museum
	Bilbao	Museum of Fine Art
	Figueres	Dali Museum
	Madrid	Museum of Madrid
		National Archaeological Museum
		National Museum of Ethnology
		National Museum of Decorative Arts
		Prado Museum
	Seville	Museum of Fine Art
		Museum of the Alcazar of Seville
	Toledo	El Greco Museum
		Museum of the Alcazar of Toledo
	Valencia	Museum of Fine Art
Sri Lanka	Colombo	Colombo National Museum
Suriname	Paramaribo	Stichting Suranaams Museum
Sweden	Stockholm	National Museum of Antiquities
		Nordic Museum
		Stockholm City Museum
Switzerland	Basel	Basel Art and Contemporary Art Museum
		Basel Historical Museum
	Geneva	Museum of Art and History
		Voltaire Museum
	Zürich	House of Art
		Swiss National Museum
Syria	Damascus	National Museum
Tajikistan	Dushanbe	Tajik Historical State Museum
Thailand	Bangkok	National Museum
Trinidad and Tobago	Port of Spain	National Museum and Art Gallery
Tunisia	Tunis	National Museum of Bardo
Turkey	Ankara	Archaeological Museum
	Istanbul	Archaeological Museum
		Hagia Sophia Museum
		Museum of the Ancient Orient
		Topkapi Palace Museum
Turkmenistan	Ashkhabad	Turkmen State United Museum of History and Ethnography
Ukraine	Kiev	Kiev State Historical Museum
United Arab Emirates	Abu Dhabi	Al-Ain Museum
United Kingdom	Bradford	National Museum of Photography, Film and Television
	Cambridge	Fitzwilliam Museum
	Cardiff	National Museum of Wales
	Edinburgh	National Gallery of Scotland
		Royal Museum of Scotland
		Scottish National Portrait Gallery
	Glasgow	Burrell Collection
		Kelvingrove Art Gallery and Museum

Country	Location	Museum/gallery
	London	British Museum
		Imperial War Museum
		National Gallery
		National Maritime Museum
		National Portrait Gallery
		Natural History Museum
		Science Museum
		Tate Britain
		Tate Modern
		Victoria and Albert Museum
	Oxford	Ashmolean Museum
Uruguay	Montevideo	National Historical Museum
USA	Boston	Museum of Fine Arts
	Chicago	Field Museum of Natural History
	Dallas	Dallas Museum of Fine Arts
	Detroit	Henry Ford Museum
	Los Angeles	John Paul Getty Museum
	New York	Metropolitan Museum of Art
		Museum of Modern Art
		Solomon R. Guggenheim Museum
	Philadelphia	Philadelphia Museum of Art
	San Francisco	M.H. de Young Memorial Museum
	Washington (Smithsonian Institute)	National Air and Space Museum
		National Museum of American Art
		National Museum of American History
Uzbekistan	Tashkent	Tashkent Historical Museum of the People of Uzbekistan
Venezuela	Los Caobos	Museum of Fine Arts
Vietnam	Hanoi	Vietnam History Museum

12
Sports and Games

12.1 *International Competition*

Olympic Games (summer)

Year held	Venue
1896	Athens (Greece)
1900	Paris (France)
1904	St Louis (USA)
1908	London (UK)
1912	Stockholm (Sweden)
1920	Antwerp (Belgium)
1924	Paris (France)
1928	Amsterdam (Netherlands)
1932	Los Angeles (USA)
1936	Berlin (Germany)
1948	London (UK)
1952	Helsinki (Finland)
1956	Melbourne (Australia)
1960	Rome (Italy)
1964	Tokyo (Japan)
1968	Mexico City (Mexico)
1972	Munich (West Germany)
1976	Montreal (Canada)
1980	Moscow (USSR)
1984	Los Angeles (USA)
1988	Seoul (South Korea)
1992	Barcelona (Spain)
1996	Atlanta (USA)
2000	Sydney (Australia)
2004	Athens (Greece)

Olympic Games (winter)

Year held	Venue
1924	Chamonix (France)
1928	St Moritz (Switzerland)
1932	Lake Placid (USA)
1936	Garmisch-Partenkirchen (Germany)
1948	St Moritz (Germany)
1952	Oslo (Norway)
1956	Cortina (Italy)
1960	Squaw Valley (USA)
1964	Innsbruck (Austria)
1968	Grenoble (France)
1972	Sapporo (Japan)
1976	Innsbruck (Austria)
1980	Lake Placid (USA)
1984	Sarajevo (Yugoslavia)
1988	Calgary (Canada)
1992	Albertville (France)
1994	Lillehammer (Norway)
1998	Nugano (Japan)
2002	Salt Lake City (USA)
2006	Turin (Italy)

Olympic medals (summer 2000)

	Country	Gold	Silver	Bronze	Total
1	USA	39	25	33	97
2	Russia	32	28	28	88
3	China	28	16	15	59
4	Australia	16	25	17	58
5	Germany	14	17	26	57
6	France	13	14	11	38
7	Italy	13	8	13	34
8	Cuba	11	11	7	29
9	Great Britain	11	10	7	28
10	Korea	8	9	11	28
11	Romania	11	6	9	26
12	Netherlands	12	9	4	25
13	Ukraine	3	10	10	23
14	Japan	5	8	5	18
15	Hungary	8	6	3	17
16	Belarus	3	3	11	17
17	Poland	6	5	3	14
18	Canada	3	3	8	14
19	Bulgaria	5	6	2	13
20	Greece	4	6	3	13

Olympic medals (winter)

	Country	Gold	Silver	Bronze	Total
1	Russia/USSR/ Unified Team	108	77	74	259
2	Norway	83	87	69	239
3	Germany/West Germany	62	53	45	160
4	USA	59	59	41	159
5	Austria	39	53	53	145
6	Finland	38	49	48	135
7	East Germany	39	36	35	110
8	Sweden	39	28	35	102
9	Switzerland	29	31	32	92
10	Canada	25	25	29	79

Note Up to and including the 1998 Winter Olympics

Commonwealth Games

Year held	Venue
1930	Hamilton (Canada)
1934	London (England)
1938	Sydney (Australia)
1950	Auckland (New Zealand)
1954	Vancouver (Canada)
1958	Cardiff (Wales)
1962	Perth (Australia)
1966	Kingston (Jamaica)
1970	Edinburgh (Scotland)
1974	Christchurch (New Zealand)
1978	Edmonton (Canada)
1982	Brisbane (Australia)
1986	Edinburgh (Scotland)
1990	Auckland (New Zealand)
1994	Victoria (Canada)
1998	Kuala Lumpur (Malaysia)
2002	Manchester (England)

Note The games were called the British Empire Games from 1930, the British Empire and Commonwealth Games from 1954, the British Commonwealth Games from 1970 and the Commonwealth Games from 1978

Commonwealth Games medals

	Country	Gold	Silver	Bronze	Total
1	Australia	563	487	426	1476
2	England	488	461	468	1417
3	Canada	356	372	384	1112
4	New Zealand	107	143	199	449

	Country	Gold	Silver	Bronze	Total
5	Scotland	65	79	126	270
6	South Africa	71	59	67	197
7	Wales	40	61	73	174
8	India	50	57	46	153
9	Kenya	49	34	46	129
10	Nigeria	30	38	39	107

Note Up to and including the 1998 Commonwealth Games

12.2 *Angling*

World Freshwater Championship (since 1981)

Individual

1981	David Thomas (England)
1982	Kevin Ashurst (England)
1983	Wolf-Rüdiger Kremkus (West Germany)
1984	Bobby Smithers (Ireland)
1985	David Roper (England)
1986	Lud Wever (Netherlands)
1987	Clive Branson (Wales)
1988	Jean-Pierre Fouquet (France)
1989	Tom Pickering (England)
1990	Bob Nudd (England)
1991	Bob Nudd (England)
1992	David Wesson (Australia)
1993	Mario Barras (Portugal)
1994	Bob Nudd (England)
1995	Pierre Jean (France)
1996	Alan Scothorne (England)
1997	Alan Scothorne (England)
1998	Alan Scothorne (England)
1999	Bob Nudd (England)

Team

1981	France
1982	Netherlands
1983	Belgium
1984	Luxembourg
1985	England
1986	Italy
1987	England
1988	England
1989	Wales

1990	France
1991	England
1992	Italy
1993	Italy
1994	Italy
1995	France
1996	Italy
1997	Italy
1998	England
1999	Spain

Note Held annually since 1957

World Fly Fishing Championship

Individual

1982	Viktor Diez y Diez (Spain)
1983	Segismondo Fernandez (Spain)
1984	Tony Pawson (England)
1985	Lesław Frasik (Poland)
1986	Slivoj Svoboda (Czechoslovakia)
1987	Brian Leadbetter (England)
1988	John Pawson (England)
1989	Wladyslaw Trzebuinia (Poland)
1990	Franciszek Szajnik (Poland)
1991	Brian Leadbetter (England)
1992	Pierluigi Cocito (Italy)
1993	Russell Owen (Wales)
1994	Pascal Cognard (France)
1995	Jeremy Herrmann (England)
1996	Pierluigi Cocito (Italy)
1997	Pascal Cognard (France)
1998	Tomas Starychsojtu (Czech Republic)
1999	Ross Stewart (Australia)

Team

1983	Italy
1984	Italy
1985	Poland
1986	Italy
1987	England
1988	England
1989	Poland
1990	Czechoslovakia
1991	New Zealand
1992	Italy
1993	England
1994	Czech Republic
1995	England
1996	Czech Republic

1997	France
1998	Czech Republic
1999	Australia
2000	France

Note Held annually since 1981

12.3 *Archery*

World Championship (since 1969)

Individual (men)

1969	Hardy Ward (USA)
1971	John Williams (USA)
1973	Viktor Sidoruk (USSR)
1975	Darrell Pace (USA)
1977	Richard McKinney (USA)
1979	Darrell Pace (USA)
1981	Kysti Laasonen (Finland)
1983	Richard McKinney (USA)
1985	Richard McKinney (USA)
1987	Vladimir Yesheyev (USSR)
1989	Stanislav Zabrodsky (USSR)
1991	Simon Fairweather (Australia)
1993	Kyung-Mo Park (South Korea)
1995	Gary Broadhead (USA)
1997	Kyung-Ho Kim (South Korea)
1999	Sung-Chil Hong (South Korea)

Team (men)

1969	USA
1971	USA
1973	USA
1975	USA
1977	USA
1979	USA
1981	USA
1983	USA
1985	South Korea
1987	South Korea
1989	USSR
1991	South Korea
1993	France
1995	USA
1997	South Korea
1999	Italy

Individual (women)

1969	Dorothy Lidstone (Canada)
1971	Emma Gapchenko (USSR)
1973	Linda Myers (USA)
1975	Zebiniso Rustamova (USSR)
1977	Luann Ryon (USA)
1979	Kim Jin-Ho (South Korea)
1981	Natalia Butuzova (USSR)
1983	Kim Jin-Ho (South Korea)
1985	Irina Soldatova (USSR)
1987	Ma Xiaojun (China)
1989	Kim Soo-Nyung (South Korea)
1991	Kim Soo-Nyung (South Korea)
1993	Kim Hyo-Jung (South Korea)
1995	Angel Moscarelly (USA)
1997	Kim Du-Ri (South Korea)
1999	Eun-Kyung Lee (South Korea)

Team (women)

1969	USSR
1971	Poland
1973	USSR
1975	USSR
1977	USA
1979	South Korea
1981	USSR
1983	South Korea
1985	USSR
1987	USSR
1989	South Korea
1991	South Korea
1993	South Korea
1995	USA
1997	South Korea
1999	Italy

Note Held annually in the years 1931–59 and since then every two years

12.4 *Athletics*

World outdoor records

Men

Event	Record	Holder	Date
100 m	9.79	Maurice Greene (USA)	1999
200 m	19.32	Michael Johnson (USA)	1996

Event	Record	Holder	Date
400 m	43.18	Michael Johnson (USA)	1999
800 m	01:41.1	Wilson Kipketer (Denmark)	1997
1000 m	02:12.0	Noah Ngeny (Kenya)	1999
1500 m	03:26.0	Hicham El Guerrouj (Morocco)	1998
Mile	03:43.1	Hicham El Guerrouj (Morocco)	1999
2000 m	04:44.8	Hicham El Guerrouj (Morocco)	1999
3000 m	07:20.7	Daniel Komen (Kenya)	1996
3000 m steeplechase	07:55.7	Bernard Barmasi (Kenya)	1997
5000 m	12:39.4	Haile Gebrselassie (Ethiopia)	1998
10000 m	26:22.7	Haile Gebrselassie (Ethiopia)	1998
20000 m	56:55.6	Arturo Barrios (Mexico)	1991
Hour	21 101 m	Arturo Barrios (Mexico)	1991
25000 m	1:13:55.8	Toshikiko Seko (Japan)	1981
30000 m	1:29:08.8	Toshikiko Seko (Japan)	1981
Marathon	02:05.4	Khalid Khannouchi (Morocco)	1999
110 m hurdles	12.91	Colin Jackson (Great Britain)	1993
400 m hurdles	46.78	Kevin Young (USA)	1992
20 km walk	17:25.6	Bernardo Segura (Mexico)	1994
30 km walk	01:44.1	Maurizio Damilano (Italy)	1992
50 km walk	40:57.9	Thierry Toutain (France)	1996
4 × 100 m relay	37.4	Jon Drummond, Leroy Burrell, Dennis Mitchell, Andre Cason (USA)	1993
4 × 200 m relay	01:18.7	Mike Marsh, Leroy Burrell, Floyd Heard, Carl Lewis (USA)	1994
4 × 400 m relay	02:54.2	Jerome Young, Antonio Pettigrew, Michael Johnson, Tyree Washington (USA)	1998
4 × 800 m relay	07:03.9	Peter Elliott, Garry Cook, Steve Cram, Sebastian Coe (Great Britain)	1982
4 × 1500 m relay	14:38.8	Thomas Wessinghage, Harald Hudak, Michael Lederer, Karl Fleschen (West Germany)	1977
High jump	2.48 m	Javier Sotomayer (Cuba)	1993
Pole vault	6.14 m	Sergey Bubka (Ukraine)	1994
Long jump	8.95 m	Mike Powell (USA)	1991
Triple jump	18.29 m	Jonathan Edwards (Great Britain)	1995
Shot	23.12 m	Randy Barnes (USA)	1990
Discus	74.08 m	Jurgen Schult (East Germany)	1986
Hammer	86.74 m	Yuri Syedikh (USSR)	1986
Javelin	98.48 m	Jan Zelezny (Czech Republic)	1996
Decathlon	8 994 points	Tomas Dvorak (Czech Republic)	1999

Women

Event	Record	Holder	Date
100 m	10.49	Florence Griffith Joyner (USA)	1988
200 m	21.34	Florence Griffith Joyner (USA)	1988
400 m	47.6	Marita Koch (East Germany)	1985
800 m	01:53.3	Jarmila Kratochvilova (Czechoslovakia)	1983
1000 m	02:29.0	Svetlana Masterkova (Russia)	1996
1500 m	03:50.5	Qu Yunxia (China)	1993
Mile	04:12.6	Svetlana Masterkova (Russia)	1996

2000 m	05:25.4	Sonia O'Sullivan (Ireland)	1994
3000 m	08:06.1	Wang Yunxia (China)	1993
5000 m	14:28.1	Jiang Bo (China)	1997
10000 m	29:31.8	Wang Yunxia (China)	1993
20000 m	1:06:48.8	Izumi Maki (Japan)	1993
Hour	18 340 m	Tegla Loroupe (Kenya)	1998
25000 m	1:29:29.2	Karolina Szab (Hungary)	1998
30000 m	1:49:05.6	Karolina Szab (Hungary)	1988
Marathon	02:20:43	Tegla Loroupe (Kenya)	1999
100 m hurdles	12.21	Yordanka Donkova (Bulgaria)	1988
400 m hurdles	52.61	Kim Batten (USA)	1995
10 km walk	41:56.2	Nadezhda Ryashkina (USSR)	1990
20 km walk	01:29:40	Kerry Saxby (Australia)	1988
50 km walk	04:50:51	Sandra Brown (Great Britain)	1991
4 × 100 m relay	41.37	Silke Gladisch, Sabine Reiger, Ingrid Auerswald, Marlies Göhr (East Germany)	1985
4 × 200 m relay	01:27.5	Latasha Jenkins, La Tasha Colander Richardson, Nanceen Perry, Marion Jones (USA)	2000
4 × 400 m relay	03:15.2	Tayana Ledovskaya, Olga Nazarove, Maria Pinigina, Olga Bryzgina (USSR)	1988
4 × 800 m relay	07:50.2	Nadezhda Olizarenko, Lyubov Gurina, Lyudmila Borisova, Irina Podyalovskaya (USSR)	1984
High jump	2.09 m	Stefka Kostadinova (Bulgaria)	1987
Pole vault	4.62 m	Stacy Dragila (USA)	2000
Long jump	7.52 m	Galina Chistyakova (USSR)	1988
Triple jump	15.50 m	Inessa Kravets (Ukraine)	1995
Shot	22.63 m	Natalya Lisovskaya (USSR)	1987
Discus	76.80 m	Gabriele Reinsch (East Germany)	1988
Hammer	76.07 m	Mihaela Melinte (Romania)	1999
Javelin	80.00 m	Petra Felke (East Germany)	1988
Heptathlon	7 291 points	Jackie Joyner-Kersee (USA)	1988

World indoor records

Men

Event	Record	Holder	Date
50 m	5.56	Donovan Bailey (Canada)	1996
60 m	6.39	Maurice Greene (USA)	1998
200 m	19.92	Frankie Fredericks (Namibia)	1996
400 m	44.63	Michael Johnson (USA)	1995
800 m	01:42.7	Wilson Kipketer (Denmark)	1997
1000 m	02:15.0	Wilson Kipketer (Denmark)	2000
1500 m	03:31.1	Hicham El Guerrouj (Morocco)	1997
Mile	03:48.5	Hicham El Guerrouj (Morocco)	1997
2000 m	04:52.9	Haile Gebrselassie (Ethiopia)	1998
3000 m	07.24.9	Daniel Komen (Kenya)	1998
5000 m	12:50.4	Haile Gebrselassie (Ethiopia)	1999
50 m hurdles	6.25	Mark McKoy (Canada)	1986

Event	Record	Holder	Date
60 m hurdles	7.3	Colin Jackson (Great Britain)	1994
5000 m walk	18:07.1	Mikhail Schennikov (Russia)	1995
4 × 200 m relay	01:22.1	Linford Christie, Darren Braithwaite, Ade Mafe, John Regis (Great Britain)	1991
4 × 400 m relay	03:02.8	Andre Morris, Dameon Johnson, Deon Minor, Milton Campbell (USA)	1999
High jump	2.43	Javier Sotomayor (Cuba)	1989
Pole vault	6.15	Sergey Bubka (Unified Team)	1993
Long jump	8.79	Carl Lewis (USA)	1984
Triple jump	17.83	Aliacer Urrutia (Cuba)	1997
Shot	22.66	Randy Barnes (USA)	1989
Pentathlon	4440 points	Christian Plaziat (France)	1990
Heptathlon	6476 points	Dan O'Brien (USA)	1993

Women

Event	Record	Holder	Date
50 m	5.96	Irina Privalova (Russia)	1995
60 m	6.92	Irina Privalova (Russia)	1995
200 m	21.87	Merlene Ottey (Jamaica)	1993
400 m	49.59	Jarmila Kratochvilova (Czechoslovakia)	1982
800 m	01:56.4	Maria Mutola (Mozambique)	1998
1000 m	02:30.9	Maria Mutola (Mozambique)	1999
1500 m	04:00.3	Doina Melinte (Romania)	1990
Mile	04:17.1	Doina Melinte (Romania)	1990
3000 m	08:33.8	Elly van Hulst (Netherlands)	1989
5000 m	14:47.4	Gabriela Szabo (Romania)	1999
50 m hurdles	6.58	Cornelia Oschkenat (East Germany)	1988
60 m hurdles	7.69	Lyudmila Narozhilenko (USSR)	1993
3000 m walk	11:44.0	Yelena Ivanova (Unified Team)	1992
4 × 200 m relay	01:32.6	Helga Arendt, Silke-Beate Knoll, Mechthild Kluth, Gisela Kinzel (West Germany)	1988
4 × 400 m relay	03:24.2	Tatyana Chebykina, Svetlana Goncharenko, Olga Kotlyarova, Natalya Nazarova (Russia)	1999
High jump	2.07 m	Heike Henkel (Germany)	1992
Pole vault	4.62 m	Stacy Dragila (USA)	2000
Long jump	7.37 m	Heike Drechsler (East Germany)	1992
Triple jump	15.16 m	Ashia Hansen (Great Britain)	1998
Shot	22.50 m	Helena Fibingerova (Czechoslovakia)	1977
Pentathlon	4 991 points	Irina Byelova (Unified Team)	1992

12.5 *Badminton*

World Championship (since 1985)

Men's singles

Year	Winner
1985	Han Jian (China)
1987	Yang Yang (China)
1989	Yang Yang (China)
1991	Zhao Jianhua (China)
1993	Joko Suprianto (Indonesia)
1995	Heryanto Arbi (Indonesia)
1997	Peter Rasmussen (Denmark)
1999	Sun Jun (China)

Women's singles

Year	Winner
1985	Han Aiping (China)
1987	Han Aiping (China)
1989	Li Lingwei (China)
1991	Tang Jiuhong (China)
1993	Susi Susanti (Indonesia)
1995	Ye Zhaoying (China)
1997	Ye Zhaoying (China)
1999	Camilla Martin (Denmark)

Note First held in 1977 and every two years since 1983

All-England Championship (since 1985)

Men's singles

Year	Winner
1985	Zhao Jianhua (China)
1986	Morten Frost (Denmark)
1987	Morten Frost (Denmark)
1988	Ib Frederikson (Denmark)
1989	Yang Yang (China)
1990	Zhao Jianhua (China)
1991	Ardi Wiranata (Indonesia)
1992	Liu Jun (China)
1993	Heryanto Arbi (Indonesia)
1994	Heryanto Arbi (Indonesia)
1995	Poul-Erik Hoyer Larsen (Denmark)
1996	Poul-Erik Hoyer Larsen (Denmark)
1997	Dong Jiong (China)

Year	Winner
1998	Sun Jun (China)
1999	Peter Gade Christensen (Denmark)
2000	Xia Xuanze (China)

Women's singles

Year	Winner
1985	Han Aiping (China)
1986	Yun-Ja Kim (Korea)
1987	Kirsten Larsen (Denmark)
1988	Gu Jiaming (China)
1989	Li Lingwei (China)
1990	Susi Susanti (Indonesia)
1991	Susi Susanti (Indonesia)
1992	Tang Jiuhong (China)
1993	Susi Susanti (Indonesia)
1994	Susi Susanti (Indonesia)
1995	Lin Xiao Qing (Sweden)
1996	Bang Soo-Hyun (South Korea)
1997	Ye Zhaoying (China)
1998	Ye Zhaoying (China)
1999	Ye Zhaoying (China)
2000	Gong Zhichao (China)

Note First held in 1899

12.6 *Baseball*

Olympic Baseball Championship

Year	Champions
1992	Cuba
1996	Cuba
2000	USA

Note Baseball became an Olympic sport in 1992

World Amateur Championship (since 1974)

Year	Champions
1974	USA
1976	Cuba
1978	Cuba
1980	Cuba

1982	South Korea
1984	Cuba
1986	Cuba
1988	Cuba
1990	Cuba
1992	Cuba
1994	Cuba
1996	Cuba
1998	Cuba

Note First held in 1938 and every two years since 1974

World Series

Year	Winners	League
1903	Boston	AL
1904	(not held)	
1905	New York	NL
1906	Chicago	AL
1907	Chicago	NL
1908	Chicago	NL
1909	Pittsburgh	NL
1910	Philadelphia	AL
1911	Philadelphia	AL
1912	Boston	AL
1913	Philadelphia	AL
1914	Boston	NL
1915	Boston	AL
1916	Boston	AL
1917	Chicago	AL
1918	Boston	AL
1919	Cincinnati	NL
1920	Cleveland	AL
1921	New York	NL
1922	New York	NL
1923	New York	AL
1924	Washington	AL
1925	Pittsburgh	NL
1926	St Louis	NL
1927	New York	AL
1928	New York	AL
1929	Philadelphia	AL
1930	Philadelphia	AL
1931	St Louis	NL
1932	New York	AL
1933	New York	NL
1934	St Louis	NL
1935	Detroit	AL
1936	New York	AL
1937	New York	AL
1938	New York	AL

Year	Winners	League
1939	New York	AL
1940	Cincinnati	NL
1941	New York	AL
1942	St Louis	NL
1943	New York	AL
1944	St Louis	NL
1945	Detroit	AL
1946	St Louis	NL
1947	New York	AL
1948	Cleveland	AL
1949	New York	AL
1950	New York	AL
1951	New York	AL
1952	New York	AL
1953	New York	AL
1954	New York	NL
1955	Brooklyn	NL
1956	New York	AL
1957	Milwaukee	NL
1958	New York	AL
1959	Los Angeles	NL
1960	Pittsburgh	NL
1961	New York	AL
1962	New York	AL
1963	Los Angeles	NL
1964	St Louis	NL
1965	Los Angeles	NL
1966	Baltimore	AL
1967	St Louis	NL
1968	Detroit	AL
1969	New York	NL
1970	Baltimore	AL
1971	Pittsburgh	NL
1972	Oakland	AL
1973	Oakland	AL
1974	Oakland	AL
1975	Cincinnati	NL
1976	Cincinnati	NL
1977	New York	AL
1978	New York	AL
1979	Pittsburgh	NL
1980	Philadelphia	NL
1981	Los Angeles	NL
1982	St Louis	NL
1983	Baltimore	AL
1984	Detroit	AL
1985	Kansas City	AL
1986	New York	NL
1987	Minnesota	AL
1988	Los Angeles	NL
1989	Oakland	AL

1990	Cincinnati	NL
1991	Minnesota	AL
1992	Toronto	AL
1993	Toronto	AL
1994	(not held)	
1995	Atlanta	NL
1996	New York	AL
1997	Florida	NL
1998	New York	AL
1999	New York	AL
2000	New York	AL

Note The World Series of seven games is played each year at the end of the season by the winners of the National League (NL) and the American League (AL)

Most Valuable Player

Year	American League	National League
1931	Lefty Grove (Philadelphia Athletics)	Frank Frisch (St Louis Cardinals)
1932	Jimmie Foxx (Philadelphia Athletics)	Charles Klein (Philadelphia Phillies)
1933	Jimmie Foxx (Philadelphia Athletics)	Carl Hubbell (New York Mets)
1934	Mickey Cochrane (Detroit Tigers)	Dizzy Dean (St Louis Cardinals)
1935	Hank Greenberg (Detroit Tigers)	Gabby Hartnett (Chicago Cubs)
1936	Lou Gehrig (New York Yankees)	Carl Hubbell (New York Mets)
1937	Charley Gehringer (Detroit Tigers)	Joe Medwick (St Louis Cardinals)
1938	Jimmie Foxx (Boston Red Sox)	Ernie Lombardi (Cincinnati Reds)
1939	Joe DiMaggio (New York Yankees)	Bucky Walters (Cincinnati Reds)
1940	Hank Greenberg (Detroit Tigers)	Frank McCormick (Cincinnati Reds)
1941	Joe DiMaggio (New York Yankees)	Dolph Carnitti (Brooklyn Dodgers)
1942	Joe Gordon (New York Yankees)	Mort Cooper (St Louis Cardinals)
1943	Spurgeon Chandler (New York Yankees)	Stan Musial (St Louis Cardinals)
1944	Hal Newhouser (Detroit Tigers)	Martin Marion (St Louis Cardinals)
1945	Hal Newhouser (Detroit Tigers)	Phil Cavarretta (Chicago Cubs)
1946	Ted Williams (Boston Red Sox)	Stan Musial (St Louis Cardinals)
1947	Joe DiMaggio (New York Yankees)	Bob Elliott (Boston Braves)
1948	Lou Boudreau (Cleveland Indians)	Stan Musial (St Louis Cardinals)
1949	Ted Williams (Boston Red Sox)	Jackie Robinson (Brooklyn Dodgers)
1950	Phil Rizzuto (New York Yankees)	Jim Konstanty (Philadelphia Phillies)
1951	Yogi Berra (New York Yankees)	Roy Campanella (Brooklyn Dodgers)
1952	Bobby Shantz (Philadelphia Athletics)	Hank Sauer (Chicago Cubs)
1953	Al Rosen (Cleveland Indians)	Roy Campanella (Brooklyn Dodgers)
1954	Yogi Berra (New York Yankees)	Willie Mays (New York Mets)
1955	Yogi Berra (New York Yankees)	Roy Campanella (Brooklyn Dodgers)
1956	Mickey Mantle (New York Yankees)	Don Newcombe (Brooklyn Dodgers)
1957	Mickey Mantle (New York Yankees)	Henry Aaron (Milwaukee Brewers)
1958	Jackie Jensen (Boston Red Sox)	Ernie Banks (Chicago Cubs)
1959	Nellie Fox (Chicago White Sox)	Ernie Banks (Chicago Cubs)
1960	Roger Maris (New York Yankees)	Dick Groat (Pittsburgh Pirates)
1961	Roger Maris (New York Yankees)	Frank Robinson (Cincinnati Reds)
1962	Mickey Mantle (New York Yankees)	Maury Wills (Los Angeles Dodgers)
1963	Elston Howard (New York Yankees)	Sandy Koufax (Los Angeles Dodgers)

Year	American League	National League
1964	Brooks Robinson (Baltimore Orioles)	Ken Boyers (St Louis Cardinals)
1965	Zoilo Versalles (Minnesota Twins)	Willie Mays (San Francisco Giants)
1966	Frank Robinson (Baltimore Orioles)	Roberto Clemente (Pittsburgh Pirates)
1967	Carl Yastrzemski (Boston Red Sox)	Orlando Cepeda (St Louis Cardinals)
1968	Denny McLain (Detroit Tigers)	Bob Gibson (St Louis Cardinals)
1969	Harmon Killebrew (Minnesota Twins)	Willie McCovey (San Francisco Giants)
1970	John (Boog) Powell (Baltimore Orioles)	Johnny Bench (Cincinnati Reds)
1971	Vida Blue (Oakland Athletics)	Joe Torre (St Louis Cardinals)
1972	Dick Allen (Chicago White Sox)	Johnny Bench (Cincinnati Reds)
1973	Reggie Jackson (Oakland Athletics)	Pete Rose (Cincinnati Reds)
1974	Jeff Burroughs (Texas Rangers)	Steve Garvey (Los Angeles Dodgers)
1975	Fred Lynn (Boston Red Sox)	Joe Morgan (Cincinnati Reds)
1976	Thurman Munson (New York Yankees)	Joe Morgan (Cincinnati Reds)
1977	Rod Carew (Minnesota Twins)	George Foster (Cincinnati Reds)
1978	Jim Rice (Boston Red Sox)	Dave Parker (Pittsburgh Pirates)
1979	Don Baylor (California Angels)	Willie Stargell (Pittsburgh Pirates)/ Keith Hernandez (St Louis Cardinals)
1980	George Brett (Kansas City Royals)	Mike Schmidt (Philadelphia Phillies)
1981	Rollie Fingers (Milwaukee Brewers)	Mike Schmidt (Philadelphia Phillies)
1982	Robin Yount (Milwaukee Brewers)	Dale Murphy (Atlanta Braves)
1983	Cal Ripken Jr (Baltimore Orioles)	Dale Murphy (Atlanta Braves)
1984	Willie Hernandez (Detroit Tigers)	Ryne Sandberg (Chicago Cubs)
1985	Don Mattingley (New York Yankees)	Willie McGee (St Louis Cardinals)
1986	Roger Clemens (Boston Red Sox)	Mike Schmidt (Philadelphia Phillies)
1987	George Bell (Toronto Blue Jays)	Andre Dawson (Chicago Cubs)
1988	Jose Canseco (Oakland Athletics)	Kirk Gibson (Los Angeles Dodgers)
1989	Robin Yount (Milwaukee Brewers)	Kevin Mitchell (San Francisco Giants)
1990	Rickey Henderson (Oakland Athletics)	Barry Bonds (Pittsburgh Pirates)
1991	Cal Ripken Jr (Baltimore Orioles)	Terry Pendleton (Atlanta Braves)
1992	Dennis Eckersley (Oakland Athletics)	Barry Bonds (Pittsburgh Pirates)
1993	Frank Thomas (Chicago White Sox)	Barry Bonds (San Francisco Giants)
1994	Frank Thomas (Chicago White Sox)	Jeff Bagwell (Houston Astros)
1995	(no award)	(no award)
1996	Juan Gonzalez (Texas Rangers)	Ken Caminiti (San Diego Padres)
1997	Ken Griffey Jr (Seattle Mariners)	Larry Walker (Colorado Rockies)
1998	Juan Gonzalez (Texas Rangers)	Sammy Sosa (Chicago Cubs)
1999	Ivan Rodriguez (Texas Rangers)	Chipper (Larry) Jones (Atlanta Braves)
2000	Jason Giambi (Oakland Athletics)	Jeff Kent (San Francisco Giants)

Cy Young Award (for outstanding pitcher)

Year	Winner
1956	Don Newcombe (Brooklyn Dodgers)
1957	Warren Spahn (Milwaukee Braves)
1958	Bob Turley (New York Yankees)
1959	Early Wynn (Chicago White Sox)
1960	Vernon Law (Pittsburgh Pirates)
1961	Whitey Ford (New York Yankees)
1962	Don Drysdale (Los Angeles Dodgers)

1963	Sandy Koufax (Los Angeles Dodgers)
1964	Dean Chance (California Angels)
1965	Sandy Koufax (Los Angeles Dodgers)
1967	Sandy Koufax (Los Angeles Dodgers)

American League

1967	Jim Lonborg (Boston Red Sox)
1968	Denny McLain (Detroit Tigers)
1969	Denny McLain (Detroit Tigers)/Mike Cuellar (Baltimore Orioles)
1970	Jim Perry (Minnesota Twins)
1971	Vida Blue (Oakland A's)
1972	Gaylord Perry (Cleveland Indians)
1973	Jim Palmer (Baltimore Orioles)
1974	Jim 'Catfish' Hunter (Oakland A's)
1975	Jim Palmer (Baltimore Orioles)
1976	Jim Palmer (Baltimore Orioles)
1977	Sparky Lyle (New York Yankees)
1978	Ron Guidry (New York Yankees)
1979	Mike Flanagan (Baltimore Orioles)
1980	Steve Stone (Baltimore Orioles)
1981	Rollie Fingers (Milwaukee Brewers)
1982	Pete Vuckovich (Milwaukee Brewers)
1983	La Marr Hoyt (Chicago White Sox)
1984	Willie Hernandez (Detroit Tigers)
1985	Bret Saberhagen (Kansas City Royals)
1986	Roger Clemens (Boston Red Sox)
1987	Roger Clemens (Boston Red Sox)
1988	Frank Viola (Minnesota Twins)
1989	Bret Saberhagen (Kansas City Royals)
1990	Bob Welch (Oakland A's)
1991	Roger Clemens (Boston Red Sox)
1992	Dennis Eckersley (Oakland A's)
1993	Jack McDowell (Chicago White Sox)
1994	David Cone (Kansas City Royals)
1995	(no award)
1996	Pat Hentgen (Toronto Blue Jays)
1997	Roger Clemens (Toronto Blue Jays)
1998	Roger Clemens (Toronto Blue Jays)
1999	Pedro Martinez (Boston Red Sox)
2000	Pedro Martinez (Boston Red Sox)

National League

1967	Mike McCormick (San Francisco Giants)
1968	Bob Gibson (St Louis Cardinals)
1969	Tom Seaver (New York Mets)
1970	Bob Gibson (St Louis Cardinals)
1971	Ferguson Jenkins (Chicago Cubs)
1972	Steve Carlton (Philadelphia Phillies)
1973	Tom Seaver (New York Mets)
1974	Mike Marshall (Los Angeles Dodgers)
1975	Tom Seaver (New York Mets)
1976	Randy Jones (San Diego Padres)
1977	Steve Carlton (Philadelphia Phillies)

Year	Winner
1978	Gaylord Perry (San Diego Padres)
1979	Bruce Sutter (Chicago Cubs)
1980	Steve Carlton (Philadelphia Phillies)
1981	Fernando Valenzuela (Los Angeles Dodgers)
1982	Steve Carlton (Philadelphia Phillies)
1983	John Denny (Philadelphia Phillies)
1984	Rick Sutcliffe (Chicago Cubs)
1985	Dwight Gooden (New York Mets)
1986	Mike Scott (Houston Astros)
1987	Steve Bedrosian (Philadelphia Phillies)
1988	Orel Hershiser (Los Angeles Dodgers)
1989	Mark Davis (San Diego Padres)
1990	Doug Drabek (Pittsburgh Pirates)
1991	Tom Glavine (Atlanta Braves)
1992	Greg Maddux (Chicago Cubs)
1993	Greg Maddux (Atlanta Braves)
1994	Greg Maddux (Atlanta Braves)
1995	(no award)
1996	John Smoltz (Atlanta Braves)
1997	Pedro Martinez (Montreal Expos)
1998	Tom Glavine (Atlanta Braves)
1999	Randy Johnson (Arizona Diamondbacks)
2000	Randy Johnson (Arizona Diamondbacks)

12.7 *Basketball*

World Championship (since 1963)

Men

Year	Champions
1963	Brazil
1967	USSR
1970	Yugoslavia
1974	USSR
1978	Yugoslavia
1982	USSR
1986	USA
1990	Yugoslavia
1994	USA
1998	Yugoslavia

Women

Year	Champions
1964	USSR
1967	USSR
1971	USSR
1975	USSR
1979	USA
1983	USSR
1987	USA
1991	USA
1994	Brazil
1998	USA

Note The Men's World Championship was first held in 1950; the Women's World Championship was first held in 1953

Olympic Games

Men

Year	Champions
1948	USA
1952	USA
1956	USA
1960	USA
1964	USA
1968	USA
1972	USSR
1976	USA
1980	Yugoslavia
1984	USA
1988	USSR
1992	USA
1996	USA
2000	USA

Women

Year	Champions
1976	USSR
1980	USSR
1984	USA
1988	USA
1992	Unified Team
1996	USA
2000	USA

Note The Men's competition became an Olympic event in 1936; the Women's competition followed in 1976

National Basketball Association Championship

Year	Champions
1947	Philadelphia Warriors
1948	Baltimore Bullets
1949	Minneapolis Lakers
1950	Minneapolis Lakers
1951	Rochester Royals
1952	Minneapolis Lakers
1953	Minneapolis Lakers
1954	Minneapolis Lakers
1955	Syracuse Nationals
1956	Philadelphia Warriors
1957	Boston Celtics
1958	St Louis Hawks
1959	Boston Celtics
1960	Boston Celtics
1961	Boston Celtics
1962	Boston Celtics
1963	Boston Celtics
1964	Boston Celtics
1965	Boston Celtics
1966	Boston Celtics
1967	Philadelphia 76ers
1968	Boston Celtics
1969	Boston Celtics
1970	New York Knickerbockers
1971	Milwaukee Bucks
1972	LA Lakers
1973	New York Knickerbockers
1974	Boston Celtics
1975	Golden State Warriors
1976	Boston Celtics
1977	Portland Trail Blazers
1978	Washington Bullets
1979	Seattle SuperSonics
1980	LA Lakers
1981	Boston Celtics
1982	LA Lakers
1983	Philadelphia 76ers
1984	Boston Celtics
1985	LA Lakers
1986	Boston Celtics
1987	LA Lakers
1988	LA Lakers
1989	Detroit Pistons
1990	Detroit Pistons
1991	Chicago Bulls
1992	Chicago Bulls
1993	Chicago Bulls
1994	Houston Rockets

1995	Houston Rockets
1996	Chicago Bulls
1997	Chicago Bulls
1998	Chicago Bulls
1999	San Antonio Spurs
2000	LA Lakers

Note The championship culminates in a play-off between the winners of the Eastern and Western Conferences of the Association

12.8 *Biathlon*

World Championship (since 1985)

Men

15 km (10 km until 1988)

Year	Champion
1985	Frank-Peter Rötsch (East Germany)
1986	Valeriy Medvetsev (USSR)
1987	Frank-Peter Rötsch (East Germany)
1988	Frank-Peter Rötsch (East Germany)
1989	Frank Luck (East Germany)
1990	Mark Kirchner (East Germany)
1991	Mark Kirchner (Germany)
1992	Mark Kirchner (Germany)
1993	Mark Kirchner (Germany)
1994	Sergei Tchepikov (Russia)
1995	Patrice Bailly-Salins (France)
1996	Vladimir Dratshev (Russia)
1997	Erik Lundström (Sweden)
1998	Ole Einar Bjoerndalen (Norway)
1999	Frank Luck (Germany)
2000	Frode Andreson (Norway)

20 km

Year	Champion
1985	Yuriy Kashkarov (USSR)
1986	Valeriy Medevetsev (USSR)
1987	Frank-Peter Rötsch (East Germany)
1988	Frank-Peter Rötsch (East Germany)
1989	Eric Kvalfoss (Norway)
1990	Valeriy Medevetsev (USSR)
1991	Mark Kirchner (Germany)
1992	Yevgeniy Redkine (Unified Team)
1993	Franz Zingerle (Austria)
1994	Sergei Tarasov (Russia)

Year	Champion
1995	Tomaz Sikora (Poland)
1996	Sergei Tarasov (Russia)
1997	Ricco Gross (Germany)
1998	Halvard Hanevold (Norway)
1999	Ricco Gross (Germany)
2000	Wolfgang Rottmann (Austria)

Women

7.5 km (5 km until 1988)

Year	Champion
1985	Sanna Gronlid (Norway)
1986	Kaya Parva (USSR)
1987	Yelena Golovina (USSR)
1988	Petra Schaaf (West Germany)
1989	Anne-Elinor Elvebakk (Norway)
1990	Anne-Elinor Elvebakk (Norway)
1991	Ingeborg Nykelmo (Norway)
1992	Anfissa Restzova (CIS)
1993	Myriam Bedard (Canada)
1994	Myriam Bedard (Canada)
1995	Anne Briand (France)
1996	Olga Romasko (Russia)
1997	Olga Romasko (Russia)
1998	Galina Koukleva (Russia)
1999	Martina Zellner (Germany)
2000	Liv Grete Skjelbreid (Norway)

15 km (10 km until 1988)

Year	Champion
1985	Kaya Parva (USSR)
1986	Eva Korpela (Sweden)
1987	Sanna Gronlid (Norway)
1988	Anne-Elinor Elvebakk (Norway)
1989	Petra Schaaf (West Germany)
1990	Svetlana Davydova (USSR)
1991	Petra Schaaf (Germany)
1992	Antje Misersky (Germany)
1993	Petra Schaaf (Germany)
1994	Myriam Bedard (Canada)
1995	Corrine Miogret (France)
1996	Emmanuelle Claret (France)
1997	Magdalena Forsberg (Sweden)
1998	Yekaterina Dafovska (Bulgaria)
1999	Olena Zubrilova (Ukraine)
2000	Corrine Niogret (France)

12.9 *Billiards*

World Professional Championship (since 1985)

Year	Champion
1985	Ray Edmonds (England)
1986	Robbie Foldvari (Australia)
1987	Norman Dagley (England)
1988	Norman Dagley (England)
1989	Mike Russell (England)
1990	(not held)
1991	Mike Russell (England)
1992	Geet Sethi (India)
1993	Geet Sethi (India)
1994	Peter Gilchrist (England)
1995	Geet Sethi (India)
1996	Mike Russell (England)
1997	Mike Russell (England)
1998	Geet Sethi (India)
1999	Mike Russell (England)

Note The World Professional Championship was first held in 1870, became a knockout event in 1909, was halted in 1934, and was revived in 1951

12.10 *Bobsleigh and Luge*

Bobsleigh World Championship (since 1985)

Two-man

Year	Champions
1985	Wolfgang Hoppe/Dietmar Schauerhammer (East Germany)
1986	Wolfgang Hoppe/Dietmar Schauerhammer (East Germany)
1987	Ralf Pichler/Celest Poltera (Switzerland)
1988	Janis Kipurs/Vladimir Kozlov (USSR)
1989	Wolfgang Hoppe/Bogdan Musiol (East Germany)
1990	Gustav Weber/Bruno Gerber (Switzerland)
1991	Rudi Lochner/Markus Zimmermann (Germany)
1992	Gustav Weber/Donat Acklin (Switzerland)
1993	Christoph Langen/Peer Joechel (Switzerland)

Year	Champions
1994	Gustav Weber/Donat Acklin (Switzerland)
1995	Christoph Langen/Olaf Hampel (Germany)
1996	Christoph Langen/Markus Zimmermann (Germany)
1997	Reto Goetschi/Guido Acklin (Switzerland)
1998	Pierre Lueders/David MacEachern (Canada) and Günter Huber/Antonio Tartaglia (Italy)
1999	Günter Huber/Ubaldo Ranzi (Italy)
2000	Christoph Langen/Markus Zimmermann (Germany)

Four-man

Year	Champions
1987	Switzerland
1988	Switzerland
1989	Switzerland
1990	Switzerland
1991	Germany
1992	Austria
1993	Switzerland
1994	Switzerland
1995	Germany
1996	Germany
1997	Germany
1998	Germany
1999	France
2000	Germany

Note The two-man competition was first held in 1930; the four-man event followed in 1931

Luge Olympic Games (since 1988)

Men's single-seater

Year	Champion
1988	Jens Müller (East Germany)
1992	Georg Hackl (Germany)
1994	Georg Hackl (Germany)
1998	Georg Hackl (Germany)

Women's single-seater

Year	Champion
1988	Steffi Martin Walter (East Germany)
1992	Doris Neuner (Austria)
1994	Gerda Weissensteiner (Italy)
1998	Silke Kraushaar (Germany)

Luge World Championship (since 1980)

Men's single-seater

Year	Champion
1980	Bernhard Glass (East Germany)
1981	Sergey Danilin (USSR)
1983	Miroslav Zajonc (Canada)
1985	Michael Walter (East Germany)
1987	Markus Prock (Austria)
1989	Georg Hackl (West Germany)
1990	Georg Hackl (West Germany)
1991	Arnold Huber (Italy)
1993	Werdel Suckow (USA)
1995	Armin Zoggeler (Italy)
1997	Georg Hackl (Germany)
1999	Armin Zoggeler (Italy)

Women's single-seater

Year	Champion
1980	Vera Sosulya (USSR)
1981	Melitta Sollman (East Germany)
1983	Steffi Martin (East Germany)
1985	Steffi Martin (East Germany)
1987	Cerstin Schmidt (East Germany)
1989	Susi Erdmann (East Germany)
1990	Gabriele Kohlisch (East Germany)
1991	Susi Erdmann (Germany)
1993	Gerda Weissensteiner (Italy)
1994	Gerda Weissensteiner (Italy)
1995	Gabriele Kohlisch (Germany)
1997	Susi Erdmann (Germany)
1999	Sonja Wiedmann (Germany)

Note First held in 1955 and every two years since 1981

12.11 *Bowls*

World Outdoor Championship (since 1972)

Men's singles

Year	Champion
1972	Maldwyn Evans (Wales)
1976	Doug Watson (South Africa)
1980	David Bryant (England)
1984	Peter Bellis (New Zealand)

Year	Champion
1988	David Bryant (England)
1992	Tony Allcock (England)
1996	Tony Allcock (England)
2000	Jeremy Henry (Ireland)

Men's pairs

Year	Champions
1976	South Africa
1980	Australia
1984	USA
1988	New Zealand
1992	Scotland
1996	Ireland
2000	Scotland

Men's triples

Year	Champions
1976	South Africa
1980	England
1984	Ireland
1988	New Zealand
1992	Israel
1996	Scotland
2000	New Zealand

Men's fours

Year	Champions
1976	South Africa
1980	Hong Kong
1984	England
1988	Ireland
1992	Scotland
1996	England
2000	Wales

Men's team (Leonard Trophy)

Year	Champions
1976	South Africa
1980	England
1984	Scotland
1988	England
1992	Scotland
1996	Scotland
2000	Australia

Women's singles

Year	Champion
1973	Elsie Wilke (New Zealand)
1977	Elsie Wilke (New Zealand)
1981	Norma Shaw (England)
1985	Merle Richardson (Australia)
1988	Janet Ackland (Wales)
1992	Margaret Johnston (Ireland)

| 1996 | Carmen Anderson (Norfolk Island) |
| 2000 | Margaret Johnston (Ireland) |

Women's pairs

Year	Champions
1977	Hong Kong
1981	Ireland
1985	Australia
1988	Ireland
1992	Ireland
1996	Ireland
2000	Scotland

Women's triples

Year	Champions
1977	Wales
1981	Hong Kong
1985	Australia
1988	Australia
1992	Scotland
1996	South Africa
2000	New Zealand

Women's fours

Year	Champions
1977	Australia
1981	England
1985	Scotland
1988	Australia
1992	Scotland
1996	Australia
2000	New Zealand

Women's team

Year	Champions
1977	Australia
1981	England
1985	Australia
1988	England
1992	Scotland
1996	South Africa
2000	England

Note The Men's World Championship was first held in 1966; the Women's Championship followed in 1969

World Indoor Championship (since 1985)

Men's singles

Year	Champion
1985	Terry Sullivan (Wales)
1986	Tony Allcock (England)
1987	Tony Allcock (England)
1988	Hugh Duff (Scotland)

Year	Champion
1989	Richard Corsie (Scotland)
1990	John Price (Wales)
1991	Richard Corsie (Scotland)
1992	Ian Schuback (Australia)
1993	Richard Corsie (Scotland)
1994	Andy Thompson (England)
1995	Andy Thompson (England)
1996	David Gourlay Jr (Scotland)
1997	Hugh Duff (Scotland)
1998	Paul Foster (Scotland)
1999	Alex Marshall (Scotland)
2000	Robert Weale (Wales)

Women's singles

Year	Champion
1995	Joyce Lindores (Scotland)
1996	Sandy Hazell (England)
1997	Norma Shaw (England)
1998	Caroline McAllister (Scotland)
1999	Caroline McAllister (Scotland)

Note The Men's competition was first held in 1979; the Women's event followed in 1988

Waterloo Handicap (since 1982)

Year	Champion
1982	Dennis Mercer
1983	Stan Frith
1984	Steve Ellis
1985	Tommy Johnstone
1986	Brian Duncan
1987	Brian Duncan
1988	Ingham Gregory
1989	Brian Duncan
1990	John Bancroft
1991	John Eccles
1992	Brian Duncan
1993	Alan Broadhurst
1994	Bill Hilton
1995	Ken Strutt
1996	Lee Heaton
1997	Andrew Cairns
1998	Michael Jagger
1999	Ian Smout
2000	Carl Armitage

Note First held in 1907 and since regarded as the leading Crown Green competition

12.12 *Boxing*

Weight divisions

Division	Maximum weight
Heavyweight	Over 86.2 kg (over 190 lb)
Cruiserweight	86.2 kg (190 lb)
Light heavyweight	79.4 kg (175 lb)
Super middleweight	76.2 kg (168 lb)
Middleweight	72.6 kg (160 lb)
Super welterweight	69.9 kg (154 lb)
Welterweight	66.7 kg (147 lb)
Junior welterweight	63.5 kg (140 lb)
Lightweight	61.2 kg (135 lb)
Junior lightweight	59.0 kg (130 lb)
Featherweight	57.2 kg (126 lb)
Junior featherweight	55.3 kg (122 lb)
Bantamweight	53.5 kg (118 lb)
Junior bantamweight	52.2 kg (115 lb)
Flyweight	50.8 kg (112 lb)
Junior flyweight	49.0 kg (108 lb)
Strawweight	47.6 kg (105 lb)

World Heavyweight Championship

Year	Champion	Recognizing body
1882	John L. Sullivan (USA)	Undisputed
1892	James J. Corbett (USA)	Undisputed
1897	Bob Fitzsimmons (Great Britain)	Undisputed
1899	James J. Jefferies (USA)	Undisputed
1905	Marvin Hart (USA)	Undisputed
1906	Tommy Burns (USA)	Undisputed
1908	Jack Johnson (USA)	Undisputed
1915	Jess Willard (USA)	Undisputed
1919	Jack Dempsey (USA)	Undisputed
1926	Gene Tunney (USA)	Undisputed
1930	Max Schmeling (Germany)	Undisputed
1932	Jack Sharkey (USA)	Undisputed
1933	Primo Carnera (Italy)	Undisputed
1934	Max Baer (USA)	Undisputed
1935	James J. Braddock (USA)	Undisputed
1937	Joe Louis (USA)	Undisputed
1949	Ezzard Charles (USA)	Undisputed
1951	Jersey Joe Walcott (USA)	Undisputed

Year	Champion	Recognizing body
1952	Rocky Marciano (USA)	Undisputed
1956	Floyd Patterson (USA)	Undisputed
1959	Ingemar Johansson (Sweden)	Undisputed
1960	Floyd Patterson (USA)	Undisputed
1962	Sonny Liston (USA)	Undisputed
1964	Cassius Clay (USA)	Undisputed
1965	Ernie Terrell (USA)	WBA
1968	Joe Frazier (USA)	New York title
1968	Jimmy Ellis (USA)	WBA
1970	Joe Frazier (USA)	Undisputed
1973	George Foreman (USA)	Undisputed
1974	Muhammad Ali (USA)	Undisputed
1978	Leon Spinks (USA)	Undisputed
1978	Ken Norton (USA)	WBC
1978	Larry Holmes (USA)	WBC
1979	John Tate (USA)	WBA
1980	Mike Weaver (USA)	WBA
1982	Michael Dokes (USA)	WBA
1983	Gerrie Coetzee (South Africa)	WBA
1984	Pinklon Thomas (USA)	WBC
1984	Greg Page (USA)	WBA
1985	Michael Spinks (USA)	IBF
1985	Tony Tubbs (USA)	WBA
1986	Tim Witherspoon (USA)	WBA
1986	Trevor Berbick (Canada)	WBC
1986	Mike Tyson (USA)	WBC
1986	James Smith (USA)	WBA
1987	Tony Tucker (USA)	IBF
1987	Mike Tyson (USA)	WBA/WBC
1987	Mike Tyson (USA)	Undisputed
1989	Francesco Damiani (Italy)	WBO
1990	James (Buster) Douglas (USA)	WBA/WBC/IBF
1990	Evander Holyfield (USA)	WBA/WBC/IBF
1991	Ray Mercer (USA)	WBO
1992	Riddick Bowe (USA)	WBA/WBC/IBF
1992	Michael Moorer (USA)	WBO
1992	Lennox Lewis (UK)	WBC
1993	Tommy Morrison (USA)	WBO
1993	Michael Bentt (USA)	WBO
1993	Evander Holyfield (USA)	WBA/IBF
1994	Oliver McCall (UK)	WBC
1994	Michael Moorer (USA)	WBA/IBF
1994	Herbie Hide (UK)	WBO
1994	George Foreman (USA)	IBF
1995	Bruce Sheldon (USA)	WBA
1995	Frank Bruno (UK)	WBC
1995	Frans Botha (South Africa)	IBF
1996	Mike Tyson (USA)	WBC
1996	Henry Akinwande (UK)	WBO
1996	Evander Holyfield (USA)	WBA

1996	Michael Moorer (USA)	IBF
1997	Lennox Lewis (UK)	WBC
1997	Herbie Hide (UK)	WBO
1997	Evander Holyfield (USA)	WBA/IBF
1998	Lennox Lewis (UK)	WBC
1999	Vitali Klitschko (Ukraine)	WBO
2000	Lennox Lewis (UK)	Undisputed
2000	Evander Holyfield (USA)	WBA
2001	Hasim Rahman (USA)	WBC/IBF/WBO

Note Cassius Clay regained the World Heavyweight title after changing his name to Muhammad Ali
IBF = International Boxing Federation; WBA = World Boxing Association; WBC = World Boxing
Council; WBO = World Boxing Organization

12.13 *Canoeing*

Olympic Games

Men's single kayak

Year	Champion
1939	Gregor Hradetzky (Austria)
1948	Gert Fredriksson (Sweden)
1952	Gert Fredriksson (Sweden)
1956	Gert Fredriksson (Sweden)
1960	Erik Hansen (Denmark)
1964	Rolf Peterson (Sweden)
1968	Mihaly Hesz (Hungary)
1972	Aleksandr Shaparenko (USSR)
1976	Rüdiger Helm (East Germany)
1980	Rüdiger Helm (East Germany)
1984	Alan Thompson (New Zealand)
1988	Greg Barton (USA)
1992	Clint Robinson (Australia)
1996	Oliver Fix (Germany)
2000	Knut Holmann (Norway)

Women's single kayak

Year	Champion
1948	Keren Hoff (Denmark)
1952	Sylvi Saimo (Finland)
1956	Elisaveta Dementyeva (USSR)
1960	Antonina Seredina (USSR)
1964	Lyudmila Khvedosyuk (USSR)
1968	Lyudmila Pinayeva (USSR)
1972	Yulia Ryabchinskaya (USSR)
1976	Carola Zirzow (East Germany)

Year	Champion
1980	Birgit Fischer (East Germany)
1984	Agneta Andersson (Sweden)
1988	Vania Gecheva (USSR)
1992	Brigit Schmidt (Germany)
1996	Stepanka Hilgertova (Czech Republic)
2000	Josefa Guerrini (Italy)

12.14 *Chess*

World Championship

Year	Champion
1866	Wilhelm Steinitz (Austria)
1894	Emanuel Lasker (Germany)
1921	José Raul Capablanca (Cuba)
1927	Alexander Alekhine (Russia)
1935	Max Euwe (Netherlands)
1937	Alexander Alekhine (Russia)
1948	Mikhail Botvinnik (USSR)
1957	Vassily Smyslov (USSR)
1958	Mikhail Botvinnik (USSR)
1960	Mikhail Tal (USSR)
1961	Mikhail Botvinnik (USSR)
1963	Tigran Petrosian (USSR)
1969	Boris Spassky (USSR)
1972	Bobby Fischer (USA)
1975	Anatoly Karpov (USSR)
1985	Garry Kasparov (USSR/Azerbaijan)
1993	Anatoly Karpov (Russia)
1999	Alexander Khalifman (Russia)

12.15 *Cricket*

World Cup

Year	Winner
1975	West Indies
1979	West Indies
1983	India
1987	Australia
1992	Pakistan
1996	Sri Lanka
1999	Australia

County Championship

Year	Champions
1864	Surrey
1865	Nottinghamshire
1866	Middlesex
1867	Yorkshire
1868	Nottinghamshire
1869	Nottinghamshire/Yorkshire
1870	Yorkshire
1871	Nottinghamshire
1872	Nottinghamshire
1873	Gloucestershire/Nottinghamshire
1874	Gloucestershire
1875	Nottinghamshire
1876	Gloucestershire
1877	Gloucestershire
1878	(Undecided)
1879	Nottinghamshire/Lancashire
1880	Nottinghamshire
1881	Lancashire
1882	Nottinghamshire/Lancashire
1883	Nottinghamshire
1884	Nottinghamshire
1885	Nottinghamshire
1886	Nottinghamshire
1887	Surrey
1888	Surrey
1889	Surrey/Lancashire/Nottinghamshire
1890	Surrey
1891	Surrey

Year	Champions
1892	Surrey
1893	Yorkshire
1894	Surrey
1895	Surrey
1896	Yorkshire
1897	Lancashire
1898	Yorkshire
1899	Surrey
1900	Yorkshire
1901	Yorkshire
1902	Yorkshire
1903	Middlesex
1904	Lancashire
1905	Yorkshire
1906	Kent
1907	Nottinghamshire
1908	Yorkshire
1909	Kent
1910	Kent
1911	Warwickshire
1912	Yorkshire
1913	Kent
1914	Surrey
1915-18	(not held)
1919	Yorkshire
1920	Middlesex
1921	Middlesex
1922	Yorkshire
1923	Yorkshire
1924	Yorkshire
1925	Yorkshire
1926	Lancashire
1927	Lancashire
1928	Lancashire
1929	Nottinghamshire
1930	Lancashire
1931	Yorkshire
1932	Yorkshire
1933	Yorkshire
1934	Lancashire
1935	Yorkshire
1936	Derbyshire
1937	Yorkshire
1938	Yorkshire
1939	Yorkshire
1940-45	(not held)
1946	Yorkshire
1947	Middlesex
1948	Glamorgan
1949	Middlesex/Yorkshire
1950	Lancashire/Surrey

1951	Warwickshire
1952	Surrey
1953	Surrey
1954	Surrey
1955	Surrey
1956	Surrey
1957	Surrey
1958	Surrey
1959	Yorkshire
1960	Yorkshire
1961	Hampshire
1962	Yorkshire
1963	Yorkshire
1964	Worcestershire
1965	Worcestershire
1966	Yorkshire
1967	Yorkshire
1968	Yorkshire
1969	Glamorgan
1970	Kent
1971	Surrey
1972	Warwickshire
1973	Hampshire
1974	Worcestershire
1975	Leicestershire
1976	Middlesex
1977	Middlesex/Kent
1978	Kent
1979	Essex
1980	Middlesex
1981	Nottinghamshire
1982	Middlesex
1983	Essex
1984	Essex
1985	Middlesex
1986	Essex
1987	Nottinghamshire
1988	Worcestershire
1989	Worcestershire
1990	Middlesex
1991	Essex
1992	Essex
1993	Middlesex
1994	Warwickshire
1995	Warwickshire
1996	Leicestershire
1997	Glamorgan
1998	Leicestershire
1999	Surrey
2000	Surrey

CGU National Cricket League

Year	Champions
1969	Lancashire
1970	Lancashire
1971	Worcestershire
1972	Kent
1973	Kent
1974	Leicestershire
1975	Hampshire
1976	Kent
1977	Leicestershire
1978	Hampshire
1979	Somerset
1980	Warwickshire
1981	Essex
1982	Sussex
1983	Yorkshire
1984	Essex
1985	Essex
1986	Hampshire
1987	Worcestershire
1988	Worcestershire
1989	Lancashire
1990	Derbyshire
1991	Nottinghamshire
1992	Middlesex
1993	Glamorgan
1994	Warwickshire
1995	Kent
1996	Surrey
1997	Warwickshire
1998	Lancashire
1999	Lancashire
2000	Gloucestershire

Note Formerly known as the John Player League (1969–86), the Refuge Assurance League (1986–91) and the AXA Equity and Law League (1991–99)

Natwest Bank Trophy

Year	Winners
1963	Sussex
1964	Sussex
1965	Yorkshire
1966	Warwickshire
1967	Kent
1968	Warwickshire
1969	Yorkshire
1970	Lancashire

1971	Lancashire
1972	Lancashire
1973	Gloucestershire
1974	Kent
1975	Lancashire
1976	Northamptonshire
1977	Middlesex
1978	Sussex
1979	Somerset
1980	Middlesex
1981	Derbyshire
1982	Surrey
1983	Somerset
1984	Middlesex
1985	Essex
1986	Sussex
1987	Nottinghamshire
1988	Middlesex
1989	Warwickshire
1990	Lancashire
1991	Hampshire
1992	Northamptonshire
1993	Warwickshire
1994	Worcestershire
1995	Warwickshire
1996	Lancashire
1997	Essex
1998	Lancashire
1999	Gloucestershire
2000	Gloucestershire

Note Known as the Gillette Cup until 1981

Benson and Hedges Cup

Year	Winners
1972	Leicestershire
1973	Kent
1974	Surrey
1975	Leicestershire
1976	Kent
1977	Gloucestershire
1978	Kent
1979	Essex
1980	Northamptonshire
1981	Somerset
1982	Somerset
1983	Middlesex
1984	Lancashire
1985	Leicestershire
1986	Middlesex

Year	Winners
1987	Yorkshire
1988	Hampshire
1989	Nottinghamshire
1990	Lancashire
1991	Worcestershire
1992	Hampshire
1993	Derbyshire
1994	Warwickshire
1995	Lancashire
1996	Lancashire
1997	Surrey
1998	Essex
1999	Gloucestershire
2000	Gloucestershire

12.16 *Croquet*

McRobertson Shield

Year	Winners
1925	Great Britain
1928	Australia
1930	Australia
1935	Australia
1937	Great Britain
1950	New Zealand
1956	Great Britain
1963	Great Britain
1969	Great Britain
1974	Great Britain
1979	New Zealand
1982	Great Britain
1986	New Zealand
1990	Great Britain
1993	Great Britain
1996	Great Britain

Note Contested by Australia, Great Britain and New Zealand

12.17 *Cross Country Running*

World Championship (since 1985)

Men (individual)

Year	Champion
1985	Carlos Lopes (Portugal)
1986	John Ngugi (Kenya)
1987	John Ngugi (Kenya)
1988	John Ngugi (Kenya)
1989	John Ngugi (Kenya)
1990	Khalid Skah (Morocco)
1991	Khalid Skah (Morocco)
1992	John Ngugi (Kenya)
1993	William Sigei (Kenya)
1994	William Sigei (Kenya)
1995	Paul Tergat (Kenya)
1996	Paul Tergat (Kenya)
1997	Paul Tergat (Kenya)
1998	Paul Tergat (Kenya)
1999	Paul Tergat (Kenya)
2000	Mohammad Mourhit (Belgium)

Men (team)

Year	Champions
1985	Ethiopia
1986	Kenya
1987	Kenya
1988	Kenya
1989	Kenya
1990	Kenya
1991	Kenya
1992	Kenya
1993	Kenya
1994	Kenya
1995	Kenya
1996	Kenya
1997	Kenya
1998	Kenya
1999	Kenya
2000	Kenya

Women (individual)

Year	Champion
1985	Zola Budd (England)
1986	Zola Budd (England)
1987	Annette Sergent (France)
1988	Ingrid Kristiansen (Norway)

Year	Champion
1989	Annette Sergent (France)
1990	Lynn Jennings (USA)
1991	Lynn Jennings (USA)
1992	Lynn Jennings (USA)
1993	Albertina Dias (Portugal)
1994	Ielen Chepngeno (Kenya)
1995	Derartu Tulu (Ethiopia)
1996	Gete Wami (Ethiopia)
1997	Derartu Tulu (Ethiopia)
1998	Sonia O'Sullivan (Ireland)
1999	Gete Wami (Ethiopia)
2000	Derartu Tulu (Ethiopia)

Women (team)

Year	Champions
1985	USA
1986	England
1987	USA
1988	USSR
1989	USSR
1990	USSR
1991	Kenya
1992	Kenya
1993	Kenya
1994	Portugal
1995	Kenya
1996	Kenya
1997	Ethiopia
1998	Kenya
1999	France
2000	Portugal

Note First international championship held in 1903

12.18 *Curling*

World Championship (since 1985)

Men

Year	Champions
1985	Canada
1986	Canada
1987	Canada
1988	Norway
1989	Canada

1990	Canada
1991	Scotland
1992	Switzerland
1993	Canada
1994	Canada
1995	Canada
1996	Canada
1997	Sweden
1998	Canada
1999	Scotland
2000	Canada

Women

Year	Champions
1985	Canada
1986	Canada
1987	Canada
1988	West Germany
1989	Canada
1990	Norway
1991	Norway
1992	Sweden
1993	Germany
1994	Canada
1995	Canada
1996	Canada
1997	Canada
1998	Sweden
1999	Sweden
2000	Canada

Note The Men's Championship was first held in 1959; the Women's Championship followed in 1979

12.19 *Cycling*

Tour de France (since 1980)

Year	Winner
1980	Joop Zoetemelk (Netherlands)
1981	Bernard Hinault (France)
1982	Bernard Hinault (France)
1983	Laurent Fignon (France)
1984	Laurent Fignon (France)
1985	Bernard Hinault (France)
1986	Greg LeMond (USA)

Year	Winner
1987	Stephen Roche (Ireland)
1988	Pedro Delgado (Spain)
1989	Greg LeMond (USA)
1990	Greg LeMond (USA)
1991	Miguel Induráin (Spain)
1992	Miguel Induráin (Spain)
1993	Miguel Induráin (Spain)
1994	Miguel Induráin (Spain)
1995	Miguel Induráin (Spain)
1996	Bjarne Riis (Denmark)
1997	Jan Ullrich (Germany)
1998	Marco Pantani (Italy)
1999	Lance Armstrong (USA)
2000	Lance Armstrong (USA)
2001	Lance Armstrong (USA)

Note First held in 1903

World Road Race Championship (since 1985)

Men

Year	Champion
1985	Joop Zoetemelk (Netherlands)
1986	Moreno Argentin (Italy)
1987	Stephen Roche (Ireland)
1988	Maurizio Fondriest (Italy)
1989	Greg LeMond (USA)
1990	Rudy Dhaemens (Belgium)
1991	Gianno Bugno (Italy)
1992	Gianno Bugno (Italy)
1993	Lance Armstrong (USA)
1994	Luc Le Blanc (France)
1995	Abraham Olano (Spain)
1996	Johan Museeuw (Belgium)
1997	Laurent Brochard (France)
1998	Oscar Camenzind (Switzerland)
1999	Oscar Freire Gomez (Spain)
2000	Romans Vainsteins (Latvia)

Women

Year	Champion
1985	Jeannie Longo (France)
1986	Jeannie Longo (France)
1987	Jeannie Longo (France)
1988	Jeannie Longo (France)
1989	Jeannie Longo (France)
1990	Catherine Marsal (France)
1991	Leontein van Moorsel (Netherlands)
1992	Kathryn Watt (Australia)
1993	Leontein van Moorsel (Netherlands)
1994	Monica Valvik (Norway)

1995	Jeannie Longo (France)
1996	Jeannie Longo (France)
1997	Alessandra Cappelloto (Italy)
1998	Diana Ziliute (Lithuania)
1999	Edita Pucinskaite (Lithuania)
2000	Zinaida Stahurskaia (Belarus)

Note The Men's Championship was first held in 1927; the Women's Championship followed in 1958

12.20 *Darts*

World Cup (since 1981)

Team

Year	Winners
1981	England
1983	England
1985	England
1987	England
1989	England
1991	England
1993	England
1995	England
1997	Wales
1999	England

Individual

Year	Winners
1981	John Lowe (England)
1983	Eric Bristow (England)
1985	Eric Bristow (England)
1987	Eric Bristow (England)
1989	Eric Bristow (England)
1991	John Lowe (England)
1993	Roland Scholten (Denmark)
1995	Martin Addams (England)
1997	Raymond Barneveld (Netherlands)
1999	Raymond Barneveld (Netherlands)

Note First held in 1977

Embassy World Professional Championship (since 1980)

Year	Champion
1980	Eric Bristow (England)
1981	Eric Bristow (England)
1982	Jocky Wilson (Scotland)
1983	Keith Deller (England)
1984	Eric Bristow (England)
1985	Eric Bristow (England)
1986	Eric Bristow (England)
1987	John Lowe (England)
1988	Bob Anderson (England)
1989	Jocky Wilson (Scotland)
1990	Phil Taylor (England)
1991	Dennis Priestley (England)
1992	Phil Taylor (England)
1993	John Lowe (England)
1994	John Part (Canada)
1995	Richie Burnett (Wales)
1996	Steve Beaton (England)
1997	Les Wallace (Scotland)
1998	Raymond Barneveld (Netherlands)
1999	Raymond Barneveld (Netherlands)
2000	Ted Hankey (England)

Note First held in 1978

12.21 *Equestrian events*

World Championship (since 1978)

Show jumping (individual)

Year	Winner
1986	Gail Greenough (Canada)
1990	Eric Navet (France)
1994	Franke Sloothaak (Germany)
1998	Rodrigo Pessoa (Brazil)

Show jumping (team)

Year	Winners
1986	USA
1990	France
1994	Germany
1998	Germany

Three-day event (individual)

Year	Winner
1978	Bruce Davidson (USA)
1982	Lucinda Green (Great Britain)
1986	Virginia Leng (Great Britain)
1990	Blyth Tait (New Zealand)
1994	Vaughn Jefferis (New Zealand)
1998	Blyth Tait (New Zealand)

Three-day event (team)

Year	Winners
1978	Canada
1982	Great Britain
1986	Great Britain
1990	New Zealand
1994	Great Britain
1998	New Zealand

Dressage (individual)

Year	Winner
1978	Christine Stückelberger (Switzerland)
1982	Reiner Klimke (West Germany)
1986	Anne Grethe Jensen (Denmark)
1990	Nicole Uphoft (West Germany)
1994	Isabell Werth (Germany)
1998	Isabell Werth (Germany)

Dressage (team)

Year	Winners
1978	West Germany
1982	West Germany
1986	West Germany
1990	West Germany
1994	Germany
1998	Germany

12.22 *Fencing*

World Championship (since 1982)

Foil (individual)

Men

Year	Champion
1982	Alexander Romankov (USSR)
1983	Alexander Romankov (USSR)
1985	Mauro Numa (Italy)
1986	Andrea Borella (Italy)
1987	Mathias Gey (West Germany)
1989	Alexander Koch (West Germany)
1990	Philippe Omnes (France)
1991	Ingo Weissenborn (Germany)
1993	Alexander Koch (Germany)
1994	Rolando Tucker (Cuba)
1995	Dimitriy Chevtchenko (Russia)
1997	Sergey Golubitsky (Ukraine)
1998	Sergey Golubitsky (Ukraine)
1999	Sergey Golubitsky (Ukraine)

Foil (team)

Men

Year	Champions
1982	USSR
1983	West Germany
1985	Italy
1986	Italy
1987	USSR
1989	USSR
1990	Italy
1991	Cuba
1993	Germany
1994	Italy
1995	Cuba
1997	France
1998	Poland
1999	France

Foil (individual)

Women

Year	Champion
1982	Naila Giliazova (USSR)
1983	Dorina Vaccaroni (Italy)
1985	Cornelia Hanisch (West Germany)
1986	Anja Fichtel (West Germany)
1987	Elisabeta Tufan (Romania)
1989	Olga Velitschko (USSR)
1990	Anja Fichtel (West Germany)
1991	Giovanna Trillini (Italy)
1993	Francesca Bortolozzi (Italy)
1994	Reka Szabo-Lazar (Romania)
1995	Laura Badea (Romania)
1997	Giovanna Trillini (Italy)
1998	Sabine Bau (Germany)
1999	Valentina Vezzali (Italy)

Foil (team)

Women

Year	Champions
1982	Italy
1983	Italy
1985	West Germany
1986	USSR
1987	Hungary
1989	West Germany
1990	Italy
1991	Cuba
1993	Germany
1994	Romania
1995	Italy
1997	Italy
1998	Italy
1999	Germany

Épée (individual)

Men

Year	Champion
1982	Jenö Pap (Hungary)
1983	Ellmar Bormann (West Germany)
1985	Philippe Boisse (France)
1986	Philippe Riboud (France)
1987	Volker Fischer (West Germany)
1989	Manuel Pereira (Spain)
1990	Thomas Gerull (West Germany)
1991	Andrei Shuvalov (USSR)
1993	Pavel Kolobov (Russia)
1994	Pavel Kolobov (Russia)

Year	Champion
1995	Eric Srecki (France)
1997	Eric Srecki (France)
1998	Hugues Obry (France)
1999	Arnd Schmitt (Germany)

Épée (team)

Men

Year	Champions
1982	France
1983	France
1985	West Germany
1986	West Germany
1987	West Germany
1989	Italy
1990	Italy
1991	USSR
1993	Italy
1994	Germany
1995	Germany
1997	Cuba
1998	Hungary
1999	France

Épée (individual)

Women

Year	Champion
1989	Anja Straub (Switzerland)
1990	Taime Chappe (Cuba)
1991	Mariann Horváth (Hungary)
1992	Mariann Horváth (Hungary)
1993	Oksana Emakova (Estonia)
1994	Laura Chiesa (Italy)
1995	Joanna Jakimiuk (Poland)
1997	Miraide Garcia-Soto (Cuba)
1998	Laura Flessel (France)
1999	Laura Flessel-Colovic (France)

Épée (team)

Women

Year	Champions
1989	Hungary
1990	West Germany
1991	Hungary
1993	Hungary
1994	Spain
1995	Hungary

1997	Hungary
1998	France
1999	Hungary

Sabre (individual)

Men

Year	Champion
1982	Viktor Krovopuskov (USSR)
1983	Vasiliy Etropolski (Bulgaria)
1985	György Nébald (Hungary)
1986	Sergey Mindirgassov (USSR)
1987	Jean-François Lamour (France)
1989	Grigoriy Kirienko (USSR)
1990	György Nébald (Hungary)
1991	Grigoriy Kirienko (USSR)
1993	Grigoriy Kirienko (Russia)
1994	Felix Becker (Germany)
1995	Grigoriy Kirienko (Russia)
1997	Stanislav Pozdnyakov (Russia)
1998	Luigo Tarantino (Italy)
1999	Damien Touya (France)

Sabre (team)

Men

Year	Champions
1982	Hungary
1983	USSR
1985	USSR
1986	USSR
1987	USSR
1989	USSR
1990	USSR
1991	Hungary
1993	Hungary
1994	Russia
1995	Italy
1997	France
1998	Hungary
1999	France

Note First held in 1921

12.23 *Football, American*

Superbowl

Year	Winners
1967	Green Bay Packers
1968	Green Bay Packers
1969	New York Jets
1970	Kansas City Chiefs
1971	Baltimore Colts
1972	Dallas Cowboys
1973	Miami Dolphins
1974	Miami Dolphins
1975	Pittsburgh Steelers
1976	Pittsburgh Steelers
1977	Oakland Raiders
1978	Dallas Cowboys
1979	Pittsburgh Steelers
1980	Pittsburgh Steelers
1981	Oakland Raiders
1982	San Francisco 49ers
1983	Washington Redskins
1984	Los Angeles Raiders
1985	San Francisco 49ers
1986	Chicago Bears
1987	New York Giants
1988	Washington Redskins
1989	San Francisco 49ers
1990	San Francisco 49ers
1991	New York Giants
1992	Washington Redskins
1993	Dallas Cowboys
1994	Dallas Cowboys
1995	San Francisco 49ers
1996	Dallas Cowboys
1997	Green Bay Packers
1998	Denver Broncos
1999	Denver Broncos
2000	St Louis Rams
2001	Baltimore Ravens

12.24 *Football, Association*

FIFA World Cup

Year	Venue	Winners
1930	Uruguay	Uruguay
1934	Italy	Italy
1938	France	Italy
1950	Brazil	Uruguay
1954	Switzerland	West Germany
1958	Sweden	Brazil
1962	Chile	Brazil
1966	England	England
1970	Mexico	Brazil
1974	West Germany	West Germany
1978	Argentina	Argentina
1982	Spain	Italy
1986	Mexico	Argentina
1990	Italy	West Germany
1994	USA	Brazil
1998	France	France

South American Championship

Year	Champions
1963	Bolivia
1967	Uruguay
1975	Peru
1979	Paraguay
1983	Uruguay
1987	Uruguay
1989	Brazil
1991	Argentina
1993	Argentina
1995	Uruguay
1997	Brazil
1999	Brazil

Note First held in 1916

European Championship

Year	Champions
1960	USSR
1964	Spain
1968	Italy
1972	West Germany
1976	Czechoslovakia
1980	West Germany
1984	France
1988	Netherlands
1992	Denmark
1996	Germany
2000	France

European Champions' Cup

Year	Winners
1956	Real Madrid
1957	Real Madrid
1958	Real Madrid
1959	Real Madrid
1960	Real Madrid
1961	Benfica
1962	Benfica
1963	AC Milan
1964	Internazionale
1965	Internazionale
1966	Real Madrid
1967	Glasgow Celtic
1968	Manchester United
1969	AC Milan
1970	Feyenoord
1971	Ajax Amsterdam
1972	Ajax Amsterdam
1973	Ajax Amsterdam
1974	Bayern Munich
1975	Bayern Munich
1976	Bayern Munich
1977	Liverpool
1978	Liverpool
1979	Nottingham Forest
1980	Nottingham Forest
1981	Liverpool
1982	Aston Villa
1983	Hamburg
1984	Liverpool
1985	Juventus
1986	Steaua Bucharest

1987	Porto
1988	PSV Eindhoven
1989	AC Milan
1990	AC Milan
1991	Red Star Belgrade
1992	Barcelona
1993	Olympique Marseille
1994	AC Milan
1995	Ajax Amsterdam
1996	Juventus
1997	Borussia Dortmund
1998	Real Madrid
1999	Manchester United
2000	Real Madrid
2001	Bayern Munich

Note Popularly known as the European Cup

European Cup-Winners' Cup (since 1986)

Year	Winners
1986	Dynamo Kiev
1987	Ajax Amsterdam
1988	Mechelen
1989	Barcelona
1990	Sampdoria
1991	Manchester United
1992	Werder Bremen
1993	Parma
1994	Arsenal
1995	Real Zaragoza
1996	Paris St Germain
1997	Barcelona
1998	Chelsea
1999	Lazio

Note First held in 1961; discontinued in 2000

UEFA Cup (from 1985)

Year	Winners
1985	Real Madrid
1986	Real Madrid
1987	IFK Gothenburg
1988	Bayer Leverkusen
1989	Napoli
1990	Juventus
1991	Inter Milan
1992	Ajax Amsterdam
1993	Juventus

Year	Winners
1994	Inter Milan
1995	Parma
1996	Bayern Munich
1997	Schalke
1998	Internazionale Milan
1999	Parma
2000	Galatasaray
2001	Liverpool

Note UEFA = Union of European Football Associations; First held in 1955

English Football League

Year	Champions
1889	Preston North End
1890	Preston North End
1891	Everton
1892	Sunderland
1893	Sunderland
1894	Aston Villa
1895	Sunderland
1896	Aston Villa
1897	Aston Villa
1898	Sheffield United
1899	Aston Villa
1900	Aston Villa
1901	Liverpool
1902	Sunderland
1903	Sheffield Wednesday
1904	Sheffield Wednesday
1905	Newcastle United
1906	Liverpool
1907	Newcastle United
1908	Manchester United
1909	Newcastle United
1910	Aston Villa
1911	Manchester United
1912	Blackburn Rovers
1913	Sunderland
1914	Blackburn Rovers
1915	Everton
1916	(not held)
1917	(not held)
1918	(not held)
1919	(not held)
1920	West Bromwich Albion
1921	Burnley
1922	Liverpool
1923	Liverpool
1924	Huddersfield Town

1925	Huddersfield Town
1926	Huddersfield Town
1927	Newcastle United
1928	Everton
1929	Sheffield Wednesday
1930	Sheffield Wednesday
1931	Arsenal
1932	Everton
1933	Arsenal
1934	Arsenal
1935	Arsenal
1936	Sunderland
1937	Manchester City
1938	Arsenal
1939	Everton
1940	(not held)
1941	(not held)
1942	(not held)
1943	(not held)
1944	(not held)
1945	(not held)
1946	(not held)
1947	Liverpool
1948	Arsenal
1949	Portsmouth
1950	Portsmouth
1951	Tottenham Hotspur
1952	Manchester United
1953	Arsenal
1954	Wolverhampton Wanderers
1955	Chelsea
1956	Manchester United
1957	Manchester United
1958	Wolverhampton Wanderers
1959	Wolverhampton Wanderers
1960	Burnley
1961	Tottenham Hotspur
1962	Ipswich Town
1963	Everton
1964	Liverpool
1965	Manchester United
1966	Liverpool
1967	Manchester United
1968	Manchester City
1969	Leeds United
1970	Everton
1971	Arsenal
1972	Derby County
1973	Liverpool
1974	Leeds United
1975	Derby County
1976	Liverpool

Year	Champions
1977	Liverpool
1978	Nottingham Forest
1979	Liverpool
1980	Liverpool
1981	Aston Villa
1982	Liverpool
1983	Liverpool
1984	Liverpool
1985	Everton
1986	Liverpool
1987	Everton
1988	Liverpool
1989	Arsenal
1990	Liverpool
1991	Arsenal
1992	Leeds United
1993	Manchester United
1994	Manchester United
1995	Blackburn Rovers
1996	Manchester United
1997	Manchester United
1998	Arsenal
1999	Manchester United
2000	Manchester United
2001	Manchester United

Note Also known as the Premier League Championship since reorganization of the league in 1992

FA Cup

Year	Winners
1872	Wanderers
1873	Wanderers
1874	Oxford University
1875	Royal Engineers
1876	Wanderers
1877	Wanderers
1878	Wanderers
1879	Old Etonians
1880	Clapham Rovers
1881	Old Carthusians
1882	Old Etonians
1883	Blackburn Olympic
1884	Blackburn Rovers
1885	Blackburn Rovers
1886	Blackburn Rovers
1887	Aston Villa
1888	West Bromwich Albion
1889	Preston North End
1890	Blackburn Rovers

1891	Blackburn Rovers
1892	West Bromwich Albion
1893	Wolverhampton Wanderers
1894	Notts County
1895	Aston Villa
1896	Sheffield Wednesday
1897	Aston Villa
1898	Nottingham Forest
1899	Sheffield United
1900	Bury
1901	Tottenham Hotspur
1902	Sheffield United
1903	Bury
1904	Manchester City
1905	Aston Villa
1906	Everton
1907	Sheffield Wednesday
1908	Wolverhampton Wanderers
1909	Manchester United
1910	Newcastle United
1911	Bradford City
1912	Barnsley
1913	Aston Villa
1914	Burnley
1915	Sheffield United
1916	(not held)
1917	(not held)
1918	(not held)
1919	(not held)
1920	Aston Villa
1921	Tottenham Hotspur
1922	Huddersfield Town
1923	Bolton Wanderers
1924	Newcastle United
1925	Sheffield United
1926	Bolton Wanderers
1927	Cardiff City
1928	Blackburn Rovers
1929	Bolton Wanderers
1930	Arsenal
1931	West Bromwich Albion
1932	Newcastle United
1933	Everton
1934	Manchester City
1935	Sheffield Wednesday
1936	Arsenal
1937	Sunderland
1938	Preston North End
1939	Portsmouth
1940	(not held)
1941	(not held)
1942	(not held)

Year	Winners
1943	(not held)
1944	(not held)
1945	(not held)
1946	Derby County
1947	Charlton Athletic
1948	Manchester United
1949	Wolverhampton Wanderers
1950	Arsenal
1951	Newcastle United
1952	Newcastle United
1953	Blackpool
1954	West Bromwich Albion
1955	Newcastle United
1956	Manchester City
1957	Aston Villa
1958	Bolton Wanderers
1959	Nottingham Forest
1960	Wolverhampton Wanderers
1961	Tottenham Hotspur
1962	Tottenham Hotspur
1963	Manchester United
1964	West Ham United
1965	Liverpool
1966	Everton
1967	Tottenham Hotspur
1968	West Bromwich Albion
1969	Manchester City
1970	Chelsea
1971	Arsenal
1972	Leeds United
1973	Sunderland
1974	Liverpool
1975	West Ham United
1976	Southampton
1977	Manchester United
1978	Ipswich Town
1979	Arsenal
1980	West Ham United
1981	Tottenham Hotspur
1982	Tottenham Hotspur
1983	Manchester United
1984	Everton
1985	Manchester United
1986	Liverpool
1987	Coventry City
1988	Wimbledon
1989	Liverpool
1990	Manchester United
1991	Tottenham Hotspur
1992	Liverpool
1993	Arsenal

1994	Manchester United
1995	Everton
1996	Manchester United
1997	Chelsea
1998	Arsenal
1999	Manchester United
2000	Chelsea
2001	Liverpool

Note FA = Football Association

Football League Cup (since 1981)

Year	Winners
1981	Liverpool
1982	Liverpool
1983	Liverpool
1984	Liverpool
1985	Norwich City
1986	Oxford United
1987	Arsenal
1988	Luton Town
1989	Nottingham Forest
1990	Nottingham Forest
1991	Sheffield Wednesday
1992	Manchester United
1993	Arsenal
1994	Aston Villa
1995	Liverpool
1996	Aston Villa
1997	Leicester City
1998	Chelsea
1999	Tottenham Hotspur
2000	Leicester City
2001	Liverpool

Note Variously known as the Milk Cup (1982–86), the Littlewoods Cup (1987–90), the Rumbelows Cup (1991–92), the Coca-Cola Cup (1993–98) and the Worthington Cup (from 1999); first held in 1961

Scottish Football League

Year	Champions
1891	Dumbarton/Rangers
1892	Dumbarton
1893	Celtic
1894	Celtic
1895	Hearts
1896	Celtic
1897	Hearts
1898	Celtic

Year	Champions
1899	Rangers
1900	Rangers
1901	Rangers
1902	Rangers
1903	Hibernian
1904	Third Lanark
1905	Celtic
1906	Celtic
1907	Celtic
1908	Celtic
1909	Celtic
1910	Celtic
1911	Rangers
1912	Rangers
1913	Rangers
1914	Celtic
1915	Celtic
1916	Celtic
1917	Celtic
1918	Rangers
1919	Celtic
1920	Rangers
1921	Rangers
1922	Celtic
1923	Rangers
1924	Rangers
1925	Rangers
1926	Celtic
1927	Rangers
1928	Rangers
1929	Rangers
1930	Rangers
1931	Rangers
1932	Motherwell
1933	Rangers
1934	Rangers
1935	Rangers
1936	Celtic
1937	Rangers
1938	Celtic
1939	Rangers
1940	(not held)
1941	(not held)
1942	(not held)
1943	(not held)
1944	(not held)
1945	(not held)
1946	(not held)
1947	Rangers
1948	Hibernian
1949	Rangers

1950	Rangers
1951	Hibernian
1952	Hibernian
1953	Rangers
1954	Celtic
1955	Aberdeen
1956	Rangers
1957	Rangers
1958	Hearts
1959	Rangers
1960	Hearts
1961	Rangers
1962	Dundee
1963	Rangers
1964	Rangers
1965	Kilmarnock
1966	Celtic
1967	Celtic
1968	Celtic
1969	Celtic
1970	Celtic
1971	Celtic
1972	Celtic
1973	Celtic
1974	Celtic
1975	Rangers
1976	Rangers
1977	Celtic
1978	Rangers
1979	Celtic
1980	Aberdeen
1981	Celtic
1982	Celtic
1983	Dundee United
1984	Aberdeen
1985	Aberdeen
1986	Celtic
1987	Rangers
1988	Celtic
1989	Rangers
1990	Rangers
1991	Rangers
1992	Rangers
1993	Rangers
1994	Rangers
1995	Rangers
1996	Rangers
1997	Rangers
1998	Celtic
1999	Rangers
2000	Rangers
2001	Celtic

Scottish FA Cup (since 1980)

Year	Winner
1980	Celtic
1981	Rangers
1982	Aberdeen
1983	Aberdeen
1984	Aberdeen
1985	Celtic
1986	Aberdeen
1987	St Mirren
1988	Celtic
1989	Celtic
1990	Aberdeen
1991	Motherwell
1992	Rangers
1993	Rangers
1994	Dundee United
1995	Celtic
1996	Rangers
1997	Kilmarnock
1998	Hearts
1999	Rangers
2000	Rangers
2001	Celtic

Note First held in 1874

Scottish League Cup (since 1989)

Year	Winners
1989	Rangers
1990	Aberdeen
1991	Rangers
1992	Hibernian
1993	Rangers
1994	Rangers
1995	Raith Rovers
1996	Aberdeen
1997	Rangers
1998	Celtic
1999	Rangers
2000	Celtic
2001	Celtic

Note First held in 1947

English Football League Clubs

Club	Nickname	Ground
Arsenal	Gunners	Arsenal Stadium, Highbury
Aston Villa	Villa	Villa Park
Barnet	Bees	Underhill
Barnsley	Tykes	Oakwell
Birmingham City	Blues	St Andrews
Blackburn Rovers	Blue-and-Whites	Ewood Park
Blackpool	Tangerines	Bloomfield Road
Bolton Wanderers	Trotters	Reebok Stadium
Bournemouth	Cherries	Dean Court
Bradford City	Bantams	Pulse Stadium
Brentford	Bees	Griffin Park
Brighton and Hove Albion	Seagulls	Priestfield
Bristol City	Robins	Ashton Gate
Bristol Rovers	Pirates	Memorial Ground
Burnley	Clarets	Turf Moor
Bury	Shakers	Gigg Lane
Cambridge United	U's	Abbey Stadium
Cardiff City	Bluebirds	Ninian Park
Carlisle United	Cumbrians	Brunton Park
Charlton Athletic	Valiants	The Valley
Chelsea	Blues	Stamford Bridge
Chester City	Cestrians	Deva Stadium
Chesterfield	Spireites	Saltergate
Colchester United	U's	Layer Road
Coventry City	Sky Blues	Highfield Road
Crewe Alexandra	Railwaymen	Gresty Road
Crystal Palace	Eagles	Selhurst Park
Darlington	Quakers	Feethams
Derby County	Rams	Pride Park
Doncaster Rovers	Rovers	Belle Vue
Everton	Toffeemen	Goodison Park
Exeter City	Grecians	St James Park
Fulham	Cottagers	Craven Cottage
Gillingham	Gills	Priestfield
Grimsby Town	Mariners	Blundell Park
Hartlepool United	Pool	Victoria Ground
Hereford United	United	Edgar Street
Huddersfield Town	Terriers	MacAlpine Stadium
Hull City	Tigers	Boothferry Park
Ipswich Town	Blues	Portman Road
Leeds United	Peacocks	Elland Road
Leicester City	Foxes	Filbert Street
Leyton Orient	O's	Brisbane Road
Lincoln City	Imps	Sincil Bank
Liverpool	Reds	Anfield
Luton Town	Hatters	Kenilworth Road
Macclesfield Town	Silkmen	Moss Rose
Manchester City	Blues	Maine Road

Club	Nickname	Ground
Manchester United	Red Devils	Old Trafford
Mansfield Town	Stags	Field Mill
Middlesbrough	Boro	Cellnet Riverside Stadium
Millwall	Lions	New Den
Newcastle United	Magpies	St James' Park
Northampton Town	Cobblers	Sixfields
Norwich City	Canaries	Carrow Road
Nottingham Forest	Reds	City Ground
Notts County	Magpies	Meadow Lane
Oldham Athletic	Latics	Boundary Park
Oxford United	U's	Manor Ground
Peterborough United	Posh	London Road
Plymouth Argyle	Pilgrims	Home Park
Portsmouth	Pompey	Fratton Park
Port Vale	Valiants	Vale Park
Preston North End	Lilywhites	Deepdale
Queen's Park Rangers	R's	Rangers Stadium
Reading	Royals	Majestic Stadium
Rochdale	Dale	Spotland
Rotherham United	Millers	Millmoor
Scarborough	Boro	Seamer Road
Scunthorpe United	Irons	Glanford Road
Sheffield United	Blades	Bramall Lane
Sheffield Wednesday	Owls	Hillsborough
Shrewsbury Town	Shrews	Gay Meadow
Southampton	Saints	The Dell
Southend United	Shrimpers	Roots Hall
Stockport County	Hatters	Edgeley Park
Stoke City	Potters	Britannia Ground
Sunderland	Rokermen	Stadium of Light
Swansea City	Swans	Vetch Field
Swindon Town	Robins	County Ground
Torquay United	Gulls	Plainmoor
Tottenham Hotspur	Spurs	White Hart Lane
Tranmere Rovers	Rovers	Prenton Park
Walsall	Saddlers	Bescot Stadium
Watford	Hornets	Vicarage Road
West Bromwich Albion	Albion	The Hawthorns
West Ham United	Hammers	Boleyn Ground
Wigan Athletic	Latics	JJB Stadium
Wimbledon	Dons	Selhurst Park Ground
Wolverhampton Wanderers	Wolves	Molineux
Wrexham	Robins	Racecourse Ground
Wycombe Wanderers	Blues	Adams Park
York City	Minstermen	Bootham Crescent

Scottish Football League Clubs

Club	Nickname	Ground
Aberdeen	Dons	Pittodrie
Airdrieonians	Diamonds	Broadwood Stadium
Albion Rovers	Wee Rovers	Cliftonhill
Alloa Athletic	Wasps	Recreation Park
Arbroath	Red Lichties	Gayfield Park
Ayr United	Honest Men	Somerset Park
Berwick Rangers	Borderers	Shielfield Park
Brechin City	City	Glebe Park
Celtic	Bhoys	Celtic Park
Clyde	Bully Wee	Broadwood Stadium
Clydebank	Bankies	Burnbrae
Cowdenbeath	Cowden	Central Park
Dumbarton	Sons	Boghead Park
Dundee	Dark Blues	Dens Park
Dundee United	Terrors	Tannadice Park
Dunfermline Athletic	Pars	East End Park
East Fife	Fifers	Bayview Park
East Stirlingshire	Shire	Firs Park
Falkirk	Bairns	Brockville Park
Forfar Athletic	Sky Blues/Loons	Station Park
Greenock Morton	Ton	Cappielow Park
Hamilton Academical	Accies	Cliftonville
Heart of Midlothian	Hearts	Tynecastle Park
Hibernian	Hibs	Easter Road
Inverness Caledonian Thistle	Caley/Thistle	Caledonian Stadium
Kilmarnock	Killie	Rugby Park
Livingston	Lions	Almondvale
Montrose	Gable Endies	Links Park
Motherwell	'Well	Fir Park
Partick Thistle	Jags	Firhill Park
Queen of the South	Doonhamers	Palmerston Park
Queen's Park	Spiders	Hampden Park
Raith Rovers	Rovers	Stark's Park
Rangers	Gers	Ibrox Stadium
Ross County	Staggies	Victoria Park
St Johnstone	Saints	McDiarmid Park
St Mirren	Buddies	St Mirren Park
Stenhousemuir	Warriors	Ochilview Park
Stirling Albion	Binos	Forthbank Stadium
Stranraer	Blues	Stair Park

12.25 *Football, Australian Rules*

Premiership Trophy (since 1980)

Year	Champions
1980	Richmond
1981	Carlton
1982	Carlton
1983	Hawthorn
1984	Essendon
1985	Essendon
1986	Hawthorn
1987	Carlton
1988	Hawthorn
1989	Hawthorn
1990	Collingwood
1991	Hawthorn
1992	West Coast
1993	Essendon
1994	West Coast
1995	Carlton Blues
1996	North Melbourne
1997	Adelaide
1998	Adelaide
1999	North Melbourne
2000	Essendon

Note First held in 1897; known as the Victoria Football League until 1987

12.26 *Football, Gaelic*

All-Ireland Championship (since 1985)

Year	Champions
1985	Kerry
1986	Kerry
1987	Meath
1988	Meath
1989	Cork

1990	Cork
1991	Down
1992	Donegal
1993	Derry
1994	Down
1995	Dublin
1996	Meath
1997	Kerry
1998	Galway
1999	Meath
2000	Kerry

Note First held in 1887

12.27 *Golf*

British Open Championship (since 1946)

Year	Winner
1946	Sam Snead (USA)
1947	Fred Daly (UK)
1948	Henry Cotton (UK)
1949	Bobby Locke (South Africa)
1950	Bobby Locke (South Africa)
1951	Max Faulkner (UK)
1952	Bobby Locke (South Africa)
1953	Ben Hogan (USA)
1954	Peter Thomson (Australia)
1955	Peter Thomson (Australia)
1956	Peter Thomson (Australia)
1957	Bobby Locke (South Africa)
1958	Peter Thomson (Australia)
1959	Gary Player (South Africa)
1960	Kel Nagle (Australia)
1961	Arnold Palmer (USA)
1962	Arnold Palmer (USA)
1963	Bob Charles (New Zealand)
1964	Tony Lema (USA)
1965	Peter Thomson (Australia)
1966	Jack Nicklaus (USA)
1967	Roberto de Vincenzo (Argentina)
1968	Gary Player (South Africa)
1969	Tony Jacklin (UK)
1970	Jack Nicklaus (USA)
1971	Lee Trevino (USA)

Year	Winner
1972	Lee Trevino (USA)
1973	Tom Weiskopf (USA)
1974	Gary Player (South Africa)
1975	Tom Watson (USA)
1976	Johnny Miller (USA)
1977	Tom Watson (USA)
1978	Jack Nicklaus (USA)
1979	Seve Ballesteros (Spain)
1980	Tom Watson (USA)
1981	Bill Rogers (USA)
1982	Tom Watson (USA)
1983	Tom Watson (USA)
1984	Seve Ballesteros (Spain)
1985	Sandy Lyle (UK)
1986	Greg Norman (Australia)
1987	Nick Faldo (UK)
1988	Seve Ballesteros (Spain)
1989	Mark Calcavecchia (USA)
1990	Nick Faldo (UK)
1991	Ian Baker-Finch (Australia)
1992	Nick Faldo (UK)
1993	Greg Norman (Australia)
1994	Nick Price (Zimbabwe)
1995	John Daly (USA)
1996	Tom Lehman (USA)
1997	Justin Leonard (USA)
1998	Mark O'Meara (USA)
1999	Paul Lawrie (UK)
2000	Tiger Woods (USA)
2001	David Duval (USA)

Note First held in 1860

US Open Championship (since 1985)

Year	Winner
1985	Andy North (USA)
1986	Ray Floyd (USA)
1987	Scott Simpson (USA)
1988	Curtis Strange (USA)
1989	Curtis Strange (USA)
1990	Hale Irwin (USA)
1991	Payne Stewart (USA)
1992	Tom Kite (USA)
1993	Lee Janzen (USA)
1994	Ernie Els (South Africa)
1995	Corey Pavin (USA)
1996	Steve Jones (USA)
1997	Ernie Els (South Africa)

1998	Lee Janzen (USA)
1999	Payne Stewart (USA)
2000	Tiger Woods (USA)
2001	Retief Goosen (South Africa)

Note First held in 1895

US Masters Championship (since 1985)

Year	Winner
1985	Bernhard Langer (West Germany)
1986	Jack Nicklaus (USA)
1987	Larry Mize (USA)
1988	Sandy Lyle (UK)
1989	Nick Faldo (UK)
1990	Nick Faldo (UK)
1991	Ian Woosnam (UK)
1992	Fred Couples (USA)
1993	Bernhard Langer (Germany)
1994	José-Maria Olazábal (Spain)
1995	Ben Crenshaw (USA)
1996	Nick Faldo (UK)
1997	Tiger Woods (USA)
1998	Mark O'Meara (USA)
1999	José-Maria Olazábal (Spain)
2000	Vijay Singh (Fiji)
2001	Tiger Woods (USA)

Note First held in 1934

US PGA Championship (since 1985)

Year	Winner
1985	Hubert Green (USA)
1986	Bob Tway (USA)
1987	Larry Nelson (USA)
1988	Jeff Sluman (USA)
1989	Payne Stewart (USA)
1990	Wayne Grady (Australia)
1991	John Daly (USA)
1992	Nick Price (Zimbabwe)
1993	Paul Azinger (USA)
1994	Nick Price (Zimbabwe)
1995	Steve Elkington (Australia)
1996	Mark Brooks (USA)
1997	Davis Love III (USA)
1998	Vijay Singh (Fiji)
1999	Tiger Woods (USA)
2000	Tiger Woods (USA)

Note PGA = Professional Golf Association; first held in 1916

Ryder Cup (since 1977)

Year	Winner
1977	USA
1979	USA
1981	USA
1983	USA
1985	Europe
1987	Europe
1989	(Drawn)
1991	USA
1993	USA
1995	Europe
1997	Europe
1999	USA

Note First held in 1927

12.28 *Gymnastics*

World Championship (since 1979)

Individual (Men)

Year	Winner
1979	Aleksandr Ditiatin (USSR)
1981	Yuriy Korolev (USSR)
1983	Dmitri Belozerchev (USSR)
1985	Yuriy Korolev (USSR)
1987	Dmitri Belozerchev (USSR)
1989	Igor Korobichensky (USSR)
1991	Grigoriy Misutin (USSR)
1993	Vitaly Shcherbo (Belarus)
1995	Li Xiaoshuang (China)
1997	Ivan Ivankova (Belarus)
1999	Nikolay Krukov (Russia)

Team (Men)

Year	Winners
1979	USSR
1981	USSR
1983	China
1985	USSR
1987	USSR

1989	USSR
1991	USSR
1993	(no team prize)
1994	China
1995	China
1997	China
1999	China

Individual (Women)

Year	Winner
1979	Nelli Kim (USSR)
1981	Olga Bitcherova (USSR)
1983	Natalia Yurchenko (USSR)
1985	Yelena Shoushounova (USSR) and Oksana Omeliantchuk (USSR)
1987	Aurelia Dobre (Romania)
1989	Svetlana Boginskaya (USSR)
1991	Kim Zmeskal (USA)
1993	Shannon Miller (USA)
1994	Shannon Miller (USA)
1995	Lilia Podkopayeva (Ukraine)
1997	Svetlana Khorkina (Russia)
1999	Maria Olaru (Romania)

Team (Women)

Year	Winners
1979	Romania
1981	USSR
1983	USSR
1985	USSR
1987	Romania
1989	USSR
1991	USSR
1994	Romania
1995	Romania
1997	Romania
1999	Romania

Note First held in 1903

12.29 *Handball*

World Championship

Men

Year	Winners
1938	Germany
1954	Sweden
1958	Sweden
1961	Romania
1964	Romania
1967	Czechoslovakia
1970	Romania
1974	Romania
1978	West Germany
1982	USSR
1986	Yugoslavia
1990	Sweden
1993	Russia
1995	France
1997	Russia
1999	Sweden

Women

Year	Winners
1962	Romania
1965	Hungary
1971	East Germany
1973	Yugoslavia
1975	East Germany
1979	East Germany
1982	USSR
1986	USSR
1990	USSR
1993	Germany
1995	Germany
1997	Denmark
1999	Norway

12.30 *Hockey*

World Cup

Men

Year	Winners
1971	Pakistan
1975	India
1978	Pakistan
1982	Pakistan
1986	Australia
1990	Netherlands
1994	Pakistan
1998	Netherlands

Women

Year	Winners
1974	Netherlands
1978	Netherlands
1981	West Germany
1983	Netherlands
1986	Netherlands
1990	Netherlands
1994	Australia
1998	Australia

Olympic Games (since 1928)

Men

Year	Winners
1928	India
1932	India
1936	India
1948	India
1952	India
1956	India
1960	Pakistan
1964	India
1968	Pakistan
1972	West Germany
1976	New Zealand
1980	India
1984	Pakistan
1988	Great Britain

Year	Winners
1992	Germany
1996	Netherlands
2000	Netherlands

Women

Year	Winners
1980	Zimbabwe
1984	Netherlands
1988	Australia
1992	Spain
1996	Australia
2000	Australia

Note The Men's event was first held in 1908; the Women's event followed in 1980

12.31 *Horseracing*

The Derby (since 1960)

Year	Winning horse	Winning jockey
1960	St Paddy	Lester Piggott
1961	Psidium	Roger Poincelet
1962	Larkspur	Neville Sellwood
1963	Relko	Yves Saint-Martin
1964	Santa Claus	Scobie Breasley
1965	Sea Bird II	Pat Glennon
1966	Charlottown	Scobie Breasley
1967	Royal Palace	George Moore
1968	Sir Ivor	Lester Piggott
1969	Blakeney	Ernie Johnson
1970	Nijinsky	Lester Piggott
1971	Mill Reef	Geoff Lewis
1972	Roberto	Lester Piggott
1973	Morston	Eddie Hide
1974	Snow Knight	Brian Taylor
1975	Grundy	Pat Eddery
1976	Empery	Lester Piggott
1977	The Minstrel	Lester Piggott
1978	Shirley Heights	Greville Starkey
1979	Troy	Willie Carson
1980	Henbit	Willie Carson
1981	Shergar	Walter Swinburn
1982	Golden Fleece	Pat Eddery
1983	Teenoso	Lester Piggott

1984	Secreto	Christy Roche
1985	Slip Anchor	Steve Cauthen
1986	Shahrastani	Walter Swinburn
1987	Reference Point	Steve Cauthen
1988	Kahyashi	Ray Cochrane
1989	Nashwan	Willie Carson
1990	Quest For Fame	Pat Eddery
1991	Generous	Alan Munro
1992	Dr Devious	John Reid
1993	Commander in Chief	Michael Kinane
1994	Erhaab	Willie Carson
1995	Lammtarra	Walter Swinburn
1996	Shaamit	Michael Hills
1997	Benny the Dip	Willie Ryan
1998	High-Rise	Olivier Peslier
1999	Oath	Kieren Fallon
2000	Sinndar	Johnny Murtagh
2001	Galileo	Michael Kinane

Note First run in 1780

The Oaks (since 1985)

Year	Winning horse	Winning jockey
1985	Oh So Sharp	Steve Cauthen
1986	Midway Lady	Ray Cochrane
1987	Unite	Walter Swinburn
1988	Diminuendo	Steve Cauthen
1989	Aliysa	Walter Swinburn
1990	Salsabil	Willie Carson
1991	Jet Ski Lady	Christy Roche
1992	User Friendly	George Duffield
1993	Intrepidity	Michael Roberts
1994	Balanchine	Frankie Dettori
1995	Moonshell	Frankie Dettori
1996	Lady Carla	Pat Eddery
1997	Reams of Verse	Kieren Fallon
1998	Shahtoush	Michael Kinane
1999	Ramruma	Kieren Fallon
2000	Love Divine	Richard Quinn

Note First held in 1779

One Thousand Guineas (since 1985)

Year	Winning horse	Winning jockey
1985	Oh So Sharp	Steve Cauthen
1986	Midway Lady	Ray Cochrane
1987	Miesque	Freddy Head
1988	Ravinella	Gary Moore

Year	Winning horse	Winning Jockey
1989	Musical Bliss	Walter Swinburn
1990	Salsabil	Willie Carson
1991	Shadayid	Willie Carson
1992	Hatoof	Walter Swinburn
1993	Sayyedati	Walter Swinburn
1994	Las Meninas	John Reid
1995	Harayir	Richard Ellis
1996	Bosra Sham	Pat Eddery
1997	Sleepytime	Kieren Fallon
1998	Cape Verdi	Frankie Dettori
1999	Wince	Kieren Fallon
2000	Lahan	Richard Hills
2001	Ameerat	Philip Robinson

Note First run in 1814

Two Thousand Guineas (since 1985)

Year	Winning horse	Winning jockey
1985	Shadeed	Lester Piggott
1986	Dancing Brave	Greville Starkey
1987	Don't Forget Me	Willie Carson
1988	Doyoun	Walter Swinburn
1989	Nashwan	Willie Carson
1990	Tirol	Michael Kinanc
1991	Mystiko	Michael Roberts
1992	Rodrigo de Triano	Lester Piggott
1993	Zafonic	Pat Eddery
1994	Mister Baileys	Jason Weaver
1995	Pennekamp	Thierry Jarnet
1996	Mark of Esteem	Frankie Dettori
1997	Entrepreneur	Michael Kinane
1998	King of Kings	Michael Kinane
1999	Island Sands	Frankie Dettori
2000	King's Best	Kieren Fallon
2001	Golan	Kieren Fallon

Note First run in 1809

St Leger (since 1985)

Year	Winning horse	Winning jockey
1985	Oh So Sharp	Steve Cauthen
1986	Moon Madness	Pat Eddery
1987	Reference Point	Steve Cauthen
1988	Minster Son	Willie Carson
1989	Michelozzo	Steve Cauthen
1990	Snurge	Richard Quinn
1991	Toulon	Pat Eddery

1992	User Friendly	George Duffield
1993	Bob's Return	Philip Robinson
1994	Moonax	Pat Eddery
1995	Classic Cliché	Frankie Dettori
1996	Shantou	Frankie Dettori
1997	Silver Patriarch	Pat Eddery
1998	Nedawi	John Reid
1999	Mustafaweq	Richard Hills
2000	Millenary	T. Quinn

Note First run in 1776

Grand National (since 1946)

Year	Winning horse	Winning jockey
1946	Lovely Cottage	Captain Bobby Petre
1947	Caughoo	Eddie Dempsey
1948	Sheila's Cottage	Arthur Thompson
1949	Russian Hero	Leo McMorrow
1950	Freebooter	Jimmy Power
1951	Nickel Coin	Johnny Bullock
1952	Teal	Arthur Thompson
1953	Early Mist	Bryan Marshall
1954	Royal Tan	Bryan Marshall
1955	Quare Times	Pat Taaffe
1956	E.S.B.	Dave Dick
1957	Sundew	Fred Winter
1958	Mr What	Arthur Freeman
1959	Oxo	Michael Scudamore
1960	Merryman II	Gerry Scott
1961	Nicolaus Silver	Bobby Beasley
1962	Kilmore	Fred Winter
1963	Ayala	Pat Buckley
1964	Team Spirit	Willie Robinson
1965	Jay Trump	Tommy Smith
1966	Anglo	Tim Norman
1967	Foinavon	John Buckingham
1968	Red Alligator	Brian Fletcher
1969	Highland Wedding	Eddie Harty
1970	Gay Trip	Pat Taaffe
1971	Specify	John Cook
1972	Well To Do	Graham Thorner
1973	Red Rum	Brian Fletcher
1974	Red Rum	Brian Fletcher
1975	L'Escargot	Tommy Carberry
1976	Rag Trade	John Burke
1977	Red Rum	Tommy Stack
1978	Lucius	Bob Davies
1979	Rubstic	Maurice Barnes
1980	Ben Nevis	Charlie Fenwick
1981	Aldaniti	Bob Champion

Year	Winning horse	Winning jockey
1982	Grittar	Dick Saunders
1983	Corbière	Ben de Haan
1984	Hallo Dandy	Neale Doughty
1985	Last Suspect	Hywel Davies
1986	West Tip	Richard Dunwoody
1987	Maori Venture	Steve Knight
1988	Rhyme N' Reason	Brendan Powell
1989	Little Polvier	Jimmy Frost
1990	Mr Frisk	Marcus Armytage
1991	Seagram	Nigel Hawke
1992	Party Politics	Carl Llewellyn
1993	(declared void)	
1994	Minnehoma	Richard Dunwoody
1995	Royal Athlete	Jason Titley
1996	Rough Quest	Mick Fitzgerald
1997	Lord Gyllene	Tony Dobbin
1998	Earth Summit	Carl Llewellyn
1999	Bobbyjo	Paul Carberry
2000	Papillon	Ruby Walsh
2001	Red Marauder	Richard Guest

Note First held in 1839

Prix de l'Arc de Triomphe (since 1985)

Year	Winning horse	Winning jockey
1985	Rainbow Quest	Pat Eddery
1986	Dancing Brave	Pat Eddery
1987	Trempolino	Pat Eddery
1988	Tony Bin	John Reid
1989	Caroll House	Michael Kinane
1990	Suamarez	Gerard Mosse
1991	Suave Dancer	Cash Asmussen
1992	Subotica	Thierry Jarnet
1993	Urban Sea	Eric Saint-Martin
1994	Carnegie	Thierry Jarnet
1995	Lammtarra	Frankie Dettori
1996	Helissio	Olivier Peslier
1997	Peintre Célèbre	Olivier Peslier
1998	Sagamix	Olivier Peslier
1999	Montjeu	Michael Kinane
2000	Sinndar	J. Murtagh

Note First run in 1920

12.32 *Hurling*

All-Ireland Championship (since 1985)

Year	Winners
1985	Offaly
1986	Cork
1987	Galway
1988	Galway
1989	Tipperary
1990	Cork
1991	Tipperary
1992	Limerick
1993	Kilkenny
1994	Offaly
1995	Clare
1996	Wexford
1997	Clare
1998	Offaly
1999	Cork
2000	Kilkenny

Note First held in 1887

12.33 *Ice Hockey*

World Championship (since 1985)

Year	Winners
1985	Czechoslovakia
1986	USSR
1987	Sweden
1988	USSR
1989	USSR
1990	USSR
1991	Sweden
1992	Sweden
1993	Russia
1994	Canada

Year	Winners
1995	Finland
1996	Czech Republic
1997	Canada
1998	Sweden
1999	Czech Republic
2000	Czech Republic

Note First held in 1930

Olympic Games (since 1976)

Year	Winners
1976	USSR
1980	USA
1984	USSR
1988	USSR
1992	Unified Team
1994	Sweden
1998 (men)	Czech Republic
1998 (women)	USA

Stanley Cup (since 1985)

Year	Winners
1985	Edmonton Oilers
1986	Montreal Canadiens
1987	Edmonton Oilers
1988	Edmonton Oilers
1989	Calgary Flames
1990	Edmonton Oilers
1991	Pittsburgh Penguins
1992	Pittsburgh Penguins
1993	Montreal Canadiens
1994	New York Rangers
1995	New Jersey Devils
1996	Colorado Avalanche
1997	Detroit Red Wings
1998	Detroit Red Wings
1999	Dallas Stars
2000	New Jersey Devils
2001	Colorado Avalanche

12.34 *Ice Skating*

World Championship (since 1985)

Individual (Men)

Year	Winner
1985	Alexander Fadeyev (USSR)
1986	Brian Boitano (USA)
1987	Brian Orser (Canada)
1988	Brian Boitano (USA)
1989	Kurt Browning (Canada)
1990	Kurt Browning (Canada)
1991	Kurt Browning (Canada)
1992	Viktor Petrenko (CIS)
1993	Kurt Browning (Canada)
1994	Elvis Stojko (Canada)
1995	Elvis Stojko (Canada)
1996	Todd Eldredge (USA)
1997	Elvis Stojko (Canada)
1998	Alexei Yagudin (Russia)
1999	Alexei Yagudin (Russia)
2000	Alexei Yagudin (Russia)

Individual (Women)

Year	Winner
1985	Katarina Witt (East Germany)
1986	Debbie Thomas (USA)
1987	Katarina Witt (East Germany)
1988	Katarina Witt (East Germany)
1989	Midori Ito (Japan)
1990	Jill Trenary (USA)
1991	Kristi Yamaguchi (USA)
1992	Kristi Yamaguchi (USA)
1993	Oksana Baiul (Ukraine)
1994	Yuka Sato (Japan)
1995	Lu Chen (China)
1996	Michelle Kwan (USA)
1997	Tara Lipinski (USA)
1998	Michelle Kwan (USA)
1999	Maria Butyrskaya (Russia)
2000	Michelle Kwan (USA)

Pairs

Year	Winners
1985	Oleg Vasiliev/Yelena Valova (USSR)
1986	Sergei Grinkov/Yekaterina Gordeeva (USSR)
1987	Sergei Grinkov/Yekaterina Gordeeva (USSR)
1988	Oleg Vasiliev/Yelena Valova (USSR)

Year	Winners
1989	Sergei Grinkov/Yekaterina Gordeeva (USSR)
1990	Sergei Grinkov/Yekaterina Gordeeva (USSR)
1991	Artur Dmtriev/Natalya Mishkutienok (USSR)
1992	Artur Dmtriev/Natalya Mishkutienok (USSR)
1993	Lloyd Eisler/Isabelle Brasseur (Canada)
1994	Vadim Naumov/Evgenia Shiskova (Russia)
1995	Rene Novotny/Radka Kovarikova (Czech Republic)
1996	Andrei Bushkov/Marina Eltsova (Russia)
1997	Ingo Steuer/Mandy Woetzel (Germany)
1998	Anton Sikharulidze/Elena Berzhnaya (Russia)
1999	Anton Sikharulidze/Elena Berzhnaya (Russia)
2000	Alexei Tikhonov/Maria Petrova (Russia)

Ice dance

Year	Winners
1985	Andrei Bukin/Natalya Bestemianova (USSR)
1986	Andrei Bukin/Natalya Bestemianova (USSR)
1987	Andrei Bukin/Natalya Bestemianova (USSR)
1988	Andrei Bukin/Natalya Bestemianova (USSR)
1989	Sergei Ponomarenko/Marina Klimova (USSR)
1990	Sergei Ponomarenko/Marina Klimova (USSR)
1991	Paul Duchesnay/Isabelle Duchesnay (France)
1992	Sergei Ponomarenko/Marina Klimova (USSR)
1993	Alesandr Zhulin/Maia Usova (Russia)
1994	Yevgeni Platov/Oksana Gritschuk (Russia)
1995	Yevgeni Platov/Oksana Gritschuk (Russia)
1996	Yevgeni Platov/Oksana Gritschuk (Russia)
1997	Yevgeni Platov/Oksana Gritschuk (Russia)
1998	Oleg Ovsyannikov/Anjelika Krylova (Russia)
1999	Oleg Ovsyannikov/Anjelika Krylova (Russia)
2000	Gwendal Peizerat/Marina Anissina (France)

Note The Men's Championship was first held in 1896, the Women's Championship followed in 1906, the Pairs Championship in 1908 and the Ice Dance Championship in 1952

12.35 *Lacrosse*

World Championship (since 1974 for Men/1969 for Women)

Men

Year	Winners
1974	USA
1978	Canada
1982	USA
1986	USA
1990	USA
1994	USA
1998	USA

Women

Year	Winners
1969	Great Britain
1974	USA
1978	Canada
1982	USA
1986	Australia
1990	USA
1994	USA
1998	USA

Note The Men's Championship was first held in 1967; the Women's Championship followed in 1969

12.36 *Modern Pentathlon*

World Championship (since 1985)

Individual

Year	Winner
1985	Attila Mizser (Hungary)
1986	Carlo Massullo (Italy)
1987	Joel Bouzou (France)
1988	Janos Martinek (Hungary)
1989	Laszlo Fabien (Hungary)
1990	Gianluca Tiberti (Italy)

Year	Winner
1991	Arkadiusz Skrzypaszek (Poland)
1992	Arkadiusz Skrzypaszek (Poland)
1993	Richard Phelps (Great Britain)
1994	Dmitri Svatovski (Russia)
1995	Dmitri Svatovski (Russia)
1996	Alexander Parygin (Kazakhstan)
1997	Sebastien Deleigne (France)
1998	Sebastien Deleigne (France)
1999	Gabor Balogh (Hungary)
2000	Andrejus Zadneprovskis (Lithuania)

Team

Year	Winners
1985	USSR
1986	Italy
1987	Hungary
1988	Hungary
1989	Hungary
1990	USSR
1991	USSR
1992	Poland
1993	Hungary
1994	France
1995	Poland
1996	Poland
1997	Hungary
1998	Mexico
1999	Hungary
2000	USA

Note First held in 1949

12.37 *Motor Cycling*

World Championship (since 1985)

Year	Winner (500 cc)
1985	Freddie Spencer (USA)
1986	Eddie Lawson (USA)
1987	Wayne Gardner (Australia)
1988	Eddie Lawson (USA)
1989	Eddie Lawson (USA)
1990	Wayne Rainey (USA)
1991	Wayne Rainey (USA)
1992	Wayne Rainey (USA)

1993	Kevin Schwantz (USA)
1994	Michael Doohan (Australia)
1995	Michael Doohan (Australia)
1996	Michael Doohan (Australia)
1997	Michael Doohan (Australia)
1998	Michael Doohan (Australia)
1999	Alex Criville (Spain)

Note First held in 1949

Isle of Man TT Race (since 1985)

Year	Winner (Senior TT)
1985	Joey Dunlop (Ireland)
1986	Roger Burnett (Great Britain)
1987	Joey Dunlop (Ireland)
1988	Joey Dunlop (Ireland)
1989	Steve Hislop (Great Britain)
1990	Carl Fogarty (Great Britain)
1991	Steve Hislop (Great Britain)
1992	Steve Hislop (Great Britain)
1993	Phil McCallen (Ireland)
1994	Steve Hislop (Great Britain)
1995	Joey Dunlop (Ireland)
1996	Phil McCallen (Ireland)
1997	Phil McCallen (Ireland)
1998	Ian Simpson (Scotland)
1999	David Jefferies (England)
2000	David Jefferies (England)
2001	(not held)

Note First held in 1907

12.38 *Motor Racing*

Formula One Drivers' World Championship

Year	Champion	Constructor
1950	Giuseppe Farina (Italy)	Alfa Romeo
1951	Juan Manuel Fangio (Argentina)	Alfa Romeo
1952	Alberto Ascari (Italy)	Ferrari
1953	Alberto Ascari (Italy)	Ferrari
1954	Juan Manuel Fangio (Argentina)	Maserati-Mercedes
1955	Juan Manuel Fangio (Argentina)	Mercedes-Benz

Year	Champion	Constructor
1956	Juan Manuel Fangio (Argentina)	Lancia-Ferrari
1957	Juan Manuel Fangio (Argentina)	Maserati
1958	Mike Hawthorn (UK)	Ferrari
1959	Jack Brabham (Australia)	Cooper-Climax
1960	Jack Brabham (Australia)	Cooper-Climax
1961	Phil Hill (USA)	Ferrari
1962	Graham Hill (UK)	BRM
1963	Jim Clark (UK)	Lotus-Climax
1964	John Surtees (UK)	Ferrari
1965	Jim Clark (UK)	Lotus-Climax
1966	Jack Brabham (Australia)	Brabham-Repco
1967	Denny Hulme (New Zealand)	Brabham-Repco
1968	Graham Hill (UK)	Lotus-Ford
1969	Jackie Stewart (UK)	Matra-Ford
1970	Jochen Rindt (Austria)	Lotus-Ford
1971	Jackie Stewart (UK)	Tyrell-Ford
1972	Emerson Fittipaldi (Brazil)	Lotus-Ford
1973	Jackie Stewart (UK)	Tyrell-Ford
1974	Emerson Fittipaldi (Brazil)	McLaren-Ford
1975	Niki Lauda (Austria)	Ferrari
1976	James Hunt (UK)	McLaren-Ford
1977	Niki Lauda (Austria)	Ferrari
1978	Mario Andretti (USA)	Lotus-Ford
1979	Jody Scheckter (South Africa)	Ferrari
1980	Alan Jones (Australia)	Williams-Ford
1981	Nelson Piquet (Brazil)	Brabham-Ford
1982	Keke Rosberg (Finland)	Williams-Ford
1983	Nelson Piquet (Brazil)	Brabham-BMW
1984	Niki Lauda (Austria)	McLaren-TAG
1985	Alain Prost (France)	McLaren-TAG
1986	Alain Prost (France)	McLaren-TAG
1987	Nelson Piquet (Brazil)	Williams-Honda
1988	Ayrton Senna (Brazil)	McLaren-Honda
1989	Alain Prost (France)	McLaren-Honda
1990	Ayrton Senna (Brazil)	McLaren-Honda
1991	Ayrton Senna (Brazil)	McLaren-Honda
1992	Nigel Mansell (UK)	Williams-Renault
1993	Alain Prost (France)	Williams-Renault
1994	Michael Schumacher (Germany)	Benetton-Ford
1995	Michael Schumacher (Germany)	Benetton-Renault
1996	Damon Hill (UK)	Williams-Renault
1997	Jacques Villeneuve (Canada)	Williams-Renault
1998	Mika Hakkinen (Finland)	McLaren-Mercedes
1999	Mika Hakkinen (Finland)	McLaren-Mercedes
2000	Michael Schumacher (Germany)	Ferrari

Formula One Constructors' Championship

Year	Constructors
1958	Vanwall
1959	Cooper-Climax
1960	Cooper-Climax
1961	Ferrari
1962	BRM
1963	Lotus-Climax
1964	Ferrari
1965	Lotus-Climax
1966	Brabham-Repco
1967	Brabham-Repco
1968	Lotus-Ford
1969	Matra-Ford
1970	Lotus-Ford
1971	Tyrell-Ford
1972	Lotus-Ford
1973	Lotus-Ford
1974	McLaren-Ford
1975	Ferrari
1976	Ferrari
1977	Ferrari
1978	Lotus-Ford
1979	Ferrari
1980	Williams-Ford
1981	Williams-Ford
1982	Ferrari
1983	Ferrari
1984	McLaren-TAG
1985	McLaren-TAG
1986	Williams-Honda
1987	Williams-Honda
1988	McLaren-Honda
1989	McLaren-Honda
1990	McLaren-Honda
1991	McLaren-Honda
1992	Williams-Renault
1993	Williams-Renault
1994	Williams-Renault
1995	Williams-Renault
1996	Williams-Renault
1997	Williams-Renault
1998	McLaren-Mercedes
1999	Ferrari
2000	Ferrari

Le Mans 24-Hour Race

Year	Champions	Car
1923	Lagache/Leonard	Chenard and Walcker
1924	Duff/Clement	Bentley
1925	De Courcelles/Rossignol	La Lorraine
1926	Bloch/Rossignol	La Lorraine
1927	Benjafield/Davis	Bentley
1928	Barnato/Rubin	Bentley
1929	Barnato/Birkin	Bentley
1930	Barnato/Kidston	Bentley
1931	Howe/Birkin	Alfa Romeo
1932	Sommer/Chinetti	Alfa Romeo
1933	Sommer/Nuvolari	Alfa Romeo
1934	Chinetti/Etancelin	Alfa Romeo
1935	Hindmarsh/Fontes	Lagonda
1936	(not held)	
1937	Wimille/Benoist	Bugatti
1938	Chaboud/Tremoulet	Delahaye
1939	Wimille/Veyron	Bugatti
1940–48	(not held)	
1949	Chinetti/Lord Selsdon	Ferrari
1950	Rosier/Rosier	Lago-Talbot
1951	Whitehead/Walker	Jaguar
1952	Lang/Riess	Mercedes-Benz
1953	Rolt/Hamilton	Jaguar
1954	Gonzalez/Trintignant	Ferrari
1955	Hawthorn/Bueb	Jaguar
1956	Flockhart/Sanderson	Jaguar
1957	Flockhart/Bueb	Jaguar
1958	Hill/Gendebien	Ferrari
1959	Salvadori/Shelby	Aston Martin
1960	Gendebien/Frere	Ferrari
1961	Gendebien/Hill	Ferrari
1962	Gendebien/Hill	Ferrari
1963	Bandini/Scarfiotti	Ferrari
1964	Guichet/Vaccarella	Ferrari
1965	Gregory/Rindt	Ferrari
1966	McLaren/Amon	Ford
1967	Foyt/Gurney	Ford
1968	Rodriguez/Bianchi	Ford
1969	Ickx/Oliver	Ford
1970	Herrmann/Attwood	Porsche
1971	Van Lennep/Marko	Porsche
1972	Hill/Pescarolo	Matra-Simca
1973	Pescarolo/Larrousse	Matra-Simca
1974	Pescarolo/Larrousse	Matra-Simca
1975	Bell/Ickx	Gulf-Cosworth
1976	Ickx/van Lennep	Porsche
1977	Ickx/Barth/Haywood	Porsche

1978	Pironi/Jaussaud	Renault-Alpine
1979	Whittington/Ludwig/Whittington	Porsche
1980	Rondeau/Jaussaud	Rondeau-Cosworth
1981	Ickx/Bell	Porsche
1982	Ickx/Bell	Porsche
1983	Schuppan/Haywood/Holbert	Porsche
1984	Ludwig/Pescarolo	Porsche
1985	Ludwig/Barilla/Winter	Porsche
1986	Stuck/Bell/Holbert	Porsche
1987	Bell/Stuck/Holbert	Porsche
1988	Lammers/Dumfries/Wallace	Jaguar
1989	Mass/Reuter/Dickens	Sauber Mercedes
1990	Brundle/Nielsen/Cobb	Jaguar
1991	Weidler/Herbert/Gachot	Mazda
1992	Warwick/Blundell/Dalmas	Peugeot
1993	Brabham/Bouchot/Helary	Peugeot
1994	Dalmas/Haywood/Baldi	Dauer Porsche
1995	Dalmas/Lehto/Sekiya	McLaren
1996	Jones/Reuter/Wurz	Porsche
1997	Alboreto/Johansson/Kristensen	Porsche
1998	McNish/Ortelli/Aiello	Porsche
1999	Dalmas/Martini/Winkelhock	BMW
2000	Biela/Kristensen/Pirro	Audi
2001	Biela/Kristensen/Pirro	Audi

Indianapolis 500

Year	Champions
1911	Ray Harroun/C. Patschke
1912	Joe Dawson/D. Herr
1913	Jules Goux
1914	Rene Thomas
1915	Ralph de Palma
1916	Dario Resta
1917–18	(not held)
1919	Howdy Wilcox
1920	Gaston Chevrolet
1921	Tommy Milton
1922	Jimmy Murphy
1923	Tommy Milton/H. Wilcox
1924	Lora Corum/J. Boyer
1925	Pete de Paolo/N. K. Batten
1926	Frank Lockhart
1927	George Souders
1928	Louis Meyer
1929	Ray Keech
1930	Billy Arnold
1931	Louis Schneider
1932	Fred Frame
1933	Louis Meyer

Year	Champions
1934	Bill Cummings
1935	Kelly Petillo
1936	Louis Meyer
1937	Wilbur Shaw
1938	Floyd Roberts
1939	Wilbur Shaw
1940	Wilbur Shaw
1941	Floyd Davis/Mauri Rose
1942–45	(not held)
1946	George Robson
1947	Mauri Rose
1948	Mauri Rose
1949	Bill Holland
1950	Johnnie Parsons
1951	L. Wallard
1952	Troy Ruttman
1953	Bill Vukovich
1954	Bill Vukovich
1955	Bob Sweikert
1956	Pat Flaherty
1957	Sam Hanks
1958	Jimmy Bryan
1959	Rodger Ward
1960	Jim Rathmann
1961	A. J. Foyt
1962	Rodger Ward
1963	Parnelli Jones
1964	A. J. Foyt
1965	Jim Clark
1966	Graham Hill
1967	A. J. Foyt
1968	Robert Unser
1969	Mario Andretti
1970	Al Unser
1971	Al Unser
1972	Mark Donohue
1973	Gordon Johncock
1974	Johnny Rutherford
1975	Robert Unser
1976	Johnny Rutherford
1977	A. J. Foyt
1978	Al Unser
1979	Rick Mears
1980	Johnny Rutherford
1981	Robert Unser
1982	Gordon Johncock
1983	Tom Sneva
1984	Rick Mears
1985	Danny Sullivan
1986	Bobby Rahal
1987	Al Unser

1988	Rick Mears
1989	Emerson Fittipaldi
1990	Arie Luyendyk
1991	Rick Mears
1992	Al Unser
1993	Emerson Fittipaldi
1994	Al Unser
1995	Jacques Villeneuve
1996	Buddy Lazier
1997	Arie Luyendyk
1998	Eddie Cheever
1999	Kenny Brack
2000	Juan Montoya
2001	Helio Castroneves

World Rally Championship (from 1994)

Year	Champion	Car
1994	Didier Auriol (France)	Toyota Celica
1995	Colin McRae (UK)	Subaru Impreza
1996	Tommi Mäkinen (Finland)	Mitsubishi Lancer
1997	Tommi Mäkinen (Finland)	Mitsubishi Lancer
1998	Tommi Mäkinen (Finland)	Mitsubishi Lancer
1999	Tommi Mäkinen (Finland)	Mitsubishi Lancer
2000	Marcus Grönholm (Finland)	Peugeot

12.39 Netball

World Championship

Year	Champions
1963	Australia
1967	New Zealand
1971	Australia
1975	Australia
1979	Australia, New Zealand, Trinidad and Tobago (shared)
1983	Australia
1987	New Zealand
1991	Australia
1995	Australia
1999	Australia

12.40 *Powerboat Racing*

World Championship

Year	Champion (Formula One)
1983	Renato Molinari (Italy)
1984	Renato Molinari (Italy)
1985	Bob Spalding (Great Britain)
1986	Gene Thibodaux (USA)
1987	Ben Robertson (USA)
1990	John Hill (Great Britain)
1991	Jonathan Jones (Great Britain)
1992	Fabrizio Bacca (Italy)
1993	Guido Capellina (Italy)
1994	Guido Capellina (Italy)
1995	Guido Capellina (Italy)
1996	Guido Capellina (Italy)
1997	Scott Gillman (USA)
1998	Scott Gillman (USA)
1999	Guido Capellina (Italy)
2000	Scott Gillman (USA)

12.41 *Rowing*

World Championship (since 1985)

Men's single sculls

Year	Champion
1985	Pertti Karppinen (Finland)
1986	Peter-Michael Kolbe (West Germany)
1987	Thomas Lange (East Germany)
1988	Thomas Lange (East Germany)
1989	Thomas Lange (East Germany)
1990	Yuri Janson (USSR)
1991	Thomas Lange (East Germany)
1992	Thomas Lange (East Germany)
1993	Derek Porter (Canada)
1994	Andre Wilms (Germany)

1995	Iztok Cop (Slovenia)
1996	Xeno Müller (Switzerland)
1997	Jamie Koven (USA)
1998	Rob Waddell (New Zealand)
1999	Rob Waddell (New Zealand)

Women's single sculls

Year	Champion
1985	Cornelia Linse (East Germany)
1986	Jutta Hampe (East Germany)
1987	Magdelena Georgieva (Bulgaria)
1988	Jutta Behrendt (East Germany)
1989	Elisabeta Lipa (Romania)
1990	Brigit Peter (East Germany)
1991	Silke Laumann (Canada)
1992	Elisabeta Lipa (Romania)
1993	Jana Phieme (Germany)
1994	Trine Hansen (Denmark)
1995	Maria Brandin (Sweden)
1996	Yekaterina Khodotovich (Belarus)
1997	Yekaterina Khodotovich (Belarus)
1998	Irina Fedotova (Russia)
1999	Ekaterina Karsten (Belarus)

Note The Men's Championship was first held in 1962; the Women's Championship followed in 1974

University Boat Race (since 1985)

Year	Winners
1985	Oxford
1986	Cambridge
1987	Oxford
1988	Oxford
1989	Oxford
1990	Oxford
1991	Oxford
1992	Oxford
1993	Cambridge
1994	Cambridge
1995	Cambridge
1996	Cambridge
1997	Cambridge
1998	Cambridge
1999	Cambridge
2000	Oxford
2001	Oxford

Note First held in 1829
Total victories (2001): 76 Cambridge, 70 Oxford (1 dead heat)

12.42 *Rugby League*

World Cup

Year	Winner
1954	Great Britain
1957	Australia
1960	Great Britain
1968	Australia
1970	Australia
1972	Great Britain
1975	Australia
1977	Australia
1988	Australia
1992	Australia
1995	Australia
2000	Australia

League Championship (since 1980)

Year	Champions
1980	Bradford Northern
1981	Bradford Northern
1982	Leigh
1983	Hull
1984	Hull Kingston Rovers
1985	Hull Kingston Rovers
1986	Halifax
1987	Wigan
1988	Widnes
1989	Widnes
1990	Wigan
1991	Wigan
1992	Wigan
1993	Wigan
1994	Wigan
1995	Wigan
1996	Wigan
1997	St Helens
1998	Bradford
1999	Wigan
2000	Wigan

Note First held in 1895–96 and variously known as the Northern Union, the JJB Super League (1996–2000) and the Tetley's Bitter Super League (from 2000)

Challenge Cup (since 1980)

Year	Winners
1980	Hull Kingston Rovers
1981	Widnes
1982	Hull
1983	Featherstone Rovers
1984	Widnes
1985	Wigan
1986	Castleford
1987	Halifax
1988	Wigan
1989	Wigan
1990	Wigan
1991	Wigan
1992	Wigan
1993	Wigan
1994	Wigan
1995	Wigan
1996	St Helens
1997	St Helens
1998	Sheffield Eagles
1999	Leeds Rhinos
2000	Bradford Bulls

Note First held in 1897

12.43 *Rugby Union*

World Cup

Year	Winner
1987	New Zealand
1991	Australia
1995	South Africa
1999	Australia

Six Nations Championship (since 1984)

Year	Champions
1984	Scotland
1985	Ireland
1986	France and Scotland
1987	France
1988	France and Wales
1989	France
1990	Scotland
1991	England
1992	England
1993	France
1994	Wales
1995	England
1996	England
1997	France
1998	France
1999	Scotland
2000	England

Note First held in 1884 and known as the Five Nations Championship (contested by England, Ireland, Scotland, Wales and France) until 2000, when Italy joined

County Championship (since 1985)

Year	Champions
1985	Middlesex
1986	Warwickshire
1987	Yorkshire
1988	Lancashire
1989	Durham
1990	Lancashire
1991	Cornwall
1992	Lancashire
1993	Lancashire
1994	Yorkshire
1995	Warwickshire
1996	Gloucestershire
1997	Cumbria
1998	Cheshire
1999	Cornwall
2000	Yorkshire

Note First held in 1889

English League Championship (since 1988)

Year	Champions
1988	Leicester
1989	Bath
1990	Wasps
1991	Bath
1992	Bath
1993	Bath
1994	Bath
1995	Leicester
1996	Bath
1997	Wasps
1998	Newcastle
1999	Leicester
2000	Leicester
2001	Leicester

Note First held in 1987–88 and variously known as the Courage League Championship (1996–97) and the Allied Dunbar Premiership (from 1997)

Tetley's Bitter Cup

Year	Winners
1972	Gloucester
1973	Coventry
1974	Coventry
1975	Bedford
1976	Gosforth
1977	Gosforth
1978	Gloucester
1979	Leicester
1980	Leicester
1981	Leicester
1982	Gloucester/Moseley
1983	Bristol
1984	Bath
1985	Bath
1986	Bath
1987	Bath
1988	Harlequins
1989	Bath
1990	Bath
1991	Harlequins
1992	Bath
1993	Leicester
1994	Bath
1995	Bath

Year	Winners
1996	Bath
1997	Leicester
1998	Saracens
1999	Wasps
2000	Wasps
2001	Newcastle

Note First held in 1971–72 and previously known as the John Player Special Cup (1971–88) and the Pilkington Cup (1988–1997)

Welsh League Premier Division Championship

Year	Champions
1991	Neath
1992	Swansea
1993	Llanelli
1994	Swansea
1995	Cardiff
1996	Neath
1997	Pontypridd
1998	Swansea
1999	Llanelli

Note First held in 1990–91

Welsh Rugby Union Challenge Cup (since 1985)

Year	Winners
1985	Llanelli
1986	Cardiff
1987	Cardiff
1988	Llanelli
1989	Neath
1990	Neath
1991	Llanelli
1992	Llanelli
1993	Llanelli
1994	Cardiff
1995	Swansea
1996	Pontypridd
1997	Cardiff
1998	Llanelli
1999	Swansea
2000	Llanelli

12.44 *Skiing*

World Cup (since 1985)

Men

Year	Overall winner
1985	Marc Girardelli (Luxembourg)
1986	Marc Girardelli (Luxembourg)
1987	Pirmin Zurbriggen (Switzerland)
1988	Pirmin Zurbriggen (Switzerland)
1989	Marc Girardelli (Luxembourg)
1990	Pirmin Zurbriggen (Switzerland)
1991	Marc Girardelli (Luxembourg)
1992	Paul Accola (Switzerland)
1993	Marc Girardelli (Luxembourg)
1994	Kjetil-Andre Aamodt (Norway)
1995	Alberto Tomba (Italy)
1996	Lasse Kjus (Norway)
1997	Luc Alphand (France)
1998	Hermann Maier (Austria)
1999	Lasse Kjus (Norway)
2000	Hermann Maier (Austria)

Women

Year	Overall winner
1985	Michela Figini (Switzerland)
1986	Maria Walliser (Switzerland)
1987	Maria Walliser (Switzerland)
1988	Michela Figini (Switzerland)
1989	Vreni Schneider (Switzerland)
1990	Petra Kronberger (Austria)
1991	Petra Kronberger (Austria)
1992	Petra Kronberger (Austria)
1993	Anita Wachter (Austria)
1994	Vreni Schneider (Switzerland)
1995	Vreni Schneider (Switzerland)
1996	Katja Seizinger (Germany)
1997	Pernilla Wiberg (Sweden)
1998	Katja Seizinger (Germany)
1999	Alexandra Meissnitzer (Austria)
2000	Renata Götschl (Austria)

Note First held in 1967

12.45 *Snooker*

World Professional Championship (since 1980)

Year	Champion
1980	Cliff Thorburn (Canada)
1981	Steve Davis (England)
1982	Alex Higgins (Northern Ireland)
1983	Steve Davis (England)
1984	Steve Davis (England)
1985	Dennis Taylor (Northern Ireland)
1986	Joe Johnson (England)
1987	Steve Davis (England)
1988	Steve Davis (England)
1989	Steve Davis (England)
1990	Stephen Hendry (Scotland)
1991	John Parrott (England)
1992	Stephen Hendry (Scotland)
1993	Stephen Hendry (Scotland)
1994	Stephen Hendry (Scotland)
1995	Stephen Hendry (Scotland)
1996	Stephen Hendry (Scotland)
1997	Ken Doherty (Northern Ireland)
1998	John Higgins (Scotland)
1999	Stephen Hendry (Scotland)
2000	Mark Williams (Wales)
2001	Ronnie O'Sullivan (England)

Note First held in 1926–27

World Amateur Championship (since 1985)

Year	Champion
1985	Paul Mifsud (Malta)
1986	Paul Mifsud (Malta)
1987	Darren Morgan (Wales)
1988	James Wattana (Thailand)
1989	Ken Doherty (Ireland)
1990	Steven O'Connor (Ireland)
1991	Noppodol Noppachorn (Thailand)
1992	Neil Moseley (England)
1993	Neil Moseley (England)
1994	Mohammed Yusuf (Pakistan)
1995	Sackai Sim-ngan (Thailand)
1996	Stuart Bingham (England)

1997	Marco Fu (Hong Kong)
1998	Luke Simmonds (England)
1999	Ian Preece (Wales)

Note First held in 1963 and annually since 1984

British Open Championship (since 1986)

Year	Winner
1986	Steve Davis (England)
1987	Jimmy White (England)
1988	Stephen Hendry (Scotland)
1989	Tony Meo (England)
1990	Bob Chaperon (Canada)
1991	Stephen Hendry (Scotland)
1992	Jimmy White (England)
1993	Steve Davis (England)
1994	Ronnie O'Sullivan (England)
1995	John Higgins (Scotland)
1996	Nigel Bond (England)
1997	Mark J. Williams (Wales)
1998	John Higgins (Scotland)
1999	Fergal O'Brien (Ireland)
2000	Stephen Hendry (Scotland)

12.46 Softball

World Championship

Men

Year	Winners
1968	USA
1972	Canada
1976	Canada, New Zealand, USA
1980	USA
1984	New Zealand
1988	USA
1992	Canada
1996	New Zealand

Women

Year	Winners
1974	USA
1978	USA
1982	New Zealand
1986	USA
1990	USA
1994	USA
1998	USA

Note The Women's Championship was first held in 1965; the Men's Championship followed in 1966

12.47 *Speedway*

World Championship (since 1985)

Individual

Year	Champion
1985	Erik Gundersen (Denmark)
1986	Hans Nielsen (Denmark)
1987	Hans Nielsen (Denmark)
1988	Erik Gundersen (Denmark)
1989	Hans Nielsen (Denmark)
1990	Per Jonsson (Sweden)
1991	Jan Pedersen (Denmark)
1992	Gary Havelock (England)
1993	Sam Ermolenko (USA)
1994	Tony Rickardsson (Sweden)
1995	Hans Nielsen (Denmark)
1996	Billy Hamill (USA)
1997	Greg Hancock (USA)
1998	Tony Rickardsson (Sweden)
1999	Tony Rickardsson (Sweden)
2000	Mark Loram (England)

Pairs/Threes

Year	Champions
1985	Erik Gundersen/Tommy Knudsen (Denmark)
1986	Erik Gundersen/Hans Nielsen (Denmark)
1987	Erik Gundersen/Hans Nielsen (Denmark)
1988	Erik Gundersen/Hans Nielsen (Denmark)
1989	Erik Gundersen/Hans Nielsen (Denmark)
1990	Hans Nielsen/Jan Pedersen (Denmark)
1991	Hans Nielsen/Jan Pedersen/Tommy Knudsen (Denmark)
1992	Greg Hancock/Sam Ermolenko/Ronnie Correy (USA)

1993	Tony Rickardsson/Per Jonsson/Henrik Gustafsson (Sweden)
1994	Per Gustaffson/Tony Rickardsson (Sweden)
1995	Hans Nielsen/Tommy Knudsen/Brian Carger (Denmark)
1996	Tomasz Gollob/Piotr Protasiewicz/Slawomir Drabik (Poland)
1997	Hans Nielsen/Tommy Knudsen/Jesper Jensen (Denmark)
1998	Greg Hancock/Billy Hamill/Sam Ermolenko (USA)
1999	Jason Crump/Jason Lyons/Leigh Adams (Australia)

Team

Year	Winners
1987	Denmark
1988	Denmark
1989	England
1990	USA
1991	Denmark
1992	USA
1993	USA
1994	Sweden
1995	Denmark
1996	Poland
1997	Denmark
1998	USA
1999	Australia

Note The Individual Championship was first held in 1936; the Team Championship followed in 1960, the Pairs/Threes in 1970 (also called the World Team Cup from 1994)

12.48 *Squash*

World Open Championship (since 1985)

Men

Year	Champion
1985	Jahangir Khan (Pakistan)
1986	Ross Norman (New Zealand)
1987	Jansher Khan (Pakistan)
1988	Jahangir Khan (Pakistan)
1989	Jansher Khan (Pakistan)
1990	Jansher Khan (Pakistan)
1991	Rodney Martin (Australia)
1992	Jansher Khan (Pakistan)
1993	Jansher Khan (Pakistan)
1994	Jansher Khan (Pakistan)
1995	Jansher Khan (Pakistan)

Year	Champion
1997	Rodney Eyles (Australia)
1998	Jonathon Power (Canada)
1999	Peter Nicol (UK)

Women

Year	Champion
1985	Sue Devoy (New Zealand)
1987	Sue Devoy (New Zealand)
1989	Martine Le Moignan (Great Britain)
1990	Sue Devoy (New Zealand)
1991	Sue Devoy (New Zealand)
1992	Sue Devoy (New Zealand)
1993	Michelle Martin (Australia)
1994	Michelle Martin (Australia)
1995	Michelle Martin (Australia)
1996	Sarah Fitzgerald (Australia)
1997	Sarah Fitzgerald (Australia)
1998	Sarah Fitzgerald (Australia)
1999	Cassie Campion (England)

Note First held in 1976

12.49 *Swimming and Diving*

Records

Men

Event	Record	Holder	Date
50 m freestyle	00:21.64	Alexander Popov (Russia)	2000
100 m freestyle	00:47.8	Pieter van den Hoogenband (Netherlands)	2000
200 m freestyle	01:45.3	Pieter van den hoogenband (Netherlands)	2000
400 m freestyle	03:40.6	Ian Thorpe (Australia)	2000
800 m freestyle	07:46.0	Kieren Perkins (Australia)	1994
1500 m freestyle	14:41.7	Kieren Perkins (Australia)	1994
100 m backstroke	00:53.6	Lenny Krayxelburg (USA)	1999
200 m backstroke	01:55.9	Lenny Krayxelburg (USA)	1999
100 m breaststroke	01:00.4	Roman Sloudnov (Russia)	2000
200 m breaststroke	02:10.2	Mike Barrowman (USA)	1992
100 m butterfly	00:51.81	Michael Klim (Australia)	1999
200 m butterfly	01:55.18	Tom A. Malchow (USA)	2000
200 m individual medley	01:58.2	Jani Sievinen (Finland)	1994
400 m individual medley	04:11.8	Tom Dolan (USA)	2000
4 × 100 m freestyle relay	03:13.7	Australia	2000

| 4 × 200 m freestyle relay | 07:07.0 | Australia | 2000 |
| 4 × 100 m medley relay | 03:34.8 | USA | 1996 |

Women

Event	Record	Holder	Date
50 m freestyle	00:24.13	Inge de Bruijn (Netherlands)	2000
100 m freestyle	00:53.8	Inge de Bruijn (Netherlands)	2000
200 m freestyle	01:56.8	Franziska Van Almsick (Germany)	1994
400 m freestyle	04:03.9	Janet Evans (USA)	1988
800 m freestyle	08:16.2	Janet Evans (USA)	1989
1500 m freestyle	15:52.1	Janet Evans (USA)	1988
100 m backstroke	01:00.2	Cihong He (China)	1994
200 m backstroke	02:06.6	Kristina Egeszegi (Hungary)	1991
100 m breaststroke	01:06.9	Penelope Heyns (South Africa)	1999
200 m breaststroke	02:24.5	Penelope Heyns (South Africa)	1999
100 m butterfly	00:56.6	Inge de Bruijn (Netherlands)	2000
200 m butterfly	02:05.8	Susann O'Neill (Australia)	2000
200 m individual medley	02:09.7	Yanyan Wu (China)	1997
400 m individual medley	04:33.6	Yana Klochkova (Ukraine)	2000
4 × 100 m freestyle relay	03:36.6	USA	2000
4 × 200 m freestyle relay	07:55.5	East Germany	1987
4 × 100 m medley relay	04:01.7	China	1994

12.50 *Tennis, Lawn*

All-England Championship (Wimbledon) (since 1946)

Men's singles

Year	Winner
1946	Yvon Petra (France)
1947	Jack Kramer (USA)
1948	Bob Falkenburg (USA)
1949	Ted Schroeder (USA)
1950	Budge Patty (USA)
1951	Dick Savitt (USA)
1952	Frank Sedgman (Australia)
1953	Vic Seixas (USA)
1954	Jaroslav Drobny (Egypt)
1955	Tony Trabert (USA)
1956	Lew Hoad (Australia)
1957	Lew Hoad (Australia)
1958	Ashley Cooper (Australia)
1959	Alex Olmedo (USA)

Year	Winner
1960	Neale Fraser (Australia)
1961	Rod Laver (Australia)
1962	Rod Laver (Australia)
1963	Chuck McKinley (USA)
1964	Roy Emerson (Australia)
1965	Roy Emerson (Australia)
1966	Manuel Santana (Spain)
1967	John Newcombe (Australia)
1968	Rod Laver (Australia)
1969	Rod Laver (Australia)
1970	John Newcombe (Australia)
1971	John Newcombe (Australia)
1972	Stan Smith (USA)
1973	Jan Kodes (Czechoslovakia)
1974	Jimmy Connors (USA)
1975	Arthur Ashe (USA)
1976	Bjorn Borg (Sweden)
1977	Bjorn Borg (Sweden)
1978	Bjorn Borg (Sweden)
1979	Bjorn Borg (Sweden)
1980	Bjorn Borg (Sweden)
1981	John McEnroe (USA)
1982	Jimmy Connors (USA)
1983	John McEnroe (USA)
1984	John McEnroe (USA)
1985	Boris Becker (West Germany)
1986	Boris Becker (West Germany)
1987	Pat Cash (Australia)
1988	Stefan Edberg (Sweden)
1989	Boris Becker (West Germany)
1990	Stefan Edberg (Sweden)
1991	Michael Stich (Germany)
1992	Andre Agassi (USA)
1993	Pete Sampras (USA)
1994	Pete Sampras (USA)
1995	Pete Sampras (USA)
1996	Richard Krajicek (Netherlands)
1997	Pete Sampras (USA)
1998	Pete Sampras (USA)
1999	Pete Sampras (USA)
2000	Pete Sampras (USA)
2001	Goran Ivanisevic (Croatia)

Women's singles

Year	Winner
1946	Pauline Betz (USA)
1947	Margaret Osborne (USA)
1948	Louise Brough (USA)
1949	Louise Brough (USA)
1950	Louise Brough (USA)
1951	Doris Hart (USA)

1952	Maureen Connolly (USA)
1953	Maureen Connolly (USA)
1954	Maureen Connolly (USA)
1955	Louise Brough (USA)
1956	Shirley Fry (USA)
1957	Althea Gibson (USA)
1958	Althea Gibson (USA)
1959	Maria Bueno (Brazil)
1960	Maria Bueno (Brazil)
1961	Angela Mortimer (UK)
1962	Karen Susman (USA)
1963	Margaret Smith (Australia)
1964	Maria Bueno (Brazil)
1965	Margaret Smith (Australia)
1966	Billie Jean King (USA)
1967	Billie Jean King (USA)
1968	Billie Jean King (USA)
1969	Ann Jones (UK)
1970	Margaret Court (Australia)
1971	Evonne Goolagong (Australia)
1972	Billie Jean King (USA)
1973	Billie Jean King (USA)
1974	Chris Evert (USA)
1975	Billie Jean King (USA)
1976	Chris Evert (USA)
1977	Virginia Wade (UK)
1978	Martina Navratilova (Czechoslovakia)
1979	Martina Navratilova (Czechoslovakia)
1980	Evonne Cawley (Australia)
1981	Chris Evert Lloyd (USA)
1982	Martina Navratilova (USA)
1983	Martina Navratilova (USA)
1984	Martina Navratilova (USA)
1985	Martina Navratilova (USA)
1986	Martina Navratilova (USA)
1987	Martina Navratilova (USA)
1988	Steffi Graf (West Germany)
1989	Steffi Graf (West Germany)
1990	Martina Navratilova (Czechoslovakia)
1991	Steffi Graf (Germany)
1992	Steffi Graf (Germany)
1993	Steffi Graf (Germany)
1994	Conchita Martinez (Spain)
1995	Steffi Graf (Germany)
1996	Steffi Graf (Germany)
1997	Martina Hingis (Switzerland)
1998	Jana Novotna (Czech Republic)
1999	Lindsay Davenport (USA)
2000	Venus Williams (USA)
2001	Venus Williams (USA)

Note The Men's Singles Championship was first held in 1877; the Women's Singles Championship followed in 1884

Evonne Goolagong regained the Women's Singles title under her married name, Evonne Cawley

United States Open Championship (since 1985)

Men's singles

Year	Winner
1985	Ivan Lendl (Czechoslovakia)
1986	Ivan Lendl (Czechoslovakia)
1987	Ivan Lendl (Czechoslovakia)
1988	Mats Wilander (Sweden)
1989	Boris Becker (West Germany)
1990	Pete Sampras (USA)
1991	Stefan Edberg (Sweden)
1992	Stefan Edberg (Sweden)
1993	Pete Sampras (USA)
1994	Andre Agassi (USA)
1995	Pete Sampras (USA)
1996	Pete Sampras (USA)
1997	Patrick Rafter (Australia)
1998	Patrick Rafter (Australia)
1999	Andre Agassi (USA)
2000	Marat Safin (Russia)

Women's singles

Year	Winner
1985	Hana Mandlikova (Czechoslovakia)
1986	Martina Navratilova (USA)
1987	Martina Navratilova (USA)
1988	Steffi Graf (West Germany)
1989	Steffi Graf (West Germany)
1990	Gabriela Sabatini (Argentina)
1991	Monica Seles (Yugoslavia)
1992	Monica Seles (Yugoslavia)
1993	Steffi Graf (Germany)
1994	Arantxa Sánchez Vicario (Spain)
1995	Steffi Graf (Germany)
1996	Steffi Graf (Gemany)
1997	Martina Hingis (Switzerland)
1998	Lindsay Davenport (USA)
1999	Serena Williams (USA)
2000	Venus Williams (USA)

Note First held in 1891

Davis Cup (since 1988)

Year	Winners
1988	West Germany
1989	West Germany
1990	USA
1991	France
1992	USA
1993	Germany

1994	Sweden
1995	USA
1996	France
1997	Sweden
1998	Sweden
1999	Australia
2000	Spain

12.51 *Table Tennis*

World Championship (since 1985)

Swaythling Cup (men's team)

Year	Winners
1985	China
1987	China
1989	Sweden
1991	Sweden
1993	Sweden
1995	China
1997	China
2000	Sweden

Corbillon Cup (women's team)

Year	Winners
1985	China
1987	China
1989	China
1991	South Korea
1993	China
1995	China
1997	China
2000	China

Men's singles

Year	Winner
1985	Jiang Jialiang (China)
1987	Jiang Jialiang (China)
1989	Jan-Ove Waldner (Sweden)
1991	Jörgen Persson (Sweden)
1993	Jean-Philippe Gatien (France)
1995	Kong Ling-Hui (China)
1997	Jan-Ove Waldner (Sweden)
1999	Liu Guoliang (China)

Men's doubles

Year	Winners
1985	Mikael Applegren/Ulf Carlsson (Sweden)
1987	Chen Longcan/Wei Quinguang (China)
1989	Joerg Rosskopf/Stefen Fetzner (West Germany)
1991	Peter Karlson/Thomas von Scheele (Sweden)
1993	Wang Tao/Lu Lin (China)
1995	Wang Tao/Lu Lin (China)
1997	Kong Linghui/Liu Guoliang (China)
1999	Kong Linghui/Liu Guoliang (China)

Women's singles

Year	Winner
1985	Cao Yanhua (China)
1987	He Zhili (China)
1989	Qiao Hong (China)
1991	Deng Yaping (China)
1993	Hyun Jung-Hwa (South Korea)
1995	Deng Yaping (China)
1997	Deng Yaping (China)
1999	Wang Nan (China)

Women's doubles

Year	Winners
1985	Dai Lili/Geng Lijuan (China)
1987	Yang Young-Ja/Hyun Jung-Hwa (Korea)
1989	Quio Hong/Deng Yaping (China)
1991	Chen Zhie/Gao Jun (China)
1993	Liu Wei/Qiao Yunping (China)
1995	Deng Yaping/Qiao Hong (China)
1997	Deng Yaping/Yang Ying (China)
1999	Wang Nan/Li Ju (China)

Mixed doubles

Year	Winners
1985	Cai Zhenua/Coa Yanhua (China)
1987	Hui Jun/Geng Lijuan (China)
1989	Yoo Nam-Kyu/Hyun Jung-Hwa (South Korea)
1991	Wang Tao/Liu Wei (China)
1993	Wang Tao/Liu Wei (China)
1995	Wang Tao/Liu Wei (China)
1997	Liu Guoliang/Wu Na (China)
1999	Ma Lin/Zhang Yingying (China)

Note First held in 1926

12.52 Volleyball

World Championship (since 1980)

Men

Year	Winners
1980	USSR
1982	USSR
1984	USA
1986	USA
1988	USA
1990	Italy
1992	Brazil
1994	Italy
1996	Netherlands
1998	Italy

Women

Year	Winners
1980	USSR
1982	China
1984	China
1986	China
1988	USSR
1990	USSR
1992	Cuba
1994	Cuba
1996	Cuba
1998	Cuba

Note The Men's Championship was first held in 1949; the Women's Championship followed in 1952

12.53 Walking

World Race Walking Cup (since 1985)

Men

Year	Winners
1985	East Germany
1987	USSR
1989	USSR

Year	Winners
1991	Italy
1993	Mexico
1995	Mexico
1997	Russia
1999	Russia

Women

Year	Winners
1985	China
1987	USSR
1989	USSR
1991	USSR
1993	Italy
1995	China
1997	Russia
1999	China

Note The Men's event was first held in 1961 and was formerly known as the Lugano Trophy; the Women's event followed in 1979 and was formerly known as the Eschborn Cup

12.54 *Water Polo*

World Championship

Men

Year	Winners
1975	USSR
1978	Italy
1982	USSR
1986	Yugoslavia
1991	Yugoslavia
1994	Italy
1998	Spain

Women

Year	Winners
1986	Australia
1990	USSR
1991	Netherlands
1994	Hungary
1998	Italy

Note The Men's Championship was first held in 1973; the Women's Championship followed in 1986

World Cup (since 1985)

Men

Year	Winners
1985	West Germany
1987	Yugoslavia
1989	Yugoslavia
1991	USA
1993	Italy
1995	Hungary
1997	USA
1999	Hungary

Women

Year	Winners
1988	Netherlands
1989	Netherlands
1991	Netherlands
1993	Netherlands
1995	Australia
1997	Netherlands
1999	Netherlands

Note The Men's event was first held in 1979; the Women's event did not win official status until 1989

12.55 *Wrestling*

World Championship (since 1985)

Freestyle super-heavyweight (over 100 kg)

Year	Winner
1985	David Gobedzhishvilli (USSR)
1986	Bruce Baumgartner (USA)
1987	Khadartsv Aslam (USSR)
1988	David Gobedzhishvilli (USSR)
1989	Ali Reiza Soleimani (Iran)
1990	David Gobedzhishvilli (USSR)
1991	Andreas Schroder (Germany)
1992	Bruce Baumgartner (USA)
1993	Mikael Ljunberg (Sweden)
1994	Mahmut Demir (Turkey)
1995	Bruce Baumgartner (USA)
1996	Mahmut Demir (Turkey)

Year	Winner
1997	Zekeriya Güglü (Turkey)
1998	Alexis Rodriguez (Cuba)
1999	Stephen Neal (USA)

Graeco-Roman super-heavyweight (over 100 kg)

Year	Winner
1985	Igor Rostozotskiy (USSR)
1986	Thomas Johansson (Sweden)
1987	Igor Rostozotskiy (USSR)
1988	Alexander Karelin (USSR)
1989	Alexander Karelin (USSR)
1990	Alexander Karelin (USSR)
1991	Alexander Karelin (USSR)
1992	Alexander Karelin (Unified Team)
1993	Alexander Karelin (Russia)
1994	Alexander Karelin (Russia)
1995	Alexander Karelin (Russia)
1996	Alexander Karelin (Russia)
1997	Alexander Karelin (Russia)
1998	Alexander Karelin (Russia)
1999	Alexander Karelin (Russia)

12.56 *Yachting*

America's Cup

Year	Winner
1870	Magic (USA)
1871	Columbia (USA)/Sappho (USA)
1876	Madeleine (USA)
1881	Mischief (USA)
1885	Puritan (USA)
1886	Mayflower (USA)
1887	Volunteer (USA)
1893	Vigilant (USA)
1895	Defender (USA)
1899	Columbia (USA)
1901	Columbia (USA)
1903	Reliance (USA)
1920	Resolute (USA)
1930	Enterprise (USA)
1934	Rainbow (USA)
1937	Ranger (USA)

1958	Columbia (USA)
1962	Weatherly (USA)
1964	Constellation (USA)
1967	Intrepid (USA)
1970	Intrepid (USA)
1974	Courageous (USA)
1977	Courageous (USA)
1980	Freedom (USA)
1983	Australia II (Australia)
1987	Stars and Stripes (USA)
1988	Stars and Stripes (USA)
1992	America 3 (USA)
1995	Black Magic (New Zealand)
2000	Black Magic (New Zealand)

Admiral's Cup (since 1969)

Year	Winner
1969	USA
1971	UK
1973	West Germany
1975	UK
1977	UK
1979	Australia
1981	UK
1983	West Germany
1985	West Germany
1987	New Zealand
1989	UK
1991	France
1993	Germany
1995	Italy
1997	USA
1999	Netherlands

Note First held in 1957